DATA STRUCTURES AND ALGORITHM ANALYSIS IN C++

MARK ALLEN WEISS
Florida International University

The Benjamin/Cummings Publishing Company, Inc.
Redwood City, California • Menlo Park, California • Reading, Massachusetts
New York • Don Mills, Ontario • Wokingham, U.K. • Amsterdam
Bonn • Sydney • Singapore • Tokyo • Madrid • San Juan

Sponsoring editor: J. Carter Shanklin
Editorial assistant: Melissa Standen
Production editor: Gail Carrigan
Freelance production management: Peter Feely, Publication Services, Inc.
Copyeditor: Richard Williamson, Publication Services, Inc.
Technical art: Publication Services, Inc.
Composition: Publication Services, Inc.
Cover design: Gary Palmatier, Ideas to Images

Library of Congress Cataloging-in-Publication Data

Weiss, Mark Allen.
  Data structures and algorithm analysis in C++ / Mark Allen Weiss.
    p.   cm.
  Includes bibliographical references and index.
  ISBN 0-8053-5443-3
  1. C++ (Computer program language)   2. Data structures (Computer
science)   3. Computer algorithms.   I. Title.
QA76.73.C153W46   1993   93-37035
005.13'3—dc20   CIP

ISBN 0-8053-5443-3

  2 3 4 5 6 7 8 9 10—CRW—97 96 95 94

The Benjamin/Cummings Publishing Company, Inc.
390 Bridge Parkway
Redwood City, California 94065

To Mona, David, and Nina Weiss

PREFACE

Purpose/Goals

This book describes *data structures*, methods of organizing large amounts of data, and *algorithm analysis*, the estimation of the running time of algorithms. As computers become faster and faster, the need for programs that can handle large amounts of input becomes more acute. Paradoxically, this requires more careful attention to efficiency, since inefficiencies in programs become most obvious when input sizes are large. By analyzing an algorithm before it is actually coded, students can decide if a particular solution will be feasible. For example, in this text students look at specific problems and see how careful implementations can reduce the time constraint for large amounts of data from 16 years to less than a second. Therefore, no algorithm or data structure is presented without an explanation of its running time. In some cases, minute details that affect the running time of the implementation are explored.

Once a solution method is determined, a program must still be written. As computers have become more powerful, the problems they solve have become larger and more complex, thus requiring development of more intricate programs to solve the problems. The goal of this text is to teach students good programming and algorithm analysis skills simultaneously so that they can develop such programs with the maximum amount of efficiency.

This book is suitable for either an advanced data structures (CS7) course or a first-year graduate course in algorithm analysis. Students should have some knowledge of intermediate programming, including such topics as pointers and recursion, and some background in discrete math.

Approach

The algorithms in this book are presented in C++, which has emerged as the fastest growing systems programming language. In addition to fixing many of the basic syntactic flaws of C, C++ provides support for *object-oriented programming*, which is discussed in more detail in Chapter 1.

The most difficult part of writing the book was deciding on the amount of C++ to include. Use too many features of C++, and one gets an incomprehensible text; use too few and you have little more than a C text which supports classes. I've picked a middle ground, choosing to include as many C++ features as I could, without terribly complicating matters. I've also tried to make the code more readable, by including, for example, explicit tests against NULL.

Each data structure is implemented as a class. We provide a complete class interface (sometimes known as the specification), as well as implementations for many, but not all, of the class functions.

Each class is implemented using templates. Some reviewers expressed reservations with this decision because it complicates the code, and also because templates are not completely supported on some older compilers. I have included templates for two reasons. First, they are a powerful feature, with a syntax, that, though sometimes cumbersome, is usually not complex. Second, it is simple enough to remove them from the code, if necessary. However, attempting to use templates without seeing examples is more difficult, and also there are a few technical points that can be brought out by including them. Even so, you should check that your compiler supports templates before attempting to directly use the sample code in the text.

A more difficult feature is inheritance, especially in conjunction with templates. We've used inheritance in a limited way to extend basic classes, and have not attempted a more thorough dicussion. We have avoided iterator classes entirely, because while they are relatively straightforward, their actual implementation tends to complicate the code too much.

All C++ reserved words and predefined symbols and functions are in lower case. All other symbols are in a mixed case, in which both the first character and character following an underscore are capitalized. The only exceptions to the rule are i, j, and k. The code has been tested using g++ 2.3.3 on an assorted group of SUN workstations running UNIX, and *Turbo C++ 3.1* running on a PC compatible workstation running MS-DOS. These compilers do not support exceptions, and so our code has not used this new feature.

Overview

Chapter 1 contains review material on discrete math and recursion. I believe the only way to be comfortable with recursion is to see good uses over and over. Therefore, recursion is prevalent in this text, with examples in every chapter except Chapter 5. Chapter 1 also contains a brief review of C++ features which are used for object-oriented programming. We implement classes for strings and complex numbers. I assume that the user knows at least the C subset of C++; though C++ is used, this is first and foremost a Data Structures, not a C++ text.

Chapter 2 deals with algorithm analysis. This chapter explains asymptotic analysis and its major weaknesses. Many examples are provided, including an in-depth explanation of logarithmic running time. Simple recursive programs are analyzed by intuitively converting them into iterative programs. More complicated divide-and-conquer programs are introduced, but some of the analysis (solving recurrence relations) is implicitly delayed until Chapter 7, where it is performed in detail.

Chapter 3 covers lists, stacks, and queues. The emphasis here is on coding these data structures using templated classes, fast implementation of these data structures, and an exposition of some of their uses. We also introduce inheritance by deriving a class for sorted linked lists from the basic linked list class. There are almost no programs (just routines), but the exercises contain plenty of ideas for programming assignments.

Chapter 4 covers trees, with an emphasis on search trees, including external search trees (B-trees). The UNIX file system and expression trees are used as examples. AVL trees and splay trees are introduced but not analyzed. Seventy-five percent of the code is written, leaving similar cases to be completed by the student. Additional coverage of trees, such as file compression and game trees, is deferred until Chapter 10. Data structures for an external medium are considered as the final topic in several chapters.

Chapter 5 is a relatively short chapter concerning hash tables. Some analysis is performed and extendible hashing is covered at the end of the chapter.

Chapter 6 is about priority queues. Binary heaps are covered, and there is additional material on some of the theoretically interesting implementations of priority queues.

Chapter 7 covers sorting. It is very specific with respect to coding details and analysis. All the important general-purpose sorting algorithms are covered and compared. Three algorithms are analyzed in detail: insertion sort, Shellsort, and quicksort. External sorting is covered at the end of the chapter.

Chapter 8 discusses the disjoint set algorithm with proof of the running time. This is a short and specific chapter that can be skipped if Kruskal's algorithm is not discussed.

Chapter 9 covers graph algorithms. Algorithms on graphs are interesting, not only because they frequently occur in practice but also because their running time is so heavily dependent on the proper use of data structures. Virtually all of the standard algorithms are presented along with appropriate data structures, pseudocode, and analysis of running time. To place these problems in a proper context, a short discussion on complexity theory (including *NP*-completeness and undecidability) is provided.

Chapter 10 covers algorithm design by examining common problem-solving techniques. This chapter is heavily fortified with examples. Pseudocode is used in these later chapters so that the student's appreciation of an example algorithm is not obscured by implementation details.

Chapter 11 deals with amortized analysis. Three data structures from Chapters 4 and 6 and the Fibonacci heap, introduced in this chapter, are analyzed.

Chapters 1–9 provide enough material for most one-semester data structures courses. If time permits, then Chapter 10 can be covered. A graduate course on algorithm analysis could cover Chapters 7–11. The advanced data structures analyzed in Chapter 11 can easily be referred to in the earlier chapters. The discussion of *NP*-completeness in Chapter 9 is far too brief to be used in such a course. Garey and Johnson's book on *NP*-completeness can be used to augment this text.

Exercises

Exercises, provided at the end of each chapter, match the order in which material is presented. The last exercises may address the chapter as a whole rather than a specific section. Difficult exercises are marked with an asterisk, and more challenging exercises have two asterisks.

A solutions manual containing solutions to almost all the exercises is available separately from The Benjamin/Cummings Publishing Company.

References

References are placed at the end of each chapter. Generally the references either are historical, representing the original source of the material, or they represent extensions and improvements to the results given in the text. Some references represent solutions to exercises.

Acknowledgments

Many, many people have helped me in the preparation of this book. The preface of the Pascal version of the text lists some of them. Additionally, I would like to thank the folks at Benjamin/Cummings, in particular my editor, Carter Shanklin, his assistants, Vivian McDougal and Melissa Standen, and Liane Shayer and Mary Tudor in marketing for answering all my questions, especially the stupid ones. Once again, Gail Carrigan did a lovely job with the production. I'd also like to thank Pete Feely and his fine staff at Publication Services for beating a tight deadline.

Gary Palmatier, as usual, is responsible for the terrific cover. He's done all four, and, unbelievably, each one is more striking than the previous.

I thank C++ reviewers who provided numerous suggestions for improvement. Alphabetically they are Owen Astrachan (Duke University), Claire Bono (University of Southern California), Asesh Das (West Virginia University), Ken Joy (UC Davis), John Marsaglia (Western Oregon State), David Teague (Western Carolina University), and Edward Wright (Western Oregon State). I would especially like to thank David Teague, who tested the original code and made many valuable suggestions.

I'd like to thank the people at FIU who helped me out with this project. First and foremost, Raimund Ege was the local C++ guru who answered all my questions. Steve Luis and Cory Tsang kept the printers running, and the computers up, and made tapes on a minute's notice.

I'd also like to thank all my friends who provided encouragement during the project. I'd especially like to thank Becky Miro for always being there to cheer me up.

I would appreciate reports of any errors you find; my e-mail address is weiss@fiu.edu.

M.A.W.

Miami, Florida
June 1991
August 1993

CONTENTS

CHAPTER 1

Introduction

In this chapter, we discuss the aims and goals of this text and briefly review programming concepts and discrete mathematics. We will

- See that how a program performs for reasonably large input is just as important as its performance on moderate amounts of input.
- Summarize the basic mathematical background needed for the rest of the book.
- Briefly review recursion.
- Summarize some important features of C++ and object-oriented programming.

1.1. What's the Book About?

Suppose you have a group of n numbers and would like to determine the kth largest. This is known as the *selection problem*. Most students who have had a programming course or two would have no difficulty writing a program to solve this problem. There are quite a few "obvious" solutions.

One way to solve this problem would be to read the n numbers into an array, sort the array in decreasing order by some simple algorithm such as bubblesort, and then return the element in position k.

A somewhat better algorithm might be to read the first k elements into an array and sort them (in decreasing order). Next, each remaining element is read one by one. As a new element arrives, it is ignored if it is smaller than the kth element in the array. Otherwise, it is placed in its correct spot in the array, bumping one element out of the array. When the algorithm ends, the element in the kth position is returned as the answer.

Both algorithms are simple to code, and you are encouraged to do so. The natural questions, then, are which algorithm is better and, more importantly, is either algorithm good enough? A simulation using a random file of 1 million

1

elements and $k = 500,000$ will show that neither algorithm finishes in a reasonable amount of time—each requires several days of computer processing to terminate (albeit eventually with a correct answer). An alternative method, discussed in Chapter 7, gives a solution in about a second. Thus, although our proposed algorithms work, they cannot be considered good algorithms, because they are entirely impractical for input sizes that a third algorithm can handle in a reasonable amount of time.

A second problem is to solve a popular word puzzle. The input consists of a two-dimensional array of letters and a list of words. The object is to find the words in the puzzle. These words may be horizontal, vertical, or diagonal in any direction. As an example, the puzzle shown in Figure 1.1 contains the words *this, two, fat,* and *that.* The word *this* begins at row 1, column 1 (1, 1) and extends to (1, 4); *two* goes from (1, 1) to (3, 1); *fat* goes from (4, 1) to (2, 3); and *that* goes from (4, 4) to (1, 1).

Again, there are at least two straightforward algorithms that solve the problem. For each word in the word list, we check each ordered triple (*row, column, orientation*) for the presence of the word. This amounts to lots of nested *for* loops but is basically straightforward.

Alternatively, for each ordered quadruple (*row, column, orientation, number of characters*) that doesn't run off an end of the puzzle, we can test whether the word indicated is in the word list. Again, this amounts to lots of nested *for* loops. It is possible to save some time if the maximum number of characters in any word is known.

It is relatively easy to code up either solution and solve many of the real-life puzzles commonly published in magazines. These typically have 16 rows, 16 columns, and 40 or so words. Suppose, however, we consider the variation where only the puzzle board is given and the word list is essentially an English dictionary. Both of the solutions proposed require considerable time to solve this problem and therefore are not acceptable. However, it is possible, even with a large word list, to solve the problem in a matter of seconds.

An important concept is that, in many problems, writing a working program is not good enough. If the program is to be run on a large data set, then the running time becomes an issue. Throughout this book we will see how to estimate the running time of a program for large inputs and, more importantly, how to compare the running times of two programs without actually coding them. We will see techniques for drastically improving the speed of a program and for determining program bottlenecks. These techniques will enable us to find the section of the code on which to concentrate our optimization efforts.

Figure 1.1 Sample word puzzle

	1	2	3	4
1	t	h	i	s
2	w	a	t	s
3	o	a	h	g
4	f	g	d	t

1.2. Mathematics Review

This section lists some of the basic formulas you need to memorize or be able to derive and reviews basic proof techniques.

1.2.1. Exponents

$$x^a x^b = x^{a+b}$$

$$\frac{x^a}{x^b} = x^{a-b}$$

$$(x^a)^b = x^{ab}$$

$$x^n + x^n = 2x^n \neq x^{2n}$$

$$2^n + 2^n = 2^{n+1}$$

1.2.2. Logarithms

In computer science, all logarithms are to base 2 unless specified otherwise.

DEFINITION: $x^a = b$ if and only if $\log_x b = a$

Several convenient equalities follow from this definition.

THEOREM 1.1.

$$\log_a b = \frac{\log_c b}{\log_c a}; \quad c > 0$$

PROOF:
Let $x = \log_c b$, $y = \log_c a$, and $z = \log_a b$. Then, by the definition of logarithms, $c^x = b$, $c^y = a$, and $a^z = b$. Combining these three equalities yields $(c^y)^z = c^x = b$. Therefore, $x = yz$, which implies $z = x/y$, proving the theorem.

THEOREM 1.2.

$$\log ab = \log a + \log b$$

PROOF:
Let $x = \log a$, $y = \log b$, $z = \log ab$. Then, assuming the default base of 2, $2^x = a$, $2^y = b$, $2^z = ab$. Combining the last three equalities yields $2^x 2^y = 2^z = ab$. Therefore, $x + y = z$, which proves the theorem.

Some other useful formulas, which can all be derived in a similar manner, follow.

$$\log a/b = \log a - \log b$$

$$\log (a^b) = b \log a$$

$$\log x < x \quad \text{for all } x > 0$$

$$\log 1 = 0, \qquad \log 2 = 1, \qquad \log 1{,}024 = 10, \qquad \log 1{,}048{,}576 = 20$$

1.2.3.   Series

The easiest formulas to remember are

$$\sum_{i=0}^{n} 2^i = 2^{n+1} - 1$$

and the companion,

$$\sum_{i=0}^{n} a^i = \frac{a^{n+1} - 1}{a - 1}$$

In the latter formula, if $0 < a < 1$, then

$$\sum_{i=0}^{n} a^i \le \frac{1}{1 - a}$$

and as n tends to ∞, the sum approaches $1/(1 - a)$. These are the "geometric series" formulas.

We can derive the last formula for $\sum_{i=0}^{\infty} a^i$ $(0 < a < 1)$ in the following manner. Let S be the sum. Then

$$S = 1 + a + a^2 + a^3 + a^4 + a^5 + \cdots$$

Then

$$aS = a + a^2 + a^3 + a^4 + a^5 + \cdots$$

If we subtract these two equations (which is permissible only for a convergent series), virtually all the terms on the right side cancel, leaving

$$S - aS = 1$$

which implies that

$$S = \frac{1}{1 - a}$$

We can use this same technique to compute $\sum_{i=1}^{\infty} i/2^i$, a sum that occurs frequently. We write

$$S = \frac{1}{2} + \frac{2}{2^2} + \frac{3}{2^3} + \frac{4}{2^4} + \frac{5}{2^5} + \cdots$$

and multiply by 2, obtaining

$$2S = 1 + \frac{2}{2} + \frac{3}{2^2} + \frac{4}{2^3} + \frac{5}{2^4} + \frac{6}{2^5} + \cdots$$

Subtracting these two equations yields

$$S = 1 + \frac{1}{2} + \frac{1}{2^2} + \frac{1}{2^3} + \frac{1}{2^4} + \frac{1}{2^5} + \cdots$$

Thus, $S = 2$.

Another type of common series in analysis is the arithmetic series. Any such series can be evaluated from the basic formula.

$$\sum_{i=1}^{N} i = \frac{N(N+1)}{2} \approx \frac{N^2}{2}$$

For instance, to find the sum $2 + 5 + 8 + \cdots + (3k - 1)$, rewrite it as $3(1 + 2 + 3 + \cdots + k) - (1 + 1 + 1 + \cdots + 1)$, which is clearly $3k(k+1)/2 - k$. Another way to remember this is to add the first and last terms (total $3k + 1$), the second and next to last terms (total $3k + 1$), and so on. Since there are $k/2$ of these pairs, the total sum is $k(3k + 1)/2$, which is the same answer as before.

The next two formulas pop up now and then but are fairly infrequent.

$$\sum_{i=1}^{N} i^2 = \frac{N(N+1)(2N+1)}{6} \approx \frac{N^3}{3}$$

$$\sum_{i=1}^{N} i^k \approx \frac{N^{k+1}}{|k+1|} \qquad k \neq -1$$

When $k = -1$, the latter formula is not valid. We then need the following formula, which is used far more in computer science than in other mathematical disciplines. The numbers, H_N, are known as the harmonic numbers, and the sum is known as a harmonic sum. The error in the following approximation tends to $\gamma \approx 0.57721566$, which is known as *Euler's constant*.

$$H_N = \sum_{i=1}^{N} \frac{1}{i} \approx \log_e N$$

These two formulas are just general algebraic manipulations.

$$\sum_{i=1}^{N} f(N) = Nf(N)$$

$$\sum_{i=n_0}^{N} f(i) = \sum_{i=1}^{N} f(i) - \sum_{i=1}^{n_0-1} f(i)$$

1.2.4. Modular Arithmetic

We say that a is congruent to b modulo n, written $a \equiv b \pmod{n}$, iff n divides $a - b$. Intuitively, this means that the remainder is the same when either a or b is divided by n. Thus, $81 \equiv 61 \equiv 1 \pmod{10}$. As with equality, if $a \equiv b \pmod{n}$, then $a + c \equiv b + c \pmod{n}$ and $ad \equiv bd \pmod{n}$.

There are a lot of theorems that apply to modular arithmetic, some of which require extraordinary proofs in number theory. We will use modular arithmetic sparingly, and the preceding theorems will suffice.

1.2.5. The P Word

The two most common ways of proving statements in data structure analysis are proof by induction and proof by contradiction (and occasionally a proof by intimidation, by professors only). The best way of proving that a theorem is false is by exhibiting a counterexample.

Proof by Induction

A proof by induction has two standard parts. The first step is proving a *base case*, that is, establishing that a theorem is true for some small (usually degenerate) value(s); this step is almost always trivial. Next, an *inductive hypothesis* is assumed. Generally this means that the theorem is assumed to be true for all cases up to some limit k. Using this assumption, the theorem is then shown to be true for the next value, which is typically $k + 1$. This proves the theorem (as long as k is finite).

As an example, we prove that the Fibonacci numbers, $F_0 = 1, F_1 = 1, F_2 = 2, F_3 = 3, F_4 = 5, \ldots, F_i = F_{i-1} + F_{i-2}$, satisfy $F_i < (5/3)^i$, for $i \geq 1$. (Some definitions have $F_0 = 0$, which shifts the series.) To do this, we first verify that the theorem is true for the trivial cases. It is easy to verify that $F_1 = 1 < 5/3$ and $F_2 = 2 < 25/9$; this proves the basis. We assume that the theorem is true for $i = 1, 2, \ldots, k$; this is the inductive hypothesis. To prove the theorem, we need to show that $F_{k+1} < (5/3)^{k+1}$. We have

$$F_{k+1} = F_k + F_{k-1}$$

by the definition, and we can use the inductive hypothesis on the right-hand side, obtaining

$$F_{k+1} < (5/3)^k + (5/3)^{k-1}$$
$$< (3/5)(5/3)^{k+1} + (3/5)^2(5/3)^{k+1}$$
$$< (3/5)(5/3)^{k+1} + (9/25)(5/3)^{k+1}$$

which simplifies to

$$F_{k+1} < (3/5 + 9/25)(5/3)^{k+1}$$
$$< (24/25)(5/3)^{k+1}$$
$$< (5/3)^{k+1}$$

proving the theorem.

As a second example, we establish the following theorem.

THEOREM 1.3.

If $n \geq 1$, then $\displaystyle\sum_{i=1}^{n} i^2 = \frac{n(n + 1)(2n + 1)}{6}$

PROOF:

The proof is by induction. For the basis, it is readily seen that the theorem is true when $n = 1$. For the inductive hypothesis, assume that the theorem is true for $1 \le k \le n$. We will establish that, under this assumption, the theorem is true for $n + 1$. We have

$$\sum_{i=1}^{n+1} i^2 = \sum_{i=1}^{n} i^2 + (n+1)^2$$

Applying the inductive hypothesis, we obtain

$$\sum_{i=1}^{n+1} i^2 = \frac{n(n+1)(2n+1)}{6} + (n+1)^2$$

$$= (n+1)\left[\frac{n(2n+1)}{6} + (n+1)\right]$$

$$= (n+1)\frac{2n^2 + 7n + 6}{6}$$

$$= \frac{(n+1)(n+2)(2n+3)}{6}$$

Thus,

$$\sum_{i=1}^{n+1} = \frac{(n+1)[(n+1)+1][2(n+1)+1]}{6}$$

proving the theorem.

Proof by Counterexample

The statement $F_k \le k^2$ is false. The easiest way to prove this is to compute $F_{11} = 144 > 11^2$.

Proof by Contradiction

Proof by contradiction proceeds by assuming that the theorem is false and showing that this assumption implies that some known property is false, and hence the original assumption was erroneous. A classic example is the proof that there is an infinite number of primes. To prove this, we assume that the theorem is false, so that there is some largest prime p_k. Let $p_1, p_2, \ldots, p_k$ be all the primes in order and consider

$$N = p_1 p_2 p_3 \cdots p_k + 1$$

Clearly, N is larger than p_k, so by assumption N is not prime. However, none of p_1, $p_2, \ldots, p_k$ divide N exactly, because there will always be a remainder of 1. This is a contradiction, because every number is either prime or a product of primes. Hence, the original assumption, that p_k is the largest prime, is false, which implies that the theorem is true.

```
/* 1*/    int
/* 2*/    F( const int X )
/* 3*/    {
/* 4*/        if( X == 0 )
/* 5*/            return 0;
/* 6*/        else
/* 7*/            return 2 * F( X - 1 ) + X * X;
/* 8*/    }
```

Figure 1.2   A recursive function

1.3.   A Brief Introduction to Recursion

Most mathematical functions that we are familiar with are described by a simple formula. For instance, we can convert temperatures from Fahrenheit to Celsius by applying the formula

$$C = 5(F - 32)/9$$

Given this formula, it is trivial to write a C++ function; with declarations and braces removed, the one-line formula translates to one line of C++.

Mathematical functions are sometimes defined in a less standard form. As an example, we can define a function f, valid on nonnegative integers, that satisfies $f(0) = 0$ and $f(x) = 2f(x - 1) + x^2$. From this definition we see that $f(1) = 1$, $f(2) = 6$, $f(3) = 21$, and $f(4) = 58$. A function that is defined in terms of itself is called *recursive*. C++ allows functions to be recursive.[†] It is important to remember that what C++ provides is merely an attempt to follow the recursive spirit. Not all mathematically recursive functions are efficiently (or correctly) implemented by C++'s simulation of recursion. The idea is that the recursive function f ought to be expressible in only a few lines, just like a nonrecursive function. Figure 1.2 shows the recursive implementation of f.

Lines 4 and 5 handle what is known as the *base case*, that is, the value for which the function is directly known without resorting to recursion. Just as declaring $f(x) = 2f(x - 1) + x^2$ is meaningless, mathematically, without including the fact that $f(0) = 0$, the recursive C++ function doesn't make sense without a base case. Line 7 makes the recursive call.

There are several important and possibly confusing points about recursion. A common question is: Isn't this just circular logic? The answer is that although we are defining a function in terms of itself, we are not defining a particular instance of the function in terms of itself. In other words, evaluating $f(5)$ by computing $f(5)$ would be circular. Evaluating $f(5)$ by computing $f(4)$ is not circular—unless, of course, $f(4)$ is evaluated by eventually computing $f(5)$. The two most important issues are probably the *how* and *why* questions. In Chapter 3, the *how* and *why* issues are formally resolved. We will give an incomplete description here.

[†] Using recursion for numerical calculations is usually a bad idea. We have done so to illustrate the basic points.

It turns out that recursive calls are handled no differently from any others. If f is called with the value of 4, then line 7 requires the computation of $2 * f(3) + 4 * 4$. Thus, a call is made to compute $f(3)$. This requires the computation of $2 * f(2) + 3 * 3$. Therefore, another call is made to compute $f(2)$. This means that $2 * f(1) + 2 * 2$ must be evaluated. To do so, $f(1)$ is computed as $2 * f(0) + 1 * 1$. Now, $f(0)$ must be evaluated. Since this is a base case, we know a priori that $f(0) = 0$. This enables the completion of the calculation for $f(1)$, which is now seen to be 1. Then $f(2)$, $f(3)$, and finally $f(4)$ can be determined. All the bookkeeping needed to keep track of pending function calls (those started but waiting for a recursive call to complete), along with their variables, is done by the computer automatically. An important point, however, is that recursive calls will keep on being made until a base case is reached. For instance, an attempt to evaluate $f(-1)$ will result in calls to $f(-2)$, $f(-3)$, and so on. Since this will never get to a base case, the program won't be able to compute the answer (which is undefined anyway). Occasionally, a much more subtle error is made, which is exhibited in Figure 1.3. The error in the program in Figure 1.3 is that $Bad(1)$ is defined, by line 7, to be $Bad(1)$. Obviously, this doesn't give any clue as to what $Bad(1)$ actually is. The computer will thus repeatedly make calls to $Bad(1)$ in an attempt to resolve its values. Eventually, its bookkeeping system will run out of space, and the program will crash. Generally, we would say that this function doesn't work for one special case but is correct otherwise. This isn't true here, since $Bad(2)$ calls $Bad(1)$. Thus, $Bad(2)$ cannot be evaluated either. Furthermore, $Bad(3)$, $Bad(4)$, and $Bad(5)$ all make calls to $Bad(2)$. Since $Bad(2)$ is unevaluable, none of these values are either. In fact, this program doesn't work for any value of n, except 0. With recursive programs, there is no such thing as a "special case."

These considerations lead to the first two fundamental rules of recursion:

1. *Base cases.* You must always have some base cases, which can be solved without recursion.

2. *Making progress.* For the cases that are to be solved recursively, the recursive call must always be to a case that makes progress toward a base case.

Throughout this book, we will use recursion to solve problems. As an example of a nonmathematical use, consider a large dictionary. Words in dictionaries are defined in terms of other words. When we look up a word, we might not always understand the definition, so we might have to look up words in the definition.

Figure 1.3   A nonterminating recursive program

```
/* 1*/    int
/* 2*/    Bad( const int N )
/* 3*/    {
/* 4*/        if( N == 0 )
/* 5*/            return 0;
/* 6*/        else
/* 7*/            return Bad( N / 3 + 1 ) + N - 1;
/* 8*/    }
```

Likewise, we might not understand some of those, so we might have to continue this search for a while. As the dictionary is finite, eventually either we will come to a point where we understand all of the words in some definition (and thus understand that definition and retrace our path through the other definitions), or we will find that the definitions are circular and we are stuck, or that some word we need to understand a definition is not in the dictionary.

Our recursive strategy to understand words is as follows: If we know the meaning of a word, then we are done; otherwise, we look the word up in the dictionary. If we understand all the words in the definition, we are done; otherwise, we figure out what the definition means by *recursively* looking up the words we don't know. This procedure will terminate if the dictionary is well defined but can loop indefinitely if a word is either not defined or circularly defined.

Printing Out Numbers

Suppose we have a positive integer, N, that we wish to print out. Our routine will have the heading *Print_Out(N)*. Assume that the only I/O routines available will take a single-digit number and output it to the terminal. We will call this routine *Print_Digit*; for example, *Print_Digit*(4) will output a 4 to the terminal.

Recursion provides a very clean solution to this problem. To print out 76234, we need to first print out 7623 and then print out 4. The second step is easily accomplished with the statement *Print_Digit*($N\%10$), but the first doesn't seem any simpler than the original problem. Indeed it is virtually the same problem, so we can solve it recursively with the statement *Print_Out*($N/10$).

This tells us how to solve the general problem, but we still need to make sure that the program doesn't loop indefinitely. Since we haven't defined a base case yet, it is clear that we still have something to do. Our base case will be *Print_Digit(N)* if $0 \le N < 10$. Now *Print_Out(N)* is defined for every positive number from 0 to 9, and larger numbers are defined in terms of a smaller positive number. Thus, there is no cycle. The entire procedure is shown in Figure 1.4.

We have made no effort to do this efficiently. We could have avoided using the % operator (which is very expensive) because $N\%10 \equiv N - \lfloor N/10 \rfloor * 10.$[†]

Recursion and Induction

Let us prove (somewhat) rigorously that the recursive number-printing program works. To do so, we'll use a proof by induction.

THEOREM 1.4.

The recursive number-printing algorithm is correct for $N \ge 0$.

PROOF (BY INDUCTION ON THE NUMBER OF DIGITS IN N):

First, if N has one digit, then the program is trivially correct, since it merely makes a call to *Print_Digit*. Assume then that *Print_Out* works for all numbers of k or fewer digits. A number of $k + 1$ digits is expressed by its first

---

[†] $\lfloor x \rfloor$ is the largest integer that is less than or equal to x.

```
/* 1*/    void
/* 2*/    Print_Out( const unsigned int N )
/* 3*/    {
/* 4*/        if( N < 10 )
/* 5*/            Print_Digit( N );
/* 6*/        else
/* 7*/        {
/* 8*/            Print_Out( N / 10 );
/* 9*/            Print_Digit( N % 10 );
/*10*/        }
/*11*/    }
```

Figure 1.4   Recursive routine to print an integer

k digits followed by its least significant digit. But the number formed by the first k digits is exactly $\lfloor N/10 \rfloor$, which, by the inductive hypothesis, is correctly printed, and the last digit is $N\%10$, so the program prints out any $(k + 1)$-digit number correctly. Thus, by induction, all numbers are correctly printed.

This proof probably seems a little strange in that it is virtually identical to the algorithm description. It illustrates that in designing a recursive program, all smaller instances of the same problem (that are on the path to a base case) may be *assumed* to work correctly. The recursive program needs only to combine solutions to smaller problems, which are "magically" obtained by recursion, into a solution for the current problem. The mathematical justification for this is proof by induction. This gives the third rule of recursion:

   3. *Design rule*. Assume that all the recursive calls work.

This rule is important because it means that when designing recursive programs, you generally don't need to know the details of the bookkeeping arrangements, and you don't have to try to trace through the myriad of recursive calls. Frequently, it is extremely difficult to track down the actual sequence of recursive calls. Of course, in many cases this is an indication of a good use of recursion, since the computer is being allowed to work out the complicated details.

The main problem with recursion is the hidden bookkeeping costs. Although these costs are almost always justifiable, because recursive programs not only simplify the algorithm design but also tend to give cleaner code, recursion should never be used as a substitute for a simple *for* loop. We'll discuss the overhead involved in recursion in more detail in Section 3.3.

When writing recursive routines, it is crucial to keep in mind the four basic rules of recursion:

   1. *Base cases*. You must always have some base cases, which can be solved without recursion.

   2. *Making progress*. For the cases that are to be solved recursively, the recursive call must always be to a case that makes progress toward a base case.

3. *Design rule*. Assume that all the recursive calls work.

4. *Compound interest rule*. Never duplicate work by solving the same instance of a problem in separate recursive calls.

The fourth rule, which will be justified (along with its nickname) in later sections, is the reason that it is generally a bad idea to use recursion to evaluate simple mathematical functions, such as the Fibonacci numbers. As long as you keep these rules in mind, recursive programming should be straightforward.

1.4. C++ at a Glance

C++ is a language developed at Bell Labs by Bjarne Stroustrup to support modern object-oriented programming constructs, while at the same time retaining the look of an already existing, and quite popular, language. Though C++ has many features that make it a much less dangerous language than C, it should not be thought of as C with bells and whistles. Moreover, some of the advanced features interact in very unusual ways, making mastery of C++ a challenging experience.

Though a complete discussion of C++ is beyond the scope of this book, it is possible to look at some of the important parts of C++.

- Unlike C, C++ is a *strongly typed language*: Every object must belong to a type, and an object of one type cannot be assigned to or compared with one of another type except by a well-defined type conversion. Indeed, function prototypes, which are now found in ANSI C, were in C++ first.

- Call by reference is supported in C++. This removes some of the difficult pointer code sometimes found in C code. A direct result is that any large structure should be passed by reference.

- The compiler directive *const* can be used in many places to imply that some object is unalterable. This is manifested in three ways. First, large structures can safely be passed as *const* and by reference, rather than using a pointer. Second, even integers that are passed by value can be specified as *const* to prevent accidental modification. For instance, $if(N = 0)$, which is the typical C mistake of using assignment instead of equality, can be detected by the compiler if N is a *const*. Third, the use of *#define* for symbolic constants is considered bad practice in C++; use *const* variables instead.

- Preprocessor macros are obsolete in C++, because *inline* functions are supported.

- I/O has been revamped in C++ to use *streams*. Though *printf* and *scanf* work, it's a bad idea to use them.

- *malloc* and *free* have been replaced by *new* and *delete*. Again, though *malloc* and *free* are still present, it's a bad idea to use them.

The features just described can at best be considered as syntactic improvements to C. The major difference is support for modern programming constructs.

Before we describe what C++ provides, let us consider a few examples. When we work with any of the basic data types in a language, such as an integer, character, or floating point number, we take certain things for granted.

First, we can declare new objects (i.e., what we think of as variables), possibly with initialization. We can always copy or test for equality, and we expect to be able to output these variables. We also know that when the function in which they are declared terminates, the variable (unless static) also goes away. We also expect that, depending on the variable, other operations are available, and that the compiler won't let us mix up objects of different types.

Finally, we view the object as an *atomic unit* that the user ought not to dissect. Most of us wouldn't even think about fiddling around with the bits that represent a floating point number and would find it completely ridiculous to try to double some floating point object by altering its internal representation ourselves. This atomicity principle is known as *information hiding*. The user gets the object but does not get access to the parts of the object. If this principle is adhered to, then each object comes with the warning "Do not open—no user-servicable parts inside."

Following are some of the specific constructs that C++ offers.

Classes

In C++, the basic structure has been extended in two major ways. We normally consider a structure to be a collection of data fields. Because we would like to hide these fields from the user, we can specify that they are stored in a *private* section. Second, these structures can also declare functions as field members. Some of these functions would describe how an instance of the structure is initialized, how it is destroyed, and how assignment and equality tests are to be performed. Other functions would be specific to the particular structure.

A class is the same as structure except that, by default, all fields are private. Because these functions are field members of the class, they are accessed by the structure member operator (.), just like any other structure member.

Overloading

Functions can have the same names, as long as the profiles (which include parameter types and number) are not identical. As a special case, the usual operators can be defined to have different meanings, depending on the type of the operands. In particular, we expect that "=" and "==" should be overloaded for each class that is created, so that the syntax for copying and comparing any two objects should be the same as if they were integers. When a function call is made, the compiler determines (if possible) which of the identically named functions is being referred to. Sometimes this decision can be deferred from compilation to run time. For example, if we have two pointers to an object and attempt to compare the dereferenced values with a "<" operator, we can arrange that the choice of which "<" operator to apply be determined at run time and depend on what types the two pointers are pointing at. This is a rather complex feature of C++ that we won't get into.

Templates

This relatively new feature of C++ allows us to write a class for an arbitrary type and specify a type when each object is declared. This allows a much more general form than the conventional use of the *typedef* facility. There are two major problems with templates. First, the syntax, as we'll see, can be a bit overwhelming. More seriously, because they are so new, many compilers don't support them, and many compilers that claim to support them don't do a complete job. If your compiler is having problems with templates, it is easy enough to remove them from the examples, but as we'll see, it's not so easy to go the other way. Thus, when reasonable, this book always uses templates, even if it slightly obscures some of the code.

Inheritance

Inheritance is the object-oriented mechanism used to derive new (sub)types from existing types. The idea is that usually the new type will have many of the same routines (perhaps completely unchanged) as the original type, so it's silly to rewrite them all. With inheritance new types inherit all of the properties of the original and can then replace or augment these properties. We'll discuss this more when appropriate.

Though classes, templates, and overloading will be widely used in the text, inheritance will be used sparingly. In the following sections we will examine two classes that illustrate many of these features. The first of these is a class to handle strings, which are not basic types in C and C++. The second is a class to handle complex numbers.

1.4.1.   A String Class

Our first example is a class that supports string operations. In C this is typically done by using a null-terminated array of characters and the well-defined routines in $< string.h >$, such as *strcmp* and *strcpy*, which operate on pointers to characters. These routines are also available in C++.

This C-style implementation has several limitations. First, copying and comparing strings looks different from copying and comparing integers. Indeed, if the " = " and " = = " operators are used, they mean something quite different from copy and compare, generally leading to errors. This can be fixed by overloading the comparison and assignment operators.

Second, there is a storage issue. When a string is dynamically allocated (rather than using a predetermined array size), the user has to remember to *free* the memory when the string is no longer needed. If the string goes out of scope (i.e., it's a local variable, and the function it's in returns) and the user has not performed a *free*, the memory is gone forever. This leakage of memory can accumulate after many calls.

Another severe limitation is error handling. If the target of *strcpy* is not pointing to a sufficiently large array, disaster will strike silently. An array index out of bounds is also silent, so assigning a value to, for instance, $S[10000]$ undoubtedly corrupts another variable. At the very least, out-of-bounds array accesses should generate a run time warning.

A more subtle problem is a lack of safety. If we have a string

```
char *S = strdup("Hello");
```

we expect

```
S[0] = 'J';
```

to alter S. However,

```
char *T = S;
T[0] = 'M';
```

also alters S, without S knowing about it. We'd like to disallow that too.

The string class consists of two parts. The first part, which defines the class *String* and would typically be placed in a file named $< string.hh >$, is shown in Figure 1.5.

Lines 4 and 5 declare the two basic parts of a *String,* namely the array and the size of the array. The array is represented in the typical C fashion by using a pointer. Because these fields are in a *private* section, they are inaccessible except to functions listed in the class. In a class, all fields are private by default, but it is a good visual reminder to restate it. Actually, that's the only difference between a class and a structure.

The routine *Get_Buffer,* declared at line 6 and shown in Figure 1.6, allocates memory (including space for a null terminator) and sets *Buffer* to point at it. The *inline* keyword is a suggestion to the compiler that the overhead of a function call should be avoided by using a safe inline macro expansion. Although the compiler is free to ignore the advice, in many cases it will inline code that is not too long. The expansion is guaranteed to be semantically equivalent to the function call, which is much difference from what you get with a preprocessor macro expansion.

Note that since it is also declared in a private section, *Get_Buffer* is local to the class and cannot be called, except by class functions. The class specification generally lists only the prototypes for the functions, reserving the actual implementation for later. In cases where an implementation is trivial, it is sometimes provided in the class specification. When this is done, the *inline* keyword is implicit.

The *public* part of the class lists operations that may be applied to an object (or objects) of type *String. public* and *private* may be used more than once in a class, as we've seen.

The first group of functions consists of *constructors.* Constructors have three main purposes. First, they specify how an object is declared. Second, they provide a method for performing type conversion. Third, a special constructor, known as the *copy constructor,* is invoked to copy an object when an object is passed by value. Our copy constructor is at line 10; this is not the same as a copy by the " = " operator.

```
/* 1*/    class String
/* 2*/    {
/* 3*/      private:
/* 4*/        unsigned int Buffer_Len;
/* 5*/        char *Buffer;

/* 6*/        inline void Get_Buffer( const unsigned int Max_Length );

/* 7*/      public:
/* 8*/        // Constructors.
/* 9*/        String ( const char * Value = NULL );
/*10*/        String ( const String & Value );

/*11*/        // Destructor.
/*12*/        ~String ( ) { delete [ ] Buffer; }

/*13*/        // Assignment operator.
/*14*/        const String & operator = ( const String & Value );
/*15*/
/*16*/        // Get a single character.
/*17*/        char & operator [ ] ( unsigned int Index ) const;

/*18*/        // Type cast to char *.
/*19*/        operator const char * const ( ) const { return Buffer; }

/*20*/        // Get the length.
/*21*/        unsigned int Length ( ) { return strlen( Buffer ); }

/*22*/      private:
/*23*/        // Friends.
/*24*/        friend int operator ==
/*25*/                ( const String & Lhs, const String & Rhs );
/*26*/        friend int operator !=
/*27*/                ( const String & Lhs, const String & Rhs );
/*28*/        friend int operator <
/*29*/                ( const String & Lhs, const String & Rhs );
/*30*/        friend int operator >
/*31*/                ( const String & Lhs, const String & Rhs );
/*32*/    };
```

Figure 1.5   String class specification

```
/* 1*/    inline void String::Get_Buffer( const unsigned int Max_Length )
/* 2*/    {
/* 3*/        Buffer_Len = Max_Length + 1;
/* 4*/        Buffer = new char [ Buffer_Len ];
/* 5*/        if( !Buffer )
/* 6*/            Error( "Out of space" );
/* 7*/    }

/* 8*/    String::String( const char * Value )
/* 9*/    {
/*10*/        if( Value == NULL )    // Use "" if Value is NULL.
/*11*/        {
/*12*/            Get_Buffer( 0 );
/*13*/            Buffer[ 0 ] = '\0';
/*14*/        }
/*15*/        else
/*16*/        {
/*17*/            Get_Buffer( strlen( Value ) );
/*18*/            for( int i = 0; i < Buffer_Len; i++ )
/*19*/                Buffer[ i ] = Value[ i ];
/*20*/        }
/*21*/    }

/*22*/    String::String( const String & Value )
/*23*/    {
/*24*/        Get_Buffer( strlen( Value.Buffer ) );
/*25*/        for( int i = 0; i < Buffer_Len; i++ )
/*26*/            Buffer[ i ] = Value.Buffer[ i ];
/*27*/    }

/*28*/    const String & String::operator = ( const String & Value )
/*29*/    {
/*30*/        const int Len = strlen( Value.Buffer );

/*31*/        if( this != &Value )    // Don't copy to yourself.
/*32*/        {
/*33*/            if( Len >= Buffer_Len )
/*34*/            {
/*35*/                delete [ ] Buffer;
/*36*/                Get_Buffer( Len );
/*37*/            }

/*39*/            for( int i = 0; i < Len; i++ )
/*40*/                Buffer[ i ] = Value.Buffer[ i ];
/*41*/            Buffer[ i ] = '\0';
/*42*/        }

/*43*/        return *this;
/*44*/    }
```

Figure 1.6 Implementation of String class

```
/*45*/   inline int operator == ( const String & Lhs, const String & Rhs )
/*46*/   {
/*47*/        return strcmp( Lhs.Buffer, Rhs.Buffer ) == 0;
/*48*/   }

/*49*/   inline int operator != ( const String & Lhs, const String & Rhs )
/*50*/   {
/*51*/        return strcmp( Lhs.Buffer, Rhs.Buffer ) != 0;
/*52*/   }

/*53*/   inline int operator < ( const String & Lhs, const String & Rhs )
/*54*/   {
/*55*/        return strcmp( Lhs.Buffer, Rhs.Buffer ) < 0;
/*56*/   }

/*57*/   inline int operator > ( const String & Lhs, const String & Rhs )
/*58*/   {
/*59*/        return strcmp( Lhs.Buffer, Rhs.Buffer ) > 0;
/*60*/   }

/*61*/   char & String::operator [ ] ( unsigned int Index ) const
/*62*/   {
/*63*/        if( Index > strlen( Buffer ) )
/*64*/            cerr << "Warning: out of bounds string access" << endl;
/*65*/        return Buffer[ Index ];
/*66*/   }
```

Figure 1.6   *(Continued)*

Line 9 says that one can declare a *String* by supplying a C-style string, and that if one is not supplied, the *NULL* C-style string will be used as a default. This is an example of *default parameter values*. The syntax would be

```
String X;
```

(Warning: Do not say *String X( )*, which has a different meaning.) C++ requires only a type in the parameter list for prototypes, but leaving out a name could be confusing.

As an example of the type-conversion use of line 9, the statement

```
Y = "test";
```

by the class user, where *Y* is a previously declared *String*, makes sense (assuming we've not disabled the " = " function for *String*), because line 9 allows the conversion of a *char*∗ to a *String*. Then a *String-to-String* copy can be performed by the " = " member function of *Y*. By the way, a type-cast in the other direction is specified at line 19. Note that the implementation of that type-cast is so trivial that it is given in the class specification.

Also notice that objects are passed by reference, using the &, instead of by value. For large objects this is important, because call by value implicitly performs a copy (using the semantics of the copy constructor at line 10), which for large structures could be expensive. One might even put a warning message in the copy constructor, to be displayed if a large object is being copied, so that, at least at run time, the program can let the designer know that a needed call by reference was omitted.

Before we continue, let us examine the two uses of *const* that we've just seen. At lines 9 and 10, the parameter is passed as a *const*. This means that the two constructors cannot alter it. This is no big deal, since we are designing the constructors ourselves, and is just meant to have the compiler warn us if perhaps we use " = " instead of " = = ". At line 19, we have a more significant use of *const*. Here we are providing direct access to an internal class field, but although we are granting viewing privileges, we still don't want to allow anybody to alter this field. Thus the return type is *const char**. The *const* here means that the data that is being pointed to cannot be modified, thus preserving the integrity of the internal *Buffer*.

Line 12 declares the *destructor* function for the class *String*. The destructor function is called automatically when the block in which a *String* is declared terminates. This is similar to a local declared integer going away when a function returns. The typical use of a destructor function is to deallocate any memory allocated by a constructor. Thus the user is freed to some extent of the burden of memory management. In our case, the *Buffer* array is freed by a call to *delete*. When an array is deallocated, the brackets must follow the *delete* reserved word; otherwise you wind up freeing only one array element.

Line 21 is typical of class functions. The function always implicitly refers to the object as an unlisted parameter. Thus, the call *Y.Length( )* would return 4. The *Length* function merely makes a call to the standard *strlen* routine.

Line 17 overloads the [ ] operator in the normal fashion, so that *Y[2]* has the value *'s'*. The index is passed as a parameter. This function is declared to return *char&* instead of just *char*. This signifies that a reference is returned instead of a value. Thus

```
Y[2] = 'n';
```

will change the value of the string to *"tent"*. Note that the compiler will complain if [ ] returns just a *char*, because the result cannot be an *lvalue* (i.e., something that appears on the left-hand side of an assignment). The *const* at the end signifies that this operator is a *constant member* function: It cannot change the field members of the object it is operating on. This function is implemented in lines 61 to 66 of Figure 1.6. (Line 64 sends an error message to the standard error stream; we'll discuss streams later).

The only other public member function is the assignment operator " = ". By default, what you get is a member-by-member copy. This is clearly the wrong way to go if any member is a pointer, because then a copy is made of the pointer, not of the data being pointed at. This results in all sorts of chaos, because two *String* objects will be sharing the same *Buffer* rather than having their own. The program may well crash, because when the first string goes out of scope, the *Buffer* array will be freed by *delete[ ]*, and when the second string goes out of scope, an attempt will be made to free an already deleted array.

Thus, one is well advised to write the assignment operator for a class. Because the operator "=" is a member function, the first operand (i.e., the one on the left) need not be specified; it is the current object. Thus the statement

```
S = T;
```

applies the = operator to object S, using T, as *Value: S.operator=(T)*. Several subtle points about assignment operators are worth discussing. First, since we'd like

```
A = B = C;
```

to make sense for strings, just as it does the integers, the assignment operator shouldn't return a *void*, but rather something of type *String*. But we don't want to do this by copying, so we use a reference for both the parameter and return value of the operator "=". On the other hand, once we return a reference, statements such as

```
(A = B) = C;
```

start to make sense, so we return a *const* reference to disallow that possibility.

Another subtle point, which isn't terribly important here but crops up a lot, is that the case

```
A = A;
```

needs to be handled correctly. A strategy that is always correct is to make it a no-op. In Figure 1.6, the assignment operation is implemented on lines 28 to 44. The reserved word *this* always points at the current object and is unmodifiable. Thus, **this* is the current object, so after the copy is complete, it is returned at line 43. By comparing *this* with the address of *Value*, we can make sure that we don't copy to ourselves.

Notice that in the implementation the member routine names are preceded by the class name and two colons. The two colons are known as the *scope resolution qualifier*.

The remaining routines are the equality and relational operators. We would like to allow both $S == "mark"$ and $"mark" == S$. As a consequence, "==" cannot be a member function, because the first parameter (the left-hand side) is implicitly a *String* object, so, since "mark" is not a *String*, there is no equality operator defined. On the other hand, if "==" is a "normal" function, both forms are acceptable, because of the automatic type conversion from *char** to *String*, specified by the constructor at line 9.

Thus, we make these operators nonmember functions. These are specified at lines 22 to 31 in the class specification and implemented in lines 45 to 60 of Figure 1.6. These are not member functions, so when they are implemented, no class name and scope resolution is required. Notice that in the implementation these routines refer to the *Buffer* field. Since the *Buffer* field is private, this isn't normally allowable, so the class grants permission to these functions to access the private section by declaring that they are *friends* of the class. This must be done in the class specification. This isn't a violation of information hiding, because the class is in complete control of deciding who is granted access.

The implementation file would typically be placed in a file named *string.C,* which would *#include* the specification file *string.hh.* Many other extensions are recognized for C++ programs, including *c++, cc, cxx, c,* and *cpp.* Some compilers will require certain extensions if you use certain features. Our Borland compiler requires *.cpp* extensions if < *iostream.h* > is used.

1.4.2. A Complex Number Class

Our second example is a class to manipulate complex numbers. Our package will define a new type, *Complex,* as well as the operations that can be performed on this type.

Recall that a complex number contains a real part and an imaginary part. It is reasonable to assume that these are floating point types, though it's not obvious whether the number should be *float, double,* or perhaps a user-defined type that has more significant digits. Thus, we'll use a type *Real,* which presumably represents the actual type. The limitation of this approach is that all complex numbers must use the same type of floating point number; if this is a problem, then the newly introduced template facility should be used. Templates are discussed in Chapter 3.

The class specification, shown in Figure 1.7, contains little that is new. The private section contains the real and imaginary parts of the complex numbers. These are inaccessible to the users, so lines 19 and 20 provide functions that can access them. Of course, even though this allows the user to examine the parts of the imaginary number, the parts cannot be changed, since no routine is provided for that.

The constructors allow us to declare a complex number. By default, a new complex number is zero. Supplying one parameter declares the real part and sets the imaginary part to zero. Supplying two parameters initializes the complex number. The destructor does nothing, since no memory is allocated by the constructors. The member operators are the assignment and the increment.

Figure 1.8 shows the implementation of these functions.

Lines 23 to 34 in Figure 1.7 show functions that are not member functions of the class. They include an output function (line 23) and normal mathematical operators.

An interesting innovation of C++ is the use of *streams* for output. For terminal I/O, the file < *iostream.h* > needs to be included. Note that this replaces the older < *stream.h* >. An output stream is declared to be of type *ostream* (input streams use *istream*); objects are tossed into the output streams by use of the "<<" operator (input streams use ">>"). Since the "<<" operator evaluates to (i.e., returns) the new state of the stream, and "<<" associates from right to left, many objects can be listed on one line, as line 23 in Figure 1.8 shows. Lines 21 to 25 in Figure 1.8 show that to place a complex number (passed by reference) onto an output stream, also passed by reference, one just puts the appropriate pieces on the stream. As mentioned above, the new state of the stream must be returned by "<<". This is done by line 24 and by the fact that line 21 declares that the returned value is by reference.

```
/* 1*/    #include <iostream.h>

/* 2*/    class Complex
/* 3*/    {
/* 4*/       private:
/* 5*/          Real Real_Part;
/* 6*/          Real Imag_Part;

/* 7*/       public:
/* 8*/          // Constructors.
/* 9*/          Complex( Real R_Part = 0.0, Real I_Part = 0.0 ) :
/*10*/                   Real_Part( R_Part ), Imag_Part( I_Part ) { }
/*11*/          Complex( const Complex & Value );

/*12*/          // Destructor.
/*13*/          ~Complex( ) { }
/*14*/
/*15*/          // Assignments.
/*16*/          const Complex & operator =  ( const Complex & Value );
/*17*/          const Complex & operator += ( const Complex & Value );

/*18*/          // Accessors.
/*19*/          Real Get_Real( ) const { return Real_Part; }
/*20*/          Real Get_Imag( ) const { return Imag_Part; }

/*21*/          // Nonmember friends.
/*22*/       private:
/*23*/          friend ostream & operator <<
/*24*/                   ( ostream & Out, const Complex & Value );
/*25*/          friend Complex operator *
/*26*/                   ( const Complex & A, const Complex & B );
/*27*/          friend Complex operator /
/*28*/                   ( const Complex & A, const Complex & B );
/*29*/          friend Complex operator +
/*30*/                   ( const Complex & A, const Complex & B );
/*31*/          friend Complex operator -
/*32*/                   ( const Complex & A, const Complex & B );
/*33*/          friend Complex operator -
/*34*/                   ( const Complex & A );
/*35*/    };
```

Figure 1.7   Complex class specification

Two output streams are normally associated with a program; *cout* is for standard output, and *cerr* is for error messages. Figure 1.9 shows how output is performed. Note that *endl* is used to output the newline character. At line 10, a complex number is output by a call to the operator "<<", defined for complex numbers. Figure 1.9 also illustrates how operator overloading makes operations on complex numbers

```
/* 1*/    Complex::Complex( const Complex & Value )
/* 2*/    {
/* 3*/        Real_Part = Value.Real_Part;
/* 4*/        Imag_Part = Value.Imag_Part;
/* 5*/    }

/* 6*/    const Complex & Complex::operator = ( const Complex & Value )
/* 7*/    {
/* 8*/        if( this != &Value )
/* 9*/        {
/*10*/            Real_Part = Value.Real_Part;
/*11*/            Imag_Part = Value.Imag_Part;
/*12*/        }
/*13*/        return *this;
/*14*/    }

/*15*/    const Complex & Complex::operator += ( const Complex & Value )
/*16*/    {
/*17*/        Real_Part += Value.Real_Part;
/*18*/        Imag_Part += Value.Imag_Part;

/*19*/        return *this;
/*20*/    }

/*21*/    ostream & operator << ( ostream & Out, const Complex & Value )
/*22*/    {
/*23*/        Out << Value.Real_Part << " + " << Value.Imag_Part << "i";
/*24*/        return Out;
/*25*/    }

/*26*/    Complex operator + ( const Complex & A, const Complex & B )
/*27*/    {
/*28*/        return Complex( A.Real_Part + B.Real_Part,
/*29*/                        A.Imag_Part + B.Imag_Part );
/*30*/    }

/*31*/    Complex operator - ( const Complex & A, const Complex & B )
/*32*/    {
/*33*/        return Complex( A.Real_Part - B.Real_Part,
/*34*/                        A.Imag_Part - B.Imag_Part );
/*35*/    }

/*36*/    Complex operator - ( const Complex & A )
/*37*/    {
/*38*/        return Complex( -A.Real_Part, -A.Imag_Part );
/*39*/    }

/*40*/    Complex operator * ( const Complex & A, const Complex & B )
/*41*/    {
/*42*/        return Complex(
```

Figure 1.8 Implementation of Complex class

```
/*43*/              A.Real_Part * B.Real_Part - A.Imag_Part * B.Imag_Part,
/*44*/              A.Real_Part * B.Imag_Part + A.Imag_Part * B.Real_Part );
/*45*/    }

/*46*/    // Assumes that B is nonzero.

/*47*/    Complex operator / ( const Complex & A, const Complex & B )
/*48*/    {
/*49*/        Real Modulus =
/*50*/            B.Real_Part * B.Real_Part + B.Imag_Part * B.Imag_Part;
/*51*/        Complex Temp( B.Real_Part / Modulus, -B.Imag_Part / Modulus );

/*52*/        return A * Temp;
/*53*/    }
```

Figure 1.8 *(Continued)*

```
/* 1*/ // Some include files: only <iostream.h> is actually needed.
/* 2*/ #include <iostream.h>
/* 3*/ #include <stdlib.h>
/* 4*/ #include <math.h>

/* 5*/ main( )
/* 6*/ {
/* 7*/     Complex C1( 6.0, 4.0 ), C2( 8.0, 2.0 );
/* 8*/     Complex C3( 1.0, 1.0 ), C4( 3.0, 2.0 ), C5;

/* 9*/     C5 = -( C1 * C2 ) / ( C3 * C4 );
/*10*/     cout << C5 << endl;

/*11*/     C5 += 3;
/*12*/     cout << C5 << endl;

/*13*/     C5 += Complex( 2, 5 ); // 2 + 5i is added to C5.
/*14*/     cout << C5 << endl;

/*15*/     C5 += C1 += C2; // C1 is adjusted by C2; C5 by new C1.
/*16*/     cout << C1 << endl << C5 << endl;

/*17*/     C5 += ( 2, 5 ); // This produces an unintended result.
/*18*/     cout << C5 << endl;

/*19*/     return 0;
/*20*/ }
```

Figure 1.9 Program illustrating the Complex class and
stream I/O

look just like operations on any other predefined types. Five complex numbers (four of which are explicitly initialized) are declared at lines 7 and 8. Line 9 evaluates a simple combination of them, and the result is output at line 10. Line 11 performs an increment operation on the complex number $C5$. This requires that the right-hand side represent a complex number. Although it represents only a single number, the constructor provides an implicit type conversion. Thus, the right-hand side is interpreted as $3 + 0i$, and the statement succeeds. Line 13 adds $2 + 5i$ to $C5$. Line 15 shows how a chain of assignment statements can be processed. Line 17 shows that unexpected results can still occur; the right-hand side evaluates to 5, because the comma is the C (and C++) comma operator, instead of the intended $2 + 5i$. The 5 is then converted to $5 + 0i$ and added to $C5$. This illustrates that although many of C's pitfalls have been eliminated or at least made significantly less virulent, many traps still exist. We've also listed some of the typical include files, though only the first is needed here.

Although this summary only scratches the surface of C++ features, many language features that we will use in the text are covered here. More details on the language can be found in the references.

Summary

This chapter sets the stage for the rest of the book. The time taken by an algorithm confronted with large amounts of input will be an important criterion for deciding if it is a good algorithm. (Of course, correctness is most important.) Speed is relative. What is fast for one problem on one machine might be slow for another problem or a different machine. We will begin to address these issues in the next chapter and will use the mathematics discussed here to establish a formal model.

Exercises

1.1 Write a program to solve the selection problem. Let $k = n/2$. Draw a table showing the running time of your program for various values of n.

1.2 Write a program to solve the word puzzle problem.

1.3 Write a procedure to output an arbitrary real number (which might be negative) using only $Print\_Digit$ for I/O.

1.4 C++ allows statements of the form

```
#include filename
```

which reads *filename* and inserts its contents in place of the *include* statement. *Include* statements may be nested; in other words, the file *filename* may itself contain an *include* statement, but, obviously, a file can't include itself in any chain. Write a program that reads in a file and outputs the file as modified by the *include* statements.

1.5 Prove the following formulas:

a. $\log x < x$　for all $x > 0$

b. $\log (a^b) = b \log a$

1.6 Evaluate the following sums:

a. $\displaystyle\sum_{i=0}^{\infty} \frac{1}{4^i}$

b. $\displaystyle\sum_{i=0}^{\infty} \frac{i}{4^i}$

*c. $\displaystyle\sum_{i=0}^{\infty} \frac{i^2}{4^i}$

**d. $\displaystyle\sum_{i=0}^{\infty} \frac{i^n}{4^i}$

1.7 Estimate

$$\sum_{i=\lfloor n/2 \rfloor}^{n} \frac{1}{i}$$

*1.8 What is $2^{100} \pmod 5$?

1.9 Let F_i be the Fibonacci numbers as defined in Section 1.2. Prove the following:

a. $\displaystyle\sum_{i=1}^{n-2} F_i = F_n - 2.$

b. $F_n < \phi^n$, with $\phi = (1 + \sqrt{5})/2.$

**c. Give a precise closed-form expression for F_n.

1.10 Prove the following formulas:

a. $\displaystyle\sum_{i=1}^{n} (2i - 1) = n^2$

b. $\displaystyle\sum_{i=1}^{n} i^3 = \left(\sum_{i=1}^{n} i \right)^2$

References

There are many good textbooks covering the mathematics reviewed in this chapter. A small subset is [1], [2], [4], [14], [20], and [22]. Reference [14] is specifically geared toward the analysis of algorithms. It is the first volume of a three-volume series that will be cited throughout this text. More advanced material is covered in [10].

Object-oriented programming is discussed in [3] and [5]. C++ reference books include [9], [15], [18], and [21]. [16] is excellent for tips on avoiding C++ trouble spots, and it's hysterical, too. We also assume familiarity with pointers and recursion (the recursion summary in this chapter is meant to be a quick review). We will attempt to provide hints on their use where appropriate throughout the book. Readers not familiar with these should consult [6], [12], [19], or any good intermediate programming textbook.

General programming style is discussed in several books. Some of the classics are [8], [11], and [13].

1. M. O. Albertson and J. P. Hutchinson, *Discrete Mathematics with Algorithms*, John Wiley & Sons, New York, 1988.
2. Z. Bavel, *Math Companion for Computer Science*, Reston Publishing Company, Reston, Va., 1982.
3. G. Booch, *Object-Oriented Design with Applications*, Benjamin/Cummings, Redwood City, Calif., 1991.
4. R. A. Brualdi, *Introductory Combinatorics*, North-Holland, New York, 1977.
5. T. Budd, *An Introduction to Object-Oriented Programming*, Benjamin/Cummings, Redwood City, Calif., 1991.
6. W. H. Burge, *Recursive Programming Techniques*, Addison-Wesley, Reading, Mass., 1975.
7. T. Cargill, *C++ Programming Style*, Addison-Wesley, Reading, Mass., 1992.
8. E. W. Dijkstra, *A Discipline of Programming*, Prentice Hall, Englewood Cliffs, N.J., 1976.
9. M. A. Ellis and B. Stroustrup, *Annotated C++ Reference Manual*, Addison-Wesley, Reading Mass., 1990.
10. R. L. Graham, D. E. Knuth, and O. Patashnik, *Concrete Mathematics*, Addison-Wesley, Reading, Mass., 1989.
11. D. Gries, *The Science of Programming*, Springer-Verlag, New York, 1981.
12. P. Helman and R. Veroff, *Walls and Mirrors: Intermediate Problem Solving and Data Structures*, 2d ed., Benjamin/Cummings Publishing, Menlo Park, Calif., 1988.
13. B. W. Kernighan and P. J. Plauger, *The Elements of Programming Style*, 2d ed., McGraw-Hill, New York, 1978.
14. D. E. Knuth, *The Art of Computer Programming, Vol. 1: Fundamental Algorithms*, 2d ed., Addison-Wesley, Reading, Mass., 1973.
15. S. Lippman, *A C++ Primer*, 2d ed., Addison-Wesley, Reading, Mass., 1991.
16. S. Meyers, *Effective C++*, Addison-Wesley, Reading, Mass., 1992.
17. J. Nissen and P. Wallis, *Portability and Style in Ada*, Cambridge University Press, 1984.
18. I. Pohl, *Object-Oriented Programming Using C++*, Benjamin/Cummings, Redwood City, Calif., 1993.
19. E. Roberts, *Thinking Recursively*, John Wiley & Sons, New York, 1986.
20. F. S. Roberts, *Applied Combinatorics*, Prentice Hall, Englewood Cliffs, N.J., 1984.
21. B. Stroustrup, *The C++ Programming Language*, 2d ed., Addison-Wesley, Reading, Mass., 1991.
22. A. Tucker, *Applied Combinatorics*, 2d ed., John Wiley & Sons, New York, 1984.

CHAPTER 2

Algorithm Analysis

An *algorithm* is a clearly specified set of simple instructions to be followed to solve a problem. Once an algorithm is given for a problem and decided (somehow) to be correct, an important step is to determine how much in the way of resources, such as time or space, the algorithm will require. An algorithm that solves a problem but requires a year is hardly of any use. Likewise, an algorithm that requires a gigabyte of main memory is not (currently) useful on most machines.

In this chapter, we shall discuss

- How to estimate the time required for a program.
- How to reduce the running time of a program from days or years to fractions of a second.
- The results of careless use of recursion.
- Very efficient algorithms to raise a number to a power and to compute the greatest common divisor of two numbers.

2.1. Mathematical Background

The analysis required to estimate the resource use of an algorithm is generally a theoretical issue, and therefore a formal framework is required. We begin with some mathematical definitions.

Throughout the book we will use the following four definitions:

DEFINITION: $T(n) = O(f(n))$ if there are *constants c and n_0* such that $T(n) \le cf(n)$ when $n \ge n_0$.

DEFINITION: $T(n) = \Omega(g(n))$ if there are *constants c and n_0* such that $T(n) \ge cg(n)$ when $n \ge n_0$.

DEFINITION: $T(n) = \Theta(h(n))$ if and only if $T(n) = O(h(n))$ and $T(n) = \Omega(h(n))$.

DEFINITION: $T(n) = o(p(n))$ if $T(n) = O(p(n))$ and $T(n) \neq \Theta(p(n))$.

The idea of these definitions is to establish a relative order among functions. Given two functions, either may be smaller than the other at a given point, so it does not make sense to claim, for instance, $f(n) < g(n)$. Thus, we compare their *relative rates of growth*. When we apply this to the analysis of algorithms, we shall see why this is the important measure.

Although $1,000n$ is larger than n^2 for small values of n, n^2 grows at a faster rate, and thus n^2 will eventually be the larger function. The turning point is $n = 1,000$ in this case. The first definition says that eventually there is some point n_0 past which $c \cdot f(n)$ is always at least as large as $T(n)$, so that if constant factors are ignored, $f(n)$ is at least as big as $T(n)$. In our case, we have $T(n) = 1,000n$, $f(n) = n^2$, $n_0 = 1,000$, and $c = 1$. We could also use $n_0 = 10$ and $c = 100$. Thus, we can say that $1,000n = O(n^2)$ (order n-squared). This notation is known as *Big-Oh* notation. Frequently, instead of saying "order...," one says "Big-Oh...."

If we use the traditional inequality operators to compare growth rates, then the first definition says that the growth rate of $T(n)$ is less than or equal to ($\leq$) that of $f(n)$. The second definition, $T(n) = \Omega(g(n))$ (pronounced "omega"), says that the growth rate of $T(n)$ is greater than or equal to ($\geq$) that of $g(n)$. The third definition, $T(n) = \Theta(h(n))$ (pronounced "theta"), says that the growth rate of $T(n)$ equals ($=$) the growth rate of $h(n)$. The last definition, $T(n) = o(p(n))$ (pronounced "little-oh"), says that the growth rate of $T(n)$ is less than ($<$) the growth rate of $p(n)$. This is different from Big-Oh, because Big-Oh allows the possibility that the growth rates are the same.

To prove that some function $T(n) = O(f(n))$, we usually do not apply these definitions formally but instead use a repertoire of known results. In general, this means that a proof (or determination that the assumption is incorrect) is a very simple calculation and should not involve calculus, except in extraordinary circumstances (not likely to occur in an algorithm analysis).

When we say that $T(n) = O(f(n))$, we are guaranteeing that the function $T(n)$ grows at a rate no faster than $f(n)$; thus $f(n)$ is an *upper bound* on $T(n)$. Since this implies that $f(n) = \Omega(T(n))$, we say that $T(n)$ is a *lower bound* on $f(n)$.

As an example, n^3 grows faster than n^2, so we can say that $n^2 = O(n^3)$ or $n^3 = \Omega(n^2)$. $f(n) = n^2$ and $g(n) = 2n^2$ grow at the same rate, so both $f(n) = O(g(n))$ and $f(n) = \Omega(g(n))$ are true. When two functions grow at the same rate, then the decision whether or not to signify this with $\Theta()$ can depend on the particular context. Intuitively, if $g(n) = 2n^2$, then $g(n) = O(n^4)$, $g(n) = O(n^3)$, and $g(n) = O(n^2)$ are all technically correct, but obviously the last option is the best answer. Writing $g(n) = \Theta(n^2)$ says not only that $g(n) = O(n^2)$, but also that the result is as good (tight) as possible.

The important things to know are

RULE 1:

If $T_1(n) = O(f(n))$ and $T_2(n) = O(g(n))$, then
   (a) $T_1(n) + T_2(n) = max(O(f(n)), O(g(n)))$,
   (b) $T_1(n) * T_2(n) = O(f(n) * g(n))$,

Function	Name
c	Constant
$\log n$	Logarithmic
$\log^2 n$	Log-squared
n	Linear
$n \log n$	
n^2	Quadratic
n^3	Cubic
2^n	Exponential

Figure 2.1 Typical growth rates

RULE 2:

If $T(x)$ is a polynomial of degree n, then $T(x) = \Theta(x^n)$.

RULE 3:

$\log^k n = O(n)$ *for any constant k. This tells us that logarithms grow very slowly.*

To see that rule 1(a) is correct, note that by definition there exist four constants c_1, c_2, n_1, and n_2 such that $T_1(n) \le c_1 f(n)$ for $n \ge n_1$ and $T_2(n) \le c_2 g(n)$ for $n \ge n_2$. Let $n_0 = \max(n_1, n_2)$. Then, for $n \ge n_0$, $T_1(n) \le c_1 f(n)$ and $T_2(n) \le c_2 g(n)$, so that $T_1(n) + T_2(n) \le c_1 f(n) + c_2 g(n)$. Let $c_3 = \max(c_1, c_2)$. Then,

$$T_1(n) + T_2(n) \le c_3 f(n) + c_3 g(n)$$
$$\le c_3(f(n) + g(n))$$
$$\le 2c_3 \max(f(n), g(n))$$
$$\le c \max(f(n), g(n))$$

for $c = 2c_3$ and $n \ge n_0$.

We leave proofs of the other relations given above as exercises for the reader. This information is sufficient to arrange most of the common functions by growth rate (see Figure 2.1).

Several points are in order. First, it is very bad style to include constants or low-order terms inside a Big-Oh. Do not say $T(n) = O(2n^2)$ or $T(n) = O(n^2 + n)$. In both cases, the correct form is $T(n) = O(n^2)$. This means that in any analysis that will require a Big-Oh answer, all sorts of shortcuts are possible. Lower-order terms can generally be ignored, and constants can be thrown away. Considerably less precision is required in these cases.

Secondly, we can always determine the relative growth rates of two functions $f(n)$ and $g(n)$ by computing $\lim_{n \to \infty} f(n)/g(n)$, using L'Hôpital's rule if necessary.[†]

[†]L'Hôpital's rule states that if $\lim_{n \to \infty} f(n) = \infty$ and $\lim_{n \to \infty} g(n) = \infty$, then $\lim_{n \to \infty} f(n)/g(n) = \lim_{n \to \infty} f'(n)/g'(n)$, where $f'(n)$ and $g'(n)$ are the derivatives of $f(n)$ and $g(n)$, respectively.

The limit can have four possible values:

- The limit is 0: This means that $f(n) = o(g(n))$.
- The limit is $c \neq 0$: This means that $f(n) = \Theta(g(n))$.
- The limit is ∞: This means that $g(n) = o(f(n))$.
- The limit oscillates: There is no relation (this will not happen in our context).

Using this method almost always amounts to overkill. Usually the relation between $f(n)$ and $g(n)$ can be derived by simple algebra. For instance, if $f(n) = n \log n$ and $g(n) = n^{1.5}$, then to decide which of $f(n)$ and $g(n)$ grows faster, one really needs to determine which of $\log n$ and $n^{0.5}$ grows faster. This is like determining which of $\log^2 n$ or n grows faster. This is a simple problem, because it is already known that n grows faster than any power of a log. Thus, $g(n)$ grows faster than $f(n)$.

One stylistic note: It is bad to say $f(n) \leq O(g(n))$, because the inequality is implied by the definition. It is wrong to write $f(n) \geq O(g(n))$, which does not make sense.

2.2.   Model

In order to analyze algorithms in a formal framework, we need a model of computation. Our model is basically a normal computer, in which instructions are executed sequentially. Our model has the standard repertoire of simple instructions, such as addition, multiplication, comparison, and assignment, but, unlike real computers, it takes exactly one time unit to do anything (simple). To be reasonable, we will assume that, like a modern computer, our model has fixed size (say 32-bit) integers and that there are no fancy operations, such as matrix inversion or sorting, that clearly cannot be done in one time unit. We also assume infinite memory.

This model clearly has some weaknesses. Obviously, in real life, not all operations take exactly the same time. In particular, in our model one disk read counts the same as an addition, even though the addition is typically several orders of magnitude faster. Also, by assuming infinite memory, we never worry about page faulting, which can be a real problem, especially for efficient algorithms. This can be a major problem in many applications.

2.3.   What to Analyze

The most important resource to analyze is generally the running time. Several factors affect the running time of a program. Some, such as the compiler and computer used, are obviously beyond the scope of any theoretical model, so, although they are important, we cannot deal with them here. The other main factors are the algorithm used and the input to the algorithm.

Typically, the size of the input is the main consideration. We define two functions, $T_{avg}(n)$ and $T_{worst}(n)$, as the average and worst-case running time, respectively, used by an algorithm on input of size n. Clearly, $T_{avg}(n) \leq T_{worst}(n)$. If there is more than one input, these functions may have more than one argument.

We remark that generally the quantity required is the worst-case time, unless otherwise specified. One reason for this is that it provides a bound for all input, including particularly bad input, that an average-case analysis does not provide. The other reason is that average-case bounds are usually much more difficult to compute. In some instances, the definition of "average" can affect the result. (For instance, what is average input for the following problem?)

As an example, in the next section, we shall consider the following problem:

MAXIMUM SUBSEQUENCE SUM PROBLEM:

Given (possibly negative) integers $a_1, a_2, \ldots, a_n$, find the maximum value of $\sum_{k=i}^{j} a_k$. (For convenience, the maximum subsequence sum is 0 if all the integers are negative.)

Example:

For input $-2, 11, -4, 13, -5, -2$, the answer is 20 (a_2 through a_4).

This problem is interesting mainly because there are so many algorithms to solve it, and the performance of these algorithms varies drastically. We will discuss four algorithms to solve this problem. The running time on some computer (the exact computer is unimportant) for these algorithms is given in Figure 2.2.

There are several important things worth noting in this table. For a small amount of input, the algorithms all run in a blink of the eye, so if only a small amount of input is expected, it might be silly to expend a great deal of effort to design a clever algorithm. On the other hand, there is a large market these days for rewriting programs that were written five years ago based on a no-longer-valid assumption of small input size. These programs are now too slow because they used poor algorithms. For large amounts of input, Algorithm 4 is clearly the best choice (although Algorithm 3 is still usable).

Figure 2.2 Running time of several algorithms for maximum subsequence sum (in seconds)

Algorithm		1	2	3	4
Time		$O(n^3)$	$O(n^2)$	$O(n \log n)$	$O(n)$
Input Size	$n = 10$	0.00103	0.00045	0.00066	0.00034
	$n = 100$	0.47015	0.01112	0.00486	0.00063
	$n = 1,000$	448.77	1.1233	0.05843	0.00333
	$n = 10,000$	NA	111.13	0.68631	0.03042
	$n = 100,000$	NA	NA	8.0113	0.29832

Second, the times given do not include the time required to read the input. For Algorithm 4, the time merely to read in the input from a disk is likely to be an order of magnitude larger than the time required to solve the problem. This is typical of many efficient algorithms. Reading the data is generally the bottleneck; once the data are read, the problem can be solved quickly. For inefficient algorithms this is not true, and significant computer resources must be used. Thus it is important that, whenever possible, algorithms be efficient enough not to be the bottleneck of a problem.

Figure 2.3 shows the growth rates of the running times of the four algorithms. Even though this graph encompasses only values of n ranging from 10 to 100, the relative growth rates are still evident. Although the graph for Algorithm 3 seems linear, it is easy to verify that it is not by using a straightedge (or piece of paper). Figure 2.4 shows the performance for larger values. It dramatically illustrates how useless inefficient algorithms are for even moderate amounts of input.

2.4. Running Time Calculations

There are several ways to estimate the running time of a program. The previous table was obtained empirically. If two programs are expected to take similar times, probably the best way to decide which is faster is to code them both up and run them!

Generally, there are several algorithmic ideas, and we would like to eliminate the bad ones early, so an analysis is usually required. Furthermore, the ability to do an analysis usually provides insight into designing efficient algorithms. The analysis also generally pinpoints the bottlenecks, which are worth coding carefully.

Figure 2.3 Plot (n vs. milliseconds) of various maximum subsequence sum algorithms

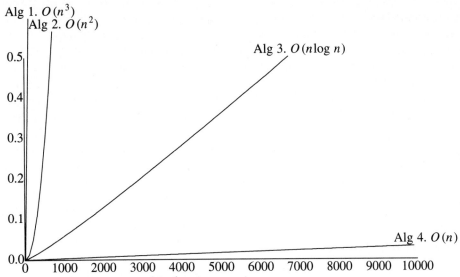

Figure 2.4 Plot (n vs. seconds) of various maximum subsequence sum algorithms

To simplify the analysis, we will adopt the convention that there are no particular units of time. Thus, we throw away leading constants. We will also throw away low-order terms, so what we are essentially doing is computing a Big-Oh running time. Since Big-Oh is an upper bound, we must be careful to never underestimate the running time of the program. In effect, the answer provided is a guarantee that the program will terminate within a certain time period. The program may stop earlier than this, but never later.

2.4.1. A Simple Example

Here is a simple program fragment to calculate $\sum_{i=1}^{n} i^3$:

```
/* 1*/     int
/* 2*/     Sum( int N )
/* 3*/     {
/* 4*/          int Partial_Sum = 0;

/* 5*/          for( int i = 1; i <= N; i++ )
/* 6*/              Partial_Sum += i * i * i;

/* 7*/          return Partial_Sum;
/* 8*/     }
```

The analysis of this program is simple. Lines 4 and 7 count for one unit each. Line 6 counts for three units per time executed (two multiplications and one addition) and is executed n times, for a total of $3n$ units. Line 5 has the hidden costs of initializing i, testing $i \leq n$, and incrementing i. The total cost of all these is 1 to initialize, $n + 1$ for all the tests, and n for all the increments, which is $2n + 2$. We ignore the costs of calling the function and returning, for a total of $5n + 4$. Thus, we say that this function is $O(n)$.

If we had to perform all this work every time we needed to analyze a program, the task would quickly become infeasible. Fortunately, since we are giving the answer in terms of Big-Oh, there are lots of shortcuts that can be taken without affecting the final answer. For instance, line 6 is obviously an $O(1)$ statement (per execution), so it is silly to count precisely whether it is two, three, or four units—it does not matter. Line 4 is obviously insignificant compared to the *for* loop, so it is silly to waste time here. This leads to several obvious general rules.

2.4.2. *General Rules*

RULE 1—LOOPS:
The running time of a loop is at most the running time of the statements inside the loop (including tests) times the number of iterations.

RULE 2—NESTED LOOPS:
Analyze these inside out. The total running time of a statement inside a group of nested loops is the running time of the statement multiplied by the product of the sizes of all the loops.

As an example, the following program fragment is $O(n^2)$:

```
/* 1*/          for( int i = 0; i < N; i++ )
/* 2*/              for( int j = 0; j < N; j++ )
/* 3*/                  k++;
```

RULE 3—CONSECUTIVE STATEMENTS:
These just add (which means that the maximum is the one that counts— see 1(a) on page 30).

As an example, the following program fragment, which has $O(n)$ work followed by $O(n^2)$ work, is also $O(n^2)$:

```
/* 1*/          for( int i = 0; i < N; i++ )
/* 2*/              A[ i ] = 0;
/* 3*/          for( i = 0; i < N; i++ )
/* 4*/              for( int j = 0; j < N; j++ )
/* 5*/                  A[ i ] += i + j;
```

RULE 4—IF-THEN-ELSE:

For the fragment

```
/* 1*/        if ( Cond )
/* 2*/            S1
/* 3*/        else
/* 4*/            S2
```

the running time of an if-then-else *statement is never more than the running time of the test plus the larger of the running times of S1 and S2.*

Clearly, this can be an over-estimate in some cases, but it is never an under-estimate.

Other rules are obvious, but a basic strategy of analyzing from the inside (or deepest part) out works. If there are function calls, obviously these must be analyzed first. If there are recursive procedures, there are several options. If the recursion is really just a thinly veiled *for* loop, the analysis is usually trivial. For instance, the following function is really just a simple loop and is obviously $O(n)$:

```
/* 1*/        unsigned long int
/* 2*/        Factorial( const unsigned long int N )
/* 3*/        {
/* 4*/            if( N <= 1 )
/* 5*/                return 1;
/* 6*/            else
/* 7*/                return N * Factorial( N - 1 );
/* 8*/        }
```

This example is really a poor use of recursion. When recursion is properly used, it is difficult to convert the recursion into a simple loop structure. In this case, the analysis will involve a recurrence relation that needs to be solved. To see what might happen, consider the following program, which turns out to be a horrible use of recursion:

```
/* 1*/        // Compute Fibonacci numbers (page 6).

/* 2*/        unsigned long int
/* 3*/        Fib( const unsigned int N )
/* 4*/        {
/* 5*/            if( N <= 1 )
/* 6*/                return 1;
/* 7*/            else
/* 8*/                return Fib( N - 1 ) + Fib( N - 2 );
/* 9*/        }
```

At first glance, this seems like a very clever use of recursion. However, if the program is coded up and run for values of *n* around 30, it becomes apparent that this program is terribly inefficient. The analysis is fairly simple. Let $T(n)$ be the running time for the function $Fib(n)$. If $n = 0$ or $n = 1$, then the running time is some constant value, which is the time to do the test at line 5 and return. We can say that $T(0) = T(1) = 1$ because constants do not matter. The running time for other values of n is then measured relative to the running time of the base case. For $n > 2$, the time to execute the function is the constant work at line 5 plus the work at line 8. Line 8 consists of an addition and two function calls. Since the function calls are not simple operations, they must be analyzed by themselves. The first function call is $Fib(n-1)$ and hence, by the definition of T, requires $T(n-1)$ units of time. A similar argument shows that the second function call requires $T(n-2)$ units of time. The total time required is then $T(n-1) + T(n-2) + 2$, where the 2 accounts for the work at line 5 plus the addition at line 8. Thus, for $n \geq 2$, we have the following formula for the running time of $Fib(n)$:

$$T(n) = T(n-1) + T(n-2) + 2$$

Since $Fib(n) = Fib(n-1) + Fib(n-2)$, it is easy to show by induction that $T(n) \geq Fib(n)$. In Section 1.2.5, we showed that $Fib(n) < (5/3)^n$. A similar calculation shows that $Fib(n) \geq (3/2)^n$, and so the running time of this program grows *exponentially*. This is about as bad as possible. By keeping a simple array and using a *for* loop, the running time can be reduced substantially.

This program is slow because there is a huge amount of redundant work being performed, violating the fourth major rule of recursion (the compound interest rule), which was discussed in Section 1.3. Notice that the first call on line 8, $Fib(n-1)$, actually computes $Fib(n-2)$ at some point. This information is thrown away and recomputed by the second call on line 8. The amount of information thrown away compounds recursively and results in the huge running time. This is perhaps the finest example of the maxim "Don't compute anything more than once" and should not scare you away from using recursion. Throughout this book, we shall see outstanding uses of recursion.

2.4.3. Solutions for the Maximum Subsequence Sum Problem

We will now present four algorithms to solve the maximum subsequence sum problem posed earlier. The first algorithm is depicted in Figure 2.5. The indices in the *for* loop reflect the fact that in C++, arrays begin at 0 instead of 1.

Convince yourself that this algorithm works (this should not take much). The running time is $O(n^3)$ and is entirely due to lines 9 and 10, which consist of an $O(1)$ statement buried inside three nested *for* loops. The loop at line 5 is of size n. The second loop has size $n - i + 1$, which could be small, but could also be of size n. We must assume the worst, with the knowledge that this could make the final bound a bit high. The third loop has size $j - i + 1$, which, again, we must assume is of size n. The total is $O(1 \cdot n \cdot n \cdot n) = O(n^3)$. Statement 4 takes only $O(1)$ total, and lines 11 and 12 take only $O(n^2)$ total, since they are easy expressions inside only two loops.

It turns out that a more precise analysis, taking into account the actual size of these loops, shows that the answer is $\Theta(n^3)$ and that our estimate above was a factor of 6 too high (which is all right, because constants do not matter). This is generally

```
/* 1*/    int
/* 2*/    Max_Subsequence_Sum( const int A[ ], const unsigned int N )
/* 3*/    {
/* 4*/        int This_Sum = 0, Max_Sum = 0;

/* 5*/        for( int i = 0; i < N; i++ )
/* 6*/            for( int j = i; j < N; j++ )
/* 7*/            {
/* 8*/                This_Sum = 0;
/* 9*/                for( int k = i; k <= j; k++ )
/*10*/                    This_Sum += A[ k ];

/*11*/                if( This_Sum > Max_Sum )
/*12*/                    Max_Sum = This_Sum;
/*13*/            }
/*14*/        return( Max_Sum );
/*15*/    }
```

Figure 2.5   Algorithm 1

true in these kinds of problems. The precise analysis is obtained from the sum $\sum_{i=1}^{n} \sum_{j=i}^{n} \sum_{k=i}^{j} 1$, which tells how many times line 10 is executed. The sum can be evaluated inside out, using formulas from Section 1.2.3. In particular, we will use the formulas for the sum of the first n integers and first n squares. First we have

$$\sum_{k=i}^{j} 1 = j - i + 1$$

Next we evaluate

$$\sum_{j=i}^{n} (j - i + 1) = \frac{(n - i + 1)(n - i + 2)}{2}$$

This sum is computed by observing that it is just the sum of the first $n - i + 1$ integers. To complete the calculation, we evaluate

$$\sum_{i=1}^{n} \frac{(n - i + 1)(n - i + 2)}{2} = \frac{1}{2} \sum_{i=1}^{n} i^2 - \left(n + \frac{3}{2}\right) \sum_{i=1}^{n} i + \frac{1}{2}(n^2 + 3n + 2) \sum_{i=1}^{n} 1$$

$$= \frac{1}{2} \frac{n(n + 1)(2n + 1)}{6} - \left(n + \frac{3}{2}\right) \frac{n(n + 1)}{2} + \frac{n^2 + 3n + 2}{2} n$$

$$= \frac{n^3 + 3n^2 + 2n}{6}$$

We can avoid the cubic running time by removing a *for* loop. Obviously, this is not always possible, but in this case there are an awful lot of unnecessary

```
/* 1*/    int
/* 2*/    Max_Subsequence_Sum( const int A[ ], const unsigned int N )
/* 3*/    {
/* 4*/        int This_Sum = 0, Max_Sum = 0;

/* 5*/        for( int i = 0; i < N; i++ )
/* 6*/        {
/* 7*/            This_Sum = 0;
/* 8*/            for( int j = i; j < N; j++ )
/* 9*/            {
/*10*/                This_Sum += A[ j ];

/*11*/                if( This_Sum > Max_Sum )
/*12*/                    Max_Sum = This_Sum;
/*13*/            }
/*14*/        }
/*15*/        return( Max_Sum );
/*16*/    }
```

Figure 2.6   Algorithm 2

computations present in the algorithm. The inefficiency that the improved algorithm corrects can be seen by noticing that $\sum_{k=i}^{j} a_k = a_j + \sum_{k=i}^{j-1} a_k$, so the computation at lines 9 and 10 in Algorithm 1 is unduly expensive. Figure 2.6 shows an improved algorithm. Algorithm 2 is clearly $O(n^2)$; the analysis is even simpler than before.

There is a recursive and relatively complicated $O(n \log n)$ solution to this problem, which we now describe. If there didn't happen to be an $O(n)$ (linear) solution, this would be an excellent example of the power of recursion. The algorithm uses a "divide-and-conquer" strategy. The idea is to split the problem into two roughly equal subproblems, each of which is half the size of the original. The subproblems are then solved recursively. This is the "divide" part. The "conquer" stage consists of patching together the two solutions of the subproblems—and possibly doing a small amount of additional work—to arrive at a solution for the whole problem.

In our case, the maximum subsequence sum can be in one of three places. Either it occurs entirely in the left half of the input, or entirely in the right half, or it crosses the middle and is in both halves. The first two cases can be solved recursively. The last case can be obtained by finding the largest sum in the first half that includes the last element in the first half and the largest sum in the second half that includes the first element in the second half. These two sums can then be added together. As an example, consider the following input:

First Half				Second Half			
4	−3	5	−2	−1	2	6	−2

The maximum subsequence sum for the first half is 6 (elements a_1 through a_3) and for the second half is 8 (elements a_6 through a_7).

The maximum sum in the first half that includes the last element in the first half is 4 (elements a_1 through a_4), and the maximum sum in the second half that includes the first element in the second half is 7 (elements a_5 though a_7). Thus, the maximum sum that spans both halves and goes through the middle is $4 + 7 = 11$ (elements a_1 through a_7).

We see, then, that among the three ways to form a large maximum subsequence, for our example, the best way is to include elements from both halves. Thus, the answer is 11. Figure 2.7 shows an implementation of this strategy. The code for Algorithm 3 deserves some comment. The general form of the call for the recursive procedure is to pass the input array along with the left and right borders, which delimit the portion of the array that is operated upon. A one-line driver program sets this up by passing the borders 0 and $n - 1$ along with the array.

Lines 7 to 11 handle the base case. If *Left* == *Right*, there is one element, and it is the maximum subsequence if the element is nonnegative. Lines 12 and 13 perform the two recursive calls. We can see that the recursive calls are always on a smaller problem than the original, although minor perturbations in the code could destroy this property. Lines 14 to 19 and then 20 to 25 calculate the two maximum sums that touch the center divider. The sum of these two values is the maximum sum that spans both halves. The pseudoroutine *Max3* returns the largest of the three possibilities.

Algorithm 3 clearly requires more effort to code than either of the two previous algorithms. However, shorter code does not always mean better code. As we have seen in the earlier table showing the running times of the algorithms, this algorithm is considerably faster than the other two for all but the smallest of input sizes.

The running time is analyzed in much the same way as for the program that computes the Fibonacci numbers. Let $T(n)$ be the time it takes to solve a maximum subsequence sum problem of size n. If $n = 1$, then the program takes some constant amount of time to execute lines 7 to 11, which we shall call one unit. Thus, $T(1) = 1$. Otherwise, the program must perform two recursive calls, the two *for* loops between lines 14 and 25, and some small amount of bookkeeping, such as line 26. The two *for* loops combine to touch every element in A, and there is constant work inside the loops, so the time expended in lines 14 to 25 is $O(n)$. The initialization in the declaration and the code in lines 7 to 11, and 26 to 27 is all a constant amount of work and can thus be ignored when compared to $O(n)$. The remainder of the work is performed in lines 12 and 13. These lines solve two subsequence problems of size $n/2$ (assuming n is even). Thus, these lines take $T(n/2)$ units of time each, for a total of $2T(n/2)$. The total time for the algorithm then is $2T(n/2) + O(n)$. This gives the equations

$$T(1) = 1$$

$$T(n) = 2T(n/2) + O(n)$$

To simplify the calculations, we can replace the $O(n)$ term in the equation above with n; since $T(n)$ will be expressed in Big-Oh notation anyway, this will not affect

```
/* 1*/    int Max_Sub_Sum( const int A[ ], const int Left, const int Right )
/* 2*/    {
/* 3*/        int Max_Left_Sum = 0, Max_Right_Sum = 0;
/* 4*/        int Max_Left_Border_Sum = 0, Max_Right_Border_Sum = 0;
/* 5*/        int Left_Border_Sum = 0, Right_Border_Sum = 0;
/* 6*/        int Center = ( Left + Right ) / 2;

/* 7*/        if( Left == Right )     // Base Case.
/* 8*/            if( A[ Left ] > 0 )
/* 9*/                return A[ Left ];
/*10*/            else
/*11*/                return 0;

/*12*/        Max_Left_Sum  = Max_Sub_Sum( A, Left, Center );
/*13*/        Max_Right_Sum = Max_Sub_Sum( A, Center + 1, Right );

/*14*/        for( int i = Center; i >= Left; i-- )
/*15*/        {
/*16*/            Left_Border_Sum += A[ i ];
/*17*/            if( Left_Border_Sum > Max_Left_Border_Sum )
/*18*/                Max_Left_Border_Sum = Left_Border_Sum;
/*19*/        }

/*20*/        for( i = Center + 1; i <= Right; i++ )
/*21*/        {
/*22*/            Right_Border_Sum += A[ i ];
/*23*/            if( Right_Border_Sum > Max_Right_Border_Sum )
/*24*/                Max_Right_Border_Sum = Right_Border_Sum;
/*25*/        }

/*26*/        return Max3( Max_Left_Sum, Max_Right_Sum,
/*27*/                        Max_Left_Border_Sum + Max_Right_Border_Sum );
/*28*/    }

/*29*/    int
/*30*/    Max_Subsequence_Sum( const int A[ ], const unsigned int N )
/*31*/    {
/*32*/        return Max_Sub_Sum( A, 0, N - 1 );
/*33*/    }
```

Figure 2.7   Algorithm 3

the answer. In Chapter 7, we shall see how to solve this equation rigorously. For now, if $T(n) = 2T(n/2) + n$, and $T(1) = 1$, then $T(2) = 4 = 2*2$, $T(4) = 12 = 4*3$, $T(8) = 32 = 8*4$, $T(16) = 80 = 16*5$. The pattern that is evident, and can be derived, is that if $n = 2^k$, then $T(n) = n*(k + 1) = n \log n + n = O(n \log n)$.

   This analysis assumes n is even, since otherwise $n/2$ is not defined. By the recursive nature of the analysis, it is really valid only when n is a power of 2, since otherwise we eventually get a subproblem that is not an even size, and the equation is invalid. When n is not a power of 2, a somewhat more complicated analysis is required, but the Big-Oh result remains unchanged.

In future chapters, we will see several clever applications of recursion. Here, we present a fourth algorithm to find the maximum subsequence sum. This algorithm is simpler to implement than the recursive algorithm and also is more efficient. It is shown in Figure 2.8.

It should be clear why the time bound is correct, but it takes a little thought to see why the algorithm actually works. This is left to the reader. An extra advantage of this algorithm is that it makes only one pass through the data, and once a_i is read and processed, it does not need to be remembered. Thus, if the array is on a disk or tape, it can be read sequentially, and there is no need to store any part of it in main memory. Furthermore, at any point in time, the algorithm can correctly give an answer to the subsequence problem for the data it has already read (the other algorithms do not share this property). Algorithms that can do this are called *on-line algorithms*. An on-line algorithm that requires only constant space and runs in linear time is just about as good as possible.

2.4.4. *Logarithms in the Running Time*

The most confusing aspect of analyzing algorithms probably centers around the logarithm. We have already seen that some divide-and-conquer algorithms will run in $O(n \log n)$ time. Besides divide-and-conquer algorithms, the most frequent

Figure 2.8 Algorithm 4

```
/* 1*/    int
/* 2*/    Max_Subsequence_Sum( const int A[ ], const unsigned int N )
/* 3*/    {
/* 4*/        int This_Sum = 0, Max_Sum = 0, Seq_Start = 0;

/* 5*/        for( int Seq_End = 0; Seq_End < N; Seq_End++ )
/* 6*/        {
/* 7*/            This_Sum += A[ Seq_End ];

/* 8*/            if( This_Sum > Max_Sum )
/* 9*/                Max_Sum = This_Sum;
/*10*/            else
/*11*/            if( This_Sum < 0 )
/*12*/            {
/*13*/                Seq_Start = Seq_End + 1;
/*14*/                This_Sum = 0;
/*15*/            }
/*16*/        }
/*17*/        return( Max_Sum );
/*18*/    }
```

appearance of logarithms centers around the following general rule: *An algorithm is* $O(\log n)$ *if it takes constant* ($O(1)$) *time to cut the problem size by a fraction (which is usually* $\frac{1}{2}$). On the other hand, if constant time is required to merely reduce the problem by a constant *amount* (such as to make the problem smaller by 1), then the algorithm is $O(n)$.

Something that should be obvious is that only special kinds of problems can be $O(\log n)$. For instance, if the input is a list of n numbers, an algorithm must take $\Omega(n)$ merely to read the input in. Thus, when we talk about $O(\log n)$ algorithms for these kinds of problems, we usually presume that the input is preread. We provide three examples of logarithmic behavior.

Binary Search

The first example is usually referred to as binary search:

> **BINARY SEARCH:**
> *Given an integer x and integers $a_0, a_1, \ldots, a_{n-1}$, which are presorted and already in memory, find i such that $a_i = x$, or return $i = -1$ if x is not in the input.*

The obvious solution consists of scanning through the list from left to right and runs in linear time. However, because this algorithm does not take advantage of the fact that the list is sorted, it is not likely to be best. The best strategy is to check if x is the middle element. If so, the answer is at hand. If x is smaller than the middle element, we can apply the same strategy to the sorted subarray to the left of the middle element; likewise, if x is larger than the middle element, we look to the right half. (There is also the case of when to stop.) Figure 2.9 shows the code for binary search. *Etype* is the basic element type; we'll use this shorthand throughout the book.

Clearly all the work done inside the loop is $O(1)$ per iteration, so the analysis requires determining the number of times around the loop. The loop starts with $High - Low = n - 1$ and finishes with $High - Low \geq -1$. Every time through the loop the value $High - Low$ must be at least halved from its previous value; thus, the number of times around the loop is at most $\lceil \log(n - 1) \rceil + 2$. (As an example, if $High - Low = 128$, then the maximum values of $High - Low$ after each iteration are 64, 32, 16, 8, 4, 2, 1, 0, -1.) Thus, the running time is $O(\log n)$. Equivalently, we could write a recursive formula for the running time, but this kind of brute-force approach is usually unnecessary when you understand what is really going on and why.

Binary search can be viewed as our first data structure. It supports the *Find* operation in $O(\log n)$ time, but all other operations (in particular *Insert*) require $O(n)$ time. In applications in which the data are static (that is, insertions and deletions are not allowed), this could be a very useful data structure. The input would then need to be sorted once, but afterward accesses would be fast. An example could be a program that needs to maintain information about the periodic table of elements (which arises in chemistry and physics). This table is relatively stable, as new elements are added infrequently. The element names could be kept sorted. Since

```
/* 1*/    // Return position of X in A.

/* 2*/    int
/* 3*/    Binary_Search( const Etype A[ ], const Etype & X, const int N )
/* 4*/    {
/* 5*/        int Low = 0, High = N - 1;
/* 6*/        int Mid;

/* 7*/        while( Low <= High )
/* 8*/        {
/* 9*/            Mid = ( Low + High ) / 2;
/*10*/            if( A[ Mid ] < X )
/*11*/                Low = Mid + 1;
/*12*/            else if( A[ Mid ] > X )
/*13*/                High = Mid - 1;
/*14*/            else
/*15*/                return Mid;
/*16*/        }

/*17*/        return Not_Found;        // Return -1.
/*18*/    }
```

Figure 2.9   Binary search

there are only about 110 elements, at most eight accesses would be required to find an element. Performing a sequential search would require many more accesses.

Euclid's Algorithm

A second example is Euclid's algorithm for computing the greatest common divisor. The greatest common divisor (gcd) of two integers is the largest integer that divides both. Thus, $gcd(50, 15) = 5$. The algorithm in Figure 2.10 computes $Gcd(M, N)$, assuming $M \geq N$. (If $N > M$, the first iteration of the loop swaps them).

The algorithm works by continually computing remainders until 0 is reached. The last nonzero remainder is the answer. Thus, if $M = 1989$ and $N = 1590$, then the sequence of remainders is 399, 393, 6, 3, 0. Therefore, $gcd(1989, 1590) = 3$. As the example shows, this is a fast algorithm.

As before, the entire running time of the algorithm depends on determining how long the sequence of remainders is. Although $\log n$ seems like a good answer, it is not at all obvious that the value of the remainder has to decrease by a constant factor, since we see that the remainder went from 399 to only 393 in the example. Indeed, the remainder *does not* decrease by a constant factor in one iteration. However, we can prove that after two iterations, the remainder is at most half of its original value. This would show that the number of iterations is at most $2 \log n = O(\log n)$ and establish the running time. This proof is easy, so we include it here. It follows directly from the following theorem.

```
/* 1*/    unsigned int
/* 2*/    Gcd( unsigned int M, unsigned int N )
/* 3*/    {
/* 4*/        unsigned int Rem;

/* 5*/        while( N > 0 )
/* 6*/        {
/* 7*/            Rem = M % N;
/* 8*/            M   = N;
/* 9*/            N   = Rem;
/*10*/        }
/*11*/        return M;
/*12*/    }
```

Figure 2.10   Euclid's algorithm

THEOREM 2.1.

If $m > n$, then $m \bmod n < m/2.0$.

PROOF:

There are two cases. If $n \le m/2$, then obviously, since the remainder is smaller than n, the theorem is true for this case. The other case is $n > m/2$. But then n goes into m once with a remainder $m - n < m/2$, proving the theorem.

One might wonder if this is the best bound possible, since $2 \log n$ is about 20 for our example, and only seven operations were performed. It turns out that the constant can be improved slightly, to roughly $1.44 \log n$, in the worst case (which is achievable if M and N are consecutive Fibonacci numbers). The average-case performance of Euclid's algorithm requires pages and pages of highly sophisticated mathematical analysis, and it turns out that the average number of iterations is about $\left(12 \ln 2 \ln n\right)/\pi^2 + 1.47$.

Exponentiation

Our last example in this section deals with raising an integer to a power (which is also an integer). Numbers that result from exponentiation are generally quite large, so an analysis works only if we can assume that we have a machine that can store such large integers (or a compiler that can simulate this). We will count the number of multiplications as the measurement of running time.

The obvious algorithm to compute x^n uses $n - 1$ multiplies. The recursive algorithm in Figure 2.11 does better. We assume that the class *Huge_Int* exists; it could always be a *long int* if we don't have this class. Lines 4 to 7 handle the base case of the recursion. Otherwise, if n is even, we have $x^n = x^{n/2} \cdot x^{n/2}$, and if n is odd, $x^n = x^{(n-1)/2} \cdot x^{(n-1)/2} \cdot x$.

```
/* 1*/    Huge_Int
/* 2*/    Pow( const Huge_Int & X, const Huge_Int & N )
/* 3*/    {
/* 4*/        if( N == 0 )
/* 5*/            return Huge_Int( 1 );
/* 6*/        if( N == 1 )
/* 7*/            return X;
/* 8*/        if( Even( N ) )
/* 9*/            return Pow( X * X, N / 2 );
/*10*/        else
/*11*/            return Pow( X * X, N / 2 ) * X;
/*12*/    }
```

Figure 2.11 Efficient exponentiation

For instance, to compute x^{62}, the algorithm does the following calculations, which involves only nine multiplications:

$$x^3 = (x^2)x, \quad x^7 = (x^3)^2 x, \quad x^{15} = (x^7)^2 x, \quad x^{31} = (x^{15})^2 x, \quad x^{62} = (x^{31})^2$$

The number of multiplications required is clearly at most $2 \log n$, because at most two multiplications (if n is odd) are required to halve the problem. Again, a recurrence formula can be written and solved. Simple intuition obviates the need for a brute-force approach.

It is sometimes interesting to see how much the code can be tweaked without affecting correctness. In Figure 2.11, lines 6 and 7 are actually unnecessary, because if n is 1, then line 11 does the right thing. Line 11 can also be rewritten as

```
/*11*/    return Pow( X, N-1 ) * X;
```

without affecting the correctness of the program. Indeed, the program will still run in $O(\log n)$, because the sequence of multiplications is the same as before. However, all of the following alternatives for line 9 are bad, even though they look correct:

```
/*9a*/    return Pow( Pow( X, 2 ), N / 2 );
/*9b*/    return Pow( Pow( X, N / 2 ), 2 );
/*9c*/    return Pow( X, N / 2 ) * Pow( X, N / 2 );
```

Both lines 9a and 9b are incorrect because when N is 2, one of the recursive calls to *Pow* has 2 as the second argument. Thus no progress is made, and an infinite loop results (with an eventual crash).

Using line 9c affects the efficiency, because there are now two recursive calls of size $N/2$ instead of only one. An analysis will show that the running time is no longer $O(\log n)$. We leave it as an exercise to the reader to determine the new running time.

2.4.5. *Checking Your Analysis*

Once an analysis has been performed, it is desirable to see if the answer is correct and as good as possible. One way to do this is to code up the program and see if the empirically observed running time matches the running time predicted by the analysis. When n doubles, the running time goes up by a factor of 2 for linear programs, 4 for quadratic programs, and 8 for cubic programs. Programs that run in logarithmic time take only an additive constant longer when n doubles, and programs that run in $O(n \log n)$ take slightly more than twice as long to run under the same circumstances. These increases can be hard to spot if the lower-order terms have relatively large coefficients and n is not large enough. An example is the jump from $n = 10$ to $n = 100$ in the running time for the various implementations of the maximum subsequence sum problem. It also can be very difficult to differentiate linear programs from $O(n \log n)$ programs purely on empirical evidence.

Another commonly used trick to verify that some program is $O(f(n))$ is to compute the values $T(n)/f(n)$ for a range of n (usually spaced out by factors of 2), where $T(n)$ is the empirically observed running time. If $f(n)$ is a tight answer for the running time, then the computed values converge to a positive constant. If $f(n)$ is an over-estimate, the values converge to zero. If $f(n)$ is an under-estimate and hence wrong, the values diverge.

As an example, the program fragment in Figure 2.12 computes the probability that two distinct positive integers, less than or equal to n and chosen randomly, are relatively prime. (As n gets large, the answer approaches $6/\pi^2$.)

You should be able to do the analysis for this program instantaneously. Figure 2.13 shows the actual observed running time for this routine on a real computer. The table shows that the last column is most likely, and thus the analysis that you should have gotten is probably correct. Notice that there is not a great deal of difference between $O(n^2)$ and $O(n^2 \log n)$, since logarithms grow so slowly.

2.4.6. *A Grain of Salt*

Sometimes the analysis is shown empirically to be an over-estimate. If this is the case, then either the analysis needs to be tightened (usually by a clever observation), or it may be the case that the *average* running time is significantly less than the worst-case running time and no improvement in the bound is possible. There are many complicated algorithms for which the worst-case bound is achievable by some bad input but is usually an over-estimate in practice. Unfortunately, for most of these problems, an average-case analysis is extremely complex (in many cases still unsolved), and a worst-case bound, even though overly pessimistic, is the best analytical result known.

Summary

This chapter gives some hints on how to analyze the complexity of programs. Unfortunately, it is not a complete guide. Simple programs usually have simple

```
/* 1*/    void
/* 2*/    Pair( const unsigned int N )
/* 3*/    {
/* 4*/        int Rel = 0, Tot = 0;

/* 5*/        for( int i = 1; i <= N; i++ )
/* 6*/            for( int j = i + 1; j <= N; j++ )
/* 7*/            {
/* 8*/                Tot++;
/* 9*/                if( Gcd( i, j ) == 1 )
/*10*/                    Rel++;
/*11*/            }

/*12*/        cout << "Fraction of relatively prime pairs is  "
/*13*/            << double( Rel ) / double( Tot ) << endl;
/*14*/    }
```

Figure 2.12 Estimate the probability that two random
numbers are relatively prime

n	CPU time (T)	T/n^2	T/n^3	$T/n^2 \log n$
100	022	.002200	.000022000	.0004777
200	056	.001400	.000007000	.0002642
300	118	.001311	.000004370	.0002299
400	207	.001294	.000003234	.0002159
500	318	.001272	.000002544	.0002047
600	466	.001294	.000002157	.0002024
700	644	.001314	.000001877	.0002006
800	846	.001322	.000001652	.0001977
900	1,086	.001341	.000001490	.0001971
1,000	1,362	.001362	.000001362	.0001972
1,500	3,240	.001440	.000000960	.0001969
2,000	5,949	.001482	.000000740	.0001947
4,000	25,720	.001608	.000000402	.0001938

Figure 2.13 Empirical running times for previous routine

analyses, but this is not always the case. As an example, we shall see, later in the text, a sorting algorithm (Shellsort, Chapter 7) and an algorithm for maintaining disjoint sets (Chapter 8) each of which requires about 20 lines of code. The analysis of Shellsort is still not complete, and the disjoint set algorithm has an analysis that is extremely difficult and requires pages and pages of intricate calculations. Most of the analysis that we will encounter here will be simple and involve counting through loops.

An interesting kind of analysis, upon which we have not touched, is lower-bound analysis. We will see an example of this in Chapter 7, where it is proved that any algorithm that sorts by using only comparisons requires $\Omega(n \log n)$ comparisons in the worst case. Lower-bound proofs are generally the most difficult, because they apply not to an algorithm but to a class of algorithms that solve a problem.

We close by mentioning that some of the algorithms described here have real-life application. The *Gcd* algorithm and the exponentiation algorithm are both used in cryptography. Specifically, a 200-digit number is raised to a large power (usually another 200-digit number), with only the low 200 or so digits retained after each multiplication. Since the calculations require dealing with 200-digit numbers, efficiency is obviously important. The straightforward algorithm for exponentiation would require about 10^{200} multiplications, whereas the algorithm presented requires only about 1,200.

Exercises

2.1 Order the following functions by growth rate: n, $\sqrt{n}$, $n^{1.5}$, n^2, $n \log n$, $n \log \log n$, $n \log^2 n$, $n \log(n^2)$, $2/n$, 2^n, $2^{n/2}$, 37, $n^2 \log n$, n^3. Indicate which functions grow at the same rate.

2.2 Suppose $T_1(n) = O(f(n))$ and $T_2(n) = O(f(n))$. Which of the following are true?

a. $T_1(n) + T_2(n) = O(f(n))$

b. $T_1(n) - T_2(n) = o(f(n))$

c. $\dfrac{T_1(n)}{T_2(n)} = O(1)$

d. $T_1(n) = O(T_2(n))$

2.3 Which function grows faster: $n \log n$ or $n^{1+\epsilon/\sqrt{\log n}}$ $\epsilon > 0$?

2.4 Prove that for any constant, k, $\log^k n = o(n)$.

2.5 Find two functions $f(n)$ and $g(n)$ such that neither $f(n) = O(g(n))$ nor $g(n) = O(f(n))$.

2.6 For each of the following six program fragments:

a. Give an analysis of the running time (Big-Oh will do).

b. Implement the code, and give the running time for several values of n.

c. Compare your analysis with the actual running times.

```
( 1 )     Sum = 0;
          for( int i = 0; i < N ; i++ )
              Sum++;
```

```
( 2 )     Sum = 0;
          for( int i = 0; i < N ; i++ )
              for( int j = 0; j < N; j++ )
                  Sum++;
```

```
( 3 )     Sum = 0;
          for( int i = 0; i < N ; i++ )
              for( int j = 0; j < N * N; j++ )
                  Sum++;
```

```
( 4 )     Sum = 0;
          for( int i = 0; i < N ; i++ )
              for( int j = 0; j < i; j++ )
                  Sum++;
```

```
( 5 )     Sum = 0;
          for( int i = 0; i < N ; i++ )
              for( int j = 0; j < i * i; j++ )
                  for( int k = 0; k < j; k++ )
                      Sum++;
```

```
( 6 )     Sum = 0;
          for( int i = 1; i <= N ; i++ )
              for( int j = 1; j <= i * i; j++ )
                  if( j % i == 0 )
                      for( int k = 0; k < j; k++ )
                          Sum++;
```

2.7 Suppose you need to generate a *random* permutation of the first n integers. For example, {4, 3, 1, 5, 2} and {3, 1, 4, 2, 5} are legal permutations, but {5, 4, 1, 2, 1} is not, because one number (1) is duplicated and another (3) is missing. This routine is often used in simulation of algorithms. We assume the existence of a random number generator, *Rand_Int(i, j)*, which generates integers between i and j with equal probability. Here are three algorithms:

1. Fill the array A from $A[0]$ to $A[N-1]$ as follows: To fill $A[i]$, generate random numbers until you get one that is not already in $A[0]$, $A[1]$,..., $A[i-1]$.

2. Same as algorithm (1), but keep an extra array called the *Used* array. When a random number, *Ran*, is first put in the array A, set *Used*[*Ran*] = 1. This means that when filling $A[i]$ with a random number, you can test in one step to see whether the random number has been used, instead of the (possibly) i steps in the first algorithm.

3. Fill the array such that $A[i] = i + 1$. Then

```
/* 1*/    for( int i = 1; i < N; i++ )
/* 2*/        Swap( A[i], A[ Rand_Int( 0, i ) ] );
          // By reference.
```

a. Prove that all three algorithms generate only legal permutations and that all permutations are equally likely.

b. Give as accurate (Big-Oh) an analysis as you can of the *expected* running time of each algorithm.

c. Write (separate) programs to execute each algorithm 10 times, to get a good average. Run program (1) for $n = 250, 500, 1,000, 2,000$; program (2) for $n = 2,500, 5,000, 10,000, 20,000, 40,000, 80,000$, and program (3) for $n = 10,000, 20,000, 40,000, 80,000, 160,000, 320,000, 640,000$.

d. Compare your analysis with the actual running times.

e. What is the worst-case running time of each algorithm?

2.8 Complete the table in Figure 2.2 with estimates for the running times that were too long to simulate. Interpolate the running times for these algorithms and estimate the time required to compute the maximum subsequence sum of one million numbers. What assumptions have you made?

2.9 How much time is required to compute $f(x) = \sum_{i=0}^{n} a_i x^i$

a. using a simple routine to perform exponentiation?

b. using the routine in Section 2.4.4?

2.10 Consider the following algorithm (known as *Horner's rule*) to evaluate $f(x) = \sum_{i=0}^{n} a_i x^i$:

```
/* 1*/    Poly = 0;
/* 2*/    for( int i = N; i >= 0; i-- )
/* 3*/        Poly = X * Poly + A[i];
```

a. Show how the steps are performed by this algorithm for $x = 3$, $f(x) = 4x^4 + 8x^3 + x + 2$.

b. Explain why this algorithm works.

c. What is the running time of this algorithm?

2.11 Give an efficient algorithm to determine if there exists an integer i such that $a_i = i$ in an array of integers $a_1 < a_2 < a_3 < \cdots < a_n$. What is the running time of your algorithm?

2.12 Give efficient algorithms (along with running time analyses) to

    a. find the minimum subsequence sum

   *b. find the minimum *positive* subsequence sum

   *c. find the maximum subsequence *product*

2.13 a. Write a program to determine if a positive integer, n, is prime.

    b. In terms of n, what is the worst-case running time of your program? (You should be able to do this in $O(\sqrt{n})$.)

    c. Let B equal the number of bits in the binary representation of n. What is the value of B?

    d. In terms of B, what is the worst-case running time of your program?

    e. Compare the running times to determine if a 20-bit and a 40-bit number are prime.

    f. Is it more reasonable to give the running time in terms of n or B? Why?

*2.14 The Sieve of Erastothenes is a method used to compute all primes less than n. We begin by making a table of integers 2 to n. We find the smallest integer, i, that is not crossed out, print i, and cross out $i, 2i, 3i, \ldots$. When $i > \sqrt{n}$, the algorithm terminates. What is the running time of this algorithm?

2.15 Show that x^{62} can be computed with only eight multiplications.

2.16 Write the fast exponentiation routine without recursion.

2.17 Give a precise count on the number of multiplications used by the fast exponentiation routine. *(Hint:* Consider the binary representation of n.)

2.18 Programs A and B are analyzed and found to have worst-case running times no greater than $150n \log_2 n$ and n^2, respectively. Answer the following questions if possible:

    a. Which program has the better guarantee on the running time, for large values of n ($n > 10,000$)?

    b. Which program has the better guarantee on the running time, for small values of n ($n < 100$)?

    c. Which program will run faster *on average* for $n = 1,000$?

    d. Is it possible that program B will run faster than program A on *all* possible inputs?

2.19 A majority element in an array, A, of size n is an element that appears more than $n/2$ times (thus, there is at most one). For example, the array

    3, 3, 4, 2, 4, 4, 2, 4, 4

has a majority element (4), whereas the array

    3, 3, 4, 2, 4, 4, 2, 4

does not. If there is no majority element, your program should indicate this. Here is a sketch of an algorithm to solve the problem:

    First, a *candidate* majority element is found (this is the harder part). This candidate is the only element that could possibly be the majority element. The second step determines if this candidate is actually the majority. This is just a sequential search through the array. To find a candidate in the array, A, form a second array, B. Then compare A_1 and A_2. If they are equal, add one of these to B; otherwise do nothing. Then compare A_3 and A_4. Again if they are equal, add one of these to B; otherwise do nothing. Continue in this fashion until the entire array is read. Then recursively find a candidate for B; this is the candidate for A (why?).

    a. How does the recursion terminate?

   *b. How is the case where n is odd handled?

   *c. What is the running time of the algorithm?

    d. How can we avoid using an extra array B?

   *e. Write a program to compute the majority element.

*2.20 Why is it important to assume that integers in our computer model have a fixed size?

2.21 Consider the word puzzle problem described in Chapter 1. Suppose we fix the size of the longest word to be 10 characters.

    a. In terms of r and c, which are the number of rows and columns in the puzzle, and W, which is the number of words, what is the running time of the algorithms described in Chapter 1?

    b. Suppose the word list is presorted. Show how to use binary search to obtain an algorithm with significantly better running time.

2.22 Suppose that line 11 in the binary search routine had the statement $Low = Mid$ instead of $Low = Mid + 1$. Would the routine still work?

2.23 Suppose that lines 12 and 13 in Algorithm 3 (Fig. 2.7) are replaced by

```
/*12*/    Max_Left_Sum  = Max_Sub_Sum( A, Left, Center-1 );
/*13*/    Max_Right_Sum = Max_Sub_Sum( A, Center, Right );
```

Would the routine still work?

*2.24 The inner loop of the cubic maximum subsequence sum algorithm performs $n(n + 1)(n + 2)/6$ iterations of the innermost code. The quadratic version performs $n(n + 1)/2$ iterations. The linear version performs n iterations. What pattern is evident? Can you give a combinatoric explanation of this phenomenon?

References

Analysis of the running time of algorithms was first made popular by Knuth in the three-part series [5], [6], and [7]. The analysis of the Gcd algorithm appears in [6]. Another early text on the subject is [1].

    Big-Oh, big-omega, big-theta, and little-oh notation were advocated by Knuth in [8]. There is still not a uniform agreement on the matter, especially when it comes to using $\Theta()$. Many people prefer to use $O()$, even though it is less expressive. Additionally, $O()$ is still used in some corners to express a lower bound, when $\Omega()$ is called for.

The maximum subsequence sum problem is from [3]. The series of books [2], [3], and [4] show how to optimize programs for speed.

1. A. V. Aho, J. E. Hopcroft, and J. D. Ullman, *The Design and Analysis of Computer Algorithms,* Addison-Wesley, Reading, Mass., 1974.
2. J. L. Bentley, *Writing Efficient Programs,* Prentice Hall, Englewood Cliffs, N.J., 1982.
3. J. L. Bentley, *Programming Pearls,* Addison-Wesley, Reading, Mass., 1986.
4. J. L. Bentley, *More Programming Pearls,* Addison-Wesley, Reading, Mass., 1988.
5. D. E. Knuth, *The Art of Computer Programming, Vol 1: Fundamental Algorithms,* 2d ed., Addison-Wesley, Reading, Mass., 1973.
6. D. E. Knuth, *The Art of Computer Programming, Vol 2: Seminumerical Algorithms,* 2d ed., Addison-Wesley, Reading, Mass., 1981.
7. D. E. Knuth, *The Art of Computer Programming, Vol 3: Sorting and Searching,* Addison-Wesley, Reading, Mass., 1975.
8. D. E. Knuth, "Big Omicron and Big Omega and Big Theta," *ACM SIGACT News, 8* (1976), 18–23.

CHAPTER 3

Lists, Stacks, and Queues

This chapter discusses three of the most simple and basic data structures. Virtually every significant program will use at least one of these structures explicitly, and a stack is always implicitly used in your program, whether or not you declare one. Among the highlights of this chapter, we will

- Introduce the concept of Abstract Data Types (ADTs), and show how they are supported by C++.
- Show how to efficiently perform operations on lists.
- Introduce the stack ADT and its use in implementing recursion.
- Introduce the queue ADT and its use in operating systems and algorithm design.

Because these data structures are so important, one might expect that they are hard to implement. In fact, they are extremely easy to code up; the main difficulty is keeping enough discipline to write good general-purpose code for routines that are generally only a few lines long.

3.1. Abstract Data Types (ADTs)

One of the basic rules concerning programming is that no routine should ever exceed a page. This is accomplished by breaking the program down into *modules*. Each module is a logical unit and does a specific job. Its size is kept small by calling other modules. Modularity has several advantages. First, it is much easier to debug small routines than large routines. Second, it is easier for several people to work on a modular program simultaneously. Third, a well-written modular program places certain dependencies in only one routine, making changes easier. The idea that global variables and side effects are bad is directly attributable to the idea that modularity is good.

An *abstract data type* (ADT) is a set of operations. Abstract data types are mathematical abstractions; nowhere in an ADT's definition is there any mention of

57

how the set of operations is implemented. This can be viewed as an extension of modular design.

Objects such as lists, sets, and graphs, along with their operations, can be viewed as abstract data types, just as integers, reals, and booleans are data types. Integers, reals, and booleans have operations associated with them, and so do abstract data types. For the set ADT, we might have such operations as *union, intersection, size,* and *complement.* Alternately, we might only want the two operations *union* and *find,* which would define a different ADT on the set.

The basic idea is that the implementation of these operations is written once in the program, and any other part of the program that needs to perform an operation on the ADT can do so by calling the appropriate function. If for some reason implementation details need to change, it should be easy to do so by merely changing the routines that perform the ADT operations. This change, in a perfect world, would be completely transparent to the rest of the program.

There is no rule telling us which operations must be supported for each ADT; this is a design decision. Error handling and tie breaking (where appropriate) are also generally up to the program designer. The three data structures that we will study in this chapter are primary examples of ADTs. We will see how each can be implemented in several ways, but if they are done correctly, the programs that use them will not need to know which implementation was used.

3.2. The List ADT

We will deal with a general list of the form $a_1, a_2, a_3, \ldots, a_n$. We say that the size of this list is n. We will call the special list of size 0 a *null list.*

For any list except the null list, we say that a_{i+1} follows (or succeeds) a_i $(i < n)$ and that a_{i-1} precedes a_i $(i > 1)$. The first element of the list is a_1, and the last element is a_n. We will not define the predecessor of a_1 or the successor of a_n. The *position* of element a_i in a list is i. Throughout this discussion, we will assume, to simplify matters, that the elements in the list are integers, but in general, arbitrarily complex elements are allowed (and easily handled in C++).

Associated with these "definitions" is a set of operations that we would like to perform on the list ADT. Some popular operations are *Print_List* and *Make_Empty,* which do the obvious things; *Find,* which returns the position of the first occurrence of a key; *Insert* and *Remove,* which generally insert and delete some key from some position in the list; and *Find_Kth,* which returns the element in some position (specified as an argument). If the list is 34, 12, 52, 16, 12, then *Find*(52) might return 3; *Insert*(x,3) might make the list into 34, 12, 52, x, 16, 12 (if we insert after the position given); and *Remove*(52) might turn that list into 34, 12, x, 16, 12.

Of course, the interpretation of what is appropriate for a function is entirely up to the programmer, as is the handling of special cases (for example, what does *Find*(1) return?). We could also add operations such as *Next* and *Previous,* which would take a position as argument and return the position of the successor and predecessor, respectively.

3.2.1. Simple Array Implementation of Lists

Obviously all of these instructions can be implemented just by using an array. Even if the array is dynamically allocated, an estimate of the maximum size of the list is required. Usually this requires a high overestimate, which wastes considerable space. This could be a serious limitation, especially if there are many lists of unknown size.

An array implementation allows *Print_List* and *Find* to be carried out in linear time, which is as good as can be expected, and the *Find_Kth* operation takes constant time. However, insertion and deletion are expensive. For example, inserting at position 0 (which amounts to making a new first element) requires first pushing the entire array down one spot to make room, whereas deleting the first element requires shifting all the elements in the list up one, so the worst case of these operations is $O(n)$. On average, half the list needs to be moved for either operation, so linear time is still required. Merely building a list by n successive inserts would require quadratic time.

Because the running time for insertions and deletions is so slow, being dominated by data movement, and the list size must be known in advance, simple arrays are generally not used to implement lists.

3.2.2. Linked Lists

In order to avoid the linear cost of insertion and deletion, we need to ensure that the list is not stored contiguously, since otherwise entire parts of the list will need to be moved. Figure 3.1 shows the general idea of a *linked list*.

The linked list consists of a series of structures, which are not necessarily adjacent in memory. Each structure contains the element and a pointer to a record containing its successor. We call this the *Next* pointer. The last cell's *Next* pointer contains zero, which is typically known as a null pointer. The symbol *NULL*, defined in <iostream.h>, will be used throughout instead of 0.

Recall that a pointer variable is just a variable that contains the address where some other data is stored. Thus, if *P* is declared to be a pointer to a record, then the value stored in *P* is interpreted as the location, in main memory, where a structure can be found. A field of that structure can be accessed by *P->Field_Name*, where *Field_Name* is the name of the field we wish to examine. Figure 3.2 shows the actual representation of the list in Figure 3.1. The list contains five structures, which happen to reside in memory locations 1000, 800, 712, 992, and 692, respectively. The *Next* pointer in the first structure has the value 800, which provides the indication of where the second structure is. The other structures each have a pointer that serves a similar purpose. Of course, in order to access this

Figure 3.1   A linked list

Figure 3.2   Linked list with actual pointer values

list, we need to know where the first cell can be found. A pointer variable can be used for this purpose. It is important to remember that a pointer is basically just a number. For the rest of this chapter, we will draw pointers with arrows, because they are more illustrative.

To execute *Print_List* or *Find(Key),* on some list *L,* we merely initialize a pointer to the first element in the list and then traverse the list by following the *Next* pointers. This operation is clearly linear-time, although the constant is likely to be larger than if an array implementation were used. The *Find_Kth* operation is no longer quite as efficient as an array implementation; *Find_Kth(i)* takes $O(i)$ time and works by traversing down the list in the obvious manner. In practice, this bound is pessimistic, because the calls to *Find_Kth* are frequently in sorted order (by i). As an example, *Find_Kth(1), Find_Kth(2), Find_Kth(3), Find_Kth(4)* can all be executed in one scan down the list.

The *Remove* command can be executed in one pointer change. Figure 3.3 shows the result of removing the third element in the original list.

The *Insert* command requires obtaining a new cell from the system by using a *new* call (more on this later) and then executing two pointer maneuvers. The general idea is shown in Figure 3.4. The dashed line represents the old pointer.

3.2.3. *Programming Details*

The description above is actually enough to get everything working, but there are several places where you are likely to go wrong. First of all, there is no really obvious way to insert at the front of the list from the definitions given. Second, deleting from the front of the list is a special case, because it changes the start of the list; careless coding will lose the list. A third problem concerns removal in general. Although the pointer moves above are simple, the removal algorithm requires us to keep track of the cell *before* the one that we want to delete.

It turns out that one simple change solves all three problems. We will keep a sentinel node, which is sometimes referred to as a *header* or *dummy* node. This is a common practice that we will see several times in the future. Our convention will be that the header is in position 0. Figure 3.5 shows a linked list with a header representing the list $a_1, a_2, \ldots, a_5$.

To avoid the problems associated with removes, we need to write a routine *Find_Previous,* which will return the position of the predecessor of the cell we wish

Figure 3.3   Deletion from a linked list

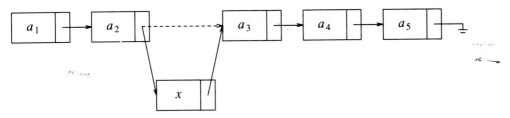

Figure 3.4   Insertion into a linked list

to delete. If we use a header, then if we wish to delete the first element in the list, *Find_Previous* will return the position of the header. The use of a header node is somewhat controversial. Some people argue that avoiding special cases is not sufficient justification for adding fictitious cells; they view the use of header nodes as little more than old-style hacking. Even so, we will use them here precisely because they allow us to show the basic pointer manipulations without obscuring the code with special cases. Otherwise, whether or not a header should be used is a matter of personal preference.

As examples, we will write the list ADT routines using a class with a template. Figure 3.6 gives the class specification. We will allow our list to hold items of arbitrary type, *Etype*. This is indicated by line 1. The keyword *protected* is similiar to *private*; the exact difference will be described later and has to do with derived classes and inheritance.

The basic list node is declared in lines 6 through 13. As described previously, a *Node* consists of an *Element* and a pointer to the *Next* node in the list. Lines 10 through 12 provide the constructor for *Node*. When a *Node* is dynamically allocated by a call to *new*, initial values to the fields can be set. The statement *new Node*; sets the initial values to zero by default. Lines 14 and 15 define the two variables associated with the *List*. One is a pointer to the header node, and the other is a pointer to the current node. "Current" can be defined in many ways; for us it is the result of the last *Find, Find_Previous, Insert* or request to reset the current position. Because all of this is in the protected section, the user of the *List* class cannot directly access the *List_Head* or the current position, nor can it even declare anything of type *Node*. The *Node* type is also hidden from the class user.

A typical C strategy would be to allow the user access to each individual cell by means of a pointer. The problem is that it is difficult to check for errors. A user could pass a pointer to something that isn't a node or to something that is a node, but in a different list. We can guarantee that this can't happen in our implementation, since all access is done by *Current*, and the user can only alter it by calling a class member function. An unfortunate consequence is that there is only one *Current*

Figure 3.5   Linked list with a header

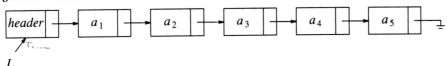

L

```
/* 1*/    template <class Etype>
/* 2*/    class List
/* 3*/    {
/* 4*/      protected:
/* 5*/        // The list is a linked list with a header node.

/* 6*/        struct Node
/* 7*/        {
/* 8*/            Etype Element;
/* 9*/            Node *Next;

/*10*/            // Constructor for node.
/*11*/            Node( Etype E = 0, Node *N = NULL ) :
/*12*/                Element( E ), Next( N ) { }
/*13*/        };

/*14*/        Node *List_Head;
/*15*/        Node *Current_Pos;

/*16*/        void Destroy_List( ); // An incorrect routine in Fig. 3.15.
/*17*/        void Delete_List( );  // The  correct routine in Fig. 3.16.

/*18*/      public:
/*19*/        // Constructors.
/*20*/        List( ) : List_Head ( new Node ), Current_Pos( List_Head ) { }
/*21*/        List( List & Value )
/*22*/            { Warn( "Call by value on list" ); operator=( Value ); }

/*23*/        // Destructor.
/*24*/        virtual ~List( ) { Delete_List( ); }

/*25*/        // Operators.
/*26*/        const List & operator = ( List & Value );
/*27*/        const List & operator ++ ( );
/*28*/        int operator ! ( ) const;
/*29*/        Etype operator ( ) ( ) const;

/*30*/        // Member functions.
/*31*/        int Is_Empty( ) const { return List_Head -> Next == NULL; }
/*32*/        virtual int Find( const Etype & X );
/*33*/        virtual int Find_Previous( const Etype & X );
/*34*/        int In_List( const Etype & X );
/*35*/        void First( ) { if( List_Head->Next != NULL )
/*36*/                              Current_Pos = List_Head->Next; }
/*37*/        void Header( ) { Current_Pos = List_Head; }
/*38*/        int Remove( const Etype & X );
/*39*/        virtual void Insert( const Etype & X );
/*40*/        virtual void Insert_As_First_Element( const Etype & X );
/*41*/    };
```

Figure 3.6 Specification for linked lists

position; thus, the case where two pointers need to independently access the list is unsupported.

A way to handle this is to do away with the concept of *Current* position and instead use an *iterator class*. One can view each instance of an iterator class as a safe pointer, on which only legal list operations, such as advancing or assignment of a node address in its list, are allowed. Access to internal list workings is granted by making the iterator class a friend of the linked list class. Though this is a better solution in general, its a bit more complicated than what we've proposed.

Returning to Figure 3.6, as we saw in Chapter 1, the *public* part, which is visible to the class user, contains constructors, a destructor, and functions that operate on an instance of *List*. The constructor at line 20 allocates a list by having *List_Head* point at a new *Node* and having *Current_Pos* point at the list header. Because we have arranged default parameters for the field members, the header's next pointer is *NULL*. The result is represented by Figure 3.7. Line 21 is a copy constructor, which is called when a temporary variable is needed or a parameter is passed by value. Because this is an expensive operation for linked lists, we've put a little warning, suggesting that the user consider using a reference variable instead.

Line 24 declares the destructor, which is indirectly provided in Figure 3.16. The destructor must go down the list and deallocate all of the list nodes. The keyword *virtual* will be discussed later; it also deals with inheritance.

Four operators are specified. The actual function bodies are all shown later. We also provide nine member functions, most of which are also shown later.

Figure 3.8 shows how to use the class. The *main* routine declares two integer lists (initially empty), *L1* and *L2*. Various operations are performed on the list, including the assignment at line 15. C++ is different from most other languages in that it allows the copy to be defined, by the class implementor, to make a physical copy of the right-hand-side list by allocating new nodes. The copy is illegal if undefined in the class specification, and it defaults to member-by-member copying if it is defined but unimplemented. This contrasts with the typical scenario in other languages, such as C, where an assignment would be sharing: *L2* would only point at the same list as *L1*, and subsequent changes in *L1* would be reflected in *L2*. In our implementation, *L1* and *L2* are really different lists (as the output of lines 18 through 22 would show). The default would give a C-like scenario and is almost always wrong when pointers are present.

The list can be printed only by accessing the list member functions. Lines 6 through 14 show a nonmember routine *Print_List*, which is written in this manner.

Figure 3.7   Empty list with header

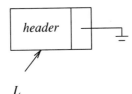

L

```
/* 1*/    // An example which instantiates two integer list classes.
/* 2*/    // The main routine does some insertions, removals, and copies,
/* 3*/    // Printing the list every now and then.
/* 4*/    // Print_List uses only the public functions.

/* 5*/    #include <iostream.h>

/* 6*/    void
/* 7*/    Print_List( List<int> & L )
/* 8*/    {
/* 9*/        if( L.Is_Empty( ) )
/*10*/            cout << "Empty list." << endl;
/*11*/        else
/*12*/            for( L.First( ); !L; ++L )
/*13*/                cout << L( ) << endl;
/*14*/    }


/* 1*/    main( )
/* 2*/    {
/* 3*/        List<int> L1, L2;

/* 4*/        cout << "( This should be empty )" << endl;
/* 5*/        Print_List( L1 );

/* 6*/        for( int i = 1; i <= 5; i++ )
/* 7*/            L1.Insert_As_First_Element( i );
/* 8*/        cout << "( This should be 5 4 3 2 1 )" << endl;
/* 9*/        Print_List( L1 );

/*10*/        for( i = 4;  i <= 6; i++ )
/*11*/            if( L1.Find( i ) )
/*12*/                cout << "Found " << L1( ) << endl;
/*13*/        else
/*14*/                cout << i << " not found." << endl;

/*15*/        L2 = L1;
/*16*/        cout << "( This should be 5 4 3 2 1 )" << endl;
/*17*/        Print_List( L2 );

/*18*/        L2.Remove( 3 );
/*19*/        cout << "( This should be 5 4 2 1 )" << endl;
/*20*/        Print_List( L2 );

/*21*/        cout << "( But list L1 should be unchanged 5 4 3 2 1 )" << endl;
/*22*/        Print_List( L1 );
/*23*/    }
```

Figure 3.8 Test program for linked lists

Lines 12 and 13 reflect the object-oriented thinking by using a natural method of iteration. *L.First* sets the current position of *L* to the first element. The operator *!*, defined in the class specification at line 28, returns true if the current position is not *NULL*, and the (prefix) operator *++* advances the current position. Finally, the operator *( )* returns the element in the current position. The code for these three operators is shown in Figure 3.9. Note: As an alternative, we could define an output function for the list class by writing an *operator* $<<$ function.

Figure 3.9 Functions to advance, retrieve, and check
whether past the end

```
/* 1*/    // Advance the current position.

/* 2*/    template <class Etype>
/* 3*/    inline const List<Etype> &
/* 4*/    List<Etype>::
/* 5*/    operator ++ ( )
/* 6*/    {
/* 7*/        if( Current_Pos != NULL )
/* 8*/            Current_Pos = Current_Pos->Next;
/* 9*/        return *this;
/*10*/    }


/* 1*/    // Retrieve element in the current position.
/* 2*/    // Return value is undefined if current position is NULL.

/* 3*/    template <class Etype>
/* 4*/    inline Etype
/* 5*/    List<Etype>::
/* 6*/    operator ( ) ( ) const
/* 7*/    {
/* 8*/        if( Current_Pos != NULL )
/* 9*/            return Current_Pos->Element;
/*10*/        else
/*11*/            return List_Head->Element;
/*12*/    }


/* 1*/    // Check if current position is not NULL.

/* 2*/    template <class Etype>
/* 3*/    inline int
/* 4*/    List<Etype>::
/* 5*/    operator ! ( ) const
/* 6*/    {
/* 7*/        return Current_Pos != NULL;
/* 8*/    }
```

Figure 3.10 shows the *Find* routine. If the item we are searching for is found, the current position is set and a nonzero value is returned. Otherwise, a zero is returned.

Next, we will *Remove* some element X (Figure 3.12). We need to decide what to do if X occurs more than once or not at all. Our routine removes that first occurence of X and returns a nonzero value if the remove succeeded. To do this, we find the cell prior to X in the list. If X is in the list, then as a result of *Find_Previous* (shown in Figure 3.11), *Current_Pos* is changed to point at the cell prior to the one we want to remove. The cell we want to remove is then bypassed and also deleted. Note that *Current_Pos* has been automatically moved, thus avoiding the subtle problem of deleting a cell but still having *Current_Pos* pointing at it.

Next comes the insertion routine, which places an item X after the current position. In Figure 3.13, line 9 sets P to point at a new node, which is spliced in after *Current_Pos* at line 14. *Current_Pos* is then changed at line 15. If *Current_Pos* is the *NULL* pointer, then this routine has the undesirable feature that it crashes. Our routines ensure that *Current_Pos* can't be *NULL*. An element can be inserted as the first element either by calling the routine *Header,* to set the current position to the header node, or by using the *Insert_As_First_Element* routine. The later method will be used in later chapters.

Finally, Figure 3.14 shows how lists are copied. Recall that for binary operators the left-hand side is the current object and the right-hand side is passed as a parameter. As a result of the copy, the current position for both lists is the first element.

Figure 3.10 *Find* routine

```
/* 1*/    // Assuming use of header node, find X.
/* 2*/    // If found, return TRUE and set the current position.

/* 3*/    template <class Etype>
/* 4*/    int
/* 5*/    List<Etype>::
/* 6*/    Find( const Etype & X )
/* 7*/    {
/* 8*/        Node *P;

/* 9*/        for( P = List_Head->Next; P != NULL; P = P->Next )
/*10*/            if( P->Element == X )
/*11*/            {
/*12*/                Current_Pos = P;
/*13*/                return 1;
/*14*/            }

/*15*/        return 0;
/*16*/    }
```

```
/* 1*/    // Assuming use of header node, find X.
/* 2*/    // If found, return TRUE and set the current position to before X.

/* 3*/    template <class Etype>
/* 4*/    int
/* 5*/    List<Etype>::
/* 6*/    Find_Previous( const Etype & X )
/* 7*/    {
/* 8*/        Node *P;

/* 9*/        for( P = List_Head; P->Next != NULL; P = P->Next )
/*10*/            if( P->Next->Element == X )
/*11*/            {
/*12*/                Current_Pos = P;
/*13*/                return 1;
/*14*/            }

/*15*/        return 0;
/*16*/    }
```

Figure 3.11   *Find_previous*—the *find* routine for use with *Remove*

```
/* 1*/    // Remove X from the list.
/* 2*/    // Return nonzero if deletion was successful.
/* 3*/    // Header node is assumed.

/* 4*/    template <class Etype>
/* 5*/    int
/* 6*/    List<Etype>::
/* 7*/    Remove( const Etype & X )
/* 8*/    {
/* 9*/        Node *Cell_To_Delete;

/*10*/        if( Find_Previous( X ) )
/*11*/        {
/*12*/            Cell_To_Delete = Current_Pos->Next;
/*13*/            Current_Pos->Next = Cell_To_Delete->Next;
/*14*/            delete Cell_To_Delete;
/*15*/            return 1;
/*16*/        }
/*17*/        return 0;
/*18*/    }
```

Figure 3.12   Remove routine for linked lists

```
/* 1*/    // Insert X after the current position.
/* 2*/    // X becomes the current element.
/* 3*/    // Header implementation assumed.

/* 4*/    template <class Etype>
/* 5*/    void
/* 6*/    List<Etype>::
/* 7*/    Insert( const Etype & X )
/* 8*/    {
/* 9*/        Node *P = new Node( X, Current_Pos->Next );

/*10*/        if( P == NULL )
/*11*/            Error( "Out of space" );
/*12*/        else
/*13*/        {
/*14*/            Current_Pos->Next = P;
/*15*/            Current_Pos = Current_Pos->Next;
/*16*/        }
/*17*/    }
```

Figure 3.13 Insertion routine for linked lists

```
/* 1*/    // Duplicate a list.
/* 2*/    // Current position becomes first element in both lists.

/* 3*/    template <class Etype>
/* 4*/    const List<Etype> &
/* 5*/    List<Etype>::
/* 6*/    operator = ( List<Etype> & Value )
/* 7*/    {
/* 8*/        if( this == &Value )  // Don't copy to yourself!.
/* 9*/            return *this;
          Delete_List( );
/*10*/        Current_Pos = List_Head = new Node;

/*11*/        for( Value.First( ); !Value; ++ Value )
/*12*/        {
/*13*/            Current_Pos->Next =
/*14*/                    new Node( Value( ), Current_Pos->Next );
/*15*/            Current_Pos = Current_Pos->Next;
/*16*/        }
/*17*/        Current_Pos->Next = 0;

/*18*/        First( );
/*19*/        Value.First( );

/*20*/        return *this;
/*21*/    }
```

Figure 3.14 Assignment operator

With the exception of the *Remove*, *Find*, *Find_Previous*, and *Copy* routines, all of the operations we have coded take $O(1)$ time. This is because in all cases only a fixed number of instructions are performed, no matter how large the list is. For the *Find* and *Find_Previous* routines, the running time is $O(n)$ in the worst case, because the entire list might need to be traversed if the element is either not found or is last in the list. On average, the running time is $O(n)$ because, on average, half the list must be traversed. The *Remove* routine is $O(1)$ plus the call to *Find_Previous*.

3.2.4. Common Errors

The most common error that you will get is that your program will crash because of a misdirected pointer. One common reason is failure to initialize the variable. We saw, for example, that many of the routines would crash if *Current_Pos* were NULL. *Whenever you do an indirection, you must make sure that the pointer is not null.*

The second common mistake concerns when and when not to use *new* to get a new cell. You must remember that declaring a pointer to a structure does not create the structure but only gives enough space to hold the address where some structure might be. The only way to create an object that is not already declared is to use the reserved word *new*. The statement $P = new\ Node$; has the system create a new object of type *Node* in accordance with the constructor for *Node*; then P is set to point to the new structure. On the other hand, if you want to use a pointer variable to access existing structures, such as to run down a list, there is no need to create a new structure; in that case the *new* command is inappropriate.

When dynamically allocated space is no longer needed, you can issue a *delete* command to inform the system that it may reclaim the space. A consequence of the *delete* command is that the referenced pointer now points to an undefined value, and the space is reclaimed by the system for later use. If the object is an array, then [] are required after the *delete* keyword.

If you never delete from a linked list, the number of calls to *new* should equal the size of the list, plus 1 if a header is used. Any less, and you cannot possibly have a working program. Any more, and you are wasting space and probably time. Occasionally, if your program uses a lot of space, the system may be unable to satisfy your request for a new cell; a *NULL* pointer is then returned.

After a deletion in a linked list, it is usually a good idea to dispose of the cell, especially if there are lots of insertions and deletions intermingled and memory might become a problem. You need to keep a temporary variable set to the cell to be disposed of, because after the pointer moves are finished, you will not have a reference to it. As an example, the code in Figure 3.15 is not the correct way to delete an entire list.

Figure 3.16 shows the correct way to do this. Disposal is not necessarily a fast thing, so you might want to check to see whether the disposal routine is causing any slow performance and comment it out if this is the case. This author has written a

```
/* 1*/    // Wrong way to destroy an entire list.
/* 2*/    // Header assumed.

/* 3*/    template <class Etype>
/* 4*/    void
/* 5*/    List<Etype>::
/* 6*/    Destroy_List( )
/* 7*/    {
/* 8*/        Node *P = List_Head->Next;
/* 9*/        while( P != NULL )
/*10*/        {
/*11*/            delete P;
/*12*/            P = P->Next;
/*13*/        }
/*14*/        delete List_Head;
/*15*/        Current_Pos = List_Head->Next;
/*16*/    }
```

Figure 3.15 Incorrect way to delete a list

program (see the exercises) that was made 25 times faster by commenting out the disposal (of 10,000 nodes). It turned out that the cells were freed in a rather peculiar order and apparently caused an otherwise linear program to spend $O(n \log n)$ time to delete n cells.

Figure 3.16 Correct way to delete a list

```
/* 1*/    // Delete an entire list.
/* 2*/    // Header assumed.

/* 3*/    template <class Etype>
/* 4*/    void
/* 5*/    List<Etype>::
/* 6*/    Delete_List( )
/* 7*/    {
/* 8*/        Node *P = List_Head->Next, *Temp;

/* 9*/        while( P != NULL )
/*10*/        {
/*11*/            Temp = P->Next;
/*12*/            delete P;
/*13*/            P = Temp;
/*14*/        }
/*15*/        delete List_Head;
/*16*/    }
```

3.2.5.   Doubly and Circularly Linked Lists

Sometimes it is convenient to traverse lists backwards. The standard implementation does not help here, but the solution is simple. Merely add an extra field containing a pointer to the previous cell to the data structure. The cost of this is an extra link, which adds to the space requirement and also doubles the cost of insertions and deletions because there are more pointers to fix. On the other hand, it simplifies deletion, because you no longer have to refer to a key by using a pointer to the previous cell; this information is now at hand. Figure 3.17 shows a doubly linked list.

A popular convention is to have the last cell keep a pointer back to the first. This can be done with or without a header (if the header is present, the last cell points to it) and can also be done with doubly linked lists (the first cell's previous pointer points to the last cell). This clearly affects some of the tests, but the structure is popular in some applications. Figure 3.18 shows a double circularly linked list with no header.

3.2.6   Sorted Linked Lists, Inheritance, and Virtual Functions

Sometimes it is desirable to keep the items in the linked list arranged in sorted order (we'll see an example in the next section). The fundamental difference between a sorted linked list and an unsorted linked list is the insertion routine. Indeed, a correct sorted list class could be obtained just by altering the insertion routine from our already written list class.

Rather than using an editor to make alterations, the object-oriented approach is to derive a new class, *Sorted_List,* from our already written *List* class. Thus, future changes in the *List* class would be reflected in the *Sorted_List* class. Figure 3.19 shows how this is done. Two routines are shown: the class specification for *Sorted_List* and then the new insertion routine.

Line 3 of the specification says that *Sorted_List* is a derived class of *List* (we must explicitly include an instantiation of the list, hence *List<Etype>*). *Sorted_List* now *inherits* everything the *List* has, including all of its functions. It is free to add new variables and new functions and even to override existing functions. By default, however, everything that is inherited is *private*, so the *public* reserved word allows users of the *Sorted_List* class to see the inherited public members of *List*. (Otherwise, for instance, *Remove* would not be visible).

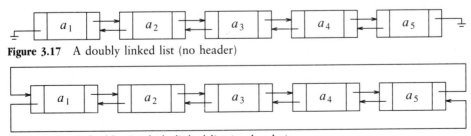

Figure 3.17   A doubly linked list (no header)

Figure 3.18   A double circularly linked list (no header)

```
/* 1*/    // Class declaration for a sorted linked list.

/* 2*/    template <class Etype>
/* 3*/    class Sorted_List : public List<Etype>
/* 4*/    {
/* 5*/      public:
/* 6*/        virtual void Insert( const Etype & X );
/* 7*/        virtual void Insert_As_First_Element( const Etype & X )
/* 8*/            { Error( "Illegal operation for sorted list." ); }
/* 9*/    };



/* 1*/    // Sorted insertion.

/* 2*/    template <class Etype>
/* 3*/    void
/* 4*/    Sorted_List<Etype>::
/* 5*/    Insert( const Etype & X )
/* 6*/    {
/* 7*/        for( Node *P = List_Head; P->Next != NULL; P = P->Next )
/* 8*/            if( P->Next->Element > X )
/* 9*/                break;

/*10*/        Current_Pos = P;
/*11*/        List<Etype>::Insert( X );
/*12*/    }
```

Figure 3.19 Sorted linked list

The class overrides two functions. *Insert_As_First_Element* no longer makes sense because performing it could destroy the sorted order. The other change is a new *Insert* routine. The routine finds the last position *P* that contains an element no larger than *X*. The current position is to set to it, and then a call to the *List* insertion is made. Warning: If line 11 doesn't explicitly qualify that the *Insert* that is being called is the *List* insertion routine, then line 11 would represent a recursive call to the *Sorted_list* routine. The explicit declaration of *Etype* shouldn't be necessary at line 11 (because it can be inferred from the type of *X*), but at the time of this writing many compilers still insist on it. Of course, *operator>* must be defined for *Etype*, or the program won't even compile.

To use the class, we declare a sorted list: *Sorted_List<int>* L. *Insert* and *Insert_As_First_Element* refer to the functions defined in Figure 3.19, while all other routines refer to the functions defined in the *base class, List*.

When an object is declared as above, things are easy because the choice of which function to use can be determined at compile time. Suppose, however, we declare a pointer to a list:

```
List<int> *L;
```

and later on we allocate either a sorted or an unsorted list to it, depending on the result of user input:

```
L = new Sorted_List;
```

or

```
L = new List;
```

This is certainly legal because *Sorted_List* is a subclass of *List*. In some other part of the code, a statement

```
L->Insert( X );
```

appears. The question is which *Insert* gets called.

The most logical alternative is to apply the function that corresponds to what *L* is actually pointing at when the call is made. Clearly, this decision cannot be at compile time and must be made at run time. The keyword *virtual* tells the compiler (more specifically the linker) that it should defer its decision on what function is implied by the call until run time. This is called *dynamic binding*. If the reserved word *virtual* is not present, then the compiler will use the function that corresponds to the type declaration of *L*, namely *List*.

In Figure 3.6 we made four member functions virtual: the two insertion routines and the two find routines (because sorted *Find* could be improved from just plain *Find* by stopping an unsuccessful search early). If a class has a virtual function, one should also ensure that the destructor is virtual too.

Delayed binding and virtual functions apply only for pointers and references to classes, so if objects are declared as in Figure 3.7 rather than dynamically allocated, there is no difference between using and omitting the *virtual* declaration.

Another approach is to make everything virtual and to have all decisions made as the program is running. A class that consists only of virtual functions (no other field members, and no bodies) can be defined. A virtual function with no body can be defined by initializing it to zero (i.e., *void F( ) = 0;*). Then the implementation is defined as a subclass of the abstract base class. Though this is popular in some circles, there are two disadvantages. First, as one might suspect, this method incurs a run-time overhead penalty, though studies have shown that it is small. Second, one also sacrifices type checking at compile time, which can frequently catch silly errors.

3.2.7. *Examples*

We provide three examples that use linked lists. The first is a simple way to represent single-variable polynomials. The second is a method to sort in linear time for some special cases. Finally, we show a complicated example of how linked lists might be used to keep track of course registration at a university.

The Polynomial ADT

We can define an abstract data type for single-variable polynomials (with nonnegative exponents) by using a list. Let $f(x) = \sum_{i=0}^{n} a_i x^i$. If most of the coefficients a_i are nonzero, we can use a simple array to store the coefficients. We could then write routines to perform addition, subtraction, multiplication, differentiation, and other operations on these polynomials. In this case, we might use the class specification given in Figure 3.20. We could then write routines to perform various operations. Two possibilities are addition and multiplication. These are shown in Figures 3.21 through 3.23.

Ignoring the time to initialize the output polynomials to zero, the running time of the multiplication routine is proportional to the product of the degree of the two input polynomials. This is adequate for dense polynomials, where most of the terms are present, but if $p_1(x) = 10x^{1000} + 5x^{14} + 1$ and $p_2(x) = 3x^{1990} - 2x^{1492} + 11x + 5$, then the running time is likely to be unacceptable. One can see that most

Figure 3.20   Class specification for array implementation of the polynomial ADT

```
/* 1*/    #include <iostream.h>

/* 2*/    static const Max_Degree = 10;
/* 3*/    class Polynomial
/* 4*/    {
/* 5*/      private:
/* 6*/        int High_Power;
/* 7*/        double *Coeff_Array;

/* 8*/        // Friends.
/* 9*/        friend Polynomial operator + ( const Polynomial & Poly1,
/*10*/                        const Polynomial & Poly2 );
/*11*/        friend Polynomial operator * ( const Polynomial & Poly1,
/*12*/                        const Polynomial & Poly2 );

/*13*/        friend ostream & operator << ( ostream & Out,
/*14*/                        const Polynomial & Value );
/*15*/        friend istream & operator >> ( istream & In,
/*16*/                        Polynomial & Value );

/*17*/      public:
/*18*/        // Constructors.
/*19*/        Polynomial( );
/*20*/        Polynomial( Polynomial & Rvalue );

/*21*/        // Destructors.
/*22*/        ~Polynomial( ) { delete [ ] Coeff_Array; }

/*23*/        // Operators.
/*24*/        const Polynomial & operator = ( const Polynomial & Rvalue );
/*25*/        int  operator == ( const Polynomial & Rvalue );
/*26*/    };
```

```
/* 1*/    Polynomial::
/* 2*/    Polynomial( )
/* 3*/    {
/* 4*/        Coeff_Array = new double[ Max_Degree + 1 ];
/* 5*/        if( Coeff_Array == NULL )
/* 6*/            Error( "Out of memory" );
/* 7*/        else
/* 8*/        {
/* 9*/            High_Power = -1;
/*10*/            for( int i = 0; i <= Max_Degree; i++ )
/*11*/                Coeff_Array[ i ] = 0.0;
/*12*/        }
/*13*/    }


/* 1*/    Polynomial::
/* 2*/    Polynomial( Polynomial & Rvalue )
/* 3*/    {
/* 4*/        High_Power = Rvalue.High_Power;
/* 5*/        Coeff_Array = new double[ Max_Degree + 1 ];
/* 6*/        for( int i = 0; i <= High_Power; i++ )
/* 7*/            Coeff_Array[ i ] = Rvalue.Coeff_Array[ i ];
/* 8*/    }
```

Figure 3.21 Constructors to initialize a polynomial to zero

```
/* 1*/    Polynomial
/* 2*/    operator + ( const Polynomial & Poly1, const Polynomial & Poly2 )
/* 3*/    {
/* 4*/        int Result_Power = Max( Poly1.High_Power, Poly2.High_Power );
/* 5*/        Polynomial Result;

/* 6*/        for( int i = 0; i <= Result_Power; i++ )
/* 7*/            Result.Coeff_Array[ i ] = Poly1.Coeff_Array[ i ] +
/* 8*/                            Poly2.Coeff_Array[ i ];

/* 9*/        Result.High_Power = Result_Power;
/*10*/        return Result;
/*11*/    }
```

Figure 3.22 Procedure to add two polynomials

```
/* 1*/    Polynomial
/* 2*/    operator * ( const Polynomial & Poly1, const Polynomial & Poly2 )
/* 3*/    {
/* 4*/        int Result_Power = Poly1.High_Power + Poly2.High_Power;
/* 5*/        Polynomial Result;

/* 6*/        for( int i = 0; i <= Poly1.High_Power; i++ )
/* 7*/            for( int j = 0; j <= Poly2.High_Power; j++ )
/* 8*/                Result.Coeff_Array[ i + j ] +=
/* 9*/                    Poly1.Coeff_Array[ i ] * Poly2.Coeff_Array[ j ];

/*10*/        Result.High_Power = Result_Power;
/*11*/        return Result;
/*12*/    }
```

Figure 3.23   Procedure to multiply two polynomials

of the time is spent multiplying zeros and stepping through what amounts to nonexistent parts of the input polynomials. This is always undesirable.

An alternative is to use a singly linked list. Each term in the polynomial is contained in one cell, and the cells are sorted in decreasing order of exponents. For instance, the linked lists in Figure 3.24 represent $p_1(x)$ and $p_2(x)$. We could then use the class specification in Figure 3.25. Notice that the public part is unchanged. A polynomial consists of a sorted linked list of *Pnodes*. Each *Pnode* represents a term, namely a coefficient and an exponent. We must define equality and comparison for the *Pnode* class because the sorted list class uses these operations. Because order in the list is based only on the exponent, and we want a list sorted in decreasing rather than increasing order, we arrive at the functions in lines 8 through 15.

Everything else is straightforward, except the destructor for the *Polynomial* class. The destructor says to do nothing, so all that happens is that the class variables are destroyed. Thus, *L* at line 20 is destroyed automatically, by implicitly calling the destructor for *Sorted_List* (which is defined by the *List* destructor).

The operations would then be straightforward to implement. The only potential difficulty is that when two polynomials are multiplied, the resultant polynomial will

Figure 3.24   Linked list representations of two polynomials

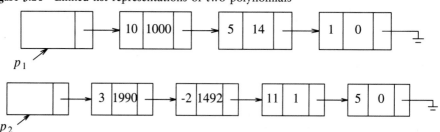

```
/* 1*/      struct Pnode
/* 2*/      {
/* 3*/          double Coefficient;
/* 4*/          unsigned int Exponent;

/* 5*/          Pnode( double C = 0.0, unsigned int E = 0 )
/* 6*/              { Coefficient = C; Exponent = E; }
/* 7*/          ~Pnode( ) { }

/* 8*/          inline int operator > ( const Pnode & Right )
/* 9*/          {
/*10*/              return Exponent < Right.Exponent;
/*11*/          }
/*12*/          inline int operator == ( const Pnode & Right )
/*13*/          {
/*14*/              return Exponent == Right.Exponent;
/*15*/          }
/*16*/      };

/*17*/      class Polynomial
/*18*/      {
/*19*/        private:
/*20*/          Sorted_List<struct Pnode> L;  // Nodes sorted by exponent.

/*21*/          friend Polynomial operator + ( const Polynomial & Poly1,
/*22*/                          const Polynomial & Poly2 );
/*23*/          friend Polynomial operator * ( const Polynomial & Poly1,
/*24*/                          const Polynomial & Poly2 );
/*25*/          friend ostream & operator << ( ostream & Out,
/*26*/                          Polynomial & Value );
/*27*/          friend istream & operator >> ( istream & In,
/*28*/                          Polynomial & Value );

/*29*/        public:
/*30*/          // Constructors.
/*31*/          Polynomial( ) { }
/*32*/          Polynomial( Polynomial & Rvalue );

/*33*/          // Destructors.
/*34*/          ~Polynomial( ) { }

/*35*/          // Operators.
/*36*/          const Polynomial & operator = ( Polynomial & Rvalue );
/*37*/          int  operator == ( const Polynomial & Rvalue );
/*38*/      };
```

Figure 3.25 Class specification for sorted linked list implementation of the Polynomial ADT have to have like terms combined. There are several ways to do this, but we will leave this as an exercise.

Radix Sort

A second example where linked lists are used is called *radix sort*. Radix sort is sometimes known as *card sort*, because it was used, until the advent of modern computers, to sort old-style punch cards.

If we have n integers in the range 1 to m (or 0 to $m - 1$), we can use this information to obtain a fast sort known as *bucket sort*. We keep an array called *Count*, of size m, which is initialized to zero. Thus, *Count* has m cells (or buckets), which are initially empty. When a_i is read, increment (by one) *Count*$[a_i]$. After all the input is read, scan the *Count* array, printing out a representation of the sorted list. This algorithm takes $O(m + n)$; the proof is left as an exercise. If $m = \Theta(n)$, then bucket sort is $O(n)$.

Radix sort is a generalization of this. The easiest way to see what happens is by example. Suppose we have 10 numbers in the range 0 to 999 that we would like to sort. In general, this is n numbers in the range 0 to $n^p - 1$ for some constant p. Obviously, we cannot use bucket sort; there would be too many buckets. The trick is to use several passes of bucket sort. The natural algorithm would be to bucket-sort by the most significant "digit" (digit is taken to base n), then next most significant, and so on. That algorithm does not work, but if we perform bucket sorts by least significant "digit" first, then the algorithm works. Of course, more than one number could fall into the same bucket, and, unlike the original bucket sort, these numbers could be different, so we keep them in a list. Notice that all the numbers could have some digit in common, so if a simple array were used for the lists, then each array would have to be of size n, for a total space requirement of $\Theta(n^2)$.

The following example shows the action of radix sort on 10 numbers. The input is 64, 8, 216, 512, 27, 729, 0, 1, 343, 125 (the first ten cubes arranged randomly). The first step bucket sorts by the least significant digit. In this case the math is in base 10 (to make things simple), but do not assume this in general. The buckets are as shown in Figure 3.26, so the list, sorted by least significant digit, is 0, 1, 512, 343, 64, 125, 216, 27, 8, 729. These are now sorted by the next least significant digit (the tens digit here) (see Fig. 3.27). Pass 2 gives output 0, 1, 8, 512, 216, 125, 27, 729, 343, 64. This list is now sorted with respect to the two least significant digits. The final pass, shown in Figure 3.28, bucket-sorts by most significant digit. The final list is 0, 1, 8, 27, 64, 125, 216, 343, 512, 729.

To see that the algorithm works, notice that the only possible failure would occur if two numbers came out of the same bucket in the wrong order. But the

Figure 3.26 Buckets after first step of radix sort

0	1	512	343	64	125	216	27	8	729
0	1	2	3	4	5	6	7	8	9

| 8 | | 729 | | | | | | | |
| 1 | 216 | 27 | | | | | | | |
0	512	125		343		64			
0	1	2	3	4	5	6	7	8	9

Figure 3.27   Buckets after the second pass of radix sort

64									
27									
8									
1									
0	125	216	343		512		729		
0	1	2	3	4	5	6	7	8	9

Figure 3.28   Buckets after the last pass of radix sort

previous passes ensure that when several numbers enter a bucket, they enter in sorted order. The running time is $O(p(n + b))$ where p is the number of passes, n is the number of elements to sort, and b is the number of buckets. In our case, $b = n$.

As an example, we could sort all integers that are representable on a computer (32 bits) by radix sort, if we did three passes over a bucket size of 2^{11}. This algorithm would always be $O(n)$ on this computer, but probably still not as efficient as some of the algorithms we shall see in Chapter 7, because of the high constant involved (remember that this algorithm would have the overhead of maintaining linked lists).

Multilists

Our last example shows a more complicated use of linked lists. A university with 40,000 students and 2,500 courses needs to be able to generate two types of reports. The first report lists the class registration for each class, and the second report lists, by student, the classes that each student is registered for.

The obvious implementation might be to use a two-dimensional array. Such an array would have 100 million entries. The average student registers for about three courses, so only 120,000 of these entries, or roughly 0.1 percent, would actually have meaningful data.

What is needed is a list for each class that contains the students in the class. We also need a list for each student that contains the classes the student is registered for. Figure 3.29 shows our implementation.

As the figure shows, we have combined two lists into one. All lists use a header and are circular. To list all of the students in class C3, we start at C3 and traverse its list (by going right). The first cell belongs to student S1. Although there is no explicit information to this effect, this can be determined by following the student's linked list until the header is reached. Once this is done, we return back to C3's list (we stored the position where we were in the course list before we traversed the

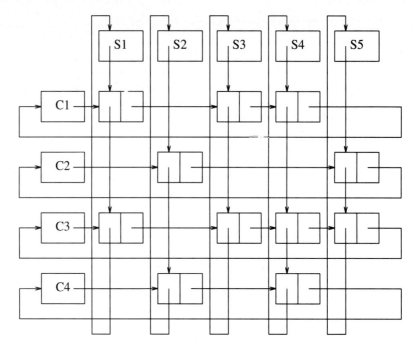

Figure 3.29   Multilist implementation for registration
problem

student's list) and find another cell, which can be determined to belong to $S3$. We can continue and find that $S4$ and $S5$ are also in this class. In a similar manner, we can determine, for any student, all of the classes in which the student is registered.

Using a circular list saves space but does so at the expense of time. In the worst case, if the first student were registered for every course, then every entry would need to be examined in order to determine all the course names for that student. Because in this application there are relatively few courses per student and few students per course, this is not likely to happen. If it were suspected that this could cause a problem, then each of the (nonheader) cells could have pointers directly back to the student and class header. This would double the space requirement but simplify and speed up the implementation.

3.2.8. *Cursor Implementation of Linked Lists*

Many languages, such as BASIC and FORTRAN, do not support pointers. If linked lists are required and pointers are not available, then an alternate implementation must be used. The alternate method we will describe is known as a *cursor* implementation.

The two important items present in a pointer implementation of linked lists are

1. The data is stored in a collection of objects. Each object contains the data and a pointer to the next object.

2. A new object can be obtained from the system's global memory by a call to *new* and released by a call to *delete*.

Our cursor implementation must be able to simulate this. The logical way to satisfy condition 1 is to have a global array of structures. For any cell in the array, its array index can be used in place of an address. Figure 3.30 gives the class specification for a cursor class. The array of structures is stored in *Cursor_Space*. We simulate condition 2 by allowing the equivalent of *new* and *delete* for cells in the *Cursor_Space* array. To do this, we will keep a list (the *freelist*) of cells that are not in any list. The list will use cell 0 as a header. The initial configuration is shown in Figure 3.31. The procedure *Init_Space* sets *Cursor_Space* to the initial configuration. *Init_Space* is called by the constructor, or by *Cnew* if necessary (we'll explain that part later).

   A value of 0 for *Next* is the equivalent of a *NULL* pointer. To perform a *new*, the first element (after the header) is removed from the freelist. To perform a *delete*, we

Figure 3.30   Class specification for cursor implementation
                 of linked lists

```
/* 1*/    #include <iostream.h>
/* 2*/    static const Default_Max_Size = 101;

/* 3*/    template <class Element_Type>
/* 4*/    class Cursor
/* 5*/    {
/* 6*/       private:
/* 7*/          unsigned int Space_Size;

/* 8*/          struct Node
/* 9*/          {
/*10*/              Element_Type Element;
/*11*/              unsigned int Next;
/*12*/          };

/*13*/          Node *Cursor_Space;
/*14*/          friend class List<Element_Type>;

/*15*/          void Init_Space( );

/*16*/       public:
/*17*/          // Constructors.
/*18*/          Cursor( unsigned int Max_Size = Default_Max_Size );

/*19*/          // Destructor.
/*20*/          ~Cursor( ) { delete [ ] Cursor_Space; }

/*21*/          // Member functions.
/*22*/          unsigned int Cnew( Element_Type E = 0, unsigned int N = 0 );
/*23*/          void Cdelete( unsigned int P );
/*24*/    };
```

Slot	Element	Next
0		1
1		2
2		3
3		4
4		5
5		6
6		7
7		8
8		9
9		10
10		0

Figure 3.31   An initialized Cursor_Space

place the cell at the front of the freelist. Figure 3.32 shows the cursor implementation of *new* and *delete*, as well as *Init_Space*. If there is no space available, our routine returns 0.

Given this, the cursor implementation of linked lists is straightforward. For consistency, we will implement our lists with a header node. As an example, in Figure 3.33, if the value of L is 5 and the value of M is 3, then L represents the list *a, b, e*; and M represents the list *c, d, f*.

Figure 3.32   *New, delete,* and initialization functions for *Cursor* class

```
/* 1*/    template <class Element_Type>
/* 2*/    void
/* 3*/    Cursor<Element_Type>::
/* 4*/    Init_Space( )
/* 5*/    {
/* 6*/        Cursor_Space = new Node [ Space_Size ];
/* 7*/        for( int i = 0; i < Space_Size; i++ )
/* 8*/            Cursor_Space[ i ].Next = i + 1;
/* 9*/        Cursor_Space[ Space_Size - 1 ].Next = 0;
/*10*/    }


/* 1*/    template <class Element_Type>
/* 2*/    Cursor<Element_Type>::
/* 3*/    Cursor( unsigned int Max_Size )
/* 4*/    {
/* 5*/        Space_Size = Max_Size;
/* 6*/        Init_Space( );
/* 7*/    }
```

```
/* 1*/    template <class Element_Type>
/* 2*/    unsigned int
/* 3*/    Cursor<Element_Type>::
/* 4*/    Cnew( Element_Type E, unsigned int N )
/* 5*/    {
/* 6*/        unsigned int P;

/* 7*/        if( Cursor_Space == NULL )
/* 8*/        {
/* 9*/            Space_Size = Default_Max_Size;
/*10*/            Init_Space( );
/*11*/        }

/*12*/        P = Cursor_Space[ 0 ].Next;
/*13*/        Cursor_Space[ 0 ].Next = Cursor_Space[ P ].Next;

/*14*/        if( P != 0 )
/*15*/        {
/*16*/            Cursor_Space[ P ].Element = E;
/*17*/            Cursor_Space[ P ].Next = N;
/*18*/        }
/*19*/        return P;
/*20*/    }

/* 1*/    template <class Element_Type>
/* 2*/    void
/* 3*/    Cursor<Element_Type>::
/* 4*/    Cdelete( unsigned int P )
/* 5*/    {
/* 6*/        Cursor_Space[ P ].Next = Cursor_Space[ 0 ].Next;
/* 7*/        Cursor_Space[ 0 ].Next = P;
/* 8*/    }
```

Figure 3.32   *(Continued)*

Slot	Element	Next
0	–	6
1	b	9
2	f	0
3	header	7
4	–	0
5	header	10
6	–	4
7	c	8
8	d	2
9	e	0
10	a	1

Figure 3.33   Example of a cursor implementation of
linked lists

To write the functions for a cursor implementation of linked lists, we must pass and return the identical parameters as the pointer implementation. Figure 3.34 shows the class specification for a cursor implementation of linked lists. Virtually everything is identical to the original implementation. At line 5, we use the keyword *static* so that all *List* classes (of a given *Element_Type*) share the same *Cursor_Space*. Unfortunately, this declaration doesn't actually allocate the *Cursor_Space*, so this must be done globally. If a list of integers is desired, the global variable declaration *Cursor<int> C;* must be used. Equally unfortunate, on our

Figure 3.34   List class specification for cursor
                 implementation

```
/* 1*/    template <class Element_Type>
/* 2*/    class List
/* 3*/    {
/* 4*/      private:
/* 5*/        static Cursor<Element_Type> C;    // C is external.

/* 6*/        // The list is a linked list with a header node.

/* 7*/        unsigned int List_Head;
/* 8*/        unsigned int Current_Pos;

/* 9*/      public:
/*10*/        // Constructors.
/*11*/        List( ) { List_Head = C.Cnew( ); }
/*12*/        List( List & Value )
/*13*/            { Warn( "List passed by value" ); operator=( Value ); }

/*14*/        // Destructor.
/*15*/        ~List( );

/*16*/        // Operators.
/*17*/        const List & operator = ( List & Value );
/*18*/        const List & operator ++ ( );
/*19*/        int operator ! ( ) const;
/*20*/        Element_Type & operator ( ) ( ) const;

/*21*/        // Member functions.
/*22*/        int Is_Empty( ) const;
/*23*/        int Find( const Element_Type & X );
/*24*/        int Find_Previous( const Element_Type & X );
/*25*/        int In_List( const Element_Type & X );
/*26*/        void First( );
/*27*/        int Remove( const Element_Type & X );
/*28*/        void Insert( const Element_Type & X );
/*29*/        void Insert_As_First_Element( const Element_Type & X );
/*30*/    };
```

machine, this means that a constructor is never called for *C*, so the first instance of *C.Cnew* would fail, unless *C* is constructed and initialized then. This explains lines 7 through 11 of the *Cnew* routine in Figure 3.32. If the *static* keyword is omitted, then each list will get its own *Cursor_Space*. Though this costs extra memory, it has the benefit of not requiring the external variable, and that the cursor constructor is called automatically for each list.

The routines are straightforward. Figure 3.35 implements a function to test whether a list is empty and another function is to go to the front of the list. Figure 3.36 implements the operators.

The function *Find* is shown in Figure 3.37. The code to implement deletion is shown in Figure 3.38. Again, the interface for the cursor implementation is identical to the pointer implementation. Finally, Figure 3.38 also shows a cursor implementation of *Insert*.

The rest of the routines are similarly coded. The crucial point is that these routines follow the ADT specification. They take specific parameters and perform specific operations. The implementation is transparent to the user. The cursor implementation could be used instead of the linked list implementation, with virtually no change required in the rest of the code. If relatively few *Find*s are performed, the cursor implementation could be significantly faster because of the lack of memory management routines. Moreover, by using a pointer for the *Next* field, we get the speed of pointers without the price of dynamic allocation.

Figure 3.35 Functions to test whether a linked list is empty and to advance to the first position—cursor implementation

```
/* 1*/    // Test for empty list, assuming header node.

/* 2*/    template <class Element_Type>
/* 3*/    inline int
/* 4*/    List<Element_Type>::
/* 5*/    Is_Empty( ) const
/* 6*/    {
/* 7*/        return C.Cursor_Space[ List_Head ].Next == 0;
/* 8*/    }


/* 1*/    // Set the current position to the first element.
/* 2*/    // Header implementation assumed.

/* 3*/    template <class Element_Type>
/* 4*/    inline void
/* 5*/    List<Element_Type>::
/* 6*/    First( )
/* 7*/    {
/* 8*/        Current_Pos = C.Cursor_Space[ List_Head ].Next;
/* 9*/    }
```

```
/* 1*/    // Advance the current position.

/* 2*/    template <class Element_Type>
/* 3*/    inline const List<Element_Type> &
/* 4*/    List<Element_Type>::
/* 5*/    operator ++ ( )
/* 6*/    {
/* 7*/        if( Current_Pos )
/* 8*/            Current_Pos = C.Cursor_Space[ Current_Pos ].Next;
/* 9*/        return *this;
/*10*/    }


/* 1*/    // Retrieve element in the current position.
/* 2*/    // Return value is undefined if current position is 0.

/* 3*/    template <class Element_Type>
/* 4*/    inline Element_Type &
/* 5*/    List<Element_Type>::
/* 6*/    operator ( ) ( ) const
/* 7*/    {
/* 8*/        if( Current_Pos != 0 )
/* 9*/            return C.Cursor_Space[ Current_Pos ].Element;
/*10*/        else
/*11*/            return C.Cursor_Space[ List_Head ].Element;
/*12*/    }


/* 1*/    // Check if current position is not 0.

/* 2*/    template <class Element_Type>
/* 3*/    inline int
/* 4*/    List<Element_Type>::
/* 5*/    operator ! ( ) const
/* 6*/    {
/* 7*/        return Current_Pos;
/* 8*/    }
```

Figure 3.36 Operators—cursor implementation

The freelist represents an interesting data structure in its own right. The cell that is removed from the freelist is the one that was most recently placed there by virtue of *Cdelete*. Thus, the last cell placed on the freelist is the first cell taken off. The data structure that also has this property is known as a *stack* and is the topic of the next section.

```
/* 1*/    // Assuming use of header node, find X.
/* 2*/    // If found, return 1 and set the current position.

/* 3*/    template <class Element_Type>
/* 4*/    int
/* 5*/    List<Element_Type>::
/* 6*/    Find( const Element_Type & X )
/* 7*/    {
/* 8*/        unsigned int P = C.Cursor_Space[ List_Head ].Next;

/* 9*/        for( ; P != 0; P = C.Cursor_Space[ P ].Next )
/*10*/            if( C.Cursor_Space[ P ].Element == X )
/*11*/            {
/*12*/                Current_Pos = P;
/*13*/                return 1;
/*14*/            }

/*15*/        return 0;
/*16*/    }
```

Figure 3.37 *Find* routine for linked lists—cursor
implementation

```
/* 1*/    // Remove X from the list.
/* 2*/    // Return nonzero if deletion was successful.
/* 3*/    // Header node is assumed.

/* 4*/    template <class Element_Type>
/* 5*/    int
/* 6*/    List<Element_Type>::
/* 7*/    Remove( const Element_Type & X )
/* 8*/    {
/* 9*/        unsigned int Cell_To_Delete;

/*10*/        if( Find_Previous( X ) )
/*11*/        {
/*12*/            Cell_To_Delete = C.Cursor_Space[ Current_Pos ].Next;
/*13*/            C.Cursor_Space[ Current_Pos ].Next =
/*14*/                        C.Cursor_Space[ Cell_To_Delete ].Next;
/*15*/            C.Cdelete( Cell_To_Delete );
/*16*/            return 1;
/*17*/        }
/*18*/        return 0;
/*19*/    }
```

Figure 3.38 Deletion and insertion routines for linked
lists—cursor implementation

```
/* 1*/   // Insert X after the current position.
/* 2*/   // X becomes the current element.
/* 3*/   // Header implementation assumed.

/* 4*/   template <class Element_Type>
/* 5*/   void
/* 6*/   List<Element_Type>::
/* 7*/   Insert( const Element_Type & X )
/* 8*/   {
/* 9*/       unsigned int P =
/*10*/               C.Cnew( X, C.Cursor_Space[ Current_Pos ].Next );

/*11*/       if( P )
/*12*/       {
/*13*/           C.Cursor_Space[ Current_Pos ].Next = P;
/*14*/           Current_Pos = C.Cursor_Space[ Current_Pos ].Next;
/*15*/       }
/*16*/       else
/*17*/           Error( "Out of space" );
/*18*/   }
```

Figure 3.38   *(Continued)*

3.3.   The Stack ADT

3.3.1.   *Stack Model*

A *stack* is a list with the restriction that *Insert*s and *Remove*s can be performed in only one position, namely the end of the list, called the *top*. The fundamental operations on a stack are *Push,* which is equivalent to an insert, and *Pop,* which removes the most recently inserted element. The most recently inserted element can be examined prior to performing a *Pop* by use of the *Top* routine. A *Pop* or *Top* on an empty stack is generally considered an error in the stack ADT. On the other hand, running out of space when performing a *Push* is an implementation error but not an ADT error.

Stacks are sometimes known as LIFO (last in, first out) lists. The model depicted in Figure 3.39 signifies only that *Push*es are input operations and *Pop*s and *Top*s are output. The usual operations to make empty stacks and test for emptiness are part of the repertoire, but essentially all that you can do to a stack is *Push* and *Pop*.

Figure 3.40 shows an abstract stack after several operations. The general model is that there is some element that is at the top of the stack, and it is the only element that is visible.

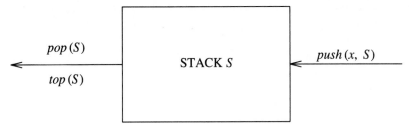

Figure 3.39   Stack model: Input to a stack is by *Push*,
output is by *Pop*

3.3.2.   *Implementation of Stacks*

Of course, since a stack is a list, any list implementation will do. We will give two
popular implementations. One uses pointers, and the other uses an array; but, as we
saw in the previous section, the calling routines do not need to know which method
is being used if we use good programming principles.

Linked List Implementation of Stacks

The first implementation of a stack uses a singly linked list. We perform a *Push* by
inserting at the front of the list. We perform a *Pop* by deleting the element at the
front of the list. A *Top* operation merely examines the element at the front of the
list, returning its value. Sometimes the *Pop* and *Top* operations are combined into
one. We could use calls to the linked list routines of the previous section, but we will
rewrite the stack routines from scratch for the sake of clarity.

First, we give the class specification in Figure 3.41. Because insertions and
deletions are so restricted, a header is not needed.

Figure 3.40   Stack model: Only the top element is accessible

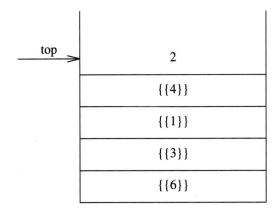

```
/* 1*/    template <class Element_Type>
/* 2*/    class Stack
/* 3*/    {
/* 4*/      private:
/* 5*/        // The stack is a linked list with no header.

/* 6*/        struct Node
/* 7*/        {
/* 8*/            Element_Type Element;
/* 9*/            Node *Next;

/*10*/            Node( Element_Type E = 0, Node *N = NULL ) :
/*11*/                Element ( E ),  Next ( N ) { }
/*12*/        };

/*13*/        Node *Stack_Top;


/*14*/      public:
/*15*/        // Default stack size is meaningless.
/*16*/        Stack( unsigned int Max_Size = 100 ) : Stack_Top ( NULL ) { };
/*17*/        Stack( Stack & Value )
/*18*/            { Warn( "Stack passed by value" ); operator=( Value ); }

/*19*/        // Destructor.
/*20*/        ~Stack( );

/*21*/        // Operators.
/*22*/        const Stack & operator = ( const Stack & Value );

/*23*/        // Member functions.
/*24*/        void Push( const Element_Type & X );
/*25*/        void Pop( );
/*26*/        Element_Type Pop_And_Top( );
/*27*/        Element_Type Top( ) const;
/*28*/        int Is_Empty( ) const { return Stack_Top == NULL; }

/*29*/    };
```

Figure 3.41 Class specification for linked list
              implementation of the stack ADT

The *Push* is implemented as an insertion into the front of a linked list, where the front of the list serves as the top of the stack (see Fig. 3.42). The *Top* is performed by examining the element in the first position of the list (see Fig. 3.43). We implement *Pop* as a remove from the front of the list (see Fig. 3.44). Figure 3.45 combines *Pop* and *Top* into one operation, and finally, the class destructor is implemented in Figure 3.46.

```
/* 1*/    template <class Element_Type>
/* 2*/    inline void
/* 3*/    Stack<Element_Type>::
/* 4*/    Push( const Element_Type & X )
/* 5*/    {
/* 6*/        Node *P = new Node( X, Stack_Top );

/* 7*/        if( P == NULL )
/* 8*/            Error( "Out of memory" );
/* 9*/        else
/*10*/            Stack_Top = P;
/*11*/    }
```

Figure 3.42   Routine to push onto a stack—Linked list
            implementation

```
/* 1*/    template <class Element_Type>
/* 2*/    inline Element_Type
/* 3*/    Stack<Element_Type>::
/* 4*/    Top( ) const
/* 5*/    {
/* 6*/        if( Is_Empty( ) )
/* 7*/            Error( "Empty stack" );

/* 8*/        return Stack_Top->Element;
/* 9*/    }
```

Figure 3.43   Routine to return top elment in a stack—
            Linked list implementation

```
/* 1*/    template <class Element_Type>
/* 2*/    inline void
/* 3*/    Stack<Element_Type>::
/* 4*/    Pop( )
/* 5*/    {
/* 6*/        Node *P;

/* 7*/        if( Is_Empty( ) )
/* 8*/            Error( "Empty stack" );
/* 9*/        else
/*10*/        {
/*11*/            P = Stack_Top->Next;
/*12*/            delete Stack_Top;
/*13*/            Stack_Top = P;
/*14*/        }
/*15*/    }
```

Figure 3.44   Routine to pop from a stack—Linked list
            implementation

```
/* 1*/    template <class Element_Type>
/* 2*/    inline Element_Type
/* 3*/    Stack<Element_Type>::
/* 4*/    Pop_And_Top( )
/* 5*/    {
/* 6*/        Element_Type Top_Element = Top( );

/* 7*/        if( !Is_Empty( ) )
/* 8*/            Pop( );

/* 9*/        return Top_Element;
/*10*/    }
```

Figure 3.45 *Pop* and *Top* combined into one—Linked list
implementation

It should be clear that all the operations (except the destructor) take constant time, because nowhere in any of the routines is there even a reference to the size of the stack (except for emptiness), much less a loop that depends on this size. The drawback of this implementation is that the calls to *new* and *delete* are expensive, especially in comparison to the pointer manipulation routines. Some of this can be avoided by using a second stack, which is initially empty. When a cell is to be disposed from the first stack, it is merely placed on the second stack. Then, when new cells are needed for the first stack, the second stack is checked first.

Array Implementation of Stacks

An alternative implementation avoids pointers and is probably the more popular solution. The only potential hazard with this strategy is that we need to declare

Figure 3.46 Stack destructor—Linked list implementation

```
/* 1*/    template <class Element_Type>
/* 2*/    Stack<Element_Type>::~Stack( )
/* 3*/    {
/* 4*/        Node *P = Stack_Top;

/* 5*/        while( P != NULL )
/* 6*/        {
/* 7*/            Node *After_P = P->Next;
/* 8*/            delete P;
/* 9*/            P = After_P;
/*10*/        }
/*11*/    }
```

an array size ahead of time. Generally this is not a problem, because in typical applications, even if there are quite a few stack operations, the actual number of elements in the stack at any time never gets too large. It is usually easy to declare the array to be large enough without wasting too much space.

If we use an array implementation, the implementation is trivial. Associated with each stack is the top of stack, *tos,* which is -1 for an empty stack (this is how an empty stack is initialized). To push some element x onto the stack, we increment *tos* and then set *Stack*[*tos*] $= x$, where *Stack* is the array representing the actual stack. To pop and obtain the popped element in one routine, we set the return value to *Stack*[*tos*] and then decrement *tos.* Of course, since there are potentially several stacks, the *Stack* array and *tos* are just members of the stack class, and these members are declared in the private part.

Notice that these operations are performed not just in constant time, but in very fast constant time. On some machines, *Push*es and *Pop*s (of integers) can be written in one machine instruction, operating on a register with auto-increment and auto-decrement addressing. The fact that most modern machines have stack operations as part of the instruction set reinforces the idea that the stack is probably the most fundamental data structure in computer science, after the array.

One problem that affects the efficiency of implementing stacks is error testing. Our linked list implementation carefully checked for errors. As described above, a *Pop* on an empty stack or a *Push* on a full stack will overflow the array bounds and lead to undesirable results, but if checks for these conditions were put in the array implementation, they would likely take as much time as the actual stack manipulation. Thus, you may be tempted to skimp on error checking. Although you can probably get away with this in most cases by declaring the stack to be large enough not to overflow and ensuring that routines that use *Pop* never attempt to *Pop* an empty stack, this can lead to code that barely works at best, especially when programs get large and are written by more than one person or at more than one time. Because stack operations take such fast constant time, it is rare that a significant part of the running time of a program is spent in these routines. This means that it is generally not justifiable to omit error checks. You should always write the error checks; if they are redundant, you can always comment them out if they really cost too much time. Having said all this, we can now write routines to implement a general stack using arrays.

For an array implementation, we will define a stack class as in Figure 3.47. Rather than pick a maximum stack size, we allow the user to specify it.[†] The simplicity of the operations is indicated in Figures 3.48 through 3.53. *Make_Empty* for the linked list implementation can be done by popping until empty (to free memory); for the array it can be done in constant time. Thus, it is a member function, implemented in Figure 3.49.

[†] It is possible to avoid this problem; see rehashing in Section 5.5. The basic idea is to start with a default size array and expand it when it becomes full.

```
/*  1*/    static const Default_Size = 100;
/*  2*/    template <class Element_Type>
/*  3*/    class Stack
/*  4*/    {
/*  5*/      private:
/*  6*/        // The stack is array based.

/*  7*/        unsigned int Full_Stack;
/*  8*/        int Top_Of_Stack;
/*  9*/        Element_Type *Stack_Array;

/*10*/      public:
/*11*/        // Constructors.
/*12*/        Stack( unsigned int Max_Size = Default_Size );
/*13*/        Stack( const Stack & Value )
/*14*/            { Warn( "Stack passed by value!" ); operator=( Value ); }

/*15*/        // Destructor.
/*16*/        ~Stack( ) { delete [ ] Stack_Array; }

/*17*/        // Operators.
/*18*/        const Stack & operator = ( const Stack & Value );

/*19*/        // Member functions.
/*20*/        void Push( const Element_Type & X );
/*21*/        void Pop( );
/*22*/        Element_Type Pop_And_Top( );
/*23*/        Element_Type Top( ) const;
/*24*/        void Make_Empty( );
/*25*/        int Is_Empty( ) const
/*26*/            { return Top_Of_Stack == -1; }
/*27*/        int Is_Full( )  const
/*28*/            { return Top_Of_Stack == Full_Stack - 1; }
/*29*/    };
```

Figure 3.47 Class specification for stack ADT—Array implementation

```
/*  1*/    template <class Element_Type>
/*  2*/    Stack<Element_Type>::
/*  3*/    Stack( unsigned int Max_Size )
/*  4*/    {
/*  5*/        Full_Stack = Max_Size;
/*  6*/        Top_Of_Stack = -1;
/*  7*/        Stack_Array = new Element_Type[ Max_Size ];
/*  8*/        if( Stack_Array == NULL )
/*  9*/            Error( "Out of space!!" );
/*10*/    }
```

Figure 3.48 Stack constructor—Array implementation

```
/* 1*/    template <class Element_Type>
/* 2*/    inline void
/* 3*/    Stack<Element_Type>::
/* 4*/    Make_Empty( )
/* 5*/    {
/* 6*/        Top_Of_Stack = -1;
/* 7*/    }
```

Figure 3.49 Routine to create an empty stack—Array
implementation

```
/* 1*/    template <class Element_Type>
/* 2*/    inline void
/* 3*/    Stack<Element_Type>::
/* 4*/    Push( const Element_Type & X )
/* 5*/    {
/* 6*/        if( Is_Full( ) )
/* 7*/            Error( "Stack is full" );
/* 8*/        else
/* 9*/            Stack_Array[ ++ Top_Of_Stack ] = X;
/*10*/    }
```

Figure 3.50 Routine to push onto a stack—Array
implementation

```
/* 1*/    template <class Element_Type>
/* 2*/    inline Element_Type
/* 3*/    Stack<Element_Type>::
/* 4*/    Top( ) const
/* 5*/    {
/* 6*/        if( Is_Empty( ) )
/* 7*/        {
/* 8*/            Error( "Empty stack" );
/* 9*/            return 0;
/*10*/        }
/*11*/        return Stack_Array[ Top_Of_Stack ];
/*12*/    }
```

Figure 3.51 Routine to return top of stack—Array
implementation

```
/* 1*/    template <class Element_Type>
/* 2*/    inline void
/* 3*/    Stack<Element_Type>::
/* 4*/    Pop( )
/* 5*/    {
/* 6*/        if( Is_Empty( ) )
/* 7*/            Error( "Empty stack" );
/* 8*/        else
/* 9*/            --Top_Of_Stack;
/*10*/    }
```

Figure 3.52   Routine to pop from a stack—Array
implementation

```
/* 1*/    template <class Element_Type>
/* 2*/    inline Element_Type
/* 3*/    Stack<Element_Type>::
/* 4*/    Pop_And_Top( )
/* 5*/    {
/* 6*/        Element_Type Top_Element;

/* 7*/        if( Is_Empty( ) )
/* 8*/        {
/* 9*/            Error( "Stack is empty" );
/*10*/            return 0;
/*11*/        }
/*12*/        return Stack_Array[ Top_Of_Stack-- ];
/*13*/    }
```

Figure 3.53   Routine to give top element and pop a
stack—Array implementation

3.3.3. Applications

It should come as no surprise that if we restrict the operations allowed on a list, those operations can be performed very quickly. The big surprise, however, is that the small number of operations left are so powerful and important. We give three of the many applications of stacks. The third application gives a deep insight into how programs are organized.

Balancing Symbols

Compilers check your programs for syntax errors, but frequently a lack of one symbol (such as a missing brace) will cause the compiler to spill out a hundred lines of diagnostics without identifying the real error.

A useful tool in this situation is a program that checks whether everything is balanced. Thus, in C++, right braces, brackets, and parentheses must correspond to their left counterparts. The sequence [()] is legal, but [(]) is wrong. Obviously, it is not worthwhile writing a huge program for this, but it turns out that it is easy to check these things. For simplicity, we will just check for balancing of parentheses, brackets, and braces and ignore any other character that appears.

The simple algorithm uses a stack and is as follows:

Make an empty stack. Read characters until end of file. If the character is an open anything, push it onto the stack. If it is a close anything, then if the stack is empty report an error. Otherwise, pop the stack. If the symbol popped is not the corresponding opening symbol, then report an error. At end of file, if the stack is not empty report an error.

You should be able to convince yourself that this algorithm works. It is clearly linear and actually makes only one pass through the input. It is thus on-line and quite fast. Extra work can be done to attempt to decide what to do when an error is reported—such as identifying the likely cause.

Postfix Expressions

Suppose we have a pocket calculator and would like to compute the cost of a shopping trip. To do so, we add a list of numbers and multiply the result by 1.06; this computes the purchase price of some items with local sales tax added. If the items are 4.99, 5.99, and 6.99, then a natural way to enter this would be the sequence

    4.99 + 5.99 + 6.99 * 1.06 =

Depending on the calculator, this produces either the intended answer, 19.05, or the scientific answer, 18.39. Most simple four-function calculators will give the first answer, but better calculators know that multiplication has higher precedence than addition.

On the other hand, some items are taxable and some are not, so if only the first and last items were actually taxable, then the sequence

    4.99 * 1.06 + 5.99 + 6.99 * 1.06 =

would give the correct answer (18.69) on a scientific calculator and the wrong answer (19.37) on a simple calculator. A scientific calculator generally comes with parentheses, so we can always get the right answer by parenthesizing, but with a simple calculator we need to remember intermediate results.

A typical evaluation sequence for this example might be to multiply 4.99 and 1.06, saving this answer as a_1. We would then add 5.99 and a_1, saving the result in a_1. Next we would multiply 6.99 and 1.06, saving the answer in a_2, and finish by adding a_1 and a_2, leaving the final answer in a_1. We can write this sequence of operations as follows:

    4.99 1.06 * 5.99 + 6.99 1.06 * +

This notation is known as *postfix* or *reverse Polish* notation and is evaluated exactly as we have described above. The easiest way to do this is to use a stack. When a number is seen, it is pushed onto the stack; when an operator is seen, the operator is applied to the two numbers (symbols) that are popped from the stack and the result is pushed onto the stack. For instance, the postfix expression

6 5 2 3 + 8 * + 3 + *

is evaluated as follows: The first four symbols are placed on the stack. The resulting stack is

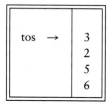

Next a '+' is read, so 3 and 2 are popped from the stack and their sum, 5, is pushed.

Next 8 is pushed.

Now a '*' is seen, so 8 and 5 are popped and 5 * 8 = 40 is pushed.

Next a '+' is seen, so 40 and 5 are popped and 5 + 40 = 45 is pushed.

Now, 3 is pushed.

Next '+' pops 3 and 45 and pushes 45 + 3 = 48.

Finally, a '*' is seen and 48 and 6 are popped; the result 6 * 48 = 288 is pushed.

The time to evaluate a postfix expression is $O(n)$, because processing each element in the input consists of stack operations and thus takes constant time. The algorithm to do so is very simple. Notice that when an expression is given in postfix notation, there is no need to know any precedence rules; this is an obvious advantage.

Infix to Postfix Conversion

Not only can a stack be used to evaluate a postfix expression, but we can also use a stack to convert an expression in standard form (otherwise known as *infix*) into postfix. We will concentrate on a small version of the general problem by allowing only the operators +, *, (,), and insisting on the usual precedence rules. We will further assume that the expression is legal. Suppose we want to convert the infix expression

$$a + b * c + (d * e + f) * g$$

into postfix. A correct answer is a b c * + d e * f + g * +.

When an operand is read, it is immediately placed onto the output. Operators are not immediately output, so they must be saved somewhere. The correct thing to do is to place operators that have been seen, but not placed on the output, onto the stack. We will also stack left parentheses when they are encountered. We start with an empty stack.

If we see a right parenthesis, then we pop the stack, writing symbols until we encounter a (corresponding) left parenthesis, which is popped but not output.

If we see any other symbol ('+', '*', '('), then we pop entries from the stack until we find an entry of lower priority. One exception is that we never remove a '(' from the stack except when processing a ')'. For the purposes of this operation, '+' has lowest priority and '(' highest. When the popping is done, we push the operator onto the stack.

Finally, if we read the end of input, we pop the stack until it is empty, writing symbols onto the output.

To see how this algorithm performs, we will convert the infix expression above into its postfix form. First, the symbol *a* is read, so it is passed through to the output. Then '+' is read and pushed onto the stack. Next *b* is read and passed through to the output. The state of affairs at this juncture is as follows:

Next '*' is read. The top entry on the operator stack has lower precedence than '*', so nothing is output and '*' is put on the stack. Next, *c* is read and output. Thus far, we have

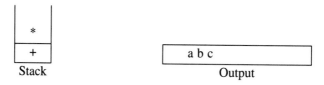

The next symbol is a '+'. Checking the stack, we find that we will pop a '*' and place it on the output, pop the other '+', which is not of *lower* but equal priority, from the stack, and then push the '+'.

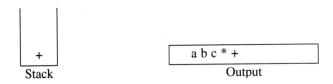

The next symbol read is an '(', which, being of highest precedence, is placed on the stack. Then *d* is read and output.

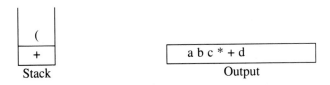

We continue by reading a '*'. Since open parentheses do not get removed except when a closed parenthesis is being processed, there is no output. Next, *e* is read and output.

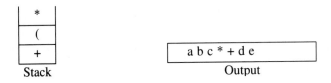

The next symbol read is a '+'. We pop and output '*' and then push '+'. Then we read and output *f*.

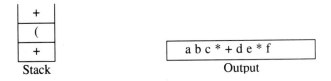

Now we read a ')', so the stack is emptied back to the '('. We output a '+'.

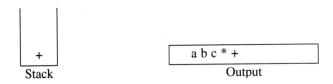

We read a '*' next; it is pushed onto the stack. Then *g* is read and output.

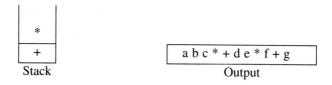

Stack   Output

The input is now empty, so we pop and output symbols from the stack until it is empty.

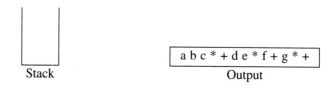

Stack   Output

As before, this conversion requires only $O(n)$ time and works in one pass through the input. We can add subtraction and division to this repertoire by assigning subtraction and addition equal priority and multiplication and division equal priority. A subtle point is that the expression $a - b - c$ will be converted to $ab - c-$ and not $abc - -$. Our algorithm does the right thing, because these operators associate from left to right. This is not necessarily the case in general, since exponentiation associates right to left: $2^{2^3} = 2^8 = 256$ not $4^3 = 64$. We leave as an exercise the problem of adding exponentiation to the repertoire of assignments.

Function Calls

The algorithm to check balanced symbols suggests a way to implement function calls. The problem here is that when a call is made to a new procedure, all the variables local to the calling routine need to be saved by the system, because otherwise the new procedure will overwrite the calling routine's variables. Furthermore, the current location in the routine must be saved so that the new function knows where to go after it is done. The variables have generally been assigned by the compiler to machine registers, and there are certain to be conflicts (usually all functions get some variables assigned to register #1), especially if recursion is involved. The reason that this problem is similar to balancing symbols is that a function call and function return are essentially the same as an open parenthesis and closed parenthesis, so the same ideas should work.

When there is a function call, all the important information that needs to be saved, such as register values (corresponding to variable names) and the return address (which can be obtained from the program counter, which is typically in a register), is saved "on a piece of paper" in an abstract way and put at the top of a pile. Then the control is transferred to the new function, which is free to replace the registers with its values. If it makes other function calls, it follows the same procedure. When the function wants to return, it looks at the "paper" at the top of the pile and restores all the registers. It then makes the return jump.

Clearly, all of this work can be done using a stack, and that is exactly what happens in virtually every programming language that implements recursion. The information saved is called either an *activation record* or *stack frame*. The stack in a real computer frequently grows from the high end of your memory partition downwards, and on many systems there is no checking for overflow. There is always the possibility that you will run out of stack space by having too many simultaneously active functions. Needless to say, running out of stack space is always a fatal error.

In normal events, you should not run out of stack space; doing so is usually an indication of runaway recursion (forgetting a base case). On the other hand, some perfectly legal and seemingly innocuous programs can cause you to run out of stack space. The routine in Figure 3.54, which prints and purges a linked list (actually our list implementation of a stack), is perfectly legal and actually correct. It properly handles the base case of an empty list, and the recursion is fine. This program can be *proven* correct. Unfortunately, if the list contains 20,000 elements, there will be a stack of 20,000 activation records representing the nested calls of line 11. Activation records are typically large because of all the information they contain, so this program is likely to run out of stack space. (If 20,000 elements are not enough to make the program crash, replace the number with a larger one.)

This program is an example of an extremely bad use of recursion known as *tail recursion*. Tail recursion refers to a recursive call at the last line. Tail recursion can be mechanically eliminated by changing the recursive call to a *goto* preceded by one assignment per function parameter. This simulates the recursive call because nothing needs to be saved—after the recursive call finishes, there is really no need to know the saved values. Because of this, we can just go to the top of the function with the values that would have been used in a recursive call. The program in Figure 3.55 shows the improved version. Keep in mind that *you* should use the more natural *while* loop construction. The *goto* is used here to show how a compiler might automatically remove the recursion.

Figure 3.54 A bad use of recursion: printing a linked list

```
/* 1*/    // Empty a Stack, printing its contents.
/* 2*/    // Bad algorithm.

/* 3*/    template<class Element_Type>
/* 4*/    void
/* 5*/    Stack<Element_Type>::
/* 6*/    Rec_Print_And_Empty( )
/* 7*/    {
/* 8*/        if( !Is_Empty( ) )
/* 9*/        {
/*10*/            cout << Pop_And_Top( ) << endl;
/*11*/            Rec_Print_And_Empty( );
/*12*/        }
/*13*/    }
```

```
/* 1*/    // Empty a Stack, printing its contents.
/* 2*/    // Nonrecursive: goto illustrates compiler's method.
/* 3*/    // Don't use it yourself.

/* 4*/    template<class Element_Type>
/* 5*/    void
/* 6*/    Stack<Element_Type>::
/* 7*/    Nor_Print_And_Empty( )
/* 8*/    {
/* 9*/    Top:
/*10*/        if( !Is_Empty( ) )
/*11*/        {
/*12*/            cout << Pop_And_Top( ) << endl;
/*13*/            goto Top;
/*14*/        }
/*15*/    }
```

Figure 3.55   Printing a list without recursion. A compiler
might do this (you should not)

Removal of tail recursion is so simple that some compilers do it automatically. Even so, it is best not to find out that yours does not.

Recursion can always be completely removed (obviously, the compiler does so in converting to assembly language), but doing so can be quite tedious. The general strategy requires using a stack and is obviously worthwhile only if you can manage to put only the bare minimum on the stack. We will not dwell on this further, except to point out that although nonrecursive programs are certainly generally faster than recursive programs, the speed advantage rarely justifies the lack of clarity that results from removing the recursion.

3.4.   The Queue ADT

Like stacks, *queues* are lists. With a queue, however, insertion is done at one end, whereas deletion is performed at the other end.

3.4.1.   Queue Model

The basic operations on a queue are *Enqueue,* which inserts an element at the end of the list (called the rear), and *Dequeue,* which deletes (and passes back) the element at the start of the list (known as the front). Figure 3.56 shows the abstract model of a queue.

Figure 3.56 Model of a queue

3.4.2. *Array Implementation of Queues*

As with stacks, any list implementation is legal for queues. Like stacks, both the linked list and array implementations give fast $O(1)$ running times for every operation. The linked list implementation is straightforward and left as an exercise. We will now discuss an array implementation of queues.

For each queue object we keep an array, *Q_Array*, and the positions *Q_Front* and *Q_Rear*, which represent the ends of the queue. We also keep track of the number of elements that are actually in the queue, *Q_Size*. All this information is part of the class, and as usual, except for the queue routines themselves, no routine should ever access these directly. The following figure shows a queue in some intermediate state. By the way, the cells that are blanks have undefined values in them. In particular, the first two cells have elements that used to be in the queue.

		5	2	7	1			

          Q_Front   Q_Rear

The operations should be clear. To *Enqueue* an element X, we increment *Q_Size* and *Q_Rear*, then set *Q_Array[Q_Rear]* = X. To *Dequeue* an element, we set the return value to *Q_Array[Q_Front]*, decrement *Q_Size*, and then increment *Q_Front*. Other strategies are possible (this is discussed later). We will comment on checking for errors presently.

There is one potential problem with this implementation. After 10 *Enqueue*s, the queue appears to be full, since *Q_Front* is now 10, and the next *Enqueue* would be in a nonexistent position. However, there might only be a few elements in the queue, because several elements may have already been dequeued. Queues, like stacks, frequently stay small even in the presence of a lot of operations.

The simple solution is that whenever *Q_Front* or *Q_Rear* gets to the end of the array, it is wrapped around to the beginning. The following figures show the queue during some operations. This is known as a *circular array* implementation.

Initial State

After *Enqueue*(1)

After *Enqueue*(3)

After *Dequeue,* Which Returns 2

After *Dequeue,* Which Returns 4

After *Dequeue,* Which Returns 1

After *Dequeue*, Which Returns 3
and Makes the Queue Empty

1	3						2	4
	^	^						

Q_Rear Q_Front

The extra code required to implement the wraparound is minimal (although it probably doubles the running time). If incrementing either *Q_Rear* or *Q_Front* causes it to go past the array, the value is reset to the first position in the array.

There are two warnings about the circular array implementation of queues. First, it is important to check the queue for emptiness, because a *Dequeue* when the queue is empty will return an undefined value silently.

Secondly, some programmers use different ways of representing the front and rear of a queue. For instance, some do not use an entry to keep track of the size, because they rely on the base case that when the queue is empty, $Q\_Rear ==$ $Q\_Front - 1$. The size is computed implicitly by comparing *Q_Rear* and *Q_Front*. This is a very tricky way to go because there are some special cases, so be very careful if you need to modify code written this way. If the size is not part of the structure, then if the array size is *A_Size*, the queue is full when there are $A\_Size - 1$ elements, since only *A_Size* different sizes can be differentiated, and one of these is 0. Pick any style you like and make sure that all your routines are consistent. Since there are a few options for implementation, it is probably worth a comment or two in the code if you don't use the size field.

In applications where you are sure that the number of *Enqueue*s is not larger than the size of the queue, obviously the wraparound is not necessary. As with stack *Pop*s, *Dequeue*s are rarely performed unless the calling routines are certain that the queue is not empty. Thus error calls are occasionally skipped for this operation, except in critical code. This is generally not justifiable, because the time savings that you are likely to achieve are too minimal.

We finish this section by writing some of the queue routines. We leave the others as an exercise to the reader. First, we give the class specification in Figure 3.57. We also provide routines to make an empty queue and perform the increment with wraparound (Figs. 3.58 and 3.59). The reader can write the function *Is_Full*, which performs the test implied by its name. Notice that *Q_Rear* is preinitialized to 1 before *Q_Front*. The final operation we will write is the *Enqueue* routine. Following the exact description above, we arrive at the implementation in Figure 3.60.

3.4.3. Applications of Queues

There are several algorithms that use queues to give efficient running times. Several of these are found in graph theory, and we will discuss them later in Chapter 9. For now, we will give some simple examples of queue usage.

```
/* 1*/    static const Default_Size = 100;

/* 2*/    template <class Element_Type>
/* 3*/    class Queue
/* 4*/    {
/* 5*/      private:
/* 6*/        unsigned int Full_Queue;
/* 7*/        int Q_Front;
/* 8*/        int Q_Rear;
/* 9*/        int Q_Size;
/*10*/        Element_Type *Q_Array;

/*11*/        void Increment( int & X );

/*12*/      public:
/*13*/        // Constructors.
/*14*/        Queue( unsigned int Max_Size = Default_Size );
/*15*/        Queue( const Queue & Value )
/*16*/            { Warn( "Queue passed by value" ); operator =( Value ); }

/*17*/        // Destructor.
/*18*/        ~Queue( ) { delete [ ] Q_Array; }

/*19*/        // Operators.
/*20*/        const Queue & operator = ( const Queue & Value );

/*21*/        // Member functions.
/*22*/        void Enqueue( const Element_Type & X );
/*23*/        Element_Type Dequeue( );
/*24*/        void Make_Empty( );
/*25*/        int Is_Empty( ) const { return Q_Size == 0; }
/*26*/        int Is_Full( )  const { return Q_Size == Full_Queue; }
/*27*/    };
```

Figure 3.57   Class specification for queue—Array
implementation

```
/* 1*/    template <class Element_Type>
/* 2*/    void
/* 3*/    Queue<Element_Type>::
/* 4*/    Make_Empty( )
/* 5*/    {
/* 6*/        Q_Front = 1;
/* 7*/        Q_Rear = 0;
/* 8*/        Q_Size = 0;
/* 9*/    }
```

Figure 3.58   Routine to make an empty queue, and a
constructor—Array implementation

```
/* 1*/     template <class Element_Type>
/* 2*/     Queue<Element_Type>::
/* 3*/     Queue( unsigned int Max_Size )
/* 4*/     {
/* 5*/         Full_Queue = Max_Size;
/* 6*/         Make_Empty();
/* 7*/         Q_Array = new Element_Type[ Max_Size ];
/* 8*/         if( Q_Array == NULL )
/* 9*/             Error( "Out of space" );
/*10*/     }
```

Figure 3.58   *(Continued)*

```
/* 1*/     template <class Element_Type>
/* 2*/     void
/* 3*/     Queue<Element_Type>::
/* 4*/     Increment( int & X )
/* 5*/     {
/* 6*/         if( ++ X == Full_Queue )
/* 7*/             X = 0;
/* 8*/     }
```

Figure 3.59   Routine to implement wraparound

```
/* 1*/     template <class Element_Type>
/* 2*/     void
/* 3*/     Queue<Element_Type>::
/* 4*/     Enqueue( const Element_Type & X )
/* 5*/     {
/* 6*/         if( Is_Full( ) )
/* 7*/             Error( "Queue is full" );
/* 8*/         else
/* 9*/         {
/*10*/             Q_Size++;
/*11*/             Increment( Q_Rear );
/*12*/             Q_Array[ Q_Rear ] = X;
/*13*/         }
/*14*/     }
```

Figure 3.60   Routines to enqueue—Array implementation

When jobs are submitted to a printer, they are arranged in order of arrival. Thus, essentially, jobs sent to a line printer are placed on a queue.[†]

Virtually every real-life line is (supposed to be) a queue. For instance, lines at ticket counters are queues, because service is first-come first-served.

Another example concerns computer networks. There are many network setups of personal computers in which the disk is attached to one machine, known as the *file server*. Users on other machines are given access to files on a first-come first-served basis, so the data structure is a queue.

Further examples include the following:

- Calls to large companies are generally placed on a queue when all operators are busy.
- In large universities, where resources are limited, students must sign a waiting list if all terminals are occupied. The student who has been at a terminal the longest is forced off first, and the student who has been waiting the longest is the next user to be allowed on.

A whole branch of mathematics, known as *queueing theory*, deals with computing, probabilistically, how long users expect to wait on a line, how long the line gets, and other such questions. The answer depends on how frequently users arrive to the line and how long it takes to process a user once the user is served. Both of these parameters are given as probability distribution functions. In simple cases, an answer can be computed analytically. An example of an easy case would be a phone line with one operator. If the operator is busy, callers are placed on a waiting line (up to some maximum limit). This problem is important for businesses, because studies have shown that people are quick to hang up the phone.

If there are k operators, then this problem is much more difficult to solve. Problems that are difficult to solve analytically are often solved by a simulation. In our case, we would need to use a queue to perform the simulation. If k is large, we also need other data structures to do this efficiently. We shall see how to do this simulation in Chapter 6. We could then run the simulation for several values of k and choose the minimum k that gives a reasonable waiting time.

Additional uses for queues abound, and, as with stacks, it is staggering that such a simple data structure can be so important.

Summary

This chapter describes the concept of ADTs and illustrates the concept with three of the most common abstract data types. The primary objective is to separate the implementation of the abstract data types from their function. The program must know what the operations do, but it is actually better off not knowing how it is done. This is very easy to do using C++ classes, templates, and inheritance.

[†]We say *essentially* a queue, because jobs can be killed. This amounts to a deletion from the middle of the queue, which is a violation of the strict definition.

Lists, stacks, and queues are perhaps the three fundamental data structures in all of computer science, and their use is documented through a host of examples. In particular, we saw how stacks are used to keep track of function calls and how recursion is actually implemented. This is important to understand, not just because it makes procedural languages possible, but because knowing how recursion is implemented removes a good deal of the mystery that surrounds its use. Although recursion is very powerful, it is not an entirely free operation; misuse and abuse of recursion can result in programs crashing.

Exercises

3.1   Write a program to print out the elements of a singly linked list.

3.2   You are given a linked list, L, and another linked list, P, containing integers sorted in ascending order. The operation *Print_Lots(L,P)* will print the elements in L that are in positions specified by P. For instance, if $P = 1, 3, 4, 6$, the first, third, fourth and sixth elements in L are printed. Write the routine *Print_Lots(L,P)*. You should use only the basic list operations. What is the running time of your routine?

3.3   Swap two adjacent elements by adjusting only the pointers (and not the data) using

    a. singly linked lists,

    b. doubly linked lists.

3.4   Given two sorted lists, L_1 and L_2, write a routine to compute $L_1 \cap L_2$ using only the basic list operations.

3.5   Given two sorted lists, L_1 and L_2, write a routine to compute $L_1 \cup L_2$ using only the basic list operations.

3.6   Write a function to add two polynomials. Do not destroy the input. Use a linked list implementation. If the polynomials have m and n terms respectively, what is the time complexity of your program?

3.7   Write a function to multiply two polynomials, using a linked list implementation. You must make sure that the output polynomial is sorted by exponent and has at most one term of any power.

    a. Give an algorithm to solve this problem in $O(m^2n^2)$ time.

    *b. Write a program to perform the multiplication in $O(m^2n)$ time, where m is the number of terms in the polynomial of fewer terms.

    *c. Write a program to perform the multiplication in $O(mn\log(mn))$ time.

    d. Which time bound above is the best?

3.8   Write a program that takes a polynomial, $f(x)$, and computes $(f(x))^p$. What is the complexity of your program? Propose at least one alternative solution that could be competitive for some plausible choices of $f(x)$ and p.

3.9 Write an arbitrary-precision integer arithmetic package. You should use a strategy similar to polynomial arithmetic. Compute the distribution of the digits 0 to 9 in 2^{4000}.

3.10 The *Josephus problem* is the following game: n people, numbered 1 to n, are sitting in a circle. Starting at person 1, a hot potato is passed. After m passes, the person holding the hot potato is eliminated, the circle closes ranks, and the game continues with the person who was sitting after the eliminated person picking up the hot potato. The last remaining person wins. Thus, if $m = 0$ and $n = 5$, players are eliminated and player 5 wins. If $m = 1$ and $n = 5$, the order of elimination is 2, 4, 1, 5.

   a. Write a program to solve the Josephus problem for general values of m and n. Try to make your program as efficient as possible. Make sure you dispose of cells.

   b. What is the running time of your program?

   c. If $m = 1$, what is the running time of your program? How is the actual speed affected by the *delete* routine for large values of n ($n > 10000$)?

3.11 Write a program to find a particular element in a singly linked list. Do this both recursively and nonrecursively, and compare the running times. How big does the list have to be before the recursive version crashes?

3.12 a. Write a nonrecursive function to reverse a singly linked list in $O(n)$ time.

  *b. Write a function to reverse a singly linked list in $O(n)$ time using constant extra space.

3.13 You have to sort an array of student records by social security number. Write a program to do this, using radix sort with 1000 buckets and three passes.

3.14 Write a program to read a graph into adjacency lists using

   a. linked lists

   b. cursors

3.15 a. Write an array implementation of self-adjusting lists. A *self-adjusting* list is like a regular list, except that all insertions are performed at the front, and when an element is accessed by a *Find,* it is moved to the front of the list without changing the relative order of the other items.

   b. Write a linked list implementation of self-adjusting lists, using inheritance.

  *c. Suppose each element has a fixed probability, p_i, of being accessed. Show that the elements with highest access probability are expected to be close to the front.

3.16 Suppose we have an array-based list A and we want to delete all duplicates. *Last_Position* is initially $N-1$, but gets smaller as elements are deleted. Consider the pseudocode program fragment in Figure 3.61. The function *Remove* deletes the element in position j and collapses the list, thus decreasing *Last_Position*.

   a. Explain how this function works.

   b. Rewrite this function using general list operations.

```
/* 1*/     for( int i = 0; i < Last_Position; i++ )
/* 2*/     {
/* 3*/         int j = i + 1;
/* 4*/         while( j < Last_Position )
/* 5*/         {
/* 6*/             if( A[ i ] == A[ j ] )
/* 7*/                 Remove( j );
/* 8*/             else
/* 9*/                 j++;
/*10*/         }
/*11*/     }
```

Figure 3.61   Routine to remove duplicates from a list—
            Array implementation

*c. Using a standard array implementation, what is the running time of this function?

d. What is the running time using a linked list implementation?

*e. Give an algorithm to solve this problem in $O(n \log n)$ time.

**f. Prove that any algorithm to solve this problem requires $\Omega(n \log n)$ comparisons if only comparisons are used. (*Hint:* Look to Chapter 7.)

*g. Prove that if we allow operations besides comparisons, and the keys are real numbers, then we can solve the problem without using comparisons between elements.

3.17 An alternative to the deletion strategy we have given is to use *lazy deletion*. To delete an element, we merely mark it deleted (using an extra bit field). The number of deleted and nondeleted elements in the list is kept as part of the data structure. If there are as many deleted elements as nondeleted elements, we traverse the entire list, performing the standard deletion algorithm on all marked nodes.

a. List the advantages and disadvantages of lazy deletion.

b. Write routines to implement the standard linked list operations using lazy deletion. Use inheritance.

3.18 Write a program to check for balancing symbols in the following languages:

a. Pascal (*begin/end,* ( ), [ ], { }).

b. C (/* */, ( ), [ ], { }).

*c. Explain how to print out an error message that is likely to reflect the probable cause.

3.19 Write a program to evaluate a postfix expression.

3.20 a. Write a program to convert an infix expression that includes '(', ')', '+', '−', '*' and '/' to postfix.

b. Add the exponentiation operator to your repertoire.

c. Write a program to convert a postfix expression to infix.

3.21 Write routines to implement two stacks using only one array. Your stack routines should not declare an overflow unless every slot in the array is used.

3.22 *a. Propose a data structure that supports the stack *Push* and *Pop* operations and a third operation *Find_Min*, which returns the smallest element in the data structure, all in $O(1)$ worst case time.

   *b. Prove that if we add the fourth operation *Delete_Min*, which finds and removes the smallest element, then at least one of the operations must take $\Omega(\log n)$ time. (This requires reading Chapter 7.)

3.23 * Show how to implement three stacks in one array.

3.24 If the recursive routine in Section 2.4 used to compute Fibonacci numbers is run for $n = 50$, is stack space likely to run out? Why or why not?

3.25 Write the routines to implement queues using

   a. linked lists

   b. arrays

3.26 A *Deque* is a data structure consisting of a list of items, on which the following operations are possible:

D.Push(X): Insert item X on the front end of deque D.

D.Pop(X): Remove the front item from deque D and place it in X.

D.Inject(X): Insert item X on the rear end of deque D.

D.Eject(X): Remove the rear item from deque D and place it in X.

Write routines to support the deque that take $O(1)$ time per operation.

CHAPTER 4

Trees

For large amounts of input, the linear access time of linked lists is prohibitive. In this chapter we look at a simple data structure for which the running time of most operations is $O(\log n)$ on average. We also sketch a conceptually simple modification to this data structure that guarantees the above time bound in the worst case and discuss a second modification that essentially gives an $O(\log n)$ running time per operation for a long sequence of instructions.

The data structure that we are referring to is known as a *binary search tree.* *Trees* in general are very useful abstractions in computer science, so we will discuss their use in other, more general applications. In this chapter, we will

- See how trees are used to implement the file system of several popular operating systems.
- See how trees can be used to evaluate arithmetic expressions.
- Show how to use trees to support searching operations in $O(\log n)$ average time, how to refine these ideas to obtain $O(\log n)$ worst-case bounds, and how to implement these operations when the data is stored on a disk.

4.1. Preliminaries

A *tree* can be defined in several ways. One natural way to define a tree is recursively. A tree is a collection of nodes. The collection can be empty, which is sometimes denoted as Λ. Otherwise, a tree consists of a distinguished node r, called the *root,* and zero or more (sub)trees $T_1, T_2, \ldots, T_k$, each of whose roots are connected by a directed *edge* to r.

The root of each subtree is said to be a *child* of r, and r is the *parent* of each subtree root. Figure 4.1 shows a typical tree using the recursive definition.

From the recursive definition, we find that a tree is a collection of n nodes, one of which is the root, and $n - 1$ edges. That there are $n - 1$ edges follows from the fact that each edge connects some node to its parent, and every node except the root has one parent (see Figure 4.2).

115

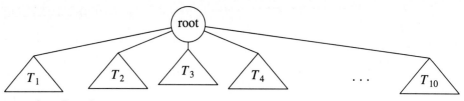

Figure 4.1 Generic tree

In the tree of Figure 4.2, the root is *A*. Node *F* has *A* as a parent and *K*, *L*, and *M* as children. Each node may have an arbitrary number of children, possibly zero. Nodes with no children are known as *leaves*; the leaves in the tree of Figure 4.2 are *B*, *C*, *H*, *I*, *P*, *Q*, *K*, *L*, *M*, and *N*. Nodes with the same parent are *siblings*; thus *K*, *L*, and *M* are all siblings. *Grandparent* and *grandchild* relations can be defined in a similar manner.

A *path* from node n_1 to n_k is defined as a sequence of nodes $n_1, n_2, \ldots, n_k$ such that n_i is the parent of n_{i+1} for $1 \le i < k$. The *length* of this path is the number of edges on the path, namely $k - 1$. There is a path of length zero from every node to itself. Notice that in a tree there is exactly one path from the root to each node.

For any node n_i, the *depth* of n_i is the length of the unique path from the root to n_i. Thus, the root is at depth 0. The *height* of n_i is the longest path from n_i to a leaf. Thus all leaves are at height 0. The height of a tree is equal to the height of the root. For the tree in Figure 4.2, *E* is at depth 1 and height 2; *F* is at depth 1 and height 1; the height of the tree is 3. The depth of a tree is equal to the depth of the deepest leaf; this is always equal to the height of the tree.

If there is a path from n_1 to n_2, then n_1 is an *ancestor* of n_2 and n_2 is a *descendant* of n_1. If $n_1 \ne n_2$, then n_1 is a *proper ancestor* of n_2 and n_2 is a *proper descendant* of n_1.

4.1.1. *Implementation of Trees*

One way to implement a tree would be to have in each node, besides its data, a pointer to each child of the node. However, since the number of children per node can vary so greatly and is not known in advance, it might be infeasible to make the

Figure 4.2 A tree

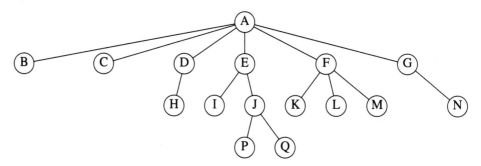

```
/* 1*/   struct Tree_Node
/* 2*/   {
/* 3*/        Element_Type Element;
/* 4*/        Tree_Node *First_Child;
/* 5*/        Tree_Node *Next_Sibling;
/* 6*/   };
```

Figure 4.3   Node declarations for trees

children direct links in the data structure, because there would be too much wasted space. The solution is simple: Keep the children of each node in a linked list of tree nodes. The declaration in Figure 4.3 is typical.

Figure 4.4 shows how a tree might be represented in this implementation. Arrows that point downward are *First_Child* pointers. Arrows that go left to right are *Next_Sibling* pointers. Null pointers are not drawn, because there are too many.

In the tree of Figure 4.4, node *E* has both a pointer to a sibling (*F*) and a pointer to a child (*I*), while some nodes have neither.

4.1.2. *Tree Traversals with an Application*

There are many applications for trees. One of the popular uses is the directory structure in many common operating systems, including UNIX, VAX/VMS, and DOS. Figure 4.5 is a typical directory in the UNIX file system.

The root of this directory is */usr*. (The asterisk next to the name indicates that */usr* is itself a directory.) */usr* has three children, *mark, alex,* and *bill*, which are themselves directories. Thus, */usr* contains three directories and no regular files. The filename */usr/mark/book/ch1.r* is obtained by following the leftmost child three times. Each / after the first indicates an edge; the result is the full *pathname*. This hierarchical file system is very popular because it allows users to organize their

Figure 4.4   First child/next sibling representation of the tree shown in Figure 4.2

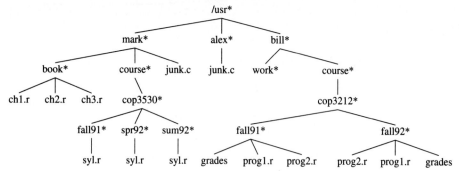

Figure 4.5 UNIX directory

data logically. Furthermore, two files in different directories can share the same name, because they must have different paths from the root and thus have different pathnames. A directory in the UNIX file system is just a file with a list of all its children, so the directories are structured almost exactly in accordance with the type declaration above.[†] Indeed, if the normal command to print a file is applied to a directory, then the names of the files in the directory can be seen in the output (along with other non-ASCII information).

Suppose we would like to list the names of all of the files in the directory. Our output format will be that files of depth d will have their names indented by d tabs. Our algorithm is given in Figure 4.6.

The recursion-function *List_Directory* needs to be started with the directory name and a depth of 0 to signify no indenting for the root. This depth is an internal

Figure 4.6   Routine to list a directory in a hierarchical file
                 system

```
/* 1*/    void
/* 2*/    List_Directory( const Directory_Or_File & D, const int Depth = 0 )
/* 3*/    {
/* 4*/        if( Is_A_Legitimate_Entry( D ) )
/* 5*/        {
/* 6*/            Print_Name( Depth, D );
/* 7*/            if( Is_Directory( D ) )
/* 8*/                for Each Child, C, Of D
/* 9*/                    List_Directory( C, Depth + 1 );
/*10*/        }
/*11*/    }
```

[†]Each directory in the UNIX file system also has one entry that points to itself and another entry that points to the parent of the directory. Thus, technically, the UNIX file system is not a tree, but is treelike.

bookkeeping variable and is hardly a parameter that a calling routine should be expected to know about. Thus, the default value of zero is provided for *Depth*.

The logic of the algorithm is simple to follow. The argument to *List_Directory* is some sort of pointer into the tree. As long as the pointer is valid, the name implied by the pointer is printed out with the appropriate number of tabs. If the entry is a directory, then we process all children recursively, one by one. These children are one level deeper and thus must be indented an extra space. The output is in Figure 4.7.

This traversal strategy is known as a *preorder* traversal. In a preorder traversal, work at a node is performed before (*pre*) its children are processed. When this program is run, it is clear that line 6 is executed exactly once per node, since each name is output once. Since line 6 is executed at most once per node, line 7 must also be executed once per node. Furthermore, line 9 can be executed at most once for each child of each node. But the number of children is exactly one less than the

Figure 4.7 The (preorder) directory listing

```
/usr
    mark
        book
            chr1.c
            chr2.c
            chr3.c
        course
            cop3530
                fall91
                    syl.r
                spr92
                    syl.r
                sum92
                    syl.r
        junk.c
    alex
        junk.c
    bill
        work
        course
            cop3212
                fall91
                    grades
                    prog1.r
                    prog2.r
                fall92
                    prog2.r
                    prog1.r
                    grades
```

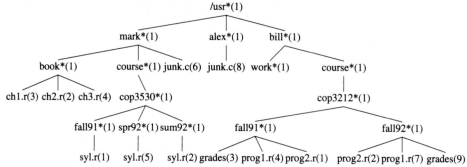

Figure 4.8   UNIX directory with file sizes obtained via
postorder traversal

number of nodes. Finally, the *for* loop iterates once per execution of line 9, plus
once each time the loop ends. Each *for* loop terminates on a *NULL* pointer, but
there is at most one of those per node. Thus, the total amount of work is constant
per node. If there are *n* file names to be output, then the running time is $O(n)$.

Another common method of traversing a tree is the *postorder* traversal. In a
postorder traversal, the work at a node is performed after (*post*) its children are
evaluated. As an example, Figure 4.8 represents the same directory structure as
before. (The numbers in parentheses represent the number of disk blocks taken up
by each file.)

Since the directories are themselves files, they have sizes too. Suppose we would
like to calculate the total number of blocks used by all the files in the tree. The
most natural way to do this would be to find the number of blocks contained in the
subdirectories */usr/mark* (30), */usr/alex* (9), and */usr/bill* (32). The total number of
blocks is then the total in the subdirectories (71) plus the one block used by */usr*,
for a total of 72. The function *Size_Directory* in Figure 4.9 implements this strategy.

Figure 4.9   Routine to calculate the size of a directory

```
/* 1*/   int
/* 2*/   Size_Directory( const Directory_Or_File & D )
/* 3*/   {
/* 4*/       int Total_Size;

/* 5*/       if( Is_A_Legitimate_Entry( D ) )
/* 6*/       {
/* 7*/           Total_Size = File_Size( D );
/* 8*/           if( Is_Directory( D ) )
/* 9*/               for Each Child, C, Of D
/*10*/                   Total_Size += Size_Directory( C );
/*11*/       }

/*12*/       return Total_Size;
/*13*/   }
```

ch1.r		3
ch2.r		2
ch3.r		4
book		10
syl.r		1
fall91		2
syl.r		5
spr92		6
syl.r		2
sum92		3
cop3530		12
course		13
junk.c		6
mark		30
junk.c		8
alex		9
work		1
grades		3
prog1.r		4
prog2.r		1
fall91		9
prog2.r		2
prog1.r		7
grades		9
fall92		19
cop3212		29
course		30
bill		32
/usr		72

Figure 4.10   Trace of the *size* function

If *D* is not a directory, *Size Directory* merely returns the number of blocks used by *D*. Otherwise, the number of blocks used by *D* is added to the number of blocks (recursively) found in all of the children. To illustrate the difference between the postorder traversal strategy and the preorder traversal strategy, Figure 4.10 shows how the size of each directory or file is produced by the algorithm.

4.2.   Binary Trees

A binary tree is a tree in which no node can have more than two children.

Figure 4.11 shows that a binary tree consists of a root and two subtrees, T_L and T_R, both of which could be empty.

A property of binary trees that is sometimes important is that the depth of an average binary tree is considerably smaller than *n*. An analysis shows that the average

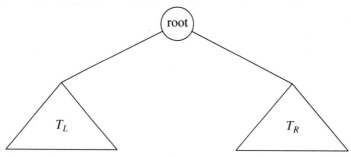

Figure 4.11   Generic binary tree

depth is $O(\sqrt{n})$, and that for a special type of binary tree, namely the *binary search tree*, the average value of the depth is $O(\log n)$. Unfortunately, the depth can be as large as $n - 1$, as the example in Figure 4.12 shows.

4.2.1.   *Implementation*

Because a binary tree has at most two children, we can keep direct pointers to them. The declaration of tree nodes is similar in structure to that for doubly linked lists, in that a node consists of the *key* information plus two pointers (*Left* and *Right*) to other nodes (see Fig. 4.13).

Many of the rules that apply to linked lists will apply to trees as well. In particular, when an insertion is performed, a node will have to be created by a call to *new*. Nodes can be freed after deletion by calling *delete*.

We could draw the binary trees using the rectangular boxes that are customary for linked lists, but trees are generally drawn as circles connected by lines because they are actually graphs. We also do not explicitly draw *NULL* pointers when referring to trees, because every binary tree with n nodes would require $n + 1$ *NULL* pointers.

Binary trees have many important uses not associated with searching. One of the principal uses of binary trees is in the area of compiler design, which we will now explore.

Figure 4.12   Worst-case binary tree

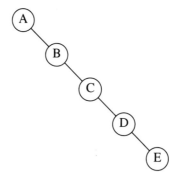

```
/* 1*/    struct Tree_Node
/* 2*/    {
/* 3*/        Element_Type Element;
/* 4*/        Tree_Node *Left;
/* 5*/        Tree_Node *Right;
/* 6*/    };
```

Figure 4.13   Binary tree node declarations

4.2.2. *Expression Trees*

Figure 4.14 shows an example of an *expression tree*. The leaves of an expression tree are *operands*, such as constants or variable names, and the other nodes contain *operators*. This particular tree happens to be binary because all of the operations are binary; although this is the simplest case, it is possible for nodes to have more than two children. It is also possible for a node to have only one child, as is the case with the *unary minus* operator. We can evaluate an expression tree, T, by applying the operator at the root to the values obtained by recursively evaluating the left and right subtrees. In our example, the left subtree evaluates to $a + (b * c)$ and the right subtree evaluates to $((d * e) + f) * g$. The entire tree therefore represents $(a + (b * c)) + (((d * e) + f) * g)$.

We can produce an (overly parenthesized) infix expression by recursively producing a parenthesized left expression, then printing out the operator at the root, and finally recursively producing a parenthesized right expression. This general strategy (left, node, right) is known as an *inorder* traversal; it is easy to remember because of the type of expression it produces.

An alternate traversal strategy is to recursively print out the left subtree, the right subtree, and then the operator. If we apply this strategy to our tree above, the output is a b c * + d e * f + g * +, which is easily seen to be the postfix representation of Section 3.3.3. This traversal strategy is generally known as a *postorder* traversal. We have seen this traversal strategy earlier, in Section 4.1.

Figure 4.14   Expression tree for $(a + b * c) + ((d * e + f) * g)$

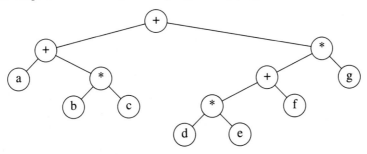

A third traversal strategy is to print out the operator first and then recursively print out the left and right subtrees. The resulting expression, $+ + a * b c * + * d e f g$, is the less useful *prefix* notation, and the traversal strategy is a *preorder* traversal, which we have also seen in Section 4.1. We will return to these traversal strategies once again later in this chapter.

Constructing an Expression Tree

We now give an algorithm to convert a postfix expression into an expression tree. Since we already have an algorithm to convert infix to postfix, we can generate expression trees from the two common types of input. The method we describe strongly resembles the postfix evaluation algorithm of Section 3.2.3. We read our expression one symbol at a time. If the symbol is an operand, we create a one-node tree and push a pointer to it onto a stack. If the symbol is an operator, we pop pointers to two trees T_1 and T_2 from the stack (T_1 is popped first) and form a new tree whose root is the operator and whose left and right children point to T_2 and T_1 respectively. A pointer to this new tree is then pushed onto the stack.

As an example, suppose the input is

a b + c d e + * *

The first two symbols are operands, so we create one-node trees and push pointers to them onto a stack.[†]

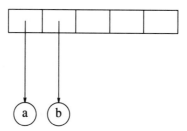

Next, a '+' is read, so two pointers to trees are popped, a new tree is formed, and a pointer to it is pushed onto the stack.

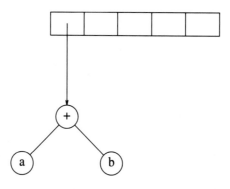

[†] For convenience, we will have the stack grow from left to right in the diagrams.

Next, *c*, *d*, and *e* are read, a one-node tree is created for each, and a pointer to the corresponding tree is pushed onto the stack.

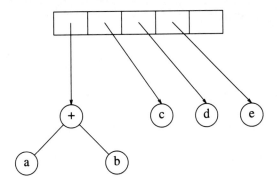

Now a '+' is read, so two trees are merged.

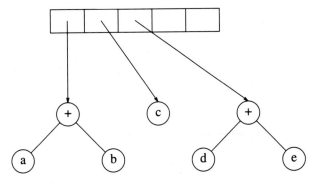

Continuing, a '*' is read, so we pop two tree pointers and form a new tree with a '*' as root.

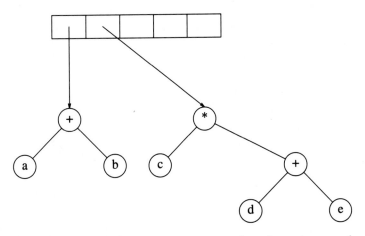

Finally, the last symbol is read, two trees are merged, and a pointer to the final tree is left on the stack.

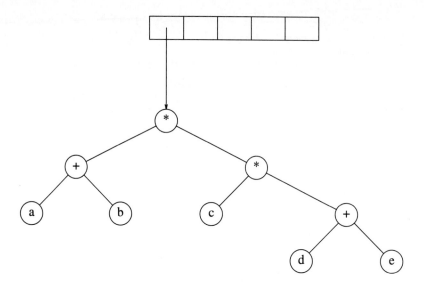

4.3. The Search Tree ADT—Binary Search Trees

An important application of binary trees is their use in searching. Let us assume that each node in the tree is assigned a key value. In our examples, we will assume for simplicity that these are integers, although arbitrarily complex keys are easily handled in C++. We will also assume that all the keys are distinct. We will deal with duplicates later.

The property that makes a binary tree into a binary search tree is that for every node, X, in the tree, the values of all the keys in the left subtree are smaller than the key value in X, and the values of all the keys in the right subtree are larger than the key value in X. Notice that this implies that all the elements in the tree can be ordered in some consistent manner. In Figure 4.15, the tree on the left is a binary search tree,

Figure 4.15 Two binary trees (only the left tree is a search tree)

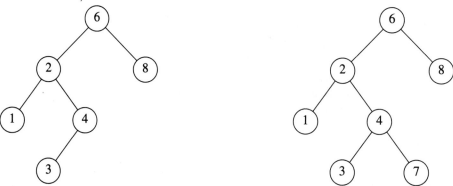

but the tree on the right is not. The tree on the right has a node with key 7 in the left subtree of a node with key 6 (which happens to be the root).

We now give brief descriptions of the operations that are usually performed on binary search trees. Note that because of the recursive definition of trees, it is common to write these routines recursively. Because the average depth of a binary search tree is $O(\log n)$, we generally do not need to worry about running out of stack space. Figure 4.16 is the class specification. Our style is similiar to the linked

Figure 4.16   Binary search tree class specifications

```
/* 1*/   #include <iostream.h>

/* 2*/   template <class Etype>
/* 3*/   class Tree_Node
/* 4*/   {
/* 5*/     protected:
/* 6*/       Etype Element;
/* 7*/       Tree_Node *Left;
/* 8*/       Tree_Node *Right;

/* 9*/       Tree_Node( Etype E = 0, Tree_Node *L = NULL,
/*10*/           Tree_Node *R = NULL ) : Element( E ),
/*11*/           Left( L ), Right( R ) { }

/*12*/       friend int Height( Tree_Node * T );

/*13*/       friend class Binary_Search_Tree<Etype>;
/*14*/   };

/*15*/   template <class Etype>
/*16*/   class Binary_Search_Tree
/*17*/   {
/*18*/     protected:
/*19*/       void Make_Empty( Tree_Node<Etype> * & T );
/*20*/       void Insert( const Etype & X, Tree_Node<Etype> * & T );
/*21*/       void Remove( const Etype & X, Tree_Node<Etype> * & T );
/*22*/       void Print_Tree( Tree_Node<Etype> * T ) const;
/*23*/       Tree_Node<Etype> *
/*24*/           Copy( const Tree_Node<Etype> * T );
/*25*/       Tree_Node<Etype> *
/*26*/           Find( const Etype & X, Tree_Node<Etype> * T ) const;
/*27*/       Tree_Node<Etype> *
/*28*/           Find_Min( Tree_Node<Etype> * T ) const;
/*29*/       Tree_Node<Etype> *
/*30*/           Find_Max( Tree_Node<Etype> * T ) const;

/*31*/       Tree_Node<Etype> *Root;
/*32*/       Tree_Node<Etype> *Last_Find;
```

```
/*33*/    public:
/*34*/      // Constructors.
/*35*/      Binary_Search_Tree( ) : Root( NULL ), Last_Find( NULL ) { }
/*36*/      Binary_Search_Tree( Binary_Search_Tree & Value )
/*37*/         { Warn( "Tree passed by value" ); operator=( Value ); }

/*38*/      // Destructor.
/*39*/      virtual ~Binary_Search_Tree( )
/*40*/         { Make_Empty( Root ); Root = Last_Find = NULL; }

/*41*/      // Operators.
/*42*/      const Binary_Search_Tree &
/*43*/         operator = ( const Binary_Search_Tree & Value );
/*44*/      Etype operator ( ) ( ) const
/*45*/         { return Last_Find != NULL ? Last_Find->Element : NULL; }

/*46*/      // Member functions.
/*47*/      void Make_Empty( )
/*48*/         { Make_Empty( Root ); Root = Last_Find = NULL; }
/*49*/      void Print_Tree( ) const
/*50*/         { Print_Tree( Root ); }

/*51*/      virtual int Find( const Etype & X )
/*52*/         { return int( Last_Find = Find( X, Root ) ); }
/*53*/      virtual int Find_Min( )
/*54*/         { return int( Last_Find = Find_Min( Root ) ); }
/*55*/      virtual int Find_Max( )
/*56*/         { return int( Last_Find = Find_Max( Root ) ); }
/*57*/      virtual void Insert( const Etype & X )
/*58*/         { Insert( X, Root ); }
/*59*/      virtual void Remove( const Etype & X )
/*60*/         { Remove( X, Root ); }
/*61*/    };
```

Figure 4.16   *(Continued)*

list routines of Chapter 3. A *Tree_Node* class is declared in lines 2 through 14 and can be instantiated with an arbitrary *Etype*. Line 12 is for a later example.

The *Binary_Search_Tree* class consists of pointers to the root and to the last node that was subjected to a *Find* (after a deletion, the latter could be undefined), as well as a variety of functions. The functions in the protected part perform operations on an arbitrary rooted subtree; they are called with the root as a parameter by the public functions. This is the most convenient way to handle recursive routines. Figure 4.17 shows a specific example: the assignment operator, which is the public function, calls the protected recursive routine, *Copy*.

As before, the use of *protected* and *virtual* reflects the fact that more fancy search trees, discussed later in the chapter, will inherit the basic binary search tree properties.

```
/* 1*/    template <class Etype>
/* 2*/    const Binary_Search_Tree<Etype> &
/* 3*/    Binary_Search_Tree<Etype>::
/* 4*/    operator = ( const Binary_Search_Tree<Etype> & Value )
/* 5*/    {
/* 6*/        if( this != &Value )
/* 7*/        {
/* 8*/            Make_Empty( Root );
/* 9*/            Root = Copy( Value.Root );    // A POINTER TO THE ROOT IS
/*10*/            Last_Find = Root;                   RETURNED
/*11*/        }
/*12*/        return *this;
/*13*/    }

/*14*/    template <class Etype>
/*15*/    Tree_Node<Etype> *
/*16*/    Binary_Search_Tree<Etype>::
/*17*/    Copy( const Tree_Node<Etype> * T )
/*18*/    {
/*19*/        if( T != NULL )
/*20*/            return new Tree_Node<Etype>
/*21*/                ( T->Element, Copy( T->Left ), Copy( T->Right ) );
/*22*/        else
/*23*/            return NULL;
/*24*/    }
```

a POINTER TO LEFT CHILD will be RETURNED

a POINTER TO Right child will be RETURNED

Figure 4.17 Copy routine for binary search trees

4.3.1. Make_Empty

This operation is mainly for initialization. Some programmers prefer to initialize the first element as a one-node tree, but our implementation follows the recursive definition of trees more closely. It is also a simple routine, as evidenced by Figure 4.18.

Figure 4.18 Routine to make an empty tree

```
/* 1*/    template <class Etype>
/* 2*/    void
/* 3*/    Binary_Search_Tree<Etype>::
/* 4*/    Make_Empty( Tree_Node<Etype> * & T )
/* 5*/    {
/* 6*/        if( T != NULL )
/* 7*/        {
/* 8*/            Make_Empty( T->Left );
/* 9*/            Make_Empty( T->Right );
/*10*/            delete T;
/*11*/            T = NULL;
/*12*/        }
/*13*/    }
```

4.3.2. Find

This operation generally requires returning a pointer to the node in tree T that has key X or NULL if there is no such node. The protected Find routine does this. The public routine then returns nonzero if the Find succeeded, and sets Last_Find. If the Find failed, zero is returned, and Last_Find points to NULL. The structure of the tree makes this simple. If T is NULL, then we return 0. Otherwise, if the key stored at T is X, we can return T. Otherwise, we make a recursive call on a subtree of T, either left or right, depending on the relationship of X to the key stored in T. The code in Figure 4.19 is an implementation of this strategy.

Notice the order of the tests. It is crucial that the test for an empty tree be performed first, since otherwise the indirections would be on a NULL pointer. The remaining tests are arranged with the least likely case last. Also, note that both recursive calls are actually tail recursions and can be easily removed with an assignment and a *goto* (or preferably by a loop). The use of tail recursion is justifiable here because the simplicity of algorithmic expression compensates for the decrease in speed, and the amount of stack space used is expected to be only $O(\log n)$.

4.3.3. Find_Min and Find_Max

Internally, these routines return the position of the smallest and largest elements in the tree, respectively. Although returning the exact values of these elements might seem more reasonable, this would be inconsistent with the Find operation. It is important that similar-looking operations do similar things. To perform a Find_Min, start at the root and go left as long as there is a left child. The stopping point is the smallest element. The Find_Max routine is the same, except that branching is to the right child. The public interface is similar to that of the Find routine.

Figure 4.19 *Find* operation for binary search trees

```
/* 1*/    template <class Etype>
/* 2*/    Tree_Node<Etype> *
/* 3*/    Binary_Search_Tree<Etype>::
/* 4*/    Find( const Etype & X, Tree_Node<Etype> * T ) const
/* 5*/    {
/* 6*/        if( T == NULL )
/* 7*/            return NULL;
/* 8*/        else
/* 9*/        if( X < T->Element )
/*10*/            return Find( X, T->Left );
/*11*/        else
/*12*/        if( X > T->Element )
/*13*/            return Find( X, T->Right );
/*14*/        else
/*15*/            return T;
/*16*/    }
```

```
/* 1*/    template <class Etype>
/* 2*/    Tree_Node<Etype> *
/* 3*/    Binary_Search_Tree<Etype>::
/* 4*/    Find_Min( Tree_Node<Etype> * T ) const
/* 5*/    {
/* 6*/        if( T == NULL )
/* 7*/            return NULL;
/* 8*/        else
/* 9*/        if( T->Left == NULL )
/*10*/            return T;
/*11*/        else
/*12*/            return Find_Min( T->Left );
/*13*/    }
```

Figure 4.20 Recursive implementation of *Find_Min* for
binary search trees

This is so easy that many programmers do not bother using recursion. We will code the routines both ways by doing *Find_Min* recursively and *Find_Max* nonrecursively (see Figs. 4.20 and 4.21).

Notice how we carefully handle the degenerate case of an empty tree. Although this is always important to do, it is especially crucial in recursive programs.

4.3.4. Insert

The insertion routine is conceptually simple. To insert X into tree T, proceed down the tree as you would with a *Find*. If X is found, do nothing (or "update" something). Otherwise, insert X at the last spot on the path traversed. Figure 4.22 shows what happens. To insert 5, we traverse the tree as though a *Find* were occurring. At the

Figure 4.21 Nonrecursive implementation of *Find_Max* for
binary search trees

```
/* 1*/    template <class Etype>
/* 2*/    Tree_Node<Etype> *
/* 3*/    Binary_Search_Tree<Etype>::
/* 4*/    Find_Max( Tree_Node<Etype> * T ) const
/* 5*/    {
/* 6*/        if( T != NULL )
/* 7*/            while( T->Right != NULL )
/* 8*/                T = T->Right;
/* 9*/        return T;
/*10*/    }
```

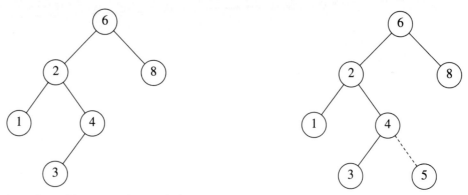

Figure 4.22 Binary search trees before and after inserting 5

node with key 4, we need to go right, but there is no subtree, so 5 is not in the tree, and this is the correct spot.

Duplicates can be handled by keeping an extra field in the node record indicating the frequency of occurrence. This adds some extra space to the entire tree but is better than putting duplicates in the tree (which tends to make the tree very deep). Of course this strategy does not work if the key is only part of a larger record. If that is the case, we can keep all of the records that have the same key in an auxiliary data structure, such as a list or another search tree.

Figure 4.23 shows the code for the insertion routine. The declaration $* \& T$ on line 4 says that T is a pointer to a node and is passed by reference. Thus, the C style of returning a pointer to the new tree, which is necessitated by call value, is avoided.

Figure 4.23 Insertion into a binary search tree

```
/* 1*/    template <class Etype>
/* 2*/    void
/* 3*/    Binary_Search_Tree<Etype>::
/* 4*/    Insert( const Etype & X, Tree_Node<Etype> * & T )
/* 5*/    {
/* 6*/        if( T == NULL )
/* 7*/        {
/* 8*/            T = new Tree_Node<Etype>( X );
/* 9*/            if( T == NULL )
/*10*/                Error( "Out of space" );
/*11*/        }
/*12*/        else
/*13*/        if( X < T->Element )
/*14*/            Insert( X, T->Left );
/*15*/        else
/*16*/        if( X > T->Element )
/*17*/            Insert( X, T->Right );
/*18*/        // Else X is in the tree already.  We'll do nothing.
/*19*/    }
```

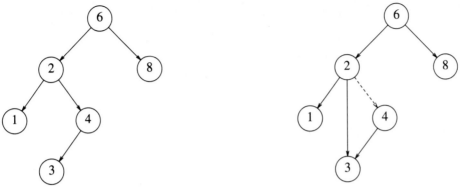

Figure 4.24 Removal of a node (4) with one child, before
and after

4.3.5. Remove

As is common with many data structures, the hardest operation is deletion. Once
we have found the node to be removed, we need to consider several possibilities.

If the node is a leaf, it can be deleted immediately. If the node has one child,
the node can be removed after its parent adjusts a pointer to bypass the node (we
will draw the pointer directions explicitly for clarity). See Figure 4.24. Notice that
the removed node is now unreferenced and can be *deleted* only if a pointer to it has
been saved.

The complicated case is when a node has two children. The general strategy
is to replace the key of this node with the smallest key of the right subtree (which
is easily found) and recursively remove that node (which is now empty). Because
the smallest node in the right subtree cannot have a left child, the second *Remove*
is an easy one. Figure 4.25 shows an initial tree and the result of a deletion. The
node to be deleted is the left child of the root; the key value is 2. It is replaced

Figure 4.25 Removal of a node (2) with two children,
before and after

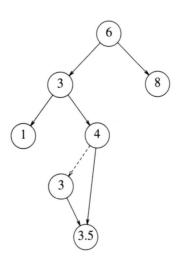

with the smallest key in its right subtree (3), and then that node is deleted as before.

The code in Figure 4.26 performs removal. It is inefficient, because it makes two passes down the tree to find and remove the smallest node in the right subtree when this is appropriate. It is easy to remove this inefficiency by writing a special *Delete_Min* function, and we have left it in only for simplicity. Be aware that the *else if* at lines 27 and 28 really is necessary.

If the number of deletions is expected to be small, then a popular strategy to use is *lazy deletion:* When an element is to be deleted, it is left in the tree and merely *marked* as being deleted. This is especially popular if duplicate keys are present, because then the field that keeps count of the frequency of appearance can

Figure 4.26   *Remove* routine for binary search trees

```
/* 1*/  template <class Etype>
/* 2*/  void
/* 3*/  Binary_Search_Tree<Etype>::
/* 4*/  Remove( const Etype & X, Tree_Node<Etype> * & T )
/* 5*/  {
/* 6*/      Tree_Node<Etype> *Tmp_Cell;

/* 7*/      if( T == NULL )
/* 8*/          Error( "Element not found" );
/* 9*/      else
/*10*/      if( X < T->Element )   // Go left.
/*11*/          Remove( X, T->Left );
/*12*/      else
/*13*/      if( X > T->Element )   // Go right.
/*14*/          Remove( X, T->Right );
/*15*/      else                          // Found element to be removed.
/*16*/      if( T->Left != NULL && T->Right != NULL )   // Two children.
/*17*/      {   // Replace with smallest in right subtree.
/*18*/          Tmp_Cell = Find_Min( T->Right );
/*19*/          T->Element = Tmp_Cell->Element;
/*20*/          Remove( T->Element, T->Right );
/*21*/      }
/*22*/      else     // One or zero child.
/*23*/      {
/*24*/          Tmp_Cell = T;
/*25*/          if( T->Left == NULL )   // Only a right child.
/*26*/              T = T->Right;
/*27*/          else
/*28*/          if( T->Right == NULL )   // Only a left child.
/*29*/              T = T->Left;
/*30*/          delete Tmp_Cell;
/*31*/      }
/*32*/  }
```

be decremented. If the number of real nodes in the tree is the same as the number of "deleted" nodes, then the expected depth of a random node in the tree is expected to go up by only a small constant (why?), so there is a very small time penalty associated with lazy deletion. Also, if a deleted key is reinserted, the overhead of allocating a new cell is avoided. Watch out, though: The other routines must be rewritten. For instance, if the maximum node is marked deleted, *Find_Max* will give the wrong answer.

4.3.6. *Average-Case Analysis*

Intuitively, we expect that all of the operations of the previous section, except *Make_Empty*, should take $O(\log n)$ time because in constant time we descend a level in the tree, thus operating on a tree that is now roughly half as large. Indeed, the running time of all the operations except *Make_Empty* is $O(d)$, where d is the depth of the node containing the accessed key.

We prove in this section that the average depth over all nodes in a tree is $O(\log n)$ on the assumption that all trees are equally likely.

The sum of the depths of all nodes in a tree is known as the *internal path length*. We will now calculate the average internal path length of a binary search tree, where the average is taken over all possible binary search trees.

Let $D(n)$ be the internal path length for some tree T of n nodes. $D(1) = 0$. An n-node tree consists of an i-node left subtree and an $(n - i - 1)$-node right subtree, plus a root at depth zero for $0 \le i < n$. $D(i)$ is the internal path length of the left subtree with respect to its root. In the main tree, all these nodes are one level deeper. The same holds for the right subtree. Thus, we get the recurrence

$$D(n) = D(i) + D(n - i - 1) + n - 1$$

If all subtree sizes are equally likely, which is true for binary search trees (since the subtree size depends only on the relative rank of the first element inserted into the tree) but not binary trees, then the average value of both $D(i)$ and $D(n - i - 1)$ is $(1/n) \sum_{j=0}^{n-1} D(j)$. This yields

$$D(n) = \frac{2}{n}\left[\sum_{j=0}^{n-1} D(j)\right] + n - 1$$

This recurrence will be encountered and solved in Chapter 7; it yields an average value of $D(n) = O(n \log n)$. Thus, the expected depth of any node is $O(\log n)$. As an example, the randomly generated 500-node tree shown in Figure 4.27 has nodes at expected depth 9.98.

It is tempting to say immediately that this result implies that the average running time of all the operations discussed in the previous section is $O(\log n)$, but this is not entirely true. The reason for this is that because of removals, it is not clear that all binary search trees are equally likely. In particular, the *Remove* algorithm described above favors making the left subtrees deeper than the right because we are always replacing a deleted node with a node from the right subtree. The exact effect of this strategy is still unknown, but it seems to be only a theoretical novelty.

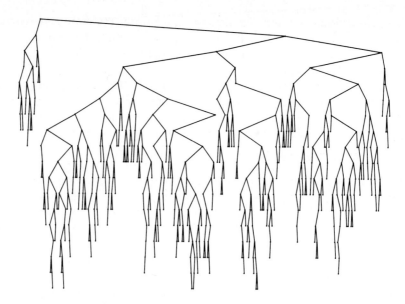

Figure 4.27   A randomly generated binary search tree

It has been shown that if we alternate insertions and deletions $\Theta(n^2)$ times, then the trees will have an expected depth of $\Theta(\sqrt{n})$. After a quarter-million random *Insert/Remove* pairs, the tree that was somewhat right-heavy in Figure 4.27 looks decidedly unbalanced (average depth = 12.51). See Figure 4.28.

We could try to eliminate the problem by randomly choosing between the smallest element in the right subtree and the largest in the left when replacing the removed element. This apparently eliminates the bias and should keep the trees

Figure 4.28   Binary search tree after $O(n^2)$ *Insert/Remove* pairs

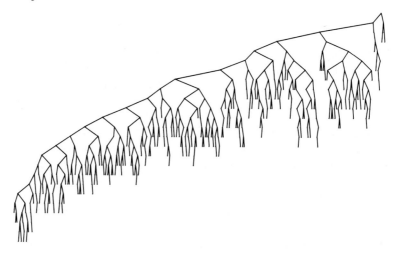

balanced, but nobody has actually proved this. In any event, this phenomenon appears to be mostly a theoretical novelty, because the effect does not show up at all for small trees, and—stranger still—if o(n^2) *Insert/Remove* pairs are used, then the tree seems to gain balance!

The main point of this discussion is that deciding what "average" means is generally extremely difficult and can require assumptions that may or may not be valid. In the absence of removals, or when lazy deletion is used, it can be shown that all binary search trees are equally likely, and we can conclude that the average running times of the operations above are $O(\log n)$. Except for strange cases like the one discussed above, this result is very consistent with observed behavior.

If the input comes into a tree presorted, then a series of *Insert*s will take quadratic time and give a very expensive implementation of a linked list, since the tree will consist only of nodes with no left children. One solution to the problem is to insist on an extra structural condition called *balance*: No node is allowed to get too deep.

There are quite a few general algorithms to implement balanced trees. Most are a good deal more complicated than a standard binary search tree, and all take longer on average. They do, however, provide protection against the embarrassingly simple cases. In the next section we will sketch one of the oldest forms of balanced search trees, the AVL tree.

A second, newer method is to forgo the balance condition and allow the tree to be arbitrarily deep, but apply a restructuring rule that tends to make future operations efficient after every operation. These types of data structures are generally classified as *self-adjusting*. In the case of a binary search tree, we can no longer guarantee an $O(\log n)$ bound on any single operation, but we can show that any *sequence* of m operations takes total time $O(m \log n)$ in the worst case. This is generally sufficient protection against a bad worst case. The data structure we will discuss is known as a *splay tree;* its analysis is fairly intricate and is discussed in Chapter 11.

4.4.   AVL Trees

An AVL (Adelson-Velskii and Landis) tree is a binary search tree with a *balance* condition. The balance condition must be easy to maintain, and it ensures that the depth of the tree is $O(\log n)$. The simplest idea is to require that the left and right subtrees have the same height. As Figure 4.29 shows, this idea does not force the tree to be shallow.

Another balance condition would insist that every node must have left and right subtrees of the same height. If the height of an empty subtree is defined to be -1 (as is usual), then only perfectly balanced trees of $2^k - 1$ nodes would satisfy this criterion. Thus, although this guarantees trees of small depth, the balance condition is too rigid to be useful and needs to be relaxed.

An AVL tree is identical to a binary search tree, except that for every node in the tree, the height of the left and right subtrees can differ by at most 1. (The height of an empty tree is defined to be -1.) In Figure 4.30 the tree on the left is an AVL

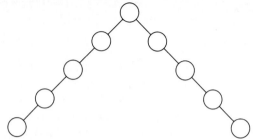

Figure 4.29   A bad binary tree. Requiring balance at the root is not enough.

tree, but the tree on the right is not. Height information is kept for each node (in the node structure). It is easy to show that the height of an AVL tree is at most roughly $1.44 \log n$, but in practice it is about $\log(n + 1) + 0.25$ (although the latter claim has not been proven). As an example, the AVL tree of height 9 with the fewest nodes (143) is shown in Figure 4.31. This tree has as a left subtree an AVL tree of height 7 of minimum size. The right subtree is an AVL tree of height 8 of minimum size. This tells us that the minimum number of nodes, $N(h)$, in an AVL tree of height h is given by $N(h) = N(h-1) + N(h-2) + 1$. For $h = 0, N(h) = 1$. For $h = 1, N(h) = 2$. The function $N(h)$ is closely related to the Fibonacci numbers, from which the bound claimed above on the height of an AVL tree follows.

Thus, all the tree operations can be performed in $O(\log n)$ time, except possibly insertion (we will assume lazy deletion). When we do an insertion, we need to update all the balancing information for the nodes on the path back to the root, but the reason that insertion is potentially difficult is that inserting a node could violate the AVL tree property. (For instance, inserting $6\frac{1}{2}$ into the AVL tree in Figure 4.30 would destroy the balance condition at the node with key 8.) If this is the case, then the property has to be restored before the insertion step is considered over. It turns out that this can always be done with a simple modification to the tree, known as a rotation. We describe this below.

Figure 4.30   Two binary search trees. Only the left tree is AVL.

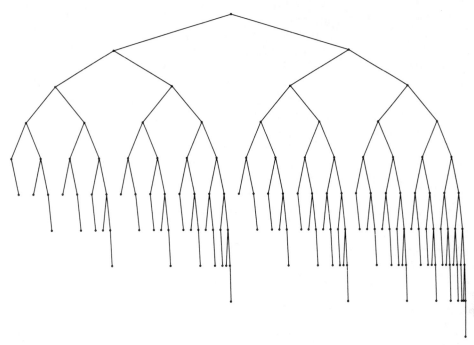

Figure 4.31   Smallest AVL tree of height 9

4.4.1.   *Single Rotation*

The two trees in Figure 4.32 contain the same elements and are both binary search trees. First of all, in both trees $k_1 < k_2$. Second, all elements in the subtree X are smaller than k_1 in both trees. Third, all elements in subtree Z are larger than k_2. Finally, all elements in subtree Y are in between k_1 and k_2. The conversion of one of the above trees to the other is known as a *rotation*. A rotation involves only a few pointer changes (we shall see exactly how many later) and changes the structure of the tree while preserving the search tree property.

The rotation does not have to be done at the root of a tree; it can be done at any node in the tree, since that node is the root of some subtree. It can transform either tree into the other. This gives a simple method to fix up an AVL tree if an insertion causes one of its nodes to lose the balance property: Do a rotation

Figure 4.32   Single rotation

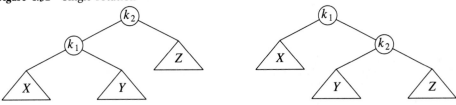

at that node. The basic algorithm is to start at the node inserted and travel up the tree, updating the balance information at every node on the path. If we get to the root without having found any badly balanced nodes, we are done. Otherwise, we do a rotation at the first bad node found, adjust its balance, and are done (we do not have to continue going to the root). In many cases, this is sufficient to rebalance the tree. For instance, in Figure 4.33, after the insertion of the $6\frac{1}{2}$ in the original AVL tree on the left, node 8 becomes unbalanced. Thus, we do a single rotation between 7 and 8, obtaining the tree on the right.

Let us work through a rather long example. Suppose we start with an empty AVL tree and insert the keys 1 through 7 in sequential order. The first problem occurs when it is time to insert key 3, because the AVL property is violated at the root. We perform a single rotation between the root and its right child to fix the problem. The tree is shown in the following figure, before and after the rotation:

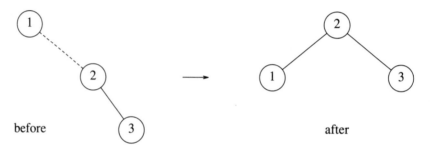

To make things clearer, a dashed line indicates the two nodes that are the subject of the rotation. Next, we insert the key 4, which causes no problems. The insertion of 5, however, creates a violation at node 3, which is fixed by a single rotation. Besides the local change caused by the rotation, the programmer must remember that the rest of the tree must be informed of this change. Here, this means that 2's right child must be reset to point to 4 instead of 3. It is easy to forget to do this, and forgetting would destroy the tree (4 would be inaccessible).

Figure 4.33 AVL property destroyed by insertion of $6\frac{1}{2}$, then fixed by a rotation

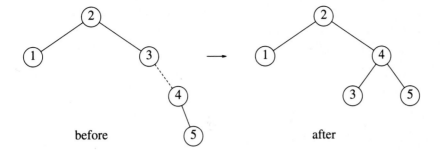

before   after

Next, we insert 6. This causes a balance problem for the root, since its left subtree is of height 0 and its right subtree would be height 2. Therefore, we perform a single rotation at the root between 2 and 4.

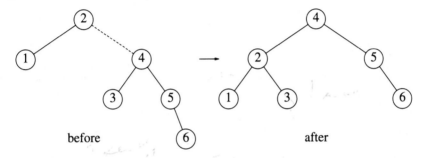

before   after

The rotation is performed by making 2 a child of 4 and making 4's original left subtree the new right subtree of 2. Every key in this subtree must lie between 2 and 4, so this transformation makes sense. The next key we insert is 7, which causes another rotation.

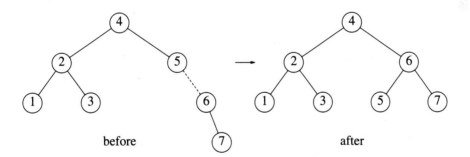

before   after

4.4.2. Double Rotation

The algorithm described in the preceding paragraphs has one problem. There is a case where the rotation does not fix the tree. Continuing our example, suppose we insert keys 8 through 15 in reverse order. Inserting 15 is easy, since it does not destroy the balance property, but inserting 14 causes a height imbalance at node 7.

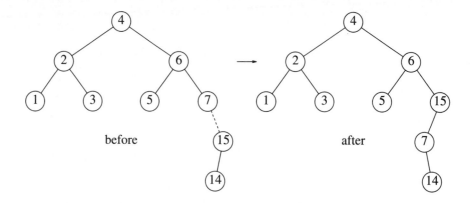

As the diagram shows, the single rotation has not fixed the height imbalance. The problem is that the height imbalance was caused by a node inserted into the tree containing the middle elements (tree Y in Fig. 4.32) at the same time as the other trees had identical heights. The case is easy to check for, and the solution is called a *double rotation*, which is similar to a single rotation but involves four subtrees instead of three. In Figure 4.34, the tree on the left is converted to the tree on the right. By the way, the effect is the same as rotating between k_1 and k_2 and then between k_2 and k_3. There is a symmetric case, which is also shown (see Fig. 4.35).

In our example, the double rotation is a right–left double rotation and involves 7, 15, and 14. Here, k_3 is the node with key 7, k_1 is the node with key 15, and k_2 is the node with key 14. Subtrees A, B, C, and D are all empty.

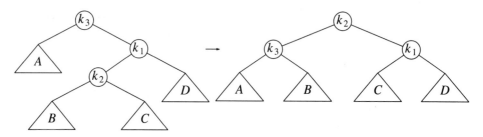

Figure 4.34 (Right–left) double rotation

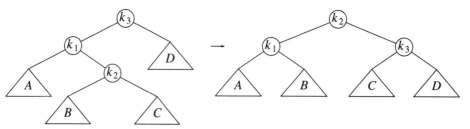

Figure 4.35 (Left–right) double rotation

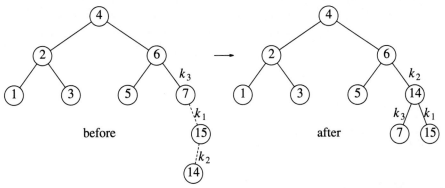

Next we insert 13, which requires a double rotation. Here the double rotation is again a right–left double rotation that will involve 6, 14, and 7 and will restore the tree. In this case, k_3 is the node with key 6, k_1 is the node with key 14, and k_2 is the node with key 7. Subtree A is the tree rooted at the node with key 5, subtree B is the empty subtree that was originally the left child of the node with key 7, subtree C is the tree rooted at the node with key 13, and finally, subtree D is the tree rooted at the node with key 15.

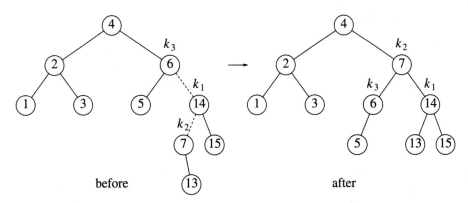

If 12 is now inserted, there is an imbalance at the root. Since 12 is not between 4 and 7, we know that the single rotation will work.

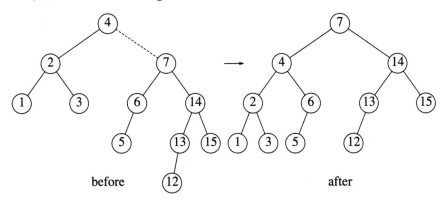

Insertion of 11 will require a single rotation:

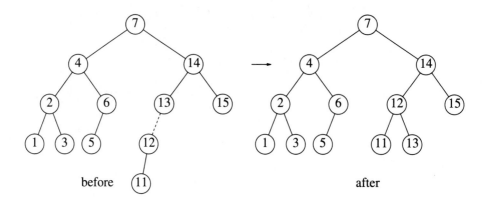

To insert 10, a single rotation needs to be performed, and the same is true for the subsequent insertion of 9. We insert 8 without a rotation, creating the almost perfectly balanced tree that follows.

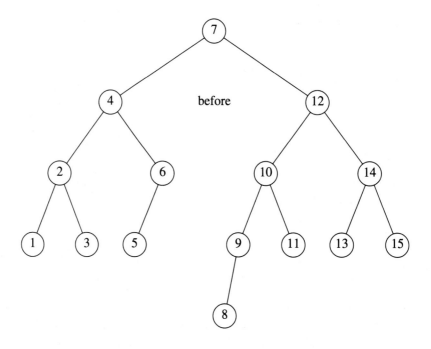

Finally, we insert $8\frac{1}{2}$ to show the symmetric case of the double rotation. This causes the node containing 9 to become unbalanced. Since $8\frac{1}{2}$ is between 9 and 8 (which is 9's child on the path to $8\frac{1}{2}$), a double rotation must be performed, yielding the following tree.

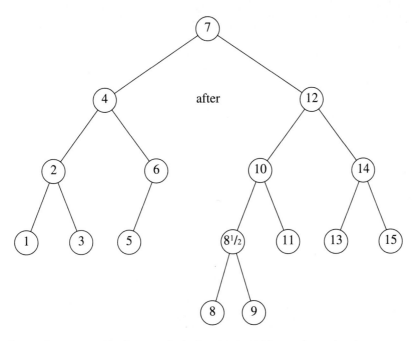

The reader can verify that any imbalance caused by an insertion into an AVL tree can always be fixed by either a single or double rotation. The programming details are fairly straightforward, except that there are several cases. To insert a new node with key x into an AVL tree T, we recursively insert x into the appropriate subtree of T (let us call this T_{lr}). If the height of T_{lr} does not change, we are done. Otherwise, if a height imbalance appears in T, we do the appropriate single or double rotation depending on x and the keys in T and T_{lr}, update the heights (making the connection from the rest of the tree above), and are done. Since one rotation always suffices, a carefully coded nonrecursive version generally turns out to be significantly faster than the recursive version. However, nonrecursive versions are quite difficult to code correctly, so many programmers implement AVL trees recursively.

Another efficiency issue concerns storage of the height information. Since all that is really required is the difference in height, which is guaranteed to be small, we could get by with two bits (to represent $+1$, 0, -1) if we really try. Doing so will avoid repetitive calculation of balance factors but results in some loss of clarity. The resulting code is somewhat more complicated than if the height were stored at each node. If a recursive routine is written, then speed is probably not the main consideration. In this case, the slight speed advantage obtained by storing balance factors hardly seems worth the loss of clarity and relative simplicity. Furthermore, since most machines will align this to at least an 8-bit boundary anyway, there is not likely to be any difference in the amount of space used. Eight bits will allow us to store absolute heights of up to 255. Since the tree is balanced, it is inconceivable that this would be insufficient (see the exercises).

With all this, we are ready to write the AVL routines. We will do only a partial job and leave the rest as an exercise. First, we need the class specification. This is given in Figure 4.36. We presume the trivial *Max* function has already been written. As

```
/* 1*/  template <class Etype>
/* 2*/  class Avl_Node : public Tree_Node<Etype>
/* 3*/  {
/* 4*/    private:
/* 5*/      int Height;

/* 6*/      friend int Node_Ht( Avl_Node * P )
/* 7*/        { return P ? P->Height : -1; }
/* 8*/      friend int Node_Ht( Tree_Node<Etype> * P )
/* 9*/        { return Node_Ht( ( Avl_Node<Etype> * ) P ); }

/*10*/      friend void Calculate_Height( Avl_Node * P )
/*11*/        { P->Height = 1 +
/*12*/            Max( Node_Ht( P->Left ), Node_Ht( P->Right ) ); }

/*13*/      friend void S_Rotate_Left( Avl_Node * & k2 );
/*14*/      friend void D_Rotate_Left( Avl_Node * & k3 );
/*15*/      friend void S_Rotate_Right( Avl_Node * & k1 );
/*16*/      friend void D_Rotate_Right( Avl_Node * & k3 );

/*17*/    protected:
/*18*/      friend class Avl_Tree<Etype>;

/*19*/    public:
/*20*/      Avl_Node( Etype E = 0, Avl_Node *L = NULL,
/*21*/          Avl_Node *R = NULL, int H = 0 ) :
/*22*/          Tree_Node<Etype>( E, L, R ), Height( H ) { }
/*23*/  };

/*24*/  template <class Etype>
/*25*/  class Avl_Tree : public Binary_Search_Tree<Etype>
/*26*/  {
/*27*/    protected:
/*28*/      Avl_Node<Etype> * Copy( const Avl_Node<Etype> * T );
/*29*/      void Insert( const Etype & X, Avl_Node<Etype> * & T );
/*30*/      void Remove( const Etype & X, Avl_Node<Etype> * & T );
/*31*/    public:
/*32*/      Avl_Tree( ) : Binary_Search_Tree<Etype>( ) { }

/*33*/      const Avl_Tree & operator = ( const Avl_Tree & Value );
/*34*/      virtual void Insert( const Etype & X )
/*35*/        { Insert( X, ( Avl_Node<Etype> * & ) Root ); }
/*36*/      virtual void Remove( const Etype & X )
/*37*/        { Remove( X, ( Avl_Node<Etype> * & ) Root ); }
/*38*/  };
```

Figure 4.36   AVL tree class specification

lines 2 and 24 show, the classes *Avl_Node* and *Avl_Tree* are derived from *Tree_Node* and *Binary_Search_Tree*, respectively.

An AVL tree node adds a fourth field, namely *Height*, to *Tree_Node*. A new constructor is provided on lines 20 through 22. The rest of the *Avl_Node* class consists of friend functions. The function at lines 8 and 9 is merely a convenience to avoid repetitive type conversions when computing node heights. A node height function is useful, because a *NULL* node is a special case. The type cast is needed because even if *T* is an *Avl_Node*, our declarations say that *T->Left* is a *Tree_Node*.

For the *Avl_Tree* class, all of the functions that don't change the tree are unchanged, so they are not listed and the *Binary_Search_Tree* functions are called. The new routines are assignment, *Insert*, and *Remove*. Line 35 is typical of one problem we must watch for. Without the type conversion, the insertion would be expected to call the *Binary_Search_Tree* insertion routine, creating a *Tree_Node*. Also, the type conversion *must* include the reference operator, or else *Root* may be passed by value on some compilers (specifically g++ 2.3.3).

Figure 4.37 implements a copy. The type conversion is necessary because if it is missing and the compiler accepts the code, the calls at lines 9 and 10 will not be recursive but will be to the *Binary_Search_Tree* routine instead. The basic insertion routine is easy to write since it consists mostly of function calls (see Fig. 4.38). Note again the reference type conversion at lines 15 and 27.

For the trees in Figure 4.39, *S_Rotate_Left* converts the tree on the left to the tree on the right. *S_Rotate_Right* is symmetric. The code is shown in Figure 4.40.

The last function we will write will perform the double rotation pictured in Figure 4.41, for which the code is shown in Figure 4.42.

Deletion in AVL trees is somewhat more complicated than insertion. Lazy deletion is probably the best strategy if deletions are relatively infrequent.

Figure 4.37 AVL tree copy routine

```
/* 1*/   template <class Etype>
/* 2*/   Avl_Node<Etype> *
/* 3*/   Avl_Tree<Etype>::
/* 4*/   Copy( const Avl_Node<Etype> * T )
/* 5*/   {
/* 6*/       if( T != NULL )
/* 7*/           return new Avl_Node<Etype> (
/* 8*/               T->Element,
/* 9*/               Copy( ( Avl_Node<Etype> * )( T->Left ) ),
/*10*/               Copy( ( Avl_Node<Etype> * )( T->Right ) ),
/*11*/               T->Height );
/*12*/       else
/*13*/           return NULL;
/*14*/   }
```

```
/* 1*/   template <class Etype>
/* 2*/   void
/* 3*/   Avl_Tree<Etype>::
/* 4*/   Insert( const Etype & X, Avl_Node<Etype> * & T )
/* 5*/   {
/* 6*/       if( T == NULL )  // Create a one node tree.
/* 7*/       {
/* 8*/           T = new Avl_Node<Etype>( X );
/* 9*/           if( T == NULL )
/*10*/               Error( "Out of space" );
/*11*/           return;
/*12*/       }

/*13*/       if( X < T->Element )
/*14*/       {
/*15*/           Insert( X, ( Avl_Node<Etype> * & ) T->Left );
/*16*/           if( Node_Ht( T->Left ) - Node_Ht( T->Right ) == 2 )
/*17*/               if( X < ( ( Avl_Node<Etype> * ) T->Left )->Element )
/*18*/                   S_Rotate_Left( T );
/*19*/               else
/*20*/                   D_Rotate_Left( T );
/*21*/           else
/*22*/               Calculate_Height( T );
/*23*/       }
/*24*/       else
/*25*/       if( X > T->Element )
/*26*/       {
/*27*/           Insert( X, ( Avl_Node<Etype> * & ) T->Right );
/*28*/           if( Node_Ht( T->Right ) - Node_Ht( T->Left ) == 2 )
/*29*/               if( X > ( ( Avl_Node<Etype> * ) T->Right )->Element )
/*30*/                   S_Rotate_Right( T );
/*31*/               else
/*32*/                   D_Rotate_Right( T );
/*33*/           else
/*34*/               Calculate_Height( T );
/*35*/       }
/*36*/       // Else X is in the tree already, so we'll do nothing.
/*37*/   }
```

Figure 4.38 Insertion into an AVL tree

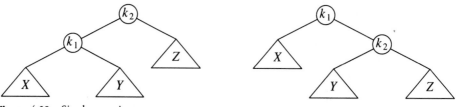

Figure 4.39 Single rotation

```
/* 1*/   // This function can be called only if k2 has a left child.
/* 2*/   // Perform a rotate between a node ( k2 ) and its left child.
/* 3*/   // Update heights.

/* 4*/   template <class Etype>
/* 5*/   void
/* 6*/   S_Rotate_Left( Avl_Node<Etype> * & k2 )
/* 7*/   {
/* 8*/        Avl_Node<Etype> *k1 = ( Avl_Node<Etype> * ) k2->Left;

/* 9*/        k2->Left = k1->Right;
/*10*/        k1->Right = k2;

/*11*/        k2->Height = Max( Node_Ht( k2->Left ),
/*12*/                             Node_Ht( k2->Right ) ) + 1;
/*13*/        k1->Height = Max( Node_Ht( k1->Left ), k2->Height ) + 1;

/*14*/        k2 = k1;
/*15*/   }
```

Figure 4.40 Routine to perform single rotation

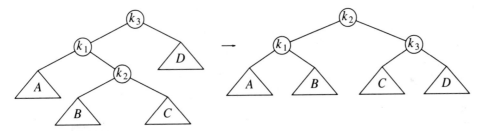

Figure 4.41 Double rotation

```
/* 1*/   // This procedure can only be called if k3 has a left child
/* 2*/   // and k3's left child has a right child.
/* 3*/   // Do the left-right double rotation.

/* 4*/   template <class Etype>
/* 5*/   void
/* 6*/   D_Rotate_Left( Avl_Node<Etype> * & k3 )
/* 7*/   {
/* 8*/        S_Rotate_Right( ( Avl_Node<Etype> * & ) k3->Left );
/* 9*/        S_Rotate_Left( k3 );
/*10*/   }
```

Figure 4.42 Routine to perform double rotation

4.5. Splay Trees

We now describe a relatively simple data structure, known as a *splay tree*, that guarantees that any m consecutive tree operations take at most $O(m \log n)$ time. Although this guarantee does not preclude the possibility that any *single* operation might take $O(n)$ time (and thus the bound is not as strong as an $O(\log n)$ worst-case bound per operation), the net effect is the same: There are no bad input sequences. Generally, when a sequence of m operations has total worst-case running time of $O(mf(n))$, we say that the *amortized* running time is $O(f(n))$. Thus, a splay tree has $O(\log n)$ amortized cost per operation. Over a long sequence of operations, some may take more, some less.

Splay trees are based on the fact that the $O(n)$ worst-case time per operation for binary search trees is not bad, as long as it occurs relatively infrequently. Any one access, even if it takes $O(n)$, is still likely to be extremely fast. The problem with binary search trees is that it is possible, and not uncommon, for a whole sequence of bad accesses to take place. The cumulative running time then becomes noticeable. A search tree data structure with $O(n)$ worst-case time, but a *guarantee* of at most $O(m \log n)$ for any m consecutive operations, is certainly satisfactory, because there are no bad sequences.

If any particular operation is allowed to have an $O(n)$ worst-case time bound, and we still want an $O(\log n)$ amortized time bound, then it is clear that whenever a node is accessed, it must be moved. Otherwise, once we find a deep node, we could keep performing *Find*s on it. If the node does not change location, and each access costs $O(n)$, then a sequence of m accesses will cost $O(m \cdot n)$.

The basic idea of the splay tree is that after a node is accessed, it is pushed to the root by a series of AVL tree rotations. Notice that if a node is deep, there are many nodes on the path that are also relatively deep, and by restructuring we can make future accesses cheaper on all these nodes. Thus, if the node is unduly deep, we want this restructuring to have the side effect of balancing the tree (to some extent). Besides giving a good time bound in theory, this method is likely to have practical utility, because in many applications, when a node is accessed, it is likely to be accessed again in the near future. Studies have shown that this happens much more often than one would expect. Splay trees also do not require the maintenance of height or balance information, thus saving space and simplifying the code to some extent (especially when careful implementations are written).

4.5.1. A Simple Idea (That Does Not Work)

One way of performing the restructuring described above is to perform single rotations, bottom up. This means that we rotate every node on the access path with its parent. As an example, consider what happens after an access (a *Find*) on k_1 in the following tree.

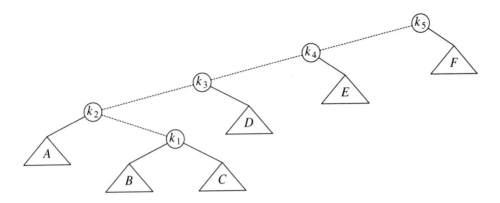

The access path is dashed. First, we would perform a single rotation between k_1 and its parent, obtaining the following tree.

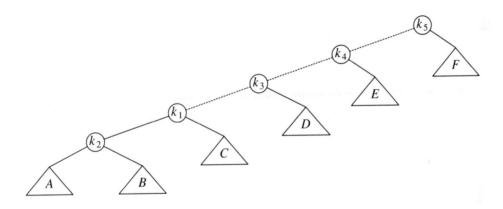

Then, we rotate between k_1 and k_3, obtaining the next tree.

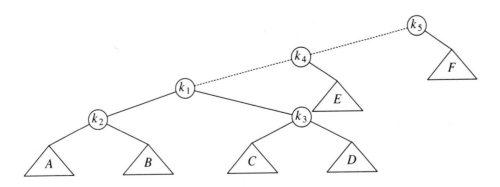

Then two more rotations are performed to reach the root.

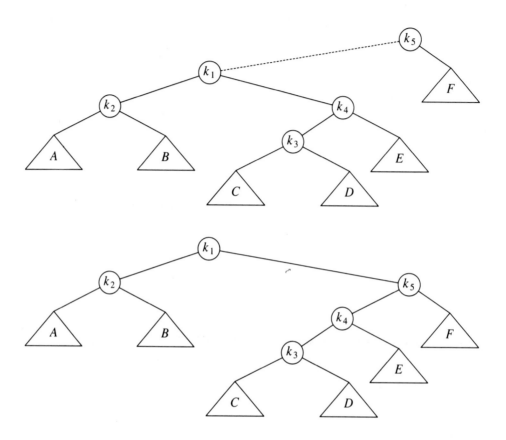

These rotations have the effect of pushing k_1 all the way to the root so that future accesses on k_1 are easy (for a while). Unfortunately, it has pushed another node (k_3) almost as deep as k_1 used to be. An access on that node will then push another node deep, and so on. Although this strategy makes future accesses of k_1 cheaper, it has not significantly improved the situation for the other nodes on the (original) access path. It turns out that it is possible to prove that using this strategy, there is a sequence of m operations requiring $\Omega(m \cdot n)$ time, so this idea is not quite good enough. The simplest way to show this is to consider the tree formed by inserting keys $1, 2, 3, \ldots, n$ into an initially empty tree (work this example out). This gives a tree consisting of only left children. This is not necessarily bad, though, since the time to build this tree is $O(n)$ total. The bad part is that accessing the node with key 1 takes $n - 1$ units of time. After the rotations are complete, an access of the node with key 2 takes $n - 2$ units of time. The total for accessing all the keys in order is $\sum_{i=1}^{n-1} i = \Omega(n^2)$. After they are accessed, the tree reverts to its original state, and we can repeat the sequence.

Figure 4.43   Zig-zag

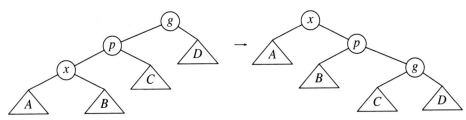

Figure 4.44   Zig-zig

4.5.2.   *Splaying*

The splaying strategy is similar to the rotation idea above except that we are a little more selective about how rotations are performed. We will still rotate bottom up along the access path. Let x be a (nonroot) node on the access path at which we are rotating. If the parent of x is the root of the tree, we merely rotate x and the root. This is the last rotation along the access path. Otherwise, x has both a parent (p) and a grandparent (g), and there are two cases, plus symmetries, to consider. The first case is the *zig-zag* case (see Fig. 4.43). Here x is a right child and p is a left child (or vice versa). If this is the case, we perform a double rotation exactly like an AVL double rotation. Otherwise, we have a *zig-zig* case: x and p are either both left children or both right children. In that case, we transform the tree on the left of Figure 4.44 to the tree on the right.

As an example, consider the tree from the last example with a *Find* on k_1:

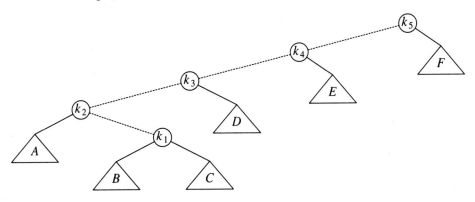

The first splay step is at k_1 and is clearly a *zig-zag*, so we perform a standard AVL double rotation using k_1, k_2, and k_3. The resulting tree follows.

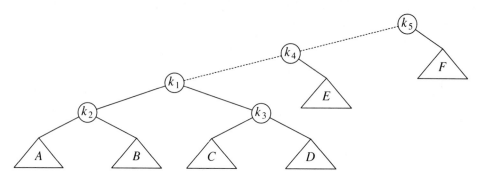

The next splay step at k_1 is a *zig-zig*, so we do the *zig-zig* rotation with k_1, k_4, and k_5, obtaining the final tree.

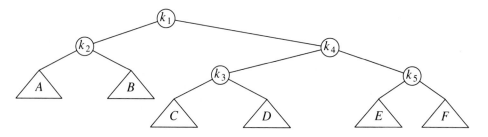

Although it is hard to see from small examples, splaying not only moves the accessed node to the root but also has the effect of roughly halving the depth of most nodes on the access path (some shallow nodes are pushed down at most two levels).

To see the difference that splaying makes over simple rotation, consider again the effect of inserting keys 1, 2, 3, ..., n into an initially empty tree. This takes a total of $O(n)$, as before, and yields the same tree as simple rotations. Figure 4.45

Figure 4.45   Result of splaying at node 1

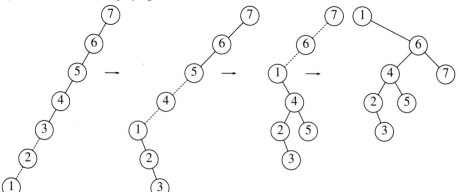

shows the result of splaying at the node with key 1. The difference is that after an access of the node with key 1, which takes $n - 1$ units, the access on the node with key 2 will take only about $n/2$ units instead of $n - 2$ units; there are no nodes quite as deep as before.

An access on the node with key 2 will bring nodes to within $n/4$ of the root, and this is repeated until the depth becomes roughly $\log n$ (an example with $n = 7$ is too small to see the effect well). Figures 4.46 to 4.54 show the result of accessing keys 1 through 9 in a 32-node tree that originally contains only left children. Thus

Figure 4.46   Result of splaying at node 1 a tree of all left children

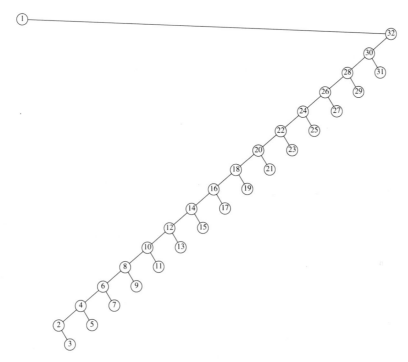

Figure 4.47   Result of splaying previous tree at node 2

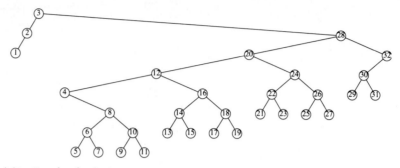

Figure 4.48   Result of splaying previous tree at node 3

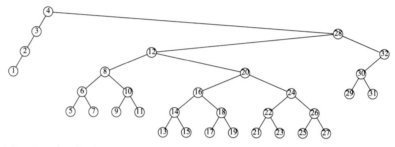

Figure 4.49   Result of splaying previous tree at node 4

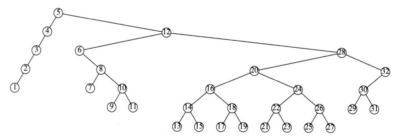

Figure 4.50   Result of splaying previous tree at node 5

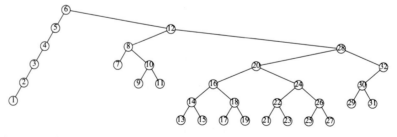

Figure 4.51   Result of splaying previous tree at node 6

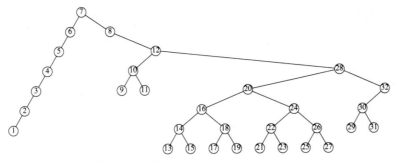

Figure 4.52   Result of splaying previous tree at node 7

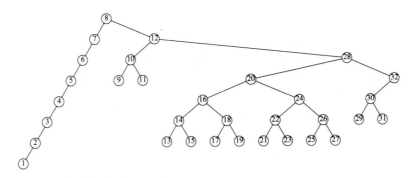

Figure 4.53   Result of splaying previous tree at node 8

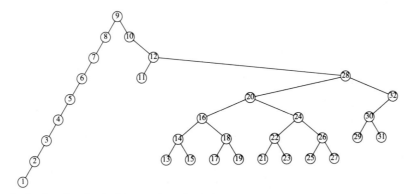

Figure 4.54   Result of splaying previous tree at node 9

we do not get the same bad behavior from splay trees that is prevalent in the simple rotation strategy. (Actually, this turns out to be a very good case. A rather complicated proof shows that for this example, the n accesses take a total of $O(n)$ time.)

These figures show off the fundamental and crucial property of splay trees. When access paths are long, thus leading to a longer-than-normal search time, the rotations tend to be good for future operations. When accesses are cheap, the rotations are not as good and can be bad. The extreme case is the initial tree formed by the insertions. All the insertions were constant-time operations leading to a bad initial tree. At that point in time, we had a very bad tree, but we were running ahead of schedule and had the compensation of less total running time. Then a couple of really horrible accesses left a nearly balanced tree, but the cost was that we had to give back some of the time that had been saved. The main theorem, which we will prove in Chapter 11, is that we never fall behind a pace of $O(\log n)$ per operation: We are always on schedule, even though occasionally there are bad operations.

Because the rotations for splay trees are performed in pairs from the bottom up, a recursive implementation does not work (although modifications to the splaying steps can be made to allow a recursive implementation). The pairs of nodes to consider are not known until the length of the path is determined to be even or odd. Thus, splay trees are coded nonrecursively and work in two passes. The first pass goes down the tree, and the second goes back up, performing rotations. This requires that the path be saved. This can be done by using a stack (which might need to store n pointers) or by adding an extra field to the node structure that will point to the parent. Neither method is particularly difficult to implement. We will provide code for the splaying routine on the assumption that each node stores its parent.

The class specification (Fig. 4.55) is simple to understand. *Find_Max*, at lines 42 through 45, is typical. After the maximum is found, a splay is performed. The

Figure 4.55   Class specification for splay trees

```
/* 1*/   template <class Etype>
/* 2*/   class Splay_Node : public Tree_Node<Etype>
/* 3*/   {
/* 4*/      protected:
/* 5*/        Splay_Node *Parent;

/* 6*/        void Single_Rotate( );
/* 7*/        void Double_Rotate( );
/* 8*/        void Zig_Left( Splay_Node * const X );
/* 9*/        void Zig_Zig_Left( Splay_Node * const X );
/*10*/        void Zig_Left_Zag_Right( Splay_Node * const X );
/*11*/        void Zig_Right( Splay_Node * const X );
/*12*/        void Zig_Zig_Right( Splay_Node * const X );
/*13*/        void Zig_Right_Zag_Left( Splay_Node * const X );

/*14*/      protected:
/*15*/        friend class Splay_Tree<Etype>;
```

```
/*16*/    public:
/*17*/      Splay_Node( Etype E = 0, Splay_Node *L = NULL,
/*18*/          Splay_Node *R = NULL, Splay_Node *P = NULL ) :
/*19*/          Tree_Node<Etype>( E, L, R ), Parent( P ) { }
/*20*/    };

/*21*/  template <class Etype>
/*22*/  class Splay_Tree : public Binary_Search_Tree<Etype>
/*23*/  {
/*24*/    protected:
/*25*/      Splay_Node<Etype> *
/*26*/          Copy( Splay_Node<Etype> * T );
/*27*/      Splay_Node<Etype> *
/*28*/          Insert( const Etype & X, Splay_Node<Etype> * & T );
/*29*/      void Remove( const Etype & X, Splay_Node<Etype> * & T );
/*30*/      int Splay( Splay_Node<Etype> * const Current );

/*31*/    public:
/*32*/      // Constructors.
/*33*/      Splay_Tree( ) : Binary_Search_Tree<Etype>( ) { }

/*34*/      // Operator.
/*35*/      const Splay_Tree & operator = ( const Splay_Tree & Value );

/*36*/      // Member functions.
/*37*/      virtual int Find( const Etype & X );

/*38*/      virtual int Find_Min( )
/*39*/          { return Splay( ( Splay_Node<Etype> * ) ( Root =
/*40*/              Last_Find = Binary_Search_Tree<Etype>::
/*41*/                          Find_Min( Root ) ) ); }

/*42*/      virtual int Find_Max( )
/*43*/          { return Splay( ( Splay_Node<Etype> * ) ( Root =
/*44*/              Last_Find = Binary_Search_Tree<Etype>::
/*45*/                          Find_Max( Root ) ) ); }

/*46*/      virtual void Insert( const Etype & X )
/*47*/          { Splay( ( Splay_Node<Etype> * )
/*48*/              ( Root = Last_Find = Splay_Tree<Etype>::
/*49*/              Insert( X, ( Splay_Node<Etype> * ) Root ) ) ); }

/*50*/      virtual void Remove( const Etype & X )
/*51*/          { Splay_Tree<Etype>::
/*52*/              Remove( X, ( Splay_Node<Etype> * ) Root ); }
/*53*/    };
```

Figure 4.55 *(Continued)*

```
/* 1*/  // Splay returns zero only if the node to splay is NULL.

/* 2*/  template <class Etype>
/* 3*/  int
/* 4*/  Splay_Tree<Etype>::
/* 5*/  Splay( Splay_Node<Etype> * const Current )
/* 6*/  {
/* 7*/      Splay_Node<Etype> *The_Parent;

/* 8*/      if( Current == NULL )
/* 9*/          return 0;

/*10*/      while( ( The_Parent = Current->Parent ) != NULL )
/*11*/          if( The_Parent->Parent )
/*12*/              Current->Double_Rotate( );
/*13*/          else
/*14*/              Current->Single_Rotate( );
/*15*/      return 1;
/*16*/  }
```

Figure 4.56   Basic splay routine

splaying routine (Fig. 4.56) takes as parameter the last node on the accessed path and makes it the new root. The *const* at line 5 means that where *Current* points may not change, though the data it is pointing at could. The routines *Single_Rotate* and *Double_Rotate* choose the correct type of rotation. We provide the code for *Single_Rotate* in Figure 4.57.

The *Splay_Node* class has member functions *Single_Rotate* and *Double_Rotate*. Thus, in Figure 4.56, since *Current* is a pointer to the *Splay_Node* class, the statement at line 14 applies *Single_Rotate* to the *Splay_Node* object that *Current* is pointing at. In Figure 4.57, we see the reserved word *this* at line 6; *this* is the address of the

Figure 4.57   Single rotation

```
/* 1*/  template <class Etype>
/* 2*/  void
/* 3*/  Splay_Node<Etype>::
/* 4*/  Single_Rotate( )
/* 5*/  {
/* 6*/      Splay_Node *X = this;

/* 7*/      if( X->Parent->Left == X )
/* 8*/          Zig_Left( X );
/* 9*/      else
/*10*/          Zig_Right( X );
/*11*/  }
```

```
/* 1*/   // Zig_Left, which connects to parent if one exists.

/* 2*/   template <class Etype>
/* 3*/   void
/* 4*/   Splay_Node<Etype>::
/* 5*/   Zig_Left( Splay_Node<Etype> * const X )
/* 6*/   {
/* 7*/        Splay_Node *P = X->Parent;
/* 8*/        Splay_Node *B = ( Splay_Node<Etype> * ) X->Right;

/* 9*/        X->Right = P;        // X's new right child is P.
/*10*/        X->Parent = P->Parent;

/*11*/        if( B != NULL )      // P's newleft subtree is B.
/*12*/            B->Parent = P;
/*13*/        P->Left = B;
/*14*/        P->Parent = X;

/*15*/        if( X->Parent != NULL )
/*16*/            if( X->Parent->Left == P )
/*17*/                X->Parent->Left = X;
/*18*/            else
/*19*/                X->Parent->Right = X;
/*20*/   }
```

Figure 4.58   Single rotation between root and its left child

object being acted upon. In our context, therefore, *this* is a pointer to the node to be splayed.

The rotation routines are similar to the AVL rotations except that the parent pointers must be maintained. Some sample routines are in the figures that follow. The code in Figure 4.58 performs a *Zig*, when *X* is a left child.

Zig-zigs and *zig-zags* are similar. We will write the routine to perform the *zig-zig* rotation (see Figure 4.59) when both *X* and *P* are left children. One way to do this is to write a *Single_Rotate* routine that includes pointer changes for the parent (as was done in Figure 4.58) and then implement the complex rotations with just two rotations. *Zig_Left_Zag_Right* in Figure 4.60 does this. This is the way the

Figure 4.59

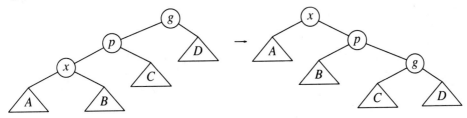

```
/* 1*/  template <class Etype>
/* 2*/  void
/* 3*/  Splay_Node<Etype>::
/* 4*/  Zig_Zig_Left( Splay_Node<Etype> * const X )
/* 5*/  {
/* 6*/      Splay_Node *P = X->Parent;
/* 7*/      Splay_Node *G = P->Parent;
/* 8*/      Splay_Node *B = ( Splay_Node<Etype> * )( X->Right );
/* 9*/      Splay_Node *C = ( Splay_Node<Etype> * )( P->Right );
/*10*/      Splay_Node *Ggp = G->Parent;

/*11*/      X->Right = P;        // X's new right child is P.
/*12*/      P->Parent = X;

/*13*/      P->Right = G;        // P's new right child is G.
/*14*/      G->Parent = P;

/*15*/      if( B != NULL )      // P's new left subtree is B.
/*16*/          B->Parent = P;
/*17*/      P->Left = B;

/*18*/      if( C != NULL )      // G's new left child is subtree C.
/*19*/          C->Parent = G;
/*20*/      G->Left = C;

/*21*/      X->Parent = Ggp;     // Connect to rest of the tree.
/*22*/      if( Ggp != NULL )
/*23*/          if( Ggp->Left == G )
/*24*/              Ggp->Left = X;
/*25*/          else
/*26*/              Ggp->Right = X;
/*27*/  }


/* 1*/  template <class Etype>
/* 2*/  void
/* 3*/  Splay_Node<Etype>::
/* 4*/  Zig_Left_Zag_Right( Splay_Node<Etype> * const X )
/* 5*/  {
/* 6*/      Zig_Right( X );
/* 7*/      Zig_Left( X );
/* 8*/  }
```

Figure 4.60 Routine to perform a *zig-zig* when both children are initially left children and a *zig-zag* when X is a right child

AVL tree routines were coded. The other way is to code the pointer changes explicitly. *Zig_Zig_Left* in Figure 4.60, which implements the rotation in Figure 4.59, does this. Figure 4.61 shows the public *Find* routine. The routine is more complex than usual because it must splay, even on an unsuccessful search, making a nonrecursive implementation necessary.

We can perform removal by accessing the node to be deleted. This puts the node at the root. If it is deleted, we get two subtrees T_L and T_R (left and right). If we find the largest element in T_L (which is easy), then this element is rotated to the root of T_L, and T_L will now have a root with no right child. We can finish the deletion by making T_R the right child.

The analysis of splay trees is difficult, because it must take into account the ever-changing structure of the tree. On the other hand, splay trees are much simpler

Figure 4.61 The *Find* routine for splay trees

```
/* 1*/   template <class Etype>
/* 2*/   int
/* 3*/   Splay_Tree<Etype>::
/* 4*/   Find( const Etype & X )
/* 5*/   {
/* 6*/       Splay_Node<Etype>
/* 7*/           *Last_On_Path,
/* 8*/           *Current = ( Splay_Node<Etype> * ) Root;

/* 9*/       if( Current == NULL )
/*10*/           return 0;

/*11*/       while( Current != NULL )
/*12*/       {
/*13*/           Last_On_Path = Current;

/*14*/           if( X < Current->Element )
/*15*/               Current = ( Splay_Node<Etype> * )( Current->Left );
/*16*/           else
/*17*/           if( X > Current->Element )
/*18*/               Current = ( Splay_Node<Etype> * )( Current->Right );
/*19*/           else
/*20*/           {   // Item is found.
/*21*/               Splay( Current );
/*22*/               Root = Last_Find = Current;
/*23*/               return 1;
/*24*/           }
/*25*/       }
/*26*/       Splay( Last_On_Path );    // Not found. Still splay, however.
/*27*/       Root = Last_On_Path;
/*28*/       return 0;
/*29*/   }
```

to program than AVL trees, since there are fewer cases to consider and no balance information to maintain. Our splay tree code may look complicated, but as pointed out before, it can be simplified; it is probably much simpler than a nonrecursive AVL implementation. Some empirical evidence suggests that this translates into faster code in practice, although the case for this is far from complete. Finally, we point out that there are several variations of splay trees that can perform even better in practice.

4.6. Tree Traversals (Revisited)

Because of the ordering information in a binary search tree, it is simple to list all the keys in sorted order. The recursive function *Print_Tree* in Figure 4.62 does this.

Convince yourself that this function works. As we have seen before, this kind of routine, when applied to trees, is known as an *inorder* traversal (which makes sense, since it lists the keys in order). The general strategy of an inorder traversal is to process the left subtree first, then perform processing at the current node, and finally process the right subtree. The interesting part about this algorithm, aside from its simplicity, is that the total running time is $O(n)$. This is because there

Figure 4.62   Routines to print a binary search tree in order and to compute the height of a tree using a postorder traversal

```
/* 1*/    template <class Etype>
/* 2*/    void
/* 3*/    Binary_Search_Tree<Etype>::
/* 4*/    Print_Tree( Tree_Node<Etype> * T ) const
/* 5*/    {
/* 6*/        if( T != NULL )
/* 7*/        {
/* 8*/            Print_Tree( T->Left );
/* 9*/            cout << T->Element << " ";
/*10*/            Print_Tree( T->Right );
/*11*/        }
/*12*/    }

/* 1*/    template <class Etype>
/* 2*/    int
/* 3*/    Height( const Tree_Node<Etype> * T )
/* 4*/    {
/* 5*/        if( T == NULL )
/* 6*/            return -1;
/* 7*/        else
/* 8*/            return 1 + Max( Height( T->Left ), Height( T->Right ) );
/* 9*/    }
```

is constant work being performed at every node in the tree. Each node is visited once, and the work performed at each node is testing against *NULL*, setting up function calls, and printing out an element. Since there is constant work per node and n nodes, the running time is $O(n)$.

Sometimes we need to process both subtrees first before we can process a node. For instance, to compute the height of a node, we need to know the height of the subtrees first. The *Height* function coded in Figure 4.62 computes this. Since it is always a good idea to check the special cases—and crucial when recursion is involved—notice that the routine will declare the height of a leaf to be zero, which is correct. This general order of traversal, which we have also seen before, is known as a *postorder* traversal. Again, the total running time is $O(n)$, because constant work is performed at each node.

The third popular traversal scheme that we have seen is *preorder* traversal. Here, the node is processed before the children. This could be useful, for example, if you wanted to label each node with its depth.

The common idea in all of these routines is that you handle the *NULL* case first and then the rest. Notice the lack of extraneous variables. These routines pass only the tree and do not declare or pass any other variables. The more compact the code, the less likely that a silly bug will turn up. A fourth, less often used, traversal (which we have not yet seen) is *level-order* traversal. In a level-order traversal, all nodes at depth d are processed before any node at depth $d + 1$. Level-order traversal differs from the other traversals in that it is not done recursively; a queue is used instead of the implied stack of recursion.

4.7.   B-Trees

Although all of the search trees we have seen so far are binary, there is a popular search tree that is not binary. This tree is known as a *B-tree*.

A B-tree of order m is a tree with the following structural properties:

• The root is either a leaf or has between 2 and m children.

• All nonleaf nodes (except the root) have between $\lceil m/2 \rceil$ and m children.

• All leaves are at the same depth.

All data is stored at the leaves. Contained in each interior node are pointers p_1, $p_2, \ldots, p_m$ to the children, and values $k_1, k_2, \ldots, k_{m-1}$, representing the smallest key found in the subtrees $p_2, p_3, \ldots, p_m$ respectively. Of course, some of these pointers might be *NULL*, and the corresponding k_i would then be undefined. For every node, all the keys in subtree p_1 are smaller than the keys in subtree p_2, and so on. The leaves contain all the actual data, which are either the keys themselves or pointers to structures containing the keys. We will assume the former to keep our examples simple. There are various definitions of B-trees that change this structure mostly in minor ways, but this definition is one of the popular forms. We will also insist (for now) that the number of keys in a leaf is also between $\lceil m/2 \rceil$ and m.

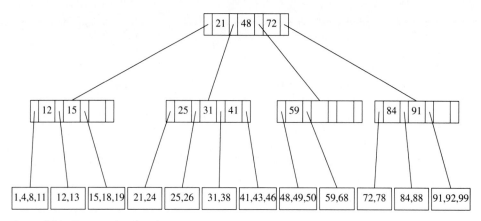

Figure 4.63   B-tree of order 4

The tree in Figure 4.63 is an example of a B-tree of order 4.

A B-tree of order 4 is more popularly known as a 2–3–4 tree, and a B-tree of order 3 is known as a 2–3 tree. We will describe the operation of B-trees by using the special case of 2–3 trees. Our starting point is the 2–3 tree that follows.

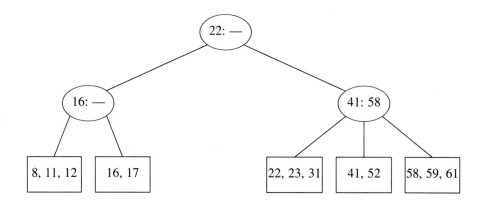

We have drawn interior nodes (nonleaves) in ellipses, which contain the two pieces of data for each node. A dash line in an interior node indicates that the node has only two children. Leaves are drawn in boxes, which contain the keys. The keys in the leaves are ordered. To perform a *Find,* we start at the root and branch in one of (at most) three directions, depending on the relation of the key we are looking for to the two (possibly one) values stored at the node.

To perform an *Insert* on a previously unseen key, *x,* we follow the path as though we were performing a *Find.* When we get to a leaf node, we have found the correct place to put *x.* Thus, to insert a node with key 18, we can just add it to a leaf without causing any violations of the 2–3 tree properties. The result is shown in the following figure.

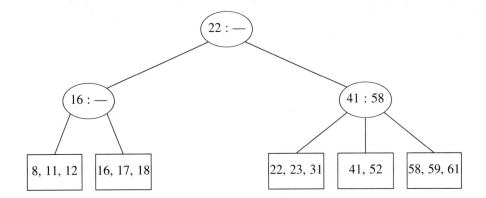

Unfortunately, since a leaf can hold only two or three keys, this might not always be possible. If we now try to insert 1 into the tree, we find that the node where it belongs is already full. Placing our new key into this node would give it a fourth element, which is not allowed. This can be solved by making two nodes of two keys each and adjusting the information in the parent.

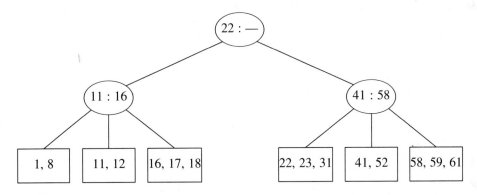

Unfortunately, this idea does not always work, as can be seen by an attempt to insert 19 into the current tree. If we make two nodes of two keys each, we obtain the following tree.

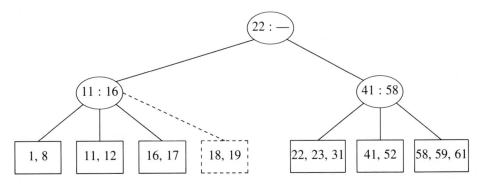

This tree has an internal node with four children, but we only allow three per node. The solution is simple. We merely split this node into two nodes with two children. Of course, this node might be one of three children itself, in which case splitting it would create a problem for its parent (which would now have four children), but we can keep on splitting nodes on the way up to the root until we either get to the root or find a node with only two children. In our case, we can get by with splitting only the first internal node we see, obtaining the following tree.

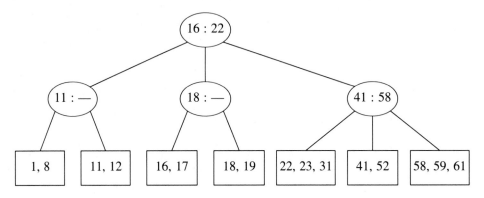

If we now insert an element with key 28, we create a leaf with four children, which is split into two leaves of two children:

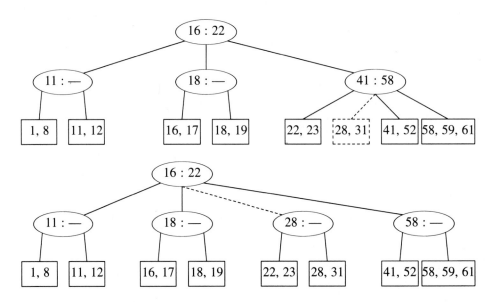

This creates an internal node with four children, which is then split into two children. What we have done here is split the root into two nodes. When we do this, we have a special case that we finish by creating a new root. This is how (the only way) a 2–3 tree gains height.

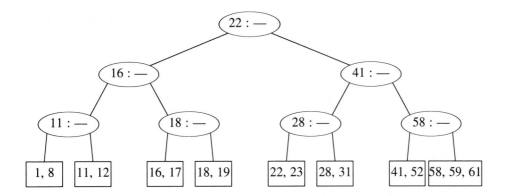

Notice also that when a key is inserted, the only changes to internal nodes occur on the access path. These changes can be made in time proportional to the length of this path, but be forewarned that there are quite a few cases to handle, and it is easy to do this wrong.

There are other ways to handle the case in which a node becomes overloaded with children, but the method we have described is probably the simplest. When attempting to add a fourth key to a leaf, we can first attempt to find a sibling with only two keys instead of splitting the node into two. For instance, to insert 70 into the tree above, we could move 58 to the leaf containing 41 and 52, place 70 with 59 and 61, and adjust the entries in the internal nodes. This strategy can also be applied to internal nodes and tends to keep more nodes full. The cost of this is slightly more complicated routines, but less space tends to be wasted.

We can perform removal by finding the key to be removed and removing it. If this key was one of only two keys in a node, then its removal leaves only one key. We can fix this by combining this node with a sibling. If the sibling has three keys, we can steal one and give both nodes two keys. If the sibling has only two keys, we combine the two nodes into a single node with three keys. The parent of this node now loses a child, so we might have to percolate this strategy all the way to the top. If the root loses its second child, then the root is also removed and the tree becomes one level shallower. As we combine nodes, we must remember to update the information kept at the internal nodes.

With general B-trees of order m, when a key is inserted, the only difficulty arises when the node that is to accept the key already has m keys. This key gives the node $m + 1$ keys, which we can split into two nodes with $\lceil (m + 1)/2 \rceil$ and $\lfloor (m + 1)/2 \rfloor$ keys respectively. As this gives the parent an extra node, we have to check whether this node can be accepted by the parent and split the parent if it already has m children. We repeat this until we find a parent with less than m children. If we split the root, we create a new root with two children.

The depth of a B-tree is at most $\lceil \log_{\lceil m/2 \rceil} n \rceil$. At each node on the path, we perform $O(\log m)$ work to determine which branch to take (using a binary search), but an *Insert* or *Remove* could require $O(m)$ work to fix up all the information at the node. The worst-case running time for each of the *Insert* and *Remove* operations is thus $O(m \log_m n) = O((m/\log m) \log n)$, but a *Find* takes only $O(\log n)$. The best (legal) choice of m for running time considerations has been shown empirically to be either $m = 3$ or $m = 4$; this agrees with the bounds above, which show that as m gets larger, the insertion and deletion times increase. If we are concerned only with main memory speed, higher order B-trees, such as 5–9 trees, are not an advantage.

The real use of B-trees lies in database systems, in which the tree is kept on a physical disk instead of main memory. Accessing a disk is typically several orders of magnitude slower than any main memory operation. If we use a B-tree of order m, then the number of *disk accesses* is $O(\log_m n)$. Although each disk access carries the overhead of $O(\log m)$ to determine the direction to branch, the time to perform this computation is typically much smaller than the time to read a block of memory and can thus be considered inconsequential (as long as m is chosen reasonably). Even if updates are performed and $O(m)$ computing time is required at each node, the time required is generally still not significant. The value of m is then chosen to be the largest value that still allows an interior node to fit into one disk block and is typically in the range $32 \le m \le 256$. The maximum number of elements that are stored in a leaf is chosen so that if the leaf is full, it fits in one block. This means that a record can always be found in very few disk accesses, since a typical B-tree will have a depth of only 2 or 3, and the root (and possibly the first level) can be kept in main memory.

Analysis suggests that a B-tree will be $\ln 2 = 69$ percent full. Better space utilization can be obtained if, instead of always splitting a node when the tree obtains its $(m + 1)$st entry, the routine searches for a sibling that can take the extra child. The details can be found in the references.

Summary

We have seen uses of trees in operating systems, compiler design, and searching. Expression trees are a small example of a more general structure known as a *parse tree*, which is a central data structure in compiler design. Parse trees are not binary, but are relatively simple extensions of expression trees (although the algorithms to build them are not quite so simple).

Search trees are of great importance in algorithm design. They support almost all the useful operations, and the logarithmic average cost is very small. Nonrecursive implementations of search trees are somewhat faster, but the recursive versions are sleeker, more elegant, and easier to understand and debug. The problem with search trees is that their performance depends heavily on the input being random. If this is not the case, the running time increases significantly, to the point where search trees become expensive linked lists.

We saw several ways to deal with this problem. AVL trees work by insisting that all nodes' left and right subtrees differ in height by at most one. This ensures that the tree cannot get too deep. The operations that do not change the tree, as insertion does, can all use the standard binary search tree code. Operations that change the tree must restore the tree. This can be somewhat complicated, especially in the case of deletion. We showed how to restore the tree after insertions in $O(\log n)$ time.

We also examined the splay tree. Nodes in splay trees can get arbitrarily deep, but the tree is adjusted in a somewhat mysterious manner after every access. The net effect is that any sequence of m operations takes $O(m \log n)$ time, which is the same as a balanced tree would take.

B-trees are balanced m-way (as opposed to 2-way or binary) trees that are well suited for disks; a special case is the 2–3 tree, which is commonly used when a balanced data structure is desired.

In practice, the running time of all the balanced tree schemes is worse (by a constant factor) than the simple binary search tree, but this is generally acceptable in view of the protection they provide against worst-case input.

A final note: By inserting elements into a search tree and then performing an inorder traversal, we obtain the elements in sorted order. This gives an $O(n \log n)$ algorithm to sort, which is a worst-case bound if any sophisticated search tree is used. We shall see better ways in Chapter 7, but none that have a lower time bound.

Exercises

Questions 4.1 to 4.3 refer to the tree in Figure 4.64.

4.1 For the tree in Figure 4.64:
   a. Which node is the root?
   b. Which nodes are leaves?

4.2 For each node in the tree of Figure 4.64:
   a. Name the parent node.
   b. List the children.
   c. List the siblings.
   d. Compute the depth.
   e. Compute the height.

4.3 What is the depth of the tree in Figure 4.64?

Figure 4.64

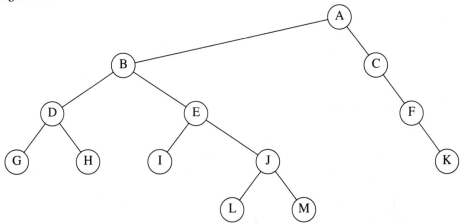

4.4 Show that in a binary tree of n nodes, there are $n + 1$ *NULL* pointers representing children.

4.5 Show that the maximum number of nodes in a binary tree of height h is $2^{h+1} - 1$.

4.6 A *full node* is a node with two children. Prove that the number of full nodes plus one is equal to the number of leaves in a binary tree.

4.7 Suppose a binary tree has leaves $l_1, l_2, \ldots, l_m$ at depth $d_1, d_2, \ldots, d_m$, respectively. Prove that $\sum_{i=1}^{m} 2^{-d_i} \leq 1$ and determine when the equality is true.

4.8 Give the prefix, infix, and postfix expressions corresponding to the tree in Figure 4.65.

4.9 a. Show the result of inserting 3, 1, 4, 6, 9, 2, 5, 7 into an empty binary search tree.

   b. Show the result of deleting the root.

4.10 Write routines to implement the basic binary search tree operations.

4.11 Binary search trees can be implemented with cursors using a strategy similar to a cursor linked list implementation. Write the basic binary search tree routines using a cursor implementation.

4.12 Suppose you want to perform an experiment to verify the problems that can be caused by random *Insert/Remove* pairs. Here is a strategy that is not perfectly random, but close enough. You build a tree with n elements by inserting n elements chosen at random from the range 1 to $m = \alpha n$. You then perform n^2 pairs of insertions followed by removals. Assume the existence of a routine, *Rand_Int(A, B)*, which returns a uniform random integer between A and B, inclusive.

   a. Explain how to generate a random integer between 1 and m that is not already in the tree (so a random insert can be performed). In terms of n and α, what is the running time of this operation?

   b. Explain how to generate a random integer between 1 and m that is already in the tree (so a random *Remove* can be performed). What is the running time of this operation?

Figure 4.65   Tree for Exercise 4.8

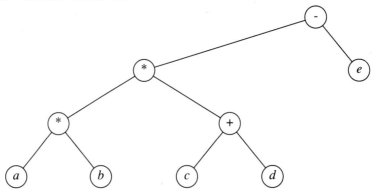

    c. What is a good choice of α? Why?

4.13 Write a program to evaluate empirically the following strategies for removing nodes with two children:

    a. Replace with the largest node, X, in T_L and recursively remove X.

    b. Alternately replace with the largest node in T_L and the smallest node in T_R, and recursively remove the appropriate node.

    c. Replace with either the largest node in T_L or the smallest node in T_R (recursively removing the appropriate node), making the choice randomly.

       Which strategy seems to give the most balance? Which takes the least CPU time to process the entire sequence?

4.14 ** Prove that the depth of a random binary search tree (depth of the deepest node) is $O(\log n)$, on average.

4.15 *a. Give a precise expression for the minimum number of nodes in an AVL tree of height h.

    b. What is the minimum number of nodes in an AVL tree of height 15?

4.16 Show the result of inserting 2, 1, 4, 5, 9, 3, 6, 7 into an empty AVL tree.

4.17 * Keys $1, 2, \ldots, 2^k - 1$ are inserted in order into an empty AVL tree. Prove that the resulting tree is perfectly balanced.

4.18 Write the remaining procedures to implement AVL single and double rotations.

4.19 Write a nonrecursive function to insert into an AVL tree.

4.20 * How can you implement (nonlazy) deletion in AVL trees?

4.21 a. How many bits are required per node to store the height of a node in an n-node AVL tree?

    b. What is the smallest AVL tree that overflows an 8-bit height counter?

4.22 Write the functions to perform double rotation without the inefficiency of doing two single rotations.

4.23 Show the result of accessing the keys 3, 9, 1, 5 in order in the splay tree in Figure 4.66.

Figure 4.66

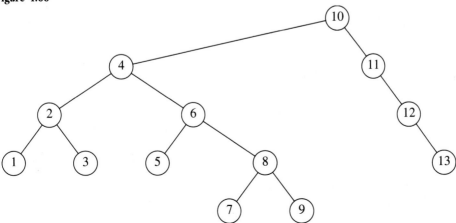

4.24 Show the result of deleting the element with key 6 in the resulting splay tree for the previous exercise.

4.25 Nodes 1 through $n = 1024$ form a splay tree of left children.

    a. What is the internal path length of the tree (exactly)?

    *b. Calculate the internal path length after each of *Find*(1), *Find*(2), *Find*(3), *Find*(4), *Find*(5), *Find*(6).

    *c. If the sequence of successive finds is continued, when is the internal path length minimized?

4.26 a. Show that if all nodes in a splay tree are accessed in sequential order, the resulting tree consists of a chain of left children.

    **b. Show that if all nodes in a splay tree are accessed in sequential order, then the total access time is $O(n)$, regardless of the initial tree.

4.27 Write a program to perform random operations on splay trees. Count the total number of rotations performed over the sequence. How does the running time compare to AVL trees and unbalanced binary search trees?

4.28 Write efficient functions that take only a pointer to a binary tree root, T, and compute

    a. the number of nodes in T.

    b. the number of leaves in T.

    c. the number of full nodes in T.

What is the running time of each of your routines?

4.29 Write a function to generate an n-node random binary search tree with distinct keys 1 through n. What is the running time of your routine?

4.30 Write a function to generate the AVL tree of height h with fewest nodes. What is the running time of your function?

4.31 Write a function to generate a perfectly balanced binary search tree of height h with keys 1 through $2^{h+1} - 1$. What is the running time of your function?

4.32 Write a function that takes as input a binary search tree, T, and two keys k_1 and k_2, which are ordered so that $k_1 \leq k_2$, and prints all elements x in the tree such that $k_1 \leq key(x) \leq k_2$. Do not assume any information about the type of keys except that they can be ordered (consistently). Your program should run in $O(K + \log n)$ average time, where K is the number of keys printed. Bound the running time of your algorithm.

4.33 The larger binary trees in this chapter were generated automatically by a program. This was done by assigning an (x, y) coordinate to each tree node, drawing a circle around each coordinate (this is hard to see in some pictures), and connecting each node to its parent. Assume you have a binary search tree stored in memory (perhaps generated by one of the routines above) and that each node has two extra fields to store the coordinates.

    a. The x coordinate can be computed by assigning the inorder traversal number. Write a routine to do this for each node in the tree.

b. The y coordinate can be computed by using the negative of the depth of the node. Write a routine to do this for each node in the tree.

c. In terms of some imaginary unit, what will the dimensions of the picture be? How can you adjust the units so that the tree is always roughly two-thirds as high as it is wide?

d. Prove that using this system no lines cross, and that for any node, X, all elements in X's left subtree appear to the left of X, and all elements in X's right subtree appear to the right of X.

4.34 Write a general-purpose tree-drawing program that will convert a tree into the following graph-assembler instructions:

a. *Circle*(x, y)

b. *Drawline*(i, j)

The first instruction draws a circle at (x, y), and the second instruction connects the ith circle to the jth circle (circles are numbered in the order drawn). You should either make this a program and define some sort of input language or make this a function that can be called from any program. What is the running time of your routine?

4.35 Write a routine to list out the nodes of a binary tree in *level-order*. List the root, then the nodes at depth 1, followed by the nodes at depth 2, and so on. You must do this in linear time. Prove your time bound.

4.36 a. Show the result of inserting the following keys into an initially empty 2–3 tree: 3, 1, 4, 5, 9, 2, 6, 8, 7, 0.

b. Show the result of deleting 0 and then 9 from the 2–3 tree created in part (a).

4.37 *a. Write a routine to perform insertion to a B-tree.

*b. Write a routine to perform deletion from a B-tree. When a key is removed, is it necessary to update information in the internal nodes?

*c. Modify your insertion routine so that if an attempt is made to add into a node that already has m entries, a search is performed for a sibling with less than m children before the node is split.

4.38 A *B*-tree* of order m is a B-tree in which each interior node has between $2m/3$ and m children. Describe a method to perform insertion into a B*-tree.

4.39 Show how the tree in Figure 4.67 is represented using a child/sibling pointer implementation.

4.40 Write a procedure to traverse a tree stored with child/sibling links.

4.41 Two binary trees are similar if they are both empty or both nonempty and have similar left and right subtrees. Write a function to decide whether two binary trees are similar. What is the running time of your program?

4.42 Two trees, T_1 and T_2, are *isomorphic* if T_1 can be transformed into T_2 by swapping left and right children of (some of the) nodes in T_1. For instance, the two trees in Figure 4.68 are isomorphic because they are the same if the children of A, B, and G, but not the other nodes, are swapped.

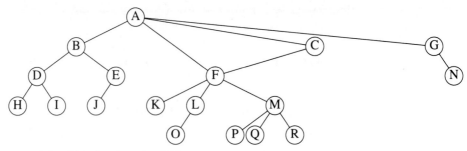

Figure 4.67   Tree for Exercise 4.39

     a. Give a polynomial time algorithm to decide if two trees are isomorphic.

    *b. What is the running time of your program? (There is a linear solution.)

4.43 *a. Show that via AVL single rotations, any binary search tree T_1 can be transformed into another search tree T_2 (with the same keys).

    *b. Give an algorithm to perform this transformation using $O(n \log n)$ rotations on average.

   **c. Show that this transformation can be done with $O(n)$ rotations, worst-case.

4.44 Suppose we want to add the operation *Find_Kth* to our repertoire. The operation *Find_Kth(T,i)* returns the element in tree T with ith smallest key. Assume all elements have distinct keys. Explain how to modify the binary search tree to support this operation in $O(\log n)$ average time without sacrificing the time bounds of any other operation.

4.45 Since a binary search tree with n nodes has $n + 1$ *NULL* pointers, half the space allocated in a binary search tree for pointer information is wasted. Suppose that if a node has a *NULL* left child, we make its left child point to its inorder predecessor, and if a node has a *NULL* right child, we make its right child point to its inorder successor. This is known as a *threaded tree*, and the extra pointers are called *threads*.

    a. How can we distinguish threads from real children pointers?

    b. Write routines to perform insertion and deletion into a tree threaded in the manner described above.

    c. What is the advantage of using threaded trees?

4.46 A binary search tree presupposes that searching is based on only one key per record. Suppose we would like to be able to perform searching based on either of two keys, key_1 or key_2.

Figure 4.68   Two isomorphic trees

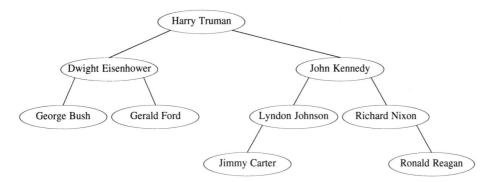

Figure 4.69   A 2-d tree

a. One method is to build two separate binary search trees. How many extra pointers does this require?

b. An alternative method is a *2-d tree*. A 2-d tree is similar to a binary search tree, except that branching at even levels is done with respect to key_1, and branching at odd levels is done with key_2. Figure 4.69 shows a 2-d tree with the first and last names of post–WWII presidents as keys. The presidents' names were inserted chronologically (Truman, Eisenhower, Kennedy, Johnson, Nixon, Ford, Carter, Reagan, Bush). (Where would Bill Clinton be inserted?) Write a routine to perform insertion into a 2-d tree.

c. Write an efficient procedure that prints all records in the tree that simultaneously satisfy the constraints $low_1 \leq key_1 \leq high_1$ and $low_2 \leq key_2 \leq high_2$.

d. Show how to extend the 2-d tree to handle more than two search keys. The resulting strategy is known as a k-d tree.

References

More information on binary search trees, and in particular the mathematical properties of trees can be found in the two books by Knuth [23] and [24].

Several papers deal with the lack of balance caused by biased deletion algorithms in binary search trees. Hibbard's paper [20] proposed the original deletion algorithm and established that one deletion preserves the randomness of the trees. A complete analysis has been performed only for trees with three nodes [21] and four nodes [5]. Eppinger's paper [15] provided early empirical evidence of nonrandomness, and the papers by Culberson and Munro, [11], [12], provide some analytical evidence (but not a complete proof for the general case of intermixed insertions and deletions).

AVL trees were proposed by Adelson-Velskii and Landis [1]. Simulation results for AVL trees and variants in which the height imbalance is allowed to be at most k for various values of k are presented in [22]. A deletion algorithm for AVL trees can be found in [24]. Analysis of the average depth of AVL trees is incomplete, but some results are contained in [25].

[3] and [9] considered self-adjusting trees like the type in Section 4.5.1. Splay trees are described in [29].

B-trees first appeared in [6]. The implementation described in the original paper allows data to be stored in internal nodes as well as leaves. The data structure we have described is sometimes known as a B^+ tree. A survey of the different types of B-trees is presented in [10]. Empirical results of the various schemes is reported in [18]. Analysis of 2–3 trees and B-trees can be found in [4], [14], and [33].

Exercise 4.14 is deceptively difficult. A solution can be found in [16]. Exercise 4.26 is from [32]. Information on B*-trees, described in Exercise 4.38, can be found in [13]. Exercise 4.42 is from [2]. A solution to Exercise 4.43 using $2n - 6$ rotations is given in [30]. Using threads, *à la* Exercise 4.45, was first proposed in [28]. *k*-d trees were first proposed in [7]. Their major drawback is that both deletion and balancing are difficult. [8] discusses *k*-d trees and other methods used for multidimensional searching.

Other popular balanced search trees are red-black trees [19] and weight-balanced trees [27]. More balanced tree schemes can be found in the books [17], [26], and [31].

1. G. M. Adelson-Velskii and E. M. Landis, "An Algorithm for the Organization of Information," *Soviet Math. Doklady* 3 (1962), 1259–1263.
2. A. V. Aho, J. E. Hopcroft, and J. D. Ullman, *The Design and Analysis of Computer Algorithms,* Addison-Wesley, Reading, Mass., 1974.
3. B. Allen and J. I. Munro, "Self Organizing Search Trees," *Journal of the ACM,* 25 (1978), 526–535.
4. R. A. Baeza-Yates, "Expected Behaviour of B^+- trees under Random Insertions," *Acta Informatica* 26 (1989), 439–471.
5. R. A. Baeza-Yates, "A Trivial Algorithm Whose Analysis Isn't: A Continuation," *BIT* 29 (1989), 88–113.
6. R. Bayer and E. M. McGreight, "Organization and Maintenance of Large Ordered Indices," *Acta Informatica* 1 (1972), 173–189.
7. J. L. Bentley, "Multidimensional Binary Search Trees Used for Associative Searching," *Communications of the ACM* 18 (1975), 509–517.
8. J. L. Bentley and J. H. Friedman, "Data Structures for Range Searching," *Computing Surveys* 11 (1979), 397–409.
9. J. R. Bitner, "Heuristics that Dynamically Organize Data Structures," *SIAM Journal on Computing* 8 (1979), 82–110.
10. D. Comer, "The Ubiquitous B-tree," *Computing Surveys* 11 (1979), 121–137.
11. J. Culberson and J. I. Munro, "Explaining the Behavior of Binary Search Trees under Prolonged Updates: A Model and Simulations," *Computer Journal* 32 (1989), 68–75.
12. J. Culberson and J. I. Munro, "Analysis of the Standard Deletion Algorithms in Exact Fit Domain Binary Search Trees," *Algorithmica* 5 (1990) 295–311.
13. K. Culik, T. Ottman, and D. Wood, "Dense Multiway Trees," *ACM Transactions on Database Systems* 6 (1981), 486–512.
14. B. Eisenbath, N. Ziviana, G. H. Gonnet, K. Melhorn, and D. Wood, "The Theory of Fringe Analysis and its Application to 2–3 Trees and B-trees," *Information and Control* 55 (1982), 125–174.
15. J. L. Eppinger, "An Empirical Study of Insertion and Deletion in Binary Search Trees," *Communications of the ACM* 26 (1983), 663–669.

16. P. Flajolet and A. Odlyzko, "The Average Height of Binary Trees and Other Simple Trees," *Journal of Computer and System Sciences* 25 (1982), 171–213.

17. G. H. Gonnet and R. Baeza-Yates, *Handbook of Algorithms and Data Structures,* second edition, Addison-Wesley, Reading, Mass., 1991.

18. E. Gudes and S. Tsur, "Experiments with B-tree Reorganization," *Proceedings of ACM SIGMOD Symposium on Management of Data* (1980), 200–206.

19. L. J. Guibas and R. Sedgewick, "A Dichromatic Framework for Balanced Trees," *Proceedings of the Nineteenth Annual IEEE Symposium on Foundations of Computer Science* (1978), 8–21.

20. T. H. Hibbard, "Some Combinatorial Properties of Certain Trees with Applications to Searching and Sorting," *Journal of the ACM 9* (1962), 13–28.

21. A. T. Jonassen and D. E. Knuth, "A Trivial Algorithm Whose Analysis Isn't," *Journal of Computer and System Sciences* 16 (1978), 301–322.

22. P. L. Karlton, S. H. Fuller, R. E. Scroggs, and E. B. Kaehler, "Performance of Height Balanced Trees," *Communications of the ACM 19* (1976), 23–28.

23. D. E. Knuth, *The Art of Computer Programming: Volume 1: Fundamental Algorithms,* second edition, Addison-Wesley, Reading, Mass., 1973.

24. D. E. Knuth, *The Art of Computer Programming: Volume 3: Sorting and Searching,* second printing, Addison-Wesley, Reading, Mass., 1975.

25. K. Melhorn, "A Partial Analysis of Height-Balanced Trees under Random Insertions and Deletions," *SIAM Journal of Computing* 11 (1982), 748–760.

26. K. Melhorn, *Data Structures and Algorithms 1: Sorting and Searching,* Springer-Verlag, Berlin, 1984.

27. J. Nievergelt and E. M. Reingold, "Binary Search Trees of Bounded Balance," *SIAM Journal on Computing* 2 (1973), 33–43.

28. A. J. Perlis and C. Thornton, "Symbol Manipulation in Threaded Lists," *Communications of the ACM 3* (1960), 195–204.

29. D. D. Sleator and R. E. Tarjan, "Self-adjusting Binary Search Trees," *Journal of ACM 32* (1985), 652–686.

30. D. D. Sleator, R. E. Tarjan, and W. P. Thurston, "Rotation Distance, Triangulations, and Hyperbolic Geometry," *Journal of AMS* (1988), 647–682.

31. H. F. Smith, *Data Structures—Form and Function,* Harcourt Brace Jovanovich, 1987.

32. R. E. Tarjan, "Sequential Access in Splay Trees Takes Linear Time," *Combinatorica 5* (1985), 367–378.

33. A. C. Yao, "On Random 2–3 trees," *Acta Informatica 9* (1978), 159–170.

CHAPTER 5

Hashing

In Chapter 4, we discussed the search tree ADT, which allowed various operations on a set of elements. In this chapter, we discuss the *hash table* ADT, which supports only a subset of the operations allowed by binary search trees.

The implementation of hash tables is frequently called *hashing*. Hashing is a technique used for performing insertions, deletions, and finds in constant average time. Tree operations that require any ordering information among the elements are not supported efficiently. Thus, operations such as *Find_Min, Find_Max,* and the printing of the entire table in sorted order in linear time are not supported.

The central data structure in this chapter is the *hash table*. We will

- See several methods of implementing the hash table.
- Compare these methods analytically.
- Show numerous applications of hashing.
- Compare hash tables with binary search trees.

5.1. General Idea

The ideal hash table data structure is merely an array of some fixed size, containing the keys. Typically, a key is a string with an associated value (for instance, salary information). We will refer to the table size as *HSize,* with the understanding that this is part of a hash data structure and not merely some variable floating around globally. The common convention is to have the table run from 0 to *HSize−1*; we will see why shortly.

Each key is mapped into some number in the range 0 to *HSize−1* and placed in the appropriate cell. The mapping is called a *hash function,* which ideally should be simple to compute and should ensure that any two distinct keys get different cells. Since there are a finite number of cells and a virtually inexhaustible supply of keys, this is clearly impossible, and thus we seek a hash function that distributes the keys evenly among the cells. Figure 5.1 is typical of a perfect situation. In this example, *john* hashes to 3, *phil* hashes to 4, *dave* hashes to 6, and *mary* hashes to 7.

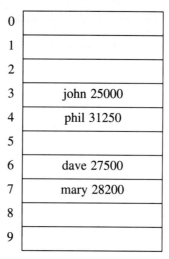

Figure 5.1   An ideal hash table

This is the basic idea of hashing. The only remaining problems deal with choosing a function, deciding what to do when two keys hash to the same value (this is known as a *collision*), and deciding on the table size.

5.2.   Hash Function

If the input keys are integers, then simply returning *Key mod HSize* is generally a reasonable strategy, unless *Key* happens to have some undesirable properties. In this case, the choice of hash function needs to be carefully considered. For instance, if the table size is 10 and the keys all end in zero, then the standard hash function is obviously a bad choice. For reasons we shall see later, and to avoid situations like the one above, it is usually a good idea to ensure that the table size is prime. When the input keys are random integers, then this function is not only very simple to compute but also distributes the keys evenly.

Usually, the keys are strings; in this case, the hash function needs to be chosen carefully. We use the *String* class defined in Chapter 1.

One option is to add up the ASCII values of the characters in the string. The routine in Figure 5.2 implements this strategy, using the typical C/C++ method of stepping through a string.

The hash function depicted in Figure 5.2 is simple to implement and computes an answer quickly. However, if the table size is large, the function does not distribute the keys well. For instance, suppose that *HSize* = 10,007 (10,007 is a prime number). Suppose all the keys are eight or fewer characters long. Since a *char* is an integer value that is always at most 127, the hash function can only assume values between 0 and 1016, which is 127 * 8. This is clearly not an equitable distribution!

Another hash function is shown in Figure 5.3. This hash function assumes that *Key* has at least length 2. 27 represents the number of letters in the English

```
/* 1*/     unsigned int
/* 2*/     Hash( const String & Key, const int H_Size )
/* 3*/     {
/* 4*/          const char *Key_Ptr = Key;
/* 5*/          unsigned int Hash_Val = 0;

/* 6*/          while( *Key_Ptr )
/* 7*/              Hash_Val += *Key_Ptr++;

/* 8*/          return Hash_Val % H_Size;
/* 9*/     }
```

Figure 5.2 A simple hash function

alphabet, plus the blank, and 729 is 27^2. This function examines only the first three characters, but if these are random, and the table size is 10,007 as before, then we would expect a reasonably equitable distribution. Unfortunately, English is not random. Although there are $26^3 = 17,576$ possible combinations of three characters (ignoring blanks), a check of a reasonably large on-line dictionary reveals that the number of different combinations is actually only 2,851. Even if none of *these* combinations collide, only 28 percent of the table can actually be hashed to. Thus this function, although easily computable, is also not appropriate if the hash table is reasonably large.

Figure 5.4 shows a third attempt at a hash function. This hash function involves all characters in the key and can generally be expected to distribute well (it computes $\sum_{i=0}^{Key\_Size-1} Key[Key\_Size - i] \cdot 32^i$, and brings the result into proper range). The code computes a polynomial function (of 32) by use of Horner's rule. For instance, another way of computing $h_k = k_1 + 27k_2 + 27^2 k_3$ is by the formula $h_k = ((k_3)*27+k_2)*27+k_1$. Horner's rule extends this to an nth degree polynomial.

We have used 32 instead of 27 because multiplication by 32 is not really a multiplication, but amounts to bit-shifting by five. In line 7, the addition could be replaced with a bitwise exclusive *or* for increased speed.

The hash function described in Figure 5.4 is not necessarily the best with respect to table distribution, but it does have the merit of extreme simplicity and speed. If the keys are very long, the hash function will take too long to compute. Furthermore, the early characters will wind up being left-shifted out of the eventual

```
/* 1*/     unsigned int
/* 2*/     Hash( const String & Key, const int H_Size )
/* 3*/     {
/* 4*/          return ( Key[ 0 ] + 27 * Key[ 1 ] + 729 * Key[ 2 ] ) % H_Size;
/* 5*/     }
```

Figure 5.3 Another possible hash function—not too good

```
/* 1*/    unsigned int
/* 2*/    Hash( const String & Key, const int H_Size )
/* 3*/    {
/* 4*/        const char *Key_Ptr = Key;
/* 5*/        unsigned int Hash_Val = 0;

/* 6*/        while( *Key_Ptr )
/* 7*/            Hash_Val = ( Hash_Val << 5 ) + *Key_Ptr++;

/* 8*/        return Hash_Val % H_Size;
/* 9*/    }
```

Figure 5.4   A good hash function

answer. A common practice in this case is to not use all the characters. The length and properties of the keys would then influence the choice. For instance, the keys could be a complete street address. The hash function might include a couple of characters from the street address and perhaps a couple of characters from the city name and ZIP code. Some programmers implement their hash function by using only the characters in the odd spaces, with the idea that the time saved computing the hash function will make up for a slightly less evenly distributed function.

The main programming detail left is collision resolution. If, when inserting an element, it hashes to the same value as an already inserted element, then we have a *collision* and need to resolve it. There are several methods for dealing with this. We will discuss two of the simplest: open hashing and closed hashing.[†]

5.3.   Open Hashing (Separate Chaining)

The first strategy, commonly known as either *open hashing* or *separate chaining,* is to keep a list of all elements that hash to the same value. For convenience, our lists have headers. This makes the list implementation the same as in Chapter 3. If space is tight, it might be preferable to avoid their use. We assume for this section that the keys are the first 10 perfect squares and that the hashing function is simply $Hash(X) = X \bmod 10$. (The table size is not prime, but is used here for simplicity.) Figure 5.5 should make this clear.

To perform a *Find,* we use the hash function to determine which list to traverse. We then traverse this list in the normal manner, returning the position where the item is found. To perform an *Insert,* we traverse down the appropriate list to check whether the element is already in place (if duplicates are expected, an extra field is usually kept, and this field would be incremented in the event of a match). If the element turns out to be new, it is inserted either at the front of the list or at the

---

[†]These are also commonly known as *separate chaining* and *open addressing*, respectively.

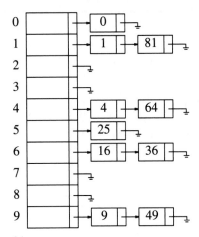

Figure 5.5   An open hash table

end of the list, whichever is easiest. This is an issue most easily addressed while the code is being written. Sometimes new elements are inserted at the front of the list, since it is convenient and also because frequently it happens that recently inserted elements are the most likely to be accessed in the near future.

The class specification required to implement open hashing is in Figure 5.6. Notice that we are using the linked list class from Chapter 3. We maintain the notion of a current list. Thus, the last item is accessed by accessing the item in the current list with the ( ) operator as shown on line 20.

Figure 5.7 shows that to construct the hash table, we merely allocate an array of lists. These lists are automatically initialized by the *List* constrictor. Routines to copy and reinitialize are also provided.

The call *Find(Key)* implemented in Figure 5.8 behaves like the linked list *Find*, and is a trivial implementation.

Next comes the insertion routine. If the item to be inserted is already present, then we do nothing; otherwise we place it at the front of the appropriate list (see Fig. 5.9).† The element can be placed anywhere in the list; this is most convenient in our case.

The deletion routine shown in Figure 5.9 is a straightforward implementation of deletion in a linked list. If the repertoire of hash routines does not include deletions, it is probably best to not use headers, since their use would provide no simplification and would waste considerable space. We leave this as an exercise, too, as it amounts to writing the linked list package without headers.

Any scheme could be used besides linked lists to resolve the collisions—a binary search tree or even another hash table would work, but we expect that if the table is large and the hash function is good, all the lists should be short, so it is not worthwhile to try anything complicated.

---

† Since the table in Figure 5.5 was created by inserting at the end of the list, the code in Figure 5.9 will produce a table with the lists in Figure 5.5 reversed.

```
/* 1*/    static const Default_Size = 101;

/* 2*/    template <class Element_Type>
/* 3*/    class Hash_Table
/* 4*/    {
/* 5*/      private:
/* 6*/        unsigned int H_Size;
/* 7*/        List<Element_Type> *The_Lists;
/* 8*/        unsigned int Current_List;   // The last list accessed.

/* 9*/        void Allocate_Lists( );

/*10*/      public:
/*11*/        // Constructors.
/*12*/        Hash_Table( unsigned int Initial_Size = Default_Size );
/*13*/        Hash_Table( Hash_Table & Value )
/*14*/            { Warn( "Hash passed by value" ); operator=( Value ); }

/*15*/        // Destructor.
/*16*/        ~Hash_Table( ) { delete [ ] The_Lists; }

/*17*/        // Operators.
/*18*/        const Hash_Table & operator = ( const Hash_Table & Value );
/*19*/        Element_Type operator ( ) ( ) const
/*20*/            { return The_Lists[ Current_List ] ( ); }

/*21*/        // Member functions.
/*22*/        void Initialize_Table( );
/*23*/        void Insert( const Element_Type & Key );
/*24*/        void Remove( const Element_Type & Key );
/*25*/        int Find( const Element_Type & Key );
/*26*/    };
```

Figure 5.6 Class specification for open hash table

We define the load factor, λ, of a hash table to be the ratio of the number of elements in the hash table to the table size. In the example above, $\lambda = 1.0$. The average length of a list is λ. The effort required to perform a search is the constant time required to evaluate the hash function plus the time to traverse the list.

In an unsuccessful search, the number of links to traverse is λ (excluding the final *NULL* link) on average. A successful search requires that about $1 + (\lambda/2)$ links be traversed, since there is a guarantee that one link must be traversed (since the search is successful), and we also expect to go halfway down a list to find our match. This analysis shows that the table size is not really important, but the load factor is. The general rule for open hashing is to make the table size about as large as the number of elements expected (in other words, let $\lambda \approx 1$). It is also a good idea, as mentioned before, to keep the table size prime to help ensure a good distribution.

```
/* 1*/    template <class Element_Type>
/* 2*/    void
/* 3*/    Hash_Table<Element_Type>::
/* 4*/    Allocate_Lists( )
/* 5*/    {
/* 6*/        The_Lists = new List<Element_Type> [ H_Size ];
/* 7*/        if( The_Lists == NULL )
/* 8*/            Error( "Out of space!!" );
/* 9*/    }

/*10*/    template <class Element_Type>
/*11*/    Hash_Table<Element_Type>::
/*12*/    Hash_Table( unsigned int Initial_Size )
/*13*/    {
/*14*/        H_Size = Initial_Size;
/*15*/        Allocate_Lists( );
/*16*/    }



/* 1*/    template <class Element_Type>
/* 2*/    void
/* 3*/    Hash_Table<Element_Type>::
/* 4*/    Initialize_Table( )
/* 5*/    {
/* 6*/        delete [ ] The_Lists;
/* 7*/        Allocate_Lists( );
/* 8*/    }



/* 1*/    template <class Element_Type>
/* 2*/    const Hash_Table<Element_Type> &
/* 3*/    Hash_Table<Element_Type>::
/* 4*/    operator = ( const Hash_Table<Element_Type> & Value )
/* 5*/    {
/* 6*/        if( this != &Value )
/* 7*/        {
/* 8*/            delete [ ] The_Lists;
/* 9*/            H_Size = Value.H_Size;
/*10*/            Allocate_Lists( );
/*11*/            for( int i = 0; i < H_Size; i++ )
/*12*/                The_Lists[ i ] = Value.The_Lists[ i ];
/*13*/        }
/*14*/        return *this;
/*15*/    }
```

Figure 5.7   Initialization and copy routines for open hash
table

```
/* 1*/    template <class Element_Type>
/* 2*/    inline int
/* 3*/    Hash_Table<Element_Type>::
/* 4*/    Find( const Element_Type & Key )
/* 5*/    {
/* 6*/        unsigned int Hash_Val = Hash( Key, H_Size );

/* 7*/        if( The_Lists[ Hash_Val ].Find( Key ) )
/* 8*/        {
/* 9*/            Current_List = Hash_Val;
/*10*/            return 1;
/*11*/        }
/*12*/        return 0;
/*13*/    }
```

Figure 5.8   *Find* routine for open hash table

Figure 5.9   *Insert* and *Remove* routine for open hash table

```
/* 1*/    template <class Element_Type>
/* 2*/    inline void
/* 3*/    Hash_Table<Element_Type>::
/* 4*/    Insert( const Element_Type & Key )
/* 5*/    {
/* 6*/        unsigned int Hash_Val = Hash( Key, H_Size );

/* 7*/        if( !The_Lists[ Hash_Val ].In_List( Key ) )
/* 8*/            The_Lists[ Hash_Val ].Insert_As_First_Element( Key );
/* 9*/    }
```

```
/* 1*/    template <class Element_Type>
/* 2*/    inline void
/* 3*/    Hash_Table<Element_Type>::
/* 4*/    Remove( const Element_Type & Key )
/* 5*/    {
/* 6*/        The_Lists[ Hash( Key, H_Size ) ].Remove( Key );
/* 7*/    }
```

5.4. Closed Hashing (Open Addressing)

Open hashing has the disadvantage of requiring pointers. This tends to slow the algorithm down a bit because of the time required to allocate new cells, and it also essentially requires the implementation of a second data structure. *Closed hashing*, also known as *open addressing*, is an alternative to resolving collisions with linked lists. In a closed hashing system, if a collision occurs, alternate cells are tried until an empty cell is found. More formally, cells $h_0(x), h_1(x), h_2(x), \ldots$ are tried in succession where $h_i(x) = (Hash(x) + f(i)) \bmod HSize$, with $f(0) = 0$. The function, f, is the collision resolution strategy. Because all the data goes inside the table, a bigger table is needed for closed hashing than for open hashing. Generally, the load factor should be below $\lambda = 0.5$ for closed hashing. We now look at three common collision resolution strategies.

5.4.1. Linear Probing

In linear probing, f is a linear function of i, typically $f(i) = i$. This amounts to trying cells sequentially (with wraparound) in search of an empty cell. Figure 5.10 shows the result of inserting keys {89, 18, 49, 58, 69} into a closed table using the same hash function as before and the collision resolution strategy, $f(i) = i$.

The first collision occurs when 49 is inserted; it is put in the next available spot, namely spot 0, which is open. 58 collides with 18, 89, and then 49 before an empty cell is found three away. The collision for 69 is handled in a similar manner. As long as the table is big enough, a free cell can always be found, but the time to do

	Empty Table	After 89	After 18	After 49	After 58	After 69
0				49	49	49
1					58	58
2						69
3						
4						
5						
6						
7						
8			18	18	18	18
9		89	89	89	89	89

Figure 5.10 Closed hash table with linear probing, after each insertion

so can get quite large. Worse, even if the table is relatively empty, blocks of occupied cells start forming. This effect, known as *primary clustering,* means that any key that hashes into the cluster will require several attempts to resolve the collision, and then it will add to the cluster.

Although we will not perform the calculations here, it can be shown that the expected number of probes using linear probing is roughly $\frac{1}{2}(1 + 1/(1 - \lambda)^2)$ for insertions and unsuccessful searches and $\frac{1}{2}(1 + 1/(1 - \lambda))$ for successful searches. The calculations are somewhat involved. It is easy to see from the code that insertions and unsuccessful searches require the same number of probes. A moment's thought suggests that on average, successful searches should take less time than unsuccessful searches.

The corresponding formulas, if clustering were not a problem, are fairly easy to derive. We will assume a very large table and that each probe is independent of the previous probes. These assumptions are satisfied by a *random* collision resolution strategy and are reasonable unless λ is very close to 1. First, we derive the expected number of probes in an unsuccessful search. This is just the expected number of probes until we find an empty cell. Since the fraction of empty cells is $1 - \lambda$, the number of cells we expect to probe is $1/(1 - \lambda)$. The number of probes for a successful search is equal to the number of probes required when the particular element was inserted. When an element is inserted, it is done as a result of an unsuccessful search. Thus, we can use the cost of an unsuccessful search to compute the average cost of a successful search.

The caveat is that λ changes from 0 to its current value, so that earlier insertions are cheaper and should bring the average down. For instance, in the table above, $\lambda = 0.5$, but the cost of accessing 18 is determined when 18 is inserted. At that point, $\lambda = 0.2$. Since 18 was inserted into a relatively empty table, accessing it should be easier than accessing a recently inserted element such as 69. We can estimate the average by using an integral to calculate the mean value of the insertion time, obtaining

$$I(\lambda) = \frac{1}{\lambda} \int_0^{\lambda} \frac{1}{1 - x} dx = \frac{1}{\lambda} \ln \frac{1}{1 - \lambda}$$

These formulas are clearly better than the corresponding formulas for linear probing. Clustering is not only a theoretical problem but actually occurs in real implementations. Figure 5.11 compares the performance of linear probing (dashed curves) with what would be expected from more random collision resolution. Successful searches are indicated by an *S,* and unsuccessful searches and insertions are marked with *U* and *I,* respectively.

If $\lambda = 0.75$, then the formula above indicates that 8.5 probes are expected for an insertion in linear probing. If $\lambda = 0.9$, then 50 probes are expected, which is unreasonable. This compares with 4 and 10 probes for the respective load factors if clustering were not a problem. We see from these formulas that linear probing can be a bad idea if the table is expected to be more than half full. If $\lambda = 0.5$, however, only 2.5 probes are required on average for insertion and only 1.5 probes are required, on average, for a successful search.

Figure 5.11 Number of probes plotted against load factor for linear probing (dashed) and random strategy. *S* is successful search, *U* is unsuccessful search, *I* is insertion

5.4.2. Quadratic Probing

Quadratic probing is a collision resolution method that eliminates the primary clustering problem of linear probing. Quadratic probing is what you would expect—the collision function is quadratic. The popular choice is $f(i) = i^2$. Figure 5.12 shows the resulting closed table with this collision function on the same input used in the linear probing example.

When 49 collides with 89, the next position attempted is one cell away. This cell is empty, so 49 is placed there. Next 58 collides at position 8. Then the cell one away is tried, but another collision occurs. A vacant cell is found at the next cell tried, which is $2^2 = 4$ away. 58 is thus placed in cell 2. The same thing happens for 69.

For linear probing it is a bad idea to let the hash table get nearly full because performance degrades. For quadratic probing, the situation is even more drastic: There is no guarantee of finding an empty cell once the table gets more than half full, or even before the table gets half full if the table size is not prime. This is because at most half of the table can be used as alternate locations to resolve collisions. Indeed, we prove now that if the table is half empty and the table size is prime, then we are always guaranteed to be able to insert a new element.

THEOREM 5.1.

If quadratic probing is used and the table size is prime, then a new element can always be inserted if the table is at least half empty.

	Empty Table	After 89	After 18	After 49	After 58	After 69
0				49	49	49
1						
2					58	58
3						69
4						
5						
6						
7						
8			18	18	18	18
9		89	89	89	89	89

Figure 5.12   Closed hash table with quadratic probing, after each insertion

PROOF:

Let the table size, *HSize,* be an (odd) prime greater than 3. We show that the first $\lfloor HSize/2 \rfloor$ alternate locations are all distinct. Two of these locations are $h(x) + i^2 (mod\ HSize)$ and $h(x) + j^2 (mod\ HSize)$, where $0 < i, j \le \lfloor HSize/2 \rfloor$. Suppose, for the sake of contradiction, that these locations are the same, but $i \ne j$. Then

$$h(x) + i^2 \equiv h(x) + j^2 \qquad (mod\ HSize)$$
$$i^2 \equiv j^2 \qquad (mod\ HSize)$$
$$i^2 - j^2 \equiv 0 \qquad (mod\ HSize)$$
$$(i - j)(i + j) \equiv 0 \qquad (mod\ HSize)$$

Since *HSize* is prime, it follows that either $(i - j)$ or $(i + j)$ is equal to 0 $(mod\ HSize)$. Since i and j are distinct, the first option is not possible. Since $0 < i, j < \lfloor HSize/2 \rfloor$, the second option is also impossible. Thus, the first $\lfloor HSize/2 \rfloor$ alternate locations are distinct. Since the element to be inserted can also be placed in the cell to which it hashes (if there are no collisions), any element has $\lceil HSize/2 \rceil$ locations into which it can go. If at most $\lfloor HSize/2 \rfloor$ positions are taken, then an empty spot can always be found.

If the table is even one more than half full, the insertion could fail (although this is extremely unlikely). Therefore, it is important to keep this in mind. It is also crucial that the table size be prime.[†] If the table size is not prime, the number of alternate locations can be severely reduced. As an example, if the table size were 16, then the only alternate locations would be at distances 1, 4, or 9 away.

Standard deletion cannot be performed in a closed hash table, because the cell might have caused a collision to go past it. For instance, if we remove 89, then virtually all of the remaining *Find*s will fail. Thus, closed hash tables require lazy deletion, although in this case there really is no laziness implied.

The class specification for closed hashing is in Figure 5.13. Initializing the table (Fig. 5.14) is performed by setting the *Info* field to *Empty*; this is implicit in the *Hash_Entry* constructor at lines 12 through 14 in Figure 5.13.

Find(Key) will set the class variable *Current_Cell* to the position of *Key* in the hash table. If *Key* is not present, then *Current_Cell* is set to the position where the *Find* last probed. We assume for convenience that the hash table is at least twice as large as the number of elements in the table, so quadratic resolution will always work. Otherwise, we would need to test *i* before line 11. In the implementation in Figure 5.15, elements that are marked as deleted count as being in the table. This can cause problems because the table can get too full prematurely. We shall discuss this item presently.

Lines 11 through 13 represent the fast way of doing quadratic resolution. From the definition of the quadratic resolution function, $f(i) = f(i-1) + 2i - 1$, so the next cell to try can be determined with a multiplication by two (really a bit shift) and a decrement. If the new location is past the array, it can be put back in range by subtracting *HSize*. This is faster than the obvious method because it avoids the multiplication and division that seem to be required. The variable name *i* is not the best one to use; we use it only to be consistent with the text. An important warning: The order of testing at lines 8 and 9 is important. The same goes for lines 15 and 16. Don't switch them!

The final routine is insertion. As with open hashing, we do nothing if *Key* is already present. It is a simple modification to do something else. Otherwise, we place it at the spot where the *Find* failed. The code is shown in Figure 5.16. Removal is also shown.

Although quadratic probing eliminates primary clustering, elements that hash to the same position will probe the same alternate cells. This is known as *secondary clustering*. Secondary clustering is a slight theoretical blemish. Simulation results suggest that it generally causes less than an extra $\frac{1}{2}$ probe per search. The following technique eliminates this, but does so at the cost of extra multiplications and divisions.

5.4.3. Double Hashing

The last collision resolution method we will examine is *double hashing*. For double hashing, one popular choice is $f(i) = i \cdot hash_2(x)$. This formula says that we apply a second hash function to *x* and probe at a distance $hash_2(x), 2hash_2(x), \ldots,$ and

---

[†]If the table size is a prime of the form $4k + 3$, and the quadratic collision resolution strategy $f(i) = \pm i^2$ is used, then the entire table can be probed. The cost is a slightly more complicated routine.

```
/* 1*/    const int Default_Size = 101;

/* 2*/    template <class Element_Type>
/* 3*/    class Hash_Table
/* 4*/    {
/* 5*/      public:
/* 6*/        enum Kind_Of_Entry { Legitimate, Empty, Deleted };

/* 7*/      protected:
/* 8*/        struct Hash_Entry
/* 9*/        {
/*10*/            Element_Type Element;
/*11*/            Kind_Of_Entry Info;

/*12*/            Hash_Entry( Element_Type E = 0,
/*13*/                Kind_Of_Entry i = Empty ) :
/*14*/                Element( E ), Info( i ) { }
/*15*/        };

/*16*/        unsigned int H_Size;
/*17*/        Hash_Entry *The_Cells;
/*18*/        unsigned int Current_Cell;    // The last cell accessed.

/*19*/        void Allocate_Cells( );

/*20*/      public:
/*21*/        // Constructors.
/*22*/        Hash_Table( unsigned int Initial_Size = Default_Size );
/*23*/        Hash_Table( Hash_Table & Value );

/*24*/        // Destructor.
/*25*/        virtual ~Hash_Table( ) { delete [ ] The_Cells; }

/*26*/        // Operators.
/*27*/        const Hash_Table & operator = ( const Hash_Table & Value );
/*28*/        Element_Type operator ( ) ( ) const
/*29*/            { return The_Cells[ Current_Cell ].Element; }

/*30*/        // Member functions.
/*31*/        virtual void Initialize_Table( );
/*32*/        virtual void Insert( const Element_Type & Key );
/*33*/        void Remove( const Element_Type & Key );
/*34*/        int Find( const Element_Type & Key );
/*35*/    };
```

Figure 5.13 Class specification for closed hash tables

```
/* 1*/    template <class Element_Type>
/* 2*/    void
/* 3*/    Hash_Table<Element_Type>::
/* 4*/    Allocate_Cells( )
/* 5*/    {
/* 6*/        The_Cells = new Hash_Entry [ H_Size ];
/* 7*/        if( The_Cells == NULL )
/* 8*/            Error( "Out of space!!" );
/* 9*/    }

/*10*/    template <class Element_Type>
/*11*/    Hash_Table<Element_Type>::
/*12*/    Hash_Table( unsigned int Initial_Size )
/*13*/    {
/*14*/        H_Size = Next_Prime( Initial_Size );
/*15*/        Allocate_Cells( );
/*16*/    }


/* 1*/    template <class Element_Type>
/* 2*/    void
/* 3*/    Hash_Table<Element_Type>::
/* 4*/    Initialize_Table( )
/* 5*/    {
/* 6*/        delete [ ] The_Cells;
/* 7*/        Allocate_Cells( );
/* 8*/    }


/* 1*/    template <class Element_Type>
/* 2*/    const Hash_Table<Element_Type> &
/* 3*/    Hash_Table<Element_Type>::
/* 4*/    operator = ( const Hash_Table<Element_Type> & Value )
/* 5*/    {
/* 6*/        if( this != &Value )
/* 7*/        {
/* 8*/            delete [ ] The_Cells;
/* 9*/            H_Size = Value.H_Size;
/*10*/            Allocate_Cells( );
/*11*/            for( int i = 0; i < H_Size; i++ )
/*12*/                The_Cells[ i ] = Value.The_Cells[ i ];
/*13*/        }
/*14*/        return *this;
/*15*/    }
```

Figure 5.14   Routines to initialize and copy closed hash
tables

```
/* 1*/    template <class Element_Type>
/* 2*/    int
/* 3*/    Hash_Table<Element_Type>::
/* 4*/    Find( const Element_Type & Key )
/* 5*/    {
/* 6*/        unsigned int i = 0;

/* 7*/        Current_Cell = Hash( Key, H_Size );
/* 8*/        while( The_Cells[ Current_Cell ].Info != Empty &&
/* 9*/            The_Cells[ Current_Cell ].Element != Key )
/*10*/        {
/*11*/            Current_Cell += 2 * ( ++i ) - 1;
/*12*/            if( Current_Cell >= H_Size )
/*13*/                Current_Cell -= H_Size;
/*14*/        }

/*15*/        return The_Cells[ Current_Cell ].Info == Legitimate &&
/*16*/            The_Cells[ Current_Cell ].Element == Key;
/*17*/    }
```

Figure 5.15 *Find* routine for closed hashing with quadratic probing

```
/* 1*/    template <class Element_Type>
/* 2*/    inline void
/* 3*/    Hash_Table<Element_Type>::
/* 4*/    Insert( const Element_Type & Key )
/* 5*/    {
/* 6*/        if( Find( Key ) == 0 )
/* 7*/            The_Cells[ Current_Cell ] = Hash_Entry( Key, Legitimate );
/* 8*/    }
```

```
/* 1*/    template <class Element_Type>
/* 2*/    inline void
/* 3*/    Hash_Table<Element_Type>::
/* 4*/    Remove( const Element_Type & Key )
/* 5*/    {
/* 6*/        if( Find( Key ) )
/* 7*/            The_Cells[ Current_Cell ].Info = Deleted;
/* 8*/        else
/* 9*/            Error( "Item not found" );
/*10*/    }
```

Figure 5.16 *Insert* and *Remove* routines for closed hash tables with quadratic probing so on. A poor choice of $hash_2(x)$ would be disastrous. For instance, the obvious choice $hash_2(x) = x \bmod 9$ would not help if 99 were inserted into the input in the previous examples. Thus, the function must never evaluate to zero. It is also important to make sure all cells can be probed (this is not possible in the following example because the table size is not prime). A function such as $hash_2(x) = R - (x \bmod R)$, with R a prime smaller than $HSize$, will work well. If we choose $R = 7$, then Figure 5.17 shows the results of inserting the same keys as before.

The first collision occurs when 49 is inserted. $hash_2(49) = 7 - 0 = 7$, so 49 is inserted in position 6. $hash_2(58) = 7 - 2 = 5$, so 58 is inserted at location 3. Finally, 69 collides and is inserted at a distance $hash_2(69) = 7 - 6 = 1$ away. If we tried to insert 60 in position 0, we would have a collision. Since $hash_2(60) = 7 - 4 = 3$, we would then try positions 3, 6, 9, and then 2 until an empty spot is found. It is generally possible to find some bad case, but there are not too many here.

As we have said before, the size of our sample hash table is not prime. We have done this for convenience in computing the hash function, but it is worth seeing why it is important to make sure the table size is prime when double hashing is used. If we attempt to insert 23 into the table, it would collide with 58. Since $hash_2(23) = 7 - 2 = 5$, and the table size is 10, we essentially have only one alternate location, and it is already taken. Thus, if the table size is not prime, it is possible to run out of alternate locations prematurely. However, if double hashing is correctly implemented, simulations imply that the expected number of probes is almost the same as for a random collision resolution strategy. This makes double hashing theoretically interesting. Quadratic probing, however, does not require the use of a second hash function and is thus likely to be simpler and faster in practice.

Figure 5.17 Closed hash table with double hashing, after each insertion

	Empty Table	After 89	After 18	After 49	After 58	After 69
0						69
1						
2						
3					58	58
4						
5						
6				49	49	49
7						
8			18	18	18	18
9		89	89	89	89	89

5.5. Rehashing

If the table gets too full, the running time for the operations will start taking too long and *Insert*s might fail for closed hashing with quadratic resolution. This can happen if there are too many removals intermixed with insertions. A solution, then, is to build another table that is about twice as big (with associated new hash function) and scan down the entire original hash table, computing the new hash value for each (nondeleted) element and inserting it in the new table.

As an example, suppose the elements 13, 15, 24, and 6 are inserted into a closed hash table of size 7. The hash function is $h(x) = x \bmod 7$. Suppose linear probing is used to resolve collisions. The resulting hash table appears in Figure 5.18.

If 23 is inserted into the table, the resulting table in Figure 5.19 will be over 70 percent full. Because the table is so full, a new table is created. The size of this table is 17, because this is the first prime that is twice as large as the old table size. The new hash function is then $h(x) = x \bmod 17$. The old table is scanned, and elements

Figure 5.18   Closed hash table with linear probing with input 13, 15, 6, 24

0	6
1	15
2	
3	24
4	
5	
6	13

Figure 5.19   Closed hash table with linear probing after 23 is inserted

0	6
1	15
2	23
3	24
4	
5	
6	13

6, 15, 23, 24, and 13 are inserted into the new table. The resulting table appears in Figure 5.20.

This entire operation is called *rehashing*. This is obviously a very expensive operation—the running time is $O(n)$ since there are n elements to rehash and the table size is roughly $2n$, but it is actually not all that bad because it happens very infrequently. In particular, there must have been $n/2$ *Inserts* prior to the last rehash, so it essentially adds a constant cost to each insertion.[†] If this data structure is part of the program, the effect is not noticeable. On the other hand, if the hashing is performed as part of an interactive system, then the unfortunate user whose insertion caused a rehash could see a slowdown.

Rehashing can be implemented in several ways with quadratic probing. One alternative is to rehash as soon as the table is half full. The other extreme is to rehash only when an insertion fails. A third, middle of the road strategy is to rehash when the table reaches a certain load factor. Since performance does degrade as the load factor increases, the third strategy, implemented with a good cutoff, could be best.

Rehashing frees the programmer from worrying about the table size and is important because hash tables cannot be made arbitrarily large in complex programs.

Figure 5.20   Closed hash table after rehashing

0	
1	
2	
3	
4	
5	
6	6
7	23
8	24
9	
10	
11	
12	
13	13
14	
15	15
16	

[†]This is why the new table is made twice as large as the old table.

The exercises ask you to investigate the use of rehashing in conjunction with lazy deletion. Rehashing can be used in other data structures as well. For instance, if the stack data structure of Chapter 3 became full, we could declare a double-sized array and copy everything over, freeing the original.

Figure 5.21 shows that rehashing can be implemented by adding a counter to the *Hash_Table* class. Figure 5.22 shows *Rehash*. In *Rehash*, *Old_Cells* points to the old array. A new, empty, double-sized hash table is allocated in lines 9 and 10. Then each element in the old array is inserted into the new table (lines 11 through 13). The old array is then freed. Figure 5.23 shows the new insertion routine. It merely calls the original insertion routine and then rehashes if appropriate.

5.6.   Extendible Hashing

Our last topic in this chapter deals with the case in which the amount of data is too large to fit in main memory. As we saw in Chapter 4, the main consideration then is the number of disk accesses required to retrieve data.

As before, we assume that at any point we have n records to store; the value of n changes over time. Furthermore, at most m records fit in one disk block. We will use $m = 4$ in this section.

If either open hashing or closed hashing is used, the major problem is that collisions could cause several blocks to be examined during a *Find*, even for a well-distributed hash table. Furthermore, when the table gets too full, an extremely expensive rehashing step must be performed, which requires $O(n)$ disk accesses.

A clever alternative, known as extendible hashing, allows a *Find* to be performed in two disk accesses. Insertions also require few disk accesses.

We recall from Chapter 4 that a B-tree has depth $O(\log_{m/2} n)$. As m increases, the depth of a B-tree decreases. We could in theory choose m to be so large that the depth of the B-tree would be 1. Then any *Find* after the first would take one disk access since, presumably, the root node could be stored in main memory. The problem with this strategy is that the branching factor is so high that it would take considerable processing to determine which leaf the data was in. If the time to perform this step could be reduced, then we would have a practical scheme. This is exactly the strategy used by extendible hashing.

Let us suppose, for the moment, that our data consists of several six-bit integers. Figure 5.24 shows an extendible hashing scheme for this data. The root of the "tree" contains four pointers determined by the leading two bits of the data. Each leaf has up to $m = 4$ elements. It happens that in each leaf the first two bits are identical; this is indicated by the number in parentheses. To be more formal, D will represent the number of bits used by the root, which is sometimes known as the *directory*. The number of entries in the directory is thus 2^D. d_l is the number of leading bits that all the elements of some leaf l have in common. d_l will depend on the particular leaf, and $d_l \leq D$.

Suppose that we want to insert the key 100100. This would go into the third leaf, but as the third leaf is already full, there is no room. We thus split this leaf into

```
/* 1*/   template <class Element_Type>
/* 2*/   class Dynamic_Hash_Table : public Hash_Table<Element_Type>
/* 3*/   {
/* 4*/     private:
/* 5*/       unsigned int Num_Elements_In_Table;
/* 6*/       void Rehash( );

/* 7*/     public:
/* 8*/       // Constructors.
/* 9*/       Dynamic_Hash_Table( unsigned int Initial_Size = Default_Size )
/*10*/       {
/*11*/           Hash_Table<Element_Type>::Hash_Table( Initial_Size );
/*12*/           Num_Elements_In_Table = 0;
/*13*/       }

/*14*/       Dynamic_Hash_Table( Dynamic_Hash_Table & Value )
/*15*/           { Warn( "Hash passed by value" ); operator=( Value ); }

/*16*/       // Operators.
/*17*/       const Dynamic_Hash_Table & operator =
/*18*/                   ( const Dynamic_Hash_Table & Value );

/*19*/       // Member functions.
/*20*/       virtual void Initialize_Table( )
/*21*/       {
/*22*/           Hash_Table<Element_Type>::Initialize_Table( );
/*23*/           Num_Elements_In_Table = 0;
/*24*/       }

/*25*/       virtual void Insert( const Element_Type & Key );
/*26*/   };

/*27*/   template <class Element_Type>
/*28*/   const Dynamic_Hash_Table<Element_Type> &
/*29*/   Dynamic_Hash_Table<Element_Type>::
/*30*/   operator = ( const Dynamic_Hash_Table<Element_Type> & Value )
/*31*/   {
/*32*/       if( this != &Value )
/*33*/       {
/*34*/           Hash_Table<Element_Type>::operator = ( Value );
/*35*/           Num_Elements_In_Table = Value.Num_Elements_In_Table;
/*36*/       }
/*37*/       return *this;
/*38*/   }
```

Figure 5.21 Declarations for rehashing

```
/* 1*/    template <class Element_Type>
/* 2*/    void
/* 3*/    Dynamic_Hash_Table<Element_Type>::
/* 4*/    Rehash( )
/* 5*/    {
/* 6*/        Hash_Entry *Old_Cells = The_Cells;
/* 7*/        unsigned int Old_Size = H_Size;

/* 8*/        Num_Elements_In_Table = 0;
/* 9*/        H_Size = Next_Prime( 2 * Old_Size );
/*10*/        Allocate_Cells( );

/*11*/        for( int i = 0; i < Old_Size; i++ )
/*12*/            if( Old_Cells[ i ].Info == Legitimate )
/*13*/                Insert( Old_Cells[ i ].Element );

/*14*/        delete [ ] Old_Cells;
/*15*/    }
```

Figure 5.22   Code to rehash

```
/* 1*/    template <class Element_Type>
/* 2*/    void
/* 3*/    Dynamic_Hash_Table<Element_Type>::
/* 4*/    Insert( const Element_Type & Key )
/* 5*/    {
/* 6*/        Hash_Table<Element_Type>::Insert( Key );
/* 7*/        if( ++Num_Elements_In_Table > H_Size / 2 )
/* 8*/            Rehash( );
/* 9*/    }
```

Figure 5.23   Insertion routine with automatic rehashing

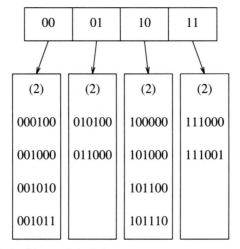

Figure 5.24   Extendible hashing: original data

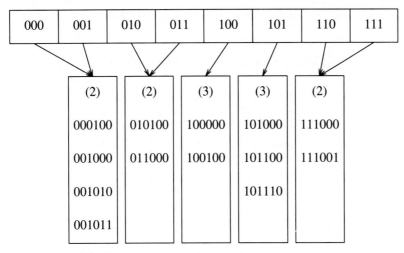

Figure 5.25 Extendible hashing: after insertion of 100100 and directory split

two leaves, which are now determined by the first *three* bits. This requires increasing the directory size to 3. These changes are reflected in Figure 5.25.

Notice that all of the leaves not involved in the split are now pointed to by two adjacent directory entries. Thus, although an entire directory is rewritten, none of the other leaves are actually accessed.

If the key 000000 is now inserted, then the first leaf is split, generating two leaves with $d_l = 3$. Since $D = 3$, the only change required in the directory is the updating of the 000 and 001 pointers. See Figure 5.26.

Figure 5.26 Extendible hashing: after insertion of 000000 and leaf split

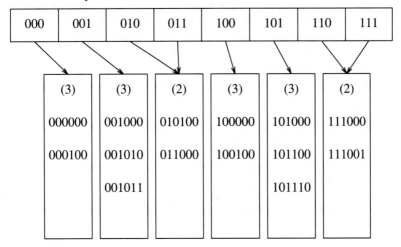

This very simple strategy provides quick access times for *Insert* and *Find* operations on large databases. There are a few important details we have not considered.

First, it is possible that several directory splits will be required if the elements in a leaf agree in more than $D + 1$ leading bits. For instance, starting at the original example, with $D = 2$, if 111010, 111011, and finally 111100 are inserted, the directory size must be increased to 4 to distinguish between the five keys. This is an easy detail to take care of, but it must not be forgotten. Second, there is the possibility of duplicate keys; if there are more than m duplicates, then this algorithm does not work at all. In this case, some other arrangements need to be made.

These possibilities suggest that it is important for the bits to be fairly random. This can be accomplished by hashing the keys into a reasonably long integer; hence the reason for the name.

We close by mentioning some of the performance properties of extendible hashing, which are derived after a very difficult analysis. These results are based on the reasonable assumption that the bit patterns are uniformly distributed.

The expected number of leaves is $(n/m) \log_2 e$. Thus the average leaf is $\ln 2 = 0.69$ full. This is the same as for B-trees, which is not entirely surprising, since for both data structures new nodes are created when the $(m + 1)$st entry is added.

The more surprising result is that the expected size of the directory (in other words, 2^D) is $O(n^{1+1/m}/m)$. If m is very small, then the directory can get unduly large. In this case, we can have the leaves contain pointers to the records instead of the actual records, thus increasing the value of m. This adds a second disk access to each *Find* operation in order to maintain a smaller directory. If the directory is too large to fit in main memory, the second disk access would be needed anyway.

Summary

Hash tables can be used to implement the *Insert* and *Find* operations in constant average time. It is especially important to pay attention to details such as load factor when using hash tables, since otherwise the time bounds are not valid. It is also important to choose the hash function carefully when the key is not a short string or integer.

For open hashing, the load factor should be close to 1, although performance does not significantly degrade unless the load factor becomes very large. For closed hashing, the load factor should not exceed 0.5 unless this is completely unavoidable. If linear probing is used, performance degenerates rapidly as the load factor approaches 1. Rehashing can be implemented to allow the table to grow (and shrink), thus maintaining a reasonable load factor. This is important if space is tight and it is not possible just to declare a huge hash table.

Binary search trees can also be used to implement *Insert* and *Find* operations. Although the resulting average time bounds are $O(\log n)$, binary search trees also support routines that require order and are thus more powerful. Using a hash table, it is not possible to find the minimum element. It is not possible to search efficiently for a string unless the exact string is known. A binary search tree could quickly find all items in a certain range; this is not supported by hash tables. Furthermore, the $O(\log n)$ bound is not necessarily that much more than $O(1)$, especially since no multiplications or divisions are required by search trees.

On the other hand, the worst case for hashing generally results from an implementation error, whereas sorted input can make binary search trees perform poorly. Balanced search trees are quite expensive to implement, so if no ordering information is required and there is any suspicion that the input might be sorted, then hashing is the data structure of choice.

Hashing applications are abundant. Compilers use hash tables to keep track of declared variables in source code. The data structure is known as a *symbol table*. Hash tables are the ideal application for this problem, because only *Insert*s and *Find*s are performed. Identifiers are typically short, so the hash function can be computed quickly.

A hash table is useful for any graph theory problem where the nodes have real names instead of numbers. Here, as the input is read, vertices are assigned integers from 1 onwards by order of appearance. Again, the input is likely to have large groups of alphabetized entries. For example, the vertices could be computers. Then if one particular installation lists its computers as *ibm1, ibm2, ibm3,* ..., there could be a dramatic effect on efficiency if a search tree is used.

A third common use of hash tables is in programs that play games. As the program searches through different lines of play, it keeps track of positions it has seen by computing a hash function based on the position (and storing its move for that position). If the same position reoccurs, usually by a simple transposition of moves, the program can avoid expensive recomputation. This general feature of all game-playing programs is known as the *transposition table*.

Yet another use of hashing is in online spelling checkers. If misspelling detection (as opposed to correction) is important, an entire dictionary can be prehashed and words can be checked in constant time. Hash tables are well suited for this because it is not important to alphabetize words; printing out misspellings in the order they occurred in the document is certainly acceptable.

We close this chapter by returning to the word puzzle problem of Chapter 1. If the second algorithm described in Chapter 1 is used, and we assume that the maximum word size is some small constant, then the time to read in the dictionary containing W words and put it in a hash table is $O(W)$. This time is likely to be dominated by the disk I/O and not the hashing routines. The rest of the algorithm would test for the presence of a word for each ordered quadruple (*row, column, orientation, number of characters*). As each lookup would be $O(1)$, and there are only a constant number of orientations (8) and characters per word, the running time of this phase would be $O(r \cdot c)$. The total running time would be $O(r \cdot c + W)$, which is a distinct improvement over the original $O(r \cdot c \cdot W)$. We could make further optimizations that would decrease the running time in practice; these are described in the exercises.

Exercises

5.1 Given input $\{4371, 1323, 6173, 4199, 4344, 9679, 1989\}$ and a hash function $h(x) = x \bmod 10$, show the resulting

    a. open hash table.

    b. closed hash table using linear probing.

    c. closed hash table using quadratic probing.

    d. closed hash table with second hash function $h_2(x) = 7 - (x \bmod 7)$.

5.2 Show the result of rehashing the hash tables in Exercise 5.1.

5.3 Write a program to compute the number of collisions required in a long random sequence of insertions using linear probing, quadratic probing, and double hashing.

5.4 A large number of deletions in an open hash table can cause the table to be fairly empty, which wastes space. In this case, we can rehash to a table half as large. Assume that we rehash to a larger table when there are twice as many elements as the table size. How empty should an open table be before we rehash to a smaller table?

5.5 An alternative collision resolution strategy is to define a sequence, $f(i) = r_i$, where $r_0 = 0$ and $r_1, r_2, \ldots, r_n$ is a random permutation of the first n integers (each integer appears exactly once).

    a. Prove that under this strategy, if the table is not full, then the collision can always be resolved.

    b. Would this strategy be expected to eliminate clustering?

    c. If the load factor of the table is λ, what is the expected time to perform an insert?

    d. If the load factor of the table is λ, what is the expected time for a successful search?

    e. Give an efficient algorithm (theoretically as well as practically) to generate the random sequence. Explain why the rules for choosing P are important.

5.6 What are the advantages and disadvantages of the various collision resolution strategies?

5.7 Write a program to implement the following strategy for multiplying two sparse polynomials P_1, P_2 of size m and n respectively. Each polynomial is represented as a linked list with cells consisting of a coefficient, an exponent, and a *next* pointer (Exercise 3.7). We multiply each term in P_1 by a term in P_2 for a total of mn operations. One method is to sort these terms and combine like terms, but this requires sorting mn records, which could be expensive, especially in small-memory environments. Alternatively, we could merge terms as they are computed and then sort the result.

    a. Write a program to implement the alternate strategy.

    b. If the output polynomial has about $O(m + n)$ terms, what is the running time of both methods?

5.8 A spelling checker reads an input file and prints out all words not in some online dictionary. Suppose the dictionary contains 30,000 words and the file is one megabyte, so that the algorithm can make only one pass through the input file. A simple strategy is to read the dictionary into a hash table and look for each input word as it is read. Assuming that an average word is seven characters and that it is possible to store words of length L in $L + 1$ bytes (so space waste is not much of a consideration), and assuming a closed table, how much space does this require?

5.9 If memory is limited and the entire dictionary cannot be stored in a hash table, we can still get an efficient algorithm that almost always works. We declare an array H_Table of bits (initialized to zeros) from 0 to $Table\_Size - 1$. As we read in a word, we set $H\_Table[Hash(Word)] = 1$. Which of the following is true?

   a. If a word hashes to a location with value 0, the word is not in the dictionary.

   b. If a word hashes to a location with value 1, the word is in the dictionary.

Suppose we choose $Table\_Size = 300,007$.

   c. How much memory does this require?

   d. What is the probability of an error in this algorithm?

   e. A typical document might have about three actual misspellings per page of 500 words. Is this algorithm usable?

5.10 *Describe a procedure that avoids initializing a hash table (at the expense of memory).

5.11 Suppose we want to find the first occurrence of a string $p_1 p_2 \ldots p_k$ in a long input string $a_1 a_2 \ldots a_n$. We can solve this problem by hashing the pattern string, obtaining a hash value h_p, and comparing this value with the hash value formed from $a_1 a_2 \ldots a_k, a_2 a_3 \ldots a_{k+1}, a_3 a_4 \ldots a_{k+2}$, and so on until $a_{n-k+1} a_{n-k+2} \ldots a_n$. If we have a match of hash values, we compare the strings character by character to verify the match. We return the position (in a) if the strings actually do match, and we continue in the unlikely event that the match is false.

   *a. Show that if the hash value of $a_i a_{i+1} \ldots a_{i+k-1}$ is known, then the hash value of $a_{i+1} a_{i+2} \ldots a_{i+k}$ can be computed in constant time.

   b. Show that the running time is $O(k + n)$ plus the time spent refuting false matches.

   *c. Show that the expected number of false matches is negligible.

   d. Write a program to implement this algorithm.

   **e. Describe an algorithm that runs in $O(k + n)$ worst-case time.

   **f. Describe an algorithm that runs in $O(n/k)$ average time.

5.12 A BASIC program consists of a series of statements, each of which is numbered in ascending order. Control is passed by use of a *goto* or *gosub* and a statement number. Write a program that reads in a legal BASIC program and renumbers the statements so that the first starts at number f and each statement has a number d higher than the previous statement. You may assume an upper limit of *n* statements, but the statement numbers in the input might be as large as a 32-bit integer. Your program must run in linear time.

5.13 a. Implement the word puzzle program using the algorithm described at the end of the chapter.

b. We can get a big speed increase by storing, in addition to each word *w*, all of *w*'s prefixes. (If one of *w*'s prefixes is another word in the dictionary, it is stored as a real word.) Although this may seem to increase the size of the hash table drastically, it does not, because many words have the same prefixes. When a scan is performed in a particular direction, if the word that is looked up is not even in the hash table as a prefix, then the scan in that direction can be terminated early. Use this idea to write an improved program to solve the word puzzle.

c. If we are willing to sacrifice the sanctity of the hash table ADT, we can speed up the program in part (b) by noting that if, for example, we have just computed the hash function for "excel," we do not need to compute the hash function for "excels" from scratch. Adjust your hash function so that it can take advantage of its previous calculation.

d. In Chapter 2, we suggested using binary search. Incorporate the idea of using prefixes into your binary search algorithm. The modification should be simple. Which algorithm is faster?

5.14 Show the result of inserting the keys 10111101, 00000010, 10011011, 10111110, 01111111, 01010001, 10010110, 00001011, 11001111, 10011110, 11011011, 00101011, 01100001, 11110000, 01101111 into an initially empty extendible hashing data structure with $m = 4$.

5.15 Write a program to implement extendible hashing. If the table is small enough to fit in main memory, how does its performance compare with open and closed hashing?

References

Despite the apparent simplicity of hashing, much of the analysis is quite difficult and there are still many unresolved questions. There are also many interesting theoretical issues, which generally attempt to make it unlikely that the worst-case possibilities of hashing arise.

An early paper on hashing is [17]. A wealth of information on the subject, including an analysis of closed hashing with linear probing can be found in [11]. An excellent survey on the subject is [14]; [15] contains suggestions, and pitfalls, for choosing hash functions. Precise analytic and simulation results for all of the methods described in this chapter can be found in [8].

An analysis of double hashing can be found in [9] and [13]. Yet another collision resolution scheme is coalesced hashing, as described in [18]. Yao [20] has shown that uniform hashing, in which no clustering exists, is optimal with respect to cost of a successful search.

If the input keys are known in advance, then perfect hash functions, which do not allow collisions, exist [2], [7]. Some more complicated hashing schemes, for which the worst case depends not on the particular input but on random numbers chosen by the algorithm, appear in [3] and [4].

Extendible hashing appears in [5], with analysis in [6] and [19].

One method of implementing Exercise 5.5 is described in [16]. Exercise 5.11 (a–d) is from [10]. Part (e) is from [12], and part (f) is from [1].

1. R. S. Boyer and J. S. Moore, "A Fast String Searching Algorithm," *Communications of the ACM* 20 (1977), 762–772.
2. J. L. Carter and M. N. Wegman, "Universal Classes of Hash Functions," *Journal of Computer and System Sciences* 18 (1979), 143–154.
3. M. Dietzfelbinger, A. R. Karlin, K. Melhorn, F. Meyer auf der Heide, H. Rohnert, and R. E. Tarjan, "Dynamic Perfect Hashing: Upper and Lower Bounds," *Proceedings of the Twenty-ninth IEEE Symposium on Foundations of Computer Science* (1988), 524–531.
4. R. J. Enbody and H. C. Du, "Dynamic Hashing Schemes," *Computing Surveys* 20 (1988), 85–113.
5. R. Fagin, J. Nievergelt, N. Pippenger, and H. R. Strong, "Extendible Hashing—A Fast Access Method for Dynamic Files," *ACM Transactions on Database Systems* 4 (1979), 315–344.
6. P. Flajolet, "On the Performance Evaluation of Extendible Hashing and Trie Searching," *Acta Informatica* 20 (1983), 345–369.
7. M. L. Fredman, J. Komlos, and E. Szemeredi, "Storing a Sparse Table with O(1) Worst Case Access Time," *Journal of the ACM* 31 (1984), 538–544.
8. G. H. Gonnet and R. Baeza-Yates, *Handbook of Algorithms and Data Structures*, second edition, Addison-Wesley, Reading, Mass., 1991.
9. L. J. Guibas and E. Szemeredi, "The Analysis of Double Hashing," *Journal of Computer and System Sciences* 16 (1978), 226–274.
10. R. M. Karp and M. O. Rabin, "Efficient Randomized Pattern-Matching Algorithms," *Aiken Computer Laboratory Report TR-31-81,* Harvard University, Cambridge, Mass., 1981.
11. D. E. Knuth, *The Art of Computer Programming, Vol 3: Sorting and Searching,* second printing, Addison-Wesley, Reading, Mass., 1975.
12. D. E. Knuth, J. H. Morris, and V. R. Pratt, "Fast Pattern Matching in Strings," *SIAM Journal on Computing* 6 (1977), 323–350.
13. G. Lueker and M. Molodowitch, "More Analysis of Double Hashing," *Proceedings of the Twentieth ACM Symposium on Theory of Computing* (1988), 354–359.
14. W. D. Maurer and T. G. Lewis, "Hash Table Methods," *Computing Surveys* 7 (1975), 5–20.
15. B. J. McKenzie, R. Harries, and T. Bell, "Selecting a Hashing Algorithm," *Software—Practice and Experience* 20 (1990), 209–224.
16. R. Morris, "Scatter Storage Techniques," *Communications of the ACM* 11 (1968), 38–44.
17. W. W. Peterson, "Addressing for Random Access Storage," *IBM Journal of Research and Development* 1 (1957), 130–146.
18. J. S. Vitter, "Implementations for Coalesced Hashing," *Communications of the ACM* 25 (1982), 911–926.
19. A. C. Yao, "A Note on The Analysis of Extendible Hashing," *Information Processing Letters* 11 (1980), 84–86.
20. A. C. Yao, "Uniform Hashing Is Optimal," *Journal of the ACM* 32 (1985), 687–693.

CHAPTER 6

Priority Queues (Heaps)

Although jobs sent to a line printer are generally placed on a queue, this might not always be the best thing to do. For instance, one job might be particularly important, so that it might be desirable to allow that job to be run as soon as the printer is available. Conversely, if, when the printer becomes available, there are several one-page jobs and one hundred-page job, it might be reasonable to make the long job go last even if it is not the last job submitted. (Unfortunately, most systems do not do this, which can be particularly annoying at times.)

Similarly, in a multiuser environment, the operating system scheduler must decide which of several processes to run. Generally a process is allowed to run only for a fixed period of time. One algorithm uses a queue. Jobs are initially placed at the end of the queue. The scheduler will repeatedly take the first job on the queue, run it until either it finishes or its time limit is up, and place it at the end of the queue if it does not finish. This strategy is generally not appropriate, because very short jobs will seem to take a long time because of the wait involved to run. Generally, it is important that short jobs finish as fast as possible, so these jobs should have preference over jobs that have already been running. Furthermore, some jobs that are not short are still very important and should also have preference.

This particular application seems to require a special kind of queue known as a *priority queue*. In this chapter, we will discuss

- Efficient implementation of the ADT priority queue.
- Uses of priority queues.
- Advanced implementations of priority queues.

The data structures we will see are among the most elegant in computer science.

6.1. Model

A priority queue is a data structure that allows at least the following two operations: *Insert,* which does the obvious thing, and *Delete_Min*, which finds, passes back, and removes the minimum element in the priority queue. The *Insert*

211

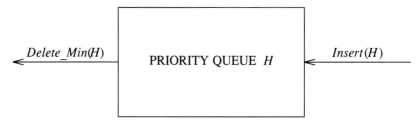

Figure 6.1   Basic model of a priority queue

operation is the equivalent of *Enqueue*, and *Delete_Min* is the priority queue equivalent of the queue's *Dequeue* operation. As with most data structures, it is sometimes possible to add other operations, but these are extensions and not part of the basic model depicted in Figure 6.1.

Priority queues have many applications besides operating systems. In Chapter 7, we will see how priority queues are used for external sorting. Priority queues are also important in the implementation of *greedy algorithms*, which operate by repeatedly finding a minimum; we will see specific examples in Chapters 9 and 10. In this chapter we will see a use of priority queues in discrete event simulation.

6.2.   Simple Implementations

There are several obvious ways to implement a priority queue. We could use a simple linked list, performing insertions at the front in $O(1)$ and traversing the list, which requires $O(n)$ time, to delete the minimum. Alternatively, we could insist that the list be always kept sorted; this makes insertions expensive ($O(n)$) and *Delete_Min*s cheap ($O(1)$). The former is probably the better idea of the two, based on the fact that there are never more *Delete_Min*s than insertions.

Another way of implementing priority queues would be to use a binary search tree. This gives an $O(\log n)$ average running time for both operations. This is true in spite of the fact that although the insertions are random, the deletions are not. Recall that the only element we ever delete is the minimum. Repeatedly removing a node that is in the left subtree would seem to hurt the balance of the tree by making the right subtree heavy. However, the right subtree is random. In the worst case, where the *Delete_Min*s have depleted the left subtree, the right subtree would have at most twice as many elements as it should. This adds only a small constant to its expected depth. Notice that the bound can be made into a worst-case bound by using a balanced tree; this protects one against bad insertion sequences.

Using a search tree could be overkill, because it supports a host of operations that are not required. The basic data structure we will use will not require pointers and will support both operations in $O(\log n)$ worst-case time. Insertion will actually take constant time on average, and our implementation will allow building a priority queue of n items in linear time if no deletions intervene. We will then discuss how to implement priority queues to support efficient merging. This additional operation seems to complicate matters a bit and apparently requires the use of pointers.

6.3. Binary Heap

The implementation we will use is known as a *binary heap*. Its use is so common for priority queue implementations that when the word *heap* is used without a qualifier, it is generally assumed to be referring to this implementation of the data structure. In this section, we will refer to binary heaps as merely *heaps*. Like binary search trees, heaps have two properties, namely, a structure property and a heap order property. As with AVL trees, an operation on a heap can destroy one of the properties, so a heap operation must not terminate until all heap properties are in order. This turns out to be simple to do.

6.3.1. Structure Property

A heap is a binary tree that is completely filled, with the possible exception of the bottom level, which is filled from left to right. Such a tree is known as a *complete binary tree*. Figure 6.2 shows an example.

It is easy to show that a complete binary tree of height h has between 2^h and $2^{h+1} - 1$ nodes. This implies that the height of a complete binary tree is $\lfloor \log n \rfloor$, which is clearly $O(\log n)$.

An important observation is that because a complete binary tree is so regular, it can be represented in an array and no pointers are necessary. The array in Figure 6.3 corresponds to the heap in Figure 6.2.

Figure 6.2   A complete binary tree

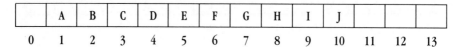

	A	B	C	D	E	F	G	H	I	J			
0	1	2	3	4	5	6	7	8	9	10	11	12	13

Figure 6.3 Array implementation of complete binary tree

For any element in array position i, the left child is in position $2i$, the right child is in the cell after the left child ($2i + 1$), and the parent is in position $\lfloor i/2 \rfloor$. Thus, not only are pointers not required, but the operations required to traverse the tree are extremely simple and likely to be very fast on most computers. The only problem with this implementation is that an estimate of the maximum heap size is required in advance, but typically this is not a problem. In Figure 6.3, the limit on the heap size is 13 elements. The array has a position 0; more on this later.

A heap data structure will, then, consist of an array (of whatever type the key is) and an integer representing the current heap size. Figure 6.4 shows the class specification for a priority queue.

Throughout this chapter, we shall draw the heaps as trees, with the implication that an actual implementation will use simple arrays.

Figure 6.4 Class specification for binary heaps

```
/* 1*/  // Note: The user must supply the routine Min_Val,
/* 2*/  // which returns the minimum value of type Element_Type,
/* 3*/  // which is used as a sentinel.

/* 4*/  static const Default_Max_Size = 10;

/* 5*/  template <class Element_Type>
/* 6*/  class Binary_Heap
/* 7*/  {
/* 8*/    private:
/* 9*/      unsigned int Max_Size;      // Maximum number of elements.
/*10*/      unsigned int Size;          // Current number of elements.
/*11*/      Element_Type *Elements;     // The array.

/*12*/    public:
/*13*/      // Constructors.
/*14*/      Binary_Heap( unsigned int Initial_Size = Default_Max_Size );
/*15*/      Binary_Heap( Binary_Heap & Value )
/*16*/          { Warn( "Heap passed by value" ); operator=( Value ); }

/*17*/      // Destructor.
/*18*/      ~Binary_Heap( ) { delete [ ] Elements; }

/*19*/      // Operator.
/*20*/      const Binary_Heap & operator = ( const Binary_Heap & Value );
```

```
/*21*/      // Member functions.
/*22*/      void Make_Empty( )          { Size = 0; }
/*23*/      int Is_Empty( ) const       { return Size == 0; }
/*24*/      int Is_Full( ) const        { return Size == Max_Size; }
/*25*/      void Insert( const Element_Type & X );
/*26*/      Element_Type Delete_Min( );
/*27*/      Element_Type Find_Min( ) const;
/*28*/      };


/* 1*/   template <class Element_Type>
/* 2*/   Binary_Heap<Element_Type>::
/* 3*/   Binary_Heap( unsigned int Initial_Size )
/* 4*/   {
/* 5*/       Size = 0;
/* 6*/       Max_Size = Initial_Size;
/* 7*/       Elements = new Element_Type [ Max_Size + 1 ];
/* 8*/       if( Elements == NULL )
/* 9*/           Error( "Out of space!!" );
/*10*/       Elements[ 0 ]= Min_Val( );
/*11*/   }
```

Figure 6.4   *(Continued)*

6.3.2.   *Heap Order Property*

The property that allows operations to be performed quickly is the *heap order* property. Since we want to be able to find the minimum quickly, it makes sense that the smallest element should be at the root. If we consider that any subtree should also be a heap, then any node should be smaller than all of its descendants.

Applying this logic, we arrive at the heap order property. In a heap, for every node X, the key in the parent of X is smaller than (or equal to) the key in X, with the obvious exception of the root (which has no parent).[†] In Figure 6.5 the tree on

Figure 6.5   Two complete trees (only the left tree is a heap)

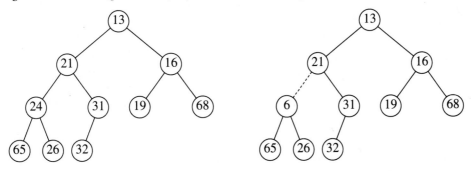

[†]Analogously, we can declare a *(max)*heap, which, by using a different heap order property, enables us to find and remove the maximum element efficiently. Thus, a heap can be used to find *either* a minimum or a maximum, but this needs to be decided ahead of time.

the left is a heap, but the tree on the right is not (the dashed line shows the violation of heap order).

By the heap order property, the minimum element can always be found at the root. Thus, we get the extra operation, *Find_Min*, in constant time.

6.3.3. Basic Heap Operations

It is easy (both conceptually and practically) to perform the two required operations. All the work involves ensuring that the heap order property is maintained.

Insert

To insert an element X into the heap, we create a hole in the next available location, since otherwise the tree will not be complete. If X can be placed in the hole without violating heap order, then we do so and are done. Otherwise we slide the element that is in the hole's parent node into the hole, thus bubbling the hole up toward the root. We continue this process until X can be placed in the hole. Figure 6.6 shows that to insert 14, we create a hole in the next available heap location. Inserting 14 in the hole would violate the heap order property, so 31 is slid down into the hole. This strategy is continued in Figure 6.7 until the correct location for 14 is found.

This general strategy is known as a *percolate up;* the new element is percolated up the heap until the correct location is found. Insertion is easily implemented with the code shown in Figure 6.8.

We could have implemented the percolation in the *Insert* routine by performing repeated swaps until the correct order was established, but a swap requires three assignment statements. If an element is percolated up d levels, the number of assignments performed by the swaps would be $3d$. Our method uses $d + 1$ assignments.

If the element to be inserted is the new minimum, it will be pushed all the way to the top. At some point, i will be 1 and we will want to break out of the *while* loop. We could do this with an explicit test, but we have chosen to put a very small value in position 0 in order to make the *while* loop terminate. This value must be guaranteed to be smaller than (or equal to) any element in the heap;

Figure 6.6   Attempt to insert 14: creating the hole, and bubbling the hole up

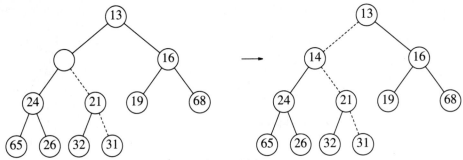

Figure 6.7   The remaining two steps to insert 14 in previous heap

it is known as a *sentinel*. The sentinel is given by a function *Min_Val*, which the user must provide for each type of priority queue. This idea is similar to the use of header nodes in linked lists. By adding a dummy piece of information, we avoid a test that is executed once per loop iteration, thus saving some time.

The time to do the insertion could be as much as $O(\log n)$ if the element to be inserted is the new minimum and is percolated all the way to the root. On average, the percolation terminates early; it has been shown that 2.607 comparisons are required on average to perform an insert, so the average *Insert* moves an element up 1.607 levels.

Figure 6.8   Procedure to insert into a binary heap

```
/* 1*/    template <class Element_Type>
/* 2*/    void
/* 3*/    Binary_Heap<Element_Type>::
/* 4*/    Insert( const Element_Type & X )
/* 5*/    {
/* 6*/        unsigned int i;

/* 7*/        if( Is_Full( ) )
/* 8*/            Error( "Priority queue is full" );
/* 9*/        else
/*10*/        {
/*11*/            i = ++ Size;
/*12*/            while( Elements[ i / 2 ] > X )    CHECK PARENT
/*13*/            {
/*14*/                Elements[ i ] = Elements[ i / 2 ];
/*15*/                i /= 2;
/*16*/            }
/*17*/            Elements[ i ] = X;
/*18*/        }
/*19*/    }
```

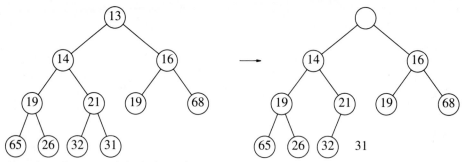

Figure 6.9   Creation of the hole at the root

Delete_Min

*Delete_Min*s are handled in a similar manner as insertions. Finding the minimum is easy; the hard part is removing it. When the minimum is removed, a hole is created at the root. Since the heap now becomes one smaller, it follows that the last element in the heap must move somewhere in the heap. If the last element can be placed in the hole, then we are done. This is unlikely, so we slide the smaller of the hole's children into the hole, thus pushing the hole down one level. We repeat this step until the last element can be placed in the hole. Thus, our action is to place the last element in its correct spot along a path from the root containing *minimum* children.

In Figure 6.9 the left figure shows a heap prior to the *Delete_Min*. After 13 is removed, we must now try to place 31 in the heap. 31 cannot be placed in the hole, because this would violate heap order. Thus, we place the smaller child (14) in the hole, sliding the hole down one level (see Fig. 6.10). We repeat this again, placing 19 into the hole and creating a new hole one level deeper. We then place 26 in the hole and create a new hole on the bottom level. Finally, we are able to place 31 in the hole (Fig. 6.11). This general strategy is known as a *percolate down*. We use the same technique as in the *Insert* routine to avoid the use of swaps in this routine.

A frequent implementation error in heaps occurs when there are an even number of elements in the heap, and the one node that has only one child is encountered. You must make sure not to assume that there are always two children. This usually involves an extra test. In the code, depicted in Figure 6.12, we've done this test at

Figure 6.10   Next two steps in *Delete_Min*

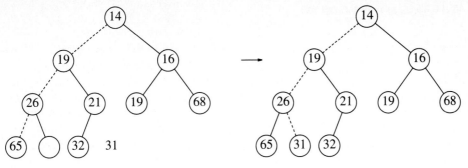

Figure 6.11 Last two steps in *Delete_Min*

```
/* 1*/    template <class Element_Type>
/* 2*/    Element_Type
/* 3*/    Binary_Heap<Element_Type>::
/* 4*/    Delete_Min( )
/* 5*/    {
/* 6*/        unsigned int Child;
/* 7*/        Element_Type Min_Element, Last_Element;

/* 8*/        if( Is_Empty( ) )
/* 9*/        {
/*10*/            Error( "Priority queue is empty" );
/*11*/            return Elements[ 0 ];    // If error is not fatal.
/*12*/        }

/*13*/        Min_Element  = Elements[ 1 ];
/*14*/        Last_Element = Elements[ Size-- ];

/*15*/        for( int i = 1; i * 2 <= Size; i = Child )
/*16*/        {
/*17*/            // Find smaller child.
/*18*/            Child = i * 2;
/*19*/            if( Child != Size )
/*20*/                if( Elements[ Child + 1 ] < Elements[ Child ] )
/*21*/                    Child++;

/*22*/            // Percolate one level.
/*23*/            if( Last_Element > Elements[ Child ] )
/*24*/                Elements[ i ] = Elements[ Child ];
/*25*/            else
/*26*/                break;
/*27*/        }
/*28*/        Elements[ i ] = Last_Element;

/*29*/        return Min_Element;
/*30*/    }
```

Figure 6.12 Function to perform *Delete_Min* in a binary
heap

line 19. One extremely tricky solution is always to ensure that your algorithm *thinks* every node has two children. Do this by placing a sentinel, of value higher than any in the heap, at the spot after the heap ends, at the start of each *percolate down* when the heap size is even. You should think very carefully before attempting this, and you must put in a prominent comment if you do use this technique. Although this eliminates the need to test for the presence of a right child, you cannot eliminate the requirement that you test when you reach the bottom, because this would require a sentinel for every leaf.

The worst-case running time for this operation is $O(\log n)$. On average, the element that is placed at the root is percolated almost to the bottom of the heap (which is the level it came from), so the average running time is $O(\log n)$.

6.3.4.   *Other Heap Operations*

Notice that although finding the minimum can be performed in constant time, a heap designed to find the minimum element (also known as a (*min*)heap) is of no help whatsoever in finding the maximum element. In fact, a heap has very little ordering information, so there is no way to find any particular key without a linear scan through the entire heap. To see this, consider the large heap structure (the elements are not shown) in Figure 6.13, where we see that the only information known about the maximum element is that it is at one of the leaves. Half the elements, though, are contained in leaves, so this is practically useless information. For this reason, if it is important to know where elements are, some other data structure, such as a hash table, must be used in addition to the heap. (Recall that the model does not allow looking inside the heap.)

If we assume that the position of every element is known by some other method, then several other operations become cheap. The three operations below all run in logarithmic worst-case time.

Figure 6.13   A very large complete binary tree

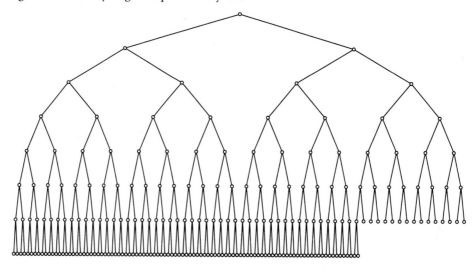

Decrease_Key

The *Decrease_Key(P, Δ)* operation lowers the value of the key at position P by a positive amount $Δ$. Since this might violate the heap order, it must be fixed by a *percolate up*. This operation could be useful to system administrators: They can make their programs run with highest priority.

Increase_Key

The *Increase_Key(P, Δ)* operation increases the value of the key at position P by a positive amount $Δ$. This is done with a *percolate down*. Many schedulers automatically drop the priority of a process that is consuming excessive CPU time.

Remove

The *Remove(I)* operation removes the node at position I from the heap. This is done by first performing *Decrease_Key(I, ∞)* and then performing *Delete_Min*. When a process is terminated by a user (instead of finishing normally), it must be removed from the priority queue.

Build_Heap

The *Build_Heap* operation takes as input n keys and places them into an empty heap. Obviously, this can be done with n successive *Inserts*. Since each *Insert* will take $O(1)$ average and $O(\log n)$ worst-case time, the total running time of this algorithm would be $O(n)$ average but $O(n \log n)$ worst-case. Since this is a special instruction and there are no other operations intervening, and we already know that the instruction can be performed in linear average time, it is reasonable to expect that with reasonable care a linear time bound can be guaranteed.

The general algorithm is to place the n keys into the tree in any order, maintaining the structure property. Then, if *Percolate_Down(P)* percolates down from node P, perform the algorithm in Figure 6.14 to create a heap-ordered tree.

The first tree in Figure 6.15 is the unordered tree. The seven remaining trees in Figures 6.15 through 6.18 show the result of each of the seven *Percolate_Downs*. Each dashed line corresponds to two comparisons: one to find the smaller child and one to compare the smaller child with the node. Notice that there are only 10 dashed lines in the entire algorithm (there could have been an 11th—where?) corresponding to 20 comparisons.

To bound the running time of *Build_Heap*, we must bound the number of dashed lines. This can be done by computing the sum of the heights of all the nodes

Figure 6.14   Sketch of *Build_Heap*

```
for ( i = N/2; i > 0; i-- )
    Percolate_Down( i );
```

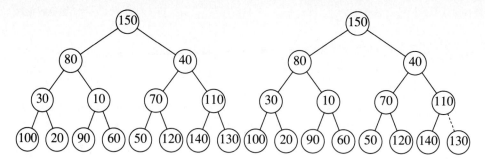

Figure 6.15 Left: initial heap; right: after
Percolate_Down(7)

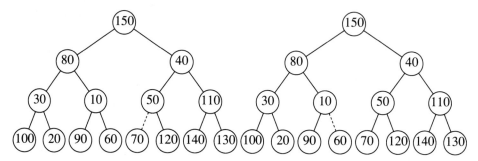

Figure 6.16 Left: after *Percolate_Down*(6); right: after
Percolate_Down(5)

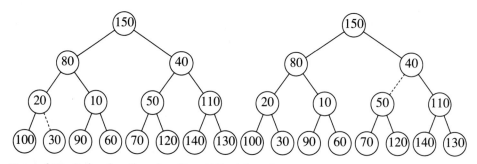

Figure 6.17 Left: after *Percolate_Down*(4); right: after
Percolate_Down(3)

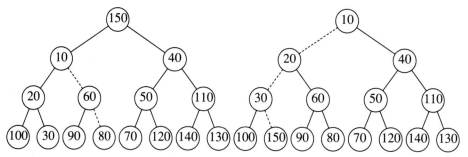

Figure 6.18 Left: after *Percolate_Down*(2); right: after
Percolate_Down(1)

in the heap, which is the maximum number of dashed lines. What we would like to show is that this sum is $O(n)$.

THEOREM 6.1.

For the perfect binary tree of height h containing $2^{h+1} - 1$ nodes, the sum of the heights of the nodes is $2^{h+1} - 1 - (h + 1)$.

PROOF:

It is easy to see that this tree consists of 1 node at height h, 2 nodes at height $h - 1$, 2^2 nodes at height $h - 2$, and in general 2^i nodes at height $h - i$. The sum of the heights of all the nodes is then

$$S = \sum_{i=0}^{h} 2^i (h - i)$$

$$= h + 2(h - 1) + 4(h - 2) + 8(h - 3) + 16(h - 4) + \cdots + 2^{h-1}(1) \quad (6.1)$$

Multiplying by 2 gives the equation

$$2S = 2h + 4(h - 1) + 8(h - 2) + 16(h - 3) + \cdots + 2^h(1) \quad (6.2)$$

We subtract these two equations and obtain equation (6.3). We find that certain terms almost cancel. For instance, we have $2h - 2(h - 1) = 2$, $4(h - 1) - 4(h - 2) = 4$, and so on. The last term in Equation (6.2), 2^h, does not appear in Equation (6.1); thus, it appears in Equation (6.3). The first term in Equation (6.1), h, does not appear in Equation (6.2); thus, $-h$ appears in Equation (6.3). We obtain

$$S = -h + 2 + 4 + 8 + \cdots + 2^{h-1} + 2^h = (2^{h+1} - 1) - (h + 1) \quad (6.3)$$

which proves the theorem.

A complete tree is not a perfect binary tree, but the result we have obtained is an upper bound on the the sum of the heights of the nodes in a complete tree. Since a complete tree has between 2^h and 2^{h+1} nodes, this theorem implies that this sum is $O(n)$, where n is the number of nodes.

Although the result we have obtained is sufficient to show that *Build_Heap* is linear, the bound on the sum of the heights is not as strong as possible. For a complete tree with $n = 2^h$ nodes, the bound we have obtained is roughly $2n$. The sum of the heights can be shown by induction to be $n - b(n)$, where $b(n)$ is the number of 1s in the binary representation of n.

6.4. Applications of Priority Queues

We have already mentioned how priority queues are used in operating systems design. In Chapter 9, we will see how priority queues are used to implement several graph algorithms efficiently. Here we will show how to use priority queues to obtain solutions to two problems.

6.4.1. The Selection Problem

The first problem we will examine is the *selection problem* from Chapter 1. Recall that the input is a list of n elements, which can be totally ordered, and an integer k. The selection problem is to find the kth largest element.

Two algorithms were given in Chapter 1, but neither is very efficient. The first algorithm, which we shall call Algorithm 1A, is to read the elements into an array and sort them, returning the appropriate element. Assuming a simple sorting algorithm, the running time is $O(n^2)$. The alternative algorithm, 1B, is to read k elements into an array and sort them. The smallest of these is in the kth position. We process the remaining elements one by one. As an element arrives, it is compared with the kth element in the array. If it is larger, then the kth element is removed, and the new element is placed in the correct place among the remaining $k-1$ elements. When the algorithm ends, the element in the kth position is the answer. The running time is $O(n \cdot k)$ (why?). If $k = \lceil n/2 \rceil$, then both algorithms are $O(n^2)$. Notice that for any k, we can solve the symmetric problem of finding the $(n-k+1)$th smallest element, so $k = \lceil n/2 \rceil$ is really the hardest case for these algorithms. This also happens to be the most interesting case, since this value of k is known as the *median*.

We give two algorithms here, both of which run in $O(n \log n)$ in the extreme case of $k = \lceil n/2 \rceil$, which is a distinct improvement.

Algorithm 6A

For simplicity, we assume that we are interested in finding the kth *smallest* element. The algorithm is simple. We read the n elements into an array. We then apply the *Build_Heap* algorithm to this array. Finally, we'll perform k *Delete_Min* operations. The last element extracted from the heap is our answer. It should be clear that by changing the heap order property, we could solve the original problem of finding the kth *largest* element.

The correctness of the algorithm should be clear. The worst-case timing is $O(n)$ to construct the heap if *Build_Heap* is used, and $O(\log n)$ for each *Delete_Min*. Since there are k *Delete_Min*s, we obtain a total running time of $O(n + k \log n)$. If $k = O(n/\log n)$, then the running time is dominated by the *Build_Heap* operation and is $O(n)$. For larger values of k, the running time is $O(k \log n)$. If $k = \lceil n/2 \rceil$, then the running time is $\Theta(n \log n)$.

Notice that if we run this program for $k = n$ and record the values as they leave the heap, we will have essentially sorted the input file in $O(n \log n)$ time. In Chapter 7, we will refine this idea to obtain a fast sorting algorithm known as *Heapsort*.

Algorithm 6B

For the second algorithm, we return to the original problem and find the kth *largest* element. We use the idea from Algorithm 1B. At any point in time we will maintain a set S of the k largest elements. After the first k elements are read, when a new element is read, it is compared with the kth largest element, which we denote by S_k. Notice that S_k is the smallest element in S. If the new element is larger, then it replaces S_k in S. S will then have a new smallest element, which may or may not be the newly added element. At the end of the input, we find the smallest element in S and return it as the answer.

This is essentially the same algorithm described in Chapter 1. Here, however, we will use a heap to implement S. The first k elements are placed into the heap in total time $O(k)$ with a call to *Build_Heap*. The time to process each of the remaining elements is $O(1)$, to test if the element goes into S, plus $O(\log k)$, to delete S_k and insert the new element if this is necessary. Thus, the total time is $O(k+(n-k)\log k) = O(n \log k)$. This algorithm also gives a bound of $\Theta(n \log n)$ for finding the median.

In Chapter 7, we will see how to solve this problem in $O(n)$ average time. In Chapter 10, we will see an elegant, albeit impractical, algorithm to solve this problem in $O(n)$ worst-case time.

6.4.2. *Event Simulation*

In Section 3.4.3, we described an important queuing problem. Recall that we have a system, such as a bank, where customers arrive and wait on a line until one of k tellers is available. Customer arrival is governed by a probability distribution function, as is the service time (the amount of time to be served once a teller is available). We are interested in statistics such as how long on average a customer has to wait or how long the line might be.

With certain probability distributions and values of k, these answers can be computed exactly. However, as k gets larger, the analysis becomes considerably more difficult, so it is appealing to use a computer to simulate the operation of the bank. In this way, the bank officers can determine how many tellers are needed to ensure reasonably smooth service.

A simulation consists of processing events. The two events here are (a) a customer arriving and (b) a customer departing, thus freeing up a teller.

We can use the probability functions to generate an input stream consisting of ordered pairs of arrival time and service time for each customer, sorted by arrival time. We do not need to use the exact time of day. Rather, we can use a quantum unit, which we will refer to as a *tick*.

One way to do this simulation is to start a simulation clock at zero ticks. We then advance the clock one tick at a time, checking to see if there is an event. If there is, then we process the event(s) and compile statistics. When there are no customers left in the input stream and all the tellers are free, then the simulation is over.

The problem with this simulation strategy is that its running time does not depend on the number of customers or events (there are two events per customer), but instead depends on the number of ticks, which is not really part of the input. To see why this is important, suppose we changed the clock units to milliticks and multiplied all the times in the input by 1,000. The result would be that the simulation would take 1,000 times longer!

The key to avoiding this problem is to advance the clock to the next event time at each stage. This is conceptually easy to do. At any point, the next event that can occur is either (a) the next customer in the input file arrives, or (b) one of the customers at a teller leaves. Since all the times when the events will happen are available, we just need to find the event that happens nearest in the future and process that event.

If the event is a departure, processing includes gathering statistics for the departing customer and checking the line (queue) to see whether there is another customer waiting. If so, we add that customer, process whatever statistics are required, compute the time when that customer will leave, and add that departure to the set of events waiting to happen.

If the event is an arrival, we check for an available teller. If there is none, we place the arrival on the line (queue); otherwise we give the customer a teller, compute the customer's departure time, and add the departure to the set of events waiting to happen.

The waiting line for customers can be implemented as a queue. Since we need to find the event *nearest* in the future, it is appropriate that the set of arrivals and departures waiting to happen be organized in a priority queue. The next event is thus the next arrival or next departure (whichever is sooner); both are easily available.

It is then straightforward, although possibly time-consuming, to write the simulation routines. If there are C customers (and thus $2C$ events) and k tellers, then the running time *of the simulation* would be $O(C \log(k + 1))^{\dagger}$ because computing and processing each event takes $O(\log H)$, where $H = k + 1$ is the size of the heap.

6.5. d-Heaps

Binary heaps are so simple that they are almost always used when priority queues are needed. A simple generalization is a *d-heap*, which is exactly like a binary heap except that all nodes have d children (thus, a binary heap is a 2-heap). Figure 6.19 shows a 3-heap.

Notice that a *d*-heap is much more shallow than a binary heap, improving the running time of *Insert*s to $O(\log_d n)$. However, the *Delete_Min* operation is more expensive because, even though the tree is shallower, the minimum of d children must be found, which takes $d - 1$ comparisons using a standard algorithm. This raises the time for this operation to $O(d \log_d n)$. If d is a constant, both running

Figure 6.19   A *d*-heap

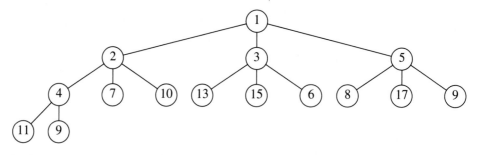

---

†We use $O(C \log(k + 1))$ instead of $O(C \log k)$ to avoid confusion for the $k = 1$ case.

times are, of course, $O(\log n)$. Furthermore, although an array can still be used, the multiplications and divisions to find children and parents are now by d, which seriously increases the running time because we can no longer implement division by a bit shift. d-heaps are interesting in theory because there are many algorithms in which the number of insertions is much greater than the number of *Delete_Min*s (and thus a theoretical speedup is possible). They are also of interest when the priority queue is too large to fit entirely in main memory. In this case, a d-heap can be advantageous in much the same way as a B-tree.

The most glaring weakness of the heap implementation, aside from the inability to perform *Find*s, is that combining two heaps into one is a hard operation. This extra operation is known as a *Merge*. There are quite a few ways of implementing heaps so that the running time of a *Merge* is $O(\log n)$. We will now discuss three data structures, of various complexity, that support the *Merge* operation efficiently. We will defer any complicated analysis until Chapter 11.

6.6. Leftist Heaps

It seems difficult to design a data structure that efficiently supports merging (that is, processes a *Merge* in o(n) time) and uses only an array, as in a binary heap. The reason for this is that merging would seem to require copying one array into another, which would take $\Theta(n)$ time for equal-sized heaps. For this reason, all the advanced data structures that support efficient merging require the use of pointers. In practice, we can expect that this will make all the other operations slower; pointer manipulation is generally more time-consuming than multiplication and division by two.

Like a binary heap, a *leftist heap* has both a structural property and an ordering property. Indeed, a leftist heap, like virtually all heaps used, has the same heap order property we have already seen. Furthermore, a leftist heap is also a binary tree. The only difference between a leftist heap and a binary heap is that leftist heaps are not perfectly balanced, but actually attempt to be very unbalanced.

6.6.1. Leftist Heap Property

We define the *null path length, Npl(X),* of any node X to be the length of the shortest path from X to a node without two children. Thus, the *Npl* of a node with zero or one child is 0, while $Npl\ (NULL) = -1$. In the tree in Figure 6.20, the null path lengths are indicated inside the tree nodes.

Notice that the null path length of any node is 1 more than the minimum of the null path lengths of its children. This applies to nodes with less than two children because the null path length of *NULL* is -1.

The leftist heap property is that for every node X in the heap, the null path length of the left child is at least as large as that of the right child. This property is satisfied by only one of the trees in Figure 6.20, namely, the tree on the left. This property actually goes out of its way to ensure that the tree is unbalanced because it clearly biases the tree to get deep towards the left. Indeed, a tree consisting of a long path of left nodes is possible (and actually preferable to facilitate merging); hence the name *leftist heap*.

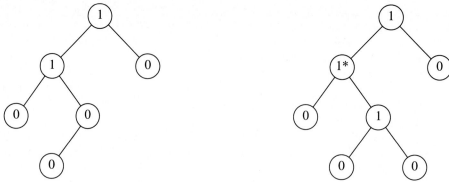

Figure 6.20 Null path lengths for two trees; only the left tree is leftist

Because leftist heaps tend to have deep left paths, it follows that the right path ought to be short. Indeed, the right path down a leftist heap is as short as any in the heap. Otherwise, there would be a path that goes through some node X and takes the left child. Then X would violate the leftist property.

THEOREM 6.2.

A leftist tree with r nodes on the right path must have at least $2^r - 1$ nodes.

PROOF:

The proof is by induction. If $r = 1$, there must be at least one tree node. Otherwise, suppose that the theorem is true for $1, 2, \ldots, r$. Consider a leftist tree with $r + 1$ nodes on the right path. Then the root has a right subtree with r nodes on the right path, and a left subtree with at least r nodes on the right path (otherwise it would not be leftist). Applying the inductive hypothesis to these subtrees yields a minimum of $2^r - 1$ nodes in each subtree. This plus the root gives at least $2^{r+1} - 1$ nodes in the tree, proving the theorem.

From this theorem, it follows immediately that a leftist tree of n nodes has a right path containing at most $\lfloor \log(n + 1) \rfloor$ nodes. The general idea for the leftist heap operations is to perform all the work on the right path, which is guaranteed to be short. The only tricky part is that performing *Inserts* and *Merges* on the right path could destroy the leftist heap property. It turns out to be extremely easy to restore the property.

6.6.2.   Leftist Heap Operations

The fundamental operation on leftist heaps is merging. Notice that insertion is merely a special case of merging since we may view an insertion as a *Merge* of a one-node heap with a larger heap. We will first give a simple recursive solution and then show how this might be done nonrecursively. Our input is the two leftist heaps, H_1 and H_2, in Figure 6.21. You should check that these heaps really are leftist. Notice that the smallest elements are at the roots. In addition to space for the data and left and right pointers, each cell will have an entry that indicates the null path length.

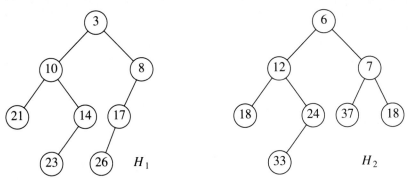

Figure 6.21 Two leftist heaps H_1 and H_2

If either of the two heaps is empty, then we can return the other heap. Otherwise, to merge the two heaps, we compare their roots. First, we recursively merge the heap with the larger root with the right subheap of the heap with the smaller root. In our example, this means we recursively merge H_2 with the subheap of H_1 rooted at 8, obtaining the heap in Figure 6.22.

Since this tree is formed recursively, and we have not yet finished the description of the algorithm, we cannot at this point show how this heap was obtained. However, it is reasonable to assume that the resulting tree is a leftist heap because it was obtained via a recursive step. This is much like the inductive hypothesis in a proof by induction. Since we can handle the base case (which occurs when one tree is empty), we can assume that the recursive step works as long as we can finish the merge; this is rule 3 of recursion, which we discussed in Chapter 1. We now make this new heap the right child of the root of H_1 (see Figure 6.23).

Although the resulting heap satisfies the heap order property, it is not leftist, because the left subtree of the root has a null path length of 1 whereas the right subtree has null path length of 2. Thus, the leftist property is violated at the root. However, it is easy to see that the remainder of the tree must be leftist. The right

Figure 6.22 Result of merging H_2 with H_1's right subheap

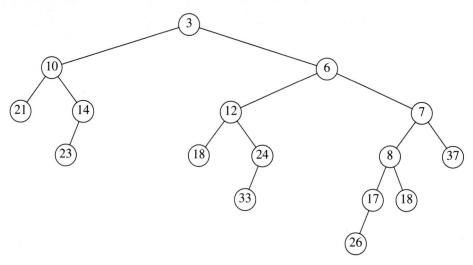

Figure 6.23 Result of attaching leftist heap of previous
figure as H_1's right child

subtree of the root is leftist because of the recursive step. The left subtree of the root
has not been changed, so it too must still be leftist. Thus, we need only to fix the
root. We can make the entire tree leftist by merely swapping the root's left and right
children (Figure 6.24) and updating the null path length—the new null path length
is 1 plus the null path length of the new right child—completing the *Merge*. Notice
that if the null path length is not updated, then all null path lengths will be 0, and
the heap will not be leftist but merely random. In this case, the algorithm will work,
but the time bound we will claim will no longer be valid.

The description of the algorithm translates directly into code. The class specification (Figure 6.25) is similiar to that of the binary search tree, except that it is

Figure 6.24 Result of swapping children of H_1's root

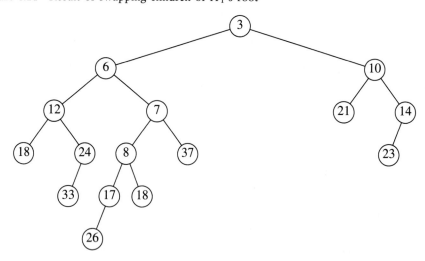

augmented with the *Npl* (null path length) field. Since this isn't a search tree, we don't use inheritance.

The routine to merge (Figure 6.26) is a driver designed to remove special cases and ensure that H_1 has the smaller root. The actual merging is performed in *Merge1* (Figure 6.27).

Figure 6.25   Leftist heap class specification

```
/* 1*/    template <class Etype>
/* 2*/    class Left_Node
/* 3*/    {
/* 4*/      protected:
/* 5*/        Etype Element;
/* 6*/        Left_Node *Left;
/* 7*/        Left_Node *Right;
/* 8*/        unsigned int Npl;

/* 9*/        Left_Node( Etype E = 0, Left_Node *L = NULL,
/*10*/            Left_Node *R = NULL, unsigned int Np = 0 ) :
/*11*/            Element( E ), Left( L ), Right( R ), Npl( Np ) { }

/*12*/        friend class Left_Heap<Etype>;
/*13*/    };

/*14*/    template <class Etype>
/*15*/    class Left_Heap
/*16*/    {
/*17*/      private:
/*18*/        Left_Node<Etype> *Root;

/*19*/        void Destroy( Left_Node<Etype> *T );
/*20*/        Left_Node<Etype> *Copy( Left_Node<Etype> *T );
/*21*/        inline void Swap( Left_Node<Etype> * & A,
/*22*/                Left_Node<Etype> * & B );
/*23*/        Left_Node<Etype> *Merge (
/*24*/                Left_Node<Etype> *H1,
/*25*/                Left_Node<Etype> *H2 );
/*26*/        Left_Node<Etype> *Merge1(
/*27*/                Left_Node<Etype> *H1,
/*28*/                Left_Node<Etype> *H2 );

/*29*/      public:
/*30*/        // Constructors.
/*31*/        Left_Heap( unsigned int Initial_Size = 0 ) : Root( NULL ) { }
/*32*/        Left_Heap( Left_Heap & Value )
/*33*/            { Warn( "Heap passed by value" ); operator=( Value ); }

/*34*/        // Destructor.
/*35*/        ~Left_Heap( ) { Destroy( Root ); }
```

```
/*36*/        // Operator.
/*37*/        const Left_Heap & operator = ( const Left_Heap & Value );

/*38*/        // Member functions.
/*39*/        void Make_Empty( )      { Destroy( Root ); Root = NULL; }
/*40*/        int Is_Empty( ) const   { return Root == NULL; }

/*41*/        inline void Insert( const Etype & X );
/*42*/        inline void Merge( Left_Heap & Value );
/*43*/        inline Etype Find_Min( ) const;

/*44*/        Etype Delete_Min( );
/*45*/   };
```

Figure 6.25 *(Continued)*

```
/* 1*/   template <class Etype>
/* 2*/   Left_Node<Etype> *
/* 3*/   Left_Heap<Etype>::
/* 4*/   Merge( Left_Node<Etype> *H1, Left_Node<Etype> *H2 )
/* 5*/   {
/* 6*/       if( H1 == NULL )
/* 7*/           return H2;
/* 8*/       if( H2 == NULL )
/* 9*/           return H1;
/*10*/       if( H2->Element > H1->Element )
/*11*/           return Merge1( H1, H2 );
/*12*/       return( Merge1( H2, H1 ) );
/*13*/   }
```

Figure 6.26 Driving routine for merging leftist heaps

```
/* 1*/   template <class Etype>
/* 2*/   Left_Node<Etype> *
/* 3*/   Left_Heap<Etype>::
/* 4*/   Merge1( Left_Node<Etype> *H1, Left_Node<Etype> *H2 )
/* 5*/   {
/* 6*/       if( H1->Left == NULL )         // Single node.
/* 7*/           H1->Left = H2;
/* 8*/       else
/* 9*/       {
/*10*/           H1->Right = Merge( H1->Right, H2 );
/*11*/           if( H1->Left->Npl < H1->Right->Npl )
/*12*/               Swap( H1->Left, H1->Right );
/*13*/           H1->Npl = H1->Right->Npl + 1;
/*14*/       }
/*15*/       return H1;
/*16*/   }
```

Figure 6.27 Actual routine to merge leftist heaps

The time to perform the merge is proportional to the sum of the length of the right paths, because constant work is performed at each node visited during the recursive calls. Thus we obtain an $O(\log n)$ time bound to merge two leftist heaps. We can also perform this operation nonrecursively by essentially performing two passes. In the first pass, we create a new tree by merging the right paths of both heaps. To do this, we arrange the nodes on the right paths of H_1 and H_2 in sorted order, keeping their respective left children. In our example, the new right path is 3, 6, 7, 8, 18 and the resulting tree is shown in Figure 6.28. A second pass is made up the heap, and child swaps are performed at nodes that violate the leftist heap property. In Figure 6.28, there is a swap at nodes 7 and 3, and the same tree as before is obtained. The nonrecursive version is simpler to visualize but harder to code. We leave it to the reader to show that the recursive and nonrecursive procedures do the same thing.

As mentioned above, we can carry out insertions by making the item to be inserted a one-node heap and performing a *Merge*. To perform a *Delete_Min*, we merely destroy the root, creating two heaps, which can then be merged. Thus, the time to perform a *Delete_Min* is $O(\log n)$. These two routines are coded in Figure 6.29 and Figure 6.30. Figure 6.29 also shows the public *Merge* routine. The leftist heap that is absorbed must be set to *NULL* to guarantee that an item is only in one heap. Otherwise, problems could result from a *delete* on a node.

Notice how the headings for these routines are identical to those for the binary heap implementation. Either priority queue package could be used, and the implementation would be completely transparent to the calling routines.

Finally, we can build a leftist heap in $O(n)$ time by building a binary heap (obviously using a pointer implementation). Although a binary heap is clearly leftist, this is not necessarily the best solution because the heap we obtain is the worst possible leftist heap. Furthermore, traversing the tree in reverse-level order is not as

Figure 6.28   Result of merging right paths of H_1 and H_2

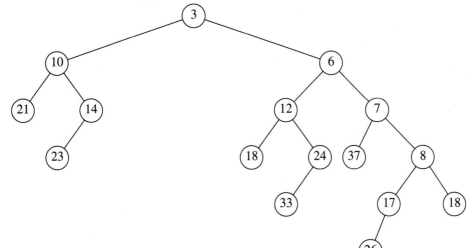

```
/* 1*/   template <class Etype>
/* 2*/   void
/* 3*/   Left_Heap<Etype>::
/* 4*/   Insert( const Etype & X )
/* 5*/   {
/* 6*/       Left_Node<Etype> *P;

/* 7*/       P = new Left_Node<Etype> ( X );
/* 8*/       if( P == NULL )
/* 9*/           Error( "Out of space!!" );
/*10*/       Root = Merge( P, Root );
/*11*/   }


/*12*/   template <class Etype>
/*13*/   void
/*14*/   Left_Heap<Etype>::
/*15*/   Merge( Left_Heap<Etype> & Value )
/*16*/   {
/*17*/       Root = Merge( Root, Value.Root );
/*18*/       Value.Root = NULL;
/*19*/   }
```

Figure 6.29   Insertion routine for leftist heaps, and public
                  Merge routine

```
/* 1*/   template <class Etype>
/* 2*/   Etype
/* 3*/   Left_Heap<Etype>::
/* 4*/   Delete_Min( )
/* 5*/   {
/* 6*/       Etype Min_Element;
/* 7*/       Left_Node<Etype> *Left_Heap, *Right_Heap;

/* 8*/       if( Is_Empty( ) )
/* 9*/       {
/*10*/           Error( "Priority queue is empty" );
/*11*/           return 0;
/*12*/       }

/*13*/       Min_Element = Root->Element;

/*14*/       Left_Heap  = Root->Left;
/*15*/       Right_Heap = Root->Right;
/*16*/       delete Root;
/*17*/       Root = Merge( Left_Heap, Right_Heap );

/*18*/       return Min_Element;
/*19*/   }
```

Figure 6.30   *Delete_Min* routine for leftist heaps

easy with pointers. The *Build_Heap* effect can be obtained by recursively building the left and right subtrees and then percolating the root down. The exercises contain an alternative solution.

6.7. Skew Heaps

A *skew heap* is a self-adjusting version of a leftist heap that is incredibly simple to implement. The relationship of skew heaps to leftist heaps is analogous to the relation between splay trees and AVL trees. Skew heaps are binary trees with heap order, but there is no structural constraint on these trees. Unlike leftist heaps, skew heaps maintain no information about the null path length of any node. The right path of a skew heap can be arbitrarily long at any time, so the worst-case running time of all operations is $O(n)$. However, as with splay trees, it can be shown (see Chapter 11) that for any m consecutive operations, the total worst-case running time is $O(m \log n)$. Thus, skew heaps have $O(\log n)$ amortized cost per operation.

As with leftist heaps, the fundamental operation on skew heaps is merging. The *Merge* routine is once again recursive, and we perform the exact same operations as before, with one exception. The difference is that for leftist heaps, we check to see whether the left and right children satisfy the leftist heap order property and swap them if they do not. For skew heaps, the swap is unconditional—we *always* do it, with the one exception that the largest of all the nodes on the right paths does not have its children swapped. This one exception is what happens in the natural recursive implementation, so it is not really a special case at all. Furthermore, it is not necessary to prove the bounds, but since this node is guaranteed not to have a right child, it would be silly to perform the swap and give it one. (In our example, there are no children of this node, so we do not worry about it.) Again, suppose our input is the same two heaps as before, Figure 6.31.

If we recursively merge H_2 with the subheap of H_1 rooted at 8, we will get the heap in Figure 6.32.

Again, this is done recursively, so by the third rule of recursion (Section 1.3) we need not worry about how it was obtained. This heap happens to be leftist, but there

Figure 6.31 Two skew heaps H_1 and H_2

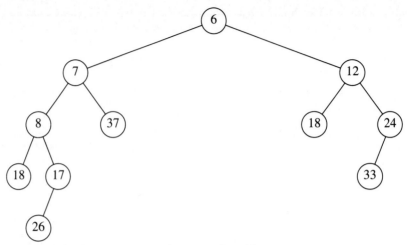

Figure 6.32   Result of merging H_2 with H_1's right subheap

is no guarantee that this is always the case. We make this heap the new left child of H_1, and the old left child of H_1 becomes the new right child (see Figure 6.33).

The entire tree is leftist, but it is easy to see that that is not always true: Inserting 15 into this new heap would destroy the leftist property.

We can perform all operations nonrecursively, as with leftist heaps, by merging the right paths and swapping left and right children for every node on the right path, with the exception of the last. After a few examples, it becomes clear that since all but the last node on the right path have their children swapped, the net effect is that this becomes the new left path (see the preceding example to convince yourself). This makes it very easy to merge two skew heaps visually.

Figure 6.33   Result of merging skew heaps H_1 and H_2

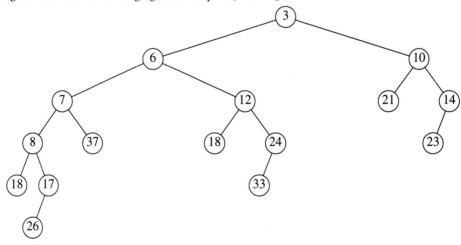

The implementation of skew heaps is left as a (trivial) exercise. Skew heaps have the advantage that no extra space is required to maintain path lengths, and no tests are required to determine when to swap children. It is an open problem to determine precisely the expected right path length of both leftist and skew heaps (the latter is undoubtedly more difficult). Such a comparison would make it easier to determine whether the slight loss of balance information is compensated by the lack of testing.

6.8. Binomial Queues

Although both leftist and skew heaps support merging, insertion, and *Delete_Min* all effectively in $O(\log n)$ time per operation, there is room for improvement because we know that binary heaps support insertion in *constant average* time per operation. Binomial queues support all three operations in $O(\log n)$ worst-case time per operation, but insertions take constant time on average.

6.8.1. *Binomial Queue Structure*

Binomial queues differ from all the priority queue implementations that we have seen in that a binomial queue is not a heap-ordered tree but rather a *collection* of heap-ordered trees, known as a *forest*. Each of the heap-ordered trees are of a constrained form known as a *binomial tree* (the name will be obvious later). There is at most one binomial tree of every height. A binomial tree of height 0 is a one-node tree; a binomial tree, B_k, of height k is formed by attaching a binomial tree, B_{k-1}, to the root of another binomial tree, B_{k-1}. Figure 6.34 shows binomial trees B_0, B_1, B_2, B_3, and B_4.

It is probably obvious from the diagram that a binomial tree, B_k, consists of a root with children B_0, B_1, . . ., B_{k-1}. Binomial trees of height k have exactly 2^k nodes, and the number of nodes at depth d is the binomial coefficient $\binom{k}{d}$. If we impose heap order on the binomial trees and allow at most one binomial tree of any height, we can uniquely represent a priority queue of any size by a collection of binomial trees. For instance, a priority queue of size 13 could be represented by the forest B_3, B_2, B_0. We might write this representation as 1101, which not only represents 13 in binary but also represents the fact that B_3, B_2 and B_0 are present in the representation and B_1 is not.

As an example, a priority queue of six elements could be represented as in Figure 6.35.

6.8.2. *Binomial Queue Operations*

The minimum element can then be found by scanning the roots of all the trees. Since there are at most $\log n$ different trees, the minimum can be found in $O(\log n)$

B_0 B_1 B_2 B_3

B_4

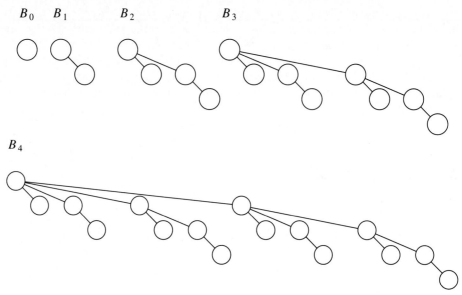

Figure 6.34   Binomial trees B_0, B_1, B_2, B_3, and B_4

time. Alternatively, we can maintain knowledge of the minimum and perform the operation in $O(1)$ time, if we remember to update the minimum when it changes during other operations.

     Merging two binomial queues is a conceptually easy operation, which we will describe by example. Consider the two binomial queues, H_1 and H_2, with six and seven elements, respectively, pictured in Figure 6.36.

     The merge is performed essentially by adding the two queues together. Let H_3 be the new binomial queue. Since H_1 has no binomial tree of height 0 and H_2 does, we can just use the binomial tree of height 0 in H_2 as part of H_3. Next, we add binomial trees of height 1. Since both H_1 and H_2 have binomial trees of height 1, we merge them by making the larger root a subtree of the smaller, creating a binomial tree of height 2, shown in Figure 6.37. Thus, H_3 will not have a binomial tree of height 1. There are now three binomial trees of height 2, namely, the original trees of H_1 and H_2 plus the tree formed by the previous step. We keep one binomial tree of height 2 in H_3 and merge the other two, creating a binomial tree of

Figure 6.35   Binomial queue H_1 with six elements

H_1:

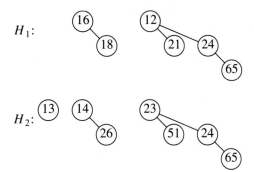

Figure 6.36   Two binomial queues H_1 and H_2

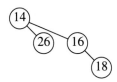

Figure 6.37   Merge of the two B_1 trees in H_1 and H_2

height 3. Since H_1 and H_2 have no trees of height 3, this tree becomes part of H_3, and we are finished. The resulting binomial queue is shown in Figure 6.38.

Since merging two binomial trees takes constant time with almost any reasonable implementation, and there are $O(\log n)$ binomial trees, the merge takes $O(\log n)$ time in the worst case. To make this operation efficient, we need to keep the trees in the binomial queue sorted by height, which is certainly a simple thing to do.

Insertion is just a special case of merging, since we merely create a one-node tree and perform a merge. The worst-case time of this operation is likewise $O(\log n)$. More precisely, if the priority queue into which the element is being inserted has the property that the smallest nonexistent binomial tree is B_i, the running time is proportional to $i + 1$. For example, H_3 (Figure 6.38) is missing a binomial tree of height 1, so the insertion will terminate in two steps. Since each tree in a binomial queue is present with probability $\frac{1}{2}$, it follows that we expect an insertion to terminate in two steps, so the average time is constant. Furthermore, an easy analysis will show that performing n *Insert*s on an initially empty binomial queue will take $O(n)$ worst-case time. Indeed, it is possible to do this operation using only $n - 1$ comparisons; we leave this as an exercise.

Figure 6.38   Binomial queue H_3: the result of merging H_1 and H_2

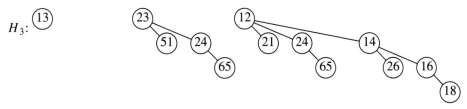

As an example, we show in Figures 6.39 through 6.45 the binomial queues that are formed by inserting 1 through 7 in order. Inserting 4 shows off a bad case. We merge 4 with B_0, obtaining a new tree of height 1. We then merge this tree with B_1, obtaining a tree of height 2, which is the new priority queue. We count this as three steps (two tree merges plus the stopping case). The next insertion after 7 is inserted is another bad case and would require three tree merges.

A *Delete_Min* can be performed by first finding the binomial tree with the smallest root. Let this tree be B_k, and let the original priority queue be H. We remove the binomial tree B_k from the forest of trees in H, forming the new binomial queue H'. We also remove the root of B_k, creating binomial trees $B_0, B_1, \ldots, B_{k-1}$, which collectively form priority queue H''. We finish the operation by merging H' and H''.

Figure 6.39   After 1 is inserted

Figure 6.40   After 2 is inserted

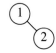

Figure 6.41   After 3 is inserted

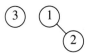

Figure 6.42   After 4 is inserted

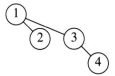

Figure 6.43   After 5 is inserted

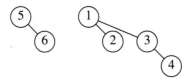

Figure 6.44   After 6 is inserted

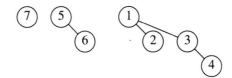

Figure 6.45   After 7 is inserted

As an example, suppose we perform a *Delete_Min* on H_3, which is shown again in Figure 6.46. The minimum root is 12, so we obtain the two priority queues H' and H'' in Figure 6.47 and Figure 6.48. The binomial queue that results from merging H' and H'' is the final answer and is shown in Figure 6.49.

For the analysis, note first that the *Delete_Min* operation breaks the original binomial queue into two. It takes $O(\log n)$ time to find the tree containing the

Figure 6.46   Binomial queue H_3

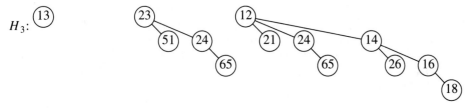

Figure 6.47   Binomial queue H', containing all the binomial trees in H_3 except B_3

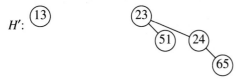

Figure 6.48   Binomial queue H'': B_3 with 12 removed

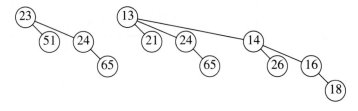

Figure 6.49 Result of *Delete_Min*(H_3)

minimum element and to create the queues H' and H''. Merging these two queues takes $O(\log n)$ time, so the entire *Delete_Min* operation takes $O(\log n)$ time.

6.8.3. Implementation of Binomial Queues

The *Delete_Min* operation requires the ability to find all the subtrees of the root quickly, so the standard representation of general trees is required: The children of each node are kept in a linked list, and each node has a pointer to its first child (if any). This operation also requires that the children be ordered by the size of their subtrees, in essentially the same way as we have been drawing them. The reason for this is that when a *Delete_Min* is performed, the children will form the binomial queue H''.

We also need to make sure that it is easy to merge two trees. Two binomial trees can be merged only if they have the same size, so if this is to be done efficiently, the size of the tree must be stored in the root. Also, when two trees are merged, one of the trees is added as a child to the other. Since this new tree will be the last child (as it will be the largest subtree), we must be able to keep track of the last child of each node efficiently. Only then will we be able to merge two binomial trees, and thus two binomial queues, efficiently. One way to do this is to use a circular doubly linked list. In this list, the left sibling of the first child will be the last child. The right sibling of the last child could be defined as the first child, but it might be easier just to define it as *NULL*. This makes it easy to test whether the child we are pointing to is the last.

To summarize, then, each node in a binomial tree will contain the data, first child, left and right sibling, and the number of children (which we will call the *rank*). Since a binomial queue is just a list of trees, we can use a pointer to the smallest tree as the reference to the data structure.

Figure 6.51 shows how the binomial queue in Figure 6.50 is represented. Figure 6.52 shows the class specifications for a node in the binomial tree and for the whole queue.

Figure 6.50 Binomial queue H_3 drawn as a forest

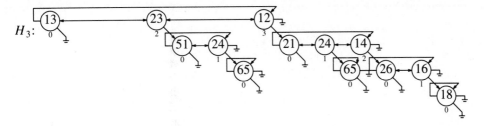

Figure 6.51 Representation of binomial queue H_3

```
/* 1*/   template <class Etype>
/* 2*/   class Binom_Node
/* 3*/   {
/* 4*/      private:
/* 5*/        Etype Element;
/* 6*/        Binom_Node *L_Sib;          // Left sibling.
/* 7*/        Binom_Node *R_Sib;          // Right sibling.
/* 8*/        Binom_Node *F_Child;        // First child.
/* 9*/        unsigned int Rank;

/*10*/        friend class Binom_Heap<Etype>;

/*11*/        Binom_Node( Etype E = 0, Binom_Node *L = NULL,
/*12*/            Binom_Node *R = NULL, Binom_Node *F = NULL,
/*13*/            unsigned int Ra = 0 ) : Element( E ), L_Sib( L ),
/*14*/            R_Sib( R ), F_Child( F ), Rank( Ra ) { }
/*15*/   };


/* 1*/   template <class Etype>
/* 2*/   class Binom_Heap
/* 3*/   {
/* 4*/      private:
/* 5*/        // Basic routines for binom_node.

/* 6*/        Binom_Node<Etype> *Merge_Tree(
/* 7*/                Binom_Node<Etype> *T1,
/* 8*/                Binom_Node<Etype> *T2 );
/* 9*/        Binom_Node<Etype> *Merge(
/*10*/                Binom_Node<Etype> *H1,
/*11*/                Binom_Node<Etype> *H2 );
/*12*/        void Extract( Binom_Node<Etype> * & T1,
/*13*/                Binom_Node<Etype> * & H1 );
```

Figure 6.52 Binomial queue class specifications

```
/*14*/        void Destroy( Binom_Node<Etype> *T );
/*15*/        Binom_Node<Etype> *Copy(
/*16*/            const Binom_Node<Etype> *T );
/*17*/        void Swap( Binom_Node<Etype> * & A,
/*18*/            Binom_Node<Etype> * & B );

/*19*/        Binom_Node<Etype> *Root;

/*20*/    public:
/*21*/        // Constructors.
/*22*/        Binom_Heap( unsigned int Initial_Size = 0 ) : Root( NULL ) { }
/*23*/        Binom_Heap( Binom_Heap & Value )
/*24*/            { Warn( "Heap passed by value" ); operator=( Value ); }

/*25*/        // Destructor.
/*26*/        ~Binom_Heap( ) { Destroy( Root ); }

/*27*/        // Operator.
/*28*/        const Binom_Heap & operator = ( const Binom_Heap & Value );

/*29*/        // Member functions.
/*30*/        void Make_Empty( ) { Destroy( Root ); Root = NULL; }
/*31*/        int Is_Empty( ) const    { return Root == NULL; }
/*32*/        void Insert( const Etype & X );
/*33*/        Etype Delete_Min( );
/*34*/        Etype Find_Min( ) const;
/*35*/        void Merge( Binom_Heap & Value );
/*36*/    };
```

Figure 6.52 *(Continued)*

In order to merge two binomial queues, we need a routine to merge two binomial trees of the same size. Figure 6.53 shows how the pointers change when two binomial trees are merged. First, the root of the new tree gains a child, so we must update its rank. We then need to change several pointers in order to splice one tree into the list of children of the root of the other tree. The code to do this is simple and shown in Figure 6.54.

The routine to merge two binomial queues is relatively simple. We use recursion to keep the code size small; a nonrecursive procedure will give better performance

Figure 6.53 Merging two binomial trees

```
/* 1*/  template <class Etype>
/* 2*/  Binom_Node<Etype>*
/* 3*/  Binom_Heap<Etype>::
/* 4*/  Merge_Tree( Binom_Node<Etype> *T1, Binom_Node<Etype> *T2 )
/* 5*/  {
/* 6*/      if( T1->Element > T2->Element )
/* 7*/          return Merge_Tree( T2, T1 );
/* 8*/      if( T1->Rank++ == 0 )
/* 9*/          T1->F_Child = T2;
/*10*/      else
/*11*/      {
/*12*/          T2->L_Sib = T1->F_Child->L_Sib;
/*13*/          T2->L_Sib->R_Sib = T2;
/*14*/          T1->F_Child->L_Sib = T2;
/*15*/      }
/*16*/      return T1;
/*17*/  }
```

Figure 6.54 Routine to merge two equal-sized binomial
trees

and is left as Exercise 6.32. We assume the routine *Extract(T,H)*, which removes
the first tree from the priority queue H, placing the tree in T. Suppose the smallest
binomial tree is contained in H_1, but not in H_2. Then, to merge H_1, we remove
the first tree in H_1 and add to it the result of merging the rest of H_1 with H_2. If
the smallest tree is contained in both H_1 and H_2, then we remove both trees and
merge them, obtaining a one-tree binomial queue H'. We then merge the remainder
of H_1 and H_2, and merge this result with H'. This strategy is implemented in Figure
6.55. The other routines are straightforward implementations, which we leave as
exercises.

Figure 6.55 Routine to merge two priority queues

```
/* 1*/  template <class Etype>
/* 2*/  Binom_Node<Etype>*
/* 3*/  Binom_Heap<Etype>::
/* 4*/  Merge( Binom_Node<Etype> *H1, Binom_Node<Etype> *H2 )
/* 5*/  {
/* 6*/      Binom_Node<Etype> *H3, *T1, *T2, *T3;

/* 7*/      if( H1 == NULL )
/* 8*/          return H2;
/* 9*/      if( H2 == NULL )
/*10*/          return H1;
/*11*/      if( H1->Rank < H2->Rank )
```

```
/*12*/        {
/*13*/              Extract( T1, H1 );
/*14*/              H3 = Merge( H1, H2 );
/*15*/              T1->L_Sib = H3->L_Sib;
/*16*/              H3->L_Sib->R_Sib = NULL;
/*17*/              T1->R_Sib = H3;
/*18*/              H3->L_Sib = T1;
/*19*/              return T1;
/*20*/        }
/*21*/        if( H2->Rank < H1->Rank )
/*22*/              return Merge( H2, H1 );

/*23*/        // Otherwise, first two trees have same rank.
/*24*/        Extract( T1, H1 );
/*25*/        Extract( T2, H2 );
/*26*/        H3 = Merge( H1, H2 );
/*27*/        T3 = Merge_Tree( T1, T2 );
/*28*/        return Merge( T3, H3 );
/*29*/  }
```

Figure 6.55   *(Continued)*

We can extend binomial queues to support some of the nonstandard operations that binary heaps allow, such as *Decrease_Key* and *Remove*, when the position of the affected element is known. A *Decrease_Key* is a *percolate up*, which can be performed in $O(\log n)$ time if we add a field to each node pointing to its parent. An arbitrary *Remove* can be performed by a combination of *Decrease_Key* and *Delete_Min* in $O(\log n)$ time.

Summary

In this chapter we have seen various implementations and uses of the priority queue ADT. The standard binary heap implementation is elegant because of its simplicity and speed. It requires no pointers and only a constant amount of extra space, yet supports the priority queue operations efficiently.

We considered the additional *Merge* operation and developed three implementations, each of which is unique in its own way. The leftist heap is a wonderful example of the power of recursion. The skew heap represents a remarkable data structure because of the lack of balance criteria. Its analysis, which we will perform in Chapter 11, is interesting in its own right. The binomial queue shows how a simple idea can be used to achieve a good time bound.

We have also seen several uses of priority queues, ranging from operating systems scheduling to simulation. We will see their use again in Chapters 7, 9, and 10.

Exercises

6.1 Suppose that we replace the *Delete_Min* routine with *Find_Min*. Can both *Insert* and *Find_Min* be implemented in constant time?

6.2 a. Show the result of inserting 10, 12, 1, 14, 6, 5, 8, 15, 3, 9, 7, 4, 11, 13, and 2, one at a time, into an initially empty binary heap.

  b. Show the result of using the linear-time algorithm to build a binary heap using the same input.

6.3 Show the result of performing three *Delete_Min* operations in the heap of the previous exercise.

6.4 Write the routines to do a *Percolate_Up* and a *Percolate_Down* in a binary heap.

6.5 Write and test a program that performs the operations *Insert, Delete_Min, Build_Heap, Find_Min, Decrease_Key, Remove,* and *Increase_Key* in a binary heap.

6.6 How many nodes are in the large heap in Figure 6.13?

6.7 a. Prove that for binary heaps, *Build_Heap* does at most $2n - 2$ comparisons between elements.

  b. Show that a heap of 8 elements can be constructed in 8 comparisons between heap elements.

  **c. Give an algorithm to build a binary heap in $\frac{13}{8}n + O(\log n)$ element comparisons.

**6.8 Show that the expected depth of the kth smallest element in a large complete heap (you may assume $n = 2^k - 1$) is bounded by $\log k$.

6.9 *a. Give an algorithm to find all nodes less than some value, x, in a binary heap. Your algorithm should run in $O(K)$, where K is the number of nodes output.

  b. Does your algorithm extend to any of the other heap structures discussed in this chapter?

**6.10 Propose an algorithm to insert m nodes into a binary heap on n elements in $O(m + \log n)$ time. Prove your time bound.

6.11 Write a program to take n elements and do the following:

  a. Insert them into a heap one by one.

  b. Build a heap in linear time.

  Compare the running time of both algorithms for sorted, reverse-ordered, and random inputs.

6.12 Each *Delete_Min* operation uses $2 \log n$ comparisons in the worst case.

  *a. Propose a scheme so that the *Delete_Min* operation uses only $\log n + \log \log n + O(1)$ comparisons between elements. This need not imply less data movement.

    **b. Extend your scheme in part (a) so that only $\log n + \log\log\log n + O(1)$ comparisons are performed.

    **c. How far can you take this idea?

    d. Do the savings in comparisons compensate for the increased complexity of your algorithm?

6.13 If a d-heap is stored as an array, for an entry located in position i, where are the parents and children?

6.14 Suppose we need to perform m *Percolate_Up*s and n *Delete_Min*s on a d-heap that initially has n elements.

    a. What is the total running time of all operations in terms of m, n, and d?

    b. If $d = 2$, what is the running time of all heap operations?

    c. If $d = \Theta(n)$, what is the total running time?

    *d. What choice of d minimizes the total running time?

6.15 A *min-max heap* is a data structure that supports both *Delete_Min* and *Delete_Max* in $O(\log n)$ per operation. The structure is identical to a binary heap, but the heap order property is that for any node, X, at even depth, the key stored at X is the smallest in its subtree, and for any node X at odd depth, the key stored at X is the largest in its subtree. See Figure 6.56.

    a. How do we find the minimum and maximum elements?

    *b. Give an algorithm to insert a new node into the min-max heap.

    *c. Give an algorithm to perform *Delete_Min* and *Delete_Max*.

    *d. Can you build a min-max heap in linear time?

    **e. Suppose we would like to support *Delete_Min*, *Delete_Max*, and *Merge*. Propose a data structure to support all operations in $O(\log n)$ time using at most two pointers per item.

Figure 6.56   Min-max heap

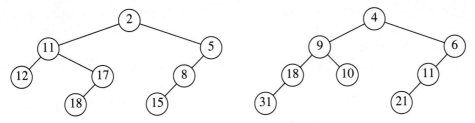

Figure 6.57

6.16 Merge the two leftist heaps in Figure 6.57.

6.17 Show the result of inserting keys 1 to 15 in order into an initially empty leftist heap.

6.18 Prove or disprove: A perfectly balanced tree forms if keys 1 to $2^k - 1$ are inserted in order into an initially empty leftist heap.

6.19 Give an example of input that generates the best leftist heap.

6.20 a. Can leftist heaps efficiently support *Decrease_Key?*

     b. What changes, if any (if possible), are required to do this?

6.21 One way to delete nodes from a known position in a leftist heap is to use a lazy strategy. To delete a node, merely mark it deleted. When a *Find_Min* or *Delete_Min* is performed, there is a potential problem if the root is marked deleted because the node then has to be actually deleted and the real minimum needs to be found, which may involve deleting other marked nodes. In this strategy, *Delete*s cost one unit, but the cost of a *Delete_Min* or *Find_Min* depends on the number of nodes that are marked deleted. Suppose that after a *Delete_Min* or *Find_Min* there are k fewer marked nodes than before the operation.

  *a. Show how to perform the *Delete_Min* in $O(k \log n)$ time.

  **b. Propose an implementation, with an analysis to show that the time to perform the *Delete_Min* is $O(k \log(2n/k))$.

6.22 We can perform *Build_Heap* in linear time for leftist heaps by considering each element as a one-node leftist heap, placing all these heaps on a queue, and performing the following step: Until only one heap is on the queue, dequeue two heaps, merge them, and enqueue the result.

     a. Prove that this algorithm is $O(n)$ in the worst case.

     b. Why might this algorithm be preferable to the algorithm described in the text?

6.23 Merge the two skew heaps in Figure 6.57.

6.24 Show the result of inserting keys 1 to 15 in order into a skew heap.

6.25 Prove or disprove: A perfectly balanced tree forms if the keys 1 to $2^k - 1$ are inserted in order into an initially empty skew heap.

6.26 A skew heap of n elements can be built using the standard binary heap algorithm. Can we use the same merging strategy described in Exercise 6.22 for skew heaps to get an $O(n)$ running time?

6.27 Prove that a binomial tree B_k has binomial trees $B_0, B_1, \ldots, B_{k-1}$ as children of the root.

6.28 Prove that a binomial tree of height k has $\binom{k}{d}$ nodes at depth d.

6.29 Merge the two binomial queues in Figure 6.58.

6.30 a. Show that n *Inserts* into an initially empty binomial queue takes $O(n)$ time in the worst case.

b. Give an algorithm to build a binomial queue of n elements, using at most $n - 1$ comparisons between elements.

*6.31 Propose an algorithm to insert m nodes into a binomial queue of n elements in $O(m + \log n)$ worst-case time. Prove your bound.

6.32 Write nonrecursive routines to perform *Merge, Insert,* and *Delete_Min* using binomial queues.

**6.33 Suppose we extend binomial queues to allow at most two trees of the same height per structure. Can we obtain $O(1)$ worst-case time for insertion while retaining $O(\log n)$ for the other operations?

6.34 Suppose you have a number of boxes, each of which can hold total weight C and items $i_1, i_2, i_3, \ldots, i_n$, which weigh $w_1, w_2, w_3, \ldots, w_n$. The object is to pack all the items without placing more weight in any box than its capacity and using as few boxes as possible. For instance, if $C = 5$, and the items have weights 2, 2, 3, 3, then we can solve the problem with two boxes.

In general, this problem is very hard, and no efficient solution is known. Write programs to implement efficiently the following approximation strategies:

*a. Place the weight in the first box for which it fits (creating a new box if there is no box with enough room). (This strategy and all that follow would give three boxes, which is suboptimal.)

Figure 6.58

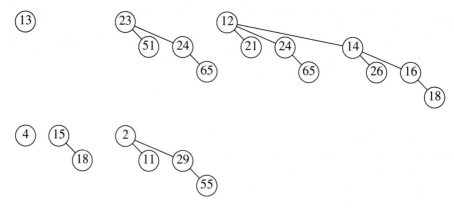

b. Place the weight in the box with the most room for it.

*c. Place the weight in the most filled box that can accept it without overflowing.

**d. Are any of these strategies enhanced by presorting the items by weight?

6.35 Suppose we want to add the *Decrease_All_Keys(Δ)* operation to the heap repertoire. The result of this operation is that all keys in the heap have their value decreased by an amount Δ. For the heap implementation of your choice, explain the necessary modifications so that all other operations retain their running times and *Decrease_All_Keys* runs in $O(1)$.

6.36 Which of the two selection algorithms has the better time bound?

References

The binary heap was first described in [24]. The linear-time algorithm for its construction is from [11].

The first description of *d*-heaps was in [16]. Leftist heaps were invented by Crane [7] and described in Knuth [17]. Skew heaps were developed by Sleator and Tarjan [19]. Binomial queues were invented by Vuillemin [23]; Brown provided a detailed analysis and empirical study showing that they perform well in practice [2], if carefully implemented.

Exercise 6.7 (b–c) is taken from [14]. A method for constructing binary heaps that uses about $1.52n$ comparisons on average is described in [18]. Lazy deletion in leftist heaps (Exercise 6.21) is from [6]. A solution to Exercise 6.33 can be found in [5].

Min-max heaps (Exercise 6.15) were originally described in [1]. A more efficient implementation of the operations is given in [15] and [20]. An alternate representation for double ended priority queues is the *deap*. Details can be found in [3] and [4]. A solution to 6.15(e) is given in [8].

A generalization of the double-ended priority queue is the multidimensional priority queue, in which items contain several keys, any one of which can be used to direct a *Delete_Min*. The first implicit multidimensional priority queue was the *interval heap*, by van Leeuwen and Wood [22]. An alternative, which is more suitable for smaller dimensions, is provided in [9].

A theoretically interesting priority queue representation is the *Fibonacci heap* [13], which we will describe in Chapter 11. The Fibonacci heap allows all operations to be performed in $O(1)$ amortized time except for deletions, which are $O(\log n)$. *Relaxed heaps* [10] achieve identical bounds in the worst case. Another interesting implementation is the *pairing heap* [12]. Finally, a priority queue that works when the data consists of small integers is described in [21].

1. M. D. Atkinson, J. R. Sack, N. Santoro, and T. Strothotte, "Min-Max Heaps and Generalized Priority Queues," *Communications of the ACM* 29 (1986), 996–1000.
2. M. R. Brown, "Implementation and Analysis of Binomial Queue Algorithms," *SIAM Journal on Computing* 7 (1978), 298–319.
3. S. Carlsson, "The Deap—A Double-ended Heap to Implement Double-ended Priority Queues," *Information Processing Letters* 26 (1987), 33–36.

4. S. Carlsson, J. Chen, and T. Strothotte, "A Note on the Construction of the Data Structure 'Deap'," *Information Processing Letters* 31 (1989), 315–317.

5. S. Carlsson, J. I. Munro, and P. V. Poblete, "An Implicit Binomial Queue with Constant Insertion Time," *Proceedings of First Scandinavian Workshop on Algorithm Theory*, 1988, 1–13.

6. D. Cheriton and R. E. Tarjan, "Finding Minimum Spanning Trees," *SIAM Journal on Computing* 5 (1976), 724–742.

7. C. A. Crane, "Linear Lists and Priority Queues as Balanced Binary Trees," *Technical Report STAN-CS-72-259*, Computer Science Department, Stanford University, Stanford, Calif., 1972.

8. Y. Ding and M. A. Weiss, "The Relaxed Min-Max Heap: A Mergeable Double-Ended Priority Queue," *Acta Informatica* 30 (1993), 215–231.

9. Y. Ding and M. A. Weiss, "The *K-D* Heap: An Efficient Multi-Dimensional Priority Queue," *Proceedings of the Third Workshop on Algorithms and Data Structures* (1993), 302–313.

10. J. R. Driscoll, H. N. Gabow, R. Shrairman, and R. E. Tarjan, "Relaxed Heaps: An Alternative to Fibonacci Heaps with Applications to Parallel Computation," *Communications of the ACM* 31 (1988), 1343–1354.

11. R. W. Floyd, "Algorithm 245: Treesort 3," *Communications of the ACM* 7 (1964), 701.

12. M. L. Fredman, R. Sedgewick, D. D. Sleator, and R. E. Tarjan, "The Pairing Heap: A New Form of Self-adjusting Heap," *Algorithmica* 1 (1986), 111–129.

13. M. L. Fredman and R. E. Tarjan, "Fibonacci Heaps and Their Uses in Improved Network Optimization Algorithms," *Journal of the ACM* 34 (1987), 596–615.

14. G. H. Gonnet and J. I. Munro, "Heaps on Heaps," *SIAM Journal on Computing* 15 (1986), 964–971.

15. A. Hasham and J. R. Sack, "Bounds for Min-max Heaps," *BIT* 27 (1987), 315–323.

16. D. B. Johnson, "Priority Queues with Update and Finding Minimum Spanning Trees," *Information Processing Letters* 4 (1975), 53–57.

17. D. E. Knuth, *The Art of Computer Programming, Vol 3: Sorting and Searching,* second printing, Addison-Wesley, Reading, Mass. 1975.

18. C. J. H. McDiarmid and B. A. Reed, "Building Heaps Fast," *Journal of Algorithms* 10 (1989), 352–365.

19. D. D. Sleator and R. E. Tarjan, "Self-adjusting Heaps," *SIAM Journal on Computing* 15 (1986), 52–69.

20. T. Strothotte, P. Eriksson, and S. Vallner, "A Note on Constructing Min-max Heaps," *BIT* 29 (1989), 251–256.

21. P. van Emde Boas, R. Kaas, E. Zijlstra, "Design and Implementation of an Efficient Priority Queue," *Mathematical Systems Theory* 10 (1977), 99–127.

22. J. van Leeuwen and D. Wood, "Interval Heaps," *The Computer Journal* 36 (1993), 209–216.

23. J. Vuillemin, "A Data Structure for Manipulating Priority Queues," *Communications of the ACM* 21 (1978), 309–314.

24. J. W. J. Williams, "Algorithm 232: Heapsort," *Communications of the ACM* 7 (1964), 347–348.

CHAPTER 7

Sorting

In this chapter we discuss the problem of sorting an array of elements. To simplify matters, we will assume in our examples that the array contains only integers, although our code will once again allow arbitrary elements. For most of this chapter, we will also assume that the entire sort can be done in main memory so that the number of elements is relatively small (less than a million). Sorts that cannot be performed in main memory and must be done on disk or tape are also quite important. This type of sorting, known as external sorting, will be discussed at the end of the chapter.

Our investigation of internal sorting will show that

- There are several easy algorithms, such as insertion sort, to sort in $O(n^2)$.
- There is an algorithm, Shellsort, that is very simple to code, runs in $o(n^2)$, and is efficient in practice.
- There are slightly more complicated $O(n \log n)$ sorting algorithms.
- Any general-purpose sorting algorithm requires $\Omega(n \log n)$ comparisons.

The rest of this chapter will describe and analyze the various sorting algorithms. These algorithms contain interesting and important ideas for code optimization as well as algorithm design. Sorting is also an example in which the analysis can be performed precisely. Be forewarned that where appropriate, we will do as much analysis as possible.

7.1. Preliminaries

The algorithms we describe will all be exchangeable. Each will be passed an array containing the elements and an integer containing the number of elements.

We will assume that N, the number of elements passed to our sorting routines, has already been checked and is legal. For some of the sorting routines, it will be convenient to place a sentinel in position 0, so we assume that the array ranges from 0 to N. The actual data will start at position 1 for all sorts.

We require the existence of the "<" and ">" operators, which can be used to place a consistent ordering on the input. Besides the assignment operator, these are the only operations allowed on the input data. Sorting under these conditions is known as *comparison-based* sorting.

7.2. Insertion Sort

7.2.1. The Algorithm

One of the simplest sorting algorithms is the *insertion sort*. Insertion sort consists of $n - 1$ *passes*. For pass $P = 2$ through n, insertion sort ensures that the elements in positions 1 through P are in sorted order. Insertion sort makes use of the fact that elements in positions 1 through $P - 1$ are already known to be in sorted order. Figure 7.1 shows a sample file after each pass of insertion sort.

Figure 7.1 shows the general strategy. In pass P, we move the Pth element left until its correct place is found among the first P elements. The code in Figure 7.2 implements this strategy. Lines 9 through 12 implement that data movement without the explicit use of swaps. The element in position P is saved in *Tmp,* and all larger elements (prior to position P) are moved one spot to the right. Then *Tmp* is placed in the correct spot. This is the same technique that was used in the implementation of binary heaps.

7.2.2. Analysis of Insertion Sort

Because of the nested loops, each of which can take n iterations, insertion sort is $O(n^2)$. Furthermore, this bound is tight because input in reverse order can actually achieve this bound. A precise calculation shows that the tests at line 10 can be executed at most P times for each value of P. Summing over all P gives a total of

$$\sum_{P=2}^{n} P = 2 + 3 + 4 + \cdots + n = \Theta(n^2)$$

On the other hand, if the input is presorted, the running time is $O(n)$ because the test at the top of the inner *for* loop always fails immediately. Indeed, if the input is almost sorted (this term will be more rigorously defined in the next section), insertion sort will run quickly. Because of this wide variation, it is worth analyzing the average-case behavior of this algorithm. It turns out that the average case is $\Theta(n^2)$ for insertion sort as well as for a variety of other sorting algorithms, as the next section shows.

Figure 7.1 Insertion sort after each pass

Original	34	8	64	51	32	21	Positions Moved
After $p = 2$	8	34	64	51	32	21	1
After $p = 3$	8	34	64	51	32	21	0
After $p = 4$	8	34	51	64	32	21	1
After $p = 5$	8	32	34	51	64	21	3
After $p = 6$	8	21	32	34	51	64	4

```
/* 1*/    template <class Etype>
/* 2*/    void
/* 3*/    Insertion_Sort( Etype A[], const unsigned int N )
/* 4*/    {
/* 5*/        Etype Tmp;

/* 6*/        A[ 0 ] = Min_Val();
/* 7*/        for( int P = 2; P <= N; P++ )
/* 8*/        {
/* 9*/            Tmp = A[ P ];
/*10*/            for( int j = P; Tmp < A[ j - 1 ]; j-- )
/*11*/                A[ j ] = A[ j - 1 ];
/*12*/            A[ j ] = Tmp;
/*13*/        }
/*14*/    }
```

Figure 7.2 Insertion sort routine

7.3. A Lower Bound for Simple Sorting Algorithms

An *inversion* in an array of numbers is any ordered pair (i, j) having the property that $i < j$ but $a[i] > a[j]$. In the example of the last section, the input list 34, 8, 64, 51, 32, 21 had nine inversions, namely (34,8), (34,32), (34,21), (64,51), (64,32), (64,21), (51,32), (51,21), and (32,21). Notice that this is exactly the number of swaps that needed to be (implicitly) performed by insertion sort. This is always the case because swapping two adjacent elements that are out of place removes exactly one inversion, and a sorted file has no inversions. Since there is $O(n)$ other work involved in the algorithm, the running time of insertion sort is $O(I + n)$, where I is the number of inversions in the original file. Thus, insertion sort runs in linear time if the number of inversions is $O(n)$.

We can compute precise bounds on the average running time of insertion sort by computing the average number of inversions in a permutation. As usual, defining *average* is a difficult proposition. We will assume that there are no duplicate elements (if we allow duplicates, it is not even clear what the average number of duplicates is). Under this assumption, we can also assume that the input is some permutation of the first n integers (since only relative ordering is important) and that all are equally likely. Under these assumptions, we have the following theorem:

THEOREM 7.1.

The average number of inversions in an array of n distinct numbers is $n(n - 1)/4$.

PROOF:
For any list, L, of numbers, consider L_r, the list in reverse order. The reverse list of the example is 21, 32, 51, 64, 8, 34. Consider any pair of two numbers in the list (x, y), with $y > x$. Clearly, in exactly one of L and L_r this ordered pair

represents an inversion. The total number of these pairs in a list L and its reverse L_r is $n(n-1)/2$. Thus, an average list has half this amount, or $n(n-1)/4$ inversions.

This theorem implies that insertion sort is quadratic on average. It also provides a very strong lower bound about any algorithm that only exchanges adjacent elements.

THEOREM 7.2.

Any algorithm that sorts by exchanging adjacent elements requires $\Omega(n^2)$ time on average.

PROOF:

The average number of inversions is initially $n(n-1)/4 = \Omega(n^2)$. Each swap removes only one inversion, so $\Omega(n^2)$ swaps are required.

This is an example of a lower-bound proof. It is valid not only for insertion sort, which performs adjacent exchanges implicitly, but also for other simple algorithms such as bubble sort and selection sort, which we will not describe here. In fact, it is valid over an entire *class* of sorting algorithms, including those undiscovered, that perform only adjacent exchanges. Because of this, this proof cannot be confirmed empirically. Although this lower-bound proof is rather simple, in general proving lower bounds is much more complicated than proving upper bounds and in some cases resembles voodoo.

This lower bound shows us that in order for a sorting algorithm to run in subquadratic, or $o(n^2)$, time, it must do comparisons and, in particular, exchanges between elements that are far apart. A sorting algorithm makes progress by eliminating inversions, and to run efficiently, it must eliminate more than just one inversion per exchange.

7.4. Shellsort

Shellsort, named after its inventor, Donald Shell, was one of the first algorithms to break the quadratic time barrier, although it was not until several years after its initial discovery that a subquadratic time bound was proven. As suggested in the previous section, it works by comparing elements that are distant; the distance between comparisons decreases as the algorithm runs until the last phase, in which adjacent elements are compared. For this reason, Shellsort is sometimes referred to as *diminishing increment* sort.

Shellsort uses a sequence, $h_1, h_2, \ldots, h_t$, called the *increment sequence*. Any increment sequence will do as long as $h_1 = 1$, but obviously some choices are better than others (we will discuss that question later). After a *phase,* using some increment h_k, for every i, we have $a[i] \le a[i + h_k]$ (where this makes sense); all elements spaced h_k apart are sorted. The file is then said to be h_k-*sorted.* For example, Figure 7.3 shows an array after several phases of Shellsort. An important property of Shellsort (which we state without proof) is that an h_k-sorted file that is

Original	81	94	11	96	12	35	17	95	28	58	41	75	15
After 5-sort	35	17	11	28	12	41	75	15	96	58	81	94	95
After 3-sort	28	12	11	35	15	41	58	17	94	75	81	96	95
After 1-sort	11	12	15	17	28	35	41	58	75	81	94	95	96

Figure 7.3   Shellsort after each pass

then h_{k-1}-sorted remains h_k-sorted. If this were not the case, the algorithm would likely be of little value, since work done by early phases would be undone by later phases.

The general strategy to h_k-sort is for each position, i, in $h_k + 1, h_k + 2, \ldots, n$, place the element in the correct spot among $i, i - h_k, i - 2h_k$, and so on. Although this does not affect the implementation, a careful examination shows that the action of an h_k-sort is to perform an insertion sort on h_k independent subarrays. This observation will be important when we analyze the running time of Shellsort.

A popular (but poor) choice for the increment sequence is to use the sequence suggested by Shell: $h_t = \lfloor n/2 \rfloor$, and $h_k = \lfloor h_{k+1}/2 \rfloor$. Figure 7.4 contains a program that implements Shellsort using this sequence. We shall see later that there are increment sequences that give a significant improvement in the algorithm's running time. The program in Figure 7.4 avoids the explicit use of swaps in the same manner as our implementation of insertion sort.

Figure 7.4   Shellsort routine using Shell's increments (better
increments are possible)

```
/* 1*/    template <class Etype>
/* 2*/    void
/* 3*/    Shell_Sort( Etype A[], const unsigned int N )
/* 4*/    {
/* 5*/        Etype Tmp;

/* 6*/        for( int Increment = N / 2; Increment > 0; Increment /= 2 )
/* 7*/            for( int i = Increment + 1; i <= N; i++ )
/* 8*/            {
/* 9*/                Tmp = A[ i ];
/*10*/                for( int j = i; j > Increment; j -= Increment )
/*11*/                    if( Tmp < A[ j - Increment ] )
/*12*/                        A[ j ] = A[ j - Increment ];
/*13*/                    else
/*14*/                        break;
/*15*/                A[ j ] = Tmp;
/*16*/            }
/*17*/    }
```

7.4.1. Worst-Case Analysis of Shellsort

Although Shellsort is simple to code, the analysis of its running time is quite another story. The running time of Shellsort depends on the choice of increment sequence, and the proofs can be rather involved. The average-case analysis of Shellsort is a long-standing open problem except for the most trivial increment sequences. We will prove tight worst-case bounds for two particular increment sequences.

THEOREM 7.3.

The worst-case running time of Shellsort, using Shell's increments, is $\Theta(n^2)$.

PROOF:

The proof requires showing not only an upper bound on the worst-case running time but also showing that there exists some input that actually takes $\Omega(n^2)$ time to run. We prove the lower bound first, by constructing a bad case. First, we choose n to be a power of 2. This makes all the increments even except for the last increment, which is 1. Now, we will give as input an array, *Input_Data*, with the $n/2$ largest numbers in the even positions and the $n/2$ smallest numbers in the odd positions. As all the increments except the last are even, when we come to the last pass, the $n/2$ largest numbers are still all in even positions and the $n/2$ smallest numbers are still all in odd positions. The ith smallest number ($i \le n/2$) is thus in position $2i - 1$ before the beginning of the last pass. Restoring the ith element to its correct place requires moving it $i - 1$ spaces in the array. Thus, to merely place the $n/2$ smallest elements in the correct place requires at least $\sum_{i=1}^{n/2} i - 1 = \Omega(n^2)$ work. As an example, Figure 7.5 shows a bad (but not the worst) input when $n = 16$. The number of inversions remaining after the 2-sort is exactly $1 + 2 + 3 + 4 + 5 + 6 + 7 = 28$; thus, the last pass will take considerable time.

To finish the proof, we show the upper bound of $O(n^2)$. As we have observed before, a pass with increment h_k consists of h_k insertion sorts of about n/h_k elements. Since insertion sort is quadratic, the total cost of a pass is $O(h_k(n/h_k)^2) = O(n^2/h_k)$. Summing over all passes gives a total bound of $O(\sum_{i=1}^{t} n^2/h_i) = O(n^2 \sum_{i=1}^{t} 1/h_i)$. Because the increments form a geometric series with common ratio 2, and the largest term in the series is $h_1 = 1$, $\sum_{i=1}^{t} 1/h_i < 2$. Thus we obtain a total bound of $O(n^2)$.

The problem with Shell's increments is that pairs of increments are not necessarily relatively prime, and thus the smaller increment can have little effect. Hib-

Figure 7.5   Bad case for Shellsort with Shell's increments

Start	1	9	2	10	3	11	4	12	5	13	6	14	7	15	8	16
After 8-sort	1	9	2	10	3	11	4	12	5	13	6	14	7	15	8	16
After 4-sort	1	9	2	10	3	11	4	12	5	13	6	14	7	15	8	16
After 2-sort	1	9	2	10	3	11	4	12	5	13	6	14	7	15	8	16
After 1-sort	1	2	3	4	5	6	7	8	9	10	11	12	13	14	15	16

bard suggested a slightly different increment sequence, which gives better results in practice (and theoretically). His increments are of the form $1, 3, 7, \ldots,$ $2^k - 1$. Although these increments are almost identical, the key difference is that consecutive increments have no common factors. We now analyze the worst-case running time of Shellsort for this increment sequence. The proof is rather complicated.

THEOREM 7.4.

The worst-case running time of Shellsort using Hibbard's increments is $\Theta(n^{3/2})$.

PROOF:

We will prove only the upper bound and leave the proof of the lower bound as an exercise. The proof requires some well-known results from additive number theory. References to these results are provided at the end of the chapter.

For the upper bound, as before, we bound the running time of each pass and sum over all passes. For increments $h_k > n^{1/2}$, we will use the bound $O(n^2/h_k)$ from the previous theorem. Although this bound holds for the other increments, it is too large to be useful. Intuitively, we must take advantage of the fact that *this* increment sequence is *special*. What we need to show is that for any element a_p in position p, when it is time to perform an h_k-sort, there are only a few elements to the left of position p that are larger than a_p.

When we come to h_k-sort the input array, we know that it has already been h_{k+1}- and h_{k+2}-sorted. Prior to the h_k-sort, consider elements in positions p and $p - i, i < p$. If i is a multiple of h_{k+1} or h_{k+2}, then clearly $a[p-i] < a[p]$. We can say more, however. If i is expressible as a linear combination (in nonnegative integers) of h_{k+1} and h_{k+2}, then $a[p - i] < a[p]$. As an example, when we come to 3-sort, the array is already 7- and 15-sorted. 52 is expressible as a linear combination of 7 and 15 because $52 = 1 * 7 + 3 * 15$. Thus, $a[100]$ cannot be larger than $a[152]$ because $a[100] \le a[107] \le a[122] \le a[137] \le a[152]$.

Now, $h_{k+2} = 2h_{k+1} + 1$, so h_{k+1} and h_{k+2} cannot share a common factor. In this case, it is possible to show that all integers that are at least as large as $(h_{k+1} - 1)(h_{k+2} - 1) = 8h_k^2 + 4h_k$ can be expressed as a linear combination of h_{k+1} and h_{k+2} (see the reference at the end of the chapter).

This tells us that the *for* loop at line 10 can be executed at most $8h_k + 4 = O(h_k)$ times for each of the $n - h_k$ positions. This gives a bound of $O(nh_k)$ per pass.

Using the fact that about half the increments satisfy $h_k < \sqrt{n}$, and assuming that t is even, the total running time is then

$$O\left(\sum_{k=1}^{t/2} nh_k + \sum_{k=t/2+1}^{t} n^2/h_k\right) = O\left(n\sum_{k=1}^{t/2} h_k + n^2 \sum_{k=t/2+1}^{t} 1/h_k\right)$$

Because both sums are geometric series, and since $h_{t/2} = \Theta(\sqrt{n})$, this simplifies to

$$= O\left(nh_{t/2}\right) + O\left(\frac{n^2}{h_{t/2}}\right) = O(n^{3/2})$$

The average-case running time of Shellsort, using Hibbard's increments, is thought to be $O(n^{5/4})$, based on simulations, but nobody has been able to prove this. Pratt has shown that the $\Theta(n^{3/2})$ bound applies to a wide range of increment sequences. One such sequence is obtained by modifying Figure 7.4 to add one to *Increment* whenever it is nonzero and even.

Sedgewick has proposed several increment sequences that give an $O(n^{4/3})$ worst-case running time (also achievable). The average running time is well approximated by $O(n^{7/6})$ for these increment sequences. Empirical studies show that these sequences perform significantly better in practice than Hibbard's. The best of these is the sequence $\{1, 5, 19, 41, 109, \ldots\}$, in which the terms are either of the form $9 \cdot 4^i - 9 \cdot 2^i + 1$ or $4^i - 3 \cdot 2^i + 1$. This is most easily implemented by placing these values in an array. This increment sequence is the best known in practice, although there is a lingering possibility that some increment sequence might exist that could give a significant improvement in the running time of Shellsort.

There are several other results on Shellsort that (generally) require difficult theorems from number theory and combinatorics and are mainly of theoretical interest. Shellsort is a fine example of a very simple algorithm with an extremely complex analysis.

The performance of Shellsort is quite acceptable in practice, even for n in the tens of thousands. The simplicity of the code makes it the algorithm of choice for sorting up to moderately large input.

7.5. Heapsort

As mentioned in Chapter 6, priority queues can be used to sort in $O(n \log n)$ time. The algorithm based on this idea is known as *heapsort* and gives the best Big-Oh running time we have seen so far. In practice, however, it is slower than a version of Shellsort that uses Sedgewick's increment sequence.

Recall, from Chapter 6, that the basic strategy is to build a binary heap of n elements. This stage takes $O(n)$ time. We then perform n *Delete_Min* operations. The elements leave the heap smallest first, in sorted order. By recording these elements in a second array and then copying the array back, we sort n elements. Since each *Delete_Min* takes $O(\log n)$ time, the total running time is $O(n \log n)$.

The main problem with this algorithm is that it uses an extra array. Thus, the memory requirement is doubled. This could be a problem in some instances. Notice that the extra time spent copying the second array back to the first is only $O(n)$, so this is not likely to affect the running *time* significantly. The problem is space.

A clever way to avoid using a second array makes use of the fact that after each *Delete_Min*, the heap shrinks by 1. Thus, the cell that was last in the heap can be used to store the element that was just deleted. As an example, suppose we have a heap with six elements. The first *Delete_Min* produces a_1. Now the heap has only five elements, so we can place a_1 in position 6. The next *Delete_Min* produces a_2. Since the heap will now only have four elements, we can place a_2 in position 5.

Using this strategy, after the last *Delete_Min* the array will contain the elements in *decreasing* sorted order. If we want the elements in the more typical *increasing*

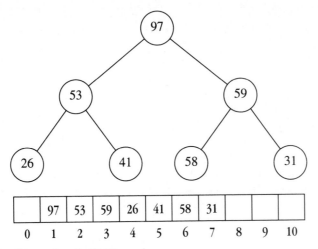

Figure 7.6 (*Max*)heap after *Build_Heap* phase

sorted order, we can change the ordering property so that the parent has a larger key than the child. Thus we have a (*max*)heap.

In our implementation, we will use a (*max*)heap, but avoid the actual ADT for the purposes of speed. As usual, everything is done in an array. The first step builds the heap in linear time. We then perform $n - 1$ *Delete_Max*es by swapping the last element in the heap with the first, decrementing the heap size, and percolating down. When the algorithm terminates, the array contains the elements in sorted order. For instance, consider the input sequence $31, 41, 59, 26, 53, 58, 97$. The resulting heap is shown in Figure 7.6.

Figure 7.7 shows the heap that results after the first *Delete_Max*. As the figures imply, the last element in the heap is 31; 97 has been placed in a part of the heap array that is technically no longer part of the heap. After 5 more *Delete_Max*

Figure 7.7 Heap after first *Delete_Max*

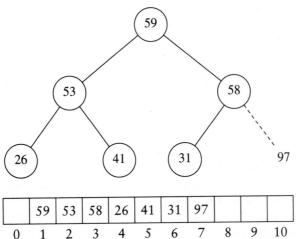

```
/* 1*/    template <class Etype>
/* 2*/    void
/* 3*/    Perc_Down( Etype A[], unsigned int i, const unsigned int N )
/* 4*/    {
/* 5*/        unsigned int Child;
/* 6*/        Etype Tmp = A[ i ];

/* 7*/        for{ ; i * 2 <= N; i = Child )
/* 8*/        {
/* 9*/            Child = i * 2;
/*10*/            if( Child != N && A[ Child + 1 ] > A[ Child ] )
/*11*/                Child++;
/*12*/            if( Tmp < A[Child ] )
/*13*/                A[ i ] = A[ Child ];
/*14*/            else
/*15*/                break;
/*16*/        }
/*17*/        A[ i ] = Tmp;
/*18*/    }


/* 1*/    template <class Etype>
/* 2*/    void
/* 3*/    Heap_Sort( Etype A[], const unsigned int N )
/* 4*/    {
/* 5*/        for( unsigned int i = N / 2; i > 0; i-- )    // Build_Heap.
/* 6*/            Perc_Down( A, i, N );

/* 7*/        for( i = N; i >= 2; i-- )
/* 8*/        {
/* 9*/            Swap( A[ 1 ], A[ i ] ); // Delete_Max.
/*10*/            Perc_Down( A, ( unsigned int ) 1, i - 1 );
/*11*/        }
/*12*/    }
```

Figure 7.8 Heapsort

operations, the heap will actually have only one element, but the elements left in the heap array will be in sorted order. The code to perform heapsort is given in Figure 7.8.

7.6. Mergesort

We now turn our attention to *mergesort*. Mergesort runs in $O(n \log n)$ worst-case running time, and the number of comparisons used is nearly optimal. It is a fine example of a recursive algorithm.

The fundamental operation in this algorithm is merging two sorted lists. Because the lists are sorted, this can be done in one pass through the input if the output is put in a third list. The basic merging algorithm takes two input arrays *a* and *b*, an output array *c*, and three counters, *aptr*, *bptr*, and *cptr*, which are initially set to the beginning of their respective arrays. The smaller of *a[aptr]* and *b[bptr]* is copied to the next entry in *c*, and the appropriate counters are advanced. When either input list is exhausted, the remainder of the other list is copied to *c*. An example of how the merge routine works is provided for the following input.

If the array *a* contains 1, 13, 24, 26, and *b* contains 2, 15, 27, 38, then the algorithm proceeds as follows: First, a comparison is done between 1 and 2. 1 is added to *c*, and then 13 and 2 are compared.

2 is added to *c*, and then 13 and 15 are compared.

13 is added to *c*, and then 24 and 15 are compared. This proceeds until 26 and 27 are compared.

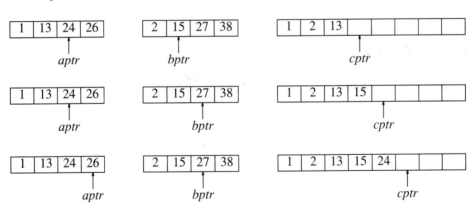

26 is added to *c*, and the *a* array is exhausted.

The remainder of the *b* array is then copied to *c*.

aptr   bptr   cptr

The time to merge two sorted lists is clearly linear, because at most $n - 1$ comparisons are made, where n is the total number of elements. To see this, note that every comparison adds an element to c except the last, which adds at least two.

The mergesort algorithm is therefore easy to describe. If $n = 1$, there is only one element to sort, and the answer is at hand. Otherwise, recursively mergesort the first half and the second half. This gives two sorted halves, which can then be merged together using the merging algorithm described above. For instance, to sort the eight-element array 24, 13, 26, 1, 2, 27, 38, 15, we recursively sort the first four and last four elements, obtaining 1, 13, 24, 26, 2, 15, 27, 38. Then we merge the two halves as above, obtaining the final list 1, 2, 13, 15, 24, 26, 27, 38. This algorithm is a classic divide-and-conquer strategy. The problem is *divided* into smaller problems and solved recursively. The *conquering* phase consists of patching together the answers. Divide-and-conquer is a very powerful use of recursion that we will see many times.

An implementation of mergesort is provided in Figure 7.9. A fair amount of work is required to make the compiler agree that all the types match. Figure 7.10 implements the *Merge* routine.

Figure 7.9 Mergesort routine

```
/* 1*/   template <class Etype>
/* 2*/   void
/* 3*/   Merge_Sort( Etype A[], const unsigned int N )
/* 4*/   {
/* 5*/       Etype *Tmp_Array = new Etype[ N + 1 ];
/* 6*/       unsigned int New_N = N;              // Non-constant, for M_Sort.

/* 7*/       if( Tmp_Array != NULL )
/* 8*/       {
/* 9*/           M_Sort( A, Tmp_Array, ( unsigned int ) 1, New_N );
/*10*/           delete [] Tmp_Array;
/*11*/       }
/*12*/       else
/*13*/           Error( "No space for tmp array" );
/*14*/   }


/* 1*/   template <class Etype>
/* 2*/   void
/* 3*/   M_Sort( Etype A[], Etype Tmp_Array[],
/* 4*/           unsigned int Left, unsigned int Right )
/* 5*/   {
/* 6*/       if( Left < Right )
/* 7*/       {
/* 8*/           unsigned int Center = ( Left + Right ) / 2;
```

```
/* 9*/              M_Sort( A, Tmp_Array, Left, Center );
/*10*/              M_Sort( A, Tmp_Array, Center + 1, Right );
/*11*/              Merge( A, Tmp_Array, Left, Center + 1, Right );
/*12*/         }
/*13*/    }
```

Figure 7.9 *(Continued)*

7.6.1. *Analysis of Mergesort*

Mergesort is a classic example of the techniques used to analyze recursive routines. It is not obvious that mergesort can easily be rewritten without recursion (it can), so we have to write a recurrence relation for the running time. We will assume that n is a power of 2 so that we always split into even halves. For $n = 1$, the time to mergesort is constant, which we will denote by 1. Otherwise, the time to mergesort n numbers is equal to the time to do two recursive mergesorts of size $n/2$, plus the time to merge, which is linear. The equations below say this exactly:

$$T(1) = 1$$
$$T(n) = 2T(n/2) + n$$

Figure 7.10 *Merge routine*

```
/* 1*/  // Left_Pos = start of left half.
/* 2*/  // Right_Pos = start of right half.

/* 3*/  template <class Etype>
/* 4*/  void
/* 5*/  Merge( Etype A[], Etype Tmp_Array[], unsigned int Left_Pos,
/* 6*/          unsigned int Right_Pos, unsigned int Right_End )
/* 7*/  {
/* 8*/      int Left_End = Right_Pos - 1;
/* 9*/      int Tmp_Pos  = Left_Pos;
/*10*/      int Num_Elements = Right_End - Left_Pos + 1;

/*11*/      // Main loop.
/*12*/      while( Left_Pos <= Left_End && Right_Pos <= Right_End )
/*13*/          if( A[ Left_Pos ] <= A [ Right_Pos ] )
/*14*/              Tmp_Array[ Tmp_Pos++ ] = A[ Left_Pos++ ];
/*15*/          else
/*16*/              Tmp_Array[ Tmp_Pos++ ] = A[ Right_Pos++ ];

/*17*/      while( Left_Pos <= Left_End )        // Copy rest of first half.
/*18*/          Tmp_Array[ Tmp_Pos++ ] = A[ Left_Pos++ ];

/*19*/      while( Right_Pos <= Right_End )      // Copy rest of second half.
/*20*/          Tmp_Array[ Tmp_Pos++ ] = A[ Right_Pos++ ];
```

```
/*21*/        // Copy Tmp_Array back.
/*22*/        for( int i = 1; i <= Num_Elements; i++, Right_End-- )
/*23*/            A[ Right_End ] = Tmp_Array[ Right_End ];
/*24*/    }
```

Figure 7.10 (*Continued*)

This is a standard recurrence relation that can be solved several ways. We will show two methods. The first idea is to divide the recurrence relation through by n. The reason for doing this will become apparent soon. This yields

$$\frac{T(n)}{n} = \frac{T(n/2)}{n/2} + 1$$

This equation is valid for any n that is a power of 2, so we may also write

$$\frac{T(n/2)}{n/2} = \frac{T(n/4)}{n/4} + 1$$

and

$$\frac{T(n/4)}{n/4} = \frac{T(n/8)}{n/8} + 1$$

$$\vdots$$

$$\frac{T(2)}{2} = \frac{T(1)}{1} + 1$$

Now add up all the equations. This means that we add all of the terms on the left-hand side and set the result equal to the sum of all of the terms on the right-hand side. Observe that the term $T(n/2)/(n/2)$ appears on both sides and thus cancels. In fact, virtually all the terms appear on both sides and cancel. This is called *telescoping* a sum. After everything is added, the final result is

$$\frac{T(n)}{n} = \frac{T(1)}{1} + \log n$$

because all of the other terms cancel and there are $\log n$ equations, and so all the 1s at the end of these equations add up to $\log n$. Multiplying through by n gives the final answer.

$$T(n) = n \log n + n = O(n \log n)$$

Notice that if we did not divide through by n at the start of the solution, the sum would not telescope. This is why it was necessary to divide through by n.

An alternative method is to substitute the recurrence relation continually on the right-hand side. We have

$$T(n) = 2T(n/2) + n$$

Since we can substitute $n/2$ into the main equation,

$$2T(n/2) = 2(2(T(n/4)) + n/2) = 4T(n/4) + n$$

we have

$$T(n) = 4T(n/4) + 2n$$

Again, by substituting $n/4$ into the main equation, we see that

$$4T(n/4) = 4(2T(n/8) + n/4) = 8T(n/8) + n$$

So we have

$$T(n) = 8T(n/8) + 3n$$

Continuing in this manner, we obtain

$$T(n) = 2^k T(n/2^k) + k \cdot n$$

Using $k = \log n$, we obtain

$$T(n) = nT(1) + n \log n = n \log n + n$$

The choice of which method to use is a matter of taste. The first method tends to produce scrap work that fits better on a standard $8\frac{1}{2} \times 11$ sheet of paper, leading to fewer mathematical errors, but it requires a certain amount of experience to apply. The second method is more of a brute force approach.

Recall that we have assumed $n = 2^k$. The analysis can be refined to handle cases in which n is not a power of 2. The answer turns out to be almost identical (this is usually the case).

Although mergesort's running time is $O(n \log n)$, it is hardly ever used for main memory sorts. The main problem is that merging two sorted lists requires linear extra memory, and the additional work spent copying to the temporary array and back, throughout the algorithm, has the effect of slowing down the sort considerably. This copying can be avoided by passing *Tmp_Array* as a parameter to merge and judiciously switching the roles of A and *Tmp_Array* at alternate levels of the recursion. A variant of mergesort can also be implemented nonrecursively (Exercise 7.13), but even so, for serious internal sorting applications, the algorithm of choice is quicksort, which is described in the next section. Nevertheless, as we will see later in this chapter, the merging routine is the cornerstone of most external sorting algorithms.

7.7. Quicksort

As its name implies, *quicksort* is the fastest known sorting algorithm in practice. Its average running time is $O(n \log n)$. It is very fast, mainly because of a very tight and highly optimized inner loop. It has $O(n^2)$ worst-case performance, but this can be made exponentially unlikely with a little effort. The quicksort algorithm is simple to understand and prove correct, although for many years it had the reputation of being an algorithm that could in theory be highly optimized but in practice was impossible to code correctly (no doubt because of FORTRAN). Like mergesort, quicksort is a divide-and-conquer recursive algorithm. The basic algorithm to sort an array S consists of the following four easy steps:

1. If the number of elements in S is 0 or 1, then return.
2. Pick any element v in S. This is called the *pivot*.
3. *Partition* $S - \{v\}$ (the remaining elements in S) into two disjoint groups: $S_1 = \{x \in S - \{v\} | x \leq v\}$, and $S_2 = \{x \in S - \{v\} | x \geq v\}$.
4. Return {quicksort (S_1) followed by v followed by quicksort(S_2)}.

Since the partition step ambiguously describes what to do with elements equal to the pivot, this becomes a design decision. Part of a good implementation is handling this case as efficiently as possible. Intuitively, we would hope that about half the keys that are equal to the pivot go into S_1 and the other half into S_2, much as we like binary search trees to be balanced.

Figure 7.11 shows the action of quicksort on a set of numbers. The pivot is chosen (by chance) to be 65. The remaining elements in the set are partitioned into two smaller sets. Recursively sorting the set of smaller numbers yields 0, 13, 26, 31, 43, 57 (by rule 3 of recursion). The set of large numbers is similarly sorted. The sorted arrangement of the entire set is then trivially obtained.

It should be clear that this algorithm works, but it is not clear why it is any faster than mergesort. Like mergesort, it recursively solves two subproblems and requires linear additional work (step 3), but, unlike mergesort, the subproblems are not guaranteed to be of equal size, which is potentially bad. The reason that quicksort is faster is that the partitioning step can actually be performed in place and very efficiently. This efficiency more than makes up for the lack of equal-sized recursive calls.

The algorithm as described so far lacks quite a few details, which we now fill in. There are many ways to implement steps 2 and 3; the method presented here is the result of extensive analysis and empirical study and represents a very efficient way to implement quicksort. Even the slightest deviations from this method can cause surprisingly bad results.

7.7.1. *Picking the Pivot*

Although the algorithm as described works no matter which element is chosen as pivot, some choices are obviously better than others.

A Wrong Way

The popular, uninformed choice is to use the first element as the pivot. This is acceptable if the input is random, but if the input is presorted or in reverse order, then the pivot provides a poor partition because virtually all the elements go into S_1 or S_2. Worse, this happens consistently throughout the recursive calls. The practical effect is that if the first element is used as the pivot and the input is presorted, then quicksort will take quadratic time to do essentially nothing at all, which is quite embarrassing. Moreover, presorted input (or input with a large presorted section) is

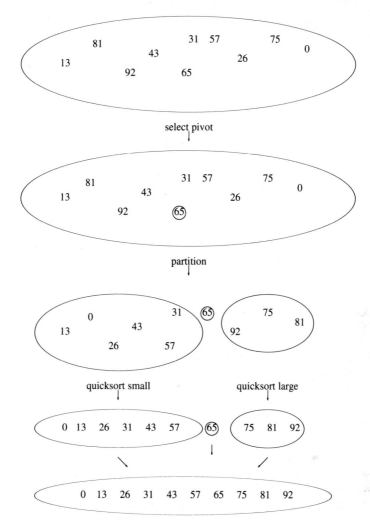

Figure 7.11 The steps of quicksort illustrated by example

quite frequent, so using the first element as pivot *is an absolutely horrible idea* and should be discarded immediately. An alternative is choosing the larger of the first two distinct keys as pivot, but this has the same bad properties as merely choosing the first key. Do not use that pivoting strategy either.

A Safe Maneuver

A safe course is merely to choose the pivot randomly. This strategy is generally perfectly safe, since it is very unlikely that a random pivot would consistently provide a poor partition unless the random number generator has a flaw (which is not as uncommon as you might think). On the other hand, random number generation is generally an expensive commodity and does not reduce the average running time of the rest of the algorithm at all.

Median-of-Three Partitioning

The median of a group of n numbers is the $\lceil n/2 \rceil$ th largest number. The best choice of pivot would be the median of the file. Unfortunately, this is hard to calculate and would slow down quicksort considerably. A good estimate can be obtained by picking three elements randomly and using the median of these three as pivot. The randomness turns out not to help much, so the common course is to use as pivot the median of the left, right, and center elements. For instance, with input 8, 1, 4, 9, 6, 3, 5, 2, 7, 0 as before, the left element is 8, the right element is 0, and the center (in position $\lfloor (left + right)/2) \rfloor$) element is 6. Thus, the pivot would be $v = 6$. Using median-of-three partitioning clearly eliminates the bad case for sorted input (the partitions become equal in this case) and actually reduces the running time of quicksort by about 5 percent.

7.7.2. *Partitioning Strategy*

There are several partitioning strategies used in practice, but the one described here is known to give good results. It is very easy, as we shall see, to do this wrong or inefficiently, but it is safe to use a known method. The first step is to get the pivot element out of the way by swapping it with the last element. The index i starts at the first element, and j starts at the next-to-last element. If the original input was the same as before, the following figure shows the current situation.

For now we will assume that all the elements are distinct. Later on we will worry about what to do in the presence of duplicates. As a limiting case, our algorithm must do the proper thing if *all* of the elements are identical. It is surprising how easy it is to do the *wrong* thing.

What our partitioning stage wants to do is to move all the small elements to the left part of the array and all the large elements to the right part. "Small" and "large" are, of course, relative to the pivot.

While i is to the left of j, we move i right, skipping over elements that are smaller than the pivot. We move j left, skipping over elements that are larger than the pivot. When i and j have stopped, i is pointing at a large element and j is pointing at a small element. If i is to the left of j, those elements are swapped. The effect is to push a large element to the right and a small element to the left. In the example above, i would not move and j would slide over one place. The situation is as follows.

We then swap the elements pointed to by i and j and repeat the process until i and j cross.

```
+-------------------------------------------------+
|                 After First Swap                |
+-------------------------------------------------+
|  2    1    4    9    0    3    5    8    7    6  |
|  ↑                             ↑                 |
|  i                             j                 |
+-------------------------------------------------+
```

```
+-------------------------------------------------+
|                Before Second Swap               |
+-------------------------------------------------+
|  2    1    4    9    0    3    5    8    7    6  |
|            ↑              ↑                      |
|            i              j                      |
+-------------------------------------------------+
```

```
+-------------------------------------------------+
|                 After Second Swap               |
+-------------------------------------------------+
|  2    1    4    5    0    3    9    8    7    6  |
|            ↑              ↑                      |
|            i              j                      |
+-------------------------------------------------+
```

```
+-------------------------------------------------+
|                 Before Third Swap               |
+-------------------------------------------------+
|  2    1    4    5    0    3    9    8    7    6  |
|                      ↑    ↑                      |
|                      j    i                      |
+-------------------------------------------------+
```

At this stage, i and j have crossed, so no swap is performed. The final part of the partitioning is to swap the pivot element with the element pointed to by i.

```
+-------------------------------------------------+
|                After Swap with Pivot            |
+-------------------------------------------------+
|  2    1    4    5    0    3    6    8    7    9  |
|                           ↑              ↑      |
|                           i            Pivot    |
+-------------------------------------------------+
```

When the pivot is swapped with i in the last step, we know that every element in a position $p < i$ must be small. This is because either position p contained a small element to start with, or the large element originally in position p was replaced during a swap. A similar argument shows that elements in positions $p > i$ must be large, with the exception of the pivot.

One important detail we must consider is how to handle keys that are equal to the pivot. The questions are whether or not i should stop when it sees a key equal to the pivot and whether or not j should stop when it sees a key equal to the pivot. Intuitively, i and j ought to do the same thing since otherwise the partitioning step is biased. For instance, if i stops and j does not, then all keys that are equal to the pivot will wind up in S_2.

To get an idea of what might be good, we consider the case in which all the keys in the array are identical. If both i and j stop, there will be many swaps between identical elements. Although this seems useless, the positive effect is that i and j will cross in the middle, so when the pivot is replaced, the partition creates two nearly equal subfiles. The mergesort analysis tells us that the total running time would then be $O(n \log n)$.

If neither i nor j stop, and code is present to prevent them from running off the end of the array, no swaps will be performed. Although this seems good, a correct implementation would then swap the pivot into the last spot that i touched, which would be the next-to-last position (or last, depending on the exact implementation). This would create very uneven subfiles. If all the keys are identical, the running time is $O(n^2)$. The effect is the same as using the first element as a pivot for presorted input. It takes quadratic time to do nothing!

Thus, we find that it is better to do the unnecessary swaps and create even subfiles than to risk wildly uneven subfiles. Therefore, we will have both i and j stop if they encounter a key equal to the pivot. This turns out to be the only one of the four possibilities that does not take quadratic time for this input.

At first glance it may seem that worrying about an array of identical elements is silly. After all, why would anyone want to sort 5,000 identical elements? However, recall that quicksort is recursive. Suppose there are 100,000 elements, of which 5,000 are identical. Eventually, quicksort will make the recursive call on only these 5,000 elements. Then it really will be important to make sure that 5,000 identical elements can be sorted efficiently.

7.7.3. Small Files

For very small files ($n \leq 20$), quicksort does not perform as well as insertion sort. Furthermore, because quicksort is recursive, these cases will occur frequently. A common solution is not to use quicksort recursively for small files, but instead use a sorting algorithm that is efficient for small arrays, such as insertion sort. An even better idea is to leave the array slightly unsorted and finish up with insertion sort. This works well because insertion sort is efficient for nearly sorted input. Using this strategy can actually save about 15 percent in the running time (over doing no cutoff at all). A good cutoff range is $n = 10$, although any cutoff between 5 and 20 is likely to produce similar results. This also saves nasty degenerate cases such as taking the median of three elements when there are only one or two. Of course, if there is a bug in the basic quicksort routine, then the insertion sort will be very, very slow.

7.7.4. Actual Quicksort Routines

The driver and swap routine for quicksort are shown in Figure 7.12.

The general form of the routines will be to pass the array and the range of the array (*Left* and *Right*) to be sorted. The first routine to deal with is pivot selection.

```
/* 1*/    template <class Etype>
/* 2*/    void
/* 3*/    Quick_Sort( Etype A[], const unsigned int N )
/* 4*/    {
/* 5*/        const unsigned int One = 1;

/* 6*/        Q_Sort( A, One, N );
/* 7*/        Insertion_Sort( A, N );
/* 8*/    }

/* 9*/    template <class Etype>
/*10*/    inline void
/*11*/    Swap( Etype & A, Etype & B )
/*12*/    {
/*13*/        Etype Tmp;

/*14*/        Tmp = A;
/*15*/        A = B;
/*16*/        B = Tmp;
/*17*/    }
```

Figure 7.12   Driver for quicksort

The easiest way to do this is to sort A[Left], A[Right], and A[Center] in place. This has the extra advantage that the smallest of the three winds up in A[Left], which is where the partitioning step would put it anyway. The largest winds up in A[Right], which is also the correct place since it is larger than the pivot. Therefore, we can place the pivot in A[Right − 1] and initialize i and j to Left + 1 and Right − 2 in the partition phase. Yet another benefit is that because A[Left] is smaller than the pivot, it will act as a sentinel for j. Thus, we do not need to worry about j running past the end. Since i will stop on keys equal to the pivot, storing the pivot in A[Right − 1] provides a sentinel for i. The code in Figure 7.13 does the median-of-three partitioning with all the side effects described. It may seem that it is only slightly inefficient to compute the pivot by a method that does not actually sort A[Left], A[Center], and A[Right], but, surprisingly, this produces bad results (see Exercise 7.37).

The real heart of the quicksort routine is in Figure 7.14. It includes the partitioning and recursive calls. There are several things worth noting in this implementation. Line 9 initializes i and j to 1 past their correct values, so that there are no special cases to consider. This initialization depends on the fact that median-of-three partitioning has some side effects; this program will not work if you try to use it without change with a simple pivoting strategy, because i and j start in the wrong place and there is no longer a sentinel for j.

The *Swap* at line 15 is a fundamental operation. For the algorithm to be fast, it is necessary to force the compiler to compile this code in-line. We have asked, in Figure 7.12, that *Swap* be expanded inline. The compiler may ignore the request, however.

```
/* 1*/   template <class Etype>
/* 2*/   Etype &
/* 3*/   Median3( Etype A[],
/* 4*/            const unsigned int Left, const unsigned int Right )
/* 5*/   {
/* 6*/       unsigned int Center = ( Left + Right ) / 2;

/* 7*/       if( A[ Left ] > A[ Center ] )
/* 8*/           Swap( A[ Left ], A[ Center ] );
/* 9*/       if( A[ Left ] > A[ Right ] )
/*10*/           Swap( A[ Left ], A[ Right ] );
/*11*/       if( A[ Center ] > A[ Right ] )
/*12*/           Swap( A[ Center ], A[ Right ] );

/*13*/       // Invariant:  A[ Left ] <= A[ Center ] <= A[ Right ].
/*14*/       // Now hide and return pivot.

/*15*/       Swap( A[ Center ], A[ Right - 1 ] );
/*16*/       return A[ Right - 1 ];
/*17*/   }
```

Figure 7.13   Code to perform median-of-three partitioning

```
/* 1*/   template <class Etype>
/* 2*/   void
/* 3*/   Q_Sort( Etype A[],
/* 4*/           const unsigned int Left, const unsigned int Right )
/* 5*/   {
/* 6*/       if( Left + Cutoff <= Right )
/* 7*/       {
/* 8*/           Etype Pivot = Median3( A, Left, Right );
/* 9*/           unsigned int i = Left, j = Right - 1;

/*10*/           for( ; ; )
/*11*/           {
/*12*/               while( A[ ++i ] < Pivot );
/*13*/               while( A[ --j ] > Pivot );
/*14*/               if(i < j )
/*15*/                   Swap( A[ i ], A[ j ] );
/*16*/               else
/*17*/                   break;
/*18*/           }

/*19*/           Swap( A[ i ], A[ Right - 1 ] ); // Restore pivot.

/*20*/           Q_Sort( A, Left, i - 1 );
/*21*/           Q_Sort( A, i + 1, Right );
/*22*/       }
/*23*/   }
```

Figure 7.14   Main quicksort routine

```
/* 9*/          unsigned int i = Left + 1, j = Right - 2;

/*10*/          for( ; ; )
/*11*/          {
/*12*/              while( A[ i ] < Pivot ) i++;
/*13*/              while( A[ j ] > Pivot ) j--;
```

Figure 7.15 A small change to quicksort that breaks the
algorithm

Finally, lines 12 through 17 show why quicksort is so fast. The inner loop
of the algorithm consists of an increment/decrement (by 1, which is fast), a test,
and a jump. There is no extra juggling as there is in mergesort. This code is still
surprisingly tricky. It is tempting to replace lines 9 through 13 with the statements
in Figure 7.15. This does not work, because there would be an infinite loop if
$A[i] == A[j]$ and $A[j] == Pivot$.

7.7.5. *Analysis of Quicksort*

Like mergesort, quicksort is recursive, and hence, its analysis requires solving a
recurrence formula. We will do the analysis for a quicksort, assuming a random
pivot (no median-of-three partitioning) and no cutoff for small files. We will take
$T(0) = T(1) = 1$, as in mergesort. The running time of quicksort is equal to the
running time of the two recursive calls plus the linear time spent in the partition (the
pivot selection takes only constant time). This gives the basic quicksort relation

$$T(n) = T(i) + T(n - i - 1) + cn \qquad (7.1)$$

where $i = |S_1|$ is the number of elements in S_1. We will look at three cases.

Worst-Case Analysis

The pivot is the smallest element all the time. Then $i = 0$ and if we ignore $T(0) = 1$,
which is insignificant, the recurrence is

$$T(n) = T(n - 1) + cn, \quad n > 1 \qquad (7.2)$$

We telescope, using Equation (7.2) repeatedly. Thus

$$T(n - 1) = T(n - 2) + c(n - 1) \qquad (7.3)$$

$$T(n - 2) = T(n - 3) + c(n - 2) \qquad (7.4)$$

$$\vdots$$

$$T(2) = T(1) + c(2) \qquad (7.5)$$

Adding up all these equations yields

$$T(n) = T(1) + c\sum_{i=2}^{n} i = O(n^2) \tag{7.6}$$

as claimed earlier.

Best-Case Analysis

In the best case, the pivot is in the middle. To simplify the math, we assume that the two subfiles are each exactly half the size of the original, and although this gives a slight overestimate, this is acceptable because we are only interested in a Big-Oh answer.

$$T(n) = 2T(n/2) + cn \tag{7.7}$$

Divide both sides of Equation (7.7) by n.

$$\frac{T(n)}{n} = \frac{T(n/2)}{n/2} + c \tag{7.8}$$

We will telescope using this equation.

$$\frac{T(n/2)}{n/2} = \frac{T(n/4)}{n/4} + c \tag{7.9}$$

$$\frac{T(n/4)}{n/4} = \frac{T(n/8)}{n/8} + c \tag{7.10}$$

$$\vdots$$

$$\frac{T(2)}{2} = \frac{T(1)}{1} + c \tag{7.11}$$

We add all the equations from (7.7) to (7.11) and note that there are $\log n$ of them:

$$\frac{T(n)}{n} = \frac{T(1)}{1} + c\log n \tag{7.12}$$

which yields

$$T(n) = cn\log n + n = O(n\log n) \tag{7.13}$$

Notice that this is the exact same analysis as that of mergesort; hence, we get the same answer.

Average-Case Analysis

This is the most difficult part. For the average case, we assume that each of the file sizes for S_1 is equally likely, and hence has probability $1/n$. This assumption is actually valid for our pivoting and partitioning strategy, but it is not valid for some others. Partitioning strategies that do not preserve the randomness of the subfiles cannot use this analysis. Interestingly, these strategies seem to result in programs that take longer to run in practice.

With this assumption, the average value of $T(i)$, and hence $T(n - i - 1)$, is $\frac{1}{n}\sum_{j=0}^{n-1} T(j)$. Equation (7.1) then becomes

$$T(n) = \frac{2}{n}\left[\sum_{j=0}^{n-1} T(j)\right] + cn \tag{7.14}$$

If Equation (7.14) is multiplied by n, it becomes

$$nT(n) = 2\left[\sum_{j=0}^{n-1} T(j)\right] + cn^2 \tag{7.15}$$

We need to remove the summation sign to simplify matters. We note that we can telescope with one more equation.

$$(n - 1)T(n - 1) = 2\left[\sum_{j=0}^{n-2} T(j)\right] + c(n - 1)^2 \tag{7.16}$$

If we subtract (7.16) from (7.15), we obtain

$$nT(n) - (n - 1)T(n - 1) = 2T(n - 1) + 2cn - c \tag{7.17}$$

We rearrange terms and drop the insignificant $-c$ on the right, obtaining

$$nT(n) = (n + 1)T(n - 1) + 2cn \tag{7.18}$$

We now have a formula for $T(n)$ in terms of $T(n - 1)$ only. Again the idea is to telescope, but Equation (7.18) is in the wrong form. Divide (7.18) by $n(n + 1)$:

$$\frac{T(n)}{n + 1} = \frac{T(n - 1)}{n} + \frac{2c}{n + 1} \tag{7.19}$$

Now we can telescope.

$$\frac{T(n - 1)}{n} = \frac{T(n - 2)}{n - 1} + \frac{2c}{n} \tag{7.20}$$

$$\frac{T(n-2)}{n-1} = \frac{T(n-3)}{n-2} + \frac{2c}{n-1} \tag{7.21}$$

$$\vdots$$

$$\frac{T(2)}{3} = \frac{T(1)}{2} + \frac{2c}{3} \tag{7.22}$$

Adding equations (7.19) through (7.22) yields

$$\frac{T(n)}{n+1} = \frac{T(1)}{2} + 2c \sum_{i=3}^{n+1} \frac{1}{i} \tag{7.23}$$

The sum is about $\log_e(n+1) + \gamma - \frac{3}{2}$, where $\gamma \approx 0.577$ is known as Euler's constant, so

$$\frac{T(n)}{n+1} = O(\log n) \tag{7.24}$$

And so

$$T(n) = O(n \log n) \tag{7.25}$$

Although this analysis seems complicated, it really is not—the steps are natural once you have seen some recurrence relations. The analysis can actually be taken further. The highly optimized version that was described above has also been analyzed, and this result gets extremely difficult, involving complicated recurrences and advanced mathematics. The effects of equal keys has also been analyzed in detail, and it turns out that the code presented does the right thing.

7.7.6. A Linear-Expected-Time Algorithm for Selection

Quicksort can be modified to solve the *selection problem*, which we have seen in chapters 1 and 6. Recall that by using a priority queue, we can find the kth largest (or smallest) element in $O(n + k \log n)$. For the special case of finding the median, this gives an $O(n \log n)$ algorithm.

Since we can sort the file in $O(n \log n)$ time, one might expect to obtain a better time bound for selection. The algorithm we present to find the kth smallest element in a set S is almost identical to quicksort. In fact, the first three steps are the same. We will call this algorithm *quickselect*. Let $|S_i|$ denote the number of elements in S_i. The steps of quickselect are

1. If $|S| = 1$, then $k = 1$ and return the element in S as the answer. If a cutoff for small files is being used and $|S| \leq CUTOFF$, then sort S and return the kth smallest element.
2. Pick a pivot element, $v \in S$.
3. Partition $S - \{v\}$ into S_1 and S_2, as was done with quicksort.
4. If $k \leq |S_1|$, then the kth smallest element must be in S_1. In this case, return quickselect (S_1, k). If $k = 1 + |S_1|$, then the pivot is the kth smallest element

and we can return it as the answer. Otherwise, the kth smallest element lies in S_2, and it is the $(k - |S_1| - 1)$st smallest element in S_2. We make a recursive call and return quickselect $(S_2, k - |S_1| - 1)$.

In contrast to quicksort, quickselect makes only one recursive call instead of two. The worst case of quickselect is identical to that of quicksort and is $O(n^2)$. Intuitively, this is because quicksort's worst case is when one of S_1 and S_2 is empty; thus, quickselect is not really saving a recursive call. The average running time, however, is $O(n)$. The analysis is similar to quicksort's and is left as an exercise.

The implementation of quickselect is even simpler than the abstract description might imply. The code to do this is shown in Figure 7.16. When the basic algorithm terminates, the kth smallest element is in position k. This destroys the original ordering; if this is undesirable, we can set up a driver routine that will call *Q_Select* with a copy of the array.

Figure 7.16 Main quickselect routine

```
/* 1*/   template <class Etype>
/* 2*/   void
/* 3*/   Q_Select( Etype A[ ], const unsigned int k,
/* 4*/             const unsigned int Left, const unsigned int Right )
/* 5*/   {
/* 6*/       if( Left + Cutoff <= Right )
/* 7*/       {
/* 8*/           Etype Pivot = Median3( A, Left, Right );
/* 9*/           unsigned int i = Left, j = Right - 1;

/*10*/           for( ; ; )
/*11*/           {
/*12*/               while( A[ ++i ] < Pivot );
/*13*/               while( A[ --j ] > Pivot );
/*14*/               if( i < j )
/*15*/                   Swap( A[ i ], A[ j ] );
/*16*/               else
/*17*/                   break;
/*18*/           }

/*19*/           Swap( A[ i ], A[ Right - 1 ] ); // Restore pivot.

/*20*/           if( k < i )
/*21*/               Q_Select( A, k, Left, i - 1 );
/*22*/           else
/*23*/           if( k > i )
/*24*/               Q_Select( A, k, i + 1, Right );
/*25*/       }
/*26*/       else
/*27*/           Insert_Sort( A, Left, Right );
/*28*/   }
```

Using a median-of-three pivoting strategy makes the chance of the worst case occurring almost negligible. By carefully choosing the pivot, however, we can eliminate the quadratic worst case and ensure an $O(n)$ algorithm. The overhead involved in doing this is considerable, so the resulting algorithm is mostly of theoretical interest. In Chapter 10, we will examine the linear-time worst-case algorithm for selection, and we shall also see an interesting technique of choosing the pivot that results in a somewhat faster selection algorithm in practice.

7.8.   Sorting Large Objects

Although our code can handle nonintegers, throughout our discussion of sorting, we have assumed that the elements to be sorted are simply integers. Frequently, we need to sort large objects by a certain key. For instance, we might have payroll objects, with each object consisting of a name, address, phone number, financial information such as salary, and tax information. We might want to sort this information by one particular field, such as the name. For all of our algorithms, the fundamental operation is the swap, but here swapping two objects can be a very expensive operation, because the objects are potentially large. If this is the case, a practical solution is to have the input array contain pointers to the objects. We sort by comparing the keys the pointers point to, swapping pointers when necessary. This means that all the data movement is essentially the same as if we were sorting integers. This is known as *indirect sorting*; we can use this technique for most of the data structures we have described. This justifies our assumption that complex objects can be handled without tremendous loss of efficiency.

7.9.   A General Lower Bound for Sorting

Although we have $O(n \log n)$ algorithms for sorting, it is not clear that this is as good as we can do. In this section, we prove that any algorithm for sorting that uses only comparisons requires $\Omega(n \log n)$ comparisons (and hence time) in the worst case, so that mergesort and heapsort are optimal to within a constant factor. The proof can be extended to show that $\Omega(n \log n)$ comparisons are required, even on average, for any sorting algorithm that uses only comparisons, which means that quicksort is optimal on average to within a constant factor.

Specifically, we will prove the following result: Any sorting algorithm that uses only comparisons requires $\lceil \log n! \rceil$ comparisons in the worst case and $\log n!$ comparisons on average. We will assume that all n elements are distinct since any sorting algorithm must work for this case.

7.9.1.   Decision Trees

A *decision tree* is an abstraction used to prove lower bounds. In our context, a decision tree is a binary tree. Each node represents a set of possible orderings,

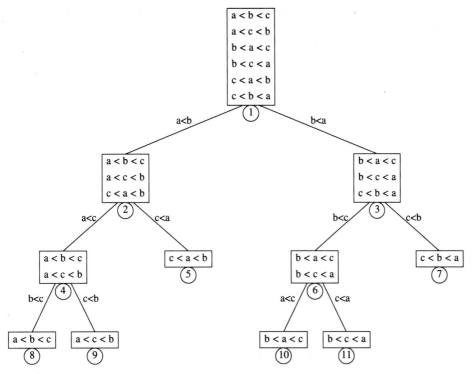

Figure 7.17 A decision tree for three-element insertion sort

consistent with comparisons that have been made, among the elements. The results of the comparisons are the tree edges.

The decision tree in Figure 7.17 represents an algorithm that sorts the three elements *a*, *b*, and *c*. The initial state of the algorithm is at the root. (We will use the terms *state* and *node* interchangeably.) No comparisons have been done, so all orderings are legal. The first comparison that *this particular* algorithm performs compares *a* and *b*. The two results lead to two possible states. If $a < b$, then only three possibilities remain. If the algorithm reaches node 2, then it will compare *a* and *c*. Other algorithms might do different things; a different algorithm would have a different decision tree. If $a > c$, the algorithm enters state 5. Since there is only one ordering that is consistent, the algorithm can terminate and report that it has completed the sort. If $a < c$, the algorithm cannot do this because there are two possible orderings and it cannot possibly be sure which is correct. In this case, the algorithm will require one more comparison.

Every algorithm that sorts by using only comparisons can be represented by a decision tree. Of course, it is feasible to draw the tree only for extremely small input sizes. The number of comparisons used by the sorting algorithm is equal to the depth of the deepest leaf. In our case, this algorithm uses three comparisons in the worst case. The average number of comparisons used is equal to the average depth of the leaves. Since a decision tree is large, it follows that there must be some long paths. To prove the lower bounds, all that needs to be shown are some basic tree properties.

LEMMA 7.1.

Let T be a binary tree of depth d. Then T has at most 2^d leaves.

PROOF:

The proof is by induction. If $d = 0$, then there is at most one leaf, so the basis is true. Otherwise, we have a root, which cannot be a leaf, and a left and right subtree, each of depth at most $d - 1$. By the induction hypothesis, they can each have at most 2^{d-1} leaves, giving a total of at most 2^d leaves. This proves the lemma.

LEMMA 7.2.

A binary tree with L leaves must have depth at least $\lceil \log L \rceil$.

PROOF:

Immediate from the preceding lemma.

THEOREM 7.5.

Any sorting algorithm that uses only comparisons between elements requires at least $\lceil \log n! \rceil$ comparisons in the worst case.

PROOF:

A decision tree to sort n elements must have at least $n!$ leaves. The theorem follows from the preceding lemma.

THEOREM 7.6.

Any sorting algorithm that uses only comparisons between elements requires $\Omega(n \log n)$ comparisons.

PROOF:

From the previous theorem, $\log n!$ comparisons are required.

$$\log n! = \log(n(n-1)(n-2)\cdots(2)(1))$$

$$= \log n + \log(n-1) + \log(n-2) + \cdots + \log 2 + \log 1$$

$$\geq \log n + \log(n-1) + \log(n-2) + \cdots + \log n/2$$

$$\geq \frac{n}{2} \log \frac{n}{2}$$

$$\geq \frac{n}{2} \log n - \frac{n}{2}$$

$$= \Omega(n \log n)$$

This type of lower-bound argument, when used to prove a worst-case result, is sometimes known as an *information-theoretic* lower bound. The general theorem says that if there are P different possible cases to distinguish, and the questions are of the form YES/NO, then $\lceil \log P \rceil$ questions are always required in some case by any algorithm to solve the problem. It is possible to prove a similar result for the average-case running time of any comparison-based sorting algorithm. This result is implied by the following lemma, which is left as an exercise: Any binary tree with L leaves has an average depth of at least $\log L$.

7.10. Bucket Sort

Although we proved in the previous section that any general sorting algorithm that uses only comparisons requires $\Omega(n \log n)$ time in the worst case, recall that it is still possible to sort in linear time in some special cases.

A simple example is bucket sort. For bucket sort to work, extra information must be available. The input $a_1, a_2, ..., a_n$ must consist of only positive integers smaller than m. (Obviously extensions to this are possible.) If this is the case, then the algorithm is simple: Keep an array called *count*, of size m, which is initialized to all 0s. Thus, *count* has m cells, or buckets, which are initially empty. When a_i is read, increment *count*$[a_i]$ by 1. After all the input is read, scan the *count* array, printing out a representation of the sorted list. This algorithm takes $O(m + n)$; the proof is left as an exercise. If m is $O(n)$, then the total is $O(n)$.

Although this algorithm seems to violate the lower bound, it turns out that it does not because it uses a more powerful operation than simple comparisons. By incrementing the appropriate bucket, the algorithm essentially performs an *m*-way comparison in unit time. This is similar to the strategy used in extendible hashing (Section 5.6). This is clearly not in the model for which the lower bound was proven.

This algorithm does, however, question the validity of the model used in proving the lower bound. The model actually is a strong model, because a *general-purpose* sorting algorithm cannot make assumptions about the type of input it can expect to see, but must make decisions based on ordering information only. Naturally, if there is extra information available, we should expect to find a more efficient algorithm, since otherwise the extra information would be wasted.

Although bucket sort seems like much too trivial an algorithm to be useful, it turns out that there are many cases in which the input is only small integers, so using a method like quicksort is really overkill.

7.11. External Sorting

So far, all the algorithms we have examined require that the input fit into main memory. There are, however, applications for which the input is much too large to fit into memory. This section will discuss *external sorting* algorithms, which are designed to handle very large inputs.

7.11.1. Why We Need New Algorithms

Most of the internal sorting algorithms take advantage of the fact that memory is directly addressable. Shellsort compares elements $A[i]$ and $A[i - h_k]$ in one time unit. Heapsort compares elements $A[i]$ and $A[i * 2]$ in one time unit. Quicksort, with median-of-three partitioning, requires comparing $A[Left]$, $A[Center]$, and $A[Right]$ in a constant number of time units. If the input is on a tape, then all these operations lose their efficiency since elements on a tape can be accessed only sequentially. Even if the data is on a disk, there is still a practical loss of efficiency because of the delay required to spin the disk and move the disk head.

To see how slow external accesses really are, create a random file that is large, but not too big to fit in main memory. Read the file in and sort it using an efficient algorithm. The time it takes to sort the input is certain to be insignificant compared to the time to read the input, even though sorting is an $O(n \log n)$ operation and reading the input is only $O(n)$.

7.11.2. Model for External Sorting

The wide variety of mass storage devices makes external sorting much more device-dependent than internal sorting. The algorithms that we will consider work on tapes, which are probably the most restrictive storage medium. Since access to an element on tape is done by winding the tape to the correct location, tapes can be efficiently accessed only in sequential order (in either direction).

We will assume that we have at least three tape drives to perform the sorting. We need two drives to do an efficient sort; the third drive simplifies matters. If only one tape drive is present, then we are in trouble: any algorithm will require $\Omega(n^2)$ tape accesses.

7.11.3. The Simple Algorithm

The basic external sorting algorithm uses the *merge* routine from mergesort. Suppose we have four tapes, T_{a1}, T_{a2}, T_{b1}, T_{b2}, which are two input and two output tapes. Depending on the point in the algorithm, the a and b tapes are either input tapes or output tapes. Suppose the data is initially on T_{a1}. Suppose further that the internal memory can hold (and sort) m records at a time. A natural first step is to read m records at a time from the input tape, sort the records internally, and then write the sorted records alternately to T_{b1} and T_{b2}. We will call each set of sorted records a *run*. When this is done, we rewind all the tapes. Suppose we have the same input as our example for Shellsort.

T_{a1}	81	94	11	96	12	35	17	99	28	58	41	75	15
T_{a2}													
T_{b1}													
T_{b2}													

If $m = 3$, then after the runs are constructed, the tapes will contain the data indicated in the following figure.

T_{a1}							
T_{a2}							
T_{b1}	11	81	94	17	28	99	15
T_{b2}	12	35	96	41	58	75	

Now T_{b1} and T_{b2} contain a group of runs. We take the first runs from each tape and merge them, writing the result, which is a run twice as long, onto T_{a1}. Then we take the next runs from each tape, merge these, and write the result to T_{a2}. We continue this process, alternating between T_{a1} and T_{a2}, until either T_{b1} or T_{b2} is empty. At this point either both are empty or there is one run left. In the latter case, we copy this run to the appropriate tape. We rewind all four tapes, and repeat the same steps, this time using the a tapes as input and the b tapes as output. This will give runs of length $4m$. We continue the process until we get one run of length n.

This algorithm will require $\lceil \log(n/m) \rceil$ passes, plus the initial run-constructing pass. For instance, if we have 10 million records of 128 bytes each, and four megabytes of internal memory, then the first pass will create 320 runs. We would then need nine more passes to complete the sort. Our example requires $\lceil \log 13/3 \rceil = 3$ more passes, which are shown in the following figure.

T_{a1}	11	12	35	81	94	96	15					
T_{a2}	17	28	41	58	75	99						
T_{b1}												
T_{b2}												

T_{a1}												
T_{a2}												
T_{b1}	11	12	17	28	35	51	58	75	81	94	96	99
T_{b2}	15											

T_{a1}	11	12	15	17	28	35	41	58	75	81	94	96	99
T_{a2}													
T_{b1}													
T_{b2}													

7.11.4. Multiway Merge

If we have extra tapes, then we can expect to reduce the number of passes required to sort our input. We do this by extending the basic (two-way) merge to a k-way merge.

Merging two runs is done by winding each input tape to the beginning of each run. Then the smaller element is found, placed on an output tape, and the appropriate input tape is advanced. If there are k input tapes, this strategy works the same way, the only difference being that it is slightly more complicated to find the smallest of the k elements. We can find the smallest of these elements by using a priority queue. To obtain the next element to write on the output tape, we perform a *Delete_Min* operation. The appropriate input tape is advanced, and if the run on the input tape is not yet completed, we *Insert* the new element into the priority queue. Using the same example as before, we distribute the input onto the three tapes.

T_{a1}						
T_{a2}						
T_{a3}						
T_{b1}	11	81	94	41	58	75
T_{b2}	12	35	96	15		
T_{b3}	17	28	99			

We then need two more passes of three-way merging to complete the sort.

T_{a1}	11	12	17	28	35	81	94	96	99
T_{a2}	15	41	58	75					
T_{a3}									
T_{b1}									
T_{b2}									
T_{b3}									

T_{a1}												
T_{a2}												
T_{a3}												
T_{b1}	11	12	15	17	28	35	41	58	75	81	94	96	99
T_{b2}												
T_{b3}												

After the initial run construction phase, the number of passes required using k-way merging is $\lceil \log_k(n/m) \rceil$, because the runs get k times as large in each pass. For the example above, the formula is verified, since $\lceil \log_3 13/3 \rceil = 2$. If we have 10 tapes, then $k = 5$, and our large example from the previous section would require $\lceil \log_5 320 \rceil = 4$ passes.

7.11.5. Polyphase Merge

The k-way merging strategy developed in the last section requires the use of $2k$ tapes. This could be prohibitive for some applications. It is possible to get by with only $k + 1$ tapes. As an example, we will show how to perform two-way merging using only three tapes.

Suppose we have three tapes, T_1, T_2, and T_3, and an input file on T_1 that will produce 34 runs. One option is to put 17 runs on each of T_2 and T_3. We could then merge this result onto T_1, obtaining one tape with 17 runs. The problem is that since all the runs are on one tape, we must now put some of these runs on T_2 to perform another merge. The logical way to do this is to copy the first eight runs from T_1 onto T_2 and then perform the merge. This has the effect of adding an extra half pass for every pass we do.

An alternative method is to split the original 34 runs unevenly. Suppose we put 21 runs on T_2 and 13 runs on T_3. We would then merge 13 runs onto T_1 before T_3 was empty. At this point, we could rewind T_1 and T_3 and merge T_1, with 13 runs, and T_2, which has 8 runs, onto T_3. We could then merge 8 runs until T_2 was empty, which would leave 5 runs left on T_1 and 8 runs on T_3. We could then merge T_1 and T_3, and so on. The following table shows the number of runs on each tape after each pass.

	Run Const.	After $T_3 + T_2$	After $T_1 + T_2$	After $T_1 + T_3$	After $T_2 + T_3$	After $T_1 + T_2$	After $T_1 + T_3$	After $T_2 + T_3$
T_1	0	13	5	0	3	1	0	1
T_2	21	8	0	5	2	0	1	0
T_3	13	0	8	3	0	2	1	0

The original distribution of runs makes a great deal of difference. For instance, if 22 runs are placed on T_2, with 12 on T_3, then after the first merge, we obtain 12 runs on T_1 and 10 runs on T_2. After another merge, there are 10 runs on T_1 and 2 runs on T_3. At this point the going gets slow because we can merge only two sets of runs before T_3 is exhausted. Then T_1 has 8 runs and T_2 has 2 runs. Again, we can merge only two sets of runs, obtaining T_1 with 6 runs and T_3 with 2 runs. After three more passes, T_2 has two runs, and the other tapes are empty. We must copy one run to another tape, and then we can finish the merge.

It turns out that the first distribution we gave is optimal. If the number of runs is a Fibonacci number F_n, then the best way to distribute them is to split them into two Fibonacci numbers F_{n-1} and F_{n-2}. Otherwise, it is necessary to pad the tape with dummy runs in order to get the number of runs up to a Fibonacci number. We leave the details of how to place the initial set of runs on the tapes as an exercise.

We can extend this to a k-way merge, in which case we need kth order Fibonacci numbers for the distribution, where the kth order Fibonacci number is defined as $F^{(k)}(n) = F^{(k)}(n - 1) + F^{(k)}(n - 2) + \cdots + F^{(k)}(n - k)$, with the appropriate initial conditions $F^{(k)}(n) = 0, 0 \le n \le k - 2, F^{(k)}(k - 1) = 1$.

7.11.6. Replacement Selection

The last item we will consider is construction of the runs. The strategy we have used so far is the simplest possible: We read as many elements as possible and sort them, writing the result to some tape. This seems like the best approach possible until one realizes that as soon as the first element is written to an output tape, the memory it used becomes available for another element. If the next element on the input tape is larger than the element we have just output, then it can be included in the run.

Using this observation, we can give an algorithm for producing runs. This technique is commonly referred to as *replacement selection*. Initially, m elements are read into memory and placed in a priority queue. We perform a *Delete_Min*, writing the smallest element to the output tape. We read the next element from the input tape. If it is larger than the element we have just written, we can add it to the priority queue. Otherwise, it cannot go into the current run. Since the priority queue is smaller by one element, we can store this new element in the dead space of the priority queue until the run is completed and use the element for the next run. Storing an element in the dead space is similar to what is done in heapsort. We continue doing this until the size of the priority queue is zero, at which point the run is over. We start a new run by building a new priority queue, using all the elements in the dead space. Figure 7.18 shows the run construction for the small example we have been using, with $m = 3$. Dead elements are indicated by an asterisk.

In this example, replacement selection produces only three runs, compared with the five runs obtained by sorting. Because of this, a three-way merge finishes in one pass instead of two. If the input is randomly distributed, replacement selection can

Figure 7.18   Example of run construction

	3 Elements In Heap Array			Output	Next Element Read
	H[1]	H[2]	H[3]		
Run 1	11	94	81	11	96
	81	94	96	81	12*
	94	96	12*	94	35*
	96	35*	12*	96	17*
	17*	35*	12*	End of Run.	Rebuild Heap
Run 2	12	35	17	12	99
	17	35	99	17	28
	28	99	35	28	58
	35	99	58	35	41
	41	99	58	41	75*
	58	99	75*	58	end of tape
	99		75*	99	
			75*	End of Run.	Rebuild Heap
Run 3	75			75	

be shown to produce runs of average length $2m$. For our large example, we would expect 160 runs instead of 320 runs, so a five-way merge would require four passes. In this case, we have not saved a pass, although we might if we get lucky and have 125 runs or less. Since external sorts take so long, every pass saved can make a significant difference in the running time.

As we have seen, it is possible for replacement selection to do no better than the standard algorithm. However, the input is frequently sorted or nearly sorted to start with, in which case replacement selection produces only a few very long runs. This kind of input is common for external sorts and makes replacement selection extremely valuable.

Summary

For most general internal sorting applications, either insertion sort, Shellsort, or quicksort will be the method of choice, and the decision of which to use will depend on the size of the input. Figure 7.19 shows the running time obtained for each algorithm on various file sizes.

The data was chosen to be random permutations of n integers, and the times given include only the actual time to sort. The code given in Figure 7.2 was used for insertion sort. Shellsort used the code in Section 7.4 modified to run with Sedgewick's increments. Based on literally millions of sorts, ranging in size from 100 to 25 million, the expected running time of Shellsort with these increments is well approximated by $O(n^{7/6})$. The heapsort routine is the same as in Section 7.5. Two versions of quicksort are given. The first uses a simple pivoting strategy and does not do a cutoff. Fortunately, the input files were random. The second uses median-of-three partitioning and a cutoff of ten. Further optimizations were possible. We could have coded the median-of-three routine in-line instead of using a function, and we could have written quicksort nonrecursively. There are some other optimizations to the code that are fairly tricky to implement, and of course we could have used an assembly language. We have made an honest attempt

Figure 7.19 Comparison of different sorting algorithms (all times are in seconds)

n	Insertion Sort $O(n^2)$	Shellsort $O(n^{7/6})(?)$	Heapsort $O(n \log n)$	Quicksort $O(n \log n)$	Quicksort (opt.) $O(n \log n)$
10	0.00044	0.00041	0.00057	0.00052	.00046
100	0.00675	0.00171	0.00420	0.00284	.00244
1000	0.59564	0.02927	0.05565	0.03153	.02587
10000	58.864	0.42998	0.71650	0.36765	.31532
100000	NA	5.7298	8.8591	4.2298	3.5882
1000000	NA	71.164	104.68	47.065	41.282

to code all routines efficiently, but obviously the performance can vary somewhat from machine to machine.

The highly optimized version of quicksort is as fast as Shellsort even for very small input sizes. The improved version of quicksort still has an $O(n^2)$ worst case (one exercise asks you to construct a small example), but the chances of this worst case appearing are so negligible as to not be a factor. If you need to sort large files, quicksort is the method of choice. But never, ever, take the easy way out and use the first element as pivot. It is just not safe to assume that the input will be random. If you do not want to worry about this, use Shellsort. Shellsort will give a small performance penalty but could also be acceptable, especially if simplicity is required. Its worst case is only $O(n^{4/3})$; the chance of that worst case occurring is likewise negligible.

Heapsort, although an $O(n \log n)$ algorithm with an apparently tight inner loop, is slower than Shellsort. A close examination of the algorithm reveals that in order to move data, heapsort does two comparisons. An improvement suggested by Floyd moves data with essentially only one comparison, but implementing this improvement makes the code somewhat longer. We leave it to the reader to decide whether the extra coding effort is worth the increased speed (Exercise 7.39).

Insertion sort is useful only for small files or very nearly sorted files. We have not included mergesort, because its performance is not as good as quicksort for main memory sorts and it is not any simpler to code. We have seen, however, that merging is the central idea of external sorts.

Exercises

7.1 Sort the sequence 3, 1, 4, 1, 5, 9, 2, 6, 5 using insertion sort.

7.2 What is the running time of insertion sort if all keys are equal?

7.3 Suppose we exchange elements $A[i]$ and $A[i + k]$, which were originally out of order. Prove that at least 1 and at most $2k - 1$ inversions are removed.

7.4 Show the result of running Shellsort on the input 9, 8, 7, 6, 5, 4, 3, 2, 1 using the increments { 1, 3, 7 }.

7.5 What is the running time of Shellsort using the two-increment sequence { 1, 2 }?

7.6*a. Prove that the running time of Shellsort is $\Omega(n^2)$ using increments of the form $1, c, c^2, ..., c^i$ for any integer c.

    **b. Prove that for these increments, the average running time is $\Theta(n^{3/2})$.

*7.7 Prove that if a k-sorted file is then h-sorted, it remains k-sorted.

**7.8 Prove that the running time of Shellsort, using the increment sequence suggested by Hibbard, is $\Omega(n^{3/2})$ in the worst case. *Hint:* You can prove the bound by considering the special case of what Shellsort does when all elements are either 0 or 1. Set $Input\_Data[i] = 1$ if i is expressible as a linear combination of $h_t, h_{t-1}, ..., h_{\lfloor t/2 \rfloor + 1}$ and 0 otherwise.

7.9 Determine the running time of Shellsort for

   a. sorted input

   *b. reverse-ordered input

7.10 Show how heapsort processes the input 142, 543, 123, 65, 453, 879, 572, 434, 111, 242, 811, 102.

7.11 a. What is the running time of heapsort for presorted input?

   **b. Is there any input for which heapsort runs in $o(n \log n)$

   (in other words, are there any particularly good inputs for heapsort)?

7.12 Sort 3, 1, 4, 1, 5, 9, 2, 6 using mergesort.

7.13 How would you implement mergesort without using recursion?

7.14 Determine the running time of mergesort for

   a. sorted input

   b. reverse-ordered input

   c. random input

7.15 In the analysis of mergesort, constants have been disregarded. Prove that the number of comparisons used in the worst case by mergesort is $n \lceil \log n \rceil - 2^{\lceil \log n \rceil} + 1$.

7.16 Sort 3, 1, 4, 1, 5, 9, 2, 6, 5, 3, 5 using quicksort with median-of-three partitioning and a cutoff of 3.

7.17 Using the quicksort implementation in this chapter, determine the running time of quicksort for

   a. sorted input

   b. reverse-ordered input

   c. random input

7.18 Repeat Exercise 7.17 when the pivot is chosen as

   a. the first element

   b. the largest of the first two nondistinct keys

   c. a random element

   *d. the average of all keys in the set

7.19 a. For the quicksort implementation in this chapter, what is the running time when all keys are equal?

   b. Suppose we change the partitioning strategy so that neither i nor j stops when an element with the same key as the pivot is found. What fixes need to be made in the code to guarantee that quicksort works, and what is the running time, when all keys are equal?

   c. Suppose we change the partitioning strategy so that i stops at an element with the same key as the pivot, but j does not stop in a similar case. What fixes need to be made in the code to guarantee that quicksort works, and when all keys are equal, what is the running time of quicksort?

7.20 Suppose we choose the middle key as pivot. Does this make it unlikely that quicksort will require quadratic time?

7.21 Construct a permutation of 20 elements that is as bad as possible for quicksort using median-of-three partitioning and a cutoff of 3.

7.22 Write a program to implement the selection algorithm.

7.23 Solve the following recurrence: $T(n) = \frac{1}{n}\left[\sum_{i=0}^{n-1} T(i)\right] + cn, \ T(0) = 0.$

7.24 A sorting algorithm is *stable* if elements with equal keys are left in the same order as they occur in the input. Which of the sorting algorithms in this chapter are stable and which are not? Why?

7.25 Suppose you are given a sorted list of n elements followed by $f(n)$ randomly ordered elements. How would you sort the entire list if

  a. $f(n) = O(1)$?

  b. $f(n) = O(\log n)$?

  c. $f(n) = O(\sqrt{n})$?

  *d. How large can $f(n)$ be for the entire list still to be sortable in $O(n)$ time?

7.26 Prove that any algorithm that finds an element x in a sorted list of n elements requires $\Omega(\log n)$ comparisons.

7.27 Using Stirling's formula, $n! \approx (n/e)^n \sqrt{2\pi n}$, give a precise estimate for $\log n!$.

7.28 *a. In how many ways can two sorted arrays of n elements be merged?

  *b. Give a nontrivial lower bound on the number of comparisons required to merge two sorted lists of n elements.

7.29 Prove that sorting n elements with integer keys in the range $1 \le key \le m$ takes $O(m + n)$ time using bucket sort.

7.30 Suppose you have an array of n elements containing only two distinct keys, *True* and *False*. Give an $O(n)$ algorithm to rearrange the list so that all *False* elements precede the *True* elements. You may use only constant extra space.

7.31 Suppose you have an array of n elements, containing three distinct keys, *True, False,* and *Maybe*. Give an $O(n)$ algorithm to rearrange the list so that all *False* elements precede *Maybe* elements, which in turn precede *True* elements. You may use only constant extra space.

7.32 a. Prove that any comparison-based algorithm to sort 4 elements requires 5 comparisons.

  b. Give an algorithm to sort 4 elements in 5 comparisons.

7.33 a. Prove that 7 comparisons are required to sort 5 elements using any comparison-based algorithm.

  *b. Give an algorithm to sort 5 elements with 7 comparisons.

7.34 Write an efficient version of Shellsort and compare performance when the following increment sequences are used:

  a. Shell's original sequence

  b. Shell's original sequence, adding 1 after line 6 if an increment is even.

  c. Hibbard's increments

  d. Knuth's increments: $h_i = \frac{1}{2}(3^i + 1)$

e. Gonnet's increments: $h_t = \lfloor \frac{n}{2.2} \rfloor$, and $h_k = \lfloor \frac{h_{k+1}}{2.2} \rfloor$ (with $h_1 = 1$ if $h_2 = 2$)

f. Sedgewick's increments.

7.35 Implement an optimized version of quicksort and experiment with combinations of the following:

a. Pivot: first element, middle element, random element, median of three, median of five.

b. Cutoff values from 0 to 20.

7.36 Write a routine that reads in two alphabetized files and merges them together, forming a third, alphabetized, file.

7.37 Suppose we implement the median of three routine as follows: Find the median of $A[Left]$, $A[Center]$, $A[Right]$, and swap it with $A[Right]$. Proceed with the normal partitioning step starting i at $Left$ and j at $Right - 1$ (instead of $Left + 1$ and $Right - 2$). Assume that $A[Left - 1] = Min\_Data$, so that sentinels are present.

a. Suppose the input is $2, 3, 4, ..., n - 1, n, 1$. What is the running time of this version of quicksort?

b. Suppose the input is in reverse order. What is the running time of this version of quicksort?

7.38 Prove that any comparison-based sorting algorithm requires $\Omega(n \log n)$ comparisons on average.

7.39 Consider the following strategy for $Percolate\_Down$. We have a hole at node X. The normal routine is to compare X's children and then move the child up to X if it is larger (in the case of a (max)heap) than the element we are trying to place, thereby pushing the hole down; we stop when it is safe to place the new element in the hole. The alternate strategy is to move elements up and the hole down as far as possible without testing whether the new cell can be inserted. This would place the new cell in a leaf and probably violate the heap order; to fix the heap order, percolate the new cell up in the normal manner. Write a routine to include this idea, and compare the running time with a standard implementation of heapsort.

7.40 Propose an algorithm to sort a large file using only two tapes.

References

Knuth's book [10] is a comprehensive, though somewhat dated, reference for sorting. Gonnet and Baeza-Yates [4] has some more recent results, as well as a huge bibliography.

The original paper detailing Shellsort is [22]. The paper by Hibbard [5] suggested the use of the increments $2^k - 1$ and tightened the code by avoiding swaps. Theorem 7.4 is from [13]. Pratt's lower bound, which uses a more complex method than that suggested in the text, can be found in [15]. Improved increment sequences and upper bounds appear in [9], [21], and [24]; matching lower bounds have been shown in [25]. A recent result shows that no increment sequence gives an $O(n \log n)$ worst-case running time [14]. The average-case running time for Shellsort is still unresolved. Yao [27] has performed an extremely complex analysis for the three-increment case. The result has yet to be extended to more increments. Experiments with various increment sequences appear in [23].

Heapsort was invented by Williams [26]; Floyd [1] provided the linear-time algorithm for heap construction. The analysis of its average case has only recently been obtained [16].

An exact average-case analysis of mergesort has been claimed in [3]; the paper detailing the results is forthcoming. An algorithm to perform merging in linear time without extra space is described in [8].

Quicksort is from Hoare [6]. This paper analyzes the basic algorithm, describes most of the improvements, and includes the selection algorithm. A detailed analysis and empirical study was the subject of Sedgewick's dissertation [20]. Many of the important results appear in the three papers [17], [18], and [19].

Decision trees and sorting optimality are discussed in Ford and Johnson [2]. This paper also provides an algorithm that almost meets the lower bound in terms of number of comparisons (but not other operations). This algorithm was eventually shown to be slightly suboptimal by Manacher [11].

External sorting is covered in detail in [10] and [12]. Stable sorting, described in Exercise 7.24, has been addressed by Horvath [7].

1. R. W. Floyd, "Algorithm 245: Treesort 3," *Communications of the ACM* 7 (1964), 701.
2. L. R. Ford and S. M. Johnson, "A Tournament Problem," *American Mathematics Monthly* 66 (1959), 387–389.
3. M. Golin and R. Sedgewick, "Exact Analysis of Mergesort," *Fourth SIAM Conference on Discrete Mathematics,* 1988.
4. G. H. Gonnet and R. Baeza-Yates, *Handbook of Algorithms and Data Structures,* second edition, Addison-Wesley, Reading, Mass., 1991.
5. T. H. Hibbard, "An Empirical Study of Minimal Storage Sorting," *Communications of the ACM* 6 (1963), 206–213.
6. C. A. R. Hoare, "Quicksort," *Computer Journal* 5 (1962), 10–15.
7. E. C. Horvath, "Stable Sorting in Asymptotically Optimal Time and Extra Space," *Journal of the ACM* 25 (1978), 177–199.
8. B. Huang and M. Langston, "Practical In-place Merging," *Communications of the ACM* 31 (1988), 348–352.
9. J. Incerpi and R. Sedgewick, "Improved Upper Bounds on Shellsort," *Journal of Computer and System Sciences* 31 (1985), 210–224.
10. D. E. Knuth, *The Art of Computer Programming. Volume 3: Sorting and Searching,* second printing, Addison-Wesley, Reading, Mass. 1975.
11. G. K. Manacher, "The Ford-Johnson Sorting Algorithm Is Not Optimal," *Journal of the ACM* 26 (1979), 441–456.
12. N. E. Miller, *File Structures Using Pascal,* Benjamin/Cummings, Redwood City, Calif. 1985.
13. A. A. Papernov and G. V. Stasevich, "A Method of Information Sorting in Computer Memories," *Problems of Information Transmission* 1 (1965), 63–75.

14. C. G. Plaxton, B. Poonen, and T. Suel, "Improved Lower Bounds for Shellsort," *Proceedings of the Thirty-Third Annual IEEE Symposium on the Foundations of Computer Science,* (1992). 226–235.
15. V. R. Pratt, *Shellsort and Sorting Networks,* Garland Publishing, New York, 1979. (Originally presented as the author's Ph.D. thesis, Stanford University, 1971.)
16. R. Schaffer and R. Sedgewick, "The Analysis of Heapsort," *Journal of Algorithms,* 14 (1993), 76–100.
17. R. Sedgewick, "Quicksort with Equal Keys," *SIAM Journal on Computing* 6 (1977), 240–267.
18. R. Sedgewick, "The Analysis of Quicksort Programs," *Acta Informatica* 7 (1977), 327–355.
19. R. Sedgewick, "Implementing Quicksort Programs," *Communications of the ACM* 21 (1978), 847–857.
20. R. Sedgewick, *Quicksort,* Garland Publishing, New York, 1978. (Originally presented as the author's Ph.D. thesis, Stanford University, 1975.)
21. R. Sedgewick, "A New Upper Bound for Shellsort," *Journal of Algorithms* 7 (1986), 159–173.
22. D. L. Shell, "A High-Speed Sorting Procedure," *Communications of the ACM* 2 (1959), 30–32.
23. M. A. Weiss, "Empirical Results on the Running Time of Shellsort," *Computer Journal* 34 (1991), 88–91.
24. M. A. Weiss and R. Sedgewick, "More on Shellsort Increment Sequences," *Information Processing Letters* 34 (1990), 267–270.
25. M. A. Weiss and R. Sedgewick, "Tight Lower Bounds for Shellsort," *Journal of Algorithms* 11 (1990), 242–251.
26. J. W. J. Williams, "Algorithm 232: Heapsort," *Communications of the ACM* 7 (1964), 347–348.
27. A. C. Yao, "An Analysis of $(h, k, 1)$ Shellsort," *Journal of Algorithms* 1 (1980), 14–50.

CHAPTER 8

The Disjoint Set ADT

In this chapter we describe an efficient data structure to solve the equivalence problem. The data structure is simple to implement. Each routine requires only a few lines of code, and a simple array can be used. The implementation is also extremely fast, requiring constant average time per operation. This data structure is also very interesting from a theoretical point of view because its analysis is extremely difficult; the functional form of the worst case is unlike any we have yet seen. For the disjoint set ADT, we will

- Show how it can be implemented with minimal coding effort.
- Greatly increase its speed using just two simple observations.
- Analyze the running time of a fast implementation.
- See a simple application.

8.1. Equivalence Relations

A *relation* R is defined on a set S if for every pair of elements (a, b), $a, b \in S$, $a \, R \, b$ is either true or false. If $a \, R \, b$ is true, then we say that a is related to b.

An *equivalence relation* is a relation R that satisfies three properties:

1. (*Reflexive*) $a \, R \, a$, for all $a \in S$.
2. (*Symmetric*) $a \, R \, b$ if and only if $b \, R \, a$.
3. (*Transitive*) $a \, R \, b$ and $b \, R \, c$ implies that $a \, R \, c$.

We'll consider several examples.

The $\leq$ relationship is not an equivalence relationship. Although it is reflexive, since $a \leq a$, and transitive, since $a \leq b$ and $b \leq c$ implies $a \leq c$, it is not symmetric, since $a \leq b$ does not imply $b \leq a$.

Electrical connectivity, where all connections are by metal wires, is an equivalence relation. The relation is clearly reflexive, as any component is connected to itself. If a is electrically connected to b, then b must be electrically connected to a,

297

so the relation is symmetric. Finally, if a is connected to b and b is connected to c, then a is connected to c. Thus electrical connectivity is an equivalence relation.

Two cities are related if they are in the same country. It is easily verified that this is an equivalence relation. Suppose town a is related to b if it is possible to travel from a to b by taking roads. This relation is an equivalence relation if all the roads are two-way.

8.2.   The Dynamic Equivalence Problem

Given an equivalence relation $\sim$, the natural problem is to decide, for any a and b, if $a \sim b$. If the relation is stored as a two-dimensional array of booleans, then, of course, this can be done in constant time. The problem is that the relation is usually not explicitly, but rather implicitly, defined.

As an example, suppose the equivalence relation is defined over the five-element set $\{a_1, a_2, a_3, a_4, a_5\}$. Then there are 25 pairs of elements, each of which is either related or not. However, the information $a_1 \sim a_2, a_3 \sim a_4, a_5 \sim a_1, a_4 \sim a_2$ implies that all pairs are related. We would like to be able to infer this quickly.

The *equivalence class* of an element $a \in S$ is the subset of S that contains all the elements that are related to a. Notice that the equivalence classes form a partition of S: Every member of S appears in exactly one equivalence class. To decide if $a \sim b$, we need only to check whether a and b are in the same equivalence class. This provides our strategy to solve the equivalence problem.

The input is initially a collection of n sets, each with one element. This initial representation is that all relations (except reflexive relations) are false. Each set has a different element, so that $S_i \cap S_j = \varnothing$; this makes the sets *disjoint*.

There are two permissible operations. The first is *Find*, which returns the name of the set (that is, the equivalence class) containing a given element. The second operation adds relations. If we want to add the relation $a \sim b$, then we first see if a and b are already related. This is done by performing *Find*s on both a and b and checking whether they are in the same equivalence class. If they are not, then we apply *Union*. This operation merges the two equivalence classes containing a and b into a new equivalence class. From a set point of view, the result of $\cup$ is to create a new set $S_k = S_i \cup S_j$, destroying the originals and preserving the disjointness of all the sets. The algorithm to do this is frequently known as the disjoint set *Union/Find algorithm* for this reason.

This algorithm is *dynamic* because, during the course of the algorithm, the sets can change via the *Union* operation. The algorithm must also operate *on-line*: When a *Find* is performed, it must give an answer before continuing. Another possibility would be an *off-line* algorithm. Such an algorithm would be allowed to see the entire sequence of *Union*s and *Find*s. The answer it provides for each *Find* must still be consistent with all the *Union*s that were performed up until the *Find*, but the algorithm can give all its answers after it has seen *all* the questions. The difference is similar to taking a written exam (which is generally off-line—you only have to give the answers before time expires), and an oral exam (which is on-line because you must answer the current question before proceeding to the next question).

Notice that we do not perform any operations comparing the relative values of elements, but merely require knowledge of their location. For this reason, we can assume that all the elements have been numbered sequentially from 1 to n and that the numbering can be determined easily by some hashing scheme. Thus, initially we have $S_i = \{i\}$ for $i = 1$ through n.

Our second observation is that the name of the set returned by *Find* is actually fairly arbitrary. All that really matters is that $Find(x) = Find(y)$ if and only if x and y are in the same set.

These operations are important in many graph theory problems and also in compilers that process equivalence (or type) declarations. We will see an application later.

There are two strategies to solve this problem. One ensures that the *Find* instruction can be executed in constant worst-case time, and the other ensures that the *Union* instruction can be executed in constant worst-case time. It has recently been shown that both cannot be done simultaneously in constant worst-case time.

We will now briefly discuss the first approach. For the *Find* operation to be fast, we could maintain, in an array, the name of the equivalence class for each element. Then *Find* is just a simple $O(1)$ lookup. Suppose we want to perform $Union(a, b)$. Suppose that a is in equivalence class i and b is in equivalence class j. Then we scan down the array, changing all is to j. Unfortunately, this scan takes $\Theta(n)$. Thus, a sequence of $n - 1$ unions (the maximum, since then everything is in one set), would take $\Theta(n^2)$ time. If there are $\Omega(n^2)$ *Find* operations, this performance is fine, since the total running time would then amount to $O(1)$ for each *Union* or *Find* operation over the course of the algorithm. If there are fewer *Find*s, this bound is not acceptable.

One idea is to keep all the elements that are in the same equivalence class in a linked list. This saves time when updating, because we do not have to search through the entire array. This by itself does not reduce the asymptotic running time, because it is still possible to perform $\Theta(n^2)$ equivalence class updates over the course of the algorithm.

If we also keep track of the size of each equivalence class, and when performing *Union*s we change the name of the smaller equivalence class to the larger, then the total time spent for $n - 1$ merges is $O(n \log n)$. The reason for this is that each element can have its equivalence class changed at most $\log n$ times, since every time its class is changed, its new equivalence class is at least twice as large as its old. Using this strategy, any sequence of m *Find*s and up to $n - 1$ *Union*s takes at most $O(m + n \log n)$ time.

In the remainder of this chapter, we will examine a solution to the *Union/Find* problem that makes *Union*s easy but *Find*s hard. Even so, the running time for any sequence of at most m *Find*s and up to $n - 1$ *Union*s will be only a little more than $O(m + n)$.

8.3. Basic Data Structure

Recall that the problem does not require that a *Find* operation return any specific name, just that *Find*s on two elements return the same answer if and only if they are in the same set. One idea might be to use a tree to represent each set, since each element in a tree has the same root. Thus, the root can be used to name the set. We will represent each set by a tree. (Recall that a collection of trees is known as a *forest*.) Initially, each set contains one element. The trees we will use are not necessarily binary trees, but their representation is easy, because the only information we will need is a parent pointer. The name of a set is given by the node at the root. Since only the name of the parent is required, we can assume that this tree is stored implicitly in an array: Each entry $p[i]$ in the array represents the parent of element i. If i is a root, then $p[i] = 0$. In the forest in Figure 8.1, $p[i] = 0$ for $1 \leq i \leq 8$. As with heaps, we will draw the trees explicitly, with the understanding that an array is being used. Figure 8.1 shows the explicit representation. We will draw the root's parent pointer vertically for convenience.

To perform a *Union* of two sets, we merge the two trees by making the root of one tree point to the root of the other. It should be clear that this operation takes constant time. Figures 8.2, 8.3, and 8.4 represent the forest after each of *Union*(5,6), *Union*(7,8), *Union*(5,7), where we have adopted the convention that the new root after the *Union* (*x,y*) is *x*. The implicit representation of the last forest is shown in Figure 8.5.

A *Find*(*x*) on element *x* is performed by returning the root of the tree containing *x*. The time to perform this operation is proportional to the depth of the node representing *x*, assuming, of course, that we can find the node representing *x* in constant time. Using the strategy above, it is possible to create a tree of depth $n - 1$, so the worst-case running time of a *Find* is $O(n)$. Typically, the running time is computed for a *sequence* of *m* intermixed instructions. In this case, *m* consecutive operations could take $O(mn)$ time in the worst case.

The code in Figures 8.6 through 8.9 represents an implementation of the basic algorithm, assuming that error checks have already been performed. We make this assumption only because the error checking would dominate and obscure the code for the algorithm. A robust program would, of course, have to check for errors. In our routine, *Union*s are performed on the roots of the trees. Sometimes the operation is performed by passing any two elements, and having the *Union* perform two *Find*s to determine the roots. (The name *Set_Union* is used to avoid confusing with the C++ keyword *union*.)

The average-case analysis is quite hard to do. The least of the problems is that the answer depends on how to define *average* (with respect to the *Union* operation). For instance, in the forest in Figure 8.4, we could say that since there are five trees, there are $5 \cdot 4 = 20$ equally likely results of the next *Union* (as any two different trees can be *Union*ed). Of course, the implication of this model is that there is only a $\frac{2}{5}$ chance that the next *Union* will involve the large tree. Another model might say that all *Union*s between any two *elements* in different trees are equally likely, so a larger tree is more likely to be involved in the next *Union* than a smaller tree. In the example above, there is an $\frac{8}{11}$ chance that the large tree is involved in the next *Union*, since (ignoring symmetries) there are 6 ways in which to merge two elements in $\{1, 2, 3, 4\}$, and 16 ways to merge an element in $\{5, 6, 7, 8\}$ with an element in $\{1, 2, 3, 4\}$. There are still more models and no general agreement on which is the best. The average running time depends on the model; $\Theta(m)$, $\Theta(m \log n)$, and $\Theta(mn)$ bounds have actually been shown for three different models, although the last bound is thought to be more realistic.

Quadratic running time for a sequence of operations is generally unacceptable. Fortunately, there are several ways of easily ensuring that this running time does not occur.

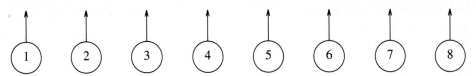

Figure 8.1 Eight elements, initially in different sets

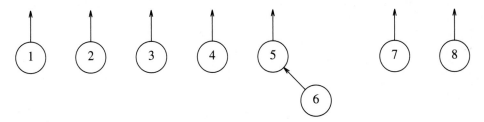

Figure 8.2 After *Union*(5, 6)

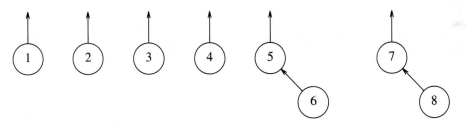

Figure 8.3 After *Union*(7, 8)

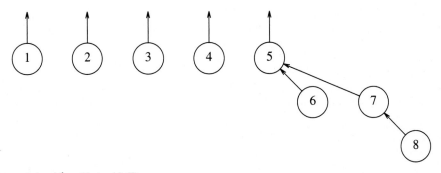

Figure 8.4 After *Union*(5, 7)

0	0	0	0	0	5	5	7
1	2	3	4	5	6	7	8

Figure 8.5 Implicit representation of previous tree

```
/* 1*/    static const Default_Size = 10;
/* 2*/    class Disj_Sets
/* 3*/    {
/* 4*/      private:
/* 5*/        int *S_Array;
/* 6*/        int S_Size;

/* 7*/      public:
/* 8*/        // Constructor.
/* 9*/        Disj_Sets( unsigned int Num_Elements = Default_Size );
/*10*/        Disj_Sets( Disj_Sets const & Value )
/*11*/            { Warn( "Sets passed by value" ); operator=( Value ); }

/*12*/        // Destructor.
/*13*/        ~Disj_Sets( ) { delete [ ] S_Array; }

/*14*/        // Operator.
/*15*/        const Disj_Sets & operator = ( Disj_Sets const & Value );

/*16*/        // Member functions.
/*17*/            // The basic routines.
/*18*/        void Set_Union( unsigned int Root1, unsigned int Root2 );
/*19*/        unsigned int Find( unsigned int X );

/*20*/            // The improved routines.
/*21*/        void Union_By_Height( unsigned int Root1,
/*22*/                                      unsigned int Root2 );
/*23*/        unsigned int Find_And_Compress( unsigned int X );
/*24*/    };
```

Figure 8.6 Disjoint set class specification

```
/* 1*/    Disj_Sets::
/* 2*/    Disj_Sets( unsigned int Num_Elements )
/* 3*/    {
/* 4*/        S_Size = Num_Elements;
/* 5*/        S_Array = new int [ S_Size + 1 ];
/* 6*/        for( int i = 0; i <= S_Size; i++ )
/* 7*/            S_Array[ i ] = 0;
/* 8*/    }
```

Figure 8.7 Disjoint set constructor

```
/* 1*/    // Union two disjoint sets.
/* 2*/    // For simplicity, we assume Root1 and Root2 are distinct
/* 3*/    // and represent set names.
/* 4*/    // Set_Union is used because union is a C++ keyword,
/* 5*/    // and thus potentially confusing.

/* 6*/    void
/* 7*/    Disj_Sets::
/* 8*/    Set_Union( unsigned int Root1, unsigned int Root2 )
/* 9*/    {
/*10*/        S_Array[ Root2 ] = Root1;
/*11*/    }
```

Figure 8.8 *Union* (not the best way)

```
/* 1*/    unsigned int
/* 2*/    Disj_Sets::
/* 3*/    Find( unsigned int X )
/* 4*/    {
/* 5*/        if( S_Array[ X ] <= 0 )
/* 6*/            return X;
/* 7*/        else
/* 8*/            return Find( S_Array[ X ] );
/* 9*/    }
```

Figure 8.9 A simple disjoint set *Find* algorithm

8.4. Smart Union Algorithms

The *Union*s above were performed rather arbitrarily, by making the second tree a subtree of the first. A simple improvement is always to make the smaller tree a subtree of the larger, breaking ties by any method; we call this approach *Union-by-size*. The three *Union*s in the preceding example were all ties, so we can consider that they were performed by size. If the next operation is *Union*(4, 5), then the forest in Figure 8.10 will form. Had the size heuristic not been used, a deeper forest would have been formed (Figure 8.11).

    We can prove that if *Union*s are done by size, the depth of any node is never more than $\log n$. To see this, note that a node is initially at depth 0. When its depth increases as a result of a *Union,* it is placed in a tree that is at least twice as large as before. Thus, its depth can be increased at most $\log n$ times. (We used this argument in the quick-find algorithm at the end of Section 8.2.) This implies that the running time for a *Find* operation is $O(\log n)$, and a sequence of m operations takes $O(m \log n)$. The tree in Figure 8.12 shows the worst tree possible after 16 *Union*s and is obtained if all *Union*s are between equal-sized trees (the worst-case trees are binomial trees, discussed in Chapter 6).

    To implement this strategy, we need to keep track of the size of each tree. Since we are really just using an array, we can have the array entry of each root contain

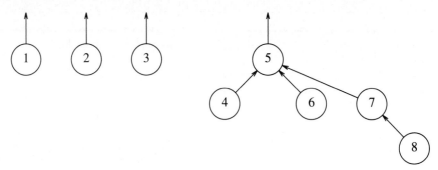

Figure 8.10   Result of union-by-size

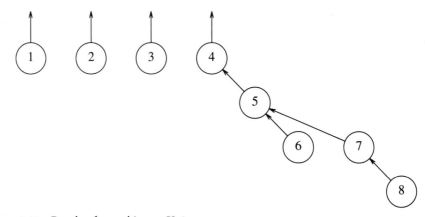

Figure 8.11   Result of an arbitrary *Union*

the *negative* of the size of its tree. Thus, initially the array representation of the tree is all −1s. When a *Union* is performed, check the sizes; the new size is the sum of the old. Thus, union-by-size is not at all difficult to implement and requires no extra space. It is also fast, on average. For virtually all reasonable models, it has been shown that a sequence of *m* operations requires $O(m)$ average time if union-by-size is used. This is because when random *Union*s are performed, generally very small (usually one-element) sets are merged with large sets throughout the algorithm.

An alternative implementation, which also guarantees that all the trees will have depth at most $O(\log n)$, is *Union-by-height*. We keep track of the height, instead of

Figure 8.12   Worst-case tree for $n = 16$

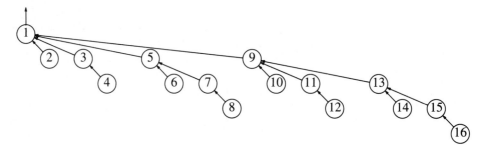

```
/* 1*/    // Union two disjoint sets using the height heuristic.
/* 2*/    // For simplicity, we assume Root1 and Root2 are distinct
/* 3*/    // and represent set names.

/* 4*/    void
/* 5*/    Disj_Sets::
/* 6*/    Union_By_Height( unsigned int Root1, unsigned int Root2 )
/* 7*/    {
/* 8*/        if( S_Array[ Root2 ] < S_Array[ Root1 ] )  // Root2 is deeper.
/* 9*/            S_Array[ Root1 ] = Root2;    // Make root2 new root.
/*10*/        else
/*11*/        {
/*12*/            if( S_Array[ Root1 ] == S_Array[ Root2 ] )
/*13*/                S_Array[ Root1 ]--;    // Update height if same.
/*14*/            S_Array[ Root2 ] = Root1;    // Make root1 new root.
/*15*/        }
/*16*/    }
```

Figure 8.13   Code for union-by-height (rank)

the size, of each tree and perform *Union*s by making the shallow tree a subtree of the deeper tree. This is an easy algorithm, since the height of a tree increases only when two equally deep trees are joined (and then the height goes up by one). Thus, union-by-height is a trivial modification of union-by-size.

The following figures show a tree and its implicit representation for both union-by-size and union-by-height. The code in Figure 8.13 implements union-by-height.

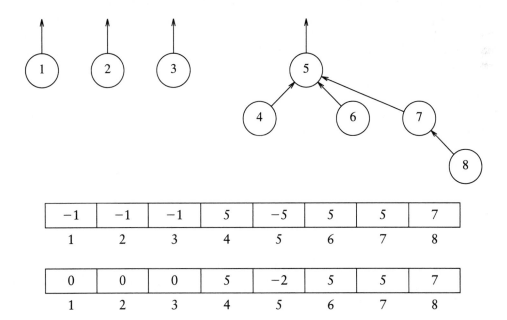

−1	−1	−1	5	−5	5	5	7
1	2	3	4	5	6	7	8

0	0	0	5	−2	5	5	7
1	2	3	4	5	6	7	8

8.5.   Path Compression

The *Union/Find* algorithm, as described so far, is quite acceptable for most cases. It is very simple and linear on average for a sequence of *m* instructions (under all models). However, the worst case of $O(m \log n)$ can occur fairly easily and naturally. For instance, if we put all the sets on a queue and repeatedly dequeue the first two sets and enqueue the union, the worst case occurs. If there are many more *Find*s than *Union*s, this running time is worse than that of the quick-find algorithm. Moreover, it should be clear that there are probably no more improvements possible for the *Union* algorithm. This is based on the observation that any method to perform the unions will yield the same worst-case trees, since it must break ties arbitrarily. Therefore, the only way to speed the algorithm up, without reworking the data structure entirely, is to do something clever on the *Find* operation.

The clever operation is known as *path compression*. Path compression is performed during a *Find* operation and is independent of the strategy used to perform *Union*s. Suppose the operation is *Find(x)*. Then the effect of path compression is that *every* node on the path from *x* to the root has its parent changed to the root. Figure 8.14 shows the effect of path compression after *Find*(15) on the generic worst tree of Figure 8.12.

The effect of path compression is that with an extra two pointer moves, nodes 13 and 14 are now one position closer to the root, and nodes 15 and 16 are now two positions closer. Thus, the fast future accesses on these nodes will pay (we hope) for the extra work to do the path compression.

As the code in Figure 8.15 shows, path compression is essentially a trivial change to the basic *Find* algorithm. The only algorithmic change to the *Find* routine is that *x*'s parent is made equal to the value returned by *Find*; thus, after the root of the set is found recursively, *x* is made to point directly to it. This occurs recursively to every node on the path to the root, so this implements path compression.

When *Union*s are done arbitrarily, path compression is a good idea because there is an abundance of deep nodes, and these are brought near the root by path

Figure 8.14   An example of path compression

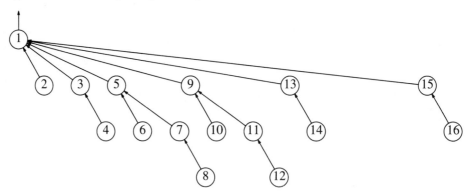

```
/* 1*/    unsigned int
/* 2*/    Disj_Sets::
/* 3*/    Find_And_Compress( unsigned int X )
/* 4*/    {
/* 5*/        if( S_Array[ X ] <= 0 )
/* 6*/            return X;
/* 7*/        else
/* 8*/            return S_Array[ X ] = Find( S_Array[ X ] );
/* 9*/    }
```

Figure 8.15 Code for disjoint set *Find* with path
compression

compression. It has been proven that when path compression is done in this case, a sequence of m operations requires at most $O(m \log n)$ time. It is still an open problem to determine what the average-case behavior is in this situation.

Path compression is perfectly compatible with union-by-size, and thus both routines can be implemented at the same time. Since doing union-by-size by itself is expected to execute a sequence of m operations in linear time, it is not clear that the extra pass involved in path compression is worthwhile on average. Indeed, this problem is still open. However, as we shall see later, the combination of path compression and a smart union rule guarantees a very efficient algorithm in all cases.

Path compression is not entirely compatible with union-by-height, because path compression can change the heights of the trees. It is not at all clear how to recompute them efficiently. The answer is do not!! Then the heights stored for each tree become estimated heights (sometimes known as *ranks*), but it turns out that union-by-rank (which is what this has now become) is just as efficient in theory as union-by-size. Furthermore, heights are updated less than sizes. As with union-by-size, it is not clear whether path compression is worthwhile on average. What we will show in the next section is that with either union heuristic, path compression significantly reduces the worst-case running time.

8.6.   Worst Case for Union-by-Rank and Path Compression

When both heuristics are used, the algorithm is almost linear in the worst case. Specifically, the time required in the worst case is $\Theta(m\alpha(m, n))$ (provided $m \geq n$), where $\alpha(m, n)$ is a functional inverse of Ackerman's function, which is defined below:[†]

$A(1, j) = 2^j$ for $j \geq 1$

$A(i, 1) = A(i - 1, 2)$ for $i \geq 2$

$A(i, j) = A(i - 1, A(i, j - 1))$ for $i, j \geq 2$

From this, we define

$$\alpha(m, n) = \min\{i \geq 1 | A(i, \lfloor m/n \rfloor) > \log n\}$$

You might want to compute some values, but for all practical purposes, $\alpha(m, n) \leq 4$, which is all that is really important here. The single-variable inverse Ackerman function, sometimes written as $\log^* n$, is the number of times the logarithm of n needs to be applied until $n \leq 1$. Thus, $\log^* 65536 = 4$, because $\log \log \log \log 65536 = 1$. $\log^* 2^{65536} = 5$, but keep in mind that 2^{65536} is a 20,000-digit number. $\alpha(m, n)$ actually grows even slower then $\log^* n$. However, $\alpha(m, n)$ is not a constant, so the running time is not linear.

In the remainder of this section, we will prove a slightly weaker result. We will show that any sequence of $m = \Omega(n)$ *Union/Find* operations takes a total of $O(m \log^* n)$ running time. The same bound holds if union-by-rank is replaced with union-by-size. This analysis is probably the most complex in the book and one of the first truly complex worst-case analyses ever performed for an algorithm that is essentially trivial to implement.

8.6.1. *Analysis of the Union/Find Algorithm*

In this section we establish a fairly tight bound on the running time of a sequence of $m = \Omega(n)$ *Union/Find* operations. The *Union*s and *Find*s may occur in any order, but *Union* is done by rank and *Find*s are done with path compression.

We begin by establishing some lemmas concerning the number of nodes of *rank r*. Intuitively, because of the union-by-rank rule, there are many more nodes of small rank than large rank. In particular, there can be at most one node of rank $\log n$. What we would like to do is to produce as precise a bound as possible on the number of nodes of any particular rank r. Since ranks change only when *Union*s are performed (and then only when the two trees have same rank), we can prove this bound by ignoring the path compression.

LEMMA 8.1.

When executing a sequence of Union instructions, a node of rank r must have 2^r descendants (including itself).

[†] Ackerman's function is frequently defined with $A(1, j) = j + 1$ for $j \geq 1$. The form in this text grows faster; thus, the inverse grows more slowly.

PROOF

By induction. The basis, $r = 0$, is clearly true. Let T be the tree of rank r with the fewest number of descendants and let x be T's root. Suppose the last *Union* x was involved in was between T_1 and T_2. Suppose T_1's root was x. If T_1 had rank r, then T_1 would be a tree of height r with fewer descendants than T, which contradicts the assumption that T is the tree with the smallest number of descendants. Hence the rank of $T_1 \leq r - 1$. The rank of $T_2 \leq$ *rank of* T_1. Since T has rank r and the rank could only increase because of T_2, it follows that the rank of $T_2 = r - 1$. Then the rank of $T_1 = r - 1$. By the induction hypothesis, each tree has at least 2^{r-1} descendants, giving a total of 2^r and establishing the lemma.

Lemma 8.1 tells us that if no path compression is performed, then any node of rank r must have at least 2^r descendants. Path compression can change this, of course, since it can remove descendants from a node. However, when *Unions* are performed, even with path compression, we are using the ranks, which are estimated heights. These ranks behave as though there is no path compression. Thus, when bounding the number of nodes of rank r, path compression can be ignored.

Thus, the next lemma is valid with or without path compression.

LEMMA 8.2.

The number of nodes of rank r is at most $n/2^r$.

PROOF

Without path compression, each node of rank r is the root of a subtree of at least 2^r nodes. No node in the subtree can have rank r. Thus all subtrees of nodes of rank r are disjoint. Therefore, there are at most $n/2^r$ disjoint subtrees and hence $n/2^r$ nodes of rank r.

The next lemma seems somewhat obvious, but is crucial in the analysis.

LEMMA 8.3.

At any point in the Union/Find algorithm, the ranks of the nodes on a path from the leaf to a root increase monotonically.

PROOF

The lemma is obvious if there is no path compression (see the example). If, after path compression, some node v is a descendant of w, then clearly v must have been a descendant of w when only *Unions* were considered. Hence the rank of v is less than the rank of w.

Let us summarize the preliminary results. Lemma 8.2 tells us how many nodes can be assigned rank r. Because ranks are assigned only by *Unions*, which have no idea of path compression, Lemma 8.2 is valid at any stage of the *Union/Find* algorithm—even in the midst of path compression. Figure 8.16 shows that while there are many nodes of ranks 0 and 1, there are fewer nodes of rank r as r gets larger.

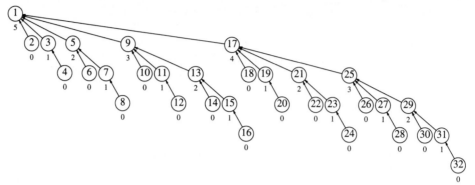

Figure 8.16 A large disjoint set tree (numbers below nodes are ranks)

Lemma 8.2 is tight, in the sense that it is possible for there to be $n/2^r$ nodes for any rank r. It is slightly loose because it is not possible for the bound to hold for all ranks r simultaneously. While Lemma 8.2 describes the *number* of nodes in a rank r, Lemma 8.3 tells us their *distribution*. As one would expect, the rank of nodes is strictly increasing along the path from a leaf to the root.

We are now ready to prove the main theorem. Our basic idea is as follows: A *Find* on any node v costs time proportional to the number of nodes on the path from v to the root. Let us, then, charge one unit of cost for every node on the path from v to the root for each *Find*. To help us count the charges, we will deposit an imaginary penny into each node on the path. This is strictly an accounting gimmick that is not part of the program. When the algorithm is over, we collect all the coins that have been deposited; this is the total cost.

As a further accounting gimmick, we deposit both American and Canadian pennies. We will show that during the execution of the algorithm, we can deposit only a certain number of American pennies during each *Find*. We will also show that we can deposit only a certain number of Canadian pennies to each node. Adding these two totals gives us a bound on the total number of pennies that can be deposited.

We now sketch our accounting scheme in a little more detail. We will divide the nodes by their ranks. We then divide the ranks into rank groups. On each *Find*, we will deposit some American coins into the general kitty and some Canadian coins into specific vertices. To compute the total number of Canadian coins deposited, we will compute the deposits per node. By adding up all the deposits for each node in rank r, we will get the total deposits per rank r. Then we will add up all the deposits for each rank r in group g and thereby obtain the total deposits for each rank group g. Finally, we add up all the deposits for each rank group g to obtain the total number of Canadian coins deposited in the forest. Adding this to the number of American coins in the kitty gives us the answer.

We will partition ranks into groups. Rank r goes into group $G(r)$, and G will be determined later. The largest rank in any rank group g is $F(g)$, where $F = G^{-1}$ is the *inverse* of G. The number of ranks in any rank group, $g > 0$, is thus $F(g) - F(g - 1)$. Clearly, $G(n)$ is a very loose upper bound on the largest rank group. As an example, suppose that we partitioned the ranks as in Figure 8.17. In

Group	Rank
0	0
1	1
2	2,3,4
3	5 through 9
4	10 through 16
i	$(i-1)^2 + 1$ through i^2

Figure 8.17   Possible partitioning of ranks into groups

this case, $G(r) = \lceil \sqrt{r} \rceil$. The largest rank in group g is $F(g) = g^2$, and observe that group $g > 0$ contains ranks $F(g-1)+1$ through $F(g)$ inclusive. This formula does not apply for rank group 0, so for convenience, we will ensure that rank group 0 contains only elements of rank 0. Notice that the groups are made of consecutive ranks.

As mentioned before, each *Union* instruction takes constant time, as long as each root keeps track of how big its subtrees are. Thus, *Union*s are essentially free, as far as this proof goes.

Each *Find(i)* takes time proportional to the number of vertices on the path from the vertex representing i to the root. We will thus deposit one penny for each vertex on the path. If this is all we do, however, we cannot expect much of a bound, because we are not taking advantage of path compression. Thus, we need to take advantage of path compression in our analysis. We will use fancy accounting.

For each vertex, v, on the path from the vertex representing i to the root, we deposit one penny under one of two accounts:

1. If v is the root, or if the parent of v is the root, or if the parent of v is in a different rank group from v, then charge one unit under this rule. This deposits an American penny into the kitty.

2. Otherwise deposit a Canadian penny into the vertex.

LEMMA 8.4.
For any Find(v), the total number of pennies deposited, either in the kitty or to a vertex, is exactly equal to the number of nodes on the path from v to the root.

PROOF
Obvious.

Thus all we need to do is to sum all the American pennies deposited under rule 1 with all the Canadian pennies deposited under rule 2.

We are doing at most m *Find*s. We need to bound the number of pennies that can be deposited into the kitty during a *Find*.

LEMMA 8.5.
Over the entire algorithm, the total deposits of American pennies under rule 1 amount to $m(G(n) + 2)$.

PROOF

This is easy. For any *Find*, at most two American pennies are deposited because of the root and its child. By Lemma 8.3, the vertices going up the path are monotonically increasing in rank, and since there are at most $G(n)$ rank groups, only $G(n)$ other vertices on the path can qualify as a rule 1 deposit for any particular *Find*. Thus, during any one *Find*, at most $G(n) + 2$ American pennies can be placed in the kitty. Thus, at most $m(G(n) + 2)$ American pennies can be deposited under rule 1 for a sequence of *m Find*s.

To get a good estimate for all the Canadian deposits under rule 2, we will add up the deposits by vertices instead of by *Find* instructions. If a coin is deposited into vertex v under rule 2, v will be moved by path compression and get a new parent of higher rank than its old parent. (This is where we are using the fact that path compression is being done.) Thus, a vertex v in rank group $g > 0$ can be moved at most $F(g) - F(g - 1)$ times before its parent gets pushed out of rank group g, since that is the size of the rank group.[†] After this happens, all future charges to v will go under rule 1.

LEMMA 8.6.

The number of vertices, $N(g)$, in rank group $g > 0$ is at most $n/2^{F(g-1)}$.

PROOF

By Lemma 8.2, there are at most $n/2^r$ vertices of rank r. Summing over the ranks in group g, we obtain

$$N(g) \leq \sum_{r=F(g-1)+1}^{F(g)} \frac{n}{2^r}$$

$$\leq \sum_{r=F(g-1)+1}^{\infty} \frac{n}{2^r}$$

$$\leq n \sum_{r=F(g-1)+1}^{\infty} \frac{1}{2^r}$$

$$\leq \frac{n}{2^{F(g-1)+1}} \sum_{s=0}^{\infty} \frac{1}{2^s}$$

$$\leq \frac{2n}{2^{F(g-1)+1}}$$

$$\leq \frac{n}{2^{F(g-1)}}$$

[†]This can be reduced by 1. We do not for the sake of clarity; the bound is not improved by being more careful here.

LEMMA 8.7.

The maximum number of Canadian pennies deposited to all vertices in rank group g is at most $nF(g)/2^{F(g-1)}$.

PROOF

Each vertex in the rank group can receive at most $F(g) - F(g - 1) \le F(g)$ Canadian pennies while its parent stays in its rank group, and Lemma 8.6 tells how many such vertices there are. The result is obtained by a simple multiplication.

LEMMA 8.8.

The total deposit under rule 2 is at most $n \sum_{g=1}^{G(n)} F(g)/2^{F(g-1)}$ Canadian pennies.

PROOF

Because rank group 0 contains only elements of rank 0, it cannot contribute to rule 2 charges (it cannot have a parent in the same rank group). The bound is obtained by summing the other rank groups.

Thus we have the deposits under rules 1 and 2. The total is

$$m(G(n) + 2) + n \sum_{g=1}^{G(n)} F(g)/2^{F(g-1)} \tag{8.1}$$

We still have not specified $G(n)$ or its inverse $F(n)$. Obviously, we are free to choose virtually anything we want, but it makes sense to choose $G(n)$ to minimize the bound above. However, if $G(n)$ is too small, then $F(n)$ will be large, hurting the bound. An apparently good choice is to choose $F(i)$ to be the function recursively defined by $F(0) = 0$ and $F(i) = 2^{F(i-1)}$. This gives $G(n) = 1 + \lfloor \log^* n \rfloor$. Figure 8.18 shows how this partitions the ranks. Notice that group 0 contains only rank 0, which we required in the previous lemma. F is very similar to the single-variable Ackerman function, which differs only in the definition of the base case ($F(0) = 1$).

Figure 8.18 Actual partitioning of ranks into groups used
in the proof

Group	Rank
0	0
1	1
2	2
3	3,4
4	5 through 16
5	17 through 2^{16}
6	65537 through 2^{65536}
7	truly huge ranks

THEOREM 8.1.

The running time of m Unions and Finds is $O(m \log^* n)$.

PROOF

Plug in the definitions of F and G into Equation (8.1). The total number of American pennies is $O(mG(n)) = O(m \log^* n)$. The total number of Canadian pennies is $n \sum_{g=1}^{G(n)} F(g)/2^{F(g-1)} = n \sum_{g=1}^{G(n)} 1 = nG(n) = O(n \log^* n)$. Since $m = \Omega(n)$, the bound follows.

What the analysis shows is that there are few nodes that could be moved frequently by path compression, and thus the total time spent is relatively small.

8.7. An Application

As an example of how this data structure might be used, consider the following problem. We have a network of computers and a list of bidirectional connections; each of these connections allows a file transfer from one computer to another. Is it possible to send a file from any computer on the network to any other? An extra restriction is that the problem must be solved *on-line*. Thus, the list of connections is presented one at a time, and the algorithm must be prepared to give an answer at any point.

An algorithm to solve this problem can initially put every computer in its own set. Our invariant is that two computers can transfer files if and only if they are in the same set. We can see that the ability to transfer files forms an equivalence relation. We then read connections one at a time. When we read some connection, say (u, v), we test to see whether u and v are the same set and do nothing if they are. If they are in different sets, we merge their sets. At the end of the algorithm, the graph is connected if and only if there is exactly one set. If there are m connections and n computers, the space requirement is $O(n)$. Using union-by-size and path compression, we obtain a worst-case running time of $O(m\alpha(m, n))$, since there are $2m$ Finds and at most $n - 1$ Unions. This running time is linear for all practical purposes.

We will see a much better application in the next chapter.

Summary

We have seen a very simple data structure to maintain disjoint sets. When the *Union* operation is performed, it does not matter, as far as correctness is concerned, which set retains its name. A valuable lesson that should be learned here is that it can be very important to consider the alternatives when a particular step is not totally specified. The *Union* step is flexible; by taking advantage of this, we are able to get a much more efficient algorithm.

Path compression is one of the earliest forms of *self-adjustment*, which we have seen elsewhere (splay trees, skew heaps). Its use is extremely interesting, especially from a theoretical point of view, because it was one of the first examples of a simple algorithm with a not-so-simple worst-case analysis.

Exercises

8.1 Show the result of the following sequence of instructions: $Union(1, 2)$, $Union(3, 4)$, $Union(3, 5)$, $Union(1, 7)$, $Union(3, 6)$, $Union(8, 9)$, $Union(1, 8)$, $Union(3, 10)$, $Union(3, 11)$, $Union(3, 12)$, $Union(3, 13)$, $Union(14, 15)$, $Union(16, 17)$, $Union(14, 16)$, $Union(1, 3)$, $Union(1, 14)$ when the $Unions$ are performed

   a. arbitrarily

   b. by height

   c. by size

8.2 For each of the trees in the previous exercise, perform a $Find$ with path compression on the deepest node.

8.3 Write a program to determine the effects of path compression and the various $Unioning$ strategies. Your program should process a long sequence of equivalence operations using all six of the possible strategies.

8.4 Show that if $Unions$ are performed by height, then the depth of any tree is $O(\log n)$.

8.5 a. Show that if $m = n^2$, then the running time of m Union/Find operations is $O(m)$.

   b. Show that if $m = n \log n$, then the running time of m Union/Find operations is $O(m)$.

   *c. Suppose $m = \Theta(n \log \log n)$. What is the running time of m Union/Find operations?

   *d. Suppose $m = \Theta(n \log^* n)$. What is the running time of m Union/Find operations?

8.6 Show the operation of the program in Section 8.7 on the following graph: (1,2), (3,4), (3,6), (5,7), (4,6), (2,4), (8,9), (5,8). What are the connected components?

8.7 Write a program to implement the algorithm in Section 8.7.

*8.8 Suppose we want to add an extra operation, $Deunion$, which undoes the last $Union$ operation that has not been already undone.

   a. Show that if we do union-by-height and $Finds$ without path compression, then $Deunion$ is easy and a sequence of m Union, Find, and Deunion operations take $O(m \log n)$ time.

   b. Why does path compression make $Deunion$ hard?

   **c. Show how to implement all three operations so that the sequence of m operations takes $O(m \log n / \log \log n)$ time.

*8.9 Suppose we want to add an extra operation, *Remove(x)*, which removes x from its current set and places it in its own. Show how to modify the *Union/Find* algorithm so that the running time of a sequence of m *Union*, *Find*, and *Remove* operations is $O(m\alpha(m, n))$.

**8.10 Give an algorithm that takes as input an n-vertex tree and a list of n pairs of vertices and determines for each pair (v, w) the closest common ancestor of v and w. Your algorithm should run in $O(n \log^* n)$.

*8.11 Show that if all of the *Union*s precede the *Find*s, then the disjoint set algorithm with path compression requires linear time, even if the *Union*s are done arbitrarily.

**8.12 Prove that if *Union*s are done arbitrarily, but path compression is performed on the *Find*s, then the worst-case running time is $\Theta(m \log n)$.

8.13 Prove that if *Union*s are done by size and path compression is performed, the worst-case running time is $O(m \log^* n)$.

8.14 Suppose we implement partial path compression on *Find(i)* by making every other node on the path from i to the root point to its grandparent (where this makes sense). This is known as *path halving*.

    a. Write a procedure to do this.

    b. Prove that if path halving is performed on the *Find*s and either union-by-height or union-by-size is used, the worst-case running time is $O(m \log^* n)$.

References

Various solutions to the *Union/Find* problem can be found in [5], [8], and [10]. Hopcroft and Ullman showed the $O(m \log^* n)$ bound of Section 8.6. Tarjan [14] obtained the bound $O(m\alpha(m, n))$. A more precise (but asymptotically identical) bound for $m < n$ appears in [2] and [17]. Various other strategies for path compression and *Union*s also achieve the same bound; see [17] for details.

A lower bound showing that under certain restrictions $\Omega(m\alpha(m, n))$ time is required to process m *Union/Find* operations was given by Tarjan [15]. Identical bounds under less restrictive conditions have been recently shown in [6] and [13].

Applications of the *Union/Find* data structure appear in [1] and [9]. Certain special cases of the *Union/Find* problem can be solved in $O(m)$ time [7]. This reduces the running time of several algorithms, such as [1], graph dominance, and reducibility (see references in Chapter 9) by a factor of $\alpha(m, n)$. Others, such as [9] and the graph connectivity problem in this chapter, are unaffected. The paper lists 10 examples. Tarjan has used path compression to obtain efficient algorithms for several graph problems [16].

Average-case results for the *Union/Find* problem appear in [4], [11], and [19]. Results bounding the running time of any single operation (as opposed to the entire sequence) appear in [3] and [12].

Exercise 8.8 is solved in [18].

1. A. V. Aho, J. E. Hopcroft, J. D. Ullman, "On Finding Lowest Common Ancestors in Trees," *SIAM Journal on Computing* 5 (1976), 115–132.
2. L. Banachowski, "A Complement to Tarjan's Result about the Lower Bound on the Complexity of the Set Union Problem," *Information Processing Letters* 11 (1980), 59–65.
3. N. Blum, "On the Single-operation Worst-case Time Complexity of the Disjoint Set Union Problem," *SIAM Journal on Computing* 15 (1986), 1021–1024.
4. J. Doyle and R. L. Rivest, "Linear Expected Time of a Simple Union Find Algorithm," *Information Processing Letters* 5 (1976), 146–148.
5. M. J. Fischer, "Efficiency of Equivalence Algorithms," *Complexity of Computer Computation* (eds. R. E. Miller and J. W. Thatcher), Plenum Press, 1972, 153–168.
6. M. L. Fredman and M. E. Saks, "The Cell Probe Complexity of Dynamic Data Structures," *Proceedings of the Twenty-first Annual Symposium on Theory of Computing* (1989), 345–354.
7. H. N. Gabow and R. E. Tarjan, "A Linear-time Algorithm for a Special Case of Disjoint Set Union," *Journal of Computer and System Sciences* 30 (1985), 209–221.
8. B. A. Galler and M. J. Fischer, "An Improved Equivalence Algorithm," *Communications of the ACM* 7 (1964), 301–303.
9. J. E. Hopcroft and R. M. Karp, "An Algorithm for Testing the Equivalence of Finite Automata," *Technical Report TR-71-114,* Department of Computer Science, Cornell University, Ithaca, N.Y., 1971.
10. J. E. Hopcroft and J. D. Ullman, "Set Merging Algorithms," *SIAM Journal on Computing* 2 (1973), 294–303.
11. D. E. Knuth and A. Schonhage, "The Expected Linearity of a Simple Equivalence Algorithm," *Theoretical Computer Science* 6 (1978), 281–315.
12. J. A. LaPoutre, "New Techniques for the Union-Find Problem," *Proceedings of the First Annual ACM–SIAM Symposium on Discrete Algorithms* (1990), 54–63.
13. J. A. LaPoutre, "Lower Bounds for the Union-Find and the Split-Find Problem on Pointer Machines," *Proceedings of the Twenty Second Annual ACM Symposium on Theory of Computing* (1990), 34–44.
14. R. E. Tarjan, "Efficiency of a Good but Not Linear Set Union Algorithm," *Journal of the ACM* 22 (1975), 215–225.
15. R. E. Tarjan, "A Class of Algorithms Which Require Nonlinear Time to Maintain Disjoint Sets," *Journal of Computer and System Sciences,* 18 (1979), 110–127.
16. R. E. Tarjan, "Applications of Path Compression on Balanced Trees," *Journal of the ACM* 26 (1979), 690–715.
17. R. E. Tarjan and J. van Leeuwen, "Worst Case Analysis of Set Union Algorithms," *Journal of the ACM* 31 (1984), 245–281.
18. J. Westbrook and R. E. Tarjan, "Amortized Analysis of Algorithms for Set Union with Backtracking," *SIAM Journal on Computing* 18 (1989), 1–11.
19. A. C. Yao, "On the Average Behavior of Set Merging Algorithms," *Proceedings of Eighth Annual ACM Symposium on the Theory of Computation,* (1976), 192–195.

CHAPTER 9

Graph Algorithms

In this chapter we discuss several common problems in graph theory. Not only are these algorithms useful in practice, they are interesting because in many real-life applications they are too slow unless careful attention is paid to the choice of data structures. We will

- Show several real-life problems that can be converted to problems on graphs.
- Give algorithms to solve several common graph problems.
- Show how the proper choice of data structures can drastically reduce the running time of these algorithms.
- See an important technique, known as depth-first search, and show how it can be used to solve several seemingly nontrivial problems in linear time.

9.1. Definitions

A *graph* $G = (V, E)$ consists of a set of *vertices*, V, and a set of *edges*, E. Each edge is a pair (v, w), where $v, w \in V$. Edges are sometimes referred to as *arcs*. If the pair is ordered, then the graph is *directed*. Directed graphs are sometimes referred to as *digraphs*. Vertex w is *adjacent* to v if and only if $(v, w) \in E$. In an undirected graph with edge (v, w), and hence (w, v), w is adjacent to v and v is adjacent to w. Sometimes an edge has a third component, known as either a *weight* or a *cost*.

A *path* in a graph is a sequence of vertices $w_1, w_2, w_3, \ldots, w_n$ such that $(w_i, w_{i+1}) \in E$ for $1 \le i < n$. The *length* of such a path is the number of edges on the path, which is equal to $n - 1$. We allow a path from a vertex to itself; if this path contains no edges, then the path length is 0. This is a convenient way to define an otherwise special case. If the graph contains an edge (v, v) from a vertex to itself, then the path v, v is sometimes referred to as a *loop*. The graphs we will consider will generally be loopless. A *simple* path is a path such that all vertices are distinct, except that the first and last could be the same.

A *cycle* in a directed graph is a path of length at least 1 such that $w_1 = w_n$; this cycle is simple if the path is simple. For undirected graphs, we require that the edges be distinct. The logic of these requirements is that the path u, v, u in an undirected graph should not be considered a cycle, because (u, v) and (v, u) are the same edge. In a directed graph these are different edges, so it makes sense to call this a cycle. A directed graph is *acyclic* if it has no cycles. A directed acyclic graph is sometimes referred to by its abbreviation DAG.

An undirected graph is connected if there is a path from every vertex to every other vertex. A directed graph with this property is called *strongly connected*. If a directed graph is not strongly connected, but the underlying graph (without direction to the arcs) is connected, then the graph is said to be *weakly connected*. A *complete graph* is a graph in which there is an edge between every pair of vertices.

An example of a real-life situation that can be modeled by a graph is the airport system. Each airport is a vertex, and two vertices are connected by an edge if there is a nonstop flight from the airports that are represented by the vertices. The edge could have a weight, representing the time, distance, or cost of the flight. It is reasonable to assume that such a graph is directed, since it might take longer or cost more (depending on local taxes, for example) to fly in different directions. We would probably like to make sure that the airport system is strongly connected, so that it is always possible to fly from any airport to any other airport. We might also like to quickly determine the best flight between any two airports. "Best" could mean the path with the fewest number of edges or could be taken with respect to one, or all, of the weight measures.

Traffic flow can be modeled by a graph. Each street intersection represents a vertex, and each street is an edge. The edge costs could represent, among other things, a speed limit or a capacity (number of lanes). We could then ask for the shortest route or use this information to find the most likely location for bottlenecks.

In the remainder of this chapter, we will see several more applications of graphs. Many of these graphs can be quite large, so it is important that the algorithms we use be efficient.

9.1.1.   *Representation of Graphs*

We will consider directed graphs (undirected graphs are similarly represented).

Suppose, for now, that we can number the vertices, starting at 1. The graph shown in Figure 9.1 represents 7 vertices and 12 edges.

One simple way to represent a graph is to use a two-dimensional array. This is known as an *adjacency matrix* representation. For each edge (u, v), we set $a[u][v]$ equal to 1; otherwise the entry in the array is 0. If the edge has a weight associated with it, then we can set $a[u][v]$ equal to the weight and use either a very large or a very small weight as a sentinel to indicate nonexistent edges. For instance, if we were looking for the cheapest airplane route, we could represent nonexistent flights with a cost of ∞. If we were looking, for some strange reason, for the most expensive airplane route, we could use $-\infty$ (or perhaps 0) to represent nonexistent edges.

Although this has the merit of extreme simplicity, the space requirement is $\Theta(|V|^2)$, which can be prohibitive if the graph does not have very many edges. An adjacency matrix is an appropriate representation if the graph is *dense*: $|E| = \Theta(|V|^2)$. In most of the applications that we shall see, this is not true. For instance, suppose the graph represents a street map. Assume a Manhattan-like orientation,

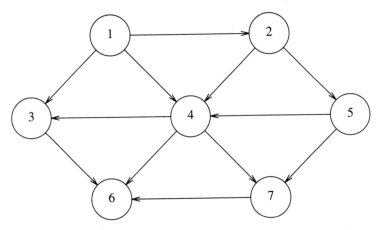

Figure 9.1   A directed graph

where almost all the streets run either north–south or east–west. Therefore, any intersection is attached to roughly four streets, so if the graph is directed and all streets are two-way, then $|E| \approx 4|V|$. If there are 3,000 intersections, then we have a 3,000-vertex graph with 12,000 edge entries, which would require an array of size nine million. Most of these entries would contain zero. This is intuitively bad, because we want our data structures to represent the data that is actually there and not the data that is not present.

If the graph is not dense—in other words, if the graph is *sparse*—a better solution is an *adjacency list* representation. For each vertex, we keep a list of all adjacent vertices. The space requirement is then $O(|E| + |V|)$. The representation should be clear from Figure 9.2; the leftmost structure in Figure 9.2 is merely an array of header cells.

Adjacency lists are the standard way to represent graphs. Undirected graphs can be similarly represented; each edge (u, v) appears in two lists, so the space usage essentially doubles. A common requirement in graph algorithms is to find all vertices adjacent to some given vertex v, and this can be done, in time proportional to the number of such vertices found, by a simple scan down the appropriate adjacency list.

In most real-life applications, the vertices have names, which are unknown at compile time, instead of numbers. Since we cannot index an array by an unknown name, we must provide a mapping of names to numbers. The easiest way to do this is to use a hash table in which we store a name and an internal number ranging from 1 to $|V|$ for each vertex. The numbers are assigned as the graph is read. The first number assigned is 1. As each edge is input, we check whether each of the two vertices has been assigned a number, by seeing if it is in the hash table. If so, we use the internal number. Otherwise, we assign to the vertex the next available number and insert the vertex name and number into the hash table.

With this transformation, all the graph algorithms will use only the internal numbers. Since eventually we will need to output the real vertex names and not the internal numbers, we must also record, for each internal number, the corresponding vertex name. One way is to use an array of strings. If the vertex names are long, this can cost considerable space because the vertex names are stored twice. An

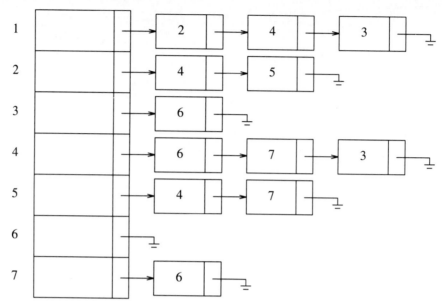

Figure 9.2   An adjacency list representation of a graph

alternative is to keep an array of pointers into the hash table. The price of this alternative is a slight loss of the sanctity of the hash table ADT.

The code that we present in this chapter will be pseudocode using previously defined classes as much as possible. We will do this to save space and, of course, to make the algorithmic presentation of the algorithms much clearer. For example, we do not define a graph class, though obviously this would be an easy extension. Our code thus bears a strong resemblence to C.

9.2.   Topological Sort

A *topological sort* is an ordering of vertices in a directed acyclic graph, such that if there is a path from v_i to v_j, then v_j appears *after* v_i in the ordering. The graph in Figure 9.3 represents the course prerequisite structure at a state university in Miami. A directed edge (v, w) indicates that course v must be completed before course w may be attempted. A topological ordering of these courses is any course sequence that does not violate the prerequisite requirement.

It is clear that a topological ordering is not possible if the graph has a cycle, since for two vertices v and w on the cycle, v precedes w and w precedes v. Furthermore, the ordering is not necessarily unique; any legal ordering will do. In the graph in Figure 9.4, $v_1, v_2, v_5, v_4, v_3, v_7, v_6$ and $v_1, v_2, v_5, v_4, v_7, v_3, v_6$ are both topological orderings.

A simple algorithm to find a topological ordering is first to find any vertex with no incoming edges. We can then print this vertex and remove it, along with its edges, from the graph. Then we apply this same strategy to the rest of the graph.

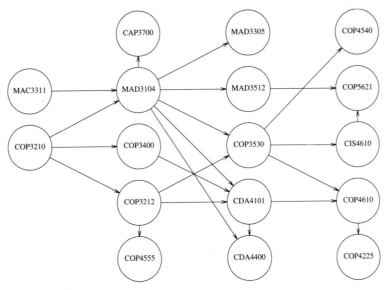

Figure 9.3 An acyclic graph representing course
prerequisite structure

To formalize this, we define the *Indegree* of a vertex v as the number of edges (u, v). We compute the indegrees of all vertices in the graph. Assuming that the *Indegree* array is initialized and that the graph is read into an adjacency list, we can then apply the algorithm in Figure 9.5 to generate a topological ordering.

The function *Find_New_Vertex_Of_Indegree_Zero* scans the *Indegree* array looking for a vertex with indegree 0 that has not already been assigned a topological number. It returns *Not_A_Vertex* (0) if no such vertex exists; this indicates that the graph has a cycle.

Because *Find_New_Vertex_Of_Indegree_Zero* is a simple sequential scan of the *Indegree* array, each call to it takes $O(|V|)$ time. Since there are $|V|$ such calls, the running time of the algorithm is $O(|V|^2)$.

Figure 9.4 An acyclic graph

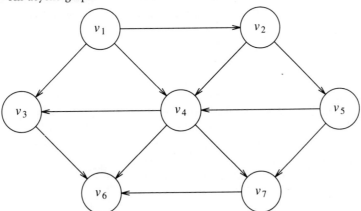

```
/* 1*/   void
/* 2*/   Topsort( Graph G )
/* 3*/   {
/* 4*/       Vertex V, W;

/* 5*/       for( int Counter = 1; Counter <= Num_Vertex; Counter++ )
/* 6*/       {
/* 7*/           V = Find_New_Vertex_Of_Indegree_Zero( );
/* 8*/           if( V == Not_A_Vertex )
/* 9*/           {
/*10*/               Error( "Graph has a cycle" );
/*11*/               return;
/*12*/           }
/*13*/           Top_Num[ V ] = Counter;
/*14*/           for Each W Adjacent To V
/*15*/               Indegree[ W ]--;
/*16*/       }
/*17*/   }
```

Figure 9.5   Simple topological sort pseudocode

By paying more careful attention to the data structures, it is possible to do better. The cause of the poor running time is the sequential scan through the *Indegree* array. If the graph is sparse, we would expect that only a few vertices have their indegrees updated during each iteration. However, in the search for a vertex of indegree 0, we look at (potentially) all the vertices, even though only a few have changed.

We can remove this inefficiency by keeping all the (unassigned) vertices of indegree 0 in a special *box*. The *Find_New_Vertex_Of_Indegree_Zero* function then returns (and removes) any vertex in the box. When we decrement the indegrees of the adjacent vertices, we check each vertex and place it in the box if its indegree falls to 0.

To implement the box, we can use either a stack or a queue. First, the indegree is computed for every vertex. Then all vertices of indegree 0 are placed on an initially empty queue. While the queue is not empty, a vertex v is removed, and all edges adjacent to v have their indegrees decremented. A vertex is put on the queue as soon as its indegree falls to 0. The topological ordering then is the order in which the vertices dequeue. Figure 9.6 shows the status after each phase.

A pseudocode implementation of this algorithm is given in Figure 9.7. As before, we will assume that the graph is already read into an adjacency list and that the indegrees are computed and placed in an array. A convenient way of doing this in practice would be to place the indegree of each vertex in the header cell. We also assume an array *Top_Num*, in which to place the topological numbering.

The time to perform this algorithm is $O(|E| + |V|)$ if adjacency lists are used. This is apparent when one realizes that the body of the *for* loop at line 14 is executed at most once per edge. The queue operations are done at most once per vertex, and the initialization steps also take time proportional to the size of the graph.

Vertex	Indegree Before Dequeue #						
	1	2	3	4	5	6	7
v_1	0	0	0	0	0	0	0
v_2	1	0	0	0	0	0	0
v_3	2	1	1	1	0	0	0
v_4	3	2	1	0	0	0	0
v_5	1	1	0	0	0	0	0
v_6	3	3	3	3	2	1	0
v_7	2	2	2	1	0	0	0
enqueue	v_1	v_2	v_5	v_4	v_3, v_7		v_6
dequeue	v_1	v_2	v_5	v_4	v_3	v_7	v_6

Figure 9.6   Result of applying topological sort to the graph
in Figure 9.4

```
/* 1*/   void
/* 2*/   Topsort( Graph G )
/* 3*/   {
/* 4*/       unsigned int Counter = 1;
/* 5*/       Vertex V, W;
/* 6*/       Queue<Vertex> Q( Num_Vertex );

/* 7*/       for Each Vertex V
/* 8*/           if ( Indegree[ V ] == 0 )
/* 9*/               Q.Enqueue( V );

/*10*/       while( !Q.Is_Empty( ) )
/*11*/       {
/*12*/           V = Q.Dequeue( );
/*13*/           Top_Num[ V ] = Counter++;

/*14*/           for Each W Adjacent To V
/*15*/               if( --Indegree[ W ] == 0 )
/*16*/                   Q.Enqueue( W );
/*17*/       }

/*18*/       if( Counter <= Num_Vertex )
/*19*/           Error( "Graph has a cycle" );
/*20*/   }
```

Figure 9.7   Pseudocode to perform topological sort

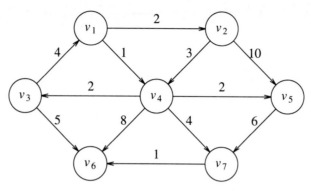

Figure 9.8   A directed graph G

1. UNWEIGHTED SHORTEST BATHS

9.3.   Shortest-Path Algorithms

In this section we examine various shortest-path problems. The input is a weighted graph: Associated with each edge (v_i, v_j) is a cost $c_{i,j}$ to traverse the arc. The cost of a path $v_1 v_2 \ldots v_n$ is $\sum_{i=1}^{n-1} c_{i,i+1}$. This is referred to as the *weighted path length*. The *unweighted path length* is merely the number of edges on the path, namely, $n - 1$.

> **SINGLE-SOURCE SHORTEST-PATH PROBLEM:**
>
> *Given as input a weighted graph, $G = (V, E)$, and a distinguished vertex, s, find the shortest weighted path from s to every other vertex in G.*

For example, in the graph in Figure 9.8 the shortest weighted path from v_1 to v_6 has a cost of 6 and goes from v_1 to v_4 to v_7 to v_6. The shortest unweighted path between these vertices is 2. Generally, when it is not specified whether we are referring to a weighted or an unweighted path, the path is weighted if the graph is. Notice also that in this graph there is no path from v_6 to v_1.

The graph in the preceding example has no edges of negative cost. The graph in Figure 9.9 shows the problems that negative edges can cause. The path from v_5

Figure 9.9   A graph with a negative-cost cycle

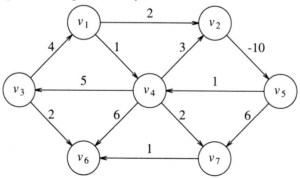

to v_4 has cost 1, but a shorter path exists by following the loop v_5, v_4, v_2, v_5, v_4, which has cost -5. This path is still not the shortest, because we could stay in the loop arbitrarily long. Thus, the shortest path between these two points is undefined. Similarly, the shortest path from v_1 to v_6 is undefined because we can get into the same loop. This loop is known as a *negative-cost cycle;* when one is present in the graph, the shortest paths are not defined. Negative-cost edges are not necessarily bad, as the cycles are, but their presence seems to make the problem harder. For convenience, in the absence of a negative-cost cycle, the shortest path from s to s is zero.

There are many situations in which we might want to solve the shortest-path problem. If the vertices represent computers, the edges represent a link between computers, and the costs represent communication costs (phone bill per 1,000 bytes of data), delay costs (number of seconds required to transmit 1,000 bytes), or a combination of these and other factors, then we can use the shortest-path algorithm to find the cheapest way to send electronic news from one computer to a set of other computers.

We can model airplane or other mass transit routes by graphs and use a shortest-path algorithm to compute the best route between two points. In this and many practical applications, we might want to find the shortest path from one vertex, s, to only one other vertex, t. Currently there are no algorithms in which finding the path from s to one vertex is any faster (by more than a constant factor) than finding the path from s to all vertices.

We will examine algorithms to solve four versions of this problem. First, we will consider the unweighted shortest-path problem and show how to solve it in $O(|E| + |V|)$. Next, we will show how to solve the weighted shortest-path problem if we assume that there are no negative edges. The running time for this algorithm is $O(|E| \log |V|)$ when implemented with reasonable data structures.

If the graph has negative edges, we will provide a simple solution, which unfortunately has a poor time bound of $O(|E| \cdot |V|)$. Finally, we will solve the weighted problem for the special case of acyclic graphs in linear time.

9.3.1. *Unweighted Shortest Paths* (Breadth First Searches)

Figure 9.10 shows an unweighted graph, G. Using some vertex, s, which is an input parameter, we would like to find the shortest path from s to all other vertices. We are only interested in the number of edges contained on the path, so there are no weights on the edges. This is clearly a special case of the weighted shortest-path problem, since we could assign all edges a weight of 1.

For now, suppose we are interested only in the length of the shortest paths, not in the actual paths themselves. Keeping track of the actual paths will turn out to be a matter of simple bookkeeping.

Suppose we choose s to be v_3. Immediately, we can tell that the shortest path from s to v_3 is then a path of length 0. We can mark this information, obtaining the graph in Figure 9.11.

Now we can start looking for all vertices that are a distance 1 away from s. These can be found by looking at the vertices that are adjacent to s. If we do this, we see that v_1 and v_6 are one edge from s. This is shown in Figure 9.12.

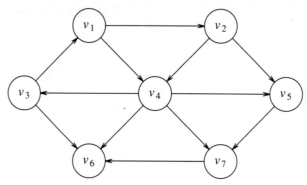

Figure 9.10 An unweighted directed graph G

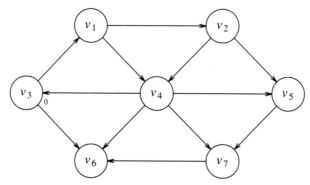

Figure 9.11 Graph after marking the start node as reachable in zero edges

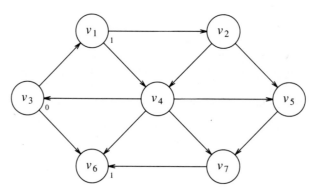

Figure 9.12 Graph after finding all vertices whose path length from s is 1

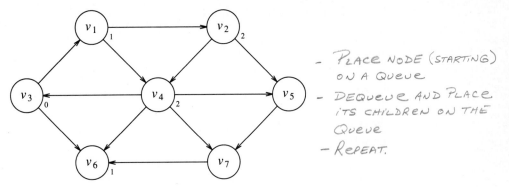

Figure 9.13   Graph after finding all vertices whose shortest path is 2

We can now find vertices whose shortest path from s is exactly 2 by finding all the vertices adjacent to v_1 and v_6 (the vertices at distance 1) whose shortest paths are not already known. This search tells us that the shortest path to v_2 and v_4 is 2. Figure 9.13 shows the progress that has been made so far.

Finally we can find, by examining vertices adjacent to the recently evaluated v_2 and v_4, that v_5 and v_7 have a shortest path of three edges. All vertices have now been calculated. Figure 9.14 shows the final result of the algorithm.

This strategy for searching a graph is known as *breadth-first search*. It operates by processing vertices in layers: the vertices closest to the start are evaluated first, and the most distant vertices are evaluated last. This is much the same as a level-order traversal for trees.

Given this strategy, we must translate it into code. Figure 9.15 shows the initial configuration of the table that our algorithm will use to keep track of its progress.

For each vertex, we will keep track of three pieces of information. First, we will keep its distance from s in the entry d_v. Initially all vertices are unreachable

Figure 9.14   Final shortest paths

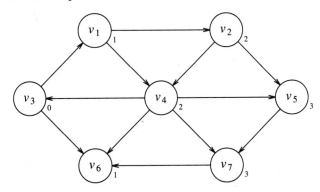

v	Known	d_v	p_v
v_1	0	∞	0
v_2	0	∞	0
v_3	0	0	0
v_4	0	∞	0
v_5	0	∞	0
v_6	0	∞	0
v_7	0	∞	0

Figure 9.15 Initial configuration of table used in unweighted shortest-path computation

except for s, whose path length is 0. The entry in p_v is the bookkeeping variable, which will allow us to print the actual paths. The entry *Known* is set to 1 after a vertex is processed. Initially, all entries are un*Known,* including the start vertex. When a vertex is *Known,* we have a guarantee that no cheaper path will ever be found, so processing for that vertex is essentially complete.

The basic algorithm can be described in Figure 9.16. The algorithm in Figure 9.16 mimics the diagrams by declaring as *Known* the vertices at distance $d = 0$,

Figure 9.16 Pseudocode for unweighted shortest-path algorithm

```
/* 1*/    void                    // T is initialized ( Fig 9.30 ).
/* 2*/    Unweighted( Table T )
/* 3*/    {
/* 4*/        Vertex V, W;

/* 5*/        for( int Curr_Dist = 0; Curr_Dist < Num_Vertex; Curr_Dist++ )
/* 6*/            for Each Vertex V
/* 7*/                if( !T[ V ].Known && T[ V ].Dist == Curr_Dist )
/* 8*/                {
/* 9*/                    T[ V ].Known = TRUE;
/*10*/                    for Each W Adjacent To V
/*11*/                        if( T[ W ].Dist == Infinity )
/*12*/                        {
/*13*/                            T[ W ].Dist = Curr_Dist + 1;
/*14*/                            T[ W ].Path = V;
/*15*/                        }
/*16*/                }
/*17*/    }
```

then $d = 1$, then $d = 2$, and so on, and setting all the adjacent vertices w that still have $d_w = \infty$ to a distance $d_w = d + 1$.

By tracing back through the p_v variable, the actual path can be printed. We will see how when we discuss the weighted case.

The running time of the algorithm is $O(|V|^2)$, because of the doubly nested *for* loops. An obvious inefficiency is that the outside loop continues until *Num_Vertex* -1, even if all the vertices become known much earlier. Although an extra test could be made to avoid this, it does not affect the worst-case running time, as can be seen by generalizing what happens when the input is the graph in Figure 9.17 with start vertex v_9.

We can remove the inefficiency in much the same way as was done for topological sort. At any point in time, there are only two types of unknown vertices that have $d_v \neq \infty$. Some have $d_v = Curr\_Dist$, and the rest have $d_v = Curr\_Dist + 1$. Because of this extra structure, it is very wasteful to search through the entire table to find a proper vertex at lines 6 and 7.

A very simple but abstract solution is to keep two boxes. Box #1 will have the unknown vertices with $d_v = Curr\_Dist$, and box #2 will have $d_v = Curr\_Dist + 1$. The test at lines 6 and 7 can be replaced by finding any vertex in box #1. After line 14 (inside the *if* block), we can add w to box #2. After the outside *for* loop terminates, box #1 is empty, and box #2 can be transferred to box #1 for the next pass of the *for* loop.

We can refine this idea even further by using just one queue. At the start of the pass, the queue contains only vertices of distance $Curr\_Dist$. When we add adjacent vertices of distance $Curr\_Dist + 1$, since they enqueue at the rear, we are guaranteed that they will not be processed until after all the vertices of distance $Curr\_Dist$ have been processed. After the last vertex at distance $Curr\_Dist$ dequeues and is processed, the queue contains only vertices of distance $Curr\_Dist + 1$, so this process perpetuates. We merely need to begin the process by placing the start node on the queue by itself.

The refined algorithm is shown in Figure 9.18. In the pseudocode, we have assumed that the start vertex, s, is known somehow and $T[s].Dist$ is 0. A C++ routine might pass s as an argument. Also, it is possible that the queue might empty prematurely, if some vertices are unreachable from the start node. In this case, a distance of *Infinity* will be reported for these nodes, which is perfectly reasonable. Finally, the *Known* field is not used; once a vertex is processed it can never enter the queue again, so the fact that it need not be reprocessed is implicitly marked. Thus, the *Known* field can be discarded. Figure 9.19 shows how the values on the graph we have been using are changed during the algorithm. We keep the *Known* field to make the table easier to follow, and for consistency with the rest of this section.

Figure 9.17 A bad case for unweighted shortest-path algorithm without data structures

```
/* 1*/    void                    // T is initialized ( Fig 9.30 ).
/* 2*/    Unweighted( Table T )
/* 3*/    {
/* 4*/        Vertex V, W;
/* 5*/        Queue<Vertex> Q( Num_Vertex );

/* 6*/        Q.Enqueue( S );    // Enqueue the start vertex S, determined
                                          elsewhere.

/* 7*/        while( ! Q.Is_Empty( ) )
/* 8*/        {
/* 9*/            V = Q.Dequeue( );
/*10*/            T[ V ].Known = TRUE;    // Not really needed anymore.
/*11*/            for Each W Adjacent To V
/*12*/                if( T[ W ].Dist == Infinity )
/*13*/                {
/*14*/                    T[ W ].Dist = T[ V ].Dist + 1;
/*15*/                    T[ W ].Path = V;
/*16*/                    Q.Enqueue( W );
/*17*/                }
/*18*/        }
/*19*/    }
```

Figure 9.18   Pseudocode for unweighted shortest-path algorithm

v	Initial State			v_3 Dequeued			v_1 Dequeued			v_6 Dequeued		
	Known	d_v	p_v	Known	d_v	p_v	Known	d_v	p_v	Known	d_v	p_v
v_1	0	∞	0	0	1	v_3	1	1	v_3	1	1	v_3
v_2	0	∞	0	0	∞	0	0	2	v_1	0	2	v_1
v_3	0	0	0	1	0	0	1	0	0	1	0	0
v_4	0	∞	0	0	∞	0	0	2	v_1	0	2	v_1
v_5	0	∞	0	0	∞	0	0	∞	0	0	∞	0
v_6	0	∞	0	0	1	v_3	0	1	v_3	1	1	v_3
v_7	0	∞	0	0	∞	0	0	∞	0	0	∞	0
Q :	v_3			v_1, v_6			v_6, v_2, v_4			v_2, v_4		

v	v_2 Dequeued			v_4 Dequeued			v_5 Dequeued			v_7 Dequeued		
	Known	d_v	p_v	Known	d_v	p_v	Known	d_v	p_v	Known	d_v	p_v
v_1	1	1	v_3	1	1	v_3	1	1	v_3	1	1	v_3
v_2	1	2	v_1	1	2	v_1	1	2	v_1	1	2	v_1
v_3	1	0	0	1	0	0	1	0	0	1	0	0
v_4	0	2	v_1	1	2	v_1	1	2	v_1	1	2	v_1
v_5	0	3	v_2	0	3	v_2	1	3	v_2	1	3	v_2
v_6	1	1	v_3	1	1	v_3	1	1	v_3	1	1	v_3
v_7	0	∞	0	0	3	v_4	0	3	v_4	1	3	v_4
Q :	v_4, v_5			v_5, v_7			v_7			empty		

Figure 9.19   How the data structure changes during the unweighted
                 shortest-path algorithm

Using the same analysis as was performed for topological sort, we see that the running time is $O(|E| + |V|)$, as long as adjacency lists are used.

9.3.2. Dijkstra's Algorithm   (FOR SHORTEST PATH IN WEIGHTED GRAPHS).

If the graph is weighted, the problem (apparently) becomes harder, but we can still use the ideas from the unweighted case.

We keep all of the same information as before. Thus, each vertex is marked as either known or unknown. A tentative distance d_v is kept for each vertex, as before. This distance turns out to be the shortest path length from s to v using only known vertices as intermediates. As before, we record p_v, which is the last vertex to cause a change to d_v.

The general method to solve the single-source shortest-path problem is known as *Dijkstra's algorithm*. This thirty-year-old solution is a prime example of a *greedy algorithm*. Greedy algorithms generally solve a problem in stages by doing what appears to be the best thing at each stage. For example, to make change in U.S. currency, most people count out the quarters first, then the dimes, nickels, and pennies. This greedy algorithm gives change using the minimum number of coins. The main problem with greedy algorithms is that they do not always work. The addition of a 12-cent piece breaks the coin-changing algorithm, because the answer it gives (one 12-cent piece and three pennies) is not optimal (one dime and one nickel).

Dijkstra's algorithm proceeds in stages, just like the unweighted shortest-path algorithm. At each stage, Dijkstra's algorithm selects a vertex v, which has the smallest d_v among all the unknown vertices, and declares that the shortest path from s to v is known. The remainder of a stage consists of updating the values of d_w.

In the unweighted case, we set $d_w = d_v + 1$ if $d_w = \infty$. Thus, we essentially lowered the value of d_w if vertex v offered a shorter path. If we apply the same logic to the weighted case, then we should set $d_w = d_v + c_{v,w}$ if this new value for d_w would be an improvement. Put simply, the algorithm decides whether or not it is a good idea to use v on the path to w. The original cost, d_w, is the cost without using v; the cost calculated above is the cheapest path using v (and only known vertices).

The graph in Figure 9.20 is our example. Figure 9.21 represents the initial configuration, assuming that the start node, s, is v_1. The first vertex selected is v_1, with path length 0. This vertex is marked known. Now that v_1 is known, some entries need to be adjusted. The vertices adjacent to v_1 are v_2 and v_4. Both these vertices get their entries adjusted, as indicated in Figure 9.22.

Next, v_4 is selected and marked known. Vertices v_3, v_5, v_6, and v_7 are adjacent, and it turns out that all require adjusting, as shown in Figure 9.23.

Next, v_2 is selected. v_4 is adjacent but already known, so no work is performed on it. v_5 is adjacent but not adjusted, because the cost of going through v_2 is $2 + 10 = 12$ and a path of length 3 is already known. Figure 9.24 shows the table after these vertices are selected.

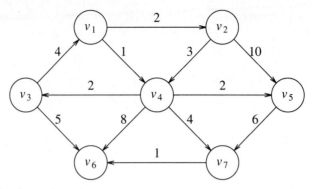

Figure 9.20   The directed graph G(again)

v	Known	d_v	p_v
v_1	0	0	0
v_2	0	∞	0
v_3	0	∞	0
v_4	0	∞	0
v_5	0	∞	0
v_6	0	∞	0
v_7	0	∞	0

Figure 9.21   Initial configuration of table used in
Dijkstra's algorithm

v	Known	d_v	p_v
v_1	1	0	0
v_2	0	2	v_1
v_3	0	∞	0
v_4	0	1	v_1
v_5	0	∞	0
v_6	0	∞	0
v_7	0	∞	0

Figure 9.22   After v_1 is declared known

v	Known	d_v	p_v
v_1	1	0	0
v_2	0	2	v_1
v_3	0	3	v_4
v_4	1	1	v_1
v_5	0	3	v_4
v_6	0	9	v_4
v_7	0	5	v_4

Figure 9.23 After v_4 is declared known

The next vertex selected is v_5 at cost 3. v_7 is the only adjacent vertex, but it is not adjusted, because $3 + 6 > 5$. Then v_3 is selected, and the distance for v_6 is adjusted down to $3 + 5 = 8$. The resulting table is depicted in Figure 9.25.

Next, v_7 is selected; v_6 gets updated down to $5 + 1 = 6$. The resulting table is Figure 9.26.

Figure 9.24 After v_2 is declared known

v	Known	d_v	p_v
v_1	1	0	0
v_2	1	2	v_1
v_3	0	3	v_4
v_4	1	1	v_1
v_5	0	3	v_4
v_6	0	9	v_4
v_7	0	5	v_4

Figure 9.25 After v_5 and then v_3 are declared known

v	Known	d_v	p_v
v_1	1	0	0
v_2	1	2	v_1
v_3	1	3	v_4
v_4	1	1	v_1
v_5	1	3	v_4
v_6	0	8	v_3
v_7	0	5	v_4

v	Known	d_v	p_v
v_1	1	0	0
v_2	1	2	v_1
v_3	1	3	v_4
v_4	1	1	v_1
v_5	1	3	v_4
v_6	0	6	v_7
v_7	1	5	v_4

Figure 9.26   After v_7 is declared known

Finally, v_6 is selected. The final table is shown in Figure 9.27. Figure 9.28 graphically shows how edges are marked known and vertices updated during Dijkstra's algorithm.

To print out the actual path from a start vertex to some vertex v, we can write a recursive routine to follow the trail left in the p array.

We now give pseudocode to implement Dijkstra's algorithm. We will assume that the vertices are numbered from 1 to *Num_Vertex* for convenience (see Figure 9.29) and that the graph can be read into an adjacency list by the routine *Read_Graph*.

In the routine in Figure 9.30, the start vertex is passed to the initialization routine. This is the only place in the code where the start vertex needs to be known.

The path can be printed out using the recursive routine in Figure 9.31. The routine recursively prints the path all the way up to the vertex before v on the path and then just prints v. This works because the path is simple.

Figure 9.32 shows the main algorithm, which is just a *for* loop to fill up the table using the greedy selection rule.

A proof by contradiction will show that this algorithm always works as long as no edge has a negative cost. If any edge has negative cost, the algorithm could produce the wrong answer (see Exercise 9.7a). The running time depends on how

Figure 9.27   After v_6 is declared known and algorithm terminates

v	Known	d_v	p_v
v_1	1	0	0
v_2	1	2	v_1
v_3	1	3	v_4
v_4	1	1	v_1
v_5	1	3	v_4
v_6	1	6	v_7
v_7	1	5	v_4

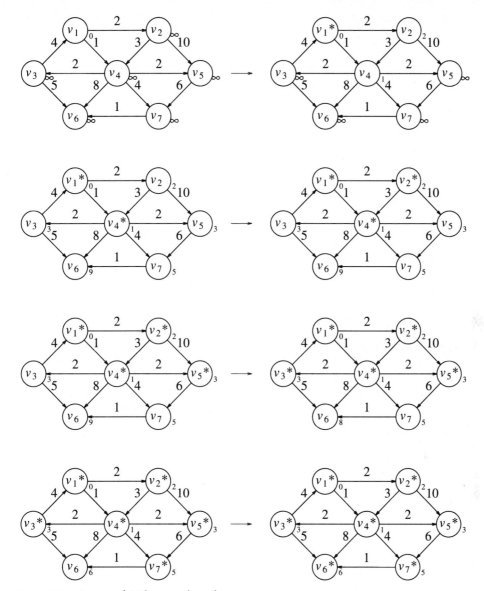

Figure 9.28 Stages of Dijkstra's algorithm

the table is manipulated, which we have yet to consider. If we use the obvious algorithm of scanning down the table to find the minimum d_v, each phase will take $O(|V|)$ time to find the minimum, and thus $O(|V|^2)$ time will be spent finding the minimum over the course of the algorithm. The time for updating d_w is constant per update, and there is at most one update per edge for a total of $O(|E|)$. Thus, the total running time is $O(|E| + |V|^2) = O(|V|^2)$. If the graph is dense, with $|E| = \Theta(|V|^2)$, this algorithm is not only simple but essentially optimal, since it runs in time linear in the number of edges.

```
/* 1*/   // Vertices are numbered starting at 1.

/* 2*/   const Not_A_Vertex = 0;
/* 3*/   typedef unsigned int Vertex;

/* 4*/   struct Adj_Vertex
/* 5*/   {
/* 6*/       Vertex W;
/* 7*/       Dist_Type V_W;
/* 8*/   };

/* 9*/   struct Table_Entry
/*10*/   {
/*11*/       List<Adj_Vertex> Adj_List;
/*12*/       int Known;
/*13*/       Dist_Type Dist;
/*14*/       Vertex Path;
/*15*/   };

/*16*/   typedef Table_Entry Table [ Num_Vertex + 1 ];
```

Figure 9.29 Declarations for Dijkstra's algorithm

```
/* 1*/   void
/* 2*/   Init_Table( Vertex Start, Graph & G, Table T )
/* 3*/   {
/* 4*/       Read_Graph( G, T );          // Read graph somehow.
/* 5*/       for( int i = 1; i <= Num_Vertex; i++ )
/* 6*/       {
/* 7*/           T[ i ].Known = FALSE;
/* 8*/           T[ i ].Dist  = Infinity;
/* 9*/           T[ i ].Path  = Not_A_Vertex;
/*10*/       }
/*11*/       T[ Start ].Dist = 0;
/*12*/   }
```

Figure 9.30 Table initialization routine

If the graph is sparse, with $|E| = \Theta(|V|)$, this algorithm is too slow. In this case, the distances would need to be kept in a priority queue. There are actually two ways to do this; both are similar.

Lines 7 and 10 combine to form a *Delete_Min* operation, since once the unknown minimum vertex is found, it is no longer unknown and must be removed from future consideration. The update at lines 16 and 17 can be implemented two ways.

```
/* 1*/    // Print shortest path to vertex V,
/* 2*/    // after procedure Dijkstra has run.
/* 3*/    // Assume that the path exists.

/* 4*/    void
/* 5*/    Print_Path( Vertex V, Table T )
/* 6*/    {
/* 7*/        if( T[ V ].Path != Not_A_Vertex )
/* 8*/        {
/* 9*/            Print_Path( T[ V ].Path, T );
/*10*/            cout << " to ";
/*11*/        }
/*12*/        cout << V;
/*13*/    }
```

Figure 9.31   Routine to print the actual shortest path

```
/* 1*/    void
/* 2*/    Dijkstra( Table T )
/* 3*/    {
/* 4*/        Vertex V, W;

/* 5*/        for( ; ; )
/* 6*/        {
/* 7*/            V = Smallest Unkown Distance Vertex;
/* 8*/            if( V == Not_A_Vertex )
/* 9*/                break;

/*10*/            T[ V ].Known = TRUE;
/*11*/            for Each W Adjacent To V
/*12*/                if( !T[ V ].Known )
/*13*/                    if( T[ V ].Dist + C ( V, W ) < T[ W ].Dist )
/*14*/                    {
/*15*/                        // Update W.
/*16*/                        decrease( T[ W ].Dist To
/*17*/                                    T[ V ].Dist + C ( V, W );
/*18*/                        T[ W ].Path = V;
/*19*/                    }
/*20*/        }
/*21*/    }
```

Figure 9.32   Pseudocode for Dijkstra's algorithm

One way treats the update as a *Decrease_Key* operation. The time to find the minimum is then $O(\log|V|)$, as is the time to perform updates, which amount to *Decrease_Key* operations. This gives a running time of $O(|E|\log|V|+ |V|\log|V|) = O(|E|\log|V|)$, an improvement over the previous bound for sparse graphs. Since priority queues do not efficiently support the *Find* operation, the location in the priority queue of each value of d_i will need to be maintained and updated whenever d_i changes in the priority queue. This is not typical of the priority queue ADT and thus is considered ugly.

The alternate method is to insert w and the new value d_w into the priority queue every time lines 16 and 17 are executed. Thus, there may be more than one representative for each vertex in the priority queue. When the *Delete_Min* operation removes the smallest vertex from the priority queue, it must be checked to make sure that it is not already known. Thus, line 7 becomes a loop performing *Delete_Min*s until an unknown vertex emerges. Although this method is superior from a software point of view and is certainly much easier to code, the size of the priority queue could get to be as big as $|E|$. This does not affect the asymptotic time bounds, since $|E| \le |V|^2$ implies that $\log|E| \le 2\log|V|$. Thus, we still get an $O(|E|\log|V|)$ algorithm. However, the space requirement does increase, and this could be important in some applications. Moreover, because this method requires $|E|$ *Delete_Min*s instead of only $|V|$, it is likely to be slower in practice.

Notice that for the typical problems, such as computer mail and mass transit commutes, the graphs are typically very sparse because most vertices have only a couple of edges, so it is important in many applications to use a priority queue to solve this problem.

There are better time bounds possible using Dijkstra's algorithm if different data structures are used. In Chapter 11, we will see another priority queue data structure called the Fibonacci heap. When this is used, the running time is $O(|E| + |V|\log|V|)$. Fibonacci heaps have good theoretical time bounds but a fair amount of overhead, so it is not clear whether using Fibonacci heaps is actually better in practice than Dijkstra's algorithm with binary heaps. Needless to say, there are no average-case results for this problem, since it is not even obvious how to model a random graph.

9.3.3. Graphs with Negative Edge Costs

If the graph has negative edge costs, then Dijkstra's algorithm does not work. The problem is that once a vertex u is declared known, it is possible that from some other, unknown vertex v there is a path back to u that is very negative. In such a case, taking a path from s to v back to u is better than going from s to u without using v.

A combination of the weighted and unweighted algorithms will solve the problem, but at the cost of a drastic increase in running time. We forget about the concept of known vertices, since our algorithm needs to be able to change its mind. We begin by placing s on a queue. Then, at each stage, we dequeue a vertex v. We find all vertices w adjacent to v such that $d_w > d_v + c_{v,w}$. We update d_w and p_w and place w on a queue if it is not already there. A bit can be set for each vertex to indicate presence in the queue. We repeat the process until the queue is empty. Figure 9.33 (almost) implements this algorithm.

Although the algorithm works if there are no negative-cost cycles, it is no longer true that the code in lines 11 through 17 is executed once per edge. Each vertex

```
/* 1*/    void                    // Assume T is initialized as in Fig 9.18.
/* 2*/    Weighted_Negative( Table T )
/* 3*/    {
/* 4*/        Vertex V, W;
/* 5*/        Queue<Vertex> Q( Num_Vertex );

/* 6*/        Q.Enqueue( S );              // Enqueue the start vertex S.
/* 7*/        while( ! Q.Is_Empty( ) )
/* 8*/        {
/* 9*/            V = Q.Dequeue( );
/*10*/            for Each W Adjacent To V
/*11*/                if( T[ V ].Dist + C ( V, W ) < T[ W ].Dist )
/*12*/                {   // Update W.
/*13*/                    T[ W ].Dist = T[ V ].Dist + C ( V, W );
/*14*/                    T[ W ].Path = V;
/*15*/                    if( ! Q.Already_In_Queue( W ) )
/*16*/                        Q.Enqueue( W );
/*17*/                }
/*18*/        }
/*19*/    }
```

Figure 9.33 Pseudocode for weighted shortest-path
             algorithm with negative edge costs

can dequeue at most $|V|$ times, so the running time is $O(|E| \cdot |V|)$ if adjacency lists are used (Exercise 9.7b). This is quite an increase from Dijkstra's algorithm, so it is fortunate that, in practice, edge costs are nonnegative. If negative-cost cycles are present, then the algorithm as written will loop indefinitely. By stopping the algorithm after any vertex has dequeued $|V| + 1$ times, we can guarantee termination.

9.3.4. Acyclic Graphs

If the graph is known to be acyclic, we can improve Dijkstra's algorithm by changing the order in which vertices are declared known, otherwise known as the *vertex selection rule*. The new rule is to select vertices in topological order. The algorithm can be done in one pass, since the selections and updates can take place as the topological sort is being performed.

This selection rule works because when a vertex v is selected, its distance, d_v, can no longer be lowered, since by the topological ordering rule it has no incoming edges emanating from unknown nodes.

There is no need for a priority queue with this selection rule; the running time is $O(|E| + |V|)$ since the selection takes constant time.

An acyclic graph could model some downhill skiing problem—we want to get from point a to b, but can only go downhill, so clearly there are no cycles. Another possible application might be the modeling of (nonreversible) chemical reactions. We could have each vertex represent a particular state of an experiment. Edges would represent a transition from one state to another, and the edge weights might

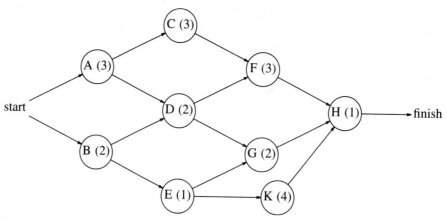

Figure 9.34   Activity-node graph

represent the energy released. If only transitions from a higher energy state to a lower are allowed, the graph is acyclic.

A more important use of acyclic graphs is *critical path analysis*. The graph in Figure 9.34 will serve as our example. Each node represents an activity that must be performed along with the time it takes to complete the activity. This graph is thus known as an *activity-node* graph. The edges represent precedence relationships: An edge (v, w) means that activity v must be completed before activity w may begin. Of course, this implies that the graph must be acyclic. We assume that any activities that do not depend (either directly or indirectly) on each other can be performed in parallel by different servers.

This type of graph could be (and frequently is) used to model construction projects. In this case, there are several important questions that would be of interest to answer. First, what is the earliest completion time for the project? We can see from the graph that 10 time units are required along the path A, C, F, H. Another important question is to determine which activities can be delayed, and by how long, without affecting the minimum completion time. For instance, delaying any of A, C, F, or H would push the completion time past 10 units. On the other hand, activity B is less critical and can be delayed up to two time units without affecting the final completion time.

To perform these calculations, we convert the activity-node graph to an *event-node* graph. Each event corresponds to the completion of an activity and all its dependent activities. Events reachable from a node v in the event-node graph may not commence until after the event v is completed. This graph can be constructed automatically or by hand. Dummy edges and nodes may need to be inserted if an activity depends on several others. This is necessary in order to avoid introducing false dependencies (or false lack of dependencies). The event-node graph corresponding to the graph in Figure 9.34 is shown in Figure 9.35.

To find the earliest completion time of the project, we merely need to find the length of the *longest* path from the first event to the last event. For general

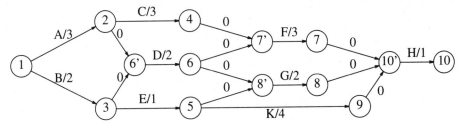

Figure 9.35 Event-node graph

graphs, the longest-path problem generally does not make sense because of the possibility of *positive-cost cycles*. These are the equivalent of negative-cost cycles in shortest-path problems. If positive-cost cycles are present, we could ask for the longest *simple* path, but no satisfactory solution is known for this problem. Since the event-node graph is acyclic, we need not worry about cycles. In this case, it is easy to adapt the shortest-path algorithm to compute the earliest completion time for all nodes in the graph. If EC_i is the earliest completion time for node i, then the applicable rules are

$$EC_1 = 0$$

$$EC_w = \max_{(v,w)\in E}(EC_v + c_{v,w})$$

Figure 9.36 shows the earliest completion time for each event in our example event-node graph.

We can also compute the latest time, LC_i, that each event can finish without affecting the final completion time. The formulas to do this are

$$LC_n = EC_n$$

$$LC_v = \min_{(v,w)\in E}(LC_w - c_{v,w})$$

These values can be computed in linear time by maintaining, for each vertex, a list of all adjacent and preceding vertices. The earliest completion times are computed for vertices by their topological order, and the latest completion times are computed by reverse topological order. The latest completion times are shown in Figure 9.37.

Figure 9.36 Earliest completion times

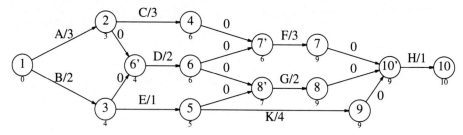

Figure 9.37   Latest completion times

The *slack* time for each edge in the event-node graph represents the amount of time that the completion of the corresponding activity can be delayed without delaying the overall completion. It is easy to see that

$$Slack_{(v,w)} = LC_w - EC_v - c_{v,w}$$

Figure 9.38 shows the slack (as the third entry) for each activity in the event-node graph. For each node, the top number is the earliest completion time and the bottom entry is the latest completion time.

Some activities have zero slack. These are critical activities, which must finish on schedule. There is at least one path consisting entirely of zero-slack edges; such a path is a *critical path*.

9.3.5.   All-Pairs Shortest Path

Sometimes it is important to find the shortest paths between all pairs of vertices in the graph. Although we could just run the appropriate single-source algorithm $|V|$ times, we might expect a somewhat faster solution, especially on a dense graph, if we compute all the information at once.

In Chapter 10, we will see an $O(|V|^3)$ algorithm to solve this problem for weighted graphs. Although, for dense graphs, this is the same bound as running a simple (non–priority queue) Dijkstra's algorithm $|V|$ times, the loops are so tight that the specialized all-pairs algorithm is likely to be faster in practice. On sparse graphs, of course, it is faster to run $|V|$ Dijkstra's algorithms coded with priority queues.

Figure 9.38   Earliest completion time, latest completion
time, and slack

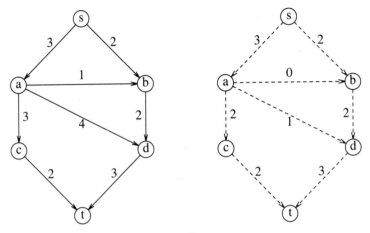

Figure 9.39 A graph (left) and its maximum flow

9.4. Network Flow Problems

Suppose we are given a directed graph $G = (V, E)$ with edge capacities $c_{v,w}$. These capacities could represent the amount of water that could flow through a pipe or the amount of traffic that could flow on a street between two intersections. We have two vertices: s, which we call the *source,* and t, which is the *sink.* Through any edge, (v, w), at most $c_{v,w}$ units of "flow" may pass. At any vertex, v, that is not either s or t, the total flow coming in must equal the total flow going out. The maximum flow problem is to determine the maximum amount of flow that can pass from s to t. As an example, for the graph in Figure 9.39 on the left the maximum flow is 5, as indicated by the graph on the right.

As required by the problem statement, no edge carries more flow than its capacity. Vertex a has three units of flow coming in, which it distributes to c and d. Vertex d takes three units of flow from a and b and combines this, sending the result to t. A vertex can combine and distribute flow in any manner that it likes, as long as edge capacities are not violated and as long as flow conservation is maintained (what goes in must come out).

9.4.1. A Simple Maximum-Flow Algorithm

A first attempt to solve the problem proceeds in stages. We start with our graph, G, and construct a flow graph G_f. G_f tells the flow that has been attained at any stage in the algorithm. Initially all edges in G_f have no flow, and we hope that when the algorithm terminates, G_f contains a maximum flow. We also construct a graph, G_r, called the *residual* graph. G_r tells, for each edge, how much more flow can be added. We can calculate this by subtracting the current flow from the capacity for each edge. An edge in G_r is known as a *residual* edge.

At each stage, we find a path in G_r from s to t. This path is known as an *augmenting path.* The minimum edge on this path is the amount of flow that can

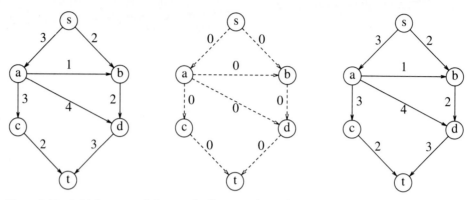

Figure 9.40 Initial stages of the graph, flow graph, and
residual graph

be added to every edge on the path. We do this by adjusting G_f and recomputing
G_r. When we find no path from s to t in G_r, we terminate. This algorithm is
nondeterministic, in that we are free to choose *any* path from s to t; obviously some
choices are better than others, and we will address this issue later. We will run
this algorithm on our example. The graphs below are G, G_f, G_r respectively. Keep
in mind that there is a slight flaw in this algorithm. The initial configuration is in
Figure 9.40.

There are many paths from s to t in the residual graph. Suppose we select s,
b, d, t. Then we can send two units of flow through every edge on this path. We
will adopt the convention that once we have filled (*saturated*) an edge, it is removed
from the residual graph. We then obtain Figure 9.41.

Next, we might select the path s, a, c, t, which also allows two units of flow.
Making the required adjustments gives the graphs in Figure 9.42.

Figure 9.41 G, G_f, G_r after two units of flow added along
s, b, d, t

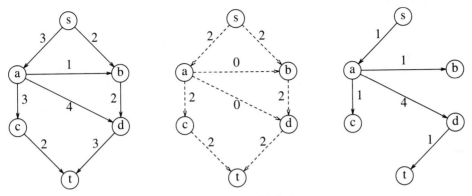

Figure 9.42 G, G_f, G_r after two units of flow added along s, a, c, t

The only path left to select is s, a, d, t, which allows one unit of flow. The resulting graphs are shown in Figure 9.43.

The algorithm terminates at this point, because t is unreachable from s. The resulting flow of 5 happens to be the maximum. To see what the problem is, suppose that with our initial graph, we chose the path s, a, d, t. This path allows 3 units of flow and thus seems to be a good choice. The result of this choice, however, is that there is now no longer any path from s to t in the residual graph, and thus, our algorithm has failed to find an optimal solution. This is an example of a greedy algorithm that does not work. Figure 9.44 shows why the algorithm fails.

In order to make this algorithm work, we need to allow the algorithm to change its mind. To do this, for every edge (v, w) with flow $f_{v,w}$ in the flow graph, we will add an edge in the residual graph (w, v) of capacity $f_{v,w}$. In effect, we are allowing the algorithm to undo its decisions by sending flow back in the opposite direction. This is best seen by example. Starting from our original graph and selecting the augmenting path s, a, d, t, we obtain the graphs in Figure 9.45.

Figure 9.43 G, G_f, G_r after one unit of flow added along s, a, d, t—algorithm terminates

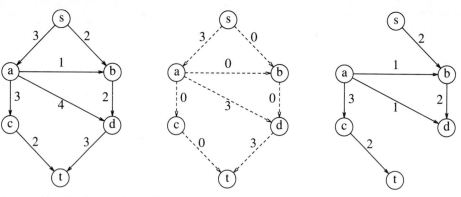

Figure 9.44 G, G_f, G_r if initial action is to add three units of flow along s, a, d, t—algorithm terminates with suboptimal solution

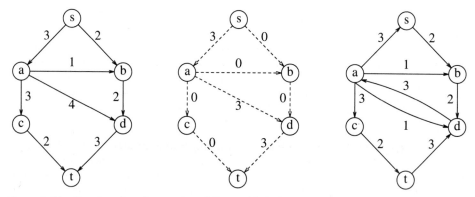

Figure 9.45   Graphs after three units of flow added along s, a, d, t using correct algorithm

Notice that in the residual graph there are edges in both directions between a and d. Either one more unit of flow can be pushed from a to d, or up to three units can be pushed back—we can undo flow. Now the algorithm finds the augmenting path s, b, d, a, c, t, of flow 2. By pushing two units of flow from d to a, the algorithm takes two units of flow away from the edge (a, d) and is essentially changing its mind. Figure 9.46 shows the new graphs.

There is no augmenting path in this graph, so the algorithm terminates. Surprisingly, it can be shown that if the edge capacities are rational numbers, this algorithm always terminates with a maximum flow. This proof is somewhat difficult and is beyond the scope of this text. Although the example happened to be acyclic, this is not a requirement for the algorithm to work. We have used acyclic graphs merely to keep things simple.

If the capacities are all integers and the maximum flow is f, then, since each augmenting path increases the flow value by at least 1, f stages suffice, and the total running time is $O(f \cdot |E|)$, since an augmenting path can be found in $O(|E|)$

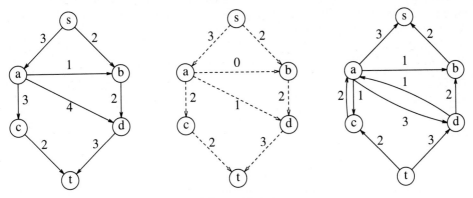

Figure 9.46 Graphs after two units of flow added along s, b, d, a, c, t using correct algorithm

time by an unweighted shortest-path algorithm. The classic example of why this is a bad running time is shown by the graph in Figure 9.47.

The maximum flow is seen by inspection to be 2,000,000 by sending 1,000,000 down each side. Random augmentations could continually augment along a path that includes the edge connected by a and b. If this were to occur repeatedly, 2,000,000 augmentations would be required, when we could get by with only 2.

A simple method to get around this problem is always to choose the augmenting path that allows the largest increase in flow. Finding such a path is similar to solving a weighted shortest-path problem, and a single-line modification to Dijkstra's algorithm will do the trick. If cap_{max} is the maximum edge capacity, then one can show that $O(|E| \log cap_{max})$ augmentations will suffice to find the maximum flow. In this case, since $O(|E| \log |V|)$ time is used for each calculation of an augmenting

Figure 9.47 The classic bad case for augmenting

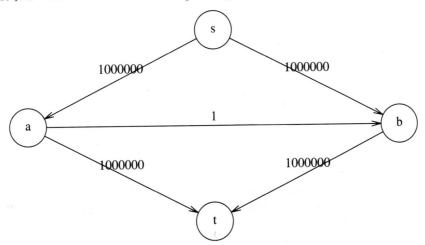

path, a total bound of $O(|E|^2 \log |V| \log cap_{max})$ is obtained. If the capacities are all small integers, this reduces to $O(|E|^2 \log |V|)$.

Another way to choose augmenting paths is always to take the path with the least number of edges, with the plausible expectation that by choosing a path in this manner, it is less likely that a small, flow-restricting edge will turn up on the path. Using this rule, it can be shown that $O(|E| \cdot |V|)$ augmenting steps are required. Each step takes $O(|E|)$, again using an unweighted shortest-path algorithm, yielding a $O(|E|^2|V|)$ bound on the running time.

Further data structure improvements to this algorithm are possible, and there are several, more complicated, algorithms. A long history of improved bounds has lowered the current best-known bound for this problem to $O(|E||V| \log(|V|^2/ |E|))$ (see the references). There are also a host of very good bounds for special cases. For instance, $O(|E||V|^{1/2})$ time finds a maximum flow in a graph having the property that all vertices except the source and sink have either a single incoming edge of capacity 1 or a single outgoing edge of capacity 1. These graphs occur in many applications.

The analyses required to produce these bounds are rather intricate, and it is not clear how the worst-case results relate to the running times encountered in practice. A related, even more difficult problem is the *min-cost flow* problem. Each edge has not only a capacity but a cost per unit of flow. The problem is to find, among all maximum flows, the one flow of minimum cost. Both of these problems are being actively researched.

9.5. Minimum Spanning Tree

The next problem we will consider is that of finding a *minimum spanning tree* in an undirected graph. The problem makes sense for directed graphs but appears to be more difficult. Informally, a minimum spanning tree of an undirected graph G is a tree formed from graph edges that connects all the vertices of G at lowest total cost. A minimum spanning tree exists if and only if G is connected. Although a robust algorithm should report the case that G is unconnected, we will assume that G is connected and leave the issue of robustness as an exercise for the reader.

In Figure 9.48 the second graph is a minimum spanning tree of the first (it happens to be unique, but this is unusual). Notice that the number of edges in the minimum spanning tree is $|V| - 1$. The minimum spanning tree is a *tree* because it is acyclic, it is *spanning* because it covers every edge, and it is *minimum* for the obvious reason. If we need to wire a house with a minimum of cable, then a minimum spanning tree problem needs to be solved. There are two basic algorithms to solve this problem; both are greedy. We now describe them.

9.5.1. Prim's Algorithm

One way to compute a minimum spanning tree is to grow the tree in successive stages. In each stage, one node is picked as the root, and we add an edge, and thus an associated vertex, to the tree.

Same as Dijkstra without cumulative cost consideration

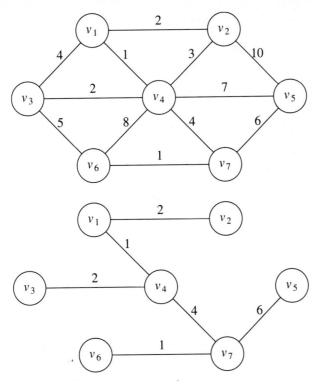

Figure 9.48   A graph G and its minimum spanning tree

At any point in the algorithm, we can see that we have a set of vertices that have already been included in the tree; the rest of the vertices have not. The algorithm then finds, at each stage, a new vertex to add to the tree by choosing the edge (u, v) such that the cost of (u, v) is the smallest among all edges where u is in the tree and v is not. Figure 9.49 shows how this algorithm would build the minimum spanning tree, starting from v_1. Initially, v_1 is in the tree as a root with no edges. Each step adds one edge and one vertex to the tree.

We can see that Prim's algorithm is essentially identical to Dijkstra's algorithm for shortest paths. As before, for each vertex we keep values d_v and p_v and an indication of whether it is known or unknown. d_v is the weight of the shortest arc connecting v to a known vertex, and p_v, as before, is the last vertex to cause a change in d_v. The rest of the algorithm is exactly the same, with the exception that since the definition of d_v is different, so is the update rule. For this problem, the update rule is even simpler than before: After a vertex v is selected, for each unknown w adjacent to v, $d_v = \min(d_w, c_{w,v})$.

The initial configuration of the table is shown in Figure 9.50. v_1 is selected, and v_2, v_3, and v_4 are updated. The table resulting from this is shown in Figure 9.51. The next vertex selected is v_4. Every vertex is adjacent to v_4. v_1 is not examined, because it is known. v_2 is unchanged, because it has $d_v = 2$ and the edge cost from v_4 to v_2 is 3; all the rest are updated. Figure 9.52 shows the resulting table. The

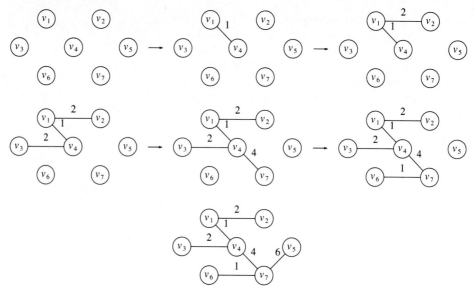

Figure 9.49   Prim's algorithm after each stage

v	Known	d_v	p_v
v_1	0	0	0
v_2	0	∞	0
v_3	0	∞	0
v_4	0	∞	0
v_5	0	∞	0
v_6	0	∞	0
v_7	0	∞	0

Figure 9.50   Initial configuration of table used in Prim's algorithm

v	Known	d_v	p_v
v_1	1	0	0
v_2	0	2	v_1
v_3	0	4	v_1
v_4	0	1	v_1
v_5	0	∞	0
v_6	0	∞	0
v_7	0	∞	0

Figure 9.51   The table after v_1 is declared known

next vertex chosen is v_2 (arbitrarily breaking a tie). This does not affect any distances. Then v_3 is chosen, which affects the distance in v_6, producing Figure 9.53. Figure 9.54 results from the selection of v_7, which forces v_6 and v_5 to be adjusted. v_6 and then v_5 are selected, completing the algorithm.

The final table is shown in Figure 9.55. The edges in the spanning tree can be read from the table: (v_2, v_1), (v_3, v_4), (v_4, v_1), (v_5, v_7), (v_6, v_7), (v_7, v_4). The total cost is 16.

Figure 9.52 The table after v_4 is declared known

v	Known	d_v	p_v
v_1	1	0	0
v_2	0	2	v_1
v_3	0	2	v_4
v_4	1	1	v_1
v_5	0	7	v_4
v_6	0	8	v_4
v_7	0	4	v_4

Figure 9.53 The table after v_2 and then v_3 are declared known

v	Known	d_v	p_v
v_1	1	0	0
v_2	1	2	v_1
v_3	1	2	v_4
v_4	1	1	v_1
v_5	0	7	v_4
v_6	0	5	v_3
v_7	0	4	v_4

Figure 9.54 The table after v_7 is declared known

v	Known	d_v	p_v
v_1	1	0	0
v_2	1	2	v_1
v_3	1	2	v_4
v_4	1	1	v_1
v_5	0	6	v_7
v_6	0	1	v_7
v_7	1	4	v_4

v	Known	d_v	p_v
v_1	1	0	0
v_2	1	2	v_1
v_3	1	2	v_4
v_4	1	1	v_1
v_5	1	6	v_7
v_6	1	1	v_7
v_7	1	4	v_4

Figure 9.55 The table after v_6 and v_5 are selected (Prim's algorithm terminates)

Edge	Weight	Action
(v_1, v_4)	1	Accepted
(v_6, v_7)	1	Accepted
(v_1, v_2)	2	Accepted
(v_3, v_4)	2	Accepted
(v_2, v_4)	3	Rejected
(v_1, v_3)	4	Rejected
(v_4, v_7)	4	Accepted
(v_3, v_6)	5	Rejected
(v_5, v_7)	6	Accepted

Figure 9.56 Action of Kruskal's algorithm on G

The entire implementation of this algorithm is virtually identical to that of Dijkstra's algorithm, and everything that was said about the analysis of Dijkstra's algorithm applies here. Be aware that Prim's algorithm runs on undirected graphs, so when coding it, remember to put every edge in two adjacency lists. The running time is $O(|V|^2)$ without heaps, which is optimal for dense graphs, and $O(|E|\log|V|)$ using binary heaps, which is good for sparse graphs.

9.5.2. Kruskal's Algorithm

A second greedy strategy is continually to select the edges in order of smallest weight and accept an edge if it does not cause a cycle. The action of the algorithm on the graph in the preceding example is shown in Figure 9.56.

Formally, Kruskal's algorithm maintains a forest—a collection of trees. Initially, there are $|V|$ single-node trees. Adding an edge merges two trees into one. When the algorithm terminates, there is only one tree, and this is the minimum spanning tree. Figure 9.57 shows the order in which edges are added to the forest.

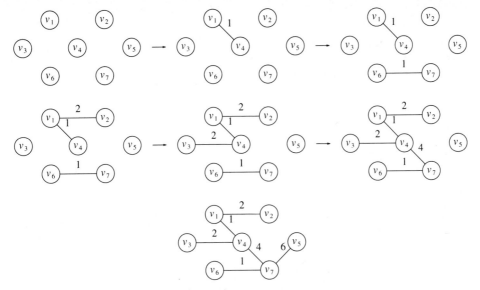

Figure 9.57 Kruskal's algorithm after each stage

The algorithm terminates when enough edges are accepted. It turns out to be simple to decide whether edge (u, v) should be accepted or rejected. The appropriate data structure is the *Union/Find* algorithm of the previous chapter.

The invariant we will use is that at any point in the process, two vertices belong to the same set if and only if they are connected in the current spanning forest. Thus, each vertex is initially in its own set. If u and v are in the same set, the edge is rejected, because since they are already connected, adding (u, v) would form a cycle. Otherwise, the edge is accepted, and a *Union* is performed on the two sets containing u and v. It is easy to see that this maintains the set invariant, because once the edge (u, v) is added to the spanning forest, if w was connected to u and x was connected to v, then x and w must now be connected, and thus belong in the same set.

The edges could be sorted to facilitate the selection, but building a heap in linear time is a much better idea. Then *Delete_Min*s give the edges to be tested in order. Typically, only a small fraction of the edges need to be tested before the algorithm can terminate, although it is always possible that all the edges must be tried. For instance, if there were an extra vertex v_8 and edge (v_5, v_8) of cost 100, all the edges would have to be examined. The function *Kruskal* in Figure 9.58 finds a minimum spanning tree. Because an edge consists of three pieces of data, on some machines it is more efficient to implement the priority queue as an array of pointers to edges, rather than as an array of edges. The effect of this implementation is that, to rearrange the heap, only pointers, not large structures, need to be moved.

The worst-case running time of this algorithm is $O(|E| \log |E|)$, which is dominated by the heap operations. Notice that since $|E| = O(|V|^2)$, this running time is actually $O(|E| \log |V|)$. In practice, the algorithm is much faster than this time bound would indicate.

★★
UNION
FROM
CHAPTER 8

```
/* 1*/     void
/* 2*/     Kruskal( Graph G )
/* 3*/     {
/* 4*/         Sets S( Num_Vertex );
/* 5*/         Binary_Heap<Edge> H( Num_Edge );
/* 6*/         Vertex U, V;
/* 7*/         Set_Type U_Set, V_Set;
/* 8*/         Edge E;
/* 9*/         int Edges_Accepted = 0;

/*10*/         Read_Graph_Into_Heap_Array( G, H );
/*11*/         H.Build_Heap( );

/*12*/         while( Edges_Accepted < Num_Vertex - 1 )
/*13*/         {
/*14*/             E = H.Delete_Min( );    // E = (U, V).
/*15*/             U_Set = S.Find_And_Compress( U );
/*16*/             V_Set = S.Find_And_Compress( V );
/*17*/             if( U_Set != V_Set )
/*18*/             {
/*19*/                 // Accept the edge.
/*20*/                 Edges_Accepted++;
/*21*/                 S.Union_By_Height( U_Set, V_Set );
/*22*/             }
/*23*/         }
/*24*/     }
```

Figure 9.58   Pseudocode for Kruskal's algorithm

9.6.   Applications of Depth-First Search

Depth-first search is a generalization of preorder traversal. Starting at some vertex, v, we process v and then recursively traverse all vertices adjacent to v. If this process is performed on a tree, then all tree vertices are systematically visited in a total of $O(|E|)$ time, since $|E| = \Theta(|V|)$. If we perform this process on an arbitrary graph, we need to be careful to avoid cycles. To do this, when we visit a vertex v, we *mark* it visited, since now we have been there, and recursively call depth-first search on all adjacent vertices that are not already marked. We implicitly assume that for undirected graphs every edge (v, w) appears twice in the adjacency lists: once as (v, w) and once as (w, v). The procedure in Figure 9.59 performs a depth-first search (and does absolutely nothing else) and is a template for the general style.

The (global) boolean array *Visited*[ ] is initialized to False. By recursively calling the procedures only on nodes that have not been visited, we guarantee that we do not loop indefinitely. If the graph is undirected and not connected, or directed and not strongly connected, this strategy might fail to visit some nodes. We then search for an unmarked node, apply a depth-first traversal there, and continue this process

```
/* 1*/   void
/* 2*/   Dfs( Vertex V )
/* 3*/   {
/* 4*/       Visited[ V ] = TRUE;
/* 5*/       for Each Vertex W Adjacent To V
/* 6*/           if( ! Visited[ W ] )
/* 7*/               Dfs( W );
/* 8*/   }
```

Figure 9.59 Template for depth-first search

until there are no unmarked nodes.[†] Because this strategy guarantees that each edge is encountered only once, the total time to perform the traversal is $O(|E| + |V|)$, as long as adjacency lists are used.

9.6.1. Undirected Graphs

An undirected graph is connected if and only if a depth-first search starting from any node visits every node. Because this test is so easy to apply, we will assume that the graphs we deal with are connected. If they are not, then we can find all the connected components and apply our algorithm on each of these in turn.

As an example of depth-first search, suppose in the graph of Figure 9.60 we start at vertex A. Then we mark A as visited and call $Dfs(B)$ recursively. $Dfs(B)$ marks B

Figure 9.60 An undirected graph

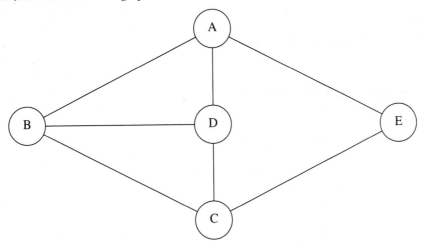

[†]An efficient way of implementing this is to begin the depth-first search at v_1. If we need to restart the depth-first search, we examine the sequence $v_k, v_{k+1}, \ldots$ for an unmarked vertex, where v_{k-1} is the vertex where the last depth-first search was started. This guarantees that throughout the algorithm, only $O(|V|)$ is spent looking for vertices where new depth-first search trees can be started.

as visited and calls *Dfs(C)* recursively. *Dfs(C)* marks *C* as visited and calls *Dfs(D)* recursively. *Dfs(D)* sees both *A* and *B*, but both these are marked, so no recursive calls are made. *Dfs(D)* also sees that *C* is adjacent but marked, so no recursive call is made there, and *Dfs(D)* returns back to *Dfs(C)*. *Dfs(C)* sees *B* adjacent, ignores it, finds a previously unseen vertex *E* adjacent, and thus calls *Dfs(E)*. *Dfs(E)* marks *E*, ignores *A* and *C*, and returns to *Dfs(C)*. *Dfs(C)* returns to *Dfs(B)*. *Dfs(B)* ignores both *A* and *D* and returns. *Dfs(A)* ignores both *D* and *E* and returns. (We have actually touched every edge twice, once as (*v, w*) and again as (*w, v*), but this is really once per adjacency list entry.)

We graphically illustrate these steps with a *depth-first spanning tree*. The root of the tree is *A*, the first vertex visited. Each edge (*v, w*) in the graph is present in the tree. If, when we process (*v, w*), we find that *w* is unmarked, or if, when we process (*w, v*), we find that *v* is unmarked, we indicate this with a tree edge. If when we process (*v, w*), we find that *w* is already marked and when processing (*w, v*) we find that *v* is already marked, we draw a dashed line, which we will call a *back edge*, to indicate that this "edge" is not really part of the tree. The depth-first search of the graph in Figure 9.60 is shown in Figure 9.61.

The tree will simulate the traversal we performed. A preorder numbering of the tree, using only tree edges, tells us the order in which the vertices were marked. If the graph is not connected, then processing all nodes (and edges) requires several calls to *Dfs*, and each generates a tree. This entire collection is a *depth-first spanning forest*, which is so named for obvious reasons.

Figure 9.61   Depth-first search of previous graph

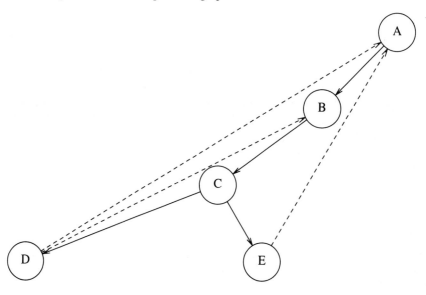

9.6.2. Biconnectivity

A connected undirected graph is *biconnected* if there are no vertices whose removal disconnects the rest of the graph. The graph in the preceding example is biconnected. If the nodes are computers and the edges are links, then if any computer goes down, network mail is unaffected, except, of course, at the down computer. Similarly, if a mass transit system is biconnected, users always have an alternate route should some terminal be disrupted.

If a graph is not biconnected, the vertices whose removal would disconnect the graph are known as *articulation points*. These nodes are critical in many applications. The graph in Figure 9.62 is not biconnected: C and D are articulation points. The removal of C would disconnect G, and the removal of D would disconnect E and F, from the rest of the graph.

Depth-first search provides a linear-time algorithm to find all articulation points in a connected graph. First, starting at any vertex, we perform a depth-first search and number the nodes as they are visited. For each vertex v, we call this preorder number $Num(v)$. Then, for every vertex v in the depth-first search spanning tree, we compute the lowest-numbered vertex, which we call $Low(v)$, that is reachable from v by taking zero or more tree edges and then possibly one back edge (in that order). The depth-first search tree in Figure 9.63 shows the preorder number first and then the lowest-numbered vertex reachable under the rule described above.

The lowest-numbered vertex reachable by A, B, and C is vertex 1 (A), because they can all take tree edges to D and then one back edge back to A. We can efficiently compute Low by performing a postorder traversal of the depth-first spanning tree. By the definition of Low, $Low(v)$ is the minimum of

1. $Num(v)$
2. the lowest $Num(w)$ among all back edges (v, w)
3. the lowest $Low(w)$ among all tree edges (v, w)

The first condition is the option of taking no edges, the second way is to choose no tree edges and a back edge, and the third way is to choose some tree edges and possibly a back edge. This third method is succinctly described with a recursive call. Since we need to evaluate Low for all the children of v before we can evaluate $Low(v)$, this is a postorder traversal. For any edge (v, w), we can tell whether it is a tree edge or a back edge merely by checking $Num(v)$ and $Num(w)$. Thus, it is easy to compute $Low(v)$: We merely scan down v's adjacency list, apply the proper rule, and keep track of the minimum. Doing all the computation takes $O(|E| + |V|)$ time.

All that is left to do is to use this information to find articulation points. The root is an articulation point if and only if it has more than one child, because if it has two children, removing the root disconnects nodes in different subtrees, and if it has only one child, removing the root merely disconnects the root. Any other vertex v is an articulation point if and only if v has some child w such that $Low(w) \geq Num(v)$. Notice that this condition is always satisfied at the root; hence the need for a special test.

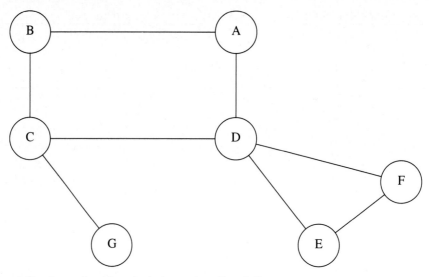

Figure 9.62   A graph with articulation points *C* and *D*

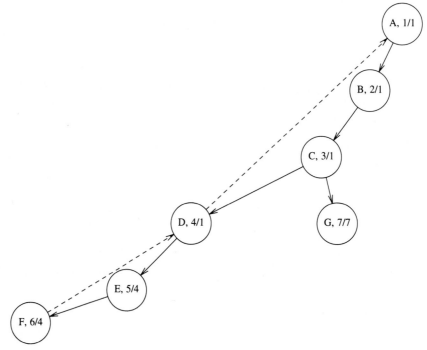

Figure 9.63   Depth-first tree for previous graph, with *Num* and *Low*

The *if* part of the proof is clear when we examine the articulation points that the algorithm determines, namely C and D. D has a child E, and $Low(E) \geq Num(D)$, since both are 4. Thus, there is only one way for E to get to any node above D, and that is by going through D. Similarly, C is an articulation point, because $Low(G) \geq Num(C)$. To prove that this algorithm is correct, one must show that the *only if* part of the assertion is true (that is, this finds *all* articulation points). We leave this as an exercise. As a second example, we show (Figure 9.64) the result of applying this algorithm on the same graph, starting the depth-first search at C.

We close by giving pseudocode to implement this algorithm. We will assume that the arrays *Visited*[ ] (initialized to False), *Num*[ ], *Low*[ ], and *Parent*[ ] are global, to keep the code simple. We will also keep a global variable called *Counter*, which is initialized to 1 to assign the preorder traversal numbers, *Num*[ ]. This is not normally good programming practice, but including all the declarations and passing the extra parameters would cloud the logic. We also leave out the easily implemented test for the root.

As we have already stated, this algorithm can be implemented by performing a preorder traversal to compute *Num* and then a postorder traversal to compute *Low*. A third traversal can be used to check which vertices satisfy the articulation point criteria. Performing three traversals, however, would be a waste. The first pass is shown in Figure 9.65.

The second and third passes, which are postorder traversals, can be implemented by the code in Figure 9.66. Line 15 handles a special case. If w is adjacent to v, then the recursive call to w will find v adjacent to w. This is not a back edge, only an edge that has already been considered and needs to be ignored. Otherwise, the procedure computes the minimum of the various *Low*[ ] and *Num*[ ] entries, as specified by the algorithm.

There is no rule that a traversal must be either preorder or postorder. It is possible to do processing both before and after the recursive calls. The function in Figure 9.67 combines the two routines *Assign_Num* and *Assign_Low* in a straightforward manner to produce the function *Find_Art*.

Figure 9.64 Depth-first tree that results if depth-first search
starts at C

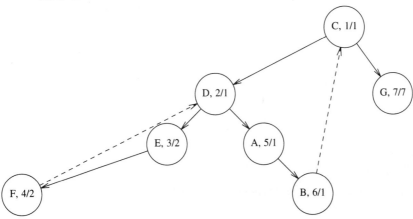

```
/* 1*/    // Assign Num and compute Parent.
/* 2*/    // Counter is global, and initialized to 1.
/* 3*/    // Num, Visited, and Parent are all global arrays.

/* 4*/    void
/* 5*/    Assign_Num( Vertex V )
/* 6*/    {
/* 7*/        Num[ V ] = Counter++;
/* 8*/        Visited[ V ] = TRUE;
/* 9*/        for Each Vertex W Adjacent To V
/*10*/            if( ! Visited[ W ] )
/*11*/            {
/*12*/                Parent[ W ] = V;
/*13*/                Assign_Num( W );
/*14*/            }
/*15*/    }
```

Figure 9.65   Routine to assign *Num* to vertices
(pseudocode)

```
/* 1*/    // Assign Low.  Also check for articulation points.

/* 2*/    void
/* 3*/    Assign_Low( Vertex V )
/* 4*/    {
/* 5*/        Low[ V ] = Num[ V ];                    // Rule 1.
/* 6*/        for Each Vertex W Adjacent To V
/* 7*/            if( Num[ W ] > Num[ V ] )           // Forward edge.
/* 8*/            {
/* 9*/                Assign_Low( W );
/*10*/                if( Low[ W ] >= Num[ V ] )
/*11*/                    cout << V << " is an articulation point" << endl;
/*12*/                Low[ V ] = Min( Low[ V ], Low[ W ] );    // Rule 3.
/*13*/            }
/*14*/            else
/*15*/            if( Parent[ V ] != W )          // Back edge.
/*16*/                Low[ V ] = Min( Low[ V ], Num[ W ] );    // Rule 2.
/*17*/    }
```

Figure 9.66   Pseudocode to compute *Low* and test for articulation points (test for the root is omitted)

```
/* 1*/  // Counter is global and initialized to 1.
/* 2*/  // Low, Num, Visited, and Parent are all global arrays.

/* 3*/  void
/* 4*/  Find_Art( Vertex V )
/* 5*/  {
/* 6*/      Visited[ V ] = TRUE;
/* 7*/      Low[ V ] = Num[ V ] = Counter++;              // Rule 1.
/* 8*/      for Each Vertex W Adjacent To V
/* 9*/          if( ! Visited[ W ] )                      // Forward edge.
/*10*/          {
/*11*/              Parent[ W ] = V;
/*12*/              Find_Art( W );
/*13*/              if( Low[ W ] >= Num[ V ] )
/*14*/                  cout << V << " is an articulation point" << endl;
/*15*/              Low[ V ] = Min( Low[ V ], Low[ W ] );     // Rule 3.
/*16*/          }
/*17*/          else
/*18*/          if( Parent[ V ] != W )                    // Back edge.
/*19*/              Low[ V ] = Min( Low[ V ], Num[ W ] );  // Rule 2.
/*20*/  }
```

Figure 9.67 Pseudocode to test for articulation points in
one depth-first search (test for the root is
omitted)

9.6.3. Euler Circuits

Consider the three figures in Figure 9.68. A popular puzzle is to reconstruct these figures using a pen, drawing each line exactly once. The pen may not be lifted from the paper while the drawing is being performed. As an extra challenge, make the pen finish at the same point at which it started. This puzzle has a surprisingly simple solution. Stop reading if you would like to try to solve it.

The first figure can be drawn only if the starting point is the lower left- or right-hand corner, and it is not possible to finish at the starting point. The second figure is easily drawn with the finishing point the same as the starting point, but the third figure cannot be drawn at all within the parameters of the puzzle.

Figure 9.68 Three drawings

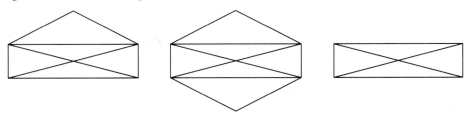

We can convert this problem to a graph theory problem by assigning a vertex to each intersection. Then the edges can be assigned in the natural manner, as in Figure 9.69.

After this conversion is performed, we must find a path in the graph that visits every edge exactly once. If we are to solve the "extra challenge," then we must find a cycle that visits every edge exactly once. This graph problem was solved in 1736 by Euler and marked the beginning of graph theory. The problem is thus commonly referred to as an *Euler path* (sometimes *Euler tour*) or *Euler circuit problem,* depending on the specific problem statement. The Euler tour and Euler circuit problems, though slightly different, have the same basic solution. Thus, we will consider the Euler circuit problem in this section.

The first observation that can be made is that an Euler circuit, which must end on its starting vertex, is possible only if the graph is connected and each vertex has an even degree (number of edges). This is because, on the Euler circuit, a vertex is entered and then left. If any vertex v has odd degree, then eventually we will reach the point where only one edge into v is unvisited, and taking it will strand us at v. If exactly two vertices have odd degree, an Euler tour, which must visit every edge but need not return to its starting vertex, is still possible if we start at one of the odd-degree vertices and finish at the other. If more than two vertices have odd degree, then an Euler tour is not possible.

The observations of the preceding paragraph provide us with a necessary condition for the existence of an Euler circuit. It does not, however, tell us that all connected graphs that satisfy this property must have an Euler circuit, nor does it give us guidance on how to find one. It turns out that the necessary condition is also sufficient. That is, any connected graph, all of whose vertices have even degree, must have an Euler circuit. Furthermore, a circuit can be found in linear time.

We can assume that we know that an Euler circuit exists, since we can test the necessary and sufficient condition in linear time. Then the basic algorithm is to perform a depth-first search. There is a surprisingly large number of "obvious" solutions that do not work. Some of these are presented in the exercises.

The main problem is that we might visit a portion of the graph and return to the starting point prematurely. If all the edges coming out of the start vertex have been used up, then part of the graph is untraversed. The easiest way to fix this is to find the first vertex on this path that has an untraversed edge, and perform

Figure 9.69   Conversion of puzzle to graph

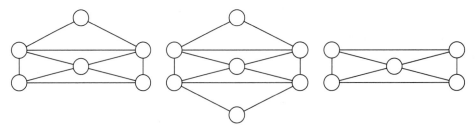

another depth-first search. This will give another circuit, which can be spliced into the original. This is continued until all edges have been traversed.

As an example, consider the graph in Figure 9.70. It is easily seen that this graph has an Euler circuit. Suppose we start at vertex 5 and traverse the circuit 5, 4, 10, 5. Then we are stuck, and most of the graph is still untraversed. The situation is shown in Figure 9.71.

We then continue from vertex 4, which still has unexplored edges. A depth-first search might come up with the path 4, 1, 3, 7, 4, 11, 10, 7, 9, 3, 4. If we splice this path into the previous path of 5, 4, 10, 5, then we get a new path of 5, 4, 1, 3, 7, 4, 11, 10, 7, 9, 3, 4, 10, 5.

The graph that remains after this is shown in Figure 9.72. Notice that in this graph all the vertices must have even degree, so we are guaranteed to find a cycle to

Figure 9.70 Graph for Euler circuit problem

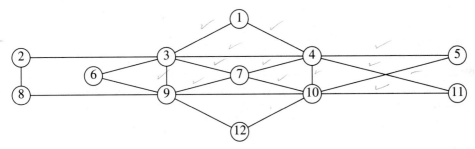

Figure 9.71 Graph remaining after 5, 4, 10, 5

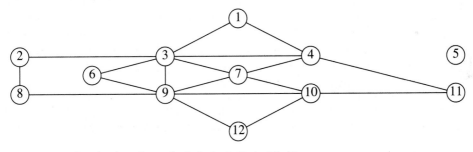

Figure 9.72 Graph after the path 5, 4, 1, 3, 7, 4, 11, 10, 7, 9, 3, 4, 10, 5

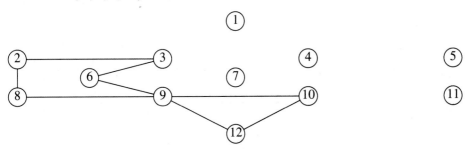

add. The remaining graph might not be connected, but this is not important. The next vertex on the path that has untraversed edges is vertex 3. A possible circuit would then be 3, 2, 8, 9, 6, 3. When spliced in, this gives the path 5, 4, 1, 3, 2, 8, 9, 6, 3, 7, 4, 11, 10, 7, 9, 3, 4, 10, 5.

The graph that remains is in Figure 9.73. On this path, the next vertex with an untraversed edge is 9, and the algorithm finds the circuit 9, 12, 10, 9. When this is added to the current path, a circuit of 5, 4, 1, 3, 2, 8, 9, 12, 10, 9, 6, 3, 7, 4, 11, 10, 7, 9, 3, 4, 10, 5 is obtained. As all the edges are traversed, the algorithm terminates with an Euler circuit.

To make this algorithm efficient, we must use appropriate data structures. We will sketch some of the ideas, leaving the implementation as an exercise. To make splicing simple, the path should be maintained as a linked list. To avoid repetitious scanning of adjacency lists, we must maintain, for each adjacency list, a pointer to the last edge scanned. When a path is spliced in, the search for a new vertex from which to perform the next *Dfs* must begin at the start of the splice point. This guarantees that the total work performed on the vertex search phase is $O(|E|)$ during the entire life of the algorithm. With the appropriate data structures, the running time of the algorithm is $O(|E| + |V|)$.

A very similar problem is to find a simple cycle, in an undirected graph, that visits every vertex. This is known as the *Hamiltonian cycle problem*. Although it seems almost identical to the Euler circuit problem, no efficient algorithm for it is known. We shall see this problem again in Section 9.7.

9.6.4. Directed Graphs

Using the same strategy as with undirected graphs, directed graphs can be traversed in linear time, using depth-first search. If the graph is not strongly connected, a depth-first search starting at some node might not visit all nodes. In this case we repeatedly perform depth-first searches, starting at some unmarked node, until all vertices have been visited. As an example, consider the directed graph in Figure 9.74.

We arbitrarily start the depth-first search at vertex B. This visits vertices B, C, A, D, E, and F. We then restart at some unvisited vertex. Arbitrarily, we start at H, which visits I and J. Finally, we start at G, which is the last vertex that needs to be visited. The corresponding depth-first search tree is shown in Figure 9.75.

Figure 9.73 Graph remaining after the path 5, 4, 1, 3, 2,
8, 9, 6, 3, 7, 4, 11, 10, 7, 9, 3, 4, 10, 5

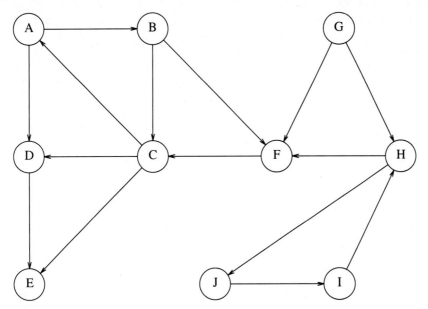

Figure 9.74 A directed graph

The dashed arrows in the depth-first spanning forest are edges (v, w) for which w was already marked at the time of consideration. In undirected graphs, these are always back edges, but, as we can see, there are three types of edges that do not lead to new vertices. First, there are *back edges*, such as (A, B) and (I, H). There are also *forward edges*, such as (C, D) and (C, E), that lead from a tree node to a descendant. Finally, there are *cross edges*, such as (F, C) and (G, F), which connect two tree nodes that are not directly related. Depth-first search forests are generally drawn with children and new trees added to the forest from left to right. In a depth-first search of a directed graph drawn in this manner, cross edges always go from right to left.

Figure 9.75 Depth-first search of previous graph

Some algorithms that use depth-first search need to distinguish between the three types of nontree edges. This is easy to check as the depth-first search is being performed, and it is left as an exercise.

One use of depth-first search is to test whether or not a directed graph is acyclic. The rule is that a directed graph is acyclic if and only if it has no back edges. (The graph above has back edges and thus is not acyclic.) The alert reader may remember that a topological sort can also be used to determine whether a graph is acyclic. Another way to perform topological sorting is to assign the vertices topological numbers $n, n - 1, \ldots, 1$ by postorder traversal of the depth-first spanning forest. As long as the graph is acyclic, this ordering will be consistent.

9.6.5. *Finding Strong Components*

By performing two depth-first searches, we can test whether a directed graph is strongly connected, and if it is not, we can actually produce the subsets of vertices that are strongly connected to themselves. This can also be done in only one depth-first search, but the method used here is much simpler to understand.

First, a depth-first search is performed on the input graph G. The vertices of G are numbered by a postorder traversal of the depth-first spanning forest, and then all edges in G are reversed, forming G_r. The graph in Figure 9.76 represents G_r for the graph G shown in Figure 9.74; the vertices are shown with their numbers.

The algorithm is completed by performing a depth-first search on G_r, always starting a new depth-first search at the highest-numbered vertex. Thus, we begin the

Figure 9.76 G_r numbered by postorder traversal of G

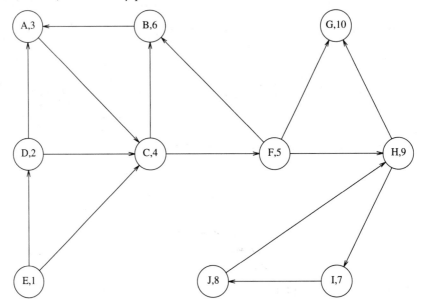

depth-first search of G_r at vertex G, which is numbered 10. This leads nowhere, so the next search is started at H. This call visits I and J. The next call starts at B and visits A, C, and F. The next calls after this are $Dfs(D)$ and finally $Dfs(E)$. The resulting depth-first spanning forest is shown in Figure 9.77.

Each of the trees (this is easier to see if you completely ignore all nontree edges) in this depth-first spanning forest forms a strongly connected component. Thus, for our example, the strongly connected components are $\{G\}$, $\{H, I, J\}$, $\{B, A, C, F\}$, $\{D\}$, and $\{E\}$.

To see why this algorithm works, first note that if two vertices v and w are in the same strongly connected component, then there are paths from v to w and from w to v in the original graph G, and hence also in G_r. Now, if two vertices v and w are not in the same depth-first spanning tree of G_r, clearly they cannot be in the same strongly connected component.

To prove that this algorithm works, we must show that if two vertices v and w are in the same depth-first spanning tree of G_r, there must be paths from v to w and from w to v. Equivalently, we can show that if x is the root of the depth-first spanning tree of G_r containing v, then there is a path from x to v and from v to x. Applying the same logic to w would then give a path from x to w and from w to x. These paths would imply paths from v to w and w to v (going through x).

Since v is a descendant of x in G_r's depth-first spanning tree, there is a path from x to v in G_r and thus a path from v to x in G. Furthermore, since x is the root, x has the higher postorder number from the first depth-first search. Therefore, during the first depth-first search, all the work processing v was completed before the work at x was completed. Since there is a path from v to x, it follows that v must be a descendant of x in the spanning tree for G—otherwise v would finish *after* x. This implies a path from x to v in G and completes the proof.

9.7. Introduction to NP-Completeness

In this chapter, we have seen solutions to a wide variety of graph theory problems. All these problems have polynomial running times, and with the exception of the network flow problem, the running time is either linear or only slightly more than

Figure 9.77 Depth-first search of G_r—strong components are $\{G\}$, $\{H, I, J\}$, $\{B, A, C, F\}$, $\{D\}$, $\{E\}$

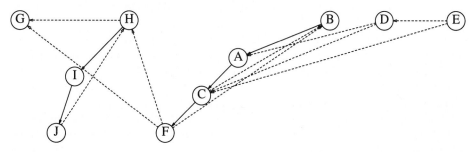

linear ($O(|E|\log|E|)$). We have also mentioned, in passing, that for some problems certain variations seem harder than the original.

Recall that the Euler circuit problem, which finds a path that touches every edge exactly once, is solvable in linear time. The Hamiltonian cycle problem asks for a simple cycle that contains every vertex. No linear algorithm is known for this problem.

The single-source unweighted shortest-path problem for directed graphs is also solvable in linear time. No linear-time algorithm is known for the corresponding longest-simple-path problem.

The situation for these problem variations is actually much worse than we have described. Not only are no linear algorithms known for these variations, but there are no known algorithms that are guaranteed to run in polynomial time. The best known algorithms for these problems could take exponential time on some inputs.

In this section we will take a brief look at this problem. This topic is rather complex, so we will take only a quick and informal look at it. Because of this, the discussion may be (necessarily) somewhat imprecise in places.

We will see that there are a host of important problems that are roughly equivalent in complexity. These problems form a class called the *NP-complete* problems. The exact complexity of these *NP*-complete problems has yet to be determined and remains the foremost open problem in theoretical computer science. Either all these problems have polynomial-time solutions or none of them do.

9.7.1.   *Easy vs. Hard*

When classifying problems, the first step is to examine the boundaries. We have already seen that many problems can be solved in linear time. We have also seen some $O(\log n)$ running times, but these either assume some preprocessing (such as input already being read or a data structure already being built) or occur on arithmetic examples. For instance, the *Gcd* algorithm, when applied on two numbers m and n, takes $O(\log n)$ time. Since the numbers consist of $\log m$ and $\log n$ bits respectively, the *Gcd* algorithm is really taking time that is linear in the *amount* or *size* of input. Thus, when we measure running time, we will be concerned with the running time as a function of the amount of input. Generally, we cannot expect better than linear running time.

At the other end of the spectrum lie some truly hard problems. These problems are so hard that they are *impossible*. This does not mean the typical exasperated moan, which means that it would take a genius to solve the problem. Just as real numbers are not sufficient to express a solution to $x^2 < 0$, one can prove that computers cannot solve every problem that happens to come along. These "impossible" problems are called *undecidable* problems.

One particular undecidable problem is the *halting problem*. Is it possible to have your C++ compiler have an extra feature that not only detects syntax errors but also infinite loops? This seems like a hard problem, but one might expect that if some very clever programmers spent enough time on it, they could produce this enhancement.

The intuitive reason that this problem is undecidable is that such a program might have a hard time checking itself. For this reason, these problems are sometimes called *recursively undecidable*.

If an infinite loop–checking program could be written, surely it could be used to check itself. We could then produce a program called *Loop*. *Loop* takes as input a program *P* and runs *P* on itself. It prints out the phrase "*Yes*" if *P* loops when run on itself. If *P* terminates when run on itself, a natural thing to do would be to print out "*No.*" Instead of doing that, we will have *Loop* go into an infinite loop.

What happens when *Loop* is given itself as input? Either *Loop* halts, or it does not halt. The problem is that both these possibilities lead to contradictions, in much the same way as does the statement "This sentence is a lie."

By our definition, *Loop(P)* goes into an infinite loop if *P(P)* terminates. Suppose that when *P* = *Loop*, *P(P)* terminates. Then, according to the *Loop* program, *Loop(P)* is obligated to go into an infinite loop. Thus, we must have *Loop(Loop)* terminating *and* entering an infinite loop, which is clearly not possible. On the other hand, suppose that when *P* = *Loop*, *P(P)* enters an infinite loop. Then *Loop(P)* must terminate, and we arrive at the same set of contradictions. Thus, we see that the program *Loop* cannot possibly exist.

9.7.2. The Class NP

Can be solved in linear
" " verified in Polynomial

A few steps down from the horrors of undecidable problems lies the class *NP*. *NP* stands for *nondeterministic polynomial-time*. A deterministic machine, at each point in time, is executing an instruction. Depending on the instruction, it then goes to some next instruction, which is unique. A nondeterministic machine has a choice of next steps. It is free to choose any that it wishes, and if one of these steps leads to a solution, it will always choose the correct one. A nondeterministic machine thus has the power of extremely good (optimal) guessing. This probably seems like a ridiculous model, since nobody could possibly build a nondeterministic computer, and because it would seem to be an incredible upgrade to your standard computer (every problem might now seem trivial). We will see that nondeterminism is a very useful theoretical construct. Furthermore, nondeterminism is not as powerful as one might think. For instance, undecidable problems are still undecidable, even if nondeterminism is allowed.

A simple way to check if a problem is in *NP* is to phrase the problem as a yes/no question. The problem is in *NP* if, in polynomial time, we can prove that any "yes" instance is correct. We do not have to worry about "no" instances, since the program always makes the right choice. Thus, for the Hamiltonian cycle problem, a "yes" instance would be any simple circuit in the graph that includes all the vertices. This is in *NP* since, given the path, it is a simple matter to check that it is really a Hamiltonian cycle. Appropriately phrased questions such as "Is there a simple path of length > *K*?" can also be checked easily and are in *NP*. Any path that satisfies this property can be checked trivially.

The class *NP* includes all problems that have polynomial-time solutions, since the solution obviously provides a check. One would expect that since it is so much easier to check an answer than to come up with one from scratch, there would be problems in *NP* that do not have polynomial-time solutions. To date no such problem has been found, so it is entirely possible, though not considered likely by experts, that nondeterminism is not such an important improvement. The problem is that proving exponential lower bounds is an extremely difficult task. The information theory bound technique, which we used to show that sorting requires $\Omega(n \log n)$ comparisons, does not seem to be adequate for the task because the decision trees are not nearly large enough.

Notice also that not all decidable problems are in *NP*. Consider the problem of determining whether a graph *does not* have a Hamiltonian cycle. To prove that a graph has a Hamiltonian cycle is a relatively simple matter—we just need to exhibit one. Nobody knows how to show, in polynomial time, that a graph does not have a Hamiltonian cycle. It seems that one must enumerate all the cycles and check them one by one. Thus the Non–Hamiltonian cycle problem is not known to be in *NP*.

9.7.3. *NP-Complete Problems*

Among all the problems known to be in *NP*, there is a subset, known as the *NP-complete* problems, that contains the hardest. An *NP*-complete problem has the property that any problem in *NP* can be *polynomially reduced* to it.

A problem P_1 can be reduced to P_2 as follows: Provide a mapping so that any instance of P_1 can be transformed to an instance of P_2. Solve P_2, and then map the answer back to the original. As an example, numbers are entered into a pocket calculator in decimal. The decimal numbers are converted to binary, and all calculations are performed in binary. Then the final answer is converted back to decimal for display. For P_1 to be polynomially reducible to P_2, all the work associated with the transformations must be performed in polynomial time.

The reason that *NP*-complete problems are the hardest *NP* problems is that a problem that is *NP*-complete can essentially be used as a subroutine for *any* problem in *NP* with only a polynomial amount of overhead. Thus, if any *NP*-complete problem has a polynomial-time solution, then *every* problem in *NP* must have a polynomial-time solution. This makes the *NP*-complete problems the hardest of all *NP* problems.

Suppose we have an *NP*-complete problem P_1. Suppose P_2 is known to be in *NP*. Suppose further that P_1 polynomially reduces to P_2, so that we can solve P_1 by using P_2 with only a polynomial time penalty. Since P_1 is *NP*-complete, every problem in *NP* polynomially reduces to P_1. By applying the closure property of polynomials, we see that every problem in *NP* is polynomially reducible to P_2: We reduce the problem to P_1 and then reduce P_1 to P_2. Thus, P_2 is *NP*-complete.

As an example, suppose that we already know that the Hamiltonian cycle problem is *NP*-complete. The *traveling salesman problem* is as follows.

> **TRAVELING SALESMAN PROBLEM:**
>
> *Given a complete graph $G = (V, E)$, with edge costs, and an integer K, is there a simple cycle that visits all vertices and has total cost $\le K$?*

The problem is different from the Hamiltonian cycle problem because all $|V|(|V| - 1)/2$ edges are present and the graph is weighted. This problem has many important applications. For instance, printed circuit boards need to have holes punched so that chips, resistors, and other electronic components can be placed. This is done mechanically. Punching the hole is a quick operation; the time-consuming step is positioning the hole puncher. The time required for positioning depends on the distance traveled from hole to hole. Since we would like to punch every hole (and then return to the start for the next board) and minimize the total amount of time spent traveling, what we have is a traveling salesman problem.

The traveling salesman problem is NP-complete. It is easy to see that a solution can be checked in polynomial time, so it is certainly in NP. To show that it is NP-complete, we polynomially reduce the Hamiltonian cycle problem to it. To do this we construct a new graph G'. G' has the same vertices as G. For G', each edge (v, w) has a weight of 1 if $(v, w) \in G$, and 2 otherwise. We choose $K = |V|$. See Figure 9.78.

It is easy to verify that G has a Hamiltonian cycle if and only if G' has a Traveling Salesman tour of total weight $|V|$.

There is now a long list of problems known to be NP-complete. To prove that some new problem is NP-complete, it must be shown to be in NP, and then an appropriate NP-complete problem must be transformed into it. Although the transformation to a traveling salesman problem was rather straightforward, most transformations are actually quite involved and require some tricky constructions. Generally, several different NP-complete problems are considered before the problem that actually provides the reduction. As we are only interested in the general ideas, we will not show any more transformations; the interested reader can consult the references.

The alert reader may be wondering how the first NP-complete problem was actually proven to be NP-complete. Since proving that a problem is NP-complete requires transforming it from another NP-complete problem, there must be some NP-complete problem for which this strategy will not work. The first problem that was proven to be NP-complete was the *satisfiability* problem. The satisfiability problem takes as input a boolean expression and asks whether the expression has an assignment to the variables that gives a value of 1.

Satisfiability is certainly in NP, since it is easy to evaluate a boolean expression and check whether the result is 1. In 1971, Cook showed that satisfiability was NP-

Figure 9.78 Hamiltonian cycle problem transformed to traveling salesman problem

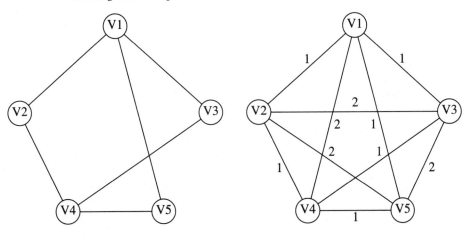

complete by directly proving that all problems that are in *NP* could be transformed to satisfiability. To do this, he used the one known fact about every problem in *NP*: Every problem in *NP* can be solved in polynomial time by a nondeterministic computer. The formal model for a computer is known as a *Turing machine*. Cook showed how the actions of this machine could be simulated by an extremely complicated and long, but still polynomial, boolean formula. This boolean formula would be true if and only if the program being run by the Turing machine produced a "yes" answer for its input.

Once satisfiability was shown to be *NP*-complete, a host of new *NP*-complete problems, including some of the most classic problems, were also shown to be *NP*-complete.

In addition to the satisfiability, Hamiltonian circuit, traveling salesman, and longest-path problems, which we have already examined, some of the more well-known *NP*-complete problems that we have not discussed are *bin packing, knapsack, graph coloring,* and *clique.* The list is quite extensive and includes problems from operating systems (scheduling and security), database systems, operations research, logic, and especially graph theory.

Summary

In this chapter we have seen how graphs can be used to model many real-life problems. Many of the graphs that occur are typically very sparse, so it is important to pay attention to the data structures that are used to implement them.

We have also seen a class of problems that do not seem to have efficient solutions. In Chapter 10, some techniques for dealing with these problems will be discussed.

Exercises

9.1 Find a topological ordering for the graph in Figure 9.79.

Figure 9.79

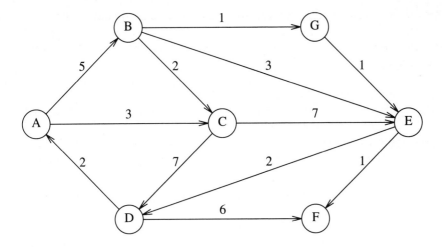

Figure 9.80

9.2 If a stack is used instead of a queue for the topological sort algorithm in Section 9.1, does a different ordering result? Why might one data structure give a "better" answer?

9.3 Write a program to perform a topological sort on a graph.

9.4 An adjacency matrix requires $O(|V|^2)$ merely to initialize using a standard double loop. Propose a method that stores a graph in an adjacency matrix (so that testing for the existence of an edge is $O(1)$) but avoids the quadratic running time.

9.5 a. Find the shortest path from A to all other vertices for the graph in Figure 9.80.

   b. Find the shortest unweighed path from B to all other vertices for the graph in Figure 9.80.

9.6 What is the worst-case running time of Dijkstra's algorithm when implemented with d-heaps (Section 6.5)?

9.7 a. Give an example in which Dijkstra's algorithm gives the wrong answer in the presence of a negative edge but no negative-cost cycle.

   **b. Show that the weighted shortest-path algorithm suggested in Section 9.3.3 works if there are negative-weight edges but no negative-cost cycles, and that the running time of this algorithm is $O(|E| \cdot |V|)$.

*9.8 Suppose all the edge weights in a graph are integers between 1 and $|E|$. How fast can Dijkstra's algorithm be implemented?

9.9 Write a program to solve the single-source shortest-path problem.

9.10 a. Explain how to modify Dijkstra's algorithm to produce a count of the number of different minimum paths from v to w.

    b. Explain how to modify Dijkstra's algorithm so that if there is more than one minimum path from v to w, a path with the fewest number of edges is chosen.

9.11 Find the maximum flow in the network of Figure 9.79.

9.12 Suppose that $G = (V, E)$ is a tree, s is the root, and we add a vertex t and edges of infinite capacity from all leaves in G to t. Give a linear-time algorithm to find a maximum flow from s to t.

9.13 A bipartite graph, $G = (V, E)$, is a graph such that V can be partitioned into two subsets V_1 and V_2, and no edge has both its vertices in the same subset.

    a. Give a linear algorithm to determine whether a graph is bipartite.

    b. The bipartite matching problem is to find the largest subset E' of E such that no vertex is included in more than one edge. A matching of four edges (indicated by dashed edges) is shown in Figure 9.81. There is a matching of five edges, which is maximum.

Show how the bipartite matching problem can be used to solve the following problem: We have a set of instructors, a set of courses, and a list of courses that each instructor is qualified to teach. If no instructor is required to teach more than one course, and only one instructor may teach a given course, what is the maximum number of courses that can be offered?

    c. Show that the network flow problem can be used to solve the bipartite matching problem.

    d. What is the time complexity of your solution to part (b)?

9.14 Give an algorithm to find an augmenting path that permits the maximum flow.

9.15 a. Find a minimum spanning tree for the graph in Figure 9.82 using both Prim's and Kruskal's algorithms.

    b. Is this minimum spanning tree unique? Why?

9.16 Does either Prim's or Kruskal's algorithm work if there are negative edge weights?

9.17 Show that a graph of V vertices can have V^{V-2} minimum spanning trees.

Figure 9.81 A bipartite graph

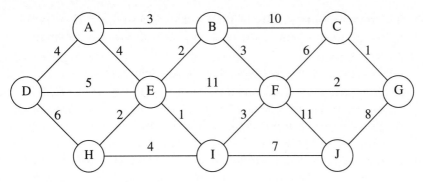

Figure 9.82

9.18 Write a program to implement Kruskal's algorithm.

9.19 If all of the edges in a graph have weights between 1 and $|E|$, how fast can the minimum spanning tree be computed?

9.20 Give an algorithm to find a *maximum* spanning tree. Is this harder than finding a minimum spanning tree?

9.21 Find all the articulation points in the graph in Figure 9.83. Show the depth-first spanning tree and the values of *Num* and *Low* for each vertex.

9.22 Prove that the algorithm to find articulation points works.

9.23 a. Give an algorithm to find the minimum number of edges that need to be removed from an undirected graph so that the resulting graph is acyclic.

   *b. Show that this problem is *NP*-complete for directed graphs.

9.24 Prove that in a depth-first spanning forest of a directed graph, all cross edges go from right to left.

9.25 Give an algorithm to decide whether an edge (v, w) in a depth-first spanning forest of a directed graph is a tree, back, cross, or forward edge.

Figure 9.83

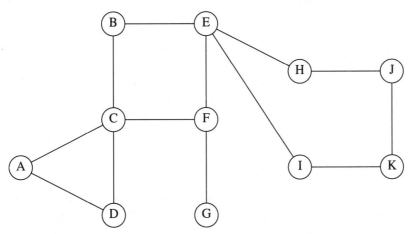

9.26 Find the strongly connected components in the graph of Figure 9.84.

9.27 Write a program to find the strongly connected components in a digraph.

*9.28 Give an algorithm that finds the strongly connected components in only one depth-first search. Use an algorithm similar to the biconnectivity algorithm.

9.29 The *biconnected components* of a graph G is a partition of the edges into sets such that the graph formed by each set of edges is biconnected. Modify the algorithm in Figure 9.67 to find the biconnected components instead of the articulation points.

9.30 Suppose we perform a breadth-first search of an undirected graph and build a breadth-first spanning tree. Show that all edges in the tree are either tree edges or cross edges.

9.31 Give an algorithm to find in an undirected (connected) graph a path that goes through every edge exactly once in each direction.

9.32 a. Write a program to find an Euler circuit in a graph if one exists.
       b. Write a program to find an Euler tour in a graph if one exists.

9.33 An Euler circuit in a directed graph is a cycle in which every edge is visited exactly once.

     *a. Prove that a directed graph has an Euler circuit if and only if it is strongly connected, and every vertex has equal indegree and outdegree.
     *b. Give a linear–time algorithm to find an Euler circuit in a directed graph where one exists.

9.34 a. Consider the following solution to the Euler circuit problem: Assume that the graph is biconnected. Perform a depth-first search, taking back edges only as a last resort. If the graph is not biconnected, apply the algorithm recursively on the biconnected components. Does this algorithm work?
       b. Suppose that when taking back edges, we take the back edge to the nearest ancestor. Does the algorithm work?

9.35 A planar graph is a graph that can be drawn in a plane without any two edges intersecting.

Figure 9.84

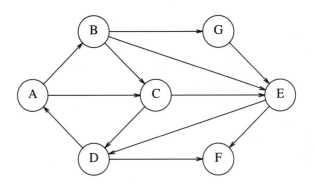

*a. Show that neither of the graphs in Figure 9.85 is planar.

b. Show that in a planar graph, there must exist some vertex that is connected to no more than five nodes.

**c. Show that in a planar graph, $|E| \le 3|V| - 6$.

9.36 A *multigraph* is a graph in which multiple edges are allowed between pairs of vertices. Which of the algorithms in this chapter work without modification for multigraphs? What modifications need to be done for the others?

*9.37 Let $G = (V, E)$ be an undirected graph. Use depth-first search to design a linear algorithm to convert each edge in G to a directed edge such that the resulting graph is strongly connected, or determine that this is not possible.

9.38 You are given a set of n sticks, which are lying on top of each other in some configuration. Each stick is specified by its two endpoints; each endpoint is an ordered triple giving its x, y, and z coordinates; no stick is vertical. A stick may be picked up only if there is no stick on top of it.

a. Explain how to write a routine that takes two sticks a and b and reports whether a is above, below, or unrelated to b. (This has nothing to do with graph theory.)

b. Give an algorithm that determines whether it is possible to pick up all the sticks, and if so, provides a sequence of stick pickups that accomplishes this.

9.39 The *clique* problem can be stated as follows: Given an undirected graph $G = (V, E)$ and an integer K, does G contain a complete subgraph of at least K vertices?

The *vertex cover* problem can be stated as follows: Given an undirected graph $G = (V, E)$ and an integer K, does G contain a subset $V' \subset V$ such that $|V'| \le K$ and every edge in G has a vertex in V'? Show that the clique problem is polynomially reducible to vertex cover.

9.40 Assume that the Hamiltonian cycle problem is *NP*-complete for undirected graphs.

a. Prove that the Hamiltonian cycle problem is *NP*-complete for directed graphs.

Figure 9.85

 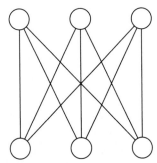

b. Prove that the unweighted simple longest-path problem is *NP*-complete for directed graphs.

9.41 The *baseball card collector* problem is as follows: Given packets P_1, $P_2, \ldots, P_m$, each of which contains a subset of the year's baseball cards, and an integer K, is it possible to collect all the baseball cards by choosing $\leq K$ packets? Show that the baseball card collector problem is *NP*-complete.

References

Good graph theory textbooks include [7], [12], [21], and [34]. More advanced topics, including the more careful attention to running times, are covered in [36], [38], and [45].

Use of adjacency lists was advocated in [23]. The topological sort algorithm is from [28], as described in [31]. Dijkstra's algorithm appeared in [8]. The improvements using d-heaps and Fibonacci heaps are described in [27] and [14], respectively. The shortest-path algorithm with negative edge weights is due to Bellman [3]; Tarjan [45] describes a more efficient way to guarantee termination.

Ford and Fulkerson's seminal work on network flow is [13]. The idea of augmenting along shortest paths or on paths admitting the largest flow increase is from [11]. Other approaches to the problem can be found in [9], [30], and [20]. An algorithm for the min-cost flow problem can be found in [18].

An early minimum spanning tree algorithm can be found in [4]. Prim's algorithm is from [39]; Kruskal's algorithm appears in [32]. Two $O(|E|\log\log|V|)$ algorithms are [5] and [46]. The theoretically best-known algorithms appear in [14] and [16]. An empirical study of these algorithms suggests that Prim's algorithm, implemented with *Decrease_Key*, is best in practice on most graphs [37].

The algorithm for biconnectivity is from [41]. The first linear-time strong components algorithm (Exercise 9.28) appears in the same paper. The algorithm presented in the text is due to Kosaraju (unpublished) and Sharir [40]. Other applications of depth-first search appear in [24], [25], [42], and [43] (as mentioned in Chapter 8, the results in [42] and [43] have been improved, but the basic algorithm is unchanged).

The classic reference work for the theory of *NP*-complete problems is [19]. Additional material can be found in [1]. The *NP*-completeness of satisfiability is shown in [6]. The other seminal paper is [29], which showed the *NP*-completeness of 21 problems. An excellent survey of complexity theory is [44]. An approximation algorithm for the traveling salesman problem, which generally gives nearly optimal results, can be found in [35].

A solution to Exercise 9.8 can be found in [2]. Solutions to the bipartite matching problem in Exercise 9.13 can be found in [22] and [33]. The problem can be generalized by adding weights to the edges and removing the restriction that the graph is bipartite. Efficient solutions for the unweighted matching problem for general graphs are quite complex. Details can be found in [10], [15], and [17].

Exercise 9.35 deals with planar graphs, which commonly arise in practice. Planar graphs are very sparse, and many difficult problems are easier on planar graphs. An example is the graph isomorphism problem, which is solvable in linear time for planar graphs [26]. No polynomial time algorithm is known for general graphs.

1. A. V. Aho, J. E. Hopcroft, and J. D. Ullman, *The Design and Analysis of Computer Algorithms,* Addison-Wesley, Reading, Mass. 1974.
2. R. K. Ahuja, K. Melhorn, J. B. Orlin, and R. E. Tarjan, "Faster Algorithms for the Shortest Path Problem," *Journal of the ACM 37* (1990), 213–223.
3. R. E. Bellman, "On a Routing Problem," *Quarterly of Applied Mathematics 16* (1958), 87–90.
4. O. Borůvka, "Ojistém problému minimálním (On a Minimal Problem)," *Práca Moravské Přirodovědecké Společnosti 3* (1926), 37–58.
5. D. Cheriton and R. E. Tarjan, "Finding Minimum Spanning Trees," *SIAM Journal on Computing 5* (1976), 724–742.
6. S. Cook, "The Complexity of Theorem Proving Procedures," *Proceedings of the Third Annual ACM Symposium on Theory of Computing* (1971), 151–158.
7. N. Deo, *Graph Theory with Applications to Engineering and Computer Science,* Prentice Hall, Englewood Cliffs, N.J., 1974.
8. E. W. Dijkstra, "A Note on Two Problems in Connexion with Graphs," *Numerische Mathematik 1* (1959), 269–271.
9. E. A. Dinic, "Algorithm for Solution of a Problem of Maximum Flow in Networks with Power Estimation," *Soviet Mathematics Doklady 11* (1970), 1277–1280.
10. J. Edmonds, "Paths, Trees, and Flowers," *Canadian Journal of Mathematics 17* (1965) 449–467.
11. J. Edmonds and R. M. Karp, "Theoretical Improvements in Algorithmic Efficiency for Network Flow Problems," *Journal of the ACM 19* (1972), 248–264.
12. S. Even, *Graph Algorithms,* Computer Science Press, Potomac, Md., 1979.
13. L. R. Ford, Jr. and D. R. Fulkerson, *Flows in Networks,* Princeton University Press, Princeton, N.J., 1962.
14. M. L. Fredman and R. E. Tarjan, "Fibonacci Heaps and Their Uses in Improved Network Optimization Algorithms," *Journal of the ACM 34* (1987), 596–615.
15. H. N. Gabow, "Data Structures for Weighted Matching and Nearest Common Ancestors with Linking," *Proceedings of First Annual ACM-SIAM Symposium on Discrete Algorithms* (1990), 434–443.
16. H. N. Gabow, Z. Galil, T. H. Spencer, and R. E. Tarjan, "Efficient Algorithms for Finding Minimum Spanning Trees on Directed and Undirected Graphs," *Combinatorica 6* (1986), 109–122.
17. Z. Galil, "Efficient Algorithms for Finding Maximum Matchings in Graphs," *ACM Computing Surveys 18* (1986), 23–38.
18. Z. Galil and E. Tardos, "An $O(n^2(m + n\log n)\log n)$ Min-Cost Flow Algorithm," *Journal of the ACM 35* (1988), 374–386.
19. M. R. Garey and D. S. Johnson, *Computers and Intractability: A Guide to the Theory of NP-Completeness,* Freeman, San Francisco, 1979.
20. A. V. Goldberg and R. E. Tarjan, "A New Approach to the Maximum-Flow Problem," *Journal of the ACM 35* (1988), 921–940.
21. F. Harary, *Graph Theory,* Addison-Wesley, Reading, Mass. 1969.
22. J. E. Hopcroft and R. M. Karp, "An $n^{5/2}$ Algorithm for Maximum Matchings in Bipartite Graphs," *SIAM Journal on Computing 2* (1973), 225–231.

23. J. E. Hopcroft and R. E. Tarjan, "Algorithm 447: Efficient Algorithms for Graph Manipulation," *Communications of the ACM 16* (1973), 372–378.

24. J. E. Hopcroft and R. E. Tarjan, "Dividing a Graph into Triconnected Components," *SIAM Journal on Computing 2* (1973), 135–158.

25. J. E. Hopcroft and R. E. Tarjan, "Efficient Planarity Testing," *Journal of the ACM 21* (1974), 549–568.

26. J. E. Hopcroft and J. K. Wong, "Linear Time Algorithm for Isomorphism of Planar Graphs," *Proceedings of the Sixth Annual ACM Symposium on Theory of Computing* (1974), 172–184.

27. D. B. Johnson, "Efficient Algorithms for Shortest Paths in Sparse Networks," *Journal of the ACM 24* (1977), 1–13.

28. A. B. Kahn, "Topological Sorting of Large Networks," *Communications of the ACM 5* (1962), 558–562.

29. R. M. Karp, "Reducibility among Combinatorial Problems," *Complexity of Computer Computations* (eds. R. E. Miller and J. W. Thatcher), Plenum Press, New York, 1972, 85–103.

30. A. V. Karzanov, "Determining the Maximal Flow in a Network by the Method of Preflows," *Soviet Mathematics Doklady 15* (1974), 434–437.

31. D. E. Knuth, *The Art of Computer Programming, Vol. 1: Fundamental Algorithms*, second edition, Addison-Wesley, Reading, Mass., 1973.

32. J. B. Kruskal, Jr. "On the Shortest Spanning Subtree of a Graph and the Traveling Salesman Problem," *Proceedings of the American Mathematical Society 7* (1956), 48–50.

33. H. W. Kuhn, "The Hungarian Method for the Assignment Problem," *Naval Research Logistics Quarterly 2* (1955), 83–97.

34. E. L. Lawler, *Combinatorial Optimization: Networks and Matroids,* Holt, Reinhart, and Winston, New York, 1976.

35. S. Lin and B. W. Kernighan, "An Effective Heuristic Algorithm for the Traveling Salesman Problem," *Operations Research 21* (1973), 498–516.

36. K. Melhorn, *Data Structures and Algorithms 2: Graph Algorithms and NP-completeness,* Springer-Verlag, Berlin, 1984.

37. B. M. E. Moret and H. D. Shapiro, "An Empirical Analysis of Algorithms for Constructing a Minimum Spanning Tree," *Proceedings of the Second Workshop on Algorithms and Data Structures* (1991), 400–411.

38. C. H. Papadimitriou and K. Steiglitz, *Combinatorial Optimization: Algorithms and Complexity,* Prentice Hall, Englewood Cliffs, N.J., 1982.

39. R. C. Prim, "Shortest Connection Networks and Some Generalizations," *Bell System Technical Journal 36* (1957), 1389–1401.

40. M. Sharir, "A Strong-Connectivity Algorithm and Its Application in Data Flow Analysis," *Computers and Mathematics with Applications 7* (1981), 67–72.

41. R. E. Tarjan, "Depth First Search and Linear Graph Algorithms," *SIAM Journal on Computing 1* (1972), 146–160.

42. R. E. Tarjan, "Testing Flow Graph Reducibility," *Journal of Computer and System Sciences 9* (1974), 355–365.

43. R. E. Tarjan, "Finding Dominators in Directed Graphs," *SIAM Journal on Computing 3* (1974), 62–89.

44. R. E. Tarjan, "Complexity of Combinatorial Algorithms," *SIAM Review 20* (1978), 457–491.

45. R. E. Tarjan, *Data Structures and Network Algorithms,* Society for Industrial and Applied Mathematics, Philadelphia, Penn., 1983.

46. A. C. Yao, "An $O(|E|\log\log|V|)$ Algorithm for Finding Minimum Spanning Trees," *Information Processing Letters 4* (1975), 21–23.

CHAPTER 10

Algorithm Design Techniques

So far, we have been concerned with the efficient implementation of algorithms. We have seen that when an algorithm is given, the actual data structures need not be specified. It is up to the programmer to choose the appropriate data structure in order to make the running time as small as possible.

In this chapter, we switch our attention from the *implementation* of algorithms to the *design* of algorithms. Most of the algorithms that we have seen so far are straightforward and simple. Chapter 9 contains some algorithms that are much more subtle, and some require an argument (in some cases lengthy) to show that they are indeed correct. In this chapter, we will focus on five of the common types of algorithms used to solve problems. For many problems, it is quite likely that at least one of these methods will work. Specifically, for each type of algorithm we will

- See the general approach.
- Look at several examples (the exercises at the end of the chapter provide many more examples).
- Discuss, in general terms, the time and space complexity, where appropriate.

With one exception, we have coded our algorithms using mostly C features, to avoid unnecessary complications.

10.1. Greedy Algorithms

The first type of algorithm we will examine is the *greedy algorithm*. We have already seen three greedy algorithms in Chapter 9: Dijkstra's, Prim's, and Kruskal's algorithms. Greedy algorithms work in phases. In each phase, a decision is made that appears to be good, without regard for future consequences. Generally, this means that some *local optimum* is chosen. This "take what you can get now" strategy is the source of the name for this class of algorithms. When the algorithm terminates, we hope that the local optimum is equal to the *global optimum*. If this is the case, then the algorithm is correct; otherwise, the algorithm has produced a suboptimal solution. If the absolute best answer is not required, then simple greedy algorithms are sometimes used to generate approximate answers, rather than using the more complicated algorithms generally required to generate an exact answer.

There are several real-life examples of greedy algorithms. The most obvious is the coin-changing problem. To make change in U.S. currency, we repeatedly dispense the largest denomination. Thus, to give out seventeen dollars and sixty-one cents in change, we give out a ten-dollar bill, a five-dollar bill, two one-dollar bills, two quarters, one dime, and one penny. By doing this, we are guaranteed to minimize the number of bills and coins. This algorithm does not work in all monetary systems, but fortunately, we can prove that it does work in the American monetary system. Indeed, it works even if two-dollar bills and fifty-cent pieces are allowed.

Traffic problems provide an example where making locally optimal choices does not always work. For example, during certain rush hour times in Miami, it is best to stay off the prime streets even if they look empty, because traffic will come to a standstill a mile down the road, and you will be stuck. Even more shocking, it is better in some cases to make a temporary detour in the direction opposite your destination in order to avoid all traffic bottlenecks.

In the remainder of this section, we will look at several applications that use greedy algorithms. The first application is a simple scheduling problem. Virtually all scheduling problems are either *NP*-complete (or of similar difficult complexity) or are solvable by a greedy algorithm. The second application deals with file compression and is one of the earliest results in computer science. Finally, we will look at an example of a greedy approximation algorithm.

10.1.1. A Simple Scheduling Problem

We are given jobs $j_1, j_2, \ldots, j_n$, all with known running times $t_1, t_2, \ldots, t_n$, respectively. We have a single processor. What is the best way to schedule these jobs in order to minimize the average completion time? In this entire section, we will assume *nonpreemptive scheduling*: Once a job is started, it must run to completion.

As an example, suppose we have the four jobs and associated running times shown in Figure 10.1. One possible schedule is shown in Figure 10.2. Because j_1 finishes in 15 (time units), j_2 in 23, j_3 in 26, and j_4 in 36, the average completion time is 25. A better schedule, which yields a mean completion time of 17.75, is shown in Figure 10.3.

Figure 10.1 Jobs and times

Job	Time
j_1	15
j_2	8
j_3	3
j_4	10

Figure 10.2 Schedule #1

Figure 10.3 Schedule #2 (optimal)

The schedule given in Figure 10.3 is arranged by shortest job first. We can show that this will always yield an optimal schedule. Let the jobs in the schedule be j_{i_1}, $j_{i_2}, \ldots, j_{i_n}$. The first job finishes in time t_{i_1}. The second job finishes after $t_{i_1} + t_{i_2}$, and the third job finishes after $t_{i_1} + t_{i_2} + t_{i_3}$. From this, we see that the total cost, C, of the schedule is

$$C = \sum_{k=1}^{n} (n - k + 1) t_{i_k} \tag{10.1}$$

$$C = (n+1) \sum_{k=1}^{n} t_{i_k} - \sum_{k=1}^{n} k \cdot t_{i_k} \tag{10.2}$$

Notice that in Equation (10.2), the first sum is independent of the job ordering, so only the second sum affects the total cost. Suppose that in an ordering there exists some $x > y$ such that $t_{i_x} < t_{i_y}$. Then a calculation shows that by swapping j_{i_x} and j_{i_y}, the second sum increases, decreasing the total cost. Thus, any schedule of jobs in which the times are not monotonically nondecreasing must be suboptimal. The only schedules left are those in which the jobs are arranged by smallest running time first, breaking ties arbitrarily.

This result indicates the reason the operating system scheduler generally gives precedence to shorter jobs.

The Multiprocessor Case

We can extend this problem to the case of several processors. Again we have jobs $j_1, j_2, \ldots, j_n$, with associated running times $t_1, t_2, \ldots, t_n$, and a number P of processors. We will assume without loss of generality that the jobs are ordered, shortest running time first. As an example, suppose $P = 3$, and the jobs are as shown in Figure 10.4.

Figure 10.5 shows an optimal arrangement to minimize mean completion time. Jobs j_1, j_4, and j_7 are run on Processor 1. Processor 2 handles j_2, j_5, and j_8, and Processor 3 runs the remaining jobs. The total time to completion is 165, for an average of $\frac{165}{9} = 18.33$.

Job	Time
j_1	3
j_2	5
j_3	6
j_4	10
j_5	11
j_6	14
j_7	15
j_8	18
j_9	20

Figure 10.4 Jobs and times

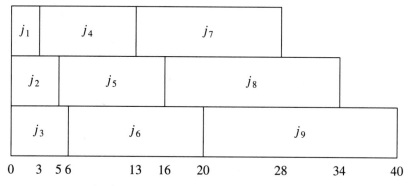

Figure 10.5 An optimal solution for the multiprocessor case

The algorithm to solve the multiprocessor case is to start jobs in order, cycling through processors. It is not hard to show that no other ordering can do better, although if the number of processors P evenly divides the number of jobs n, there are many optimal orderings. This is obtained by, for each $0 \le i < n/P$, placing each of the jobs j_{iP+1} through $j_{(i+1)P}$ on a different processor. In our case, Figure 10.6 shows a second optimal solution.

Even if P does not divide n exactly, there can still be many optimal solutions, even if all the job times are distinct. We leave further investigation of this as an exercise.

Minimizing the Final Completion Time

We close this section by considering a very similar problem. Suppose we are only concerned with when the last job finishes. In our two examples above, these completion times are 40 and 38, respectively. Figure 10.7 shows that the minimum final completion time is 34, and this clearly cannot be improved, because every processor is always busy.

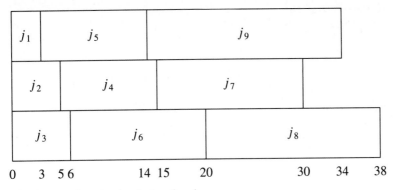

Figure 10.6 A second optimal solution for the multiprocessor case

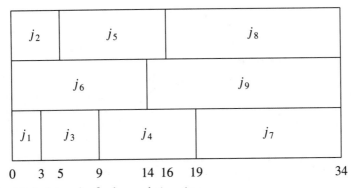

Figure 10.7 Minimizing the final completion time

Although this schedule does not have minimum mean completion time, it has merit in that the completion time of the entire sequence is earlier. If the same user owns all these jobs, then this is the preferable method of scheduling. Although these problems are very similar, this new problem turns out to be *NP*-complete; it is just another way of phrasing the knapsack or bin-packing problems, which we will encounter later in this section. Thus, minimizing the final completion time is apparently much harder than minimizing the mean completion time.

10.1.2. Huffman Codes

In this section, we consider a second application of greedy algorithms, known as *file compression*.

The normal ASCII character set consists of roughly 100 "printable" characters. In order to distinguish these characters, $\lceil \log 100 \rceil = 7$ bits are required. Seven bits allow the representation of 128 characters, so the ASCII character set adds some other "nonprintable" characters. An eighth bit is added as a parity check. The important point, however, is that if the size of the character set is C, then $\lceil \log C \rceil$ bits are needed in a standard encoding.

Character	Code	Frequency	Total Bits
a	000	10	30
e	001	15	45
i	010	12	36
s	011	3	9
t	100	4	12
space	101	13	39
newline	110	1	3
Total			174

Figure 10.8   Using a standard coding scheme

Suppose we have a file that contains only the characters *a*, *e*, *i*, *s*, *t*, plus blank spaces and *newlines*. Suppose further, that the file has ten *a*'s, fifteen *e*'s, twelve *i*'s, three *s*'s, four *t*'s, thirteen blanks, and one *newline*. As the table in Figure 10.8 shows, this file requires 174 bits to represent, since there are 58 characters and each character requires three bits.

In real life, files can be quite large. Many of the very large files are output of some program, and there is usually a big disparity between the most frequent and least frequent characters. For instance, many large data files have an inordinately large amount of digits, blanks, and *newlines*, but few *q*'s and *x*'s. We might be interested in reducing the file size if, for example, we are transmitting it over a slow phone line. Also, since disk space is precious on virtually every machine, one might wonder if it would be possible to provide a better code and reduce the total number of bits required.

The answer is that this is possible, and a simple strategy achieves 25 percent savings on typical large files and as much as 50 to 60 percent savings on many large data files. The general strategy is to allow the code length to vary from character to character and to ensure that the frequently occurring characters have short codes. Notice that if all the characters occur with the same frequency, then there is not likely to be any savings.

The binary code that represents the alphabet can be represented by the binary tree shown in Figure 10.9.

The tree in Figure 10.9 has data only at the leaves. The representation of each character can be found by starting at the root and recording the path, using a 0

Figure 10.9   Representation of the original code in a tree

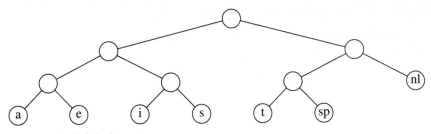

Figure 10.10   A slightly better tree

to indicate the left branch and a 1 to indicate the right branch. For instance, s is reached by going left, then right, and finally right. This is encoded as 011. This data structure is sometimes referred to as a *trie*. If character c_i is at depth d_i and occurs f_i times, then the *cost* of the code is equal to $\sum d_i f_i$.

A better code than the one given in Figure 10.9 can be obtained by noticing that the *newline* is an only child. By placing the *newline* symbol one level higher (in place of its parent), we obtain the new tree in Figure 10.10. This new tree has cost of 173, but is still far from optimal.

Notice that the tree in Figure 10.10 is a *full tree*: All nodes either are leaves or have two children. An optimal code will always have this property since otherwise, as we have already seen, nodes with only one child could move up a level.

If the characters are placed only at the leaves, any sequence of bits can always be decoded unambiguously. For instance, suppose the encoded string is 01001111000010110001000111. 0 is not a character code, 01 is not a character code, but 010 represents i, so the first character is i. Then 011 follows, giving a t. Then 11 follows, which is a *newline*. The remainder of the code is a, *space*, t, i, e, and *newline*. Thus, it does not matter if the character codes are different lengths, as long as no character code is a prefix of another character code. Such an encoding is known as a *prefix code*. Conversely, if a character is contained in a nonleaf node, it is no longer possible to guarantee that the decoding will be unambiguous.

Putting these facts together, we see that our basic problem is to find the full binary tree of minimum total cost (as defined above), in which all characters are contained in the leaves. The tree in Figure 10.11 shows the optimal tree

Figure 10.11   Optimal prefix code

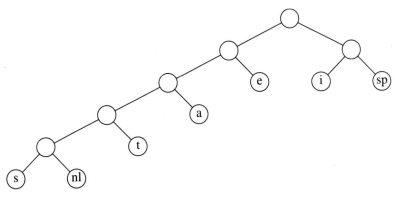

Character	Code	Frequency	Total Bits
a	001	10	30
e	01	15	30
i	10	12	24
s	00000	3	15
t	0001	4	16
space	11	13	26
newline	00001	1	5
Total			146

Figure 10.12   Optimal prefix code

for our sample alphabet. As can be seen in Figure 10.12, this code uses only 146 bits.

Notice that there are many optimal codes. These can be obtained by swapping children in the encoding tree. The main unresolved question, then, is how the coding tree is constructed. The algorithm to do this was given by Huffman in 1952. Thus, this coding system is commonly referred to as a Huffman code.

Huffman's Algorithm

Throughout this section we will assume that the number of characters is C. Huffman's algorithm can be described as follows: We maintain a forest of trees. The *weight* of a tree is equal to the sum of the frequencies of its leaves. $C - 1$ times, select the two trees, T_1 and T_2, of smallest weight, breaking ties arbitrarily, and form a new tree with subtrees T_1 and T_2. At the beginning of the algorithm, there are C single-node trees—one for each character. At the end of the algorithm there is one tree, and this is the optimal Huffman coding tree.

A worked example will make the operation of the algorithm clear. Figure 10.13 shows the initial forest; the weight of each tree is shown in small type at the root. The two trees of lowest weight are merged together, creating the forest shown in Figure 10.14. We will name the new root $T1$, so that future merges can be stated

Figure 10.13   Initial stage of Huffman's algorithm

Figure 10.14   Huffman's algorithm after the first merge unambiguously. We have made *s* the left child arbitrarily; any tiebreaking procedure can be used. The total weight of the new tree is just the sum of the weights of the old trees, and can thus be easily computed. It is also a simple matter to create the new tree, since we merely need to get a new node, set the left and right pointers, and record the weight.

Now there are six trees, and we again select the two trees of smallest weight. These happen to be $T1$ and t, which are then merged into a new tree with root $T2$ and weight 8. This is shown in Figure 10.15. The third step merges $T2$ and a, creating $T3$, with weight $10 + 8 = 18$. Figure 10.16 shows the result of this operation.

After the third merge is completed, the two trees of lowest weight are the single-node trees representing i and the blank space. Figure 10.17 shows how these trees are merged into the new tree with root $T4$. The fifth step is to merge the trees with roots e and $T3$, since these trees have the two smallest weights. The result of this step is shown in Figure 10.18.

Finally, the optimal tree, which was shown in Figure 10.11, is obtained by merging the two remaining trees. Figure 10.19 shows this optimal tree, with root $T6$.

Figure 10.15 Huffman's algorithm after the second merge

Figure 10.16 Huffman's algorithm after the third merge

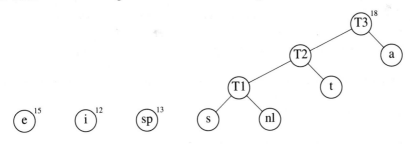

Figure 10.17 Huffman's algorithm after the fourth merge

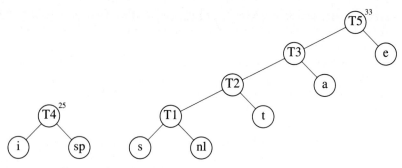

Figure 10.18   Huffman's algorithm after the fifth merge

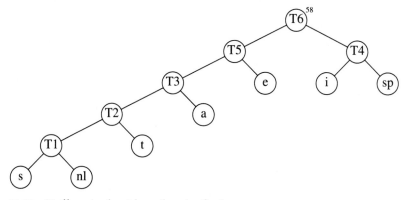

Figure 10.19   Huffman's algorithm after the final merge

We will sketch the ideas involved in proving that Huffman's algorithm yields an optimal code; we will leave the details as an exercise. First, it is not hard to show by contradiction that the tree must be full, since we have already seen how a tree that is not full is improved.

Next, we must show that the two least frequent characters α and β must be the two deepest nodes (although other nodes may be as deep). Again, this is easy to show by contradiction, since if either α or β is not a deepest node, then there must be some γ that is (recall that the tree is full). If α is less frequent than γ, then we can improve the cost by swapping them in the tree.

We can then argue that the characters in any two nodes at the same depth can be swapped without affecting optimality. This shows that an optimal tree can always be found that contains the two least frequent symbols as siblings; thus the first step is not a mistake.

The proof can be completed by using an induction argument. As trees are merged, we consider the new character set to be the characters in the roots. Thus, in our example, after four merges, we can view the character set as consisting of e and the metacharacters $T3$ and $T4$. This is probably the trickiest part of the proof; you are urged to fill in all of the details.

The reason that this is a greedy algorithm is that at each stage we perform a merge without regard to global considerations. We merely select the two smallest trees.

If we maintain the trees in a priority queue, ordered by weight, then the running time is $O(C \log C)$, since there will be one *Build_Heap*, $2C - 2$ *Delete_Min*s, and $C - 2$ *Insert*s on a priority queue that never has more than C elements. A simple implementation of the priority queue, using a linked list, would give an $O(C^2)$ algorithm. The choice of priority queue implementation depends on how large C is. In the typical case of an ASCII character set, C is small enough that the quadratic running time is acceptable. In such an application, virtually all the running time will be spent on the disk I/O required to read the input file and write out the compressed version.

There are two details that must be considered. First, the encoding information must be transmitted at the start of the compressed file, since otherwise it will be impossible to decode. There are several ways of doing this; see Exercise 10.4. For small files, the cost of transmitting this table will override any possible savings in compression, and the result will probably be file expansion. Of course, this can be detected and the original left intact. For large files, the size of the table is not significant.

The second problem is that as described, this is a two-pass algorithm. The first pass collects the frequency data, and the second pass does the encoding. This is obviously not a desirable property for a program dealing with large files. Some alternatives are described in the references.

10.1.3. *Approximate Bin Packing*

In this section, we will consider some algorithms to solve the *bin packing* problem. These algorithms will run quickly but will not necessarily produce optimal solutions. We will prove, however, that the solutions that are produced are not too far from optimal.

We are given n items of sizes $s_1, s_2, \ldots, s_n$. All sizes satisfy $0 < s_i \le 1$. The problem is to pack these items in the fewest number of bins, given that each bin has unit capacity. As an example, Figure 10.20 shows an optimal packing for an item list with sizes 0.2, 0.5, 0.4, 0.7, 0.1, 0.3, 0.8.

Figure 10.20   Optimal packing for 0.2, 0.5, 0.4, 0.7, 0.1, 0.3, 0.8

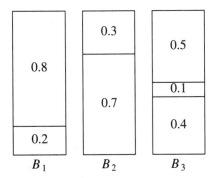

There are two versions of the bin packing problem. The first version is *on-line* bin packing. In this version, each item must be placed in a bin before the next item can be processed. The second version is the *off-line* bin packing problem. In an off-line algorithm, we do not need to do anything until all the input has been read. The distinction between on-line and off-line algorithms was discussed in Section 8.2.

On-line Algorithms

The first issue to consider is whether or not an on-line algorithm can actually always give an optimal answer, even if it is allowed unlimited computation. Remember that even though unlimited computation is allowed, an on-line algorithm must place an item before processing the next item and cannot change its decision.

To show that an on-line algorithm cannot always give an optimal solution, we will give it particularly difficult data to work on. Consider an input sequence I_1 of m small items of weight $\frac{1}{2} - \epsilon$ followed by m large items of weight $\frac{1}{2} + \epsilon, 0 < \epsilon < 0.01$. It is clear that these items can be packed in m bins if we place one small item and one large item in each bin. Suppose there were an optimal on-line algorithm A that could perform this packing. Consider the operation of algorithm A on the sequence I_2, consisting of only m small items of weight $\frac{1}{2} - \epsilon$. I_2 can be packed in $\lceil m/2 \rceil$ bins. However, A will place each item in a separate bin, since A must yield the same results on I_2 as it does for the first half of I_1, since the first half of I_1 is exactly the same input as I_2. This means that A will use twice as many bins as is optimal for I_2. What we have proven is that there is no optimal algorithm for on-line bin packing.

What the argument above shows is that an on-line algorithm never knows when the input might end, so any performance guarantees it provides must hold at every instant throughout the algorithm. If we follow the foregoing strategy, we can prove the following.

THEOREM 10.1.

There are inputs that force any on-line bin-packing algorithm to use at least $\frac{4}{3}$ the optimal number of bins.

PROOF:

Suppose otherwise, and suppose for simplicity that m is even. Consider any on-line algorithm A running on the input sequence I_1, above. Recall that this sequence consists of m small items followed by m large items. Let us consider what the algorithm A has done after processing the mth item. Suppose A has already used b bins. At this point in the algorithm, the optimal number of bins is $m/2$, because we can place two elements in each bin. Thus we know that $2b/m < \frac{4}{3}$, by our assumption of a better-than-$\frac{4}{3}$ performance guarantee.

Now consider the performance of algorithm A after all items have been packed. All bins created after the bth bin must contain exactly one item, since all small items are placed in the first b bins, and two large items will not fit in a bin. Since the first b bins can have at most two items each, and the remaining bins have one item each, we see that packing $2m$ items will require at least

$2m - b$ bins. Since the $2m$ items can be optimally packed using m bins, our performance guarantee assures us that $(2m - b)/m < \frac{4}{3}$.

The first inequality implies that $b/m < \frac{2}{3}$, and the second inequality implies that $b/m > \frac{2}{3}$, which is a contradiction. Thus, no on-line algorithm can guarantee that it will produce a packing with less than $\frac{4}{3}$ the optimal number of bins.

There are three simple algorithms that guarantee that the number of bins used is no more than twice optimal. There are also quite a few more complicated algorithms with better guarantees.

Next Fit

Probably the simplest algorithm is *next fit*. When processing any item, we check to see whether it fits in the same bin as the last item. If it does, it is placed there; otherwise, a new bin is created. This algorithm is incredibly simple to implement and runs in linear time. Figure 10.21 shows the packing produced for the same input as Figure 10.20.

Not only is next fit simple to program; its worst-case behavior is also easy to analyze.

THEOREM 10.2.

Let m be the optimal number of bins required to pack a list I of items. Then next fit never uses more than $2m$ bins. There exist sequences such that next fit uses $2m - 2$ bins.

PROOF:

Consider any adjacent bins B_j and B_{j+1}. The sum of the sizes of all items in B_j and B_{j+1} must be larger than 1, since otherwise all of these items would have been placed in B_j. If we apply this result to all pairs of adjacent bins, we see that at most half of the space is wasted. Thus, next fit uses at most twice the number of bins.

To see that this bound is tight, suppose that the n items have size $s_i = 0.5$ if i is odd and $s_i = 2/n$ if i is even. Assume n is divisible by 4. The optimal

Figure 10.21 Next fit for 0.2, 0.5, 0.4, 0.7, 0.1, 0.3, 0.8

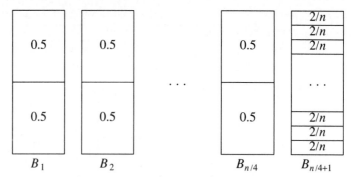

Figure 10.22 Optimal packing for 0.5, $2/n$, 0.5, $2/n$, 0.5, $2/n$,...

packing, shown in Figure 10.22, consists of $n/4$ bins, each containing 2 elements of size 0.5, and one bin containing the $n/2$ elements of size $2/n$, for a total of $(n/4) + 1$. Figure 10.23 shows that next fit uses $n/2$ bins. Thus, next fit can be forced to use almost twice as many bins as optimal.

First Fit

Although next fit has a reasonable performance guarantee, it performs poorly in practice because it creates new bins when it does not need to. In the sample run, it could have placed the item of size 0.3 in either B_1 or B_2 rather than create a new bin.

The *first fit* strategy is to scan the bins in order and place the new item in the first bin that is large enough to hold it. Thus, a new bin is created only when the results of previous placements have left no other alternative. Figure 10.24 shows the packing that results from first fit on our standard input.

A simple method of implementing first fit would process each item by scanning down the list of bins sequentially. This would take $O(n^2)$. It is possible to implement first fit to run in $O(n \log n)$; we leave this as an exercise.

A moment's thought will convince you that at any point, at most one bin can be more than half empty, since if a second bin were also half empty, its contents would

Figure 10.23 Next fit packing for 0.5, $2/n$, 0.5, $2/n$, 0.5, $2/n$,...

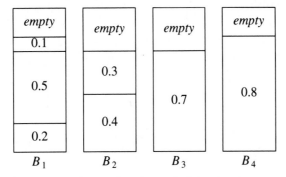

Figure 10.24 First fit for 0.2, 0.5, 0.4, 0.7, 0.1, 0.3, 0.8

fit into the first bin. Thus, we can immediately conclude that first fit guarantees a solution with at most twice the optimal number of bins.

On the other hand, the bad case that we used in the proof of next fit's performance bound does not apply for first fit. Thus, one might wonder if a better bound can be proven. The answer is yes, but the proof is complicated.

THEOREM 10.3.

Let m be the optimal number of bins required to pack a list I of items. Then first fit never uses more than $\lceil \frac{17}{10}m \rceil$ bins. There exist sequences such that first fit uses $\frac{17}{10}(m-1)$ bins.

PROOF:
See the references at the end of the chapter.

An example in which first fit does almost as poorly as the previous theorem would indicate is shown in Figure 10.25. The input consists of $6m$ items of size $\frac{1}{7} + \epsilon$, followed by $6m$ items of size $\frac{1}{3} + \epsilon$, followed by $6m$ items of size $\frac{1}{2} + \epsilon$. One simple packing places one item of each size in a bin and requires $6m$ bins. First fit requires $10m$ bins.

Figure 10.25 A case where first fit uses $10m$ bins instead of $6m$ bins

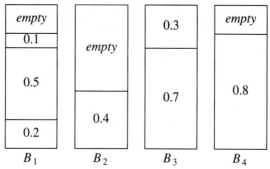

Figure 10.26   Best fit for 0.2, 0.5, 0.4, 0.7, 0.1, 0.3, 0.8

When first fit is run on a large number of items with sizes uniformly distributed between 0 and 1, empirical results show that first fit uses roughly 2 percent more bins than optimal. In many cases, this is quite acceptable.

Best Fit

The third on-line strategy we will examine is *best fit*. Instead of placing a new item in the first spot that is found, it is placed in the tightest spot among all bins. A typical packing is shown in Figure 10.26.

Notice that the item of size 0.3 is placed in B_3, where it fits perfectly, instead of B_2. One might expect that since we are now making a more educated choice of bins, the performance would improve. This is not the case, because the generic bad cases are the same. Best fit is never more than roughly 1.7 times as bad as optimal, and there are inputs for which it (nearly) achieves this bound. Nevertheless, best fit is also simple to code, especially if an $O(n \log n)$ algorithm is required.

Off-line Algorithms

If we are allowed to view the entire item list before producing an answer, then we should expect to do better. Indeed, since we can eventually find the optimal packing by exhaustive search, we already have a theoretical improvement over the on-line case.

The major problem with all the on-line algorithms is that it is hard to pack the large items, especially when they occur late in the input. The natural way around this is to sort the items, placing the largest items first. We can then apply first fit or best fit, yielding the algorithms *first fit decreasing* and *best fit decreasing,* respectively. Figure 10.27 shows that in our case this yields an optimal solution (although, of course, this is not true in general).

In this section, we will deal with first fit decreasing. The results for best fit decreasing are almost identical. Since it is possible that the item sizes are not distinct, some authors prefer to call the algorithm *first fit nonincreasing*. We will stay with the original name. We will also assume, without loss of generality, that input sizes are already sorted.

The first remark we can make is that the bad case, which showed first fit using 10*m* bins instead of 6*m* bins, does not apply when the items are sorted. We will

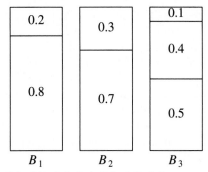

Figure 10.27 First fit for 0.8, 0.7, 0.5, 0.4, 0.3, 0.2, 0.1

show that if an optimal packing uses m bins, then first fit decreasing never uses more than $(4m + 1)/3$ bins.

The result depends on two observations. First, all the items with weight larger than $\frac{1}{3}$ will be placed in the first m bins. This implies that all the items in the extra bins have weight at most $\frac{1}{3}$. The second observation is that the number of items in the extra bins can be at most $m - 1$. Combining these two results, we find that at most $\lceil (m - 1)/3 \rceil$ extra bins can be required. We now prove these two observations.

LEMMA 10.1.

Let the n items have (sorted in decreasing order) input sizes s_1, $s_2, \ldots$, s_n, respectively, and suppose that the optimal packing is m bins. Then all items that first fit decreasing places in extra bins have size at most $\frac{1}{3}$.

PROOF:

Suppose the ith item is the first placed in bin $m + 1$. We need to show that $s_i \leq \frac{1}{3}$. We will prove this by contradiction. Assume $s_i > \frac{1}{3}$.

It follows that $s_1, s_2, \ldots, s_{i-1} > \frac{1}{3}$ since the sizes are arranged in sorted order. From this it follows that all bins $B_1, B_2, \ldots, B_m$ have at most two items each.

Consider the state of the system after the $(i - 1)$st item is placed in a bin, but before the ith item is placed. We now want to show that (under the assumption that $s_i > \frac{1}{3}$) the first m bins are arranged as follows: First there are some bins with exactly one element, and then the remaining bins have two elements.

Suppose there were two bins B_x and B_y, such that $1 \leq x < y \leq m$, B_x has two items, and B_y has one item. Let x_1 and x_2 be the two items in B_x, and let y_1 be the item in B_y. $x_1 \geq y_1$ since x was placed in the earlier bin. $x_2 \geq s_i$ by similar reasoning. Thus, $x_1 + x_2 \geq y_1 + s_i$. This implies that s_i could be placed in B_y. By our assumption this is not possible. Thus, if $s_i > \frac{1}{3}$, then, at the time that we try to process s_i, the first m bins are arranged such that the first j have one element and the next $m - j$ have two elements.

To prove the lemma we will show that there is no way to place all the items in m bins, which contradicts the premise of the lemma.

Clearly, no two items $s_1, s_2, \ldots, s_j$ can be placed in one bin by any algorithm, since if they could, first fit would have done so too. We also know that first fit has not placed any of the items of size $s_{j+1}, s_{j+2}, \ldots, s_i$ into the first j bins, so none of them fit. Thus, in any packing, specifically the optimal packing, there must be j bins that do not contain these items. It follows that the items of size $s_{j+1}, s_{j+2}, \ldots, s_{i-1}$ must be contained in some set of $m - j$ bins, and from previous considerations, the total number of such items is $2(m - j)$.[†]

The proof is completed by noting that if $s_i > \frac{1}{3}$, there is no way for s_i to be placed in one of these m bins. Clearly, it cannot go in one of the j bins, since if it could, then first fit would have done so too. To place it in one of the remaining $m - j$ bins requires distributing $2(m - j) + 1$ items into the $m - j$ bins. Thus, some bin would have to have three items, each of which is larger than $\frac{1}{3}$, a clear impossibility.

This contradicts the fact that all the sizes can be placed in m bins, so the original assumption must be incorrect. Thus, $s_i \leq \frac{1}{3}$.

LEMMA 10.2.

The number of objects placed in extra bins is at most $m - 1$.

PROOF:

Assume that there are at least m objects placed in extra bins. We know that $\sum_{i=1}^{n} s_i \leq m$ since all the objects fit in m bins. Suppose that B_j is filled with W_j total weight for $1 \leq j \leq m$. Suppose the first m extra objects have sizes $x_1, x_2, \ldots, x_m$. Then, since the items in the first m bins plus the first m extra items are a subset of all the items, it follows that

$$\sum_{i=1}^{n} s_i \geq \sum_{j=1}^{m} W_j + \sum_{j=1}^{m} x_j \geq \sum_{j=1}^{m} (W_j + x_j)$$

Now $W_j + x_j > 1$ since otherwise the item corresponding to x_j would have been placed in B_j. Thus

$$\sum_{i=1}^{n} s_i > \sum_{j=1}^{m} 1 > m$$

But this is impossible if the n items can be packed in m bins. Thus, there can be at most $m - 1$ extra items.

THEOREM 10.4.

Let m be the optimal number of bins required to pack a list I of items. Then first fit decreasing never uses more than $(4m + 1)/3$ bins.

PROOF:

There are $m - 1$ extra items of size at most $\frac{1}{3}$. Thus, there can be at most $\lceil (m - 1)/3 \rceil$ extra bins. The total number of bins used by first fit decreasing is thus at most $\lceil (4m - 1)/3 \rceil \leq (4m + 1)/3$.

[†] Recall that first fit packed these elements into $m - j$ bins and placed two items in each bin. Thus, there are $2(m - j)$ items.

Optimal			First Fit Decreasing			
$1/4 - 2\varepsilon$	$1/4 - 2\varepsilon$		*empty*	*empty*	$1/4 - 2\varepsilon$
$1/4 + \varepsilon$	$1/4 - 2\varepsilon$		$1/4 + 2\varepsilon$	$1/4 + \varepsilon$	$1/4 - 2\varepsilon$
$1/2 + \varepsilon$	$1/4 + 2\varepsilon$		$1/2 + \varepsilon$	$1/4 + \varepsilon$	$1/4 - 2\varepsilon$
	$1/4 + 2\varepsilon$			$1/4 + \varepsilon$	$1/4 - 2\varepsilon$
$B_1 \rightarrow B_{6m}$	$B_{6m+1} \rightarrow B_{9m}$		$B_m \rightarrow B_{6m}$	$B_{6m+1} \rightarrow B_{8m}$	$B_{8m+1} \rightarrow B_{11m}$

Figure 10.28 Example in which first fit decreasing uses $11m$ bins, but only $9m$ bins are required

It is possible to prove a much tighter bound for both first fit decreasing and next fit decreasing.

THEOREM 10.5.

Let m be the optimal number of bins required to pack a list I of items. Then first fit decreasing never uses more than $\frac{11}{9}m + 4$ bins. There exist sequences such that first fit decreasing uses $\frac{11}{9}m$ bins.

PROOF:

The upper bound requires a very complicated analysis. The lower bound is exhibited by a sequence consisting of $6m$ elements of size $\frac{1}{2} + \epsilon$, followed by $6m$ elements of size $\frac{1}{4} + 2\epsilon$, followed by $6m$ elements of size $\frac{1}{4} + \epsilon$, followed by $12m$ elements of size $\frac{1}{4} - 2\epsilon$. Figure 10.28 shows that the optimal packing requires $9m$ bins, but first fit decreasing uses $11m$ bins.

In practice, first fit decreasing performs extremely well. If points are chosen uniformly over the unit interval, then the expected number of extra bins is $\Theta(\sqrt{m})$. Bin packing is a fine example of how simple greedy heuristics can give good results.

10.2. Divide and Conquer

Another common technique used to design algorithms is *divide and conquer*. Divide and conquer algorithms consist of two parts:

Divide: Smaller problems are solved recursively (except, of course, base cases).

Conquer: The solution to the original problem is then formed from the solutions to the subproblems.

Traditionally, routines in which the text contains at least two recursive calls are called divide and conquer algorithms, while routines whose text contains only one recursive call are not. We generally insist that the subproblems be disjoint (that is, essentially nonoverlapping). Let us review some of the recursive algorithms that have been covered in this text.

We have already seen several divide and conquer algorithms. In Section 2.4.3, we saw an $O(n \log n)$ solution to the maximum subsequence sum problem. In Chapter 4, we saw linear-time tree traversal strategies. In Chapter 7, we saw the classic examples of divide and conquer, namely mergesort and quicksort, which have $O(n \log n)$ worst-case and average-case bounds, respectively.

We have also seen several examples of recursive algorithms that probably do not classify as divide and conquer, but merely reduce to a single simpler case. In Section 1.3, we saw a simple routine to print a number. In Chapter 2, we used recursion to perform efficient exponentiation. In Chapter 4, we examined simple search routines for binary search trees. In Section 6.6, we saw simple recursion used to merge leftist heaps. In Section 7.7, an algorithm that takes linear average time was given for selection. The disjoint set *Find* operation was written recursively in Chapter 8. Chapter 9 showed routines to recover the shortest path in Dijkstra's algorithm and other procedures to perform depth-first search in graphs. None of these algorithms are really divide and conquer algorithms, because only one recursive call is performed.

We have also seen, in Section 2.4, a very bad recursive routine to compute the Fibonacci numbers. This could be called a divide and conquer algorithm, but it is terribly inefficient because the problem really is not divided at all.

In this section, we will see more examples of the divide and conquer paradigm. Our first application is a problem in *computational geometry*. Given n points in a plane, we will show that the closest pair of points can be found in $O(n \log n)$ time. The exercises describe some other problems in computational geometry that can be solved by divide and conquer. The remainder of the section shows some extremely interesting, but mostly theoretical, results. We provide an algorithm that solves the selection problem in $O(n)$ worst-case time. We also show that two n-bit numbers can be multiplied in $o(n^2)$ operations and that two $n \times n$ matrices can be multiplied in $o(n^3)$ operations. Unfortunately, even though these algorithms have better worst-case bounds than the conventional algorithms, none are practical except for very large inputs.

10.2.1. *Running Time of Divide and Conquer Algorithms*

All the efficient divide and conquer algorithms we will see divide the problems into subproblems, each of which is some fraction of the original problem, and then perform some additional work to compute the final answer. As an example, we have seen that mergesort operates on two problems, each of which is half the size of the original, and then uses $O(n)$ additional work. This yields the running time equation (with appropriate initial conditions)

$$T(n) = 2T(n/2) + O(n)$$

We saw in Chapter 7 that the solution to this equation is $O(n \log n)$. The following theorem can be used to determine the running time of most divide and conquer algorithms.

THEOREM 10.6.

The solution to the equation $T(n) = aT(n/b) + \Theta(n^k)$, *where* $a \geq 1$ *and* $b > 1$, *is*

$$T(n) = \begin{cases} O(n^{\log_b a}) & \text{if } a > b^k \\ O(n^k \log n) & \text{if } a = b^k \\ O(n^k) & \text{if } a < b^k \end{cases}$$

PROOF:
Following the analysis of mergesort in Chapter 7, we will assume that n is a power of b; thus, let $n = b^m$. Then $n/b = b^{m-1}$ and $n^k = \left(b^m\right)^k = b^{mk} = b^{km} = (b^k)^m$. Let us assume $T(1) = 1$ and ignore the constant factor in $\Theta(n^k)$. Then we have

$$T(b^m) = aT(b^{m-1}) + (b^k)^m$$

If we divide through by a^m, we obtain the equation

$$\frac{T(b^m)}{a^m} = \frac{T(b^{m-1})}{a^{m-1}} + \left\{ \frac{b^k}{a} \right\}^m \tag{10.3}$$

We can apply this equation for other values of m, obtaining

$$\frac{T(b^{m-1})}{a^{m-1}} = \frac{T(b^{m-2})}{a^{m-2}} + \left\{ \frac{b^k}{a} \right\}^{m-1} \tag{10.4}$$

$$\frac{T(b^{m-2})}{a^{m-2}} = \frac{T(b^{m-3})}{a^{m-3}} + \left\{ \frac{b^k}{a} \right\}^{m-2} \tag{10.5}$$

$$\vdots$$

$$\frac{T(b^1)}{a^1} = \frac{T(b^0)}{a^0} + \left\{ \frac{b^k}{a} \right\}^1 \tag{10.6}$$

We use our standard trick of adding up the telescoping equations (10.3) through (10.6). Virtually all the terms on the left cancel the leading terms on the right, yielding

$$\frac{T(b^m)}{a^m} = 1 + \sum_{i=1}^{m} \left\{ \frac{b^k}{a} \right\}^i \tag{10.7}$$

$$= \sum_{i=0}^{m} \left\{ \frac{b^k}{a} \right\}^i \tag{10.8}$$

Thus

$$T(n) = T(b^m) = a^m \sum_{i=0}^{m} \left\{ \frac{b^k}{a} \right\}^i \tag{10.9}$$

If $a > b^k$, then the sum is a geometric series with ratio smaller than 1. Since the sum of infinite series would converge to a constant, this finite sum is also bounded by a constant, and thus Equation (10.10) applies:

$$T(n) = O(a^m) = O(a^{\log_b n}) = O(n^{\log_b a}) \tag{10.10}$$

If $a = b^k$, then each term in the sum is 1. Since the sum contains $1 + \log_b n$ terms and $a = b^k$ implies that $\log_b a = k$,

$$T(n) = O(a^m \log_b n) = O(n^{\log_b a} \log_b n) = O(n^k \log_b n)$$

$$= O(n^k \log n) \tag{10.11}$$

Finally, if $a < b^k$, then the terms in the geometric series are larger than 1, and the second formula in Section 1.2.3 applies. We obtain

$$T(n) = a^m \frac{(b^k/a)^{m+1} - 1}{(b^k/a) - 1} = O(a^m(b^k/a)^m) = O((b^k)^m) = O(n^k)$$

proving the last case of the theorem.

As an example, mergesort has $a = b = 2$ and $k = 1$. The second case applies, giving the answer $O(n \log n)$. If we solve three problems, each of which is half the original size, and combine the solutions with $O(n)$ additional work, then $a = 3$, $b = 2$, and $k = 1$. Case 1 applies here, giving a bound of $O(n^{\log_2 3}) = O(n^{1.59})$. An algorithm that solved three half-sized problems, but required $O(n^2)$ work to merge the solution, would have an $O(n^2)$ running time, since the third case would apply.

There are two important cases that are not covered by Theorem 10.6. We state two more theorems, leaving the proofs as exercises. Theorem 10.7 generalizes the previous theorem.

THEOREM 10.7.

The solution to the equation $T(n) = aT(n/b) + \Theta(n^k \log^p n)$, *where* $a \geq 1$, $b > 1$, *and* $p \geq 0$ *is*

$$T(n) = \begin{cases} O(n^{\log_b a}) & \text{if } a > b^k \\ O(n^k \log^{p+1} n) & \text{if } a = b^k \\ O(n^k \log^p n) & \text{if } a < b^k \end{cases} \tag{10.12}$$

THEOREM 10.8.

If $\sum_{i=1}^{k} \alpha_i < 1$, *then the solution to the equation* $T(n) = \sum_{i=1}^{k} T(\alpha_i n) + O(n)$ *is* $T(n) = O(n)$.

10.2.2. Closest-Points Problem

The input to our first problem is a list P of points in a plane. If $p_1 = (x_1, y_1)$ and $p_2 = (x_2, y_2)$, then the Euclidean distance between p_1 and p_2 is $[(x_1 - x_2)^2 + (y_1 - y_2)^2]^{1/2}$. We are required to find the closest pair of points. It is possible that two points have the same position; in that case that pair is the closest, with distance zero.

Figure 10.29 A small point set

If there are n points, then there are $n(n-1)/2$ pairs of distances. We can check all of these, obtaining a very short program, but at the expense of an $O(n^2)$ algorithm. Since this approach is just an exhaustive search, we should expect to do better.

Let us assume that the points have been sorted by x coordinate. At worst, this adds $O(n \log n)$ to the final time bound. Since we will show an $O(n \log n)$ bound for the entire algorithm, this sort is essentially free, from a complexity standpoint.

Figure 10.29 shows a small sample point set P. Since the points are sorted by x coordinate, we can draw an imaginary vertical line that partitions the point set into two halves, P_l and P_r. This is certainly simple to do. Now we have almost exactly the same situation as we saw in the maximum subsequence sum problem in Section 2.4.3. Either the closest points are both in P_l, or they are both in P_r, or one is in P_l and the other is in P_r. Let us call these distances d_l, d_r, and d_c. Figure 10.30 shows the partition of the point set and these three distances.

Figure 10.30 P partitioned into P_1 and P_2; shortest distances are shown

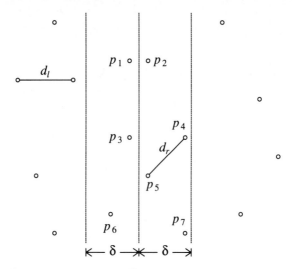

Figure 10.31   Two-lane strip, containing all points
considered for d_c strip

We can compute d_l and d_r recursively. The problem, then, is to compute d_c.
Since we would like an $O(n \log n)$ solution, we must be able to compute d_c with
only $O(n)$ additional work. We have already seen that if a procedure consists of
two half-sized recursive calls and $O(n)$ additional work, then the total time will be
$O(n \log n)$.

Let $\delta = \min(d_l, d_r)$. The first observation is that we need to compute d_c only
if d_c improves on δ. If d_c is such a distance, then the two points that define d_c must
be within δ of the dividing line; we will refer to this area as a *strip*. As shown in
Figure 10.31, this observation limits the number of points that need to be considered
(in our case, $\delta = d_r$).

There are two strategies that can be tried to compute d_c. For large point sets
that are uniformly distributed, the number of points that are expected to be in the
strip is very small. Indeed, it is easy to argue that only $O(\sqrt{n})$ points are in the strip
on average. Thus, we could perform a brute force calculation on these points in
$O(n)$ time. The pseudocode in Figure 10.32 implements this strategy, assuming the
C++ convention that the points are indexed starting at 0.

Figure 10.32   Brute force calculation of $min\ (\delta, d_c)$

```
// Points are all in the strip

for( i = 0; i < Num_Points_In_Strip; i++ )
    for( j = i + 1; j<Num_Points_In_Strip; j++ )
        if( dist(Pᵢ, Pⱼ) < δ )
            δ = dist(Pᵢ, Pⱼ);
```

```
// Points are all in the strip and sorted by y coordinate.

for( i = 0; i < Num_Points_In_Strip; i++ )
    for( j = i + 1; j < Num_Points_In_Strip; j++ )
        if( Pᵢ and Pⱼ's y coordinates differ by more than δ )
            break; // Go to next Pᵢ.
        else
        if( dist(Pᵢ, Pⱼ) < δ )
            δ = dist(Pᵢ, Pⱼ);
```

Figure 10.33   Refined calculation of $Min\ (\delta, d_c)$

In the worst case, all the points could be in the strip, so this strategy does not always work in linear time. We can improve this algorithm with the following observation: The y coordinates of the two points that define d_c can differ by at most δ. Otherwise, $d_c > \delta$. Suppose that the points in the strip are sorted by their y coordinates. Therefore, if p_i and p_j's y coordinates differ by more than δ, then we can proceed to p_{i+1}. This simple modification is implemented in Figure 10.33.

This extra test has a significant effect on the running time because for each p_i only a few points p_j are examined before p_i's and p_j's y coordinates differ by more than δ and force an exit from the inner *for* loop. Figure 10.34 shows, for instance, that for point p_3, only the two points p_4 and p_5 lie in the strip within δ vertical distance.

In the worst case, for any point p_i, at most seven points p_j are considered. This is because these points must lie either in the δ by δ square in the left half of the

Figure 10.34   Only p_4 and p_5 are considered in the
second *for* loop

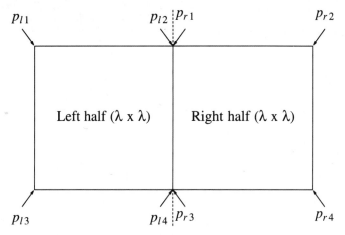

p_{l1} p_{l2} p_{r1} p_{r2}

Left half (λ x λ)   Right half (λ x λ)

p_{l3} p_{l4} p_{r3} p_{r4}

Figure 10.35   At most eight points fit in the rectangle; there are two coordinates shared by two points each

strip or in the δ by δ square in the right half of the strip. On the other hand, all the points in each δ by δ square are separated by at least δ. In the worst case, each square contains four points, one at each corner. One of these points is p_i, leaving at most seven points to be considered. This worst-case situation is shown in Figure 10.35. Notice that even though p_{l2} and p_{r1} have the same coordinates, they could be different points. For the actual analysis, it is only important that the number of points in the λ by 2λ rectangle be $O(1)$, and this much is certainly clear.

Because at most seven points are considered for each p_i, the time to compute a d_c that is better than δ is $O(n)$. Thus, we appear to have an $O(n \log n)$ solution to the closest-points problem, based on the two half-sized recursive calls plus the linear extra work to combine the two results. However, we do not quite have an $O(n \log n)$ solution yet.

The problem is that we have assumed that a list of points sorted by y coordinate is available. If we perform this sort for each recursive call, then we have $O(n \log n)$ extra work: this gives an $O(n \log^2 n)$ algorithm. This is not all that bad, especially when compared to the brute force $O(n^2)$. However, it is not hard to reduce the work for each recursive call to $O(n)$, thus ensuring an $O(n \log n)$ algorithm.

We will maintain two lists. One is the point list sorted by x coordinate, and the other is the point list sorted by y coordinate. We will call these lists P and Q, respectively. These can be obtained by a preprocessing sorting step at cost $O(n \log n)$ and thus does not affect the time bound. P_l and Q_l are the lists passed to the left-half recursive call, and P_r and Q_r are the lists passed to the right-half recursive call. We have already seen that P is easily split in the middle. Once the dividing line is known, we step through Q sequentially, placing each element in Q_l or Q_r, as appropriate. It is easy to see that Q_l and Q_r will be automatically sorted by y coordinate. When the recursive calls return, we scan through the Q list and discard all the points whose x coordinates are not within the strip. Then Q contains only points in the strip, and these points are guaranteed to be sorted by their y coordinates.

This strategy ensures that the entire algorithm is $O(n \log n)$, because only $O(n)$ extra work is performed.

10.2.3.   *The Selection Problem*

The *selection problem* requires us to find the kth smallest element in a list S of n elements. Of particular interest is the special case of finding the median. This occurs when $k = \lceil n/2 \rceil$.

In Chapters 1, 6, and 7 we have seen several solutions to the selection problem. The solution in Chapter 7 uses a variation of quicksort and runs in $O(n)$ average time. Indeed, it is described in Hoare's original paper on quicksort.

Although this algorithm runs in linear average time, it has a worst case of $O(n^2)$. Selection can easily be solved in $O(n \log n)$ worst-case time by sorting the elements, but for a long time it was unknown whether or not selection could be accomplished in $O(n)$ worst-case time. The *quickselect* algorithm outlined in Section 7.7.6 is quite efficient in practice, so this was mostly a question of theoretical interest.

Recall that the basic algorithm is a simple recursive strategy. Assuming that n is larger than the cutoff point where elements are simply sorted, an element v, known as the pivot, is chosen. The remaining elements are placed into two sets, S_1 and S_2. S_1 contains elements that are guaranteed to be no larger than v, and S_2 contains elements that are no smaller than v. Finally, if $k \le |S_1|$, then the kth smallest element in S can be found by recursively computing the kth smallest element in S_1. If $k = |S_1| + 1$, then the pivot is the kth smallest element. Otherwise, the kth smallest element in S is the $(k - |S_1| - 1)$st smallest element in S_2. The main difference between this algorithm and *quicksort* is that there is only one subproblem to solve instead of two.

In order to obtain a linear algorithm, we must ensure that the subproblem is only a fraction of the original and not merely only a few elements smaller than the original. Of course, we can always find such an element if we are willing to spend some time to do so. The difficult problem is that we cannot spend too much time finding the pivot.

For quicksort, we saw that a good choice for pivot was to pick three elements and use their median. This gives some expectation that the pivot is not too bad, but does not provide a guarantee. We could choose 21 elements at random, sort them in constant time, use the 11th largest as pivot, and get a pivot that is even more likely to be good. However, if these 21 elements were the 21 largest, then the pivot would still be poor. Extending this, we could use up to $O(n/\log n)$ elements, sort them using heapsort in $O(n)$ total time, and be almost certain, from a statistical point of view, of obtaining a good pivot. In the worst case, however, this does not work because we might select the $O(n/\log n)$ largest elements, and then the pivot would be the $[n - O(n/\log n)]$th largest element, which is not a constant fraction of n.

The basic idea is still useful. Indeed, we will see that we can use it to improve the expected number of comparisons that quickselect makes. To get a good worst case, however, the key idea is to use one more level of indirection. Instead of finding the median from a sample of random elements, we will find the median from a *sample of medians*.

The basic pivot selection algorithm is as follows:

1. Arrange the n elements into $\lfloor n/5 \rfloor$ groups of 5 elements, ignoring the (at most four) extra elements.
2. Find the median of each group. This gives a list M of $\lfloor n/5 \rfloor$ medians.
3. Find the median of M. Return this as the pivot, v.

We will use the term *median-of-median-of-five partitioning* to describe the quickselect algorithm that uses the pivot selection rule given above. We will now show that median-of-median-of-five partitioning guarantees that each recursive sub-problem is at most roughly 70 percent as large as the original. We will also show that the pivot can be computed quickly enough to guarantee an $O(n)$ running time for the entire selection algorithm.

Let us assume for the moment that n is divisible by 5, so there are no extra elements. Suppose also that $n/5$ is odd, so that the set M contains an odd number of elements. This provides some symmetry, as we shall see. We are thus assuming, for convenience, that n is of the form $10k + 5$. We will also assume that all the elements are distinct. The actual algorithm must make sure to handle the case in which this is not true. Figure 10.36 shows how the pivot might be chosen when $n = 45$.

In Figure 10.36, v represents the element that is selected by the algorithm as pivot. Since v is the median of nine elements, and we are assuming that all elements are distinct, there must be four medians that are larger than v and four that are smaller. We denote these by L and S, respectively. Consider a group of five elements with a large median (type L). The median of the group is smaller than two elements in the group and larger than two elements in the group. We will let H represent the *huge* elements. These are elements that are known to be larger than a large median. Similarly, T represents the *tiny* elements, which are smaller than a small

Figure 10.36   How the pivot is chosen

Sorted groups of five elements

Medians

median. There are 10 elements of type H: Two are in each of the groups with an L type median, and two elements are in the same group as v. Similarly, there are 10 elements of type T.

Elements of type L or H are guaranteed to be larger than v, and elements of type S or T are guaranteed to be smaller than v. There are thus guaranteed to be 14 large and 14 small elements in our problem. Therefore, a recursive call could be on at most $45 - 14 - 1 = 30$ elements.

Let us extend this analysis to general n of the form $10k + 5$. In this case, there are k elements of type L and k elements of type S. There are $2k + 2$ elements of type H, and also $2k + 2$ elements of type T. Thus, there are $3k + 2$ elements that are guaranteed to be larger than v and $3k + 2$ elements that are guaranteed to be smaller. Thus, in this case, the recursive call can contain at most $7k + 2 < 0.7n$ elements. If n is not of the form $10k + 5$, similar arguments can be made without affecting the basic result.

It remains to bound the running time to obtain the pivot element. There are two basic steps. We can find the median of five elements in constant time. For instance, it is not hard to sort five elements in eight comparisons. We must do this $\lfloor n/5 \rfloor$ times, so this step takes $O(n)$ time. We must then compute the median of a group of $\lfloor n/5 \rfloor$ elements. The obvious way to do this is to sort the group and return the element in the middle. But this takes $O(\lfloor n/5 \rfloor \log \lfloor n/5 \rfloor) = O(n \log n)$ time, so this does not work. The solution is to call the selection algorithm recursively on the $\lfloor n/5 \rfloor$ elements.

This completes the description of the basic algorithm. There are still some details that need to be filled in if an actual implementation is desired. For instance, duplicates must be handled correctly, and the algorithm needs a cutoff large enough to ensure that the recursive calls make progress. There is quite a large amount of overhead involved, and this algorithm is not practical at all, so we will not describe any more of the details that need to be considered. Even so, from a theoretical standpoint, the algorithm is a major breakthrough, because, as the following theorem shows, the running time is linear in the worst case.

THEOREM 10.9.

The running time of quickselect using median-of-median-of-five partitioning is $O(n)$.

PROOF:

The algorithm consists of two recursive calls of size $0.7n$ and $0.2n$, plus linear extra work. By Theorem 10.8, the running time is linear.

Reducing the Average Number of Comparisons

Divide and conquer can also be used to reduce the expected number of comparisons required by the selection algorithm. Let us look at a concrete example. Suppose we have a group S of 1,000 numbers and are looking for the 100th smallest number, which we will call x. We choose a subset S' of S consisting of 100 numbers. We would expect that the value of x is similar in size to the 10th smallest number in S'. More specifically, the fifth smallest number in S' is almost certainly less than x, and the 15th smallest number in S' is almost certainly greater than x.

More generally, a sample S' of s elements is chosen from the n elements. Let δ be some number, which we will choose later so as to minimize the average number of comparisons used by the procedure. We find the $(v_1 = ks/n - \delta)$th and $(v_2 = ks/n + \delta)$th smallest elements in S'. Almost certainly, the kth smallest element in S will fall between v_1 and v_2, so we are left with a selection problem on 2δ elements. With low probability, the kth smallest element does not fall in this range, and we have considerable work to do. However, with a good choice of s and δ, we can ensure, by the laws of probability, that the second case does not adversely affect the total work.

If an analysis is performed, we find that if $s = n^{2/3} \log^{1/3} n$ and $\delta = n^{1/3} \log^{2/3} n$, then the expected number of comparisons is $n + k + O(n^{2/3} \log^{1/3} n)$, which is optimal except for the low-order term. (If $k > n/2$, we can consider the symmetric problem of finding the $(n - k)$th largest element.)

Most of the analysis is easy to do. The last term represents the cost of performing the two selections to determine v_1 and v_2. The average cost of the partitioning, assuming a reasonably clever strategy, is equal to n plus the expected rank of v_2 in S, which is $n + k + O(n\delta/s)$. If the kth element winds up in S', the cost of finishing the algorithm is equal to the cost of selection on S', namely $O(s)$. If the kth smallest element doesn't wind up in S', the cost is $O(n)$. However, s and δ have been chosen to guarantee that this happens with very low probability $o(1/n)$, so the expected cost of this possibility is $o(1)$, which is a term that goes to zero as n gets large. An exact calculation is left as Exercise 10.21.

This analysis shows that finding the median requires about $1.5n$ comparisons on average. Of course, this algorithm requires some floating-point arithmetic to compute s, which can slow down the algorithm on some machines. Even so, experiments have shown that if correctly implemented, this algorithm compares favorably with the quickselect implementation in Chapter 7.

10.2.4. Theoretical Improvements for Arithmetic Problems

In this section we describe a divide and conquer algorithm that multiplies two n-digit numbers. Our previous model of computation assumed that multiplication was done in constant time because the numbers were small. For large numbers, this assumption is no longer valid. If we measure multiplication in terms of the size of numbers being multiplied, then the natural multiplication algorithm takes quadratic time. The divide and conquer algorithm runs in subquadratic time. We also present the classic divide and conquer algorithm that multiplies two n by n matrices in subcubic time.

Multiplying Integers

Suppose we want to multiply two n-digit numbers x and y. If exactly one of x and y is negative, then the answer is negative; otherwise it is positive. Thus, we can perform this check and then assume that $x, y \geq 0$. The algorithm that almost everyone uses when multiplying by hand requires $\Theta(n^2)$ operations because each digit in x is multiplied by each digit in y.

If $x = 61{,}438{,}521$ and $y = 94{,}736{,}407$, $xy = 5{,}820{,}464{,}730{,}934{,}047$. Let us break x and y into two halves consisting of the most significant and least significant digits, respectively. Then $x_l = 6{,}143$, $x_r = 8{,}521$, $y_l = 9{,}473$, and $y_r = 6{,}407$. We also have $x = x_l 10^4 + x_r$ and $y = y_l 10^4 + y_r$. It follows that

$$xy = x_l y_l 10^8 + (x_l y_r + x_r y_l) 10^4 + x_r y_r$$

Notice that this equation consists of four multiplications, $x_l y_l$, $x_l y_r$, $x_r y_l$, and $x_r y_r$, which are each half the size of the original problem ($n/2$ digits). The multiplications by 10^8 and 10^4 amount to the placing of zeros. This and the subsequent additions add only $O(n)$ additional work. If we perform these four multiplications recursively using this algorithm, stopping at an appropriate base case, then we obtain the recurrence

$$T(n) = 4T(n/2) + O(n)$$

From Theorem 10.6, we see that $T(n) = O(n^2)$, so, unfortunately, we have not improved the algorithm. To achieve a subquadratic algorithm, we must use less than four recursive calls. The key observation is that

$$x_l y_r + x_r y_l = (x_l - x_r)(y_r - y_l) + x_l y_l + x_r y_r$$

Thus, instead of using two multiplications to compute the coefficient of 10^4, we can use one multiplication, plus the result of two multiplications that have already been performed. Figure 10.37 shows how only three recursive subproblems need to be solved.

It is easy to see that now the recurrence equation satisfies

$$T(n) = 3T(n/2) + O(n),$$

and so we obtain $T(n) = O(n^{\log_2 3}) = O(n^{1.59})$. To complete the algorithm, we must have a base case that can be solved without recursion.

When both numbers are one-digit, we can do the multiplication by table lookup. If one number has zero digits, then we return zero. In practice, if we were to use this algorithm, we would choose the base case to be that which is most convenient for the machine.

Although this algorithm has better asymptotic performance than the standard quadratic algorithm, it is rarely used because for small n the overhead is significant, and for larger n there are even better algorithms. These algorithms also make extensive use of divide and conquer.

Matrix Multiplication

A fundamental numerical problem is the multiplication of two matrices. Figure 10.38 gives a simple $O(n^3)$ algorithm to compute $C = AB$, where A, B, and C are $n \times n$ matrices. The algorithm follows directly from the definition of matrix multiplication. To compute $C_{i,j}$, we compute the dot product of the ith row in A with the jth column in B. As usual, arrays begin at 0; we make no attempt to use features of C++.

Function	Value	Computational Complexity
x_l	6,143	Given
x_r	8,521	Given
y_l	9,473	Given
y_r	6,407	Given
$d_1 = x_l - x_r$	$-2,378$	$O(n)$
$d_2 = y_r - y_l$	$-3,066$	$O(n)$
$x_l y_l$	58,192,639	$T(n/2)$
$x_r y_r$	54,594,047	$T(n/2)$
$d_1 d_2$	7,290,948	$T(n/2)$
$d_3 = d_1 d_2 + x_l y_l + x_r y_r$	120,077,634	$O(n)$
$x_r y_r$	54,594,047	Computed above
$d_3 10^4$	1,200,776,340,000	$O(n)$
$x_l y_l 10^8$	5,819,263,900,000,000	$O(n)$
$x_l y_l 10^8 + d_3 10^4 + x_r y_r$	5,820,464,730,934,047	$O(n)$

Figure 10.37   The divide and conquer algorithm in action

```
/* 1*/   // Standard matrix multiplication.
/* 2*/   // Arrays start at zero.

/* 3*/   void
/* 4*/   Matrix_Multiply( Matrix A, Matrix B, Matrix C, unsigned int N )
/* 5*/   {
/* 6*/       int i, j, k;

/* 7*/       for( i = 0; i < N; i++ )              // Initialization.
/* 8*/           for( j = 0; j < N; j++ )
/* 9*/               C[ i ][ j ] = 0.0;

/*10*/       for( i = 0; i < N; i++ )
/*11*/           for( j = 0; j < N; j++ )
/*12*/               for( k = 0; k < N; k++ )
/*13*/                   C[ i ][ j ] += A[ i ][ k ] * B[ k ][ j ];
/*14*/   }
```

Figure 10.38   Simple $O(n^3)$ matrix multiplication

$$\begin{bmatrix} A_{1,1} & A_{1,2} \\ A_{2,1} & A_{2,2} \end{bmatrix} \begin{bmatrix} B_{1,1} & B_{1,2} \\ B_{2,1} & B_{2,2} \end{bmatrix} = \begin{bmatrix} C_{1,1} & C_{1,2} \\ C_{2,1} & C_{2,2} \end{bmatrix}$$

Figure 10.39 Decomposing $\mathbf{AB} = \mathbf{C}$ into four quadrants

For a long time it was assumed that $\Omega(n^3)$ was required for matrix multiplication. However, in the late sixties Strassen showed how to break the $\Omega(n^3)$ barrier. The basic idea of Strassen's algorithm is to divide each matrix into four quadrants as shown in Figure 10.39. Then it is easy to show that

$$C_{1,1} = A_{1,1}B_{1,1} + A_{1,2}B_{2,1}$$

$$C_{1,2} = A_{1,1}B_{1,2} + A_{1,2}B_{2,2}$$

$$C_{2,1} = A_{2,1}B_{1,1} + A_{2,2}B_{2,1}$$

$$C_{2,2} = A_{2,1}B_{1,2} + A_{2,2}B_{2,2}$$

As an example, to perform the multiplication $\mathbf{AB}$

$$\mathbf{AB} = \begin{bmatrix} 3 & 4 & 1 & 6 \\ 1 & 2 & 5 & 7 \\ 5 & 1 & 2 & 9 \\ 4 & 3 & 5 & 6 \end{bmatrix} \begin{bmatrix} 5 & 6 & 9 & 3 \\ 4 & 5 & 3 & 1 \\ 1 & 1 & 8 & 4 \\ 3 & 1 & 4 & 1 \end{bmatrix}$$

we define the following eight $n/2$ by $n/2$ matrices:

$$A_{1,1} = \begin{bmatrix} 3 & 4 \\ 1 & 2 \end{bmatrix} \quad A_{1,2} = \begin{bmatrix} 1 & 6 \\ 5 & 7 \end{bmatrix} \quad B_{1,1} = \begin{bmatrix} 5 & 6 \\ 4 & 5 \end{bmatrix} \quad B_{1,2} = \begin{bmatrix} 9 & 3 \\ 3 & 1 \end{bmatrix}$$

$$A_{2,1} = \begin{bmatrix} 5 & 1 \\ 4 & 3 \end{bmatrix} \quad A_{2,2} = \begin{bmatrix} 2 & 9 \\ 5 & 6 \end{bmatrix} \quad B_{2,1} = \begin{bmatrix} 1 & 1 \\ 3 & 1 \end{bmatrix} \quad B_{2,2} = \begin{bmatrix} 8 & 4 \\ 4 & 1 \end{bmatrix}$$

We could then perform eight $n/2$ by $n/2$ matrix multiplications and four $n/2$ by $n/2$ matrix additions. The matrix additions take $O(n^2)$ time. If the matrix multiplications are done recursively, then the running time satisfies

$$T(n) = 8T(n/2) + O(n^2).$$

From Theorem 10.6, we see that $T(n) = O(n^3)$, so we do not have an improvement. As we saw with integer multiplication, we must reduce the number of subproblems below 8. Strassen used a strategy similar to the integer multiplication divide and conquer algorithm and showed how to use only seven recursive calls by carefully arranging the computations. The seven multiplications are

$$M_1 = (A_{1,2} - A_{2,2})(B_{2,1} + B_{2,2})$$

$$M_2 = (A_{1,1} + A_{2,2})(B_{1,1} + B_{2,2})$$

$$M_3 = (A_{1,1} - A_{2,1})(B_{1,1} + B_{1,2})$$

$$M_4 = (A_{1,1} + A_{1,2})B_{2,2}$$

$$M_5 = A_{1,1}(B_{1,2} - B_{2,2})$$

$$M_6 = A_{2,2}(B_{2,1} - B_{1,1})$$

$$M_7 = (A_{2,1} + A_{2,2})B_{1,1}$$

Once the multiplications are performed, the final answer can be obtained with eight more additions.

$$C_{1,1} = M_1 + M_2 - M_4 + M_6$$

$$C_{1,2} = M_4 + M_5$$

$$C_{1,3} = M_6 + M_7$$

$$C_{1,4} = M_2 - M_3 + M_5 - M_7$$

It is straightforward to verify that this tricky ordering produces the desired values. The running time now satisfies the recurrence

$$T(n) = 7T(n/2) + O(n^2).$$

The solution of this recurrence is $T(n) = O(n^{\log_2 7}) = O(n^{2.81})$.

As usual, there are details to consider, such as the case when n is not a power of two, but these are basically minor nuisances. Strassen's algorithm is worse than the straightforward algorithm until n is fairly large. It does not generalize for the case in which the matrices are sparse (contain many zero entries), and it does not easily parallelize. When run with floating point entries, it is less stable numerically than the classic algorithm. Thus, it is has only limited applicability. Nevertheless, it represents an important theoretical milestone and certainly shows that in computer science, as in many other fields, even though a problem seems to have an intrinsic complexity, nothing is certain until proven.

10.3. Dynamic Programming

In the previous section, we have seen that a problem that can be mathematically expressed recursively can also be expressed as a recursive algorithm, in many cases yielding a significant performance improvement over a more naïve exhaustive search.

Any recursive mathematical formula could be directly translated to a recursive algorithm, but the underlying reality is that often the compiler will not do justice to the recursive algorithm, and an inefficient program results. When we suspect that this is likely to be the case, we must provide a little more help to the compiler by rewriting the recursive algorithm as a nonrecursive algorithm that systematically records the answers to the subproblems in a table. One technique that makes use of this approach is known as *dynamic programming*.

10.3.1. Using a Table Instead of Recursion

In Chapter 2, we saw that the natural recursive program to compute the Fibonacci numbers is very inefficient. Recall that the program shown in Figure 10.40 has a running time $T(n)$ that satisfies $T(n) \geq T(n-1) + T(n-2)$. Since $T(n)$ satisfies the same recurrence relation as the Fibonacci numbers and has the same initial

```
/* 1*/    // Compute Fibonacci numbers as described in Chapter 1.
/* 2*/    // Assume N >= 0.

/* 3*/    int
/* 4*/    Fib( const unsigned int N )
/* 5*/    {
/* 6*/        if( N <= 1 )
/* 7*/            return 1;
/* 8*/        else
/* 9*/            return Fib( N - 1 ) + Fib( N - 2 );
/*10*/    }
```

Figure 10.40   Inefficient algorithm to compute Fibonacci numbers

conditions, $T(n)$ in fact grows at the same rate as the Fibonacci numbers and is thus exponential.

On the other hand, since all that is needed to compute F_n is F_{n-1} and F_{n-2}, we need only to record the two most recently computed Fibonacci numbers. This yields the $O(n)$ algorithm in Figure 10.41.

The reason that the recursive algorithm is so slow is because of the algorithm used to simulate recursion. To compute F_n, there is one call to F_{n-1} and F_{n-2}. However, since F_{n-1} recursively makes a call to F_{n-2} and F_{n-3}, there are actually two separate calls to compute F_{n-2}. If we trace out the entire algorithm, then we can see that F_{n-3} is computed three times, F_{n-4} is computed five times, F_{n-5} is computed eight times, and so on. As Figure 10.42 shows, the growth of redundant

Figure 10.41   Linear algorithm to compute Fibonacci numbers

```
/* 1*/    int
/* 2*/    Fibonacci( const unsigned int N )
/* 3*/    {
/* 4*/        unsigned int Last = 1, Next_To_Last = 1, Answer;

/* 5*/        if( N <= 1 )
/* 6*/            return 1;

/* 7*/        for( int i = 2; i <= N; i++ )
/* 8*/        {
/* 9*/            Answer = Last + Next_To_Last;
/* 10*/           Next_To_Last = Last;
/* 11*/           Last = Answer;
/* 12*/        }

/* 13*/       return Answer;
/* 14*/    }
```

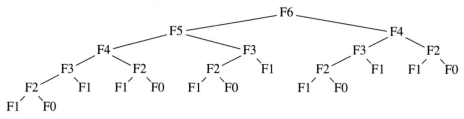

Figure 10.42   Trace of the recursive calculation of
Fibonacci numbers

calculations is explosive. If the compiler's recursion simulation algorithm were able to keep a list of all precomputed values and not make a recursive call for an already solved subproblem, then this exponential explosion would be avoided. This is why the program in Figure 10.41 is so much more efficient.

As a second example, we saw in Chapter 7 how to solve the recurrence $C(n) = 2/n \sum_{i=0}^{n-1} C(i) + n$, with $C(0) = 1$. Suppose that we want to check, numerically, whether the solution we obtained is correct. We could then write the simple program in Figure 10.43 to evaluate the recursion.

Once again, the recursive calls duplicate work. In this case, the running time $T(n)$ satisfies $T(n) = \sum_{i=0}^{n-1} T(i) + n$ because, as shown in Figure 10.44, there is one (direct) recursive call of each size from 0 to $n-1$, plus $O(n)$ additional work (where else have we seen the tree shown in Figure 10.44?). Solving for $T(n)$, we find that it grows exponentially. By using a table, we obtain the program in Figure 10.45. This program avoids the redundant recursive calls and runs in $O(n^2)$. It is not a perfect program; as an exercise, you should make the simple change that reduces its running time to $O(n)$.

Figure 10.43   Recursive program to evaluate
$C(n) = 2/n \sum_{i=0}^{n-1} C(i) + n$

```
/* 1*/      double
/* 2*/      Eval( const unsigned int N )
/* 3*/      {
/* 4*/          double Sum = 0.0;

/* 5*/          if( N == 0 )
/* 6*/              return 1.0;

/* 7*/          for( int i = 0; i < N; i++ )
/* 8*/              Sum += Eval( i );

/* 9*/          return 2.0 * Sum / double( N ) + double( N );
/*10*/      }
```

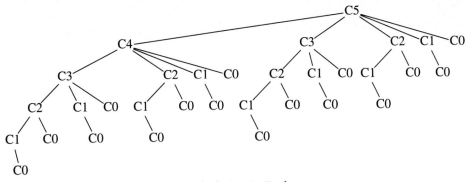

Figure 10.44 Trace of the recursive calculation in *Eval*

```
/* 1*/    double
/* 2*/    Eval( const unsigned int N )
/* 3*/    {
/* 4*/        double Sum = 0.0;
/* 5*/        double *C = new double [ N + 1 ];
/* 6*/        double Answer;

/* 7*/        C[ 0 ] = 1.0;

/* 8*/        for( int i = 1; i <= N; i++ )
/* 9*/        {
/*10*/            Sum = 0.0;
/*11*/            for( int j = 0; j < i; j++ )
/*12*/                Sum += C[ j ];

/*13*/            C[ i ] = 2.0 * Sum / double( i ) + double( i );
/*14*/        }

/*15*/        Answer = C[ N ];
/*16*/        delete [ ] C;
/*17*/        return Answer;
/*18*/    }
```

Figure 10.45 Evaluating $C(n) = 2/n \sum_{i=0}^{n-1} C(i) + n$ with a table

10.3.2. *Ordering Matrix Multiplications*

Suppose we are given four matrices, **A**, **B**, **C**, and **D**, of dimensions **A** $= 50 \times 10$, **B** $= 10 \times 40$, **C** $= 40 \times 30$, and **D** $= 30 \times 5$. Although matrix multiplication is not commutative, it is associative, which means that the matrix product **ABCD** can be parenthesized, and thus evaluated, in any order. The obvious way to multiply two matrices of dimensions $p \times q$ and $q \times r$, respectively, uses pqr scalar multiplications. (Using a theoretically superior algorithm such as Strassen's algorithm does not significantly alter the problem we will consider, so we will assume this performance bound.) What is the best way to perform the three matrix multiplications required to compute **ABCD**?

In the case of four matrices, it is simple to solve the problem by exhaustive search, since there are only five ways to order the multiplications. We evaluate each case as follows:

- **(A((BC)D))**: Evaluating **BC** requires $10 \times 40 \times 30 = 12,000$ multiplications. Evaluating **(BC)D** requires the 12,000 multiplications to compute **BC**, plus an additional $10 \times 30 \times 5 = 1,500$ multiplications, for a total of 13,500. Evaluating **A((BC)D)** requires 13,500 multiplications for **(BC)D**, plus an additional $50 \times 10 \times 5 = 2,500$ multiplications, for a grand total of 16,000 multiplications.

- **(A(B(CD)))**: Evaluating **CD** requires $40 \times 30 \times 5 = 6,000$ multiplications. Evaluating **B(CD)** requires the 6,000 multiplications to compute **CD**, plus an additional $10 \times 40 \times 5 = 2,000$ multiplications, for a total of 8,000. Evaluating **(A(B(CD)))** requires 8,000 multiplications for **B(CD)**, plus an additional $50 \times 10 \times 5 = 2,500$ multiplications, for a grand total of 10,500 multiplications.

- **((AB)(CD))**: Evaluating **CD** requires $40 \times 30 \times 5 = 6,000$ multiplications. Evaluating **AB** requires $50 \times 10 \times 40 = 20,000$ multiplications. Evaluating **((AB)(CD))** requires 6,000 multiplications for **CD**, 20,000 multiplications for **AB**, plus an additional $50 \times 40 \times 5 = 10,000$ multiplications for a grand total of 36,000 multiplications.

- **(((AB)C)D)**: Evaluating **AB** requires $50 \times 10 \times 40 = 20,000$ multiplications. Evaluating **(AB)C** requires the 20,000 multiplications to compute **AB**, plus an additional $50 \times 40 \times 30 = 60,000$ multiplications, for a total of 80,000. Evaluating **(((AB)C)D)** requires 80,000 multiplications for **(AB)C**, plus an additional $50 \times 30 \times 5 = 7,500$ multiplications, for a grand total of 87,500 multiplications.

- **((A(BC))D)**: Evaluating **BC** requires $10 \times 40 \times 30 = 12,000$ multiplications. Evaluating **A(BC)** requires the 12,000 multiplications to compute **BC**, plus an additional $50 \times 10 \times 30 = 15,000$ multiplications, for a total of 27,000. Evaluating **((A(BC))D)** requires 27,000 multiplications for **A(BC)**, plus an additional $50 \times 30 \times 5 = 7,500$ multiplications, for a grand total of 34,500 multiplications.

The calculations show that the best ordering uses roughly one-ninth the number of multiplications as the worst ordering. Thus, it might be worthwhile to perform a few calculations to determine the optimal ordering. Unfortunately, none of the obvious greedy strategies seems to work. Moreover, the number of possible orderings grows quickly. Suppose we define $T(n)$ to be this number. Then $T(1) = T(2) = 1$, $T(3) = 2$, and $T(4) = 5$, as we have seen. In general,

$$T(n) = \sum_{i=1}^{n-1} T(i)T(n-i).$$

To see this, suppose that the matrices are $A_1, A_2, \ldots, A_n$, and the last multiplication performed is $(A_1 A_2 \cdots A_i)(A_{i+1}A_{i+2}\cdots A_n)$. Then there are $T(i)$ ways to compute $(A_1 A_2 \cdots A_i)$ and $T(n-i)$ ways to compute $(A_{i+1}A_{i+2}\cdots A_n)$. Thus, there are $T(i)T(n-i)$ ways to compute $(A_1 A_2 \cdots A_i)(A_{i+1}A_{i+2}\cdots A_n)$ for each possible i.

The solution of this recurrence is the well-known Catalan numbers, which grow exponentially. Thus, for large n, an exhaustive search through all possible orderings is useless. Nevertheless, this counting argument provides a basis for a solution that is substantially better than exponential. Let c_i be the number of columns in matrix A_i for $1 \le i \le n$. Then A_i has c_{i-1} rows since otherwise the multiplications are not valid. We will define c_0 to be the number of rows in the first matrix, A_1.

Suppose $m_{Left,Right}$ is the number of multiplications required to multiply $A_{Left}A_{Left+1}\cdots A_{Right-1}A_{Right}$. For consistency, $m_{Left,Left} = 0$. Suppose the last multiplication is $(A_{Left}\cdots A_i)(A_{i+1}\cdots A_{Right})$, where $Left \le i < Right$. Then the number of multiplications used is $m_{Left,i} + m_{i+1,Right} + c_{Left-1}c_i c_{Right}$. These three terms represent the multiplications required to compute $(A_{Left}\cdots A_i)$, $(A_{i+1}\cdots A_{Right})$, and their product, respectively.

If we define $M_{Left,Right}$ to be the number of multiplications required in an *optimal* ordering, then, if $Left < Right$,

$$M_{Left,Right} = \min_{Left \le i < Right} \left\{ M_{Left,i} + M_{i+1,Right} + c_{Left-1}c_i c_{Right} \right\}$$

This equation implies that if we have an optimal multiplication arrangement of $A_{Left}\cdots A_{Right}$, the subproblems $A_{Left}\cdots A_i$ and $A_{i+1}\cdots A_{Right}$ cannot be performed suboptimally. This should be clear since otherwise we could improve the entire result by replacing the suboptimal computation by an optimal computation.

The formula translates directly to a recursive program, but, as we have seen in the last section, such a program would be blatantly inefficient. However, since there are only approximately $n^2/2$ values of $M_{Left,Right}$ that ever need to be computed, it is clear that a table can be used to store these values. Further examination shows that if $Right - Left = k$, then the only values $M_{x,y}$ that are needed in the computation of $M_{Left,Right}$ satisfy $y - x < k$. This tells us the order in which we need to compute the table.

If we want to print out the actual ordering of the multiplications in addition to the final answer $M_{1,n}$, then we can use the ideas from the shortest-path algorithms in Chapter 9. Whenever we make a change to $M_{Left,Right}$, we record the value of i that is responsible. This gives the simple program shown in Figure 10.46.

Although the emphasis of this chapter is not coding, it is worth noting that many programmers tend to shorten variable names to a single letter. c, i, and k are used as single-letter variables because this agrees with the names we have used in the description of the algorithm, which is very mathematical. However, it is generally best to avoid l as a variable name because "l" looks too much like 1 and can make for very difficult debugging if you make a transcription error.

Returning to the algorithmic issues, this program contains a triply nested loop and is easily seen to run in $O(n^3)$ time. The references describe a faster algorithm,

```
/* 1*/     // Compute optimal ordering of matrix multiplication.
/* 2*/     // C contains number of columns for each of the N matrices.
/* 3*/     // C[ 0 ] is the number of rows in matrix 1.
/* 4*/     // Minimum number of multiplications is left in M[ 1 ][ N ].
/* 5*/     // Actual ordering can be computed via
/* 6*/     // another procedure using Last_Change.
/* 7*/     // M and Last_Change are indexed starting at 1, instead of zero.

/* 8*/     void
/* 9*/     Opt_Matrix( long int C[ ], unsigned int N,
/*10*/                         Two_D_Array M, Two_D_Array Last_Change )
/*11*/     {
/*12*/         long int i, k, Left, Right, This_M;

/*13*/         for( Left = 1; Left <= N; Left++ )
/*14*/             M[ Left ][ Left ] = 0;
/*15*/         for( k = 1; k < N; k++ )                    // K is Right-Left.
/*16*/             for( Left = 1; Left <= N-k; Left++ ) // For each position.
/*17*/             {
/*18*/                 Right = Left + k;
/*19*/                 M[ Left ][ Right ] = Int_Max;
/*20*/                 for( i = Left; i < Right; i++ )
/*21*/                 {
/*22*/                     This_M = M[ Left ][ i ] + M[ i+1 ][ Right ]
/*23*/                                 + C[ Left-1 ] * C[ i ] * C[ Right ];
/*24*/                     if( This_M < M[ Left ][ Right ] )  // Update min.
/*25*/                     {
/*26*/                         M[ Left ][ Right ] = This_M;
/*27*/                         Last_Change[ Left ][ Right ] = i;
/*28*/                     }
/*29*/                 }
/*30*/             }
/*31*/     }
```

Figure 10.46   Program to find optimal ordering of matrix
multiplications

but since the time to perform the actual matrix multiplication is still likely to be
much larger than the time to compute the optimal ordering, this algorithm is still
quite practical.

10.3.3.   Optimal Binary Search Tree

Our second dynamic programming example considers the following input: We are
given a list of words, $w_1, w_2, \ldots, w_n$, and *fixed* probabilities $p_1, p_2, \ldots, p_n$ of their
occurrence. The problem is to arrange these words in a binary search tree in a way
that minimizes the expected total access time. In a binary search tree, the number of

Word	Probability
a	0.22
am	0.18
and	0.20
egg	0.05
if	0.25
the	0.02
two	0.08

Figure 10.47 Sample input for optimal binary search tree problem

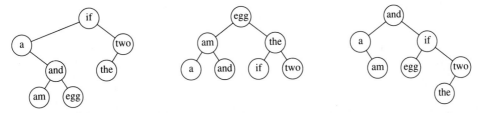

Figure 10.48 Three possible binary search trees for data in previous table

Input		Tree #1		Tree #2		Tree #3	
		Access Cost		Access Cost		Access Cost	
Word w_i	Probability p_i	Once	Sequence	Once	Sequence	Once	Sequence
a	0.22	2	0.44	3	0.66	2	0.44
am	0.18	4	0.72	2	0.36	3	0.54
and	0.20	3	0.60	3	0.60	1	0.20
egg	0.05	4	0.20	1	0.05	3	0.15
if	0.25	1	0.25	3	0.75	2	0.50
the	0.02	3	0.06	2	0.04	4	0.08
two	0.08	2	0.16	3	0.24	3	0.24
Totals	1.00		2.43		2.70		2.15

Figure 10.49 Comparison of the three binary search trees

comparisons needed to access an element at depth d is $d + 1$, so if w_i is placed at depth d_i, then we want to minimize $\sum_{i=1}^{n} p_i(1 + d_i)$.

As an example, Figure 10.47 shows seven words along with their probability of occurrence in some context. Figure 10.48 shows three possible binary search trees. Their searching costs are shown in Figure 10.49.

The first tree was formed using a greedy strategy. The word with the highest probability of being accessed was placed at the root. The left and right subtrees were then formed recursively. The second tree is the perfectly balanced search tree.

Neither of these trees is optimal, as demonstrated by the existence of the third tree. From this we can see that neither of the obvious solutions works.

This is initially surprising since the problem appears to be very similar to the construction of a Huffman encoding tree, which, as we have already seen, can be solved by a greedy algorithm. Construction of an optimal binary search tree is harder, because the data is not constrained to appear only at the leaves and also because the tree must satisfy the binary search tree property.

A dynamic programming solution follows from two observations. Once again, suppose we are trying to place the (sorted) words $w_{Left}, w_{Left+1}, \ldots, w_{Right-1}, w_{Right}$ into a binary search tree. Suppose the optimal binary search tree has w_i as the root, where $Left \le i \le Right$. Then the left subtree must contain $w_{Left}, \ldots, w_{i-1}$, and the right subtree must contain $w_{i+1} \ldots, w_{Right}$ (by the binary search tree property). Further, both of these subtrees must also be optimal, since otherwise they could be replaced by optimal subtrees, which would give a better solution for $w_{Left} \ldots, w_{Right}$. Thus, we can write a formula for the cost $C_{Left,Right}$ of an optimal binary search tree. Figure 10.50 may be helpful.

If $Left > Right$, then the cost of the tree is 0; this is the *null* case, which we always have for binary search trees. Otherwise, the root costs p_i. The left subtree has a cost of $C_{Left,i-1}$ relative to its root, and the right subtree has a cost of $C_{i+1,Right}$ relative to its root. As Figure 10.50 shows, each node in these subtrees is one level deeper from w_i than from their respective roots, so we must add $\sum_{j=Left}^{i-1} p_j$ and $\sum_{j=i+1}^{Right} p_j$. This gives the formula

$$C_{Left,Right} = \min_{Left \le i \le Right} \left\{ p_i + C_{Left,i-1} + C_{i+1,Right} + \sum_{j=Left}^{i-1} p_j + \sum_{j=i+1}^{Right} p_j \right\}$$

$$= \min_{Left \le i \le Right} \left\{ C_{Left,i-1} + C_{i+1,Right} + \sum_{j=Left}^{Right} p_j \right\}$$

From this equation, it is straightforward to write a program to compute the cost of the optimal binary search tree. As usual, the actual search tree can be maintained by saving the value of i that minimizes $C_{Left,Right}$. The standard recursive routine can be used to print the actual tree.

Figure 10.50 Structure of an optimal binary search tree

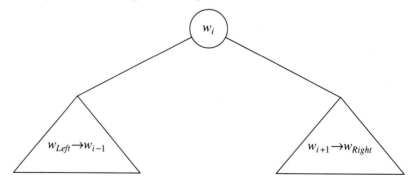

Figure 10.51 shows the table that will be produced by the algorithm. For each subrange of words, the cost and root of the optimal binary search tree are maintained. The bottommost entry, of course, computes the optimal binary search tree for the entire set of words in the input. The optimal tree is the third tree shown in Fig. 10.48.

The precise computation for the optimal binary search tree for a particular subrange, namely *am..if*, is shown in Figure 10.52. It is obtained by computing the minimum-cost tree obtained by placing *am, and, egg,* and *if* at the root. For instance, when *and* is placed at the root, the left subtree contains *am..am* (of cost 0.18, via previous calculation), the right subtree contains *egg..if* (of cost 0.35), and $p_{am} + p_{and} + p_{egg} + p_{if} = 0.68$, for a total cost of 1.21.

The running time of this algorithm is $O(n^3)$ because when it is implemented, we obtain a triple loop. An $O(n^2)$ algorithm for the problem is sketched in the exercises.

10.3.4. All-Pairs Shortest Path

Our third and final dynamic programming application is an algorithm to compute shortest weighted paths between every pair of points in a directed graph $G = (V, E)$. In Chapter 9, we saw an algorithm for the *single-source shortest-path* problem, which finds the shortest path from some arbitrary vertex s to all others. That algorithm (Dijkstra's) runs in $O(|V|^2)$ time on dense graphs, but substantially faster on sparse graphs. We will give a short algorithm to solve the all-pairs problem for dense graphs. The running time of the algorithm is $O(|V|^3)$, which is not an asymptotic improvement over $|V|$ iterations of Dijkstra's algorithm but could be faster on a very

Figure 10.51 Computation of the optimal binary search tree for sample input

	Left=1		Left=2		Left=3		Left=4		Left=5		Left=6		Left=7	
Iteration=1	a..a		am..am		and..and		egg..egg		if..if		the..the		two..two	
	.22	a	.18	am	.20	and	.05	egg	.25	if	.02	the	.08	two
Iteration=2	a..am		am..and		and..egg		egg..if		if..the		the..two			
	.58	a	.56	and	.30	and	.35	if	.29	if	.12	two		
Iteration=3	a..and		am..egg		and..if		egg..the		if..two					
	1.02	am	.66	and	.80	if	.39	if	.47	if				
Iteration=4	a..egg		am..if		and..the		egg..two							
	1.17	am	1.21	and	.84	if	.57	if						
Iteration=5	a..if		am..the		and..two									
	1.83	and	1.27	and	1.02	if								
Iteration=6	a..the		am..two											
	1.89	and	1.53	and										
Iteration=7	a..two													
	2.15	and												

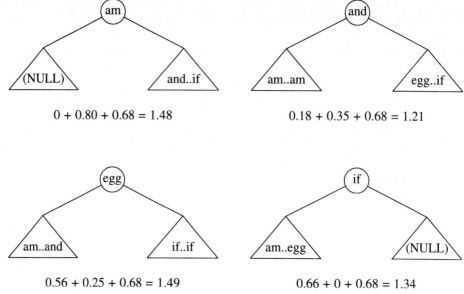

Figure 10.52   Computation of table entry (1.21, *and*) for *am..if*

dense graph because its loops are tighter. The algorithm also performs correctly if there are negative edge costs but no negative-cost cycles; Dijkstra's algorithm fails in this case.

Let us recall the important details of Dijkstra's algorithm (the reader may wish to review Section 9.3). Dijkstra's algorithm starts at a vertex s and works in stages. Each vertex in the graph is eventually selected as an intermediate vertex. If the current selected vertex is v, then for each $w \in V$, we set $d_w = \min(d_w, d_v + c_{v,w})$. This formula says that the best distance to w (from s) is either the previously known distance to w from s, or the result of going from s to v (optimally) and then directly from v to w.

Dijkstra's algorithm provides the idea for the dynamic programming algorithm: We select the vertices in sequential order. We will define $D_{k,i,j}$ to be the weight of the shortest path from v_i to v_j that uses only $v_1, v_2, \ldots, v_k$ as intermediates. By this definition, $D_{0,i,j} = c_{i,j}$, where $c_{i,j}$ is ∞ if (v_i, v_j) is not an edge in the graph. Also, by definition, $D_{|V|,i,j}$ is the shortest path from v_i to v_j in the graph.

As Figure 10.53 shows, when $k > 0$ we can write a simple formula for $D_{k,i,j}$. The shortest path from v_i to v_j that uses only $v_1, v_2, \ldots, v_k$ as intermediates is the shortest path that either does not use v_k as an intermediate at all or consists of the merging of the two paths $v_i \rightarrow v_k$ and $v_k \rightarrow v_j$, each of which uses only the first $k - 1$ vertices as intermediates. This leads to the formula

$$D_{k,i,j} = \min\left\{ D_{k-1,i,j}, D_{k-1,i,k} + D_{k-1,k,j} \right\}$$

The time requirement is once again $O(|V|^3)$. Unlike the two previous dynamic programming examples, this time bound has not been substantially lowered by another approach. Because the kth stage depends only on the $(k - 1)$st stage, it appears that only two $|V| \times |V|$ matrices need to be maintained.

```
/* 1*/    // Compute All-Shortest Paths.
/* 2*/    // A[ ] contains the adjacency matrix with.
/* 3*/    // A[ i ][ i ] presumed to be zero.
/* 4*/    // D[ ] contains the values of the shortest path.
/* 5*/    // N is the number of vertices.
/* 6*/    // A negative cycle exists iff
/* 7*/    // D[ i ][ i ] is set to a negative value.
/* 8*/    // Actual path can be computed using Path[ ].
/* 9*/    // All arrays are indexed starting at 0.
/*10*/    // Not_A_Vertex is -1.

/*11*/    void
/*12*/    All_Pairs( const Two_D_Array A, Two_D_Array D,
/*13*/                     Two_D_Array Path, const int N )
/*14*/    {
/*15*/        int i, j, k;

/*16*/        for( i = 0; i < N; i++ )     // Initialize D and Path.
/*17*/            for( j = 0; j < N; j++ )
/*18*/            {
/*19*/                D[ i ][ j ] = A[ i ][ j ];
/*20*/                Path[ i ][ j ] = Not_A_Vertex;
/*21*/            }

/*22*/        for( k = 0; k < N; k++ )
/*23*/            //  Consider each vertex as an intermediate.
/*24*/            for( i = 0; i < N; i++ )
/*25*/                for( j = 0; j < N; j++ )
/*26*/                    if( D[ i ][ k ] + D[ k ][ j ] < D[ i ][ j ] )
/*27*/                    {      // Update min.
/*28*/                        D[ i ][ j ] = D[ i ][ k ] + D[ k ][ j ];
/*29*/                        Path[ i ][ j ] = k;
/*30*/                    }
/*31*/    }
```

Figure 10.53 All-pairs shortest path

However, using k as an *intermediate* vertex on a path that starts or finishes with k does not improve the result unless there is a negative cycle. Thus, only one matrix is necessary, because $D_{k-1,i,k} = D_{k,i,k}$ and $D_{k-1,k,j} = D_{k,k,j}$, which implies that none of the terms on the right change values and need to be saved. This observation leads to the simple program in Figure 10.53, which numbers vertices starting at zero to conform with C++'s conventions.

On a complete graph, where every pair of vertices is connected (in both directions), this algorithm is almost certain to be faster than $|V|$ iterations of Dijkstra's algorithm because the loops are so tight. Lines 16 through 21 can be executed in parallel, as can lines 24 through 30. Thus, this algorithm seems to be well-suited for parallel computation.

Dynamic programming is a powerful algorithm design technique that provides a starting point for a solution. It is essentially the divide and conquer paradigm of solving simpler problems first. The important difference is that the simpler problems are not a clear division of the original. Because subproblems are repeatedly solved, it is important to record their solutions in a table rather than recompute them. In some cases, the solution can be improved (although it is certainly not always obvious and frequently difficult), and in other cases, the dynamic programming technique is the best approach known.

In some sense, if you have seen one dynamic programming problem, you have seen them all. More examples of dynamic programming can be found in the exercises and references.

10.4.   Randomized Algorithms

Suppose you are a professor who is giving weekly programming assignments. You want to make sure that the students are doing their own programs or, at the very least, understand the code they are submitting. One solution is to give a quiz on the day that each program is due. On the other hand, these quizzes take time out of class, so it might be practical to do this for only roughly half of the programs. Your problem is to decide when to give the quizzes.

Of course, if the quizzes are announced in advance, that could be interpreted as an implicit license to cheat for the 50 percent of the programs that will not get a quiz. One could adopt the unannounced strategy of giving quizzes on alternate programs, but students would figure out the strategy before too long. Another possibility is to give quizzes on what seems like the important programs, but this would likely lead to similar quiz patterns from semester to semester. Student grapevines being what they are, this strategy would probably be worthless after a semester.

One method that seems to eliminate these problems is to use a coin. A quiz is made for every program (making quizzes is not nearly as time-consuming as grading them), and at the start of class, the professor will flip a coin to decide whether the quiz is to be given. This way, it is impossible to know before class whether or not the quiz will occur, and these patterns do not repeat from semester to semester. Thus, the students will have to expect that a quiz will occur with 50 percent probability, regardless of previous quiz patterns. The disadvantage is that it is possible that there is no quiz for an entire semester. This is not a likely occurrence unless the coin is suspect. Each semester, the expected number of quizzes is half the number of programs, and, with high probability, the number of quizzes will not deviate much from this.

This example illustrates what we call *randomized algorithms*. At least once during the algorithm, a random number is used to make a decision. The running time of the algorithm depends not only on the particular input but also on the random numbers that occur.

The worst-case running time of a randomized algorithm is almost always the same as the worst-case running time of the nonrandomized algorithm. The important difference is that a good randomized algorithm has no bad inputs, but only bad random numbers (relative to the particular input). This may seem like only a philosophical difference, but actually it is quite important, as the following example shows.

Consider two variants of quicksort. Variant A uses the first element as pivot, whereas variant B uses a randomly chosen element as pivot. In both cases, the worst case running time is $\Theta(n^2)$ because it is possible at each step that the largest element is chosen as pivot. The difference between these worst cases is that there is a particular input that can always be presented to variant A to cause the bad running time. Variant A will run in $\Theta(n^2)$ time every single time it is given an already sorted list. If variant B is presented with the same input twice, it will have two different running times, depending on what random numbers occur.

Throughout the text, in our calculations of running times, we have assumed that all inputs are equally likely. This is not true, because nearly sorted input, for instance, occurs much more often than is statistically expected, and this causes problems, particularly for quicksort and binary search trees. By using a randomized algorithm, the particular input is no longer important. The random numbers are important, and we can get an *expected* running time, where we now average over all possible random numbers instead of over all possible inputs. Using quicksort with a random pivot gives an $O(n \log n)$-expected-time algorithm. This means that for any input, including already sorted input, the running time is expected to be $O(n \log n)$, based on the statistics of random numbers. An expected running time bound is somewhat stronger than an average-case bound but, of course, is weaker than the corresponding worst-case bound. On the other hand, as we saw in the selection problem, solutions that obtain the worst-case bound are frequently not as practical as their average-case counterparts. Randomized algorithms usually are.

In this section we will examine two uses of randomization. First, we will see a novel scheme for supporting the binary search tree operations in $O(\log n)$ expected time. Once again, this means that there are no bad inputs, just bad random numbers. From a theoretical point of view, this is not terribly exciting since balanced search trees achieve this bound in the worst case. Nevertheless, the use of randomization leads to relatively simple algorithms for searching, inserting, and especially deleting.

Our second application is a randomized algorithm to test the primality of large numbers. No efficient polynomial-time nonrandomized algorithms are known for this problem. The algorithm we present runs quickly but occasionally makes an error. The probability of error can, however, be made negligibly small.

10.4.1. *Random Number Generators*

Since our algorithms require random numbers, we must have a method to generate them. Actually, true randomness is virtually impossible to do on a computer since these numbers will depend on the algorithm and, thus, cannot possibly be random. Generally, it suffices to produce *pseudorandom* numbers, which are numbers that appear to be random. Random numbers have many known statistical properties; pseudorandom numbers satisfy most of these properties. Surprisingly, this too is much easier said than done.

Suppose we only need to flip a coin; thus, we must generate a 0 or 1 randomly. One way to do this is to examine the system clock. The clock might record time as an integer that counts the number of seconds since some starting time. We could then use the lowest bit. The problem is that this does not work well if a sequence of random numbers is needed. One second is a long time, and the clock might not change at all while the program is running. Even if the time were recorded in units of microseconds, if the program were running by itself, the sequence of numbers that would be generated would be far from random since the time between calls to the generator would be essentially identical on every program invocation. We see, then, that what is really needed is a *sequence* of random numbers.[†] These numbers should appear independent. If a coin is flipped and heads appears, the next coin flip should still be equally likely to come up heads or tails.

The standard method to generate random numbers is the linear congruential generator, which was first described by Lehmer in 1951. Numbers $x_1, x_2, \ldots$ are generated satisfying

$$x_{i+1} = ax_i \bmod m.$$

To start the sequence, some value of x_0 must be given. This value is known as the *seed*. If $x_0 = 0$, then the sequence is far from random, but if a and m are correctly chosen, then any other $1 \le x_0 < m$ is equally valid. If m is prime, then x_i is never 0. As an example, if $m = 11$, $a = 7$, and $x_0 = 1$, then the numbers generated are

$$7, 5, 2, 3, 10, 4, 6, 9, 8, 1, 7, 5, 2, \ldots$$

Notice that after $m - 1 = 10$ numbers, the sequence repeats. Thus, this sequence has a period of $m - 1$, which is as large as possible (by the pigeonhole principle). If m is prime, there are always choices of a that give a full period of $m - 1$. Some choices of a do not; if $a = 5$ and $x_0 = 1$, the sequence has a short period of 5.

$$5, 3, 4, 9, 1, 5, 3, 4, \ldots$$

Obviously, if m is chosen to be a large, 31-bit prime, the period should be significantly large for most applications. Lehmer suggested the use of the 31-bit prime $m = 2^{31} - 1 = 2{,}147{,}483{,}647$. For this prime, $a = 7^5 = 16{,}807$ is one of the many values that gives a full-period generator. Its use has been well studied and is recommended by experts in the field. We will see later that with random number generators, tinkering usually means breaking, so one is well advised to stick with this formula until told otherwise.

This seems like a simple routine to implement. Generally, a global variable is used to hold the current value in the sequence of x's. In C++, we can make this variable inaccessible to users by placing it in the private part of a class specification. This global variable is initialized by some routine. When debugging a program that uses random numbers, it is probably best to set $x_0 = 1$ so that the same random sequence occurs all the time. When the program seems to work, either the system clock can be used or the user can be asked to input a value for the seed.

[†] We will use random in place of pseudorandom in the rest of this section.

It is also common to return a random real number in the open interval $(0, 1)$ (0 and 1 are not possible values); this can be done by dividing by m. From this, a random number in any closed interval $[a, b]$ can be computed by normalizing. This yields the "obvious" class in Figure 10.54 which, unfortunately, works on few machines.

The problem with this routine is that the multiplication could overflow and thus affect the result. Schrage gave a procedure in which all of the calculations can be done on a 32-bit machine without overflow. We compute the quotient and remainder of m/a and define these as q and r, respectively. In our case, $q = 127,773$, $r = 2,836$, and $r < q$. We have

$$x_{i+1} = ax_i \bmod m$$

$$= ax_i - m \left\lfloor \frac{ax_i}{m} \right\rfloor$$

$$= ax_i - m \left\lfloor \frac{x_i}{q} \right\rfloor + m \left\lfloor \frac{x_i}{q} \right\rfloor - m \left\lfloor \frac{ax_i}{m} \right\rfloor$$

$$= ax_i - m \left\lfloor \frac{x_i}{q} \right\rfloor + m \left(\left\lfloor \frac{x_i}{q} \right\rfloor - \left\lfloor \frac{ax_i}{m} \right\rfloor \right)$$

Figure 10.54   Random number generator that does not
work

```
/* 1*/      static const long int A = 16807;        // 7^5.
/* 2*/      static const long int M = 2147483647;    // 2^31 - 1.

/* 3*/      class Random
/* 4*/      {
/* 5*/        private:
/* 6*/          unsigned long int Seed;

/* 7*/        public:
/* 8*/          Random( unsigned long int Init_Val = 1 ) :
/* 9*/             Seed( Init_Val ) { }

/*10*/          ~Random( ) { }

/*11*/          double Rand0_1( );
/*12*/      };

/*13*/      double
/*14*/      Random::Rand0_1( )
/*15*/      {
/*16*/          Seed = ( A * Seed ) % M;
/*17*/          return( double( Seed ) / M );
/*18*/      }
```

Since $x_i = q \lfloor x_i/q \rfloor + x_i \bmod q$, we can replace the leading ax_i and obtain

$$x_{i+1} = a \left(q \left\lfloor \frac{x_i}{q} \right\rfloor + x_i \bmod q \right) - m \left\lfloor \frac{x_i}{q} \right\rfloor + m \left(\left\lfloor \frac{x_i}{q} \right\rfloor - \left\lfloor \frac{ax_i}{m} \right\rfloor \right)$$

$$= (aq - m) \left\lfloor \frac{x_i}{q} \right\rfloor + a(x_i \bmod q) + m \left(\left\lfloor \frac{x_i}{q} \right\rfloor - \left\lfloor \frac{ax_i}{m} \right\rfloor \right)$$

Since $m = aq + r$, it follows that $aq - m = -r$. Thus we obtain

$$x_{i+1} = a(x_i \bmod q) - r \left\lfloor \frac{x_i}{q} \right\rfloor + m \left(\left\lfloor \frac{x_i}{q} \right\rfloor - \left\lfloor \frac{ax_i}{m} \right\rfloor \right)$$

The term $\delta(x_i) = \lfloor x_i/q \rfloor - \lfloor ax_i/m \rfloor$ is either 0 or 1 because both terms are integers, and their difference lies between 0 and 1. Thus we have

$$x_{i+1} = a(x_i \bmod q) - r \left\lfloor \frac{x_i}{q} \right\rfloor + m\delta(x_i)$$

A quick check shows that because $r < q$, all the remaining terms can be calculated without overflow (this is one of the reasons for choosing $a = 7^5$). Furthermore, $\delta(x_i) = 1$ only if the remaining terms evaluate to less than zero. Thus $\delta(x_i)$ does not need to be explicitly computed but can be determined by a simple test. This leads to the program in Figure 10.55.

This program works as long as $LONG\_INT\_MAX \leq 2^{31} - 1$. One might be tempted to assume that all machines have a random number generator at least as good as the one in Figure 10.55 in their standard library. Sadly, this is not true. Many libraries have generators based on the function

$$x_{i+1} = (ax_i + c) \bmod 2^b$$

where b is chosen to match the number of bits in the machine's integer, and c is odd. These libraries also return x_i, instead of a value between 0 and 1. Unfortunately, these generators always produce values of x_i that alternate between even and odd— hardly a desirable property. Indeed, the lower k bits cycle with period 2^k (at best). Many other random number generators have much smaller cycles than the one provided in Figure 10.55. These are not suitable for the case in which long sequences of random numbers are needed. Finally, it may seem that we can get a better random number generator by adding a constant to the equation. For instance, it seems that

$$x_{i+1} = (16807x_i + 1) \bmod (2^{31} - 1)$$

would somehow be even more random. This illustrates how fragile these generators are.

$$[16807(1319592028) + 1] \bmod (2^{31} - 1) = 1319592028,$$

so if the seed is 1,319,592,028, the generator gets stuck in a cycle of period 1.

```
/* 1*/    static const long int A = 16807;         // 7^5.
/* 2*/    static const long int M = 2147483647;    // 2^31 - 1.
/* 3*/    static const long int Q = 127773;        // M / A.
/* 4*/    static const long int R = 2836;          // M % A.

/* 5*/    class Random
/* 6*/    {
/* 7*/      private:
/* 8*/        unsigned long int Seed;

/* 9*/      public:
/*10*/        Random( unsigned long int Init_Val = 1 ) :
/*11*/            Seed( Init_Val ) { }

/*12*/        ~Random( ) { }

/*13*/        double Rand0_1( );
/*14*/    };

/*15*/    double
/*16*/    Random::Rand0_1( )
/*17*/    {
/*18*/        long int Tmp_Seed;

/*19*/        Tmp_Seed = A * ( Seed % Q ) - R * ( Seed / Q );
/*20*/        if( Tmp_Seed >= 0 )
/*21*/            Seed = Tmp_Seed;
/*22*/        else
/*23*/            Seed = Tmp_Seed + M;

/*24*/        return( double( Seed ) / M );
/*25*/    }
```

Figure 10.55   Random number generator that works
on 32-bit machines

10.4.2.   Skip Lists

Our first use of randomization is a data structure that supports both searching
and insertion in $O(\log n)$ expected time. As mentioned in the introduction to this
section, this means that the running time for each operation on *any input sequence*
has expected value $O(\log n)$, where the expectation is based on the random number
generator. It is possible to add deletion and all the operations that involve ordering
and obtain expected time bounds that match the average time bounds of binary
search trees.

The simplest possible data structure to support searching is the linked list.
Figure 10.56 shows a simple linked list. The time to perform a search is proportional
to the number of nodes that have to be examined, which is at most n.

Figure 10.56 Simple linked list

Figure 10.57 Linked list with pointers to two cells ahead

Figure 10.57 shows a linked list in which every other node has an additional pointer to the node two ahead of it in the list. Because of this, at most $\lceil n/2 \rceil + 1$ nodes are examined in the worst case.

We can extend this idea and obtain Figure 10.58. Here, every fourth node has a pointer to the node four ahead. Only $\lceil n/4 \rceil + 2$ nodes are examined.

The limiting case of this argument is shown in Figure 10.59. Every 2^ith node has a pointer to the node 2^i ahead of it. The total number of pointers has only doubled, but now at most $\lceil \log n \rceil$ nodes are examined during a search. It is not hard to see that the total time spent for a search is $O(\log n)$ because the search consists of either advancing to a new node or dropping to a lower pointer in the same node. Each of these steps consumes at most $O(\log n)$ total time during a search. Notice that the search in this data structure is essentially a binary search.

The problem with this data structure is that it is much too rigid to allow efficient insertion. The key to making this data structure usable is to relax the structure conditions slightly. We define a *level k node* to be a node that has k pointers. As Figure 10.59 shows, the ith pointer in any level k node ($k \geq i$) points to the next node with at least i levels. This is an easy property to maintain; however, Figure 10.59 shows a more restrictive property than this. We thus drop the restriction that the ith pointer points to the node 2^i ahead, and we replace it with the less restrictive condition above.

When it comes time to insert a new element, we allocate a new node for it. We must at this point decide what level the node should be. Examining Figure 10.59,

Figure 10.58 Linked list with pointers to four cells ahead

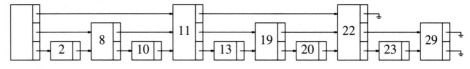

Figure 10.59 Linked list with pointers to 2^i cells ahead

Figure 10.60 A skip list

we find that roughly half the nodes are level 1 nodes, roughly a quarter are level 2, and, in general, approximately $1/2^i$ nodes are level i. We choose the level of the node randomly, in accordance with this probability distribution. The easiest way to do this is to flip a coin until a head occurs and use the total number of flips as the node level. Figure 10.60 shows a typical skip list.

Given this, the skip list algorithms are simple to describe. To perform a *Find*, we start at the highest pointer at the header. We traverse along this level until we find that the next node is larger than the one we are looking for (or *null*). When this occurs, we go to the next lower level and continue the strategy. When progress is stopped at level 1, we are either in front of the node we are looking for, or it is not in the list. To perform an *Insert*, we proceed as in a *Find*, and keep track of each point where we switch to a lower level. The new node, whose level is determined randomly, is then spliced into the list. This operation is shown in Figure 10.61.

A cursory analysis shows that since the expected number of nodes at each level is unchanged from the original (nonrandomized) algorithm, the total amount of work that is expected to be performed traversing to nodes on the same level is unchanged. This tells us that these operations have O($\log n$) *expected* costs. Of course, a more formal proof is required, but it is not much different from this.

Skip lists are similar to hash tables in that they require an estimate of the number of elements that will be in the list (so that the number of levels can be determined). If an estimate is not available, we can assume a large number or use a technique similar to rehashing. Experiments have shown that skip lists are as efficient as many balanced search tree implementations and are certainly much simpler to implement in many languages.

Figure 10.61 Before and after an insertion

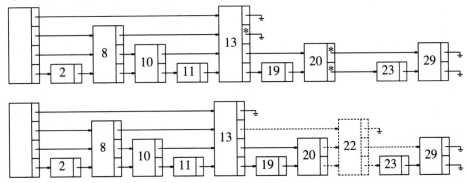

10.4.3. Primality Testing

In this section we examine the problem of determining whether or not a large number is prime. As was mentioned at the end of Chapter 2, some cryptography schemes depend on the difficulty of factoring a large, 200-digit number into two 100-digit primes. In order to implement this scheme, we need a method of generating these two primes. The problem is of major theoretical interest because nobody now knows how to test whether a d-digit number n is prime in time polynomial in d. For instance, the obvious method of testing for the divisibility by odd numbers from 3 to $\sqrt{n}$ requires roughly $\frac{1}{2}\sqrt{n}$ divisions, which is about $2^{d/2}$. On the other hand, this problem is not thought to be NP-complete; thus, it is one of the few problems on the fringe—its complexity is unknown at the time of this writing.

In this chapter, we will give a polynomial-time algorithm that can test for primality. If the algorithm declares that the number is not prime, we can be certain that the number is not prime. If the algorithm declares that the number is prime, then, with high probability but not 100 percent certainty, the number is prime. The error probability does not depend on the particular number that is being tested but instead depends on random choices made by the algorithm. Thus, this algorithm occasionally makes a mistake, but we will see that the error ratio can be made arbitrarily negligible.

The key to the algorithm is a well-known theorem due to Fermat.

THEOREM 10.10.

Fermat's Lesser Theorem: If p is prime, and $0 < a < p$, then $a^{p-1} \equiv 1 \pmod{p}$.

PROOF:

A proof of this theorem can be found in any textbook on number theory.

For instance, since 67 is prime, $2^{66} \equiv 1 \pmod{67}$. This suggests an algorithm to test whether a number n is prime. Merely check whether $2^{n-1} \equiv 1 \pmod{n}$. If $2^{n-1} \not\equiv 1 \pmod{n}$, then we can be certain that n is not prime. On the other hand, if the equality holds, then n is probably prime. For instance, the smallest n that satisfies $2^{n-1} \equiv 1 \pmod{n}$ but is not prime is $n = 341$.

This algorithm will occasionally make errors, but the problem is that it will always make the same errors. Put another way, there is a fixed set of n for which it does not work. We can attempt to randomize the algorithm as follows: Pick $1 < a < n - 1$ at random. If $a^{n-1} \equiv 1 \pmod{n}$, declare that n is probably prime, otherwise, declare that n is definitely not prime. If $n = 341$, and $a = 3$, we find that $3^{340} \equiv 56 \pmod{341}$. Thus, if the algorithm happens to choose $a = 3$, it will get the correct answer for $n = 341$.

Although this seems to work, there are numbers that fool even this algorithm for most choices of a. One such set of numbers is known as the *Carmichael numbers*. These are not prime but satisfy $a^{n-1} \equiv 1 \pmod{n}$ for *all* $0 < a < n$ that are relatively prime to n. The smallest such number is 561. Thus, we need an additional test to improve the chances of not making an error.

In Chapter 7, we proved a theorem related to quadratic probing. A special case of this theorem is the following:

THEOREM 10.11.

If p is prime and $0 < x < p$, the only solutions to $x^2 \equiv 1 \pmod{p}$ are $x = 1, p - 1$.

PROOF:

$x^2 \equiv 1 \pmod{p}$ implies that $x^2 - 1 \equiv 0 \pmod{p}$. This implies $(x - 1)(x + 1) \equiv 0 \pmod{p}$. Since p is prime, $0 \le x < p$, and p must divide either $(x - 1)$ or $(x + 1)$, the theorem follows.

Therefore, if at any point in the computation of $a^{n-1} \bmod n$ we discover a violation of this theorem, we can conclude that n is definitely not prime. If we use *Power*, from Section 2.4.4, we see that there will be several opportunities to apply this test. We modify this routine to perform operations $\bmod n$ and apply the test of Theorem 10.11. This strategy is implemented in Figure 10.62.

Recall that if *Test_Prime* returns *Definitely_Composite*, it has *proven* that n cannot be prime. The proof is nonconstructive because it gives no method of actually

Figure 10.62 A probabilistic primality-testing algorithm

```
/* 1*/    enum Test_Result { Probably_Prime, Definitely_Composite };

/* 2*/    // Compute Result = A^P mod N.
/* 3*/    // If at any point X^2 == 1 ( mod N ) is detected,
/* 4*/    // with X != 1 and X != N-1,
/* 5*/    // then set What_N_Is to Definitely_Composite.

/* 6*/    void
/* 7*/    Power( const Huge_Int & A, const Huge_Int & P, const Huge_Int & N,
/* 8*/               Huge_Int & Result, Test_Result & What_N_Is )
/* 9*/    {
/*10*/        Huge_Int X;

/*11*/        if( P == 0 )           // Base case.
/*12*/            Result = 1;
/*13*/        else
/*14*/        {
/*15*/            Power( A, P/2, N, X, What_N_Is );
/*16*/            Result = ( X * X ) % N;

/*17*/            // Check whether X^2 == 1 ( mod N ), with X != 1 or  N-1.
/*18*/            if( ( Result == 1 ) && ( X != 1 ) && ( X != N-1 ) )
/*19*/                What_N_Is = Definitely_Composite;

/*20*/            // If P is odd, we need one more A.
/*21*/            if( ( P % 2 ) == 1 )
/*22*/                Result = ( Result * A ) % N;
/*23*/        }
/*24*/    }
```

```
/* 1*/    // Test whether N >= 3 is prime using one value of A.
/* 2*/    // Repeat as many times as needed for desired error rate.

/* 3*/    Test_Result
/* 4*/    Test_Prime( const Huge_Int & N )
/* 5*/    {
/* 6*/        Huge_Int A, Result;
/* 7*/        Test_Result What_N_Is;

/* 8*/        A = Rand_Int( 2, N - 2 );
/* 9*/        What_N_Is = Probably_Prime;
/*10*/        Power( A, N-1, N, Result, What_N_Is );
/*11*/        if( ( Result != 1 ) || ( What_N_Is == Definitely_Composite ) )
/*12*/            return Definitely_Composite;
/*13*/        else
/*14*/            return Probably_Prime;
/*15*/    }
```

Figure 10.62   *(Continued)*

finding the factors. It has been shown that for any (sufficiently large) n, at most $(n - 9)/4$ values of a fool this algorithm. Thus, if a is chosen at random, and the algorithm answers *Probably_Prime*, then the algorithm is correct at least 75 percent of the time. Suppose *Test_Prime* is run 50 times. The probability that the algorithm is fooled once is at most $\frac{1}{4}$. Thus, the probability that 50 independent random trials fool the algorithm is never more than $1/4^{50} = 2^{-100}$. This is actually a very conservative estimate, which holds for only a few choices of n. Even so, one is more likely to see a hardware error than an incorrect claim of primality.

10.5.   Backtracking Algorithms

The last algorithm design technique we will examine is *backtracking*. In many cases, a backtracking algorithm amounts to a clever implementation of exhaustive search, with generally unfavorable performance. This is not always the case, however, and even so, in some cases, the savings over a brute force exhaustive search can be significant. Performance is, of course, relative: An $O(n^2)$ algorithm for sorting is pretty bad, but an $O(n^5)$ algorithm for the traveling salesman (or any *NP*-complete) problem would be a landmark result.

A practical example of a backtracking algorithm is the problem of arranging furniture in a new house. There are many possibilities to try, but typically only a few are actually considered. Starting with no arrangement, each piece of furniture is placed in some part of the room. If all the furniture is placed and the owner is happy, then the algorithm terminates. If we reach a point where all subsequent placement of furniture is undesirable, we have to undo the last step and try an alternative. Of course, this might force another undo, and so forth.

If we find that we undo all possible first steps, then there is no placement of furniture that is satisfactory. Otherwise, we eventually terminate with a satisfactory arrangement. Notice that although this algorithm is essentially brute force, it does not try all possibilities directly. For instance, arrangements that consider placing the sofa in the kitchen are never tried. Many other bad arrangements are discarded early because an undesirable subset of the arrangement is detected. The elimination of a large group of possibilities in one step is known as *pruning*.

We will see two examples of backtracking algorithms. The first is a problem in computational geometry. Our second example shows how computers select moves in games such as chess and checkers.

10.5.1. The Turnpike Reconstruction Problem

Suppose we are given n points, $p_1, p_2, \ldots, p_n$, located on the x-axis. x_i is the x coordinate of p_i. Let us further assume that $x_1 = 0$ and the points are given from left to right. These n points determine $n(n-1)/2$ (not necessarily unique) distances d_1, $d_2, \ldots, d_n$ between every pair of points of the form $|x_i - x_j| \, (i \neq j)$. It is clear that if we are given the set of points, it is easy to *construct* the set of distances in $O(n^2)$ time. This set will not be sorted, but if we are willing to settle for an $O(n^2 \log n)$ time bound, the distances can be sorted, too. The *turnpike reconstruction problem* is to reconstruct a point set from the distances. This finds applications in physics and molecular biology (see the references for pointers to more specific information). The name derives from the analogy of points to turnpike exits on East Coast highways. Just as factoring seems harder than multiplication, the reconstruction problem seems harder than the construction problem. Nobody has been able to give an algorithm that is guaranteed to work in polynomial time. The algorithm that we will present seems to run in $O(n^2 \log n)$; no counterexample to this conjecture is known, but it is still just that—a conjecture.

Of course, given one solution to the problem, an infinite number of others can be constructed by adding an offset to all the points. This is why we insist that the first point is anchored at 0 and that the point set that constitutes a solution is output in nondecreasing order.

Let D be the set of distances, and assume that $|D| = m = n(n-1)/2$. As an example, suppose that

$$D = \{1, 2, 2, 2, 3, 3, 3, 4, 5, 5, 5, 6, 7, 8, 10\}$$

Since $|D| = 15$, we know that $n = 6$. We start the algorithm by setting $x_1 = 0$. Clearly, $x_6 = 10$, since 10 is the largest element in D. We remove 10 from D. The points that we have placed and the remaining distances are as shown in the following figure.

$$D = \{1, 2, 2, 2, 3, 3, 3, 4, 5, 5, 5, 6, 7, 8\}.$$

The largest remaining distance is 8, which means that either $x_2 = 2$ or $x_5 = 8$. By symmetry, we can conclude that the choice is unimportant since either both choices lead to solutions (which are mirror images of each other), or neither do, so we can set $x_5 = 8$ without affecting the solution. We then remove the distances $x_6 - x_5 = 2$ and $x_5 - x_1 = 8$ from D, obtaining

$$D = \{ 1, 2, 2, 3, 3, 3, 4, 5, 5, 5, 6, 7 \}.$$

The next step is not obvious. Since 7 is the largest value in D, either $x_4 = 7$ or $x_2 = 3$. If $x_4 = 7$, then the distances $x_6 - 7 = 3$ and $x_5 - 7 = 1$ must also be present in D. A quick check shows that indeed they are. On the other hand, if we set $x_2 = 3$, then $3 - x_1 = 3$ and $x_5 - 3 = 5$ must be present in D. These distances are also in D, so we have no guidance on which choice to make. Thus, we try one and see if it leads to a solution. If it turns out that it does not, we can come back and try the other. Trying the first choice, we set $x_4 = 7$, which leaves

$$D = \{ 2, 2, 3, 3, 4, 5, 5, 5, 6 \}.$$

At this point, we have $x_1 = 0$, $x_4 = 7$, $x_5 = 8$, and $x_6 = 10$. Now the largest distance is 6, so either $x_3 = 6$ or $x_2 = 4$. But if $x_3 = 6$, then $x_4 - x_3 = 1$, which is impossible, since 1 is no longer in D. On the other hand, if $x_2 = 4$ then $x_2 - x_0 = 4$, and $x_5 - x_2 = 4$. This is also impossible, since 4 appears only once in D. Thus, this line of reasoning leaves no solution, so we backtrack.

Since $x_4 = 7$ failed to produce a solution, we try $x_2 = 3$. If this also fails, we give up and report no solution. We now have

$$D = \{ 1, 2, 2, 3, 3, 4, 5, 5, 6 \}.$$

Once again, we have to choose between $x_4 = 6$ and $x_3 = 4$. $x_3 = 4$ is impossible, because D only has one occurrence of 4, and two would be implied by this choice. $x_4 = 6$ is possible, so we obtain

$$D = \{ 1, 2, 3, 5, 5 \}.$$

The only remaining choice is to assign $x_3 = 5$; this works because it leaves D empty, and so we have a solution.

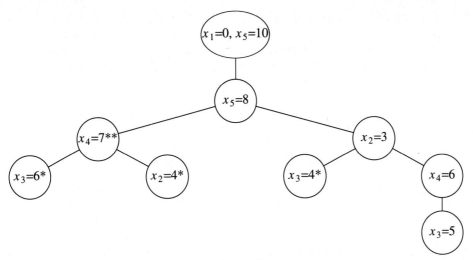

Figure 10.63 Decision tree for the worked turnpike
reconstruction example

$$x_1 = 0 \qquad x_2 = 3 \quad x_3 = 5 \; x_4 = 6 \quad x_5 = 8 \quad x_6 = 10$$

$$D = \{\}.$$

Figure 10.63 shows a decision tree representing the actions taken to arrive at the solution. Instead of labeling the branches, we have placed the labels in the branches' destination nodes. A node with an asterisk indicates that the points chosen are inconsistent with the given distances; nodes with two asterisks have only impossible nodes as children, and thus represent an incorrect path.

The pseudocode to implement this algorithm is mostly straightforward. The driving routine, *Turnpike,* is shown in Figure 10.64. It receives the point array X (which need not be initialized) and the distance array D.[†] If a solution is discovered, then *True* will be returned, the answer will be placed in X, and D will be empty. Otherwise, *False* will be returned and X will be undefined. The distance array D will be untouched. The routine sets X_1, X_{n-1}, and X_n, as described above, alters D, and calls the backtracking algorithm *Place* to place the other points. We presume that a check has already been made to ensure that $|D| = N(N-1)/2$.

The more difficult part is the backtracking algorithm, which is shown in Figure 10.65. Like most backtracking algorithms, the most convenient implementation

---

[†]We have used one-letter variable names, which is generally poor style, for consistency with the worked example. We also, for simplicity, do not give the type of variables.

```
          int
          Turnpike( int X[ ], Dist_Set D, unsigned int N )
          {
/* 1*/        X[ 1 ] = 0;
/* 2*/        X[ N ] = Delete_Max( D );
/* 3*/        X[ N - 1 ] = Delete_Max( D );
/* 4*/        if ( X[ N ] - X[ N - 1 ] ∈ D )
              {
/* 5*/            Remove( X[ N ] - X[ N - 1 ], D );
/* 6*/            return Place( X, D, N, 2, N - 2 );
              }
          else
/* 7*/            return False;
          }
```

Figure 10.64   Turnpike reconstruction algorithm: driver
routine

is recursive. We pass the same arguments plus the boundaries *Left* and *Right*;
$X_{Left}, \dots, X_{Right}$ are the x coordinates of points that we are trying to place.
If D is empty (or *Left* > *Right*), then a solution has been found, and we can return.
Otherwise, we first try to place $X_{Right} = D_{max}$. If all the appropriate distances are
present (in the correct quantity), then we tentatively place this point, remove these
distances, and try to fill from *Left* to *Right* − 1. If the distances are not present, or
the attempt to fill *Left* to *Right* − 1 fails, then we try setting $X_{Left} = X_n - D_{max}$,
using a similar strategy. If this does not work, then there is no solution; otherwise a
solution has been found, and this information is eventually passed back to *Turnpike*
by the *Found* and *X* variables.

The analysis of the algorithm involves two factors. Suppose lines 9 through 11
and 18 through 20 are never executed. We can maintain D as a balanced binary
search (or splay) tree. If we never backtrack, there are at most $O(n^2)$ operations
involving D, such as deletion and the *Find*s implied at lines 4 and 12 to 13. This
claim is obvious for deletions, since D has $O(n^2)$ elements, and no element is ever
reinserted. Each call to *Place* uses at most 2*n Find*s, and since *Place* never backtracks
in this analysis, there can be at most $2n^2$ *Find*s. Thus, if there is no backtracking,
the running time is $O(n^2 \log n)$.

Of course, backtracking happens, and if it happens repeatedly, then the performance of the algorithm is affected. No polynomial bound on the amount of
backtracking is known, but on the other hand, there are no pathological examples
that show that backtracking must occur more than $O(1)$ times. Thus, it is entirely
possible that this algorithm is $O(n^2 \log n)$. Experiments have shown that if the points
have integer coordinates distributed uniformly and randomly from $[0, D_{max}]$, where
$D_{max} = \Theta(n^2)$, then, almost certainly, at most one backtrack is performed during
the entire algorithm.

```
        // Backtracking algorithm to place the points
        // X[ Left..Right ].
        // X[ 1..Left-1 ] and X[ Right+1..N ]
        // are already tentatively placed.
        // if Place returns True, then X[ Left..Right ] will have values.

        int
        Place( int X[ ], Dist_Set D, unsigned int N, int Left, int Right )
        {
            int D_Max, Found = False;

/* 1*/      if D is Empty then
/* 2*/          return True;
/* 3*/      D_Max = Find_Max( D );

            // Check if setting X[ Right ] = D_Max is feasible.
/* 4*/      if( | X[ j ] - D_Max | ∈ D for all 1≤j<Left and Right<j≤N )
            {
/* 5*/          X[ Right ] = D_Max;          // Try X[ Right ] = D_Max.
/* 6*/          for( 1≤j<Left, Right<j≤N )
/* 7*/              Remove( | X[ j ] - D_Max |, D );
/* 8*/          Found = Place( X, D, N, Left, Right - 1 );

/* 9*/          if ( !Found )      // Backtrack.
/*10*/              for( 1≤j<Left, Right<j≤N ) // Undo the deletion.
/*11*/                  Insert( | X[ j ] - D_Max |, D );
            }

            // If first attempt failed, try to see if setting
            // X[ Left ] = X[ N ] - D_Max is feasible.
/*12*/      if( !Found && ( | X[ N ] - D_Max - X[ j ] | ∈ D
/*13*/              for all 1≤j<Left and Right<j≤N ) )
            {
/*14*/          X[ Left ] = X[ N ] - D_Max;    // Same logic as before.
/*15*/          for( 1≤j<Left, Right<j≤N )
/*16*/              Remove( | X[ N ] - D_Max - X[ j ] |, D );
/*17*/          Found = Place( X, D, N, Left + 1, Right );

/*18*/          if( !Found )    // Backtrack.
/*19*/              for( 1≤j<Left, Right<j≤N )    // Undo the deletion.
/*20*/                  Insert( | X[ N ] - D_Max - X[ j ] |, D );
            }
/*21*/      return Found;
        }
```

Figure 10.65 Turnpike reconstruction algorithm: backtracking steps

10.5.2. Games

As our last application, we will consider the strategy that a computer might use to play a strategic game such as checkers or chess. We will use, as an example, the much simpler game of tic-tac-toe because it makes the points easier to illustrate.

Tic-tac-toe is, of course, a draw if both sides play optimally. By performing a careful case-by-case analysis, it is not a difficult matter to construct an algorithm that never loses and always wins when presented the opportunity. This can be done because certain positions are known traps and can be handled by a lookup table. Other strategies, such as taking the center square when it is available, make the analysis simpler. If this is done, then we can always choose a move based only on the current position by using a table. Of course, this strategy requires the programmer, and not the computer, to do most of the thinking.

Minimax Strategy

The general strategy is to use an evaluation function to quantify the "goodness" of a position. A position that is a win for a computer might get the value of $+1$; a draw could get 0; and a position that the computer has lost would get a -1. A position for which this assignment can be determined by examining the board is known as a *terminal* position.

If a position is not terminal, the value of the position is determined by recursively assuming optimal play by both sides. This is known as a *minimax* strategy because one player (the human) is trying to minimize the value of the position while the other player (the computer) is trying to maximize it.

A *successor position* of P is any position P_s that is reachable from P by playing one move. If the computer is to move when in some position P, it recursively evaluates the value of all the successor positions. The computer chooses the move with the largest value; this is the value of P. To evaluate any successor position P_s, all of P_s's successors are recursively evaluated, and the smallest value is chosen. This smallest value represents the most favorable reply for the human player.

The code in Figure 10.66 makes the computer's strategy more clear. Lines 10 through 14 evaluate immediate wins or draws. If neither of these cases apply, then the position is nonterminal. Recalling that *Value* should contain the maximum of all possible successor positions, line 17 initializes it to the smallest possible value, and the loop in lines 20 through 30 searches for improvements. Each successor position is recursively evaluated in turn by lines 22 through 24. This is recursive, because, as we will see, the function *Find_Human_Move* calls *Find_Comp_Move*. If the human's response to a move leaves the computer with a more favorable position than that obtained with the previously best computer move, then the *Value* and *Best_Move* are updated. Figure 10.67 shows the code for the human's move selection. The logic is virtually identical, except that the human player chooses the move that leads to the lowest-valued position. Indeed, it is not difficult to combine these two procedures into one by passing an extra variable that indicates whose turn it is to move. This does make the code somewhat less readable, so we have stayed with separate routines. An object-oriented approach would certainly make *Board* an object; this is a simple improvement to implement.

```
/* 1*/        // Supporting types.
/* 2*/    enum Value_Type  { Comp_Loss, Draw, Comp_Win };
/* 3*/    enum Player_Type { Comp, Human };
/* 4*/    typedef int Board_Type[ 10 ];

/* 5*/        // Supporting routines.
/* 6*/    int Full_Board( Board_Type B );
/* 7*/    int Immediate_Win( Board_Type B, int & Move, Player_Type P );
/* 8*/    void Place( Board_Type B, int Square, Player_Type P );
/* 9*/    int Is_Empty( Board_Type B, int Square );
/*10*/    void Unplace( Board_Type B, int Square );
/*11*/    void Find_Human_Move( Board_Type & B, int &, int & Value );


/* 1*/    // Recursive procedure to find best move for computer.
/* 2*/    // Best_Move is a number from 1-9 indicating square.
/* 3*/    // Possible evaluations satisfy Comp_Loss < Draw < Comp_Win.
/* 4*/    // Complementary routine Find_Human_Move is in Fig. 10.67.
/* 5*/    // Board_Type is an array; thus Board can be changed by Place( ).

/* 6*/    void
/* 7*/    Find_Comp_Move( Board_Type & Board, int & Best_Move, int & Value )
/* 8*/    {
/* 9*/        int Dc, i, Response;                    // Dc means don't care.

/*10*/        if( Full_Board( Board ) )
/*11*/            Value = Draw;
/*12*/        else
/*13*/        if( Immediate_Win( Board, Best_Move, Comp ) )
/*14*/            Value = Comp_Win;
/*15*/        else
/*16*/        {
/*17*/            Value = Comp_Loss;
/*18*/            for( i = 1; i <= 9; i++ )        // Try each square.
/*19*/            {
/*20*/                if( Is_Empty( Board, i ) )
/*21*/                {
/*22*/                    Place( Board, i, Comp );
/*23*/                    Find_Human_Move( Board, Dc, Response );
/*24*/                    Unplace( Board, i );    // Restore board.

/*25*/                    if( Response > Value )  // Update best move.
/*26*/                    {
/*27*/                        Value = Response;
/*28*/                        Best_Move = i;
/*29*/                    }
/*30*/                }
/*31*/            }
/*32*/        }
/*33*/    }
```

Figure 10.66 Minimax tic-tac-toe algorithm: computer selection

```
/* 1*/    void
/* 2*/    Find_Human_Move( Board_Type & Board, int & Best_Move, int & Value )
/* 3*/    {
/* 4*/        int Dc, i, Response;                // Dc means don't care.

/* 5*/        if( Full_Board( Board ) )
/* 6*/            Value = Draw;
/* 7*/        else
/* 8*/        if( Immediate_Win( Board, Best_Move, Human ) )
/* 9*/            Value = Comp_Loss;
/*10*/        else
/*11*/        {
/*12*/            Value = Comp_Win;
/*13*/            for( i = 1; i <= 9; i++ )        // Try each square.
/*14*/            {
/*15*/                if( Is_Empty( Board, i ) )
/*16*/                {
/*17*/                    Place( Board, i, Human );
/*18*/                    Find_Comp_Move( Board, Dc, Response );
/*19*/                    Unplace( Board, i );    // Restore board.

/*20*/                    if( Response < Value )   // Update best move.
/*21*/                    {
/*22*/                        Value = Response;
/*23*/                        Best_Move = i;
/*24*/                    }
/*25*/                }
/*26*/            }
/*27*/        }
/*28*/    }
```

Figure 10.67   Min-max tic-tac-toe algorithm: human
                    selection

We leave supporting routines as an exercise. The most costly computation is the case in which the computer is asked to pick the opening move. Since at this stage the game is a forced draw, the computer selects square 1.[†] A total of 97,162 positions were examined, and the calculation took 2.5 seconds on a VAX 8800. No attempt was made to optimize the code. When the computer moves second, the number of positions examined is 5,185 if the human selects the center square, 9,761 when a corner square is selected, and 13,233 when a noncorner edge square is selected.

For more complex games, such as checkers and chess, it is obviously infeasible to search all the way to the terminal nodes.[‡] In this case, we have to stop the search

---

[†]We numbered the squares starting from the top left and moving right. However, this is only important for the supporting routines.

[‡]It is estimated that if this search were conducted for chess, at least 10^{100} positions would be examined for the first move. Even if the improvements described later in this section were incorporated, this number could not be reduced to a practical level.

after a certain depth of recursion is reached. The nodes where the recursion is stopped become terminal nodes. These terminal nodes are evaluated with a function that estimates the value of the position. For instance, in a chess program, the evaluation function measures such variables as the relative amount and strength of pieces and positional factors. The evaluation function is crucial for success because the computer's move selection is based on maximizing this function. The best computer chess programs have surprisingly sophisticated evaluation functions.

Nevertheless, for computer chess, the single most important factor seems to be number of moves of look-ahead the program is capable of. This is sometimes known as *ply;* it is equal to the depth of the recursion. To implement this, an extra parameter is given to the search routines.

The basic method to increase the look-ahead factor in game programs is to come up with methods that evaluate fewer nodes without losing any information. One method that we have already seen is to use a table to keep track of all positions that have been evaluated. For instance, in the course of searching for the first move, the program will examine the positions in Figure 10.68. If the values of the positions are saved, the second occurrence of a position need not be recomputed; it essentially becomes a terminal position. The data structure that records this is known as a *transposition table;* it is almost always implemented by hashing. In many cases, this can save considerable computation. For instance, in a chess endgame, in which there are relatively few pieces, the time savings can allow a search to go several levels deeper.

α–β Pruning

Probably the most significant improvement one can obtain in general is known as α–β pruning. Figure 10.69 shows the trace of the recursive calls used to evaluate some hypothetical position in a hypothetical game. This is commonly referred to as a *game tree.* (We have avoided the use of this term until now because it is somewhat misleading: no tree is actually constructed by the algorithm. The game tree is just an abstract concept.) The value of the game tree is 44.

Figure 10.68   Two searches that arrive at identical position

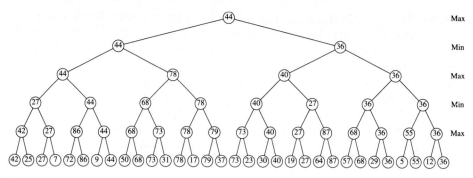

Figure 10.69   A hypothetical game tree

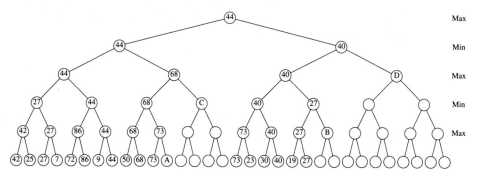

Figure 10.70   A pruned game tree

Figure 10.70 shows the evaluation of the same game tree with several unevaluated nodes. Almost half of the terminal nodes have not been checked. We show that evaluating them would not change the value at the root.

First, consider node *D*. Figure 10.71 shows the information that has been gathered when it is time to evaluate *D*. At this point, we are still in *Find_Human_Move* and are contemplating a call to *Find_Comp_Move* on *D*. However, we already know that *Find_Human_Move* will return at most 40, since it is a *min* node. On the

Figure 10.71   The node marked ? is unimportant

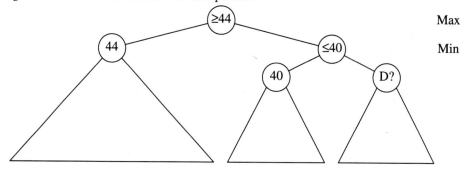

other hand, its *max* node parent has already found a sequence that guarantees 44. Nothing that *D* does can possibly increase this value. Therefore, *D* does not need to be evaluated. This pruning of the tree is known as α pruning. An identical situation occurs at node *B*. To implement α pruning, *Get_Comp_Move* passes its tentative maximum (α) to *Get_Human_Move*. If the tentative minimum of *Get_Human_Move* falls below this value, then *Get_Human_Move* returns immediately.

A similar thing happens at nodes *A* and *C*. This time, we are in the middle of a *Find_Comp_Move* and are about to make a call to *Find_Human_Move* to evaluate *C*. Figure 10.72 shows the situation that is encountered at node *C*. However, the *Find_Human_Move*, at the *min* level, which has called *Find_Comp_Move*, has already determined that it can force a value of at most 44 (recall that low values are good for the human side). Since *Find_Comp_Move* has a tentative maximum of 68, nothing that *C* does will affect the result at the *min* level. Therefore, *C* should not be evaluated. This type of pruning is known as β pruning; it is the symmetric version of α pruning. When both techniques are combined, we have α–β pruning.

Implementing α–β pruning requires surprisingly little code. It is not as difficult as one might think, although many programmers have a very hard time doing it without looking at a reference book. Figure 10.73 shows half of the α–β pruning scheme (minus type declarations); you should have no trouble coding the other half.

To take full advantage of α–β pruning, game programs usually try to apply the evaluation function to nonterminal nodes in an attempt to place the best moves early in the search. The result is even more pruning than one would expect from a random ordering of the nodes. Other techniques, such as searching deeper in more active lines of play, are also employed.

In practice, α–β pruning limits the searching to only $O(\sqrt{n})$ nodes, where n is the size of the full game tree. This is a huge saving and means that searches using α–β pruning can go twice as deep as compared to an unpruned tree. Our tic-tac-toe example is not ideal because there are so many identical values, but even so, the initial search of 97,162 nodes is reduced to 4,493 nodes. (These counts include nonterminal nodes).

In many games, computers are among the best players in the world. The techniques used are very interesting, and can be applied to more serious problems. More details can be found in the references.

Figure 10.72   The node marked ? is unimportant

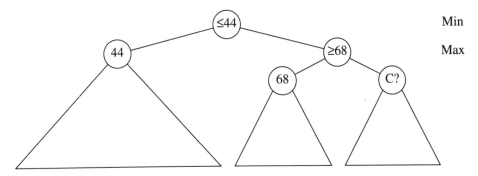

```
/* 1*/     // Same as before, but perform alpha-beta pruning.
/* 2*/     // The main routine should make the call with:
/* 3*/     // Alpha = Comp_Loss, Beta = Comp_Win.

/* 4*/     void
/* 5*/     Find_Comp_Move( Board_Type & Board, int & Best_Move, int & Value,
/* 6*/                                          int Alpha, int Beta )
/* 7*/     {
/* 8*/         int Dc, i, Reply;               // Dc means don't care.

/* 9*/         if( Full_Board( Board ) )
/*10*/             Value = Draw;
/*11*/         else
/*12*/         if( Immediate_Win( Board, Best_Move, Comp ) )
/*13*/             Value = Comp_Win;
/*14*/         else
/*15*/         {
/*16*/             Value = Alpha;
/*17*/             for( i = 1; i <= 9 && Value < Beta; i++ )
/*18*/             {         // Try each square.
/*19*/                 if( Is_Empty( Board, i ) )
/*20*/                 {
/*21*/                     Place( Board, i, Comp );
/*22*/                     Find_Human_Move( Board, Dc, Reply, Value, Beta );
/*23*/                     Unplace( Board, i );        // Restore Board.

/*24*/                     if( Reply > Value )         // Update best move.
/*25*/                     {
/*26*/                         Value = Reply;
/*27*/                         Best_Move = i;
/*28*/                     }
/*29*/                 }
/*30*/             }
/*31*/         }
/*32*/     }
```

Figure 10.73   Min-max tic-tac-toe algorithm with α–β pruning: computer selection

Summary

This chapter illustrates five of the most common techniques found in algorithm design. When confronted with a problem, it is worthwhile to see if any of these methods apply. A proper choice of algorithm, combined with judicious use of data structures, can often lead quickly to efficient solutions.

Exercises

10.1 Show that the greedy algorithm to minimize the mean completion time for multiprocessor job scheduling works.

10.2 The input is a set of jobs $j_1, j_2, \ldots, j_n$, each of which takes one time unit to complete. Each job j_i earns d_i dollars if it is completed by the time limit t_i, but no money if completed after the time limit.

    a. Give an $O(n^2)$ greedy algorithm to solve the problem.

  b. Modify your algorithm to obtain an $O(n \log n)$ time bound. *Hint: The time bound is due entirely to sorting the jobs by money. The rest of the algorithm can be implemented, in $o(n \log n)$ using the disjoint set data structure.*

10.3 A file contains only colons, spaces, newlines, commas, and digits in the following frequency: colon (100), space (605), newline (100), comma (705), 0 (431), 1 (242), 2 (176), 3 (59), 4 (185), 5 (250), 6 (174), 7 (199), 8 (205), 9 (217). Construct the Huffman code.

10.4 Part of the encoded file must be a header indicating the Huffman code. Give a method for constructing the header of size at most $O(n)$ (in addition to the symbols), where n is the number of symbols.

10.5 Complete the proof that Huffman's algorithm generates an optimal prefix code.

10.6 Show that if the symbols are sorted by frequency, Huffman's algorithm can be implemented in linear time.

10.7 Write a program to implement file compression (and uncompression) using Huffman's algorithm.

*10.8 Show that any on-line bin-packing algorithm can be forced to use at least $\frac{3}{2}$ the optimal number of bins by considering the following sequence of items: n items of size $\frac{1}{6} - 2\epsilon$, n items of size $\frac{1}{3} + \epsilon$, n items of size $\frac{1}{2} + \epsilon$.

10.9 Explain how to implement first fit and best fit in $O(n \log n)$ time.

10.10 Show the operation of all of the bin-packing strategies discussed in Section 10.1.3 on the input 0.42, 0.25, 0.27, 0.07, 0.72, 0.86, 0.09, 0.44, 0.50, 0.68, 0.73, 0.31, 0.78, 0.17, 0.79, 0.37, 0.73, 0.23, 0.30.

10.11 Write a program that compares the performance (both in time and number of bins used) of the various bin packing heuristics.

10.12 Prove Theorem 10.7.

10.13 Prove Theorem 10.8.

*10.14 n points are placed in a unit square. Show that the distance between the closest pair is $O(n^{-1/2})$.

*10.15 Argue that for the closest-points algorithm, the average number of points in the strip is $O(\sqrt{n})$. *Hint: Use the result of the previous exercise.*

10.16 Write a program to implement the closest-pair algorithm.

10.17 What is the asymptotic running time of quickselect, using a median-of-median-of-three partitioning strategy?

10.18 Show that quickselect with median-of-median-of-seven partitioning is linear. Why is median-of-median-of-seven partitioning not used in the proof?

10.19 Implement the quickselect algorithm in Chapter 7, quickselect using median-of-median-of-five partitioning, and the sampling algorithm at the end of Section 10.2.3. Compare the running times.

10.20 Much of the information used to compute the median-of-median-of-five is thrown away. Show how the number of comparisons can be reduced by more careful use of the information.

*10.21 Complete the analysis of the sampling algorithm described at the end of Section 10.2.3, and explain how the values of δ and s are chosen.

10.22 Show how the recursive multiplication algorithm computes xy, where $x = 1234$ and $y = 4321$. Include all recursive computations.

10.23 Show how to multiply two complex numbers $x = a + bi$ and $y = c + di$ using only three multiplications.

10.24 a. Show that
$$x_l y_r + x_r y_l = (x_l + x_r)(y_l + y_r) - x_l y_l - x_r y_r$$
  b. This gives an $O(n^{1.59})$ algorithm to multiply n-bit numbers. Compare this method to the solution in the text.

10.25 *a. Show how to multiply two numbers by solving five problems that are roughly one-third of the original size.

  **b. Generalize this problem to obtain an $O(n^{1+\epsilon})$ algorithm for any constant $\epsilon > 0$.

  c. Is the algorithm in part (b) better than $O(n \log n)$?

10.26 Why is it important that Strassen's algorithm does not use commutativity in the multiplication of two 2×2 matrices?

10.27 Two 70×70 matrices can be multiplied using 143,640 multiplications. Show how this can be used to improve the bound given by Strassen's algorithm.

10.28 What is the optimal way to compute $A_1 A_2 A_3 A_4 A_5 A_6$, where the dimensions of the matrices are: $A_1 : 10 \times 20$, $A_2 : 20 \times 1$, $A_3 : 1 \times 40$, $A_4 : 40 \times 5$, $A_5 : 5 \times 30$, $A_6 : 30 \times 15$?

10.29 Show that none of the following greedy algorithms for chained matrix multiplication work. At each step

  a. Compute the cheapest multiplication.

  b. Compute the most expensive multiplication.

  c. Compute the multiplication between the two matrices M_i and M_{i+1}, such that the number of columns in M_i is minimized (breaking ties by one of the rules above).

10.30 Write a program to compute the best ordering of matrix multiplication. Include the routine to print out the actual ordering.

10.31 Show the optimal binary search tree for the following words, where the frequency of occurrence is in parentheses: a (0.18), and (0.19), I (0.23), it (0.21), or (0.19).

*10.32 Extend the optimal binary search tree algorithm to allow for unsuccessful searches. In this case, q_j, for $1 \leq j < n$, is the probability that a search is performed for any word W satisfying $w_j < W < w_{j+1}$. q_0 is the probability of performing a search for $W < w_1$, and q_n is the probability of performing a search for $W > w_n$. Notice that $\sum_{i=1}^{n} p_i + \sum_{j=0}^{n} q_j = 1$.

*10.33 Suppose $C_{i,i} = 0$ and that otherwise

$$C_{i,j} = W_{i,j} + \min_{i < k \leq j}(C_{i,k-1} + C_{k,j})$$

Suppose that W satisfies the *quadrangle inequality*, namely, for all $i \leq i' \leq j \leq j'$,

$$W_{i,j} + W_{i',j'} \leq W_{i',j} + W_{i,j'}$$

Suppose further, that W is *monotone*: If $i \leq i'$ and $j \leq j'$, then $W_{i,j} \leq W_{i',j'}$.

   a. Prove that C satisfies the quadrangle inequality.
   b. Let $R_{i,j}$ be the largest k that achieves the minimum $C_{i,k-1} + C_{k,j}$. (That is, in case of ties, choose the largest k). Prove that

$$R_{i,j} \leq R_{i,j+1} \leq R_{i+1,j+1}$$

   c. Show that R is nondecreasing along each row and column.
   d. Use this to show that all entries in C can be computed in $O(n^2)$ time.
   e. Which of the dynamic programming algorithms can be solved in $O(n^2)$ using these techniques?

10.34 Write a routine to reconstruct the shortest paths from the algorithm in Section 10.3.4.

10.35 Examine the random number generator on your system. How random is it?

10.36 Write the routines to perform insertion, deletion, and searching in skip lists.

10.37 Give a formal proof that the expected time for the skip list operations is $O(\log n)$.

10.38 Figure 10.74 shows a routine to flip a coin, assuming that *Rand* returns an integer (which is prevalent in many systems). What is the expected performance of the skip list algorithms if the random number generator uses a modulus of the form $m = 2^b$ (which is unfortunately prevalent on many systems)?

10.39 a. Use the exponentiation algorithm to prove that $2^{340} \equiv 1(\mod 341)$.
       b. Show how the randomized primality test works for $n = 561$ with several choices of a.

10.40 Implement the turnpike reconstruction algorithm.

```
/* 1*/    enum Coin_Side { Heads, Tails };

/* 2*/    Coin_Side
/* 3*/    Flip( )
/* 4*/    {
/* 5*/        if( ( Rand( ) % 2 ) == 0 )
/* 6*/            return Heads;
/* 7*/        else
/* 8*/            return Tails;
/* 9*/    }
```

Figure 10.74   Questionable coin flipper

10.41 Two point sets are *homometric* if they yield the same distance set and are not rotations of each other. The following distance set gives two distinct point sets: 1, 2, 3, 4, 5, 6, 7, 8, 9, 10, 11, 12, 13, 16, 17. Find the two point sets.

10.42 Extend the reconstruction algorithm to find *all* homometric point sets given a distance set.

10.43 Show the result of $\alpha-\beta$ pruning the tree in Figure 10.75.

10.44   a. Does the code in Figure 10.73 implement α pruning or β pruning?

   b. Implement the complementary routine.

10.45 Write the remaining procedures for tic-tac-toe.

10.46 The *one-dimensional circle packing problem* is as follows: You have n circles of radii $r_1, r_2, \ldots, r_n$. These circles are packed in a box such that each circle is tangent to the bottom of the box and are arranged in the original order. The problem is to find the width of the minimum-sized box. Figure 10.76 shows an example with circles of radii 2, 1, 2, respectively. The minimum-sized box has width $4 + 4\sqrt{2}$.

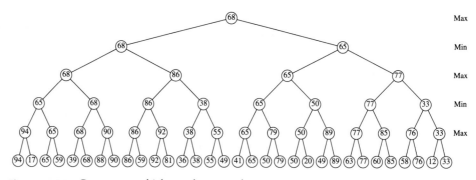

Figure 10.75   Game tree, which can be pruned

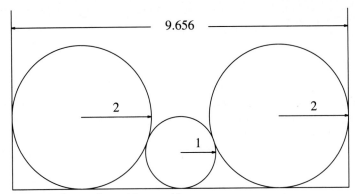

Figure 10.76 Sample for circle packing problem

*10.47 Suppose that the edges in an undirected graph G satisfy the triangle inequality: $c_{u,v} + c_{v,w} \geq c_{u,w}$. Show how to compute a traveling salesman tour of cost at most twice optimal. *Hint: Construct a minimum spanning tree.*

*10.48 You are a tournament director and need to arrange a round robin tournament among $n = 2^k$ players. In this tournament, everyone plays exactly one game each day; after $n - 1$ days, a match has occurred between every pair of players. Give an algorithm to do this.

10.49 *a. Prove that in a round robin tournament it is always possible to arrange the players in an order $p_{i_1}, p_{i_2}, \ldots, p_{i_n}$ such that for all $1 \leq j < n$, p_{i_j} has won the match against $p_{i_{j+1}}$.

    b. Give an $O(n \log n)$ algorithm to find one such arrangement. Your algorithm may serve as a proof for part (a).

*10.50 We are given a set $P = p_1, p_2, \ldots, p_n$ of n points in a plane. A *Voronoi diagram* is a partition of the plane into n regions R_i such that all points in R_i are closer to p_i than any other point in P. Figure 10.77 shows a sample

Figure 10.77 Voronoi diagram

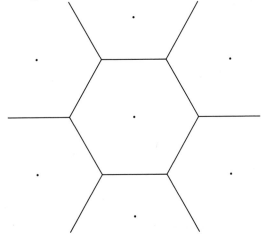

Voronoi diagram for seven (nicely arranged) points. Give an $O(n \log n)$ algorithm to construct the Voronoi diagram.

*10.51 A *convex polygon* is a polygon with the property that any line segment whose endpoints are on the polygon lies entirely within the polygon. The *convex hull* problem consists of finding the smallest (area) convex polygon that encloses a set of points in the plane. Figure 10.78 shows the convex hull for a set of 40 points. Give an $O(n \log n)$ algorithm to find the convex hull.

*10.52 Consider the problem of right-justifying a paragraph. The paragraph contains a sequence of words $w_1, w_2, \ldots, w_n$ of length $a_1, a_2, \ldots, a_n$, which we wish to break into lines of length L. Words are separated by blanks whose ideal length is b (millimeters), but blanks can stretch or shrink as necessary (but must be >0), so that a line $w_i w_{i+1} \ldots w_j$ has length exactly L. However, for each blank b' we charge $|b' - b|$ *ugliness points*. The exception to this is the last line, for which we charge only if $b' < b$ (in other words, we charge only for shrinking), since the last line does not need to be justified. Thus, if b_i is the length of the blank between a_i and a_{i+1}, then the *ugliness* of setting any line (but the last) $w_i w_{i+1} \ldots w_j$ for $j > i$ is $\sum_{k=i}^{j-1}|b_k - b| = (j - i)|b' - b|$, where b' is the average size of a blank on this line. This is true of the last line only if $b' < b$, otherwise the last line is not ugly at all.

   a. Give a dynamic programming algorithm to find the least ugly setting of $w_1, w_2, \ldots, w_n$ into lines of length L. *Hint: For $i = n, n - 1, \ldots, 1$, compute the best way to set $w_i, w_{i+1}, \ldots, w_n$.*

   b. Give the time and space complexities for your algorithm (as a function of the number of words, n).

   c. Consider the special case in which we are using a line printer instead of a laser printer, and assume the optimal value of b is 1 (space). In this case, no shrinking of blanks is allowed since the next smallest blank space would be 0. Give a linear-time algorithm to generate the least ugly setting on a line printer.

*10.53 The *longest increasing subsequence* problem is as follows: Given numbers $a_1, a_2, \ldots, a_n$, find the maximum value of k such that $a_{i_1} < a_{i_2} < \cdots < a_{i_k}$,

Figure 10.78 Example of a convex hull

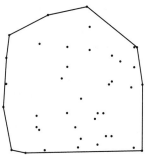

and $i_1 < i_2 < \cdots < i_k$. As an example, if the input is 3, 1, 4, 1, 5, 9, 2, 6, 5, the maximum increasing subsequence has length four (1, 4, 5, 9 among others). Give an $O(n^2)$ algorithm to solve the longest increasing subsequence problem.

*10.54 The *longest common subsequence* problem is as follows: Given two sequences $A = a_1, a_2, \ldots, a_m$, and $B = b_1, b_2, \ldots, b_n$, find the length, k, of the longest sequence $C = c_1, c_2, \ldots, c_k$ such that C is a subsequence of both A and B. As an example, if

$$A = \text{d, y, n, a, m, i, c}$$

and

$$B = \text{p, r, o, g, r, a, m, m, i, n, g,}$$

then the longest common subsequence is a,m and has length 2. Give an algorithm to solve the longest common subsequence problem. Your algorithm should run in $O(mn)$ time.

*10.55 The *pattern matching problem* is as follows: Given a string S of text and a pattern P, find the first occurrence of P in S. *Approximate pattern matching* allows k mismatches of three types:

1. A character can be in S that is not in P.
2. A character can be in P that is not in S.
3. P and S can differ in a position.

As an example, if we are searching for the pattern "textbook" with at most three mismatches in the string "data structures txtborkk", we find a match (insert an e, change an r to an o, delete a k). Give an $O(mn)$ algorithm to solve the approximate string matching problem, where $m = |P|$ and $n = |S|$.

*10.56 One form of the *knapsack problem* is as follows: We are given a set of integers $A = \{a_1, a_2, \ldots, a_n\}$ and an integer K. Is there a subset of A whose sum is exactly K?

a. Give an algorithm that solves the knapsack problem in $O(nK)$ time.

b. Why does this not show that $P = NP$?

*10.57 You are given a currency system with coins of (decreasing) value $c_1, c_2, \ldots, c_n$ cents.

a. Give an algorithm that computes the minimum number of coins required to give K cents in change.

b. Give an algorithm that computes the number of different ways to give K cents in change.

*10.58 Consider the problem of placing eight queens on an (eight by eight) chess board. Two queens are said to attack each other if they are on the same row, column, or (not necessarily main) diagonal.

a. Give a randomized algorithm to place eight nonattacking queens on the board.

```
distance
shortest( s, t, G )
{
    distance d_t , Tmp;

    if( s == t )
        return 0;

    d_t = ∞ ;
    for each vertex v adjacent to s
    {
        Tmp = shortest( v, t, G );
        if( c_{s,v} + Tmp < d_t )
                d_t = c_{s,v} + Tmp;
    }
    return d_t ;
}
```

Figure 10.79   Recursive shortest path algorithm

b. Give a backtracking algorithm to solve the same problem.

c. Implement both algorithms and compare the running time.

*10.59 In the game of chess, a knight in row r and column c may move to row $1 \le r' \le B$ and column $1 \le c' \le B$ (where B is the size of the board) provided that either

$$|r - r'| = 2 \text{ and } |c - c'| = 1$$

or

$$|r - r'| = 1 \text{ and } |c - c'| = 2$$

A *knight's tour* is a sequence of moves that visits all squares exactly once before returning to the starting point.

a. If B is odd, show that a knight's tour cannot exist.

b. Give a backtracking algorithm to find a knight's tour.

10.60 Consider the recursive algorithm in Figure 10.79 for finding the shortest weighted path in an acyclic graph from s to t.

a. Why does this algorithm not work for general graphs?

b. Prove that this algorithm terminates for acyclic graphs.

c. What is the worst-case running time of the algorithm?

References

The original paper on Huffman codes is [20]. Variations on the algorithm are discussed in [28], [30], and [31]. Another popular compression scheme is Ziv–

Lempel encoding [51], [52]. Here the codes have a fixed length but represent strings instead of characters. [3] and [33] are good surveys of the common compression schemes.

The analysis of bin-packing heuristics first appeared in Johnson's Ph.D. thesis and was published in [21]. The improved lower bound for on-line bin packing given in Exercise 10.8 is from [49]; this result has been improved further in [34]. [43] describes another approach to on-line bin packing.

Theorem 10.7 is from [6]. The closest points algorithm appeared in [44]. [46] describes the turnpike reconstruction problem and its applications. Two books on the relatively new field of computational geometry are [13] and [39]. [2] contains the lecture notes for a computational geometry course taught at MIT; it includes an extensive bibliography.

The linear-time selection algorithm appeared in [8]. [16] discusses the sampling approach that finds the median in $1.5n$ expected comparisons. The $O(n^{1.59})$ multiplication is from [22]. Generalizations are discussed in [9] and [23]. Strassen's algorithm appears in the short paper [47]. The paper states the results and not much else. Pan [37] gives several divide and conquer algorithms, including the one in Exercise 10.27. The best known bound is $O(n^{2.376})$, which is due to Coppersmith and Winograd [12].

The classic references on dynamic programming are the books [4] and [5]. The matrix ordering problem was first studied in [18]. It was shown in [19] that the problem can be solved in $O(n \log n)$ time.

An $O(n^2)$ algorithm was provided for the construction of optimal binary search trees by Knuth [24]. The all-pairs shortest-path algorithm is from Floyd [15]. A theoretically better $O(n^3 (\log \log n / \log n)^{1/3})$ algorithm is given by Fredman [17], but not surprisingly, it is not practical. Under certain conditions, the running time of dynamic programs can automatically be improved by a factor of n or more. This is discussed in Exercise 10.33, [14], and [50].

The discussion of random number generators is based on [38]. Park and Miller attribute the portable implementation to Schrage [45]. Skip lists are discussed by Pugh in [40]. The randomized primality-testing algorithm is due to Miller [35] and Rabin [42]. The theorem that at most $(n - 9)/4$ values of a fool the algorithm is from Monier [36]. Other randomized algorithms are discussed in [41].

More information on α–β pruning can be found in [1], [25], and [26]. The top programs that play chess, checkers, Othello, and backgammon have all achieved world class status. [32] describes an Othello program. The paper appears in a special issue on computer games (mostly chess); this issue is a gold mine of ideas. One of the papers describes the use of dynamic programming to solve chess endgames completely when only a few pieces are left on the board. Related research has resulted in the change of the 50-move rule in certain cases.

Exercise 10.41 is solved in [7]. It is the minimal case of a homometric point set with no duplicate distances. Determining whether any others exist for $n > 6$ is open. Christofides [11] gives a solution to Exercise 10.47 and also an algorithm that generates a tour at most $\frac{3}{2}$ optimal. Exercise 10.52 is discussed in [27]. Exercise 10.55 is solved in [48]. An $O(kn)$ algorithm is given in [29]. Exercise 10.57 is discussed in [10], but do not be misled by the title of the paper.

1. B. Abramson, "Control Strategies for Two-Player Games," *ACM Computing Surveys,* 21 (1989), 137–161.

2. A. Aggarwal and J. Wein, *Computational Geometry: Lecture Notes for 18.409,* MIT Laboratory for Computer Science, 1988.

3. T. Bell, I. H. Witten, and J. G. Cleary, "Modeling for Text Compression," *ACM Computing Surveys,* 21 (1989), 557–591.

4. R. E. Bellman, *Dynamic Programming,* Princeton University Press, Princeton, NJ, 1957.

5. R. E. Bellman and S. E. Dreyfus, *Applied Dynamic Programming,* Princeton University Press, Princeton, N.J., 1962.

6. J. L. Bentley, D. Haken, and J. B. Saxe, "A General Method for Solving Divide-and-Conquer Recurrences," *SIGACT News,* 12 (1980), 36–44.

7. G. S. Bloom, "A Counterexample to the Theorem of Piccard," *Journal of Combinatorial Theory A* (1977), 378–379.

8. M. Blum, R. W. Floyd, V. R. Pratt, R. L. Rivest, and R. E. Tarjan, "Time Bounds for Selection," *Journal of Computer and System Sciences* 7 (1973), 448–461.

9. A. Borodin and J. I. Munro, *The Computational Complexity of Algebraic and Numerical Problems,* American Elsevier, New York, 1975.

10. L. Chang and J. Korsh, "Canonical Coin Changing and Greedy Solutions," *Journal of the ACM* 23 (1976), 418–422.

11. N. Christofides, "Worst-case Analysis of a New Heuristic for the Traveling Salesman Problem," *Management Science Research Report #388,* Carnegie-Mellon University, Pittsburgh, Penna., 1976.

12. D. Coppersmith and S. Winograd, "Matrix Multiplication via Arithmetic Progressions," *Proceedings of the Nineteenth Annual ACM Symposium of the Theory of Computing* (1987), 1–6.

13. H. Edelsbrunner, *Algorithms in Combinatorial Geometry,* Springer-Verlag, Berlin, 1987.

14. D. Eppstein, Z. Galil, R. Giancarlo, "Speeding up Dynamic Programming," *Proceedings of the Twenty-ninth Annual IEEE Symposium on the Foundations of Computer Science,* (1988), 488–495.

15. R. W. Floyd, "Algorithm 97: Shortest Path," *Communications of the ACM* 5 (1962), 345.

16. R. W. Floyd and R. L. Rivest, "Expected Time Bounds for Selection," *Communications of the ACM* 18 (1975), 165–172.

17. M. L. Fredman, "New Bounds on the Complexity of the Shortest Path Problem," *SIAM Journal on Computing* 5 (1976), 83–89.

18. S. Godbole, "On Efficient Computation of Matrix Chain Products," *IEEE Transactions on Computers* 9 (1973), 864–866.

19. T. C. Hu and M. R. Shing, "Computations of Matrix Chain Products, Part I," *SIAM Journal on Computing* 11 (1982), 362–373.

20. D. A. Huffman, "A Method for the Construction of Minimum Redundancy Codes," *Proceedings of the IRE* 40 (1952), 1098–1101.

21. D. S. Johnson, A. Demers, J. D. Ullman, M. R. Garey, and R. L. Graham, "Worst-case Performance Bounds for Simple One-Dimensional Packing Algorithms," *SIAM Journal on Computing,* 3 (1974), 299–325.

22. A. Karatsuba and Y. Ofman, "Multiplication of Multi-digit Numbers on Automata," *Doklady Akademii Nauk SSSR* 145 (1962), 293–294.

23. D. E. Knuth, *The Art of Computer Programming, Vol 2: Seminumerical Algorithms,* second edition, Addison-Wesley, Reading, Mass., 1981.

24. D. E. Knuth, "Optimum Binary Search Trees," *Acta Informatica* 1 (1971), 14–25.

25. D. E. Knuth and R. W. Moore, "Estimating the Efficiency of Backtrack Programs," *Mathematics of Computation* 29, (1975) 121–136.

26. D. E. Knuth, "An Analysis of Alpha-Beta Cutoffs," *Artificial Intelligence* 6 (1975), 293–326.

27. D. E. Knuth, *TEX and Metafont, New Directions in Typesetting,* Digital Press, Bedford, Mass., 1981.

28. D. E. Knuth, "Dynamic Huffman Coding," *Journal of Algorithms* 6 (1985), 163–180.

29. G. M. Landau and U. Vishkin, "Introducing Efficient Parallelism into Approximate String Matching and a New Serial Algorithm," *Proceedings of the Eighteenth Annual ACM Symposium on Theory of Computing* (1986), 220–230.

30. L. L. Larmore, "Height-Restricted Optimal Binary Trees," *SIAM Journal on Computing* 16 (1987), 1115–1123.

31. L. L. Larmore and D. S. Hirschberg, "A Fast Algorithm for Optimal Length-Limited Huffman Codes," *Journal of the ACM* 37 (1990), 464–473.

32. K. Lee and S. Mahajan, "The Development of a World Class Othello Program," *Artificial Intelligence* 43 (1990), 21–36.

33. D. A. Lelewer and D. S. Hirschberg, "Data Compression," *ACM Computing Surveys* 19 (1987), 261–296.

34. F. M. Liang, "A Lower Bound for On-line Bin Packing," *Information Processing Letters* 10 (1980), 76–79.

35. G. L. Miller, "Riemann's Hypothesis and Tests for Primality," *Journal of Computer and System Sciences* 13 (1976), 300–317.

36. L. Monier, "Evaluation and Comparison of Two Efficient Probabilistic Primality Testing Algorithms," *Theoretical Computer Science* 12 (1980), 97–108.

37. V. Pan, "Strassen's Algorithm is Not Optimal," *Proceedings of the Nineteenth Annual IEEE Symposium on the Foundations of Computer Science* (1978), 166–176.

38. S. K. Park and K. W. Miller, "Random Number Generators: Good Ones are Hard To Find," *Communications of the ACM* 31 (1988), 1192–1201.

39. F. P. Preparata and M. I. Shamos, *Computational Geometry: An Introduction,* Springer-Verlag, New York, 1985.

40. W. Pugh, "Skip Lists: A Probabilistic Alternative to Balanced Trees," *Communications of the ACM* 33 (1990), 668–676.

41. M. O. Rabin, "Probabilistic Algorithms," in *Algorithms and Complexity, Recent Results and New Directions* (J. F. Traub, ed.), Academic Press, New York, 1976, 21–39.

42. M. O. Rabin, "Probabilistic Algorithms for Testing Primality," *Journal of Number Theory,* 12 (1980), 128–138.

43. P. Ramanan, D. J. Brown, C. C. Lee, and D. T. Lee, "On-line Bin Packing in Linear Time," *Journal of Algorithms* 10 (1989), 305–326.

44. M. I. Shamos and D. Hoey, "Closest-Point Problems," *Proceedings of the Sixteenth Annual IEEE Symposium on the Foundations of Computer Science* (1975), 151–162.

45. L. Schrage, "A More Portable FORTRAN Random Number Generator," *ACM Transactions on Mathematics Software* 5 (1979), 132–138.

46. S. S. Skiena, W. D. Smith, and P. Lemke, "Reconstructing Sets From Interpoint Distances," *Proceeding of the Sixth Annual ACM Symposium on Computational Geometry* (1990), 332–339.

47. V. Strassen, "Gaussian Elimination is Not Optimal," *Numerische Mathematik* 13 (1969), 354–356.

48. R. A. Wagner and M. J. Fischer, "The String-to-String Correction Problem," *Journal of the ACM* 21 (1974), 168–173.

49. A. C. Yao, "New Algorithms for Bin Packing," *Journal of the ACM* 27 (1980), 207–227.

50. F. F. Yao, "Efficient Dynamic Programming Using Quadrangle Inequalities," *Proceedings of the Twelfth Annual ACM Symposium on the Theory of Computing* (1980), 429–435.
51. J. Ziv and A. Lempel, "A Universal Algorithm for Sequential Data Compression," *IEEE Transactions on Information Theory* IT23 (1977), 337–343.
52. J. Ziv and A. Lempel, "Compression of Individual Sequences via Variable-rate Coding," *IEEE Transactions on Information Theory* IT24 (1978), 530–536.

CHAPTER 11

Amortized Analysis

In this chapter, we will analyze the running time for several of the advanced data structures that have been presented in Chapters 4 and 6. In particular, we will consider the worst-case running time for any sequence of m operations. This contrasts with the more typical analysis, in which a worst-case bound is given for any *single* operation.

As an example, we have seen that AVL trees support the standard tree operations in $O(\log n)$ worst-case time per operation. AVL trees are somewhat complicated to implement, not only because there are a host of cases, but also because height balance information must be maintained and updated correctly. The reason that AVL trees are used is that a sequence of $\Theta(n)$ operations on an unbalanced search tree could require $\Theta(n^2)$ time, which would be expensive. For search trees, the $O(n)$ worst-case running time of an operation is not the real problem. The major problem is that this could happen repeatedly. Splay trees offer a pleasant alternative. Although any operation can still require $\Theta(n)$ time, this degenerate behavior cannot occur repeatedly, and we can prove that any sequence of m operations takes $O(m \log n)$ worst-case time (total). Thus, in the long run this data structure behaves as though each operation takes $O(\log n)$. We call this an *amortized time bound*.

Amortized bounds are weaker than the corresponding worst-case bounds because there is no guarantee for any single operation. Since this is generally not important, we are willing to sacrifice the bound on a single operation if we can retain the same bound for the sequence of operations and at the same time simplify the data structure. Amortized bounds are stronger than the equivalent average-case bound. For instance, binary search trees have $O(\log n)$ average time per operation, but it is still possible for a sequence of m operations to take $O(mn)$ time.

Because deriving an amortized bound requires us to look at an entire sequence of operations instead of just one, we expect that the analysis will be more tricky. We will see that this expectation is generally realized.

In this chapter we shall

- Analyze the binomial queue operations.
- Analyze skew heaps.
- Introduce and analyze the Fibonacci heap.
- Analyze splay trees.

11.1.   An Unrelated Puzzle

Consider the following puzzle: Two kittens are placed on opposite ends of a football field, 100 yards apart. They walk toward each other at the speed of ten yards per minute. At the same time, their mother is at one end of the field. She can run at 100 yards per minute. The mother runs from one kitten to the other, making turns with no loss of speed, until the kittens (and thus the mother) meet at midfield. How far does the mother run?

It is not hard to solve this puzzle with a brute force calculation. We leave the details to you, but one expects that this calculation will involve computing the sum of an infinite geometric series. Although this straightforward calculation will lead to an answer, it turns out that a much simpler solution can be arrived at by introducing an extra variable, namely, time.

Because the kittens are 100 yards apart and approach each other at a combined velocity of 20 yards per minute, it takes them five minutes to get to midfield. Since the mother runs 100 yards per minute, her total is 500 yards.

This puzzle illustrates the point that sometimes it is easier to solve a problem indirectly than directly. The amortized analyses that we will perform will use this idea. We will introduce an extra variable, known as the *potential*, to allow us to prove results that seem very difficult to establish otherwise.

11.2.   Binomial Queues

The first data structure we will look at is the binomial queue of Chapter 6, which we now review briefly. Recall that a *binomial tree* B_0 is a one-node tree, and for $k > 0$, the binomial tree B_k is built by melding two binomial trees B_{k-1} together. Binomial trees B_0 through B_4 are shown in Figure 11.1.

The *rank* of a node in a binomial tree is equal to the number of children; in particular, the rank of the root of B_k is k. A *binomial queue* is a collection of heap-ordered binomial trees in which there can be at most one binomial tree B_k for any k. Two binomial queues, H_1 and H_2, are shown in Figure 11.2.

The most important operation is *Merge*. To merge two binomial queues, an operation similar to addition of binary integers is performed: At any stage we may have zero, one, two, or possibly three B_k trees, depending on whether or not the two priority queues contain a B_k tree and whether or not a B_k tree is carried over from the previous step. If there is zero or one B_k tree, it is placed as a tree in the resultant binomial queue. If there are two B_k trees, they are melded into a B_{k+1} tree and carried over; if there are three B_k trees, one is placed as a tree in the binomial queue, and the other two are melded and carried over. The result of merging H_1 and H_2 is shown in Figure 11.3.

Insertion is performed by creating a one-node binomial queue and performing a *Merge*. The time to do this is $m + 1$, where m represents the smallest type of binomial tree B_m not present in the binomial queue. Thus, insertion into a binomial queue that has a B_0 tree but no B_1 tree requires two steps. Deletion of the minimum is

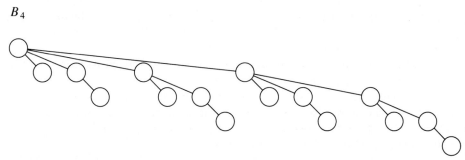

Figure 11.1 Binomial trees B_0, B_1, B_2, B_3, and B_4

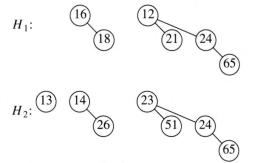

Figure 11.2 Two binomial queues H_1 and H_2

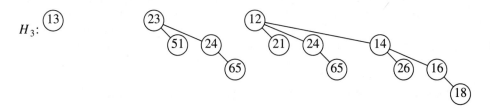

Figure 11.3 Binomial queue H_3: the result of merging H_1 and H_2

accomplished by removing the minimum and splitting the original binomial queue into two binomial queues, which are then merged. A less terse explanation of these operations is given in Chapter 6.

We consider a very simple problem first. Suppose we want to build a binomial queue of n elements. We know that building a binary heap of n elements can be done in $O(n)$, so we expect a similar bound for binomial queues.

CLAIM:

A binomial queue of n elements can be built by n successive insertions in $O(n)$ time.

The claim, if true, would give an extremely simple algorithm. Since the worst-case time for each insertion is $O(\log n)$, it is not obvious that the claim is true. Recall that if this algorithm were applied to binary heaps, the running time would be $O(n \log n)$.

To prove the claim, we could do a direct calculation. To measure the running time, we define the cost of each insertion to be one time unit plus an extra unit for each linking step. Summing this cost over all insertions gives the total running time. This total is n units plus the total number of linking steps. The 1st, 3rd, 5th, and all odd-numbered steps require no linking steps, since there is no B_0 present at the time of insertion. Thus, half of the insertions require no linking steps. A quarter of the insertions require only one linking step (2nd, 6th, 10th, and so on). An eighth require two, and so on. We could add this all up and bound the number of linking steps by n, proving the claim. This brute force calculation will not help when we try to analyze a sequence of operations that include more than just insertions, so we will use another approach to prove this result.

Consider the result of an insertion. If there is no B_0 tree present at the time of the insertion, then the insertion costs a total of one unit, by using the same accounting as above. The result of the insertion is that there is now a B_0 tree, and thus, we have added one tree to the forest of binomial trees. If there is a B_0 tree but no B_1 tree, then the insertion costs two units. The new forest will have a B_1 tree but will no longer have a B_0 tree, so the number of trees in the forest is unchanged. An insertion that costs three units will create a B_2 tree but destroy a B_0 and B_1 tree, yielding a net loss of one tree in the forest. In fact, it is easy to see, in general, that an insertion that costs c units results in a net increase of $2 - c$ trees in the forest because a B_{c-1} tree is created, but all B_i trees $0 \le i < c - 1$ are removed. Thus, expensive insertions remove trees, while cheap insertions create trees.

Let C_i be the cost of the ith insertion. Let T_i be the number of trees *after* the ith insertion. $T_0 = 0$ is the number of trees initially. Then we have the invariant

$$C_i + (T_i - T_{i-1}) = 2 \qquad (11.1)$$

We then have

$$C_1 + (T_1 - T_0) = 2$$

$$C_2 + (T_2 - T_1) = 2$$

$$\vdots$$

$$C_{n-1} + (T_{n-1} - T_{n-2}) = 2$$

$$C_n + (T_n - T_{n-1}) = 2$$

If we add all these equations, most of the T_i terms cancel, leaving

$$\sum_{i=1}^{n} C_i + T_n - T_0 = 2n$$

or equivalently,

$$\sum_{i=1}^{n} C_i = 2n - (T_n - T_0)$$

Recall that $T_0 = 0$ and T_n, the number of trees after the n insertions, is certainly not negative, so $(T_n - T_0)$ is not negative. Thus

$$\sum_{i=1}^{n} C_i \leq 2n$$

which proves the claim.

During the *Build_Binomial_Queue* routine, each insertion had a worst-case time of $O(\log n)$, but since the entire routine used at most $2n$ units of time, the insertions behaved as though each used no more than 2 units each.

This example illustrates the general technique we will use. The state of the data structure at any time is given by a function known as the *potential*. The potential function is not maintained by the program, but rather is an accounting device that will help with the analysis. When operations take less time than we have allocated for them, the unused time is "saved" in the form of a higher potential. In our example, the potential of the data structure is simply the number of trees. In the analysis above, when we have insertions that use only one unit instead of the two units that are allocated, the extra unit is saved for later by an increase in potential. When operations occur that exceed the allotted time, then the excess time is accounted for by a decrease in potential. One may view the potential as representing a savings account. If an operation uses less than its allotted time, the difference is saved for use later on by more expensive operations. Figure 11.4 shows the cumulative running time used by *Build_Binomial_Queue* over a sequence of insertions. Observe that the running time never exceeds $2n$ and that the potential in the binomial queue after any insertion measures the amount of savings.

Once a potential function is chosen, we write the main equation:

$$T_{\text{actual}} + \Delta Potential = T_{\text{amortized}} \tag{11.2}$$

T_{actual}, the *actual time* of an operation, represents the exact (observed) amount of time required to execute a particular operation. In a binary search tree, for example, the actual time to perform a *Find(x)* is 1 plus the depth of the node containing x. If we sum the basic equation over the entire sequence and the final potential is at least as large as the initial potential, then the amortized time is an upper bound on

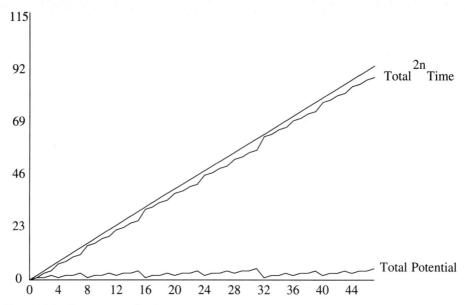

Figure 11.4   A sequence of n *Insert*s

the actual time used during the execution of the sequence. Notice that while T_{actual} varies from operation to operation, $T_{amortized}$ is stable.

Picking a potential function that proves a meaningful bound is a very tricky task; there is no one method that is used. Generally, many potential functions are tried before the one that works is found. Nevertheless, the discussion above suggests a few rules that tell us the properties that good potential functions have. The potential function should

- Always assume its minimum at the start of the sequence. A popular method of choosing potential functions is to ensure that the potential function is initially 0 and always nonnegative. All of the examples that we will encounter use this strategy.
- Cancel a term in the actual time. In our case, if the actual cost was c, then the potential change was $2 - c$. When these add, an amortized cost of 2 is obtained. This is shown in Figure 11.5.

We can now perform a complete analysis of binomial queue operations.

THEOREM 11.1.

The amortized running times of Insert, Delete_Min, and Merge are $O(1)$, $O(\log n)$, *and* $O(\log n)$, *respectively, for binomial queues.*

PROOF:

The potential function is the number of trees. The initial potential is 0, and the potential is always nonnegative, so the amortized time is an upper bound on the actual time. The analysis for *Insert* follows from the argument above. For *Merge*, assume the two trees have n_1 and n_2 nodes with T_1 and T_2 trees, respectively. Let $n = n_1 + n_2$. The actual time to perform the merge is

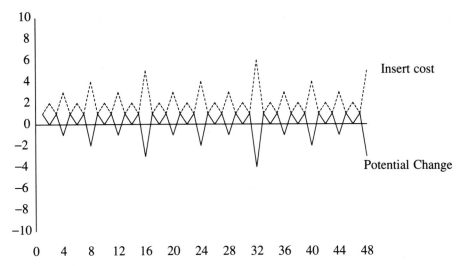

Figure 11.5 The insertion cost and potential change for each operation in a sequence

$O(\log(n_1) + \log(n_2)) = O(\log n)$. After the merge, there can be at most $\log n$ trees, so the potential can increase by at most $O(\log n)$. This gives an amortized bound of $O(\log n)$. The *Delete_Min* bound follows in a similar manner.

11.3. Skew Heaps

The analysis of binomial queues is a fairly easy example of an amortized analysis. We now look at skew heaps. As is common with many of our examples, once the right potential function is found, the analysis is easy. The difficult part is choosing a meaningful potential function.

Recall that for skew heaps, the key operation is merging. To merge two skew heaps, we merge their right paths and make this the new left path. For each node on the new path, except the last, the old left subtree is attached as the right subtree. The last node on the new left path is known to not have a right subtree, so it is silly to give it one. The bound does not depend on this exception, and if the routine is coded recursively, this is what will happen naturally. Figure 11.6 shows the result of merging two skew heaps.

Figure 11.6 Merging of two skew heaps

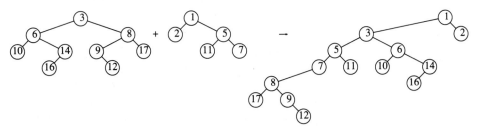

Suppose we have two heaps, H_1 and H_2, and there are r_1 and r_2 nodes on their respective right paths. Then the actual time to perform the merge is proportional to $r_1 + r_2$, so we will drop the Big-Oh notation and charge one unit of time for each node on the paths. Since the heaps have no structure, it is possible that all the nodes in both heaps lie on the right path, and this would give a $\Theta(n)$ worst-case bound to merge the heaps (Exercise 11.3 asks you to construct an example). We will show that the amortized time to merge two skew heaps is $O(\log n)$.

What is needed is some sort of a potential function that captures the effect of skew heap operations. Recall that the effect of a *Merge* is that every node on the right path is moved to the left path, and its old left child becomes the new right child. One idea might be to classify each node as a right node or left node, depending on whether or not it is a right child, and use the number of right nodes as a potential function. Although the potential is initially 0 and always nonnegative, the problem is that the potential does not decrease after a merge and thus does not adequately reflect the savings in the data structure. The result is that this potential function cannot be used to prove the desired bound.

A similar idea is to classify nodes as either heavy or light, depending on whether or not the right subtree of any node has more nodes than the left subtree.

DEFINITION: A node p is *heavy* if the number of descendants of p's right subtree is at least half of the number of descendants of p, and *light* otherwise. Note that the number of descendants of a node includes the node itself.

As an example, Figure 11.7 shows a skew heap. The nodes with keys 15, 3, 6, 12, and 7 are heavy, and all other nodes are light.

The potential function we will use is the number of heavy nodes in the (collection) of heaps. This seems like a good choice because a long right path will contain an inordinate number of heavy nodes. Because nodes on this path have their children swapped, these nodes will be converted to light nodes as a result of the merge.

Figure 11.7 Skew heap—heavy nodes are 3, 6, 7, 12, and 15

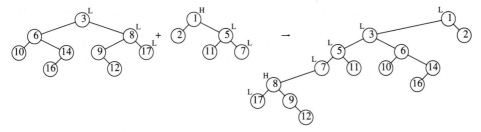

Figure 11.8 Change in heavy/light status after a merge

THEOREM 11.2.

The amortized time to merge two skew heaps is $O(\log n)$.

PROOF:

Let H_1 and H_2 be the two heaps, with n_1 and n_2 nodes, respectively. Suppose the right path of H_1 has l_1 light nodes and h_1 heavy nodes, for a total of $l_1 + h_1$. Likewise, H_2 has l_2 light and h_2 heavy nodes on its right path, for a total of $l_2 + h_2$ nodes.

If we adopt the convention that the cost of merging two skew heaps is the total number of nodes on their right paths, then the actual time to perform the merge is $l_1 + l_2 + h_1 + h_2$. Now the only nodes whose heavy/light status can change are nodes that are initially on the right path (and wind up on the left path) since no other nodes have their subtrees altered. This is shown by the example in Figure 11.8.

If a heavy node is initially on the right path, then after the merge it must become a light node. The other nodes that were on the right path were light and may or may not become heavy, but since we are proving an upper bound, we will have to assume the worst, which is that they become heavy and increase the potential. Then the net change in the number of heavy nodes is at most $l_1 + l_2 - h_1 - h_2$. Adding the actual time and the potential change (Equation 11.2) gives an amortized bound of $2(l_1 + l_2)$.

Now we must show that $l_1 + l_2 = O(\log n)$. Since l_1 and l_2 are the number of light nodes on the original right paths, and the right subtree of a light node is less than half the size of the tree rooted at the light node, it follows directly that the number of light nodes on the right path is at most $\log n_1 + \log n_2$, which is $O(\log n)$.

The proof is completed by noting that the initial potential is 0 and that the potential is always nonnegative. It is important to verify this, since otherwise the amortized time does not bound the actual time and is meaningless.

Since the *Insert* and *Delete_Min* operations are basically just *Merges*, they also have $O(\log n)$ amortized bounds.

11.4. Fibonacci Heaps

In Section 9.3.2, we showed how to use priority queues to improve on the naive $O(|V|^2)$ running time of Dijkstra's shortest-path algorithm. The important observation was that the running time was dominated by $|E|$ *Decrease_Key* operations and $|V|$ *Insert* and *Delete_Min* operations. These operations take place on a set of size at most $|V|$. By using a binary heap, all these operations take $O(\log |V|)$ time, so the resulting bound for Dijkstra's algorithm can be reduced to $O(|E| \log |V|)$.

In order to lower this time bound, the time required to perform the *Decrease_Key* operation must be improved. *d*-heaps, which were described in Section 6.5, give an $O(\log_d |V|)$ time bound for the *Decrease_Key* operation as well as for *Insert*, but an $O(d \log_d |V|)$ bound for *Delete_Min*. By choosing d to balance the costs of $|E|$ *Decrease_Key* operations with $|V|$ *Delete_Min* operations, and remembering that d must always be at least 2, we see that a good choice for d is

$$d = \max(2, \lfloor |E|/|V| \rfloor).$$

This improves the time bound for Dijkstra's algorithm to

$$O(|E| \log_{(2 + \lfloor |E|/|V| \rfloor)} |V|).$$

The *Fibonacci heap* is a data structure that supports all the basic heap operations in $O(1)$ amortized time, with the exception of *Delete_Min* and *Remove*, which take $O(\log n)$ amortized time. It immediately follows that the heap operations in Dijkstra's algorithm will require a total of $O(|E| + |V| \log |V|)$ time.

Fibonacci heaps[†] generalize binomial queues by adding two new concepts:

A different implementation of Decrease_Key: The method we have seen before is to percolate the element up toward the root. It does not seem reasonable to expect an $O(1)$ amortized bound for this strategy, so a new method is needed.

Lazy merging: Two heaps are merged only when it is required to do so. This is similar to lazy deletion. For lazy merging, *Merges* are cheap, but because lazy merging does not actually combine trees, the *Delete_Min* operation could encounter lots of trees, making that operation expensive. Any one *Delete_Min* could take linear time, but it is always possible to charge the time to previous *Merge* operations. In particular, an expensive *Delete_Min* must have been preceded by a large number of unduly cheap *Merges*, which have been able to store up extra potential.

11.4.1. Cutting Nodes in Leftist Heaps

In binary heaps, the *Decrease_Key* operation is implemented by lowering the value at a node and then percolating it up toward the root until heap order is established. In the worst case, this can take $O(\log n)$ time, which is the length of the longest path toward the root in a balanced tree.

This strategy does not work if the tree that represents the priority queue does not have $O(\log n)$ depth. As an example, if this strategy is applied to leftist heaps, then the *Decrease_Key* operation could take $\Theta(n)$ time, as the example in Figure 11.9 shows.

[†]The name comes from a property of this data structure that we will prove later in the section.

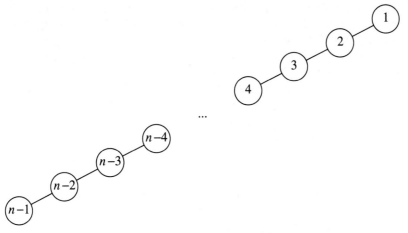

Figure 11.9   Decreasing $n - 1$ to 0 via percolate up would take $\Theta(n)$ time

We see that for leftist heaps, another strategy is needed for the *Decrease_Key* operation. Our example will be the leftist heap in Figure 11.10. Suppose we want to decrease the key with value 9 down to 0. If we make the change, we find that we have created a violation of heap order, which is indicated by a dashed line in Figure 11.11.

We do not want to percolate the 0 to the root because, as we have seen, there are cases in which this could be expensive. The solution is to *cut* the heap along the dashed line, thus creating two trees, and then merge the two trees back into one. Let x be the node to which the *Decrease_Key* operation is being applied, and let p be its parent. After the cut, we have two trees, namely, H_1 with root x, and T_2, which is the original tree with H_1 removed. The situation is shown in Figure 11.12.

If these two trees were both leftist heaps, then they could be merged in $O(\log n)$ time, and we would be done. It is easy to see that H_1 is a leftist heap since none of its nodes have had any changes in their descendants. Thus, since all of its nodes originally satisfied the leftist property, they still must.

Figure 11.10   Sample leftist heap H

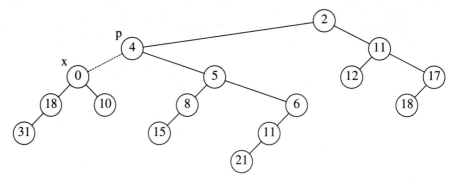

Figure 11.11   Decreasing 9 to 0 creates a heap order
violation

Nevertheless, it seems that this scheme will not work because T_2 is not necessarily leftist. However, it is easy to reinstate the leftist heap property by using two observations:

- Only nodes on the path from p to the root of T_2 can be in violation of the leftist heap property; these can be fixed by swapping children.
- Since the maximum right path length has at most $\lfloor \log(n + 1) \rfloor$ nodes, we need only to check the first $\lfloor \log(n + 1) \rfloor$ nodes on the path from p to the root of T_2. Figure 11.13 shows H_1 and T_2 after T_2 is converted to a leftist heap.

Because we can convert T_2 to the leftist heap H_2 in $O(\log n)$ steps, and then merge H_1 and H_2, we have an $O(\log n)$ algorithm for performing the *Decrease_Key* operation in leftist heaps. The heap that results in our example is shown in Figure 11.14.

11.4.2.   *Lazy Merging for Binomial Queues*

The second idea that is used by Fibonacci heaps is *lazy merging*. We will apply this idea to binomial queues and show that the amortized time to perform a *Merge*

Figure 11.12   The two trees after the cut

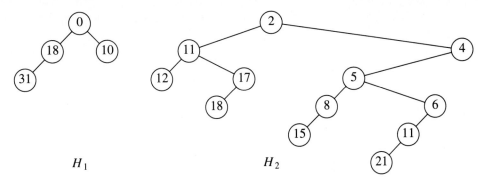

Figure 11.13 T_2 converted to the leftist heap H_2

operation (as well as insertion, which is a special case) is $O(1)$. The amortized time for *Delete_Min* will still be $O(\log n)$.

The idea is as follows: To merge two binomial queues, merely concatenate the two lists of binomial trees, creating a new binomial queue. This new queue may have several trees of the same size, so it violates the binomial queue property. We will call this a *lazy binomial queue* in order to maintain consistency. This is a fast operation, which always takes constant (worst-case) time. As before, an insertion is done by creating a one-node binomial queue and merging. The difference is that the *Merge* is lazy.

The *Delete_Min* operation is much more painful because it is where we finally convert the lazy binomial queue back into a standard binomial queue, but, as we will show, it is still $O(\log n)$ amortized time—but not $O(\log n)$ worst-case time, as before. To perform a *Delete_Min*, we find (and eventually return) the minimum element. As before, we delete it from the queue, making each of its children new trees. We then merge all the trees into a binomial queue by merging two equal-sized trees until it is no longer possible.

Figure 11.14   *Decrease_Key(H, x, 9)* completed by merg-
                  ing H_1 and H_2

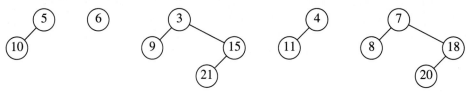

Figure 11.15   Lazy binomial queue

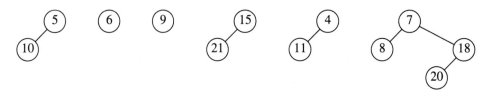

Figure 11.16   Lazy binomial queue after removing the
smallest element (3)

As an example, Figure 11.15 shows a lazy binomial queue. In a lazy binomial queue, there can be more than one tree of the same size. We can tell the size of a tree by examining the root's *rank* field, which gives the number of children (and thus implicitly the type of tree). To perform the *Delete_Min,* we remove the smallest element, as before, and obtain the tree in Figure 11.16.

We now have to merge all the trees and obtain a standard binomial queue. A standard binomial queue has at most one tree of each rank. In order to do this efficiently, we must be able to perform the *Merge* in time proportional to the number of trees present (T) (or $\log n$, whichever is larger). To do this, we form an array of lists, $L_0, L_1, \ldots, L_{R_{\max}+1}$, where $R_{\max}$ is the rank of the largest tree. Each list L_r contains all of the trees of rank r. The procedure in Figure 11.17 is then applied.

Each time through the loop, at lines 3 through 5, the total number of trees is reduced by 1. This means that this part of the code, which takes constant time per execution, can be performed only $T - 1$ times, where T is the number of trees. The *for* loop counters and the tests at the end of the *while* loop take $O(\log n)$ time, so the running time is $O(T + \log n)$, as required. Figure 11.18 shows the execution of this algorithm on the previous collection of binomial trees.

Figure 11.17   Procedure to reinstate a binomial queue

```
/* 1*/ for( int r = 0;r <= ⌊ log n⌋; r++ )
/* 2*/     while( |Lr| ≥ 2 )
           {
/* 3*/         Remove two trees from Lr;
/* 4*/         Merge the two trees into a new tree;
/* 5*/         Add the new tree to Lr+1;
           }
```

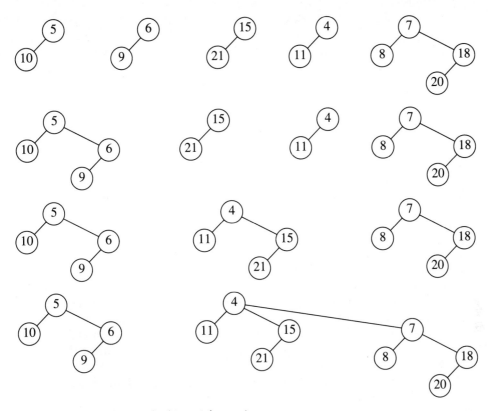

Figure 11.18 Combining the binomial trees into a binomial queue

Amortized Analysis of Lazy Binomial Queues

To carry out the amortized analysis of lazy binomial queues, we will use the same potential function that was used for standard binomial queues. Thus, the potential of a lazy binomial queue is the number of trees.

> **THEOREM 11.3.**
> *The amortized running times of Merge and Insert are both O(1) for lazy binomial queues. The amortized running time of Delete_Min is O(\log n).*

> **PROOF:**
> The potential function is the number of trees in the collection of binomial queues. The initial potential is 0, and the potential is always nonnegative. Thus, over a sequence of operations, the total amortized time is an upper bound on the total actual time.
>
> For the *Merge* operation, the actual time is constant, and the number of trees in the collection of binomial queues is unchanged, so, by Equation (11.2), the amortized time is O(1).
>
> For the *Insert* operation, the actual time is constant, and the number of trees can increase by at most 1, so the amortized time is O(1).

The *Delete_Min* operation is more complicated. Let r be the rank of the tree that contains the minimum element, and let T be the number of trees. Thus, the potential at the start of the *Delete_Min* operation is T. To perform a *Delete_Min*, the children of the smallest node are split off into separate trees. This creates $T + r$ trees, which must be merged into a standard binomial queue. The actual time to perform this is $T + r + \log n$, if we ignore the constant in the Big-Oh notation, by the argument above.[†] On the other hand, once this is done, there can be at most $\log n$ trees remaining, so the potential function can increase by at most $(\log n) - T$. Adding the actual time and the change in potential gives an amortized bound of $2 \log n + r$. Since all the trees are binomial trees, we know that $r \leq \log n$. Thus we arrive at an $O(\log n)$ amortized time bound for the *Delete_Min* operation.

11.4.3. *The Fibonacci Heap Operations*

As we mentioned before, the Fibonacci heap combines the leftist heap *Decrease_Key* operation with the lazy binomial queue *Merge* operation. Unfortunately, we cannot use both operations without a slight modification. The problem is that if arbitrary cuts are made in the binomial trees, the resulting forest will no longer be a collection of binomial trees. Because of this, it will no longer be true that the rank of every tree is at most $\lfloor \log n \rfloor$. Since the amortized bound for *Delete_Min* in lazy binomial queues was shown to be $2 \log n + r$, we need $r = O(\log n)$ for the *Delete_Min* bound to hold.

In order to ensure that $r = O(\log n)$, we apply the following rules to all nonroot nodes:

* Mark a (nonroot) node the first time that it loses a child (because of a cut).
* If a marked node loses another child, then cut it from its parent. This node now becomes the root of a separate tree and is no longer marked. This is called a *cascading cut*, because several of these could occur in one *Decrease_Key* operation.

Figure 11.19 shows one tree in a Fibonacci heap prior to a *Decrease_Key* operation.

When the node with key 39 is changed to 12, the heap order is violated. Therefore, the node is cut from its parent, becoming the root of a new tree. Since the node containing 33 is marked, this is its second lost child, and thus it is cut from its parent (10). Now 10 has lost its second child, so it is cut from 5. The process stops here since 5 was unmarked. 5 is now marked. The result is shown in Figure 11.20.

Notice that 10 and 33, which used to be marked nodes, are no longer marked, because they are now root nodes. This will be a crucial observation in our proof of the time bound.

[†]We can do this because we can place the constant implied by the Big-Oh notation in the potential function and still get the cancellation of terms, which is needed in the proof.

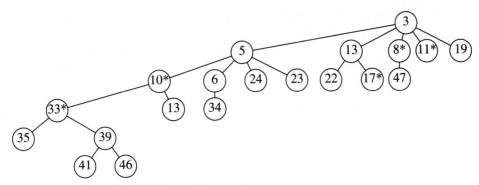

Figure 11.19   A tree in the Fibonacci heap prior to decreasing 39 to 12

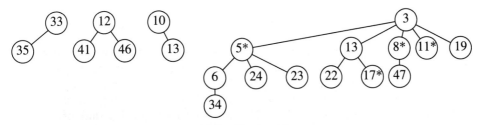

Figure 11.20   The resulting segment of the Fibonacci heap after the *Decrease_Key* operation

11.4.4.   Proof of the Time Bound

Recall that the reason for marking nodes is that we needed to bound the rank (number of children) r of any node. We will now show that any node with n descendants has rank $O(\log n)$.

LEMMA 11.1.

Let x be any node in a Fibonacci heap. Let c_i be the ith youngest child of x. Then the rank of c_i is at least $i - 2$.

PROOF:

At the time when c_i was linked to x, x already had (older) children c_1, c_2, ..., c_{i-1}. Thus, x had at least $i - 1$ children when it linked to c_i. Since nodes are only linked if they have the same rank, it follows that at the time that c_i was linked to x, c_i had at least $i - 1$ children. Since that time, it could have lost at most one child, or else it would have been cut from x. Thus, c_i has at least $i - 2$ children.

From Lemma 11.1, it is easy to show that any node of rank r must have a lot of descendants.

LEMMA 11.2.

Let F_k be the Fibonacci numbers defined (in Section 1.2) by $F_0 = 1$, $F_1 = 1$, and $F_k = F_{k-1} + F_{k-2}$. Any node of rank $r \geq 1$ has at least F_{r+1} descendants (including itself).

PROOF:

Let S_r be the smallest tree of rank r. Clearly, $S_0 = 1$ and $S_1 = 2$. By Lemma 11.1, a tree of rank r must have subtrees of rank at least $r - 2, r - 3, \ldots, 1$, and 0, plus another subtree, which has at least one node. Along with the root of S_r itself, this gives a minimum value for $S_{r>1}$ of $S_r = 2 + \sum_{i=0}^{r-2} S_i$. It is easy to show that $S_r = F_{r+1}$ (Exercise 1.9a).

Because it is well known that the Fibonacci numbers grow exponentially, it immediately follows that any node with s descendants has rank at most $O(\log s)$. Thus, we have

LEMMA 11.3.

The rank of any node in a Fibonacci heap is $O(\log n)$.

PROOF:

Immediate from the discussion above.

If all we were concerned about was the time bounds for the *Merge*, *Insert*, and *Delete_Min* operations, then we could stop here and prove the desired amortized time bounds. Of course, the whole point of Fibonacci heaps is to obtain an $O(1)$ time bound for *Decrease_Key* as well.

The actual time required for a *Decrease_Key* operation is 1 plus the number of cascading cuts that are performed during the operation. Since the number of cascading cuts could be much more than $O(1)$, we will need to pay for this with a loss in potential. If we look at Figure 11.20, we see that the number of trees actually increases with each cascading cut, so we will have to enhance the potential function to include something that decreases during cascading cuts. Notice that we cannot just throw out the number of trees from the potential function, since then we will not be able to prove the time bound for the *Merge* operation. Looking at Figure 11.20 again, we see that a cascading cut causes a decrease in the number of marked nodes because each node that is the victim of a cascading cut becomes an unmarked root. Since each cascading cut costs 1 unit of actual time and increases the tree potential by 1, we will count each marked node as two units of potential. This way, we have a chance of canceling out the number of cascading cuts.

THEOREM 11.4.

The amortized time bounds for Fibonacci heaps are $O(1)$ *for Insert, Merge, and Decrease_Key and* $O(\log n)$ *for Delete_Min.*

PROOF:

The potential is the number of trees in the collection of Fibonacci heaps plus twice the number of marked nodes. As usual, the initial potential is 0 and is always nonnegative. Thus, over a sequence of operations, the total amortized time is an upper bound on the total actual time.

For the *Merge* operation, the actual time is constant, and the number of trees and marked nodes is unchanged, so by Equation (11.2), the amortized time is $O(1)$.

For the *Insert* operation, the actual time is constant, the number of trees increases by 1, and the number of marked nodes is unchanged. Thus, the potential increases by at most 1, so the amortized time is $O(1)$.

For the *Delete_Min* operation, let r be the rank of the tree that contains the minimum element, and let T be the number of trees before the operation. To perform a *Delete_Min*, we once again split the children of a tree, creating an additional r new trees. Notice that, although this can remove marked nodes (by making them unmarked roots), this cannot create any additional marked nodes. These r new trees, along with the other T trees, must now be merged, at a cost of $T + r + \log n = T + O(\log n)$, by Lemma 11.3. Since there can be at most $O(\log n)$ trees, and the number of marked nodes cannot increase, the potential change is at most $O(\log n) - T$. Adding the actual time and potential change gives the $O(\log n)$ amortized bound for *Delete_Min*.

Finally, for the *Decrease_Key* operation, let C be the number of cascading cuts. The actual cost of a *Decrease_Key* is $C + 1$, which is the total number of cuts performed. The first (noncascading) cut creates a new tree and thus increases the potential by 1. Each cascading cut creates a new tree, but converts a marked node to an unmarked (root) node for a net loss of one unit per cascading cut. The last cut also can convert an unmarked node (in Figure 11.20 it is node 5) into a marked node, thus increasing the potential by 2. The total change in potential is thus $3 - C$. Adding the actual time and the potential change gives a total of 4, which is $O(1)$.

11.5. Splay Trees

As a final example, we analyze the running time of splay trees. Recall, from Chapter 4, that after an access of some item x is performed, a splaying step moves x to the root by a series of three operations: *zig, zig-zag,* and *zig-zig.* These tree rotations are shown in Figure 11.21. We adopt the convention that if a tree rotation is being performed at node x, then prior to the rotation p is its parent and g is its grandparent (if x is not the child of the root).

Recall that the time required for any tree operation on node x is proportional to the number of nodes on the path from the root to x. If we count each *zig* operation as one rotation and each *zig-zig* or *zig-zag* as two rotations, then the cost of any access is equal to 1 plus the number of rotations.

In order to show an $O(\log n)$ amortized bound for the splaying step, we need a potential function that can increase by at most $O(\log n)$ over the entire splaying step but which will also cancel out the number of rotations performed during the step. It is not at all easy to find a potential function that satisfies these criteria. A simple first guess at a potential function might be the sum of the depths of all the nodes in the tree. This does not work because the potential can increase by $\Theta(n)$ during an access. A canonical example of this occurs when elements are inserted in sequential order.

A potential function Φ, which does work, is defined as

$$\Phi(T) = \sum_{i \in T} \log S(i).$$

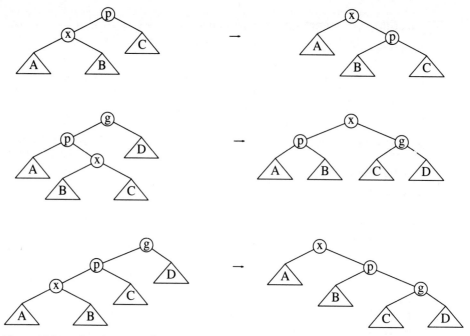

Figure 11.21 *zig, zig-zag,* and *zig-zig* operations; each has a
symmetric case (not shown)

$S(i)$ represents the number of descendants of i (including i itself). The potential
function is the sum, over all nodes i in the tree T, of the logarithm of $S(i)$.

To simplify the notation, we will define

$$R(i) = \log S(i).$$

This makes

$$\Phi(T) = \sum_{i \in T} R(i)$$

$R(i)$ represents the *rank* of node i. The terminology is similar to what we
used in the analysis of the disjoint set algorithm, binomial queues, and Fibonacci
heaps. In all these data structures, the meaning of *rank* is somewhat different, but
is generally meant to be on the order (magnitude) of the logarithm of the size of
the tree. For a tree T with n nodes, the rank of the root is simply $R(T) = \log n$.
Using the sum of ranks as a potential function is similar to using the sum of
heights as a potential function. The important difference is that while a rotation can
change the heights of many nodes in the tree, only x, p, and g can have their ranks
changed.

Before proving the main theorem, we need the following lemma.

LEMMA 11.4.

If $a + b \le c$, and a and b are both positive integers, then

$$\log a + \log b \le 2 \log c - 2.$$

PROOF:

By the arithmetic-geometric mean inequality,

$$\sqrt{ab} \le (a+b)/2.$$

Thus

$$\sqrt{ab} \le c/2$$

Squaring both sides gives

$$ab \le c^2/4$$

Taking logarithms of both sides proves the lemma.

With the preliminaries taken care of, we are ready to prove the main theorem.

THEOREM 11.5.

The amortized time to splay a tree with root T at node x is at most $3(R(T) - R(x)) + 1 = O(\log n)$.

PROOF:

The potential function is the sum of the ranks of the nodes in T.

If x is the root of T, then there are no rotations, so there is no potential change. The actual time is 1 to access the node, thus the amortized time is 1 and the theorem is true. Thus, we may assume that there is at least one rotation.

For any splaying step, let $R_i(x)$ and $S_i(x)$ be the rank and size of x before the step, and let $R_f(x)$ and $S_f(x)$ be the rank and size of x immediately after the splaying step. We will show that the amortized time required for a *zig* is at most $3(R_f(x) - R_i(x)) + 1$ and that the amortized time for either a *zig-zag* or *zig-zig* is at most $3(R_f(x) - R_i(x))$. We will show that when we add over all steps, the sum telescopes to the desired time bound.

Zig step: For the *zig* step, the actual time is 1 (for the single rotation), and the potential change is $R_f(x) + R_f(p) - R_i(x) - R_i(p)$. Notice that the potential change is easy to compute, because only x and p's trees change size. Thus

$$AT_{\text{zig}} = 1 + R_f(x) + R_f(p) - R_i(x) - R_i(p)$$

From Figure 11.21 we see that $S_i(p) \ge S_f(p)$; thus, it follows that $R_i(p) \ge R_f(p)$. Thus,

$$AT_{\text{zig}} \le 1 + R_f(x) - R_i(x).$$

Since $S_f(x) \ge S_i(x)$, it follows that $R_f(x) - R_i(x) \ge 0$, so we may increase the right side, obtaining

$$AT_{\text{zig}} \le 1 + 3(R_f(x) - R_i(x)).$$

Zig-zag step: For the *zig-zag* case, the actual cost is 2, and the potential change is $R_f(x) + R_f(p) + R_f(g) - R_i(x) - R_i(p) - R_i(g)$. This gives an amortized time bound of

$$AT_{\text{zig-zag}} = 2 + R_f(x) + R_f(p) + R_f(g) - R_i(x) - R_i(p) - R_i(g).$$

From Figure 11.21 we see that $S_f(x) = S_i(g)$, so their ranks must be equal. Thus, we obtain

$$AT_{\text{zig-zag}} = 2 + R_f(p) + R_f(g) - R_i(x) - R_i(p).$$

We also see that $S_i(p) \geq S_i(x)$. Consequently, $R_i(x) \leq R_i(p)$. Making this substitution gives

$$AT_{\text{zig-zag}} \leq 2 + R_f(p) + R_f(g) - 2R_i(x).$$

From Figure 11.21 we see that $S_f(p) + S_f(g) \leq S_f(x)$. If we apply Lemma 11.4, we obtain

$$\log S_f(p) + \log S_f(g) \leq 2 \log S_f(x) - 2.$$

By definition of *rank*, this becomes

$$R_f(p) + R_f(g) \leq 2R_f(x) - 2.$$

Substituting this we obtain

$$AT_{\text{zig-zag}} \leq 2R_f(x) - 2R_i(x)$$
$$\leq 2(R_f(x) - R_i(x))$$

Since $R_f(x) \geq R_i(x)$, we obtain

$$AT_{\text{zig-zag}} \leq 3(R_f(x) - R_i(x)).$$

Zig-zig step: The third case is the *zig-zig*. The proof of this case is very similar to the *zig-zag* case. The important inequalities are $R_f(x) = R_i(g)$, $R_f(x) \geq R_f(p)$, $R_i(x) \leq R_i(p)$, and $S_i(x) + S_f(g) \leq S_f(x)$. We leave the details as Exercise 11.8.

The amortized cost of an entire splay is the sum of the amortized costs of each splay step. Figure 11.22 shows the steps that are performed in a splay at node 2. Let $R_1(2)$, $R_2(2)$, $R_3(2)$, and $R_4(2)$ be the rank of node 2 in each of the four trees. The cost of the first step, which is a *zig-zag*, is at most $3(R_2(2) - R_1(2))$. The cost of the second step, which is a *zig-zig*, is $3(R_3(2) - R_2(2))$. The last step is a *zig* and has cost no larger than $3(R_4(2) - R_3(2)) + 1$. The total cost thus telescopes to $3(R_4(2) - R_1(2)) + 1$.

In general, by adding up the amortized costs of all the rotations, of which at most one can be a *zig*, we see that the total amortized cost to splay at node x is at most $3(R_f(x) - R_i(x)) + 1$, where $R_i(x)$ is the rank of x before the first splaying step and $R_f(x)$ is the rank of x after the last splaying step. Since the last splaying step leaves x at the root, we obtain an amortized bound of $3(R_f(T) - R_i(x)) + 1$, which is $O(\log n)$.

Because every operation on a splay tree requires a splay, the amortized cost of any operation is within a constant factor of the amortized cost of a splay. Thus, all splay tree operations take $O(\log n)$ amortized time. By using a more general potential function, it is possible to show that splay trees have several remarkable properties. This is discussed in more detail in the exercises.

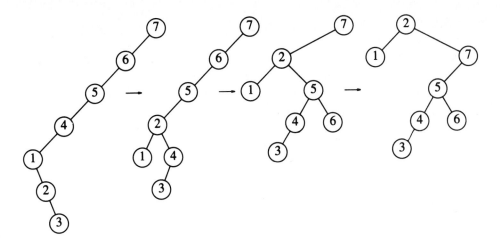

Figure 11.22   The splaying steps involved in splaying at node 2

Summary

In this chapter, we have seen how an amortized analysis can be used to apportion charges among operations. To perform the analysis, we invent a fictitious potential function. The potential function measures the state of the system. A high-potential data structure is volatile, having been built on relatively cheap operations. When the expensive bill comes for an operation, it is paid for by the savings of previous operations. One can view potential as standing for *potential for disaster,* in that very expensive operations can occur only when the data structure has a high potential and has used considerably less time than has been allocated.

Low potential in a data structure means that the cost of each operation has been roughly equal to the amount allocated for it. Negative potential means debt—more time has been spent than has been allocated, so the allocated (or amortized) time is not a meaningful bound.

As expressed by Equation (11.2), the amortized time for an operation is equal to the sum of the actual time and potential change. Taken over an entire sequence of operations, the amortized time for the sequence is equal to the total sequence time plus the net change in potential. As long as this net change is positive, then the amortized bound provides an *upper bound* for the actual time spent and is meaningful.

The keys to choosing a potential function are to guarantee that the minimum potential occurs at the beginning of the algorithm and to have the potential increase for cheap operations and decrease for expensive operations. It is important that the excess or saved time be measured by an opposite change in potential. Unfortunately, this is sometimes easier said than done.

Exercises

11.1   When do m consecutive insertions into a binomial queue take less than $2m$ time units?

11.2   Suppose a binomial queue of $n = 2^k - 1$ elements is built. Alternately perform m *Insert* and *Delete_Min* pairs. Clearly, each operation takes $O(\log n)$ time. Why does this not contradict the amortized bound of $O(1)$ for insertion?

*11.3   Show that the amortized bound of $O(\log n)$ for the skew heap operations described in the text cannot be converted to a worst-case bound, by giving a sequence of operations that lead to a *Merge* requiring $\Theta(n)$ time.

*11.4   Show how to merge two skew heaps with one top-down pass and reduce the *Merge* cost to $O(1)$ amortized time.

11.5   Extend skew heaps to support the *Decrease_Key* operation in $O(\log n)$ amortized time.

11.6   Implement Fibonacci heaps and compare their performance with binary heaps when used in Dijkstra's algorithm.

11.7   A standard implementation of Fibonacci heaps requires four pointers per node (parent, child, and two siblings). Show how to reduce the number of pointers at the cost of at most a constant factor in the running time.

11.8   Show that the amortized time of a *zig-zig* splay is at most $3(R_f(x) - R_i(x))$.

11.9   By changing the potential function, it is possible to prove different bounds for splaying. Let the *weight function* $W(i)$ be some function assigned to each node in the tree, and let $S(i)$ be the sum of the weights of all the nodes in the subtree rooted at i, including i itself. The special case $W(i) = 1$ for all nodes corresponds to the function used in the proof of the splaying bound. Let n be the number of nodes in the tree, and let m be the number of accesses. Prove the following two theorems:

   a.   The total access time is $O(m + (m + n) \log n)$.

   *b.   If q_i is the number of times that item i is accessed, and $q_i > 0$ for all i, then the total access time is

$$O\left(m + \sum_{i=1}^{n} q_i \log(m/q_i)\right)$$

11.10   a.   Show how to implement the *Merge* operation on splay trees so that a sequence of $n - 1$ *Merges* starting from n single-element trees takes $O(n \log^2 n)$ time.

   *b.   Improve the bound to $O(n \log n)$.

11.11   In Chapter 5, we described *rehashing*: When a table becomes more than half full, a new table twice as large is constructed, and the entire old table is rehashed. Give a formal amortized analysis, with potential function, to show that the amortized cost of an insertion is still $O(1)$.

11.12 Show that if deletions are not allowed, then any sequence of m insertions into an n node 2–3 tree produces $O(m + n)$ node splits.

11.13 A *deque* with *heap order* is a data structure consisting of a list of items on which the following operations are possible:

D. *Push(X):* Insert item X on the front end of deque D.

D. *Pop(X):* Remove the front item from deque D and place it in X.

D. *Inject(X):* Insert item X on the rear end of deque D.

D. *Eject(X):* Remove the rear item from deque D and place it in X.

D. *Find_Min:* Return the smallest item from deque D (breaking ties arbitrarily).

　a. Describe how to support these operations in constant amortized time per operation.

**b. Describe how to support these operations in constant worst-case time per operation.

References

An excellent survey of amortized analysis is provided in [9].

Most of the references below duplicate citations in earlier chapters. We cite them again for convenience and completeness. Binomial queues were first described in [10] and analyzed in [1]. Solutions to 11.3 and 11.4 appear in [8]. Fibonacci heaps are described in [3]. Exercise 11.9a shows that splay trees are optimal to within a constant factor of the the best static search trees. 11.9b shows that splay trees are optimal to within a constant factor of the best optimal search trees. These, as well as two other strong results, are proved in the original splay tree paper [6].

The *Merge* operation for splay trees is described in [5]. Exercise 11.12 is solved, with an implicit use of amortization, in [2]. The paper also shows how to merge 2–3 trees efficiently. A solution to 11.13 can be found in [4].

Amortized analysis is used in [7] to design an on-line algorithm that processes a series of queries in time only a constant factor larger than any off-line algorithm in its class.

1. M. R. Brown, "Implementation and Analysis of Binomial Queue Algorithms," *SIAM Journal on Computing* 7 (1978), 298–319.
2. M. R. Brown and R. E. Tarjan, "Design and Analysis of a Data Structure for Representing Sorted Lists," *SIAM Journal on Computing* 9 (1980), 594–614.
3. M. L. Fredman and R. E. Tarjan, "Fibonacci Heaps and Their Uses in Improved Network Optimization Algorithms," *Journal of the ACM* 34 (1987), 596–615.
4. H. Gajewska and R. E. Tarjan, "Deques with Heap Order," *Information Processing Letters* 22 (1986), 197–200.
5. G. Port and A. Moffat, "A Fast Algorithm for Melding Splay Trees," *Proceedings of First Workshop on Algorithms and Data Structures*, 1989, 450–459.

6. D. D. Sleator and R. E. Tarjan, "Self-adjusting Binary Search Trees," *Journal of the ACM* 32 (1985), 652–686.

7. D. D. Sleator and R. E. Tarjan, "Amortized Efficiency of List Update and Paging Rules," *Communications of the ACM* 28 (1985), 202–208.

8. D. D. Sleator and R. E. Tarjan, "Self-adjusting Heaps," *SIAM Journal on Computing* 15 (1986), 52–69.

9. R. E. Tarjan, "Amortized Computational Complexity," *SIAM Journal on Algebraic and Discrete Methods* 6 (1985), 306–318.

10. J. Vuillemin, "A Data Structure for Manipulating Priority Queues," *Communications of the ACM* 21 (1978), 309–314.

Index

489